FOREST FLORA
OF THE
SIWALIK AND JAUNSAR FOREST DIVISIONS OF THE UNITED PROVINCES OF AGRA AND OUDH

FOREST FLORA

OF THE

SIWALIK AND JAUNSAR FOREST DIVISIONS OF THE UNITED PROVINCES OF AGRA AND OUDH,

BEING A REVISED AND ENLARGED EDITION

OF

THE FOREST FLORA OF THE SCHOOL CIRCLE, N.-W. P.,

WITH

ANALYSES,

COMPILED FOR THE USE OF THE STUDENTS OF THE IMPERIAL FOREST COLLEGE, DEHRA DUN

BY

UPENDRANATH KANJILAL,

RAI BAHADUR, F.L.S.,

EXTRA-DEPUTY CONSERVATOR OF FORESTS.

GYAN

Published by

Gyan Publishing House
5, Ansari Road
Daryaganj, New Delhi-110002
Phone: 011-47034999, 9811692060
E-mail: books@gyanbooks.com

Distribution Network
gyanbooks.com
India, USA, Canada, UK, Australia, France

ISBN : 978-81-212-2095-8 (HB)
First Published, 1911

2nd Impression 2021

Printed at: Gyan Press, Delhi.

Forest Flora
of the
Siwalik and Jaunsar Forest Divisions of the United Provinces of Agra and Oudh
Author: Upendranath Kanjilal

FOREST FLORA

OF THE

SIWALIK AND JAUNSAR FOREST DIVISIONS OF THE UNITED PROVINCES OF AGRA AND OUDH,

BEING A REVISED AND ENLARGED EDITION

OF

THE FOREST FLORA OF THE SCHOOL CIRCLE, N.-W. P.,

WITH

ANALYSES,

COMPILED FOR THE USE OF THE

STUDENTS OF THE IMPERIAL FOREST COLLEGE, DEHRA DÚN,

BY

UPENDRANATH KANJILAL, RAI BAHADUR, F.L.S.,

EXTRA-DEPUTY CONSERVATOR OF FORESTS.

Published by Authority

CALCUTTA

SUPERINTENDENT GOVERNMENT PRINTING, INDIA

1911

Price Re. 1-14 for Public and Re. 1-4 for Students.

Agents for the sale of Books published by the Superintendent of Government Printing, India, Calcutta.

IN ENGLAND.

E. A. Arnold, 41 and 43, Maddox Street, Bond Street, London, W.

Constable & Co., 10, Orange Street, Leicester Square, W.C.

Kegan Paul, Trench, Trübner & Co., 43, Gerrard Street, Soho, London, W.

Bernard Quaritch, 11, Grafton Street, New Bond Street, London, W.

B. H. Blackwell, 50 and 51, Broad Street, Oxford.

Deighton, Bell & Co., Cambridge.

P. S. King & Son, 2 & 4, Great Smith Street, Westminster, London, S. W.

H. S. King & Co., 65, Cornhill, and 9, Pall Mall, London.

Grindlay & Co., 54, Parliament Street, London, S.W.

T. Fisher Unwin, 1, Adelphi Terrace, London, W.C.

W. Thacker & Co., 2, Creed Lane, London, E.C.

Luzac & Co., 46, Great Russell Street, London, W.C.

ON THE CONTINENT.

Otto Harrassowitz, Leipzig, Germany.

Karl W. Hiersemann, Leipzig, Germany.

R. Friedlander & Sohn, Berlin, W. N. Carlstrasse, 11.

Ernest Leroux, 28, Rue Bonaparte, Paris, France.

Martinus Nijhoff, The Hague, Holland.

Rudolf Haupt, 1, Dorrienstrasse, Leipzig, Germany.

IN INDIA.

Thacker, Spink & Co., Calcutta and Simla.

Newman & Co., Calcutta.

R. Cambray & Co., Calcutta.

S. K. Lahiri & Co., Calcutta.

B. Banerjee & Co., Calcutta.

Higginbotham & Co., Madras.

V. Kalyanarama Iyer & Co., Madras.

G. A. Natesan & Co., Madras.

S. Murthy & Co., Madras.

Thompson & Co., Madras.

Temple & Co., Madras.

Combridge & Co., Madras.

P. R. Rama Iyer & Co., Madras.

A. R. Pillai & Co., Trivandrum.

Thacker & Co., Ld., Bombay.

A. J. Combridge & Co., Bombay.

D. B. Taraporevala, Sons & Co., Bombay.

Radhabai Atmaram Sagoon, Bombay.

Sunder Pandurang, Bombay.

Gopal Narayan & Co., Bombay.

Superintendent, American Baptist Mission Press, Rangoon.

Rai Sahib M. Gulab Singh and Sons, Mufid-i-Am Press, Lahore and Calcutta.

A. Chand & Co., Lahore, Punjab.

N. B. Mathur, Superintendent, Nazair Kanun Hind Press, Allahabad.

A. M. & J. Ferguson, Ceylon.

S. C. Talukdar, Proprietor, Students and Company, Cooch Behar.

INTRODUCTION TO THE FIRST EDITION.

THIS work is due to the necessity, which has made itself much felt of late, of having a simple Flora for the use of the students of the Imperial Forest School to assist them in identifying the trees and shrubs, etc., which they meet with when engaged on excursions and on practical work in the forests of the School Circle of the North-Western Provinces, which are their training ground. Had it been possible to provide a new and cheaper edition of the splendid "Forest Flora of North-West and Central India," by SIR D. BRANDIS, K.C.I.E., F.R.S., this work might not have been required, but circumstances have prevented the issue of that new edition, and a Forest Flora of our own became a necessity. It was with very great pleasure that I was able to advise an old Dehra Dún student, and a native of India, to undertake a task which he was really the first fully to represent to me as urgently wanted for students' use. He was at first very diffident about it, but, on my urging him to take it up, he agreed to try and carry it out. He has worked very hard at it, in the intervals of the arduous duties of instruction of the Lower or Vernacular Class at the School, and I have every hope that the results of his labours will prove satisfactory and that his Flora will be useful, not only to the students who are qualifying for the provincial service, but to all officers of either service whose work lies in the School Circle and the Circles adjoining.

I believe this to be the first botanical work of any importance which has ever been prepared by a native of India, and the Imperial Forest School may well be proud of having educated at least one native gentleman who has taken up Botany as a study, and botanical work as a labour of love.

The book does not, of course, pretend to be original: it is based upon the "Flora of British India," the monumental work which we owe to the indefatigable labour of Sir JOSEPH HOOKER, G.C.S.I., etc., and which took from 1872 to 1898 to complete, and which, as its author distinctly says in his "Preface," was intended "to facilitate the compilation of local Indian Floras." Babu UPENDRANATH has also had before him the clear and accurate descriptions and the lucid analyses of the "Forest Flora of North-West and Central India" already referred to, and he has been able to consult many other books and writings of importance in the Library of the Forest School. This alone, however, would not have sufficed: it was necessary to examine, dissect and describe the plants themselves either living as they were met with in the forests, or dried and preserved in the Herbarium at Dehra Dún which contains now an excellent collection of specimens of the plants of India, and more especially of the trees, shrubs, climbers and herbs of economic forest value.

The real test of the value of Babu UPENDRANATH's work well be afforded by the experience of some years' use of it in the field. That I myself shall be unable to use it and test it in that way, I must regret; but I am confident that the test of experience will be a successful one, and that this Flora will prove valuable to many successive classes of Forest Students and many successive Forest Officers, whose duties may call them to the beautiful forests of the Dún and the splendid scenery of the adjoining Himalayan Mountains.

Besides such help as I have been able to give him myself, Babu UPENDRANATH has had great assistance from Mr. J. F. DUTHIE, B.A., F.L.S., the present Director of the Botanical Department of Northern India, who has now during the whole of the twenty years since the Imperial Forest School was founded, taught Systematic Botany to successive classes, both in the lecture room and in the field. Among other officers whose work either in the way of published writings, list of plants, etc., or of collecting specimens for the School Herbarium, has contributed to the present Flora, may especially be mentioned Messrs. A. SMYTHIES, N. HEARLE, and Pandit KESHAVÁNAND, all of them at one time or another connected with the School.

The area taken up in the Flora is the area of the School Circle Conservatorship, *i.e.*, the district of Sahá-ranpur, especially the Siwalik portion; the district of Dehra Dún, including the hills of Málkōt and Mussoorie and the parganas of Jaunsar-Bawar; the portion of the State of Tehri-Garhwal in the valley of the Upper Tons and its tributaries, the Pábar and Rupin, the forests of which are leased by Government for purposes of Forest

Conservancy; and the similar leased forests in the territories of the Thakurs of Raiengarh and Dádi of the Simla Hill States. In elevation, this area passes from only a few hundred feet above the sea at Sahâranpur, to the extreme limit of vegetation in the Himalayas; it is consequently not entirely a correct geographical field, but a field of study whose limits are fixed by the same political reasons that fix the area controlled by the Conservator of the School Circle.

It has not been considered necessary to enter at length into synonymy in this work. Those who desire to do so can always consult the "Flora of British India" which has invariably been quoted. Nor has it been thought advisable usually to give vernacular names from regions outside the School Circle area; or to quote uses and information, unless they are likely to be useful in that area.

The work has run to rather a greater length than was at first contemplated; but it is hoped that this will prove rather an advantage than a drawback.

J. S. GAMBLE,

Conservator of Forests, School Circle, N.-W. P. and Oudh, and Director of the Imperial Forest School, Dehra Dún.

DEHRA DÚN;
4th February 1899.

COMPILER'S PREFACE TO THE FIRST EDITION.

ALTHOUGH in the Introduction which he has so kindly written for me, Mr. GAMBLE has explained the circumstances under which this book came to be written, he has said nothing about its general plan and the way in which it is intended to be used, and I think it best, therefore, to add a few further words in explanation.

The chief object has been to render the work of any one consulting the book as easy as possible, by giving him analyses based on the most obvious characters of the Orders, the Genera and the Species. To those who are fairly good botanists, the Order and perhaps the Genus will suggest themselves at once, and so the key to the Species will alone come into use; sometimes the Order will be known but not the Genus, and then recourse will be had to the Generic key, to be followed when the Genus is ascertained, by that to the Species; often the Order itself will not be known, and then the searcher must look in the analyses of Orders; and finally there may be cases where the Division, or even the Section, of the Vegetable Kingdom is not apparent, and he will have to begin from the very beginning of all.

In using the keys, the student should bear in mind that identification is arrived at by a continued process of elimination. Thus he should first of all determine, from the key given in page 1, the Section and the Division of the Vegetable Kingdom under which the plant he wants to identify is likely to come. This primary division, it will be seen, is based exclusively on the characters of the flowers; leaf and fruit characters do not enter into it. Next follow the analyses of the great Divisions into Natural Orders. It will become evident at this stage how important it is to have a specimen complete with leaves, flowers, and fruit,—for all these characters have been employed in drawing up these and subsequent keys. To facilitate reference, the Natural Orders have been numbered consecutively all through, and the numbers and names have been repeated at the top of each page in the body of the Flora. The key to the Natural Orders was the one the most difficult to prepare, and I am fully conscious that it may have defects; but I can only hope they are few.

Having arrived at the Natural Order that seems the most likely, the student should at once turn to its description in the proper place, and compare the characters given there with those of his specimen; for the characters given in the keys usually occur with considerable variation, or are difficult of determination, and are therefore not always quite a safe guide.

When fully satisfied as to the Natural Order, the student should proceed to the Genus, and last of all, to the Species, in exactly the same way as above, *viz.*, first by the keys and then by comparing his plant with the descriptions. Generic characters have not, however, been separately given in the case of such Genera as have only one Species.

In describing characters the same sequence has been followed throughout the book. Adhering to the same principle, the several items in the description of the leaves—the most obvious of all organs for the purpose of identification—have been given, as much as possible, in a definite order. This indeed can be claimed as a special feature of the book, and it may not be out of place to state it here :—

1. *Disposition*, *i.e.*, opposite, alternate, or whorled.
2. *Form*, *i.e.*, simple or compound.
3. *Dimensions*, of the blade only.
4. *Shape*, including the termination.
5. *Margins*, whether entire, wavy or cut in any way.
6. *Consistence*, *i.e.*, whether membranous or coriaceous, tough, fleshy, soft or hard.
7. The *Surfaces*, including their indumentum.
8. *Venation*.
9. The *Base*, –any peculiarity regarding it not brought out in item 4.
10. The *Petiole*, its length, etc.
11. The *Stipules*, if present.

In the case of compound leaves, the leaflets have been described separately, generally beginning with item 3 if the leaf is digitate, or only omitting item 2 if it is pinnate. The advantages of such an arrangement are too obvious to require any further remark.

The descriptions of leaves are followed by those of the inflorescences, flowers and fruits. Sometimes it may happen that either flower or fruit is missing, and then the work will be more difficult, but a little thought may often lead the searcher into the right track, and he may be enabled to make, at any rate, a shrewd guess at his plant. To those, who, like the officers and students at or near Dehra, have the opportunity of doing so, it is strongly to be recommended that having arrived at what they conceive to be their plant, they should take an early opportunity of making sure by comparing their specimens with the named sheets in the collection. To facilitate this, the numbers of Natural Orders and Genera have invariably been quoted from HOOKER & BENTHAM's "Genera Plantarum," and the Species under each Genus have been arranged in the sequence in which they occur in the "Flora of British India."

A glossary of Botanical Terms has been added, in the preparation of which I have been greatly helped by the lately published Glossary of Mr. R. L. HEINIG, from which useful book some of the definitions have been taken *verbatim*,—and also by Mr. A. F. GRADON, the Botany Instructor at Dehra Dún, who has kindly examined and verified my draft.

It seems proper to mention that a few plants have been included that are not exactly woody, and also a few that are, properly speaking, not indigenous, although successfully cultivated in the School Circle. In either case, their economic value or botanical importance, or both, have been considered sufficient to warrant this deviation.

I hope I may be allowed to add here my own acknowledgments for the encouragement they have given me, to the Inspectors General of Forests, Mr. B. RIBBENTROP, C.I.E., and Mr. H. C. HILL, and to the Directors of the Imperial Forest School under whom I have served,—Mr. H. C. HILL, Mr. J. W. OLIVER, and more especially to Mr. J. S. GAMBLE, M.A., F.R.S., C.I.E., as it was during his tenure of office, and under his guidance, that the first draft was completed. But for his constant encouragement and ever ready help, I might have been content with a much smaller effort. My thanks are also due to Mr. DUTHIE, who, as my Instructor in Systematic Botany, has always evinced a special interest in my undertaking. I am also greatly obliged to Pandit KESHAVÁNAND, now Conservator of Forests in the Tehri-Garhwal State, for considerable help in supplementing and verifying the vernacular names collected by Messrs. HEARLE, SMYTHIES, FERNANDEZ and others. Not being myself an inhabitant of the North-Western Provinces, some such help was much wanted, and I could not have found it in any one better than in my friend Pandit KESHAVÁNAND.

I am fully conscious of many defects, and that, in spite of my best endeavours, many errors,—technical, literary and typographical,—must have crept in. If those, who may use this book, will kindly inform me of them from time to time, with a view to their correction in any subsequent edition, they will lay me under a great obligation.

UPENDRANATH KANJILAL,
Extra-Assistant Conservator of Forests.

DEHRA DÚN;
26th March 1900.

PREFACE TO THE REVISED EDITION.

In this edition, besides the usual corrections, many important changes have been introduced and attempts have been made to effect some improvements. First of all the title of the book had to be changed, the area to which it applied having changed its name, in respect of both general and forest administration, since the publication of the first edition in 1901. Then, following the recommendations of the International Conference held at Vienna in 1905, the word Family has been used in this edition to indicate what were described as Natural Orders in its predecessor, while Cohorts have been called Orders. The names of some Families also have undergone slight or complete changes in deference to the rules laid down at the above Conference.

It was found out at actual teaching that the keys to the Families, although of considerable use in the field for the practical purpose of quickly 'running down' a plant to its Family, were nevertheless essentially of an artificial nature, and therefore could not convey to the student a clear idea of the distinctive characters and relative positions of the Families. To remedy this defect an analytical synopsis has been added in which the Families have been grouped first under Orders, and again the Orders themselves under the Classes and Divisions, care being taken throughout to avoid repetition and duplication in stating their chief characters. Although in the matter of grouping PRANTL and VINE's system has been generally followed, the characters of Orders have almost in all cases been amplified or modified with special reference to Indian Families of plants, and more particularly to those actually comprised under each in this Flora. It is hoped that this synopsis will prove useful to students. To make their work easy the Orders have been indicated in their proper places in the body of the Flora. All the keys throughout the book have been revised and in some cases recast, generally in the light of further experience gained at actual teaching. The Glossary also has been considerably added to, so that it may now be more confidently said that no technical term has been used in the text that has not been defined in the Glossary.

The sequence of HOOKER & BENTHAM's "Genera Plantarum" and the "Flora of British India" has been deviated from towards the end of the book inasmuch as the Monocotyledons and the Gymnosperms have been made to change places with a view to assigning to them their more correct morphological position, and the last four Families of the Apetalæ have been rearranged to make them fit properly into their respective Orders.

The descriptive part of the Flora has been increased by the inclusion of ten additional species, *viz.*, *Delphinium vestitum*, *Rhus succedanea*, *Siegesbeckia orientalis*, *Diospyros Kanjilali*, *Linociera intermedia*, *Tylophora tenuis*, *Asparagus adscendens*, *Smilax macrophylla*,

Acorus Calamus, and *Coix Lachryma Jobi*, while three species, *viz.*, *Grewia tiliæfolia*, *Smilax elegans* and *Typha Laxmanni*, have been deleted as their inclusion did not appear to have been based on sufficient grounds. The claims of Teak for a fuller description than was given it in the first edition having been recognised, *Tectona* has been included in the generic key under VERBENACEÆ; also the generic description of *Juniperus* has been added. For the rest, besides the incorporation of corrections and of such additional information as has since been gathered, the descriptions themselves have been thoroughly revised, especially with a view to making them clearer than in the former edition. In all other respects, however, this part of the book has remained unchanged.

Only a few of the synonyms have been changed, but to the references quoted in the first edition has been added the "Indian Trees," the late Sir D. BRANDIS' monumental work, while the quotations for Mr. Gamble's classical work, the "Manual of Indian Timbers," have been corrected throughout to refer to his much enlarged new edition of 1902. Mr. DUTHIE'S excellent "Flora of the Upper Gangetic Plain" and Col. PRAIN'S critical monographs on Dalbergia and Additional Leguminosæ have also been quoted in a few cases.

MR. GAMBLE has again laid me under a debt of obligation by kindly looking through a part of the proofs and assisting me with very valuable suggestions and advice, and I take this opportunity to give expression to my thankfulness to the Inspector-General of Forests to the Government of India for entrusting me with the preparation of this revised edition of the Flora. I am also much indebted to Mr. R. S. HOLE, F.C.H., F.E.S., F.L.S., the Imperial Forest Botanist, for necessary guidance and many valuable suggestions and also to my friend and former pupil Mr. V. SUBRAMANIA IYER, M.A., F.L.S., officiating Forest Zoologist, for supplying me with a very comprehensive list of corrections and suggestions, many of which were most valuable. In fact, it is very gratifying that the request expressed in the last sentence of my preface to the first edition has generally been responded to with great alacrity, especially by those whom I had the honour of teaching Systematic Botany at what was then the Imperial Forest School. I cannot, therefore, do better than conclude this preface with an expression of gratitude to these gentlemen, coupled with a repetition of the same request in respect of the present edition, which, having had to be prepared under somewhat unfavourable circumstances far away from a library and a herbarium, cannot be expected to be entirely faultless.

UPENDRANATH KANJILAL,
Extra-Deputy Conservator of Forests.

SIBSAGAR;
22nd November 1909.

GLOSSARY

OF THE

BOTANICAL TERMS

USED IN THE TEXT.

Accrescent, increasing in size with age; usually said of parts of the calyx or corolla that persist and enlarge after flowering.

Achene, a small dry indehiscent 1-celled 1-seeded fruit, or a 1-seeded carpel of an apocarpous fruit.

Acicular, *needle*-shaped; long and slender.

Acorn, fruit of the oak, *i.e.*, a nut enclosed within a cup formed of an involucre of thickened bracts.

Acumen, a sharp tapering point more or less prolonged. Acuminate, terminating in an *acumen*.

Acute, evenly tapering and ending in a narrow angle, but without a prolongation.

Adnate, said of dissimilar organs when congenitally united.

Adpressed, lying close against the producing surface.

Adventitious, occurring in an unusual position.

Æstivation, the mode in which the parts of a flower are folded in the bud; also their relative position.

Albumen, the nutritive substance found within the seed-coats of some seeds and outside the embryo.

Amplexicaul, said of a sessile leaf or the base of a petiole when *clasping* the *stem*.

Anastomosing, reticulately united.

Anatropous, said of an inverted ovule, *i.e.*, one with the foramen close to the hilum, and the chalaza at the opposite end, the axis of the ovule itself remaining straight.

Androgynous, said of an inflorescence bearing both male and female flowers.

Annulate, marked transversely by *rings*.

Anterior, said of that part of a flower which is inserted away from the axis of inflorescence; inferior.

Anther, the part of a stamen that bears the pollen.

Apiculate, with a short pointed tip.

Apocarpous, with the carpels free and distinct.

Arcuate, shaped like a *bow*, *i.e.*, moderately curved.

Aril, **arillus**, an accessory seed-*covering* or an appendage growing from or about the hilum of a seed. **Arillate**, having an *aril*. **Arillode**, a false *aril*.

Arista, an *awn* or bristle. **Aristate**, bearing or terminating in an *arista*.

Articulate, jointed in such a manner as to separate at maturity.

Ascending, directed obliquely upward.

Auriculate, having a flat lateral expansion like the lobe of the ear.

Awn, a *bristle*-like appendage, especially of the glumes of grasses.

Axil, the upper angle formed by a leaf or a similar organ and the supporting stem or axis. **Axillary**, in or relating to the *axil*.

Axile, relating to the *axis*, generally said of a kind of placentation in which the ovules are borne on the central *axis* of the ovary.

Baccate, *berry-like*, pulpy.

Basifixed, *fixed* by the *base*, especially said of an anther attached at its lower end to the top of the filament; innate.

Bast, fibrous inner bark.

Berry, a simple fruit succulent throughout, without a stone, and generally with more than one seed.

Bifarious, in two opposite vertical *rows*.

Bifid, divided into *two* segments to about the middle with a narrow sinus.

Bifurcate, *two-forked*, having two prongs or branches.

Bilabiate, having *two lips*.

Bipartite, divided into *two segments* almost to the base.

Bipinnate, *twice pinnate*.

Biseriate, in *two series* or rows, generally one above or within the other.

Bisexual, having both stamens and pistil in the same flower; hermaphrodite.

Biternate, *twice ternate*.

Bole, the main axis or trunk of a tree.

Bract, a rudimentary or modified leaf subtending a flower or an inflorescence. **Bracteate**, having *bracts*.

Bracteole, a secondary *bract* or one of the ultimate grade subtending each flower of an inflorescence. **Bracteolate**, having *bracteoles*.

Bulb, a short stem, more or less conical above and flattened at the base, and usually underground, which bears a bud or buds concealed in fleshy scales or coats. **Bulbiform**, formed like a *bulb*. **Bulbous**, of the nature of the *bulb*.

Buttressed, said of stems with vertical ridges or projections, *e.g.*, the stems of Semal, Sundri, etc.

Caducous, falling off very early.

Cæspitose, tufted or growing in tufts, *e.g.*, many species of bamboos.

Callus, the new tissue which forms over the wounds of plants.

Calyx, the outer whorl of floral leaves, immediately below or outside the corolla. **Calycine**, relating to the *calyx*.

Calyptra, a *cap*, hood or veil.

Cambium, a zone of tender thin-walled cells separating the wood from the bark in Dicotyledons and Gymnosperms, by the division and growth of which new cells are formed.

Campanulate, *bell-shaped*, deeper than cup-shaped.

Canescent, with very short grey hairs or pubescence giving the epidermis a greyish-white hue.

Capitate, having a globose *head*.

Capsule, a dry syncarpous fruit the carpels of which open or separate at maturity.

Carpel, the ovary of an apocarpous pistil, or one of the component parts of a syncarpous ovary. **Carpellary**, relating to a *carpel*.

Cartilaginous, firm and tough like parchment.

Caryopsis, a *grain*; the seed-like fruit of Gramineæ with thin pericarp, which is usually adnate to the contained seed.

Catkin, a scaly spike or raceme of unisexual flowers, pendulous or drooping, and generally deciduous.

Caudate, furnished with a *tail*, or with a slender *tail*-like terminal appendage.

Cell, the living vegetable unit; the structural unit in the formation of a plant. Also one of the *cavities* of an ovary or of an anther.

Chalaza, that part of the ovule where the base of the nucleus is confluent with the coats.

Chartaceous, having the texture of writing *paper*; thin and flexible.

Ciliate, fringed with thick marginal hairs like the *eyelashes*.

Cirrhose, bearing *tendrils*.

Cladode, a branch, more or less flattened which assumes the form and functions of a leaf.

Clavate, *club*-shaped; slender below and gradually thickened upward.

Cocci, pl. of coccus, the seed-like and generally 1-seeded lobes of a syncarpous ovary which become more or less dry, and separate at maturity.

Cogener, one of the *same genus*.

Coma, a tuft of soft hairs or cotton borne on a seed. **Comose**, having a *coma*.

Concolor, of the same *colour* throughout.

Conduplicate, folded once upon itself lengthwise.

Cone, the multiple fruit of Conifers formed mostly of imbricated scales by which the seeds are subtended.

Connate, said of similar organs or parts of the same organ when congenitally united.

Connective, the portion of a stamen that *connects* the two lobes or cells of an anther.

Connivent, conniving, said of sepals, petals or anthers having the apex arching over or converging in the centre of the flower.

Contorted, **convolute**, said of leaves or petals with one margin within, and the other margin without, the whorl.

Cordate, *heart-shaped*, *i.e.*, with the base shaped like the figure of a *heart* on cards.

Coriaceous, *leathery;* tough and thick.

Corm, a solid fleshy underground stem more or less jointed and naked or within thin scales, such as is characteristic of certain families, *e.g.*, Aroideæ.

Corolla, the inner whorl of floral leaves.

Corona, a *crown;* the *crown*-like process from the inner face of petals or the throat of a corolla, or from stamens.

Cortical, relating to the *cortex* or *bark*.

Corymb, an inflorescence of the indefinite or centripetal kind in which the branches or pedicels, although starting from different points, all attain almost the same level.

Cotyledons, the seed-lobes or first leaves of an embryo.

Crenate, with rounded teeth.

Cruciform, in the form of a *cross;* generally said of flowers with four petals arranged crosswise.

Crustaceous, hard and brittle; said of a covering which splits and breaks off easily.

Culm, the hollow and jointed stem of grasses, especially of bamboos.

Cuneate, *wedge-shaped*, acute-angled at the base.

Cupula, cupule, a *cup*-like involucre of thickened bracts supporting the nut of the oak.

Cupular, belonging to, or shaped like, the involucre-cup.

Cusp, a long and tapering rigid *point*. **Cuspidate**, furnished with a *cusp*.

Cuticle, the outermost layer of the epidermis.

Cyme, an inflorescence of the definite or centrifugal type.

Cypsela, a dry interior achene invested with the adnate calyx; the fruit of Compositæ.

Decandrous, with *ten stamens*.

Deciduous, said of trees or shrubs which are leafless for a part of the year; also of the leaves of such plants.

Declinate, bent to one side.

Decompound, compound or divided more than once.

Decurrent, *running down* into; said of a sessile leaf when the blade is prolonged below the insertion and so *runs down* the stem.

Decussate, in pairs alternately crossing at right angles.

Dehiscence, the mode of opening of a capsule or of an anther.

Deltoid, triangular in outline or in section like the Greek letter Δ.

Dentate, with margins cut into triangular salient teeth directed outward. **Denticulate**, minutely toothed.

Dextrorse, turning or twining from left to *right*, *i.e.*, in the anti-clockwise direction.

Diadelphous, said of stamens united by their filaments into *two sets* or bundles.

Dichotomous, forked in pairs.

Didynamous, said of a flower with two long and two short stamens, and also of stamens when they are such.

Digitate, *finger-like;* said of a compound leaf with the leaflets all borne on the apex of the common petiole.

Dimorphic, **dimorphous**, having *two forms*, generally said of hermaphrodite flowers having one form with long styles and short stamens, and another with short styles and long stamens; also of leaves if of two widely different shapes on the same stem.

Diœcious, unisexual with the male and female flowers on separate individuals.

Disk, a circular enlargement of the receptacle in the form of a cup, or of a cushion. **Discoid**, *disk*-like; circular and flat or depressed in the centre.

Dissepiment, a partition in an ovary or pericarp in the direction of its length.

Distichous, arranged in two opposite vertical rows.

Divaricate, spreading widely apart.

Dorsal, relating to, inserted on, or opening by, the *back* or outer suture.

Drupe, a stone-fruit, *i.e.*, one with a fleshy or pulpy pericarp and a bony or crustaceous endocarp. **Drupaceous**, like a *drupe*.

Ebracteate, without *bracts*. **Ebracteolate**, without *bracteoles*.

Echinate, set all round with sharp bristles like a *hedge hog*.

Eglandular, without *glands*.

Elliptic, **elliptical**, oblong or oval with rounded ends. **Ellipsoid**, a solid with an elliptical outline.

Emarginate, with a notch at the apex.

Embryo, the rudimentary plantlet formed in a seed.

Endocarp, the inner layer of the pericarp.

Endosperm, the albumen of a seed.

Ensiform, in the shape of a *sword*.

Epicalyx, a whorl of bracts below the *calyx* proper and somewhat resembling it in shape and colour.

Epicarp, the outer layer of a pericarp.

Epidermis, the outermost layer of tissue or skin of a plant.

Epigynous, inserted on the top of the *ovary*.

Epipetalous, said of stamens which are borne on, or adnate to, the *petals* or corolla.

Epiphyllous, growing *on leaves* or perianths.

Epiphyte, a plant growing on, but not nourished by, another plant. **Epiphytic**, having the habit of an *epiphyte*.

Evolution, the mode and particularly the sequence in which flowers open on the same inflorescence.

Exalbuminous, without *albumen*.

Excavate, hollowed into broad deep pits.

Exocarp, the external layer of the pericarp when an endocarp is present.

Exstipulate, without *stipules*.

Extrorse, applied to anthers that dehisce towards the circumference of the flower.

Falcate, curved like the blade of a *sickle* or *scythe*.

Family, a group of co-related genera which are sometimes grouped into tribes.

Farina, *starch*, or anything resembling it or analogous to it.

Farinaceous, consisting of or resembling *starch*.

Fascicled, fasciculate, in dense clusters.

Ferruginous, coloured like *iron-rust*.

Fibrovascular, said of a tissue consisting of woody fibres and ducts or vessels.

Filament, the stalk of an anther.

Filiform, *thread-like*; long and slender.

Fimbriate, having a *fringe* or border of fine thread-like processes.

Floccose, woolly with locks of dense soft hairs that are easily detached.

Foliaceous, of the form or texture of a leaf.

Follicle, a fruit of a single carpel opening by only one, usually the inner, suture. **Follicular**, pertaining to or resembling *a follicle*.

Foramen, the minute *aperture* in the coats of an ovule corresponding to the micropyle of a seed.

Free, distinct, not adnate to any other organ. **Free-central**, said of the placenta of a one-celled ovary when it is like a column in the centre bearing ovules on the upper extremity.

Fugacious, falling off or fading very early.

Funicle, the stalk of an ovule or seed.

Fusiform, *spindle-shaped*; solid and tapering at both ends.

Gamopetalous, having *combined petals*.

Gamophyllous, said of a flower having a perianth of *united leaves* or segments; also applied to such a perianth.

Gamosepalous, having *combined sepals*.

Genus, pl. **genera**, a group of closely related species indicated by the first name of a plant.

Gibbous, having a *pouch*-like swelling or protuberance on one side.

Glabrous, without hairs of any kind. **Glabrate**, somewhat *glabrous*. **Glabrescent**, becoming *glabrous*.

Glands, small *wart*-like bodies or round *excrescences* of any kind found on stems, petioles, etc., or inside flowers. Small raised superficial *dots*, or minute *vescicles* imbedded in the substance of leaves, etc., usually filled with oil. **Glandular**, having *glands*, or relating to *glands*.

Glaucous, of a bluish-grey colour, often covered with a fine bloom.

Glumes, the chaffy bract-like *scales* of the inflorescence of grasses and their allies. **Glumaceous**, resembling or relating to *glumes*.

Gonophore, a stipe or stalk supporting both stamens and ovary in a flower.

Gynobase, a short and broad elongation of the torus on which the pistil rests. **Gynobasic**, resting on a *gynobase*.

Gynophore, the stipe or stalk *supporting* an *ovary*.

Haustorium, pl. **haustoria**, a sucker-like root by means of which a flowering parasite draws nourishment from its host.

Head, a form of inflorescence consisting of a more or less dense cluster of sessile flowers which are centripetal in evolution.

Hermaphrodite, bisexual; having both stamens and pistil in the same flower.

Heterogamous, said of flower-heads when male, female, bisexual and neuter florets, or any two or three of these, are borne on the same head.

Hilum, the place of attachment of an ovule or seed to the placenta or funicle.

Hirsute, thickly covered with long and rather coarse hairs.

Hispid, beset with rigid or bristly hairs.

Homogamous, said of a flower-head with the florets all of the same sex.

Hyaline, transparent or translucent and colourless.

Hypocrateriform, *salver-shaped;* said of a corolla with a slender tube abruptly expanded into a flat horizontal limb.

Hypogynous, inserted *below* the *ovary*.

Imbricate, overlapping so as to break joints like *tiles* on a roof.

Imparipinnate, *unequally pinnate;* pinnate with a terminal leaflet or pinna.

Incomplete, said of a flower wanting calyx or corolla or both.

Indumentum, a general term for any kind of hairy *covering* or coating produced by the epidermis.

Induplicate-valvate, said of members of a whorl when they touch one another with the margins of each folded inward.

Inferior, inserted below the ovary and free from it, if said of the calyx; adnate to, or situated below the calyx, if said of the ovary; also anterior, when said of the relative position of the parts of a flower in an inflorescence.

Inflorescence, the mode in which flowers are arranged on the stem. Also used as a collective term for the whole flowering portion of the stem of a plant with its branches, bracts, bracteoles and flowers.

Innate, said of an anther borne on the appex of the filament and with usually marginal dehiscence.

Integuments, the *coats* of an ovule or seed.

Interpetiolar, said of stipules of opposite leaves and inflorescences when they are inserted *between the petioles*, *i.e.*, across the stem.

Intrapetiolar, is applied to stipules of single leaves when they are connate by their margins so as to form apparently one stipule.

Introrse, applied to anthers that dehisce towards the pistil.

Intruded, projecting inward.

Involucre, a circle of bracts subtending a flower-cluster.

Involute, *rolled* inward.

Irregular, wanting in symmetry of form, said of flowers with the petals or perianth-segments unequal in size and shape.

Keel, the central dorsal ridge; like the prow of a boat, formed by the two anterior and innermost petals of a papilionaceous corolla.

Kernel, the contents of the putamen of a drupe.

Labiate, two-*lipped*.

Laciniate, irregularly cut or fringed into narrow lobes or segments with narrow sinuses.

Lanceolate, shaped like a *lance-head*, *i.e.*, 2-4 times as long as broad, narrowed at both ends, especially towards the apex, and broadest below the middle.

Lax, *diffuse*, said of an inflorescence when the flowers or fruits are notclosely arranged on it.

Legume, a fruit of a single carpel usually opening by both sutures when ripe. See **Pod**.

Lenticel, a *lentil*-shaped corky process developed on the bark of some trees. **Lenticellate**, having *lenticels*.

Lenticular, *lentil*-shaped; like a double-convex *lens*.

Ligule, anything shaped like a *strap*, such as the limb of the ray-corolla in some Compositæ. The thin and scarious projection from the summit of the sheath of the leaf of grasses. **Ligulate**, *strap*-shaped, usually applied to the ray-flowers of Compositæ.

Linear, narrower than lanceolate,—at least five times as long as broad.

Lobulate, divided into *small lobes*.

Loculicidal, applied to a kind of dehiscence in which the splitting takes place through the *cells*.

Loculus, the cell of an ovary; pl. **loculi**.

Lodicule, one of the small scales which represent the perianth in the flower of a grass, occurring usually in pairs.

Lyrate, pinnately lobed with a large terminal lobe and one or more pairs of small basal lobes, so as to resemble a *lyre*.

Mammillate, having *nipple*-like prominences.

Median, relating to the *middle*; in a plane radial to the axis of a plant.

Medullary rays, vertical plates of cellular tissue which radiate from the centre of a dicotyledonous plant towards the cambium.

Mesocarp, the middle layer of the pericarp.

Micropyle, the *minute orifice* in the coats of a seed represented by a scar, corresponding to the foramen of an ovule.

Monadelphous, said of stamens united by their filaments into *one set* forming a tube or column or sheath.

Moniliform, cylindrical and constricted at regular intervals so as to resemble a *necklace* of beads.

Monœcious, unisexual with the male and female flowers on the same individual.

Monopodial, pertaining to or of the nature of a *monopodium*, *i.e.*, a simple axis prolonged by means of a terminal bud.

Mucronate, abruptly terminating in a short straight stiff and sharp point.

Multifarious, in *many* vertical *rows*.

Multifid, cleft into *many* lobes or

Multiseriate, in *many series* or rows.

Needles, the acicular leaves of conifers.

Nerves, the principal lateral ribs of a leaf. **Nervose**, with nerves strongly developed.

Nucleus, the central part of an ovule or cell; pl. **nuclei**.

Nut, a hard indehiscent 1-seeded fruit resulting from a syncarpous ovary.

Obconic, inversely *conical*, *i.e.*, with the attachment at the pointed end.

Obcordate, inversely *cordate*, *i.e.*, broadly two-lobed with a notch at the apex.

Oblanceolate, inversely *lanceolate*, *i.e.*, long, narrow and tapering at both ends, but broadest above the middle. **Oblanceoloid**, said of a solid having an *oblanceolate* outline.

Oblong, much longer than broad with the sides nearly parallel.

Obovate, inversely *ovate*, *i.e.*, egg-shaped in outline with the broad end towards the apex.

Obovoid, said of a solid which is inversely egg-shaped in outline.

Obsolete, rudimentary, imperfectly developed.

Obtriangular, in the shape of an isosceles *triangle* with the attachment at the apex.

Operculum, a *lid*; a top which separates by a transverse line of separation.

Orbicular, **orbiculate**, flat with the outline circular or nearly so.

Order, a group of closely related Families of plants.

Ovary, that portion of the pistil which includes one or more cavities or cells containing one or more *ovules*.

Ovate, *egg-shaped* in outline with the broad end towards the base.

Ovoid, said of a solid with an ovate or oval longitudinal section.

Ovule, the immature or undeveloped seed in the *ovary*.

Palea, the innermost glume of the flower of a grass, or the chaffy scales on the receptacles of many Compositæ. **Paleaceous**, *chaff*-like.

Palmate, with the midribs of the lobes or leaflets all radiating from the apex of the petiole.

Palmatilobed, *palmately lobed*.

Palminerved, with nerves radiating like the ribs of a palmate leaf. **Palmatipartite**, with segments palmately separated almost to the base.

Pandurate, *fiddle*-shaped.

Panicle, an inflorescence in which the axis is divided into branches bearing two or more flowers; a compound raceme or compound irregular corymb.

Papilionaceous, *butterfly*-like; applied to the kind of corolla characteristic of the Pea tribe of Leguminosæ; like the flower of the Pea tribe. See **Keel**, **Wings** and **Standard**.

Papillose, bearing minute *nipple*-shaped projections.

Pappus, thistle-down; the hairy tufts on achenes and other fruits.

Paraboloidal, said of a solid having a *parabolic*, *i.e.*, ovate-oblong outline.

Parasite, a plant that grows on or in another plant, and draws nourishment from it.

Parietal, attached to the inner *wall* of an ovary.

Paripinnate, syn. abruptly pinnate, *evenly pinnate*; pinnate without the terminal leaflet or pinna.

Patent, widely *spreading*.

Pedate, like a bird's *foot*; palmately divided with the lateral divisions 2-cleft.

Pedicel, the ultimate stalk supporting a single flower in an inflorescence. **Pedicellate**, having a *pedicel*.

Peduncle, the stalk supporting a solitary flower or fruit or a cluster of flowers or fruits. **Pedunculate**, having a *peduncle*.

Pellucid, transparent or translucent.

Peltate, *target-shaped*; said of a flat body, generally a leaf, a bract or a stigma, attached to the stalk by the lower surface.

Penninerved, *pinnately nerved*; with nerves spreading laterally from various points on the midrib.

Pentafid, divided into *five* parts with broad notches extending from the margin to about half-way towards the common axis.

Pentamerous, having the members in each whorl of the flower in *fives*.

Penultimate, next to the *ultimate*.

Perianth, a floral envelope; a term especially used when the calyx and corolla are similar in form and texture, or are represented by a single whorl.

Pericarp, the portion of the fruit formed of the ovary and whatever adheres to it, exclusive of, and outside, the seeds.

Perigynous, inserted *around* but away from the *ovary*.

Persistent, remaining attached; generally said of a calyx or a corolla which remains attached until the fruit is mature.

Petal, one of the parts or leaves of the corolla, whether free or combined. **Petaloid**, resembling or having *petals*.

Petiole, the stalk of a leaf. **Petiolate**, having a *petiole*. **Petiolule**, the stalk of a leaflet. **Petiolulate**, having a *petiolule*.

Phloëm, the soft tissue of the inner bark which is formed by the outer portion of a vascular bundle.

Pilose, thinly sprinkled with long soft simple hairs.

Pinna, pl. pinnæ, the primary division of a bipinnate or tripinnate leaf. **Pinnule**, the secondary division of a tripinnate leaf.

Pinnate, a compound leaf is so called when the leaflets are arranged on either side of a common axis in the same way as are the webs of a *feather* on its shaft.

Pinnatisect, *pinnately cut* nearly to the common axis.

Pistil, the female organ of a flower consisting normally of ovary style and stigma. **Pistillode**, a rudimentary or barren pistil.

Placenta, that portion of the interior of an ovary on which the ovules are borne.

Plaited, plicate, folded in longitudinal *plaits*.

Plumose, *feathered;* said of bristles having fine hairs on either side like the *plume* or webs of a feather.

Pod, the same as Legume, but has a wider application, being used to denote any dry dehiscent many-seeded fruit, especially when it is much longer than broad.

Pollen, minute *powder*-like grains contained in the anther-cells,—the fertilizing agent of a plant.

Polyadelphous, having the stamens united by the filaments into *many sets* or bundles.

Polygamous, with hermaphrodite and unisexual flowers on one or different plants.

Polyphyllous, said of a perianth having *distinct leaves* or segments.

Pome, a succulent fruit with seeds in many cartilaginous dry cells, *e.g.*, the apple and the pear.

Pore, a minute passage or orifice.

Posterior, said of that part of a flower which is nearest to the axis of inflorescence; superior.

Prickle, a sharply-pointed stiff outgrowth of the epidermis.

Procumbent, **Prostrate**, lying flat or close to the ground.

Pruinose, covered with a *hoarfrost*-like bloom or powder.

Pseudocarp, a *false fruit;* one which has some portion other than the ovary so developed as to resemble a fruit.

Pubescent, covered with short soft straight simple *hairs*.

Puberulous, puberulent, minutely *pubescent*.

Punctate, dotted with small *punctures* or glands. **Punctulate**, minutely *punctate*.

Pungent, terminating in, or tapering gradually to, a hard sharp point.

Pustular, with small *blister*-like elevations.

Putamen, the shell of a nut; the hard endocarp of a drupe.

Pyrene, one of the small stones of a drupaceous fruit having more than one stone.

Pyriform, *pear-shaped;* obovoid with a tapering base.

Quadrangular, *four cornered*.

Quinquefoliolate, with *five leaflets*.

Raceme, an inflorescence of the indefinite kind in which the flowers are borne on pedicels of more or less the same length along a single undivided axis or rachis.

Rachis, the principal axis of a pinnate leaf or of an inflorescence. **Rachillum**, pl. **rachilla**, the *secondary rachis* of a compound spike; the *rachis* of a spikelet of grass.

Radicle, the axis of an embryo below the cotyledons.

Raphe, the cord or ridge which connects the hilum with the chalaza in an anatropous ovule.

Raphides, needle-shaped crystals found in the cells of some plants.

Ray, one of the radiating branches of an umbel. Ray-flowers, the marginal ligulate flowers of a head or circular flower-cluster.

Receptacle, the torus of a flower; hence also what is commonly known as the *fruit* of figs.

Regular, symmetrical; generally said of flowers with the petals or perianth-segments alike in size and shape.

Reniform, *kidney-shaped*; i.e., broader than long, broadly cordate at the base, and with the auricles rounded.

Repand, having a wavy margin.

Reticulate, having the veins connected together like the meshes of a *net*.

Retuse, with a small shallow notch in a rounded or truncate apex.

Revolute, having the margins or apex rolled backward upon the under surface.

Rhizome, an underground or prostrate jointed stem which sends off roots at the nodes and bears, like a true stem, buds, leaves, or scales.

Rhomboid, rhomboidal, with four sides more or less equal, and the lateral angles obtuse.

Rostrate, *beaked*; narrowed into a slender tip or process.

Rotate, *wheel-shaped*; said of a regular gamopetalous corolla with a short tube and a flat spreading limb.

Rotundate, circular or nearly so in outline.

Rugose, full of wrinkles. Rugulose, minutely wrinkled.

Ruminate, mottled; marked by transverse lines or divisions.

Sagittate, shaped like an *arrow-head*; tapering towards the apex, bifurcate at the base, with the lobes pointed and directed downward.

Samara, an indehiscent dry winged fruit.

Sarmentose, producing long straggling woody branches.

Scabrous, rough to the touch owing to short stiff hairs. Scaberulous, somewhat *scabrous*.

Scape, a leafless and generally unbranched flower-stem rising from the ground.

Scarious, scariose, thin, dry, membranous, somewhat stiff and not green.

Scorpioid, said of a form of unilateral inflorescence which is coiled inward from the apex in the bud like the tail of a *scorpion*.

Sepal, one of the parts or leaves of the calyx, especially when not combined.

Septicidal, dehiscing through the dissepiments or lines of junction.

Septifragal, opening by the valves breaking away from the dissepiments.

Septum, pl. Septa, see Dissepiment. Septate, divided by one or more partitions.

Serrate, toothed like a *saw* with the teeth directed forward. Serrulate, minutely *serrate*.

Sessile, attached directly without a stalk.

Setaceous, *bristle like*.

Sheath, a close-fitting tubular or enrolled case, e.g., the lower portion of the leaf of grasses,

Sigmoid, curved in two opposite directions like the Greek letter *sigma* or ς.

Simple, undivided; consisting of one blade when said of a leaf; resulting from a single pistil when said of a fruit; unbranched when said of a stem or tendril.

Sinistrorse, turning or twining from right to *left*, *i.e.*, in the clock-wise direction.

Sinus, the space between the divisions or lobes of a leaf. Sinuate, with an irregular wavy margin.

Spadix, a spike with a thickened or fleshy axis bearing 1-sexual flowers, generally sheathed in a *spathe*.

Spathe, a large sheath-like bract enclosing a spadix. Spathaceous, *spathe-like*.

Spathulate, shaped like a *spatula*, *i.e.*, broad and rounded at the apex but gradually narrowed towards the base.

Species, a group of individuals alike in all essential particulars; the subdivisions of a genus.

Spike, a form of indefinite inflorescence bearing sessile flowers on an undivided elongated common axis. Spicate, in the form of or resembling a *spike*, or disposed in *spikes*. Spikelet, a secondary *spike*; the ultimate flower-bearing stem of grasses including its glumes and flowers.

Spine, a strongly pointed woody process generally originating from the wood-tissue. Spinescent, terminating in, or resembling, a *spine-like* sharp point; also becoming spinous. Spinose, spinous, furnished with, or of the nature of, *spines*.

Spore, a minute unicellular body which detaches at maturity and performs, practically speaking, the same function in Cryptogams as the *seed* in Phanerogams.

Stamen, the male organ of a flower, consisting of a filament and an anther. Staminode, an abortive or antherless stamen.

Standard, the posterior or odd petal of a papilionaceous corolla.

Stellate, *star*-shaped; with radiating rays like the points of a star.

Stigma, that part of the pistil which receives the pollen for the fertilization of the ovules.

Stigmatic, relating to the *stigma*.

Stigmatose, resembling or of the nature of the *stigma*.

Stipe, any stalk-like support; the stalk of an ovary above the floral whorls. Syn. gynophore. Stipitate, having a *stipe*.

Stipule, an appendage of a leaf, usually one on either side of the petiole. Stipulate, having *stipules*. Stipel, a secondary *stipule*, the appendage of a leaflet. Stipellate, having *stipels*.

Stomata, pl. of Stoma, openings in the epidermis of plants with adaptations for regulating the passage of air and moisture.

Stone, the hard endocarp of a drupe. Syn. Putamen.

Striate, marked with thin longitudinal lines or minute furrows.

Strigose, covered with sharp-pointed straight stiff hairs of unequal length lying close along the surface, and all in the same direction.

Style, a *stalk* proceeding from the submit of the ovary and supporting the stigma.

Subulate, shaped like a cobbler's *awl;* narrow, tapering and somewhat stiff.

Superior, inserted on the ovary or adnate to it, if said of the calyx; above the calyx and free from it, if said of the ovary; also posterior in position.

Superposed, *placed* one *above* other.

Suture, a *seam* indicating the line of union of two parts; a line of opening.

Symmetrical, said of a flower having the same number of members in each whorl.

Syncarpous, composed of two or more *combined carpels*.

Syngenesious, said of stamens united by their anthers, as in Compositæ.

Tap-root, primary root resulting from the direct prolongation of the radicle.

Tendril, a slender process usually belonging to the axis and serving as a support in climbing.

Terete, cylindrical, *rounded* in cross section.

Ternate, arranged in *threes* in a cluster or whorl.

Testa, the outermost *coat* of a seed.

Tetramerous, said of a flower having the parts or members in each whorl in *fours*.

Tetrandrous, with *four stamens*.

Thalamus, that part of the axis of a flower which supports the floral whorls and the pistil. Syn. torus, receptacle.

Thyrsus or **thyrse**, a panicle, ovate or lanceolate in outline usually with cymose branches. **Thyrsiform**, of the shape of a *thyrsus*. **Thyrsoid** somewhat like a *thyrsus*.

Tissue, an aggregation of cells indicating differentiation from surrounding aggregations.

Tomentose, covered with hairs which are very short, soft, rather dense and more or less intricate.

Torulose, cylindrical with contractions at regular intervals.

Torus, same as receptacle or thalamus.

Tribe, a division of a Family, comprising a number of closely related genera.

Trichotomous, with the divisions always in *threes* and of more or less the same length.

Trimerous, said of a flower having the parts or members in each whorl in *threes*.

Trimorphic, having *three forms* of hermaphrodite flowers produced by the same species, but generally on different individuals. See dimorphic.

Triplinerved, with a strong secondary nerve on either side of the midrib proceeding from near the base.

Triquetrous, sharply *three-cornered*.

Tristichous, in *three* vertical *rows*.

Truncate, ending abruptly, as if with the end *cut off*.

Tuber, a thickened underground stem bearing buds or 'eyes.' **Tuberous**, swollen like a *tuber*.

Tumid, swollen.

Turbinate, *top-shaped;* like an inverted cone.

Turgid, *swollen* and more or less firm.

Umbel, a form of indefinite inflorescence in which several branches or pedicels radiate from the top of a common peduncle and are of nearly the same length.

Undulate, with a wavy margin.

Unicellular, formed of, or consisting of, only *one cell*.

Unisexual, of *one sex;* having the stamens and the pistil in separate flowers.

Urceolate, *urn-shaped;* tubular and contracted at or below the mouth.

Utricle, a 1-celled 1-seeded fruit with a thin and more or less loose pericarp.

Valvate, with the margins of the members of a whorl only meeting without overlapping. Also dehiscing by *valves*.

Variety, a group of individuals differing from others of the same species in certain striking particulars which, however, are not of a nature to justify specific rank; sub-divisions of a species.

Venation, the mode in which the *veins* are disposed in a leaf.

Ventral, relating to, inserted on, or opening by, the inner suture of a carpel.

Ventricle, a lateral swelling or bulging out. **Ventricose**, having a *ventricle;* unequally swollen.

Verrucose, covered with *wart*-like excrescences.

Versatile, swinging to and fro; said of an anther attached by the back to the top of the filament.

Verticillate, arranged in whorls.

Villous, more or less thickly covered with long soft simple hairs.

Viviparous, said of plants the seeds of which germinate before falling; also sometimes of such seeds.

Whorl, a collective name for all similar members that are arranged in a circle round an axis.

Wing, any thin membranous appendage. **Wings**, the side petals of a papilionaceous corolla.

Xylem, woody tissue which is formed by the inner portion of a fibrovascular bundle.

FOREST FLORA OF THE SIWALIK AND JAUNSAR FOREST DIVISIONS.

VEGETABLE KINGDOM.

Seed-bearing plants. Fertilization effected by pollen-tubes	I. PHANEROGAMS.
Ovules in closed ovary, fertilized through stigma. . . .	A. ANGIOSPERMS.
Cotyledons two; radicle elongated to form the primary root . . .	*a.* DICOTYLEDONS.
Calyx and corolla both present.[1]	
Corolla of distinct petals [2] . .	i. POLYPETALÆ.
Calyx of distinct sepals [3]; petals hypogynous.	
Torus small or elongated, not expanded . . .	1. Thalamifloræ
Torus thickened or expanded into a fleshy disk [4] . .	2. Discifloræ.
Calyx of combined sepals; disk thin; petals and stamens inserted on the calyx . .	3. Calycifloræ.
Corolla of combined petals [5] .	ii. GAMOPETALÆ.
Perianth single (and generally calycine), or none [6] . . .	iii. APETALÆ.
Cotyledon one; radicle not elongated to form the primary root . .	*b.* MONOCOTYLEDONS.
Ovules exposed, fertilized by direct contact with pollen-tubes . .	B. GYMMNOSPERMS
Spore-bearing plants. Fertilization not effected by pollen-tubes . .	II. CRYPTOGAMS.

---

1 *Exceptions.*—Petals wanting in some RANUNCULACEÆ, BIXACEÆ and STERCULIACEÆ among the THLAMIFLORÆ; in some RUTACEÆ, CELASTRACEÆ and RHAMNACEÆ among the DISCIFLORÆ; and in a few COMBRETACEÆ, MYRTACEÆ and SAMYDACEÆ among the CALYCIFLORÆ.

2 *Exceptions.*—Petals more or less combined in some TAMARICACEÆ and TERNSTRŒMIACEÆ among the THALAMIFLORÆ; in some OLACACEÆ, AQUIFOLIACEÆ and VITACEÆ among the DISCIFLORÆ; and in Sub-Family *MIMOSEÆ* of LEGUMINOSÆ among the CALYCIFLORÆ.

3 *Exceptions.*—Sepals combined in DIPTEROCARPACEÆ; MALVACEÆ and STERCULIACEÆ among the THALAMIFLORÆ and in BURSERACEÆ, MELIACEÆ, SAPINDACEÆ and some RUTACEÆ; RHAMNACEÆ and AQUIFOLIACEÆ among the DISCIFLORÆ.

4 *Exceptions.*—Disk obsolete in AQUIFOLIACEÆ, obscure in LINACEÆ and MALPIGHIACEÆ and wanting in CORIARIACEÆ.

5 *Exceptions.*—Petals free in some MYRSINACEÆ and STYRACEÆ.

6 *Exceptions.*—A few plants of Family EUPHORBIACEÆ and the female flowers of Genus *Juglans* of Family JUGLANDACEÆ have both calyx and corolla, and the perianth is double in Genus *Loranthus* of LORANTHACEÆ.

* The CRYPTOGAMS are not treated of in this Flora.

A. ANGIOSPERMS.—

a. DICOTYLEDONS.—

i. POLYPETALÆ.—

I. Thalamifloræ.

Stamens indefinite.
  Carpels more or less distinct or solitary [1]; stamens free.
    Herbs or soft-wooded climbing shrubs . 1. RANUNCULACEÆ.
    Generally trees or woody shrubs, rarely climbing (*e.g.*, *Schizandra* of Order 3).
      Sepals and petals usually 5, each in a single whorl, the former persistent 2. DILLENIACEÆ.
      Sepals and petals in threes, the latter in several whorls, both deciduous.
        Stipules [2] convolute; albumen even . 3 MAGNOLIACEÆ.
        Stipules 0; albumen ruminate . 4. ANONACEÆ.
  Carpels combined.
    Calyx-lobes imbricate in bud.
      Lvs. opposite, gland-dotted; stamens 3-or 5-adelphous . . . 11. HYPERICACEÆ.
      Lvs. alternate, not dotted; stamens usually free.
        Placentas axile . . . . 12 TERNSTRŒMIACEÆ.
        Placentas parietal
          Ovary long-stipitate; seeds exalbuminous . . 7. CAPPARIDACEÆ.
          Ovary sessile; seeds albuminous 8. BIXACEÆ.
    Calyx lobes valvate in bud.
      Calyx irregular, adnate to the ovary, lobes enlarged in fruit . 13. DIPTEROCARPACEÆ.
      Calyx regular, free, lobes not enlarged.
        Stamens monadelphous.
          Anthers 1-celled . . . . 14. MALVACEÆ.
          Anthers 2-celled . . . . 15. STERCULIACEÆ.
        Stamens distinct; anthers 2-celled . 16. TILIACEÆ.
Stamens few,—never more than 10.
  (Carpels more or less distinct in fruit.)
  Flowers 3-merous.
    Flowers minute; seeds curved . . 5. MENISPERMACEÆ.
    Flowers conspicuous; seeds not curved 6. BERBERIDACEÆ.
  Flowers 5-merous.
    Leaves fairly large; seeds not winged 9. PITTOSPORACEÆ.
    Leaves minute (scale-like); seeds winged . . . . 10. TAMARICACEÆ.

---

[1] Carpels combined in Genus *Anona* of Family ANONACEÆ.
[2] Stipules absent in Genus *Schizandra*.

A. ANGIOSPERMS.—

a. DICOTYLEDONS.—

i. POLYPETALÆ.—

2. Disciforæ.

Placentas axile; fruit not elongated.
Styles 1-5, quite free; filaments often connate at the base.
Leaves alternate; fruit not winged . 17. LINACEÆ.
Leaves opposite; fruit winged . . 18. MALPIGHIACEÆ.
Styles more or less combined or solitary; stamens generally free.
Flowers symmetrical.
Calyx imbricate.
Torus elongated in fr. below the ovary.
Lvs. dotted, aromatic; carpels combined (except in *Zanthoxylum*) 19. RUTACEÆ.
Lvs. not dotted, bitter or astringent; carpels distinct.
Lvs. alternate; stem terete . 20. SIMARUBACEÆ.
Lvs. opposite; stem 4-angular . 31. CORIARIACEÆ.
Torus not elongated below the ovary.
Plants resinous.
Lvs. dotted; fruit usually with more than one seed . . 21. BURSERACEÆ.
Lvs. not dotted; fruit 1-seeded (except in *Spondias*) . . 30. ANACARDIACEÆ.
Plants not resinous.
Stamens opposite to the petals . 29. SABIACEÆ.
Stamens alternating with the petals.
Disk obsolete . . . . 24. AQUIFOLIACEÆ.
Disk conspicuous . . . 25. CELASTRACEÆ.
Calyx valvate.
(Disk prominent; stamens opposite to the petals.)
Wood usually hard and close-grained, joints not swollen . . 26. RHAMNACEÆ.
Wood always soft and porous, joints swollen . . . . . 27. VITACEÆ.
Flowers not symmetrical (except in *Staphylea*), calyx imbricate . . . 28. SAPINDACEÆ.
Style solitary; stamens monadelphous (except in *Cedrela*); flowers symmetrical; calyx imbricate . . . . 22. MELIACEÆ.
Placentas free-central; fruit not elongated . 23. OLACACEÆ.
Placentas parietal; fruit a 3-valved elongated pod-like capsule . . . . . 32. MORINGACEÆ

A. ANGIOSPERMS.—

a. DICOTYLEDONS.—

i. POLYPETALÆ.—

3. Calycifloræ.

Calyx inferior, free[1]; leaves with or without stipules.
- Leaves stipulate.
  - Carpels distinct or solitary[2].
    - Fruit, a pod; calyx with the odd lobe inferior, *i.e.*, anterior . . . 33. LEGUMINOSÆ.
    - Fruit various, not a pod; calyx with the odd lobe superior, *i.e.*, posterior . . . . . 34. ROSACEÆ.
  - Carpels more or less combined.
    - Leaves alternate, usually dotted . 41. SAMYDACEÆ.
    - Leaves opposite, not dotted . 36. RHIZOPHORACEÆ.
- Leaves exstipulate; carpels combined . 40. LYTHRACEÆ.

Calyx superior or more or less adnate to the ovary; leaves exstipulate.
- Style simple.
  - Connective of anthers without any appendage.
    - Leaves aromatic, gland-dotted . 38. MYRTACEÆ.
    - Leaves not aromatic, not dotted.
      - Ovary 1-celled; fruit angled or winged . . 37. COMBRETACEÆ.
      - Ovary 1-4-celled; fruit not angled or winged . . . 43. CORNACEÆ.
  - Connective of anthers tubercled or spurred . . . . . 39. MELASTOMACEÆ.
- Styles 2 or more.
  - Stamens usually 10[3]; ovules numerous in each cell . . . 35. SAXIFRAGACEÆ.
  - Stamens rarely more than 5; ovule solitary in each cell . 42. ARALIACEÆ.

---

[1] Calyx ultimately superior and adnate to the ovary in *Rosa*, *Pyrus*, *Cratægus* and *Cotoneaster* of Family ROSACEÆ.

[2] Carpels combined in *Pyrus*, *Cratægus* and *Cotoneaster* of Family ROSACEÆ.

[3] Excepting *Itea* and *Ribes* which have 4-5 stamens.

A. ANGIOSPERMS.—
a. DICOTYLEDONS.—
ii. GAMOPETALÆ.

Ovary inferior or adnate to the calyx—*Ser. 1. EPIGYNÆ.*

- Ovary usually with more than 1 cell; anthers not united.
  - Lvs. opposite; stamens 4-5.
    - Lvs. usually exstipulate . . . 44. CAPRIFOLIACEÆ.
    - Lvs. always stipulate (unless whorled) . 45. RUBIACEÆ.
  - Lvs. alternate, (exstip.); stamens 8 or more 51. STYRACEÆ.
- Ovary 1-celled; anthers united . . . 46. COMPOSITÆ.

Ovary superior or free.[1]—*Ser. 2. HYPOGYNÆ.*

- Leaves alternate.
  - Stamens inserted on the receptacle.
    - Anthers opening at the apex . . . 47. ERICACEÆ.
    - Anthers opening inwards . . . 50. EBENACEÆ.
  - Stamens inserted on the corolla.
    - Ovules indefinite; inforescence often extra-axillary . . . 58. SOLANACEÆ.
    - Ovules definite; inflorescence axillary (often terminal in Order 56).
      - Lvs. dotted; juice not milky . . 48. MYRSINACEÆ.
      - Lvs. not dotted; juice often milky .
        - Prostrate or climbing plants . . 57. CONVOLVULACEÆ.
        - Large erect shrubs or trees . . 49. SAPOTACEÆ
      - Lvs. not dotted; juice not milky . 56. BORAGINACEÆ.
- Leaves opposite.[2]
  - Flowers regular; ovary of 2 carpels.
    - Stamens 2 . . . . 52. OLEACEÆ.
    - Stamens 5. Juice generally milky.
      - Filaments united into a tube, anthers adnate to the stigma . . . 54. ASCLEPIADACEÆ.
      - Filaments free, anthers not adnate to the stigma . . . 53. APOCYNACEÆ.
    - Stamens 4 or 5. Juice not milky . 55. LOGANIACEÆ.
  - Flowers irregular; ovary of 2 to 4 carpels.
    - Fruit elongated, seeds winged . . 59. BIGNONIACEÆ.
    - Fruit not elongated, seeds not winged.
      - Bracts conspicuous; stem with swollen joints . 60. ACANTHACEÆ.
      - Bracts minute or absent; joints of stem not swollen.
        - Ovary entire, style terminal . 61. VERBENACEÆ
        - Ovary 4-lobed, style gynobasic . 62. LABIATÆ.

---

[1] Ovary half-inferior in *Mæsa*, Family MYRSINACEÆ.

[2] Leaves alternate in *Jasminum humile*, Family OLEACEÆ.

A. ANGIOSPERMS.—

a. DICOTYLEDONS.—

iii. APETALÆ.

Flowers 2-sexual.[1]
- Ovary superior, 1-celled.
  - Stamens opening by valves. (Aromatic plants) . . . . . 65. LAURACEÆ.
  - Stamens opening by longitudinal slits.
    - Flowers bracteate.
      - Leaves stipulate. Plants prostrate or climbing, aromatic 64. PIPERACEÆ.
      - Leaves exstipulate. Plants usually herbaceous, not aromatic . 63. AMARANTACEÆ.
    - Flowers ebracteate [2].
      - Plants covered with silvery scales 67. ELÆAGNACEÆ.
      - Plants not covered with silvery scales . . . . . . 66. THYMELÆACEÆ.
- Ovary inferior, 1-celled.
  - Plants parasitic on stems; ovule solitary, erect . . . . 68. LORANTHACEÆ. (*Loranthus*)
  - Plants often parasitic on roots; ovules 2-5, pendulous . . . . . 69. SANTALACEÆ.

Flowers 1-sexual.
- Flowers not in catkins or spikes (except in *Morus*, URTICACEÆ).
  - Ovary 1-celled, 1-ovuled.
    - Leaves opposite and exstipulate, or 0; ovary inferior. Parasitic plants . 68. LORANTHACEÆ. (*Viscum*.)
    - Leaves usually alternate, stipulate; ovary superior. Not parasitic . 71. URTICACEÆ.
  - Ovary 3-celled with 1 or 2 ovules in each cell, superior . . . . 70. EUPHORBIACEÆ.
- Male (sometimes also female) flowers in catkins or spikes.
  - Leaves simple, exstipulate; ovary superior . . . . . 72. MYRICACEÆ.
  - Leaves pinnate, exstipulate; (flowers monœcious); ovary inferior. . 74. JUGLANDACEÆ.
  - Leaves simple, stipulate.
    - Flowers diœcious; ovary superior; seeds hairy . . . . . 73. SALICACEÆ.
    - Flowers monœcious; ovary inferior; seeds not hairy . . . . 75. FAGACEÆ.

---

[1] Flowers 1-sexual and diœcious in *Piper*, Family PIPERACEÆ, and in *Litsœa*, Family LAURACEÆ.

[2] Flowers bracteate in *Daphne cannabina*, Family THYMELÆACEÆ.

A. ANGIOSPERMS.—

b. MONOCOTYLEDONS.

Flowers with a coloured perianth, solitary umbelled or racemed; fruit a capsule or a berry.—Sub-class i. *PETALOIDEÆ.*

Flowers irregular; ovary inferior . . 76. SCITAMINEÆ.
Flowers regular; ovary superior . . 77. LILIACEÆ.

Flowers not coloured, arranged in a spadix; fruit a berry or a drupe.—Sub-class ii. *SPADICIFLORÆ.*

Perianth biseriately 6-lobed; plants usually woody . . 78. PALMÆ.
Perianth none or rudimentary; plants herbaceous.
Inflorescence naked; leaves sessile, linear . . . . 79. TYPHACEÆ.
Inflorescence inside a spathe; leaves usually long-petioled and broad . 80. ARACEÆ.

Flowers glumaceous, arranged in spikelets; fruit a caryopsis.—Sub-class iii. *GLUMIFLORÆ.*

Sheath of leaf entire; stem 3-quetrous; flower subtended by a single glume 81. CYPERACEÆ.
Sheath of leaf usually split: stem terete; flower subtended by several glumes 82. GRAMINEÆ.

B. GYMNOSPERMS.—

Branches articulate; leaves opposite, rudimentary or broad . . . . 83. GNETACEÆ.
Branches not articulate; leaves alternate or fascicled, usually acicular or linear . . . . . 84. CONIFERÆ.

ANALYTICAL SYNOPSIS OF THE ORDERS AND FAMILIES.

I. PHANEROGAMS.

Plants representing the greatest morphological differentiation and generally the highest vegetative development, and producing *seeds*, as distinct from *spores*, for the purpose of reproduction.

A. ANGIOSPERMS.

Plants representing the highest evolution of the flower. *Anthers* borne normally on well-developed *filaments*. *Ovary* closed, crowned by a *stigma* which is in most cases borne by a *style*. *Fertilization* is effected by the pollen-tubes reaching the egg-cell of the ovule after penetrating the stigmatic tissue.

a. DICOTYLEDONS.

Plants with roots which usually branch from the prolongation of the radicle; wood and bark separated by a cambium layer. *Leaves* reticulately veined. *Flowers* usually 4- or 5-merous. ***Embryo with two cotyledons.***

i. POLYPETALÆ.

Flowers with both *calyx* and *corolla*, ***the latter of distinct petals.***

I. THALAMIFLORÆ.

Torus not expanded. *Flowers* generally regular. *Calyx* inferior, usually of distinct *sepals*. *Corolla* hypogynous, usually of distinct *petals*. *Stamens* hypogynous. *Ovary* superior.

Order 1. Ranales.

Flowers usually regular, sometimes apetalous. *Stamens* generally indefinite. *Ovary* apocarpous. *Seeds* albuminous.

1. **Ranunculaceæ.** Generally erect herbs (rarely climbing shrubs) *Sepals* deciduous, often petaloid. *Petals* sometimes wanting. *Stamens* indefinite. *Carpels* numerous, usually free.

2. **Dilleniaceæ.** Usually trees or shrubs. *Leaves* alternate, simple, exstipulate. *Sepals* 5, fleshy, imbricate; persistent. *Petals* 5, caducous. *Stamens* ndefinite, in many series. *Seeds* usually arillate.

3. **Magnoliaceæ.** Trees or shrubs. *Leaves* alternate, simple, generally with convolute deciduous stipules. *Sepals* and *petals* alike, in whorls of three, imbricate, deciduous. *Stamens* indefinite, free or monadelphous. *Carpels* numerous, usually on an elongated torus. *Albumen* uniform.

4. **Anonaceæ.** Trees or shrubs. *Leaves* alternate, simple, exstipulate. *Flowers* 3-merous. *Sepals* 3, valvate. *Petals* fleshy, valvate, usually in two 3-merous series. *Stamens* usually indefinite. *Albumen* ruminated.

5. **Menispermaceæ.** Generally climbing shrubs. *Leaves* alternate, exstipulate. *Flowers* trimerous, small, usually 1-sexual and diœcious. *Stamens* generally 6 in two series, opposite to the petals. *Carpels* usually 3; style usually lateral in fruit. *Seed* crescent-shaped. *Albumen* even or ruminated.

6. **Berberidaceæ.** *Leaves* alternate or fascicled, glabrous. *Sepals* and *petals* alike, generally 3-merous, caducous. *Stamens* opposite to the petals; anthers opening usually by valves. *Fruit* usually of one carpel. *Seeds* not curved.

Order 2. Parietales.

Leaves usually alternate. *Flowers* with both *sepals* and *petals*. *Ovary* syncarpous, 1-2- or more-celled; ovules numerous. *Placentation* parietal.

7. **Capparidaceæ.** *Flowers* 4-merous, often irregular. *Stamens* 4-8, or numerous. *Ovary* 1-celled; usually long-stipitate. *Seeds* exalbuminous.

8. **Bixaceæ.** *Leaves* simple. *Flowers* regular, sometimes unisexual. *Sepals* 4-5. *Petals* 4-5; or 0. *Stamens* numerous. *Ovary* normally 1-celled. *Seeds* albuminous.

Order 3. Ploygales.

Leaves alternate, simple, entire. *Calyx* and *Corolla* both present. *Stamens* not indefinite. *Ovary* syncarpous. *Placentation* usually axile.

9. **Pittosporaceæ.** Shrubs or small trees. *Leaves* simple, entire, exstipulate. *Flowers* regular, 5-merous. *Stamens* 5, alternating with the petals. *Ovary* normally 1-celled. *Fruit* a 2-valved capsule. *Seeds* albuminous.

Order 4. Caryophyllales.

Leaves simple, opposite or alternate. *Flowers* generally 5-merous. *Calyx* often gamosepalous. *Stamens* usually definite. *Ovary* 1-celled. *Placenta* central, ultimately free. *Seeds* usually albuminous.

10. **Tamaricaceæ.** Shrubs or small trees. *Leaves* alternate, reduced to minute scales. *Flowers* regular, generally 5-merous. *Sepals* and *petals* imbricate, free or connate below. *Stamens* 5 or 10, rarely 4 or 8; anthers versatile. *Fruit* a capsule. *Seeds* hairy or winged.

Order 5. Guttiferales.

Generally erect shrubs or trees. *Leaves* simple. *Flowers* regular, 2-sexual, generally 5-merous. *Calyx* imbricate. *Stamens* usually indefinite. *Ovary* syncarpous. *Placenta* axile. *Seeds* exalbuminous.

11. **Hypericaceæ.** Erect shrubs. *Leaves* opposite, exstipulate, generally gland-dotted. *Sepals* and *petals* 5. *Stamens* indefinite, 3-5-adelphous. *Fruit* a capsule. *Seeds* numerous.

12. **Ternstrœmiaceæ.** Shrubs, rarely climbing, or trees. *Leaves* alternate, exstipulate. *Sepals* 5, imbricate. *Petals* 5, often more or less united at the base. *Filaments* often connate or adnate to the base of the corolla. *Ovary* 3-5-celled.

13. **Dipterocarpaceæ.** Resinous trees. *Leaves* alternate; stipules generally inconspicuous and early caducous. *Sepals* 5, connate in flower, persistent, 2 or more accrescent in fruit. *Petals* 5, twisted. *Stamens* numerous (in *Shorea*); anthers with an aristate connective. *Fruit* indehiscent, 1-seeded, generally winged with enlarged calyx-lobes. *Cotyledons* fleshy.

Order 6. Malvales.

Usually erect shrubs or herbs, or trees, with mucilaginous and fibrous bark. *Leaves* alternate, simple palmately lobed or digitate, stipulate, usually stellately hirsute. *Flowers* regular, generally 2-sexual, often bracteate. *Sepals* 5, valvate. *Petals* 5, rarely 4. *Stamens* usually many. *Ovary* generally syncarpous, sometimes stipitate. *Albumen* scanty or 0.

14. **Malvaceæ.** Young parts usually stellate-hairy. *Flowers* supported by bracteoles which generally form an epicalyx. *Petals* twistedly imbricate. *Stamens* 1-adelphous, rarely 5-adelphous; anthers 1-celled. *Carpels* usually many; styles more or less connate.

15. **Sterculiaceæ.** Young parts more or less pubescent. *Flowers* sometimes 1-sexual. *Sepals* 5, valvate, more or less connate. *Petals* 5, connate at the base or 0. *Filaments* monadelphous with 5-many 2-celled extrorse anthers. *Ovary* stipitate or sessile; syncarpous or apocarpous. *Fruit* a capsule or of distinct follicles.

16. **Tiliaceæ.** *Sepals* 3-5, free or connate; valvate. *Petals* 3-5, usually free rarely absent. *Stamens* indefinite, distinct; anthers 2-celled, introrse. *Ovary* free, 2-10-celled. *Fruit* a drupe or a capsule.

2. DISCIFLORÆ.

Torus generally expanded into a fleshy disk between the petals and the ovary. *Sepals* distinct or connate, generally small. *Petals* distinct or more or less coherent at the base or at the apex (as in some VITACEÆ), inserted on or outside the hypogynous *disk*. *Ovary* superior.

Order 1. Geraniales.

Flowers usually 5-merous. *Stamens* generally twice the number of petals. *Disk* sometimes wanting. *Ovules* 1 or 2 in each cell, pendulous; raphe ventral.

* *Leaves simple, generally stipulate. Flowers regular or irregular.*

17. **Linaceæ.** *Leaves* alternate, usually entire. *Flowers* regular, 2-sexual. *Sepals* entire, imbricate. *Petals* contorted in bud, each with a gland at the base, representing the *disk*. *Stamens* 5 and alternating with as many staminodes, or 10, adnate to the glands of the disk; anthers versatile. *Ovary* 3-5-celled; styles 3-5. *Fruit* a capsule. *Seeds* often albuminous.

18. **Malpighiaceæ.** Usually climbing shrubs. *Leaves* opposite, generally exstipulate. *Flowers* 2-sexual, often irregular. *Calyx* 5-partite, usually with a large gland outside. *Petals* 5, imbricate. *Disk* obscure. *Ovary* 3-celled; styles 1-3. *Fruit* of 1-3 samaras. *Seeds* exalbuminous.

** *Leaves pinnately compound, generally exstipulate. Flowers regular.*

19. **Rutaceæ.** *Leaves* usually alternate, pellucid-punctate. Calyx small, of 4-5 imbricate lobes. *Petals* 4-5, generally imbricate. *Stamens* up to 10, rarely more. *Disk* annular or cylindical, within the stamens. *Ovary* of 4-5 free or connate carpels; styles 1-5. *Fruit* various.

20. **Simarubaceæ.** Trees or erect shrubs with bitter bark. *Leaves* alternate. *Flowers* usually 1-sexual. *Calyx* small; 3-5 lobed. *Petals* valvate or imbricate. *Stamens* up to 10, inserted at the base of the disk. *Ovary* often deeply lobed. *Fruit* drupaceous or samaroid. *Seeds* usually albuminous.

21. **Burseraceæ.** Resinous trees or erect shrubs. *Leaves* alternate. *Flowers* 2-sexual or polygamous. *Calyx* 3-7-lobed: often minute. *Petals* 3-7, imbricate or valvate. *Disk* annular or cupular. *Stamens* up to 10, inserted at the base or on the margin of the disk. *Ovary* 2-5-celled; style simple. *Fruit* a drupe. *Seeds* exalbuminous.

22. **Meliaceæ.** Mostly trees. *Leaves* alternate. *Flowers* generally 2-sexual. *Calyx* 3-6-lobed. *Petals* 3-6, generally imbricate. *Stamens* up to 12; filaments usually connate into a tube. *Disk* hypogynous, inside the staminal tube. *Ovary* 2-5-celled; style single. *Fruit* various. *Seeds* albuminous in the local species.

Order 2. Olacales.

Leaves simple, usually alternate; stipules 0 or inconspicuous. *Flowers* regular, often 1-sexual, usually 5-merous. *Calyx* generally persistent. *Filaments* more or less connate, often adnate to the petals. *Disk* sometimes wanting. *Style* simple or 0. *Ovules* pendulous; raphe dorsal. *Fruit* drupaceous. *Seeds* albuminous.

23. **Olacaceæ.** *Leaves* exstipulate. *Petals* valvate. *Disk* cup-shaped. *Fertile stamens* 3-5. *Ovary* spuriously 3-5-celled; placenta central. *Fruit* 1-celled, 1-seeded.

24. **Aquifoliaceæ.** *Leaves* alternate; stipules minute and caducous. *Flowers* usually 1-sexual, often diœcious; sepals and petals more or less connate at the base. *Filaments* subulate, generally free in the female or 2-sexual flowers, adnate to the base of the corolla in male flowers. *Disk* 0. *Style* short or 0. *Fruit* a drupe with 2 or more stones.

Order 3. Celastrales.

Trees or shrubs. *Leaves* mostly simple, stipulate. *Flowers* regular, 4-5-merous, cymose. *Stamens* as many as petals. *Disk* conspicuous. *Ovary* 2-6-celled, sometimes sunk in the disk; style simple, rarely 0. *Ovules* erect; raphe ventral. *Seeds* usually albuminous.

25. **Celastraceæ.** *Leaves* opposite or alternate. *Flowers* 2-sexual or polygamous. *Calyx* imbricate, persistent. *Petals* imbricate, often 0. *Stamens* alternating with the petals or (if petals 0) opposite to the calyx-lobes. *Ovules* usually 2 in each cell. *Seeds* mostly arillate, sometimes winged.

26. **Rhamnaceæ.** *Leaves* generally alternate; stipules sometimes turned into prickles. *Flowers* small, greenish or pale. *Calyx* sometimes superior; lobes valvate, triangular. *Petals* generally involute, usually shorter than the calyx-lobes, sometimes 0. *Disk* fleshy. *Stamens* opposite to the petals or (when petals 0) alternating with the calyx-lobes; anthers versatile. *Ovary* usually 3-celled, with 1 ovule in each cell.

27. **Vitaceæ.** Mostly cirrhose climbing shrubs. *Leaves* alternate, simple or variously compound. *Flowers* usually 2-sexual. *Calyx-lobes* and petals valvate, the latter often cohering and caducous. *Disk* fleshy. *Stamens* opposite to the petals; filaments subulate; anthers introrse. *Style* short or 0. *Ovules* 1-2 in each cell. *Fruit* a berry.

Order 4. Sapindales.

Generally erect shrubs or trees. *Leaves* alternate (except in *Acer*, *Staphylea* and *Coriaria*) and exstipulate (except in *Staphylea*). *Flowers* regular or irregular, sometimes 1-sexual. *Calyx-lobes* imbricate. *Petals* free. *Stamens* free, generally some wanting or barren. *Disk* present (except in *Coriaria*). *Ovules* ascending or pendulous from an erect funicle; raphe ventral. *Seeds* generally exalbuminous.

28. **Sapindaceæ.** *Flowers* often irregular. *Petals* 4-5, sometimes 0. *Disk* complete or one-sided. *Stamens* hypogynous, generally 8. *Ovary* generally 3 celled, sometimes eccentric; style usually terminal. *Seeds* sometimes arillate, usually with a large hilum.

29. **Sabiaceæ.** *Flowers* generally small, usually 2-sexual. *Petals* often unequal. *Disk* small, annular. *Stamens* opposite to the petals; sometimes unequal and then only 2 or 3 perfect. *Seeds* with a broad hilum, sometimes compressed.

30. **Anacardiaceæ.** Trees or shrubs, usually resinous. *Flowers* regular, small. *Petals* free. *Disk* annular. *Stamens* sometimes not all perfect. *Ovary* 1-celled. *Fruit* usually a 1-seeded drupe.

31. **Coriariaceæ.** Erect shrubs with quadrangular branches. *Leaves* opposite or whorled, simple. *Flowers* regular, 2-sexual. *Sepals* 5, spreading. *Petals* 5, keeled, accrescent in fruit. *Disk* 0. *Stamens* 10; anthers exserted. *Carpels* usually 5, free, embraced by the fleshy petals.

32. **Moringaceæ.** Trees with soft wood. *Leaves* 2- or 3-pinnate, glandular at the base. *Flowers* irregular, 2-sexual. *Calyx* petaloid, segments deciduous. *Petals* 5, unequal. *Disk* lining the calyx-tube. *Stamens* on the edge of the disk, declinate, 5 fertile and opposite to the petals alternating with 5 antherless filaments. *Ovary* stalked, 1-celled; ovules on 3 parietal placentas. *Fruit* a pod-like 3-angled loculicidal capsule. *Seeds* usually winged.

3. CALYCIFLORÆ.

Calyx gamosepalous. Disk thin, often lining the calyx-tube. *Petals* and *stamens* inserted on the calyx or on the disk when it is adnate to the calyx. *Ovary* superior or inferior.

Order 1. Rosales.

Leaves generally alternate, stipulate (*Leguminosæ* and *Rosaceæ*) or exstipulate (*Saxifragaceæ*, etc.). *Ovary* of one or more free or connate carpels; styles usually as many as carpels. *Seeds* generally exalbuminous in the first two Families, albuminous in the others.

33. **Leguminosæ.** *Leaves* alternate, stipulate, usually compound. *Flowers* 2-sexual, generally irregular. *Calyx* often 2-lipped with the odd lobe inferior. *Petals* normally 5, usually free, sometimes very unequal. *Stamens* normally 10 and declinate, or numerous and straight. *Ovary* quite free, 1-celled ovules one or more on the ventral suture. *Fruit* a 1-many-seeded pod. *Seeds* exalbuminous except in some *Cæsalpinieæ*.

34. **Rosaceæ.** *Leaves* alternate, stipulate, simple or compound. *Flowers* regular, usually 2-sexual. *Calyx* with the odd lobe superior. *Stamens* many, distinct. *Ovary* of 1 or more free or connate carpels · ovules not more than 2 in each carpel. *Fruit* various, but never a pod or a berry, usually 1-seeded.

35. **Saxifragaceæ.** Herbs or shrubs. *Leaves* opposite or alternate, simple, exstipulate. *Flowers* regular; generally 2-sexual. *Calyx* more or less adnate to the ovary. *Petals* 5, rarely 4 or 0. *Stamens* 5, or 10, or numerous. *Ovary* 2-5-celled; styles as many as the carpels. *Fruit* a berry or a capsule. *Seeds* many, albuminous.

Order 2. Myrtales.

Leaves simple, generally exstipulate. *Flowers* regular, usually 2-sexual. *Stamens* at least twice the number of petals. *Ovary* generally inferior; style 1; ovules as a rule pendulous. *Seeds* exalbuminous (in the local Families).

36. **Rhizophoraceæ.** *Leaves* opposite, with caducous stipules. *Flowers* 2-sexual. *Calyx* 4-14-toothed. *Petals* as many as the calyx-teeth. *Stamens* 2-4-times the number of petals. *Ovary* 5-1-celled; ovules 2 in each cell, pendulous. *Fruit* 1-celled, 1-seeded.

37. **Combretaceæ.** *Leaves* opposite or alternate, exstipulate. *Flowers* rarely 1-sexual. *Calyx-lobes* 4-5, valvate. *Petals* 4-5 or 0. *Stamens* as many or twice as many as the petals. *Ovary* 1-celled; ovules pendulous. *Fruit* usually a 1-seeded drupe.

38. **Myrtaceæ.** *Leaves* typically opposite and then gland-dotted. *Calyx-limb* short, 4-5 toothed or entire. *Petals* generally 4, free or united in a calyptra. *Stamens* indefinite; anthers often versatile. *Ovary* 1-many-celled, with one, few or many ovules. *Seeds* generally angular.

39. **Melastomaceæ.** *Leaves* opposite or whorled, entire, 3-7-nerved from the base. *Flowers* generally showy; 2-sexual. *Calyx-tube* constricted above, limb 3-5-lobed. *Petals* 3-5, twisted in bud. *Stamens* 4-10; anthers usually opening by pores; connective tubercled or spurred. *Ovary* 3-5-celled; ovules many; style simple. *Fruit* a many-seeded capsule.

40. **Lythraceæ.** *Leaves* entire, generally opposite, exstipulate. *Flowers* 2-sexual *Calyx* inferior (except in *Punica*), lobes 3-6; valvate. *Petals* as many as calyx-lobes or 0. *Stamens* definite or indefinite. *Ovary* superior (except in *Punica*); style simple, persistent; ovules many on an axile placenta. *Fruit* a capsule; seeds numerous.

Order 3. Passiflorales.

Mostly herbaceous plants. *Leaves* alternate, simple, often lobed, stipulate. *Flowers* regular, 2-sexual or 1-sexual, showy except in *Samydaceæ*. *Ovary* superior or inferior, 1-3-celled, exceptionally 5-celled; style single or 2-4; placentas parietal. *Fruit* 1-celled. *Seeds* generally arillate, usually albuminous.

41. **Samydaceæ.** Generally trees. *Leaves* often punctate. *Flowers* small. *Calyx* inferior, 4-5-lobed. *Petals* generally 0. *Stamens* definite or indefinite, usually united into a hypogynous tube. *Ovary* superior, 1-celled; style single, placentas 3. *Fruit* a capsule. *Seeds* arillate and albuminous.

Order 4. Umbellales.

Leaves mostly alternate, simple or compound, usually exstipulate. *Flowers* regular, usually 2-sexual, often in heads or umbels. *Calyx-tube* adnate to the ovary. *Petals* 5, rarely more or 0, generally valvate. *Disk* epigynous, conspicuous. *Ovary* inferior, generally 2-celled, with one ovule in each cell; style solitary or as many as the cells. *Fruit* various. *Seeds* pendulous, albuminous.

42. **Araliaceæ.** *Petioles* long, usually clasping the stem; stipules adnate to the petiole or 0. *Flowers* small, 2-sexual or polygamous. *Calyx-limb* short,

truncate or with small teeth. *Petals* usually 5, normally valvate, deciduous. *Stamens* as many as the petals, inserted on the disk; anthers versatile. *Ovary* 2-5-celled; styles as many as the cells. *Fruit* a drupe or a berry.

43. **Cornaceae.** Shrubs or trees. *Leaves* simple, opposite or alternate, entire. *Flowers* in heads, cymes or panicles. *Calyx-limb* truncate or with small teeth. *Petals* 4-5, valvate, or none. *Stamens* generally as many as the petals, rarely more. *Ovary* 1-4-celled; style single. *Fruit* usually a succulent drupe.

ii. GAMOPETALÆ.

Flowers usually 2-sexual. ***Calyx and corolla both present, the latter with the petals more or less connate,*** rarely completely free. *Stamens* usually inserted on the corolla.

Series i. EPIGYNÆ.

Stamens epipetalous, alternating with the corolla-lobes. *Ovary* inferior.

Order 1. Rubiales.

Leaves simple, opposite or whorled. *Flowers* 4-5-merous, generally regular, 2-sexual. *Calyx* incised. *Corolla-tube* generally not short. *Ovary* 2-8-celled; style simple; ovules pendulous. *Seeds* albuminous.

44. **Caprifoliaceae.** *Leaves* as a rule exstipulate. *Flowers* 5-merous, bracteate, in corymbose or panicled cymes, sometimes in pairs; æstivation imbricate. *Stamens* inserted on the corolla-tube between the lobes; anthers versatile. *Ovary* 1-6-celled; ovules solitary and pendulous or many on axile placentas.

45. **Rubiaceae.** *Leaves* opposite and with interpetiolar stipules, or whorled. *Flowers* 4-5-merous, regular. *Corolla* tubular or rotate, lobes sometimes valvate. *Stamens* 4-5, inserted on the corolla-tube and alternating with the corolla-lobes. *Ovary* generally 2-celled, less often 3-5-celled, rarely 1-celled; ovules anatropous, 1 or more in each cell.

Order 2. Asterales.

Mostly herbs. *Leaves* opposite or alternate, generally exstipulate. *Flowers* usually sessile. *Calyx* generally inconspicuous. *Corolla* regular or irregular. *Stamens* on the corolla-tube. *Ovary* usually 1-celled, 1-ovuled. *Seeds* erect and exalbuminous in *Compositæ*, pendulous and often albuminous in other Orders.

46. **Compositae.** Herbs or shrubs. *Leaves* generally alternate, exstipulate. *Flowers* sessile in heads. *Calyx-limb* represented by hairs or scales or absent,

Corolla-lobes 5 and valvate in disk-flowers, ligulate in ray-flowers. *Disk* epigynous. *Stamens* 4-5, on the corolla-tube; filaments usually free; anthers usually syngenesious. *Ovary* 1-celled, with one erect ovule; style slender, 2-fid. *Fruit* a cypsela. *Seeds* exalbuminous.

Series ii. *HYPOGYNÆ.*

Stamens epipetalous, or free and hypogynous, 4-5 or more. *Ovary* superior.

* *Carpels more than two.* (*Leaves simple, generally exstipulate. Flowers regular.*)

Order 3. Ericales.

Leaves alternate, exstipulate. *Flowers* regular. *Stamens* usually hypogynous, often twice the number of corolla-lobes; filaments free. *Fruit* generally a capsule. *Seeds* many, albuminous.

47. **Ericaceæ.** *Flowers* solitary, fascicled or racemed. *Calyx* free, usually 5-lobed. *Corolla* campanulate or urceolate. *Stamens* generally twice as many as the corolla-lobes; anthers usually opening at top by pores or slits. *Ovary* 4-5-many-celled; ovules many. *Seeds* small.

Order 4. Primulales.

Leaves generally alternate, exstipulate. *Corolla*-tube generally short, or petals almost free. *Stamens* usually on the corolla-tube, always opposite to the lobes. *Style* solitary (except in PLUMBAGINEÆ).[1] *Ovary* 1-celled; placentation free-central. *Seeds* usually albuminous.

48. **Myrsinaceæ.** *Leaves* alternate, gland-dotted. *Flowers* small, inflorescence generally axile. *Calyx* sometimes adnate to the ovary; lobes persistent. *Petals* nearly or completely free. *Anthers* free or united by their margins. *Fruit* a berry. *Seeds* generally solitary and excavate at the base.

Order 5. Ebenales.

Trees or shrubs. *Leaves* alternate, exstipulate. *Flowers* usually 4-merous. *Calyx* generally persistent. *Corolla-tube* short. *Stamens* epipetalous, as many as the corolla-lobes and opposite to them or 2-3 times as many in several series, sometimes indefinite. *Ovary* 2-8-celled; ovules 1 or 2 in each cell, generally pendulous. *Fruit* a drupe or a berry. *Seeds* generally albuminous.

[1] Not described in this Flora.

49. **Sapotaceæ.** Young parts rusty-tomentose; juice often milky. *Leaves* entire, exceptionally with caducous stipules. *Calyx-lobes* 4-8, the outer whorl valvate. *Corolla-lobes* 2-24, in two series if more than 14. *Stamens* as many as the corolla-lobes or numerous in several series; filaments short; anthers extrorse with the connective often produced. *Ovary* usually 6-8-celled, with a solitary anatropous ovule in each cell; style simple. *Fruit* a berry. *Seeds* generally albuminous (exalbuminous in *Bassia*).

50. **Ebenaceæ.** *Leaves* exceptionally subopposite, entire. *Flowers* diœcious, rarely polygamous. *Calyx* often accrescent. *Corolla-lobes* generally twisted. MALE FLS.: *stamens* 4-16; anthers narrow. FEM. FLS. *staminodes* 2-10, or 0. *Ovary* 2-more-celled; ovule generally solitary, anatropous; styles 2-8. *Fruit* a berry, 1-10-seeded. *Seeds* with copious albumen.

51. **Styraceæ.** *Leaves* alternate, usually serrate or crenate. *Flowers* 2-sexual, generally white. *Calyx* adnate to the ovary; limb persistent. *Corolla* of 4-5 almost free petals. *Stamens* usually indefinite, attached to the corolla-tube or base of the petals in one or several series. *Ovary* half-superior, 2-5-celled; ovules usually 2 in each cell, pendulous (in *Symplocos*). *Fruit* drupaceous. *Seeds* albuminous.

** *Carpels never exceeding two. (Leaves as a rule exstipulate.)*

A. Flowers regular. Stamens 2 or 5, rarely 4.

Order 6. Gentianales.

Leaves normally opposite if not whorled. *Flowers* usually 2-sexual. *Stamens* between the corolla lobes. *Carpels* distinct or connate; style generally simple.

52. **Oleaceæ.** *Leaves* simple, 3-foliolate or imparipinnate. *Calyx* 4-5-or more-toothed, or truncate. *Corolla-lobes* 4-5 or more. *Stamens* 2, on the corolla-tube or hypogynous; filaments generally short. *Ovary-cells* 1-2-ovuled; style simple; stigma simple or 2-lobed. *Fruit* a capsule, berry or drupe, 2-celled with 1 or 2 seeds in each cell. *Seeds* albuminous or exalbuminous.

53. **Apocynaceæ.** Trees or shrubs with milky juice. *Leaves* opposite or whorled, very rarely alternate, simple, quite entire. *Calyx-lobes* 5, generally imbricate. *Corolla* rotate or salver-shaped; lobes twistedly imbricate. *Stamens* 5, on the corolla-tube, sometimes adherent to the stigma by the connectives; anthers sometimes spurred downwards; pollen granular. *Ovary* of 2 distinct or connate carpels. *Fruit* of 2 distinct or connate follicles, or a drupe, or a berry. *Seeds* usually albuminous, those of follicular fruits usually comose or winged.

54. **Asclepiadaceæ.** Herbs or shrubs with milky juice. *Leaves* opposite, simple, entire, sometimes 0. *Calyx-lobes* 5, imbricate. *Corolla-tube* short, often with a ring of scales at the mouth; lobes valvate or imbricate. *Stamens* 5, rarely free, generally connate into a fleshy column with the anthers adhering to the stigma by broad connectives; pollen in 1 or 2 granular or waxy masses in each cell at the angles of the stigma. *Styles* 2, connate; stigma 5-angled. *Fruit* normally of 2 follicles. *Seeds* comose at the hilum, albuminous.

55. **Loganiaceæ.** Trees, shrubs or herbs. *Leaves* opposite, simple; stipules obsolete. *Flowers* 4-5-merous. *Stamens* on the corolla-tube; filaments distinct. *Ovules* usually many in each cell; style simple. *Fruit* a berry or a capsule, 1-many-seeded. *Seeds* albuminous.

Order 7. Polemoniales.

Leaves usually alternate, simple, exstipulate. *Flowers* 5-merous, usually 2-sexual, generally cymose, often showy. *Calyx* generally persistent, often accrescent. *Stamens* 5, on the corolla-tube, alternating with the corolla-lobes. *Style* generally simple, terminal or gynobasic.

56. **Boraginaceæ.** Herbs, shrubs or trees. *Leaves* alternate, sometimes subopposite or opposite. *Calyx-lobes* valvate. *Ovary* sometimes spuriously 4-celled ; ovules usually 4 altogether ; style simple or forked, terminal or gynobasic. *Fruit* a drupe or of 2-4 nutlets. *Seeds* erect or oblique.

57. **Convolvulaceæ.** Herbs or shrubs, usually twining. *Leaves* alternate, rarely 0. *Flowers* 2-sexual. *Calyx-lobes* imbricate. *Corolla* campanulate or funnel-shaped, often 5-plaited in bud. *Ovary* sometimes spuriously 4-celled ; ovules 2 in each carpel. *Style* usually simple. *Seeds* generally exalbuminous ; cotyledons plaited or 0 (as in *Cuscuta*).

58. **Solanaceæ.** Herbs or shrubs. *Leaves* alternate. *Flowers* solitary or in cymes, axillary, extra-axillary or terminal. *Corolla* rotate or campanulate, often plaited in bud. *Ovules* many on large peltate placentas. *Style* simple. *Fruit* a many-seeded berry or a capsule. *Seeds* albuminous ; embryo curved.

B. Flowers irregular. Stamens usually 4 (by the suppression of the odd one), often 2 long and 2 short, or only 2. Leaves usually opposite.

Order 8. Personales.

Flowers usually 2-sexual. *Corolla* generally 2-labiate with the neck of the tube more or less constricted. *Stamens* epipetalous, 4 with the posterior one abortive, or 2. *Carpels* 2, median ; ovules generally indefinite ; style simple. *Fruit* capsular. *Seeds* without albumen.

59. **Bignoniaceæ.** Usually trees. *Leaves* pinnately compound. *Flowers* generally in terminal panicles or racemes. *Calyx* truncate or spathaceous ; lobes valvate. *Corolla* unequally 5-lobed imbricate in bud. *Stamens* usually 4 and didynamous, rarely 5 and nearly equal. *Ovary* more or less stipitate and supported by an annular disc. *Fruit* an elongated capsule. *Seeds* winged.

60. **Acanthaceæ.** Usually shrubs or herbs with swollen joints. *Leaves* opposite, usually simple. *Flowers* bracteate and bracteolate. *Calyx* usually 5-partite. *Corolla* 2-lipped or subequally 5-lobed ; lobes imbricate or twisted. *Stamens* 4 or 2. *Ovules* 1 or more, superposed in each cell of the ovary ; style 2-fid with one arm usually sterile. *Fruit* a loculicidal capsule. *Seeds* compressed, usually hairy.

Order 9. Lamiales.

Stem more or less quadrangular. *Leaves* opposite and decussate. *Flowers* 5-merous, usually 2-labiate and didynamous. *Stamens* epipetalous. *Carpels* 2, median. *Ovary* 2- or falsely 4-celled. *Fruit* with 1-4 seeds.

61. **Verbenaceæ.** Herbs, shrubs or trees. *Leaves* simple or digitate. *Flowers* cymose and bracteate, rarely regular. *Calyx* 4-5-toothed, often persistent and accrescent, sometimes coloured. *Corolla* 2-lipped or more or less equally lobed. *Stamens* usually 4, one pair longer than the other in 2-labiate flowers, more or less equal in regular flowers. *Ovary* 2-4-celled, entire; style terminal. *Fruit* usually a drupe, rarely a capsule. *Seeds* exalbuminous.

62. **Labiatæ.** Mostly herbs, rarely shrubs, glandular-hairy and more or less aromatic. *Flowers* always 2-labiate, in verticelled cymes which are arranged in simple or panicled spikes. *Calyx* persistent. *Stamens* 4, one pair longer than the other. *Disk* prominent. *Ovary* 4-lobed, 4-celled; style gynobasic. *Fruit* of 4 1-seeded nutlets.

iii. APETALÆ.

Perianth single and generally calycine, rarely double or none. *Flowers* in many cases unisexual.

Series 1.—*Flowers usually 2-sexual and generally regular. Ovary as a rule 1-celled and 1-ovuled. Leaves simple, generally entire.*

* *Ovary superior.*

Order 1. Chenopodiales.

Generally herbaceous. *Perianth* regular, green or coloured. *Style* in most cases solitary. *Fruit* as a rule nut-like. *Embryo* curved.

63. **Amarantaceæ.** *Leaves* generally alternate, exstipulate. *Flowers* bracteate and bracteolate. *Perianth* scarious, persistent. *Stamens* up to 5, opposite the sepals. *Fruit* usually a utricle (although baccate in the two species described in this Flora). *Seed* albuminous.

Order 2. Piperales.

Aromatic herbs or shrubs. *Flowers* usually without a perianth, bracteate, arranged in a spike or a spadix. *Ovule* orthotropous. *Embryo* minute, not curved, imbedded in copious albumen.

64. **Piperaceæ.** *Leaves* entire, often punctate. *Flowers* supported by peltate bracts in catkin-like spikes. *Fruit* small.

Order 3. Daphnales.

Leaves usually alternate, entire, exstipulate. *Flowers* regular, mostly 2-sexual, 3-4-5-merous. *Stamens* typically in two whorls, perigynous. *Ovule* anatropous. *Embryo* straight.

65. **Lauraceæ.** Aromatic plants. *Perianth* usually 3-merous, often persistent; segments imbricate. *Stamens* perigynous, up to 12 in 3 or 4 series, the innermost series often reduced to staminodes; filaments often with 2 glands at the base; anther-cells opening by deciduous valves. *Ovule* pendulous. *Seeds* pendulous, exalbuminous.

66. **Thymelæaceæ.** Shrubs or trees with very fine tenacious bast. *Leaves* alternate or opposite. *Flowers* 2-sexual; perianth tubular or campanulate; lobes usually 4, imbricate. *Stamens* epiphyllous, usually twice as many as the corolla-lobes and then in 2 series one above the other. *Style* long or short or 0. *Ovule* pendulous. *Fruit* usually indehiscent. *Seeds* generally exalbuminous.

67. **Elæagnaceæ.** *Leaves* alternate. Flowers 1-2-sexual, generally 2- or 4-merous; perianth tubular, lobes valvate. *Stamens* 4, epiphyllous. *Ovule* erect. *Fruit* indehiscent, enclosed in the accrescent perianth-tube. *Albumen* scanty or 0.

** *Ovary inferior.*

Order 4. Santalales.

Generally parasitic shrubs or trees. *Leaves* in most cases opposite, entire, exstipulate. *Stamens* as many as the perianth-lobes and inserted on and opposite to them. *Ovules* without integuments. *Fruit* 1-seeded, generally drupaceous. *Seeds* albuminous.

68. **Loranthaceæ.** Parasitic on branches of trees. *Leaves* sometimes wanting when the branches are articulate and more or less flattened. *Flowers* 1-2-sexual; perianth sometimes double, the outer then is short and truncate, and the inner usually long; lobes always valvate. *Ovule* solitary, erect.

69. **Santalaceæ.** Parasitic on roots. *Leaves* opposite or alternate. *Flowers* generally 2-sexual; sometimes polygamous. *Placentation* free-central; ovules 1-4, pendulous. *Fruit* a drupe. *Seed* solitary.

Series 2.—*Flowers 1-sexual. Perianth regular or irregular, sometimes wanting. Ovary 1-6-celled. Leaves mostly simple and alternate.*

* *Ovary superior.*

Order 5. Euphorbiales.

Trees, shrubs or herbs, sometimes with milky juice. *Leaves* generally simple and stipulate. *Perianth* usually single, rarely double or none. *Ovary* as a rule 3-celled with 1 or 2 suspended ovules in each cell; styles as many as the carpels. *Fruit* various. *Seeds* albuminous.

70. **Euphorbiaceæ.** Same characters as of the Order.

Order 6. Urticales.

Leaves simple, stipulate, generally hirsute. *Perianth* simple, of 3-5 free or connate segments, regular, rarely absent. *Stamens* usually opposite to the perianth-segments. *Ovary* usually 1-celled, 1-ovuled; style often eccentric. *Fruit* various, never a capsule. *Seeds* with or without albumen.

71. **Urticaceæ.** Trees, shrubs or herbs, sometimes with milky juice. *Flowers* monœcious or diœcious; perianth always present. *Stamens* often inflexed in bud with reversed anthers. *Embryo* straight.

Order 7. Amentales.

Trees or shrubs. *Leaves* simple and sometimes reduced to scales. *Flowers*, both male and female, in catkins or spikes, usually bracteate. *Perianth*, if present, of 4-6 segments with the stamens inserted on them. *Ovary* 1-celled; ovules few or numerous. *Seeds* exalbuminous.

72. **Myricaceæ.** *Leaves* exstipulate. *Flowers* monœcious or diœcious; perianth none. *Stamens* inserted on bracts. *Ovary* sessile, of 2 carpels but 1-celled, 1-ovuled; style 2-fid. *Ovule* erect, orthotropous.

73. **Salicaceæ.** *Leaves* stipulate; buds enclosed in scales. *Flowers* diœcious, each in the axil of a bract; perianth none. *Stamens* 2-6 on a glandular disk. *Ovary* often stipitate, of 2 carpels but 1-celled; style simple or 0. *Ovules* many; generally on parietal placentas. *Fruit* a loculicidal capsule. *Seeds* comose.

** *Ovary inferior.*

Order 8. Quernales.

Trees or shrubs. *Leaves* alternate. *Flowers* monœcious, male in catkins, female solitary or spicate. *Perianth* green, generally gamophyllous. *Ovary* 1-6-celled; ovule solitary, pendulous or basal. *Seeds* without albumen.

74. **Juglandaceæ.** *Leaves* imparipinnate, without stipules. *Flowers* bracteate. *Perianth* in male flowers flat and adnate to the supporting bract which is stipitate, in the female flowers imperfectly double. *Stamens* indefinite. *Female flowers* solitary or spicate. *Style* 2-fid. *Fruit* a drupe or nut; cotyledons contorted or corrugated.

75. **Fagaceæ.** *Leaves* simple, stipulate, coriaceous. *Flowers* generally bracteate. *Male perianth* with 1-5 segments or wanting, female tubular, adnate to the ovary and supported by an involucre of bracts. *Ovary* 3- or 4-5-celled with 1 or 2 pendulous ovules in each cell; style 3-5-armed. *Fruit* usually a 1-celled nut included within; or supported by enlarged bracts. *Seeds* pendulous

b. MONOCOTYLEDONS.

Roots usually fibrous and often fascicled at the base of the plants. There is no separable *bark*, and no continuous *cambium layer*. *Leaves* sheathing, and usually with parallel veins. *Flowers* as a rule 3-merous. ***Embryo with only one cotyledon.***

Sub-Class i. *PETALOIDEÆ.*

Flowers with a coloured perianth, solitary or in umbels or racemes. *Fruit* a capsule or a berry.

Series 1.—*Ovary inferior.*

Order 1. Amomales.

Herbaceous plants. *Leaves* pinnately parallel-veined. *Flowers* 2-sexual, very irregular. *Perianth* of 6 segments in two series. *Stamens* 1 to 5, others reduced to petaloid staminodes. *Ovary* 3-celled. *Fruit* a capsule or a berry. *Seeds* often arillate, albuminous.

76. **Scitamineæ.** Generally the characters of the Cohort. *Flowers* solitary or in spikes or panicles. *Fertile stamen* only 1 (except in *Musa*).

Series 2.—*Ovary superior.*

Order 2. Liliales.

Herbaceous plants usually with bulbous or creeping root-stocks. *Flowers* regular. *Calyx* and *corolla* similar, both coloured. *Fruit* a capsule or a berry. *Seeds* albuminous.

77. **Liliaceæ.** Generally the characters of the Cohort. *Leaves* sometimes more or less net-veined.

Sub-Class ii. *SPADICIFLORÆ.*

Flowers not coloured, arranged on a more or less fleshy *spadix*. *Ovary* superior. *Fruit* a berry or a drupe. *Seeds* with copious albumen.

Order 1. Palmales.

Flowers generally 1-sexual, monœcious or diœcious. *Stem* erect or scandent, sometimes very long. *Inflorescence* at first enclosed in a coriaceous spathe. *Perianth* of 2 series, each of 3 coriaceous segments. *Stamens* 6, on base of the perianth; anthers usually versatile. *Ovary* 1-3-celled or of 3 distinct carpels; stigmas 3, usually sessile.

78. **Palmæ.** Essential characters as above. *Leaves* alternate, pinnatisect or palmatilobed, sometimes armed.

Order 2. Arales.

Generally fleshy plants. *Flowers* small and numerous, usually monœcious, borne on a spadix or a panicle with thick branches, generally enclosed in a much developed spathe. *Perianth* polyphyllous or wanting. *Ovary* syncarpous or apocarpous. *Embryo* minute, straight.

79. **Typhaceæ.** Aquatic herbs. *Leaves* linear, sessile. *Flowers* monœcious, minute, densely crowded on bracteate spikes. *Male flowers* with usually 1 stamen; filament capillary. *Ovary* 1-2-celled. *Fruit* a minute drupe.

80. **Araceæ.** Fleshy plants, sometimes scandent. *Flowers* usually without a perianth. *Anthers* sessile, 2-4-celled. *Ovary* sessile, 1-3-celled. *Fruit* a berry.

Sub-Class iii. *GLUMIFLORÆ*.

Flowers supported by glumes in variously arranged spikelets. *Fruit* a caryopsis. *Seeds* albuminous.

Order 1. Glumales.

Ovary superior, 1-celled. *Ovule* erect.

81. **Cyperaceæ.** Grass-like herbs, generally with 3-quetrous stems. *Leaves* tristichous; sheaths entire. *Flowers* subtended by a single glume. *Perianth* reduced to bristles or scales, or 0. *Stamens* 1-3; anthers innate. *Style* with 2-3 stigmatose branches. *Fruit* 3-gonous. *Embryo* central.

82. **Gramineæ.** Herbs, shrubs or trees, generally with terete jointed stems. *Leaves* alternate, usually narrow; sheaths split in front to the base, distinct from the blade, often with a ligule at the apex. *Flowers* 1-2-sexual, subtended by several distichous imbricate glumes. *Perianth* of 2 or 3 minute hypogynous scales (lodicules) or 0. *Stamens* in most cases 3, rarely 6 or more, hypogynous; anthers versatile. *Styles* 2-3, stigmatose throughout. *Fruit* terete or compressed. *Embryo* basal and generally lateral.

B. GYMNOSPERMS.

Shrubs or trees with *separable bark* and imperfectly developed unisexual *flowers*. *Anthers* usually borne on the back of scales, the *filaments* not being developed. *Ovules* are produced in an open ovary formed by a scale, and are fertilized by the direct application of the *pollen*, the *style* and *stigma* being absent. *Cotyledons* 2 or more.

83. **Gnetaceæ.** Trees or shrubs with articulated branches. *Leaves* opposite, minute or large. *Flowers* in spikes or cones. *Anthers* 2-8 on a column of combined filaments. *Ovule* exposed, erect, one of its coats forming a protruding tube resembling a style. *Cotyledons* 2.

84. **Coniferæ.** Generally large evergreen trees with monopodial stems; wood without pores. *Leaves* alternate or fascicled, generally acicular. *Flowers* generally monœcious. *Male flowers* in deciduous catkins. *Female flowers* of one or more exposed ovules borne on a carpellary scale, arranged spirally round an axis to form a cone. *Seeds* usually variously winged. *Cotyledons* generally more than 2.

DICOTYLEDONS.

THALAMIFLORÆ.

Order I.—RANALES.

Fam. 1. RANUNCULACEÆ; G. P. n. 1.*

Herbs or climbing shrubs. *Leaves* alternate, rarely opposite, usually exstipulate, simple much divided or compound. *Flowers* usually regular, generally ebracteate. *Sepals* 4-5 or more, usually deciduous, often coloured. *Petals* 3-5 or more, often minute or deformed, or totally absent. *Stamens* usually numerous, hypogynous, free. *Carpels* many or few, free, 1-celled, 1- or more-ovuled. *Stigma* simple. *Fruit* either of many achenes, or of follicles, rarely a berry. *Seeds* albuminous.

1. Clematis, Linn.; G. P. n. 1.*

Climbing shrubs. *Leaves* opposite, exstipulate, usually compound. *Flowers* in axillary or terminal fascicles or panicles, rarely solitary. *Sepals* usually 4, valvate, petaloid. *Petals* 0. *Stamens* and *carpels* indefinite. *Fruit* a head of achenes usually with feathery styles.

---

* Serial number in Bentham & Hooker's 'Genera Plantarum.'

Analysis of the Species.

Flowers in axillary fascicles.
  Flowers white or cream-coloured.
    Seps. erect; pedicels with 2 connate bracts . . . . 1. *C. napaulensis.*
    Seps. spreading; pedicels without bracts. 2. *C. montana.*
  Flowers dull-purple. . . . . . 3. *C. barbellata.*
Flowers in axillary panicles.
  Sepals spreading.
    Glabrous. Panicles many-flowered . 4. *C. Gouriana.*
    Pubescent. Panicles few-flowered. . 5. *C. puberula.*
  Sepals erect.
    Petioles connate into a flat cup . . 6. *C. connata.*
    Petioles not so connate.
      Leaves decompoundly pinnate . . 7. *C. nutans.*
      Leaves simply pinnate . . . 8. *C. Buchananiana*

1. **C. napaulensis,** DC.; Fl. Br. Ind. i. 2.

A slender climber. *Leaves* ternately divided; common petiole 1-1·5 in.; terminal leaflet or lobe 2-3 by ·3-·5 in., lateral half as long or shorter, sessile or very shortly petioluled. *Flowers* many; pedicels 1-2 in. long, with two hyaline bracts joined into a cup, pubescent above the cup. *Sepals* 4, erect, cream-coloured. *Filaments* glabrous, base broad. *Achenes* flat, hairy; style 1·5 in. long in fruit.

Valleys in HIGHER HILLS above 6,000 ft., scarce.—Matkángrá, Deotá, Mussoorie, etc.

Fl. Cold season. Fr. May.

2. **C. montana,** Ham.; Fl. Br. Ind. i. 2; Brandis Ind. Trees I; Gamble Man. Ind. Timb. 2. Vern. *Kauniá-báli*, Jaunsar.

Stem thick, often 3 in. in diameter; young parts pubescent. *Leaves* 3-foliolate, fascicled at the nodes, glabrescent; petiole 1·5-3 in. long. *Leaflets* 1-3 in. long, ovate, toothed; petiolule ·1-·3 in. *Flowers* 2-3 in. diam., white; peduncles 2-4 in. long, generally exceeding the leaves. *Sepals* 4, sometimes connate, 1-2 in. long, elliptical, spreading, pure-white. *Filaments* linear, short. *Carpels* hairy; style ·6-1 in. long, rather stout, densely hairy.

JAUNSAR and TEHRI-GARHWAL, 6,-9,000 ft., fairly common. A very conspicuous plant during the month of May on account of its beautiful sprays of large white flowers, trailing over the tallest trees and very frequently over Deodar.

Fl. Apr., May.

3. **C. barbellata,** Edgew.; Fl. Br. Ind. i. 3; Gamble Man. Ind. Timb. 2. Vern. *Kauni*, Jaunsar.

Stem rather thin. *Leaves* 3-foliolate, much like those of the last species. *Fowers* dull-purple, in axillary fascicles; pedicels 1·5-3 in. long. *Sepals* ·6-·8 in. long, erect, pubescent on both surfaces, greyish-purple outside, villous at the margins. *Filaments* linear, often hairy, as long as the sepals or shorter; anthers bearded at the back (whence the specific name). *Athenes* glabrous or puberulent; style 1·5-1·8 in. long, brown-hairy.

JAUNSAR, TEHRI-GARHWAL and OUTER HIMALAYA, above 7,000 ft., in shady places.—Mundáli, Deoban; Deotá; Mussoorie, etc.

Fl. May, June.

4. **C. Gouriana,** Roxb.; Fl. Br. Ind. i. 4; Brandis Ind. Trees 2. Vern. *Bel Kúm*, *Bel Kangu*, Dún.

Stem thick, striate; branches purple. *Leaves* bipinnate or biternate. *Leaflets*, 2-3·5 in. long, ovate, oblong or lanceolate, acuminate, entire or distantly toothed, cordate or rounded at the base, rather coriaceous, wholly glabrous or rarely pubescent beneath. *Flowers* greenish-white, small, in dense axillary panicles. *Sepals* ·2-·3 in. long, oblong, revolute; margins tomentose. *Filaments* narrow. *Achenes* lanceolate; style 1·5-2 in. long in fruit, very slender.

Common in the DÚN and up to 4,000 ft. in the OUTER HIMALAYA. Also found in the SIWALIKS.

Fl. Aug., Sept.

5. **C. puberula,** Hook. f. & T.; Fl. Br. Ind. i. 4.

Stem grooved, moderately thick, downy. *Leaves* pinnate. *Leaflets* 1-1·5 in. long, ovate-lanceolate, entire or toothed. *Panicles* shorter than the leaves, few-flowered; branches opposite, subtended by leaf-like green bracts. *Sepals* 5, ·5 in. long, silky without. *Achenes* ovoid, silky; style about 1 in. long in fruit.

Valleys in the HIMALAYA, at 2,-4,000 ft.: Tiuni, Májog, Dhármigádh, etc.

Fl. Sept., Oct.

6. **C. connata,** DC.; Fl. Br. Ind. i. 6. Vern. *Káuni-báli*, Jaunsar.

Stem thick; young parts with scattered hairs. *Leaves* pinnate or 3-foliolate, glabrous; petiole connate into a large flat cup (whence the specific name). *Leaflets* 2-4 in. long, broad-ovate, serrate or lobed; base cordate. *Panicles* many-flowered. *Flowers* white, large. *Sepals* oblong, hairy, not ribbed. *Filaments* tapering, hairy. *Achenes* ovate, pubescent; style 1·5-2 in. long in fruit.

Forests of UPPER HILLS above 5,000 ft., not very common: Bhújkōti, Mundáli, Konáin, etc.

Fl. May, June. Fr. Sept., Oct.

7. **C. nutans,** Royle; Fl. Br. Ind. i. 5; Gamble Man. Ind. Timb. 2. Vern. *Nák-chhikni, Kánqúli,* Málkōt; *Káuni,* Jaunsar.

Stem slender, woody, furrowed, very pungent to the taste. *Leaves* decompoundly pinnate. *Leaflets* 1-3 in. long, ovate or lanceolate, usually 3-5-lobed, silky. *Flowers* cream-coloured, in much-branched panicles; pedicels with a pair of green bracts which are often leaf-like and subtend flower-buds. *Sepals* ·5-·7 in. long, oblong, closely nerved, silky outside. *Filaments* tapering, silky near the base. *Achenes* large, silky-hairy; style 1-1·5 in. in fruit, very slender.

OUTER HIMALAYAN slopes, 3,-5,000 ft.: Málkōt, above Ráj-pur. Bindál Nadi near Dehra Dún (*Mr. C. W. Hope*).

The leaves are very pungent to the taste and produce violent sneezing if smelt after bruising.

Fl. Nov., Dec.

8. **C. Buchananiana,** DC.; Fl. Br. Ind. i. 6; Brandis Ind. Trees 2; Gamble Man. Ind. Timb. 2. Vern. *Káuni Báli,* Jaunsar.

Stem thick, woody; branches widely climbing, pubescent when young. *Leaves* simply pinnate. *Leaflets* 2-4 in. long, ovate or orbiculate, coarsely lobed or serrate, pubescent; base cordate. *Flowers* large, cream-coloured, sweet-scented, in many-flowered panicles. *Sepals* thick, ribbed, softly silky-tomentose. *Filaments* and *achenes* densely hairy.

Villages in the HIMALAYA above 4,000 ft. Scarce in JAUNSAR, but common in parts of TEHRI-GARHWAL, *e.g.*, Mautárgádh.

Fl. Oct., Nov.

C. acuminata, DC.; Fl. Br. Ind. i. 5; Brandis Ind. Trees 2; has been found at the Bear-garden near Chakrata. It is a slender climber with glabrous leaves and cream-coloured flowers. *Roots* thick, fleshy, tuberous.

C. grata, Wall.; Fl. Br. Ind. i. 3—probably also occurs. It is a woody climber with a furrowed stem. *Panicles* decompound.

The following plants of herbaceous Genera are commonly met with and deserve mention :—

1. *Anemone vitifolia*, Ham.; Fl. Br. Ind. i. 8.—A perennial herb with 5-lobed radical leaves. *Flowers* large, white, in many-flowered scapes. *Seeds* white, woolly. Chakrata and the hills beyond, also Mussoorie and Málkot.—*G. P. n. 4.*

2. *A. obtusiloba*, Don ; Fl. Br. Ind. i. 8. Vern. *Ageli*, Jaunsar. A herb with a thick densely white-woolly root-stock. *Radical leaves* 3-lobed, deeply cordate, densely silky-pubescent. *Flowers* varying in colour from blue to white. Above 8,000 ft. : Mundáli, Deoban, etc.

3. *A rivularis*, Ham. ; Fl. Br. Ind. i. 9. *Stem* branched. *Radical leaves* 3-lobed. *Flowers* in many-flowered compound cymes, bluish outside. *Achenes* dark-brown, lanceolate, hooked at the tip. In damp places and snow gullies in the HILLS, above 5,000 ft.

4. *Delphinium denudatum*, Wall. ; Fl. Br. Ind. i. 25. The Larkspur. Vern. *Main*, Jaunsar. Very conspicuous in the spring season on dry grassy slopes in the hills up to 8,500 ft. *Stem* branched. *Radical leaves* 5-9-partite, orbicular. *Flowers* pale-blue, with a subulate spur. *Fruit* of 3 follicles.—*G. P. n. 25.*

5. *D. vestitum*, Wall. ; Fl. Br. Ind. i. 26. Common in the Tutuagádh near Mundáli and on the northern slopes of Rikhshin, generally in shady ravines, 6,-12,000 ft. *Stem* 1·5-3 ft. long, hispid. *Radical leaves* 6-12 in. in diam., 5-7-lobed ; lobes rounded, cut or toothed. *Flowers* dense, bluish-white ; spur inflated, conical, incurved. *Fruit* of 3 follicles.

6 *Actæa spicata*, Linn. ; Fl. Br. Ind. i. 29. An erect perennial herb with 3-nately compound leaves and small white flowers in crowded racemes. *Sepals* and *petals* similar. *Fruit* a berry. Shady ravines in JAUNSAR and TEHRI-GARHWAL.—*G. P. n. 27.*

6. *Pæonia emodi*, Wall. ; Fl. Br. Ind. i. 30. A tall almost shrubby plant, remarkable for its large showy white or pink flowers, found in the upper Tons Valley, as in ravines above Naintwár and at Dátmir and elsewhere from 7,000 to 10,000 ft.—*G. P. n. 30.*

FAM. 2. DILLENIACEÆ; G. P. N. 2.

Trees or shrubs, rarely herbs. *Leaves* alternate, simple, generally without stipules. *Flowers* large, showy.

Sepals 5, imbricate, persistent. *Petals* 5, rarely 3 or 4, deciduous. *Stamens* numerous, hypogynous, in many series. *Carpels* solitary or numerous, free or cohering at the base on the axis. *Styles* distinct. *Seeds* solitary or many, albuminous, arillate or immersed in pulp.

1. Dillenia, Linn.; G. P. n. 10.

1. **D. indica**, Linn.; Fl. Br. Ind. i. 36; Brandis For. Flora 1, Ind. Trees 3; Gamble Man. Ind. Timb. 4. Vern. *Chálta*, Hind.

An evergreen tree in its habitat but generally leafless for a short time in June at Dehra Dún; bark reddish-grey, red inside, peeling off in hard flakes. *Leaves* generally approximate at the ends of the branches, 8-12 in. long, oblanceolate or oblong-lanceolate, sharply serrate, acute or acuminate, glabrous above, usually pubescent beneath; lateral nerves very numerous, parallel, prominent; petiole sheathing at the base. *Flowers* terminal, solitary, 6-8 in. across. *Sepals* orbicular, thick and fleshy, with membranous margins, spreading in flower, accrescent and enclosing the ovary in fruit. *Petals* 3-4 in. long, obovate, white, very tender. *Inner stamens* recurved. *Styles* bent outwards in radiating white rays ·7 in. long. *Fruit* a pseudocarp, 3-5 in. diam., fleshy, enclosed in the much thickened concave sepals. *Carpels* 16-20; seeds reniform, sunk in a glutinous pulp.

Commonly cultivated at DEHRA and SAHÁRANPUR.

Wood reddish-brown, mottled with white specks, weighing about 45 lbs. per c. ft., fairly durable; medullary rays broad and shining. The fleshy calyx has an agreeable acid taste, and is eaten raw or cooked.

Fl. June, July. Fr. ripens in the cold season.

FAM. 3. MAGNOLIACEÆ; G. P. N. 4.

Trees or shrubs, sometimes climbing; wood-tissue with glandular markings. *Leaves* alternate, simple, entire or toothed, usually stipulate; stipules convolute, deciduous. *Flowers* axillary or terminal, trimerous, often large. *Sepals* and *petals* usually similar, hypogynous, deciduous. *Stamens* indefinite, free or monadelphous; filaments usually flattened. *Carpels* indefinite, often arranged on an elongated torus; style usually short. *Fruit* of berry-like or follicular carpels, or like a woody cone. *Albumen* fleshy, uniform.

Analysis of the Genera.

Trees. Stipules conspicuous; stamens free . 1. MICHELIA.
Climbing shrubs. Stipules none; stamens monadelphous . . . . . . 2. SCHIZANDRA.

1. Michelia, Linn.; G. P. n. 6.

1. **M. Champaca,** Linn.; Fl. Br. Ind. i. 42; Brandis For. Flora 3, Ind. Trees 8; Gamble Man. Ind. Timb. 12. Vern. *Champá*, Hind.

A tall, graceful, evergreen tree with dark-grey bark. *Leaves* 6-8 by 2-3·5 in., ovate or oblong-lanceolate, coriaceous, entire, glabrous, dark-green and shining above, enveloped in convolute stipules in bud; main lateral nerves 8-14 pairs; base acute; petiole 1-1·2 in. long. *Flowers* solitary, axillary, bracteate, pale-yellow, very fragrant; peduncle short, stout; bracts small, deciduous. *Sepals* and *petals* 15-21, in several series, those of the inner series gradually narrower. *Fruit* 3-4 in. long; carpels ·5-·7 in. long, subsessile, dark-coloured, with white specks.

Cultivated in the DÚN, and also in the SAHÁRANPUR DISTRICT.

Heartwood light olive-brown, very durable, seasons and polishes well; weight about 38 lbs. per c.ft. It is used for furniture. The flowers are used by Hindus in religious ceremonies and are indispensable on certain occasions.

Fl. chiefly Apr.-June, but occasionally throughout the year.

2. Schizandra, Michaux; G. P. n. 8.

Sinistrorsely climbing glabrous shrubs. *Leaves* exstipulate. *Flowers* axillary, 1-sexual and diœcious, white, yellow or orange. *Sepals* and *petals* 9-12, generally in 3 series. *Stamens* 5-15 or more, spirally arranged; filaments usually monadelphous and short or wholly connate into a fleshy head; anthers free, or sessile and half-buried in the head of connate filaments; cells small, remote. *Carpels* many, densely imbricated; stigma sessile; ovules 2, pendulous. *Fruit* an elongated spike of 1-seeded globose carpels. *Seeds* with copious albumen.

Analysis of the Species.

Filaments free above; anthers free . . . 1. *S. grandiflora.*
Filaments connate into a fleshy head; anthers imbedded in the head . . . . 2. *S. propinqua.*

1. **S. grandiflora,** Hook. f. & T.; Fl. Br. Ind. i. 44; Brandis For. Flora 571, Ind. Trees 9; Gamble Man. Ind. Timb. 14. Vern. *Bûllon, Bánoı*, Jaunsar.

A climber with dark-brown smooth bark and short leaf-bearing branches at the nodes. *Leaves* 3-6 in. long, elliptic to oblong-lanceolate, acuminate, distantly glandular-toothed, rather soft and fleshy, shining above, pale beneath; lateral nerves 6-8 pairs, faint; base acute; petiole ·5-1 in. long. *Flowers* diœcious, axillary, white, fragrant, about 1 in. diam.; pedicels 1-2 in. long, of male flowers somewhat shorter. *Sepals* and *petals* 9-12, imbricate. *Stamens* in a spiral series, monadelphous below, free and tubular above. *Ovaries* imbricated on a conical receptacle which lengthens in fruit into a fleshy axis 6-9 in. long, bearing numerous scarlet carpels.

JAUNSAR and TEHRI-GARHWAL, 6,-10,000 ft., affecting shady places: Deoban, Mundáli; Bámsu, Deotá, etc. Common but not abundant.

Fl. May, June. Fr. July, Aug.

2. **S. propinqua,** Hook. f. & T.; Fl. Br. Ind. i. 45; Brandis Ind. Trees 9; Gamble Man. Ind. Timb. 14.

A stout climber with dark-brown stem and rough verrucose branches. *Leaves* 4-6 by 1·5-2 in., ovate-lanceolate, acuminate, obscurely gland-toothed, subcoriaceous, dark-green; lateral nerves 10-12 pairs, not prominent; base rounded; petiole ·4-·6 in. long, rather stout. *Flowers* ·5-·7 in. diam., yellowish; pedicels ·4-·7 in.

long, bracteolate. *Sepals* and *petals* imbricate, concave in bud. *Stamens* connate into a globose head about ·3 in. diam.; anthers sessile, half-exserted. *Ovaries* and *fruit* as in the preceding species.

Very scarce. Korwá forests, JAUNSAR; also below MUSSOORIE. About 5,-6,000 ft.

Fl. June, July.

FAM. 4. ANONACEÆ; G. P. N. 5.

Trees or shrubs, often aromatic. *Leaves* alternate, simple, entire, exstipulate. *Flowers* usually 2-sexual. *Sepals* 3, free or connate, generally valvate. *Petals* 6, hypogynous, in two series, the inner sometimes absent. *Stamens* indefinite, filaments short or none; anthers adnate, with a connective enlarged to form a dilated or truncate head. *Ovaries* usually numerous, apocarpous, (syncarpous in *Anona*); style short or stigma sessile. *Fruit* of dry or succulent usually indehiscent carpels. *Seeds* large; testa horny; albumen ruminate.

1. Miliusa, Leschen.: G. P. n. 34.

1. **M. velutina,** Hook. f. & T.; Fl. Br. Ind. i. 87; Brandis For. Flora 6, Ind. Trees 11; Gamble Man. Ind. Timb. 21. Vern. *Dōm Sál,* Hind.; *Guá Sál,* Garhwal.

A middle-sized deciduous tree; young branches tomentose; bark dark-grey, rough; inner substance dirty brown. *Leaves* 6-10 by 3·5-6 in., ovate elliptic or oblong, acute or acuminate, entire, softly tomentose on both surfaces, aromatic; base cordate; petiole ·1-·2 in. *Flowers* pale-yellow, in 3-6-flowered lax leaf-opposed racemes; peduncles ·5-1 in. long, pedicles 2-4 in., slender. *Sepals* and *outer petals* similar, ·1 in. long, ovate, valvate in bud; *inner petals* longer, broad-ovate, dark-brown, densely tomentose outside. *Stamens* on a cylindrical torus; anthers distinct. *Fruit* of a number of black dry 1-2-seeded berry-like carpels, on short stipes.

Common in the Sál forests of DEHRA DÚN and SAHÁRANPUR, generally in ravines, or in open scrubby jungles.

Heartwood not distinct. The seasoned wood is fairly hard, light, of pretty grain; weight 40-50 lbs. per. c. ft. It is used for agricultural implements, and in constructions of a temporary character.

Fl. Mar.-May. Fr. June, July.

To this Family belong—

1. *Anona squamosa*, Linn.; Fl. Br. Ind. i. 78; Brandis Ind. Trees 22. Vern. *Sharífá, Sitáphal*, Hind., the Custard-apple; and

2. *A. reticulata*, Linn.; Fl. Br. Ind. i. 78; Brandis Ind. Trees 22. Vern, *Noná, Rámphal*, Hind, the Bullock's heart.

Both occasionally, but not commonly, cultivated in the DÚN, more frequently in SAHÁRANPUR.—*G. P. n. 30.*

FAM. 5. MENISPERMACEÆ; G. P. N. 6.

Climbing or twining, rarely erect shrubs. *Leaves* alternate, simple, entire or lobed, usually palminerved, exstipulate. *Flowers* small, usually dicœcious. *Sepals* and *petals* similar, generally 6 each, in series of 3, the outermost whorl of sepals very minute. MALE FLS.: *Stamens* usually 6, opposite to the petals, hypogynous; filaments or anthers free or connate. FEM. FLS.: *Carpels* 3, rarely 1, 6, or more; styles ultimately lateral or sub-basal; ovules solitary. *Fruit* a 1-seeded drupe. *Seed* curved into a crescent shape (whence the name of the Order), enclosed in a woody endocarp, usually with copious albumen.

1. Cocculus, DC.; G. P. n. 16.

Climbing or erect shrubs. *Flowers* panicled. *Sepals* 6, in two series. *Petals* 6, concave, embracing the stamens in the male flowers. *Styles* usually cylindrical. *Drupes* circular, laterally compressed; endocarp horse-shoe-shaped, tubercled.

Analysis of the Species.

A large erect shrub. Leaves glabrous . . 1. *C. laurifolius.*
A climbing shrub. Leaves villous . . . 2. *C. villosus.*

1. **C. laurifolius**, DC.; Fl. Br. Ind. i. 101; Brandis For. Flora 9, Ind. Trees 26; Gamble Man. Ind. Timb. 25. Vern. *Tilphára*, Dún and Garhwal.

A large evergreen shrub with a short trunk and thin grey bark; branchlets with tufts of hairs at the base. *Leaves* 3-6 in. long; lanceolate, entire, dark-green and shining above, slightly pale beneath; base 3-nerved, acute; petiole ·1-·3 in. *Panicles* axillary, solitary or 2 together, corymbose. *Flowers* minute; petals 2-lobed. *Styles* reflexed. *Drupe* ·15 in. diam., black when ripe.

Shady woods and moist places up to 4,000 ft. Banks of the Sông opposite Káluwála, Nakraunda, Bindál nálá, etc., in the DÚN. JUMNA VALLEY down to Dákhpathár. Moist ravines in the LOWER HILLS.

The wood is of a curious structure, having belts of corky tissue alternating with woody bands and looking like annual rings, which they obviously are not, as they frequently anastomose. It is used only for fuel.

Fl. Apr.-June.

2. **C. villosus**, DC.; Fl. Br. Ind. i. 101; Brandis For. Flora 9.

A climbing undershrub with tomentose branchlets. *Leaves* very variable in size, the largest 3 by 2 in., ovate or ovate-oblong, mucronate, clothed with grey tomentum; petiole up to ·5 in. *Male fls.* in axillary panicles; *fem. fls.* 1-3 together on short axillary pedicels. *Drupe* ·2 in. diam., dark-purple.

Foot of the HIMALAYA and SIWALIK FORESTS, not very common.

"The juice of the ripe berries makes a durable bluish-purple ink."—*Sir D. Brandis.* The roots and leaves are used medicinally.

Fl. Feb., March.

2. Tinospora, Miers.

T. malabarica, Miers; Fl. Br. Ind. i. 96; Brandis Ind. Trees 24; vern *Gurch*, *Giloe*, *Gulancha*, Hind.

A large climber; *stems* about 2·5 in. diameter, smooth and shining, lenticellate, with light-coloured, papery bark; branchlets pubescent. *Leaves* 4-8 in. in diameter, broadly ovate or orbicular, deeply cordate, 7-nerved, shortly acuminate, pubescent above, tomentose beneath; *petiole* 2·5-6 in. long, thickened and twisted at the base. *Flowers* greenish yellow, in racemes 3-6 in. long, usually from the old wood; pedicels slender, usually solitary in the female, clustered in the male. *Male flowers*: *Sepals* 6 in two series, the outer small, ovate-oblong, obtuse, concave, the inner larger, suborbicular, membranous, flat, ·15 in. long. *Petals* 6, clawed membranous, smaller than the sepals. *Stamens* 6; *filaments* free, thickened at the apex. *Female flowers*: *Sepals* and *Petals* as in the male flower. *Staminodes* 6. *Ovaries* 3. *Drupes* 1-3, ovoid, smooth, crimson; endocarp tubercled.

On trees in shady places in the Dun and Saharanpur forests, fairly common.

This plant has long been taken for *Tinospora cordifolia*, Miers, which is perfectly glabrous and of which there are no specimens from the Dun in the Dehra Herbarium.

The root and stems are used in medicine as substitutes for *T. cordifolia*, Miers and are largely collected for this purpose.

Fl. Mar.-June; Fr. Cold season.

3. Stephania, Lour.

Perennial glabrous climbing shrubs. *Leaves* peltate, orbicular or more or less triangular; basal nerves numerous. *Flowers* small, umbellate; *Male flowers*: *Sepals* 6-10, free. *Petals* 3-5, fleshy. *Stamens* 6, *filaments* united in a column, the *anthers* connate forming a ring round the dilated top of the column, bursting transversely. *Female flowers*: *Sepals* 3-5. *Petals* as in the male. *Ovary* 1. *Style* 3-6-partite. *Drupe* glabrous; endocarp horse-shoe-shaped, compressed, dorsally tubercled.

1. **S. glabra**, Miers.; Syn.—*S. rotunda*, Hook. f. & Thoms. ex-parte (non Lour); Fl. Br. Ind. 1,103; Brandis Ind. Trees 23 (non Lour.); Gamble Man. Ind. Timb. 26 (non Lour.); vern. *Parhá*, Dun.

A tuberous-rooted climbing shrub; twigs ribbed. *Leaves* 3-7 in. diameter, broadly ovate or suborbicular often sinuate, peltate, with 9-11 radiating nerves, glabrous, pale beneath; *petiole* 3-8 in. long. *Flowers* ·2 in. diam., greenish-yellow, in axillary compound pedunculate umbels; peduncle 1·5-3 in. long. *Sepals* 6, the three outer linear-oblong, the three inner spathulate. *Petals* shorter than the sepals. *Drupe* pisiform, red.

Common in ravines in the Dun and the Lower Hills; Dehra Dun; Rajpore, etc.

Fl. Rainy season.

S. elegans, Hook. f. & Thoms.; Fl. Br. Ind. i. 103; Brandis Trees 23; Gamble Man. Ind. Timb. 26, has been found at Mussoorie and may also occur elsewhere. It is a slender climber with elongate-deltoid, entire leaves and red fruits.

4. Cissampelos, Linn.

C. Pareira, Linn.; Fl. Br. Ind. i. 103; Brandis Ind. Trees 23; Gamble Man. Ind. Timb. 26. Vern. *Hárjori*, *Dakh-nirbisi*. Hind; *Parhé*, Dun and Garhwal.

A slender climber with a perennial root-stock, which annually throws out long twining branches covered with grey tomentum. *Leaves* 1·5-4 in. long, triangularly broad-ovate, or orbicular, usually peltate, obtuse, mucronate, base cordate or truncate, more or less tomentose on both sides, ultimately glabrous above, glaucous beneath; *petiole* 1·5-4 in. long, pubescent. *Flowers* minute. *Male* flowers in pedunculate, branched cymes, clustered in the leaf-axils or on long axillary, raceme-like shoots, each cyme in the axil of a small leaf; *pedicels* filiform. *Sepals* 4, obovate-oblong, hairy outside. *Petals* 4, united into a 4-lobed cup, hairy outside. *Stamens* 4; *filaments* united in a very short column; *anthers* connate encircling the top of the column. *Female* flowers clustered in the axils of orbicular, hoary, imbricate bracts, arranged in long, axillary racemes. *Sepal* 1, ovate-oblong, pubescent outside. *Petal* 1, about half the length of the sepal. *Ovary* 1, hairy; *style* shortly 3-fid. *Drupe* ·2 in. diameter, subglobose, compressed, hairy, red when ripe; endocarp transversely ridged.

Common in hedges in the Dun and at low levels in the hills. The leaves and roots are used in medicine, and the stem yields a strong fibre.

Fl. Rainy season.

VI. BERBERIDACEÆ.

Erect or climbing shrubs, rarely herbs, glabrous. *Leaves* alternate or fascicled, simple or compound, usually exstipulate. *Flowers* regular, yellow or white. *Sepals* and *petals* free, hypogynous, caducous, in 2-4 series, usually imbricate. *Stamens* hypogynous, usually as many as the petals and opposite to them. *Carpels* 1-3, rarely more, oblong; style short or 0; stigma dilated. *Fruit* baccate or dry.

Analysis of the Genera.

Climbing shrubs with digitate leaves	1. HOLBŒLLIA.
Erect shrubs—	
Leaves simple	2. BERBERIS.
Leaves pinnate . . .	3. MAHONIA.

1. Holbœllia, Wall.

1. **H. latifolia,** Wall.; Fl. Br. Ind. i. 108; Brandis For. Flora 13, Ind. Trees 28; Gamble Man. Ind. Timb. 27. Vern. *Gophlá, Janglí Sharifá*, Mussoorie.

A climbing shrub; stem corky when old. *Leaves* alternate, digitate, 3-9-foliolate. *Leaflets* very variable in size and shape, 3-5 by ·5-2 in., broadly or narrowly ovate, oblong or ovate-lanceolate, entire, acuminate, generally coriaceous, shining above, pale beneath; common petiole 3-4 in., petiolule ·3-1 in. long. *Flowers* monœcious, in axillary fascicles or racemes, purplish-green, sweet-scented. *Sepals* 6, in two series. *Petals* 6, minute. *Stamens* 6; anthers dehiscing by slits. *Berries* oblong, 2-3 in. long.

Shady ravines in the HILLS; above 5,500 ft.; Korwá Chakrata, Deotá, etc.

Fl. April-May. Fr. Sept.-Oct.

There are two distinct varieties of this plant:—

Var. *latifolia*, sp. Wall., with 3-5 ovate or oblong leaflets, common in the OUTER HILLS; and

Var. *angustifolia*, sp. Wall., with 5-9 linear-lanceolate leaflets, which occurs at and beyond Deotá.

2. Berberis, Linn.

The Barberries.

Spinous shrubs; wood yellow. *Leaves* pinnate and alternate, or simple and fasciculate. *Flowers* yellow, bisexual, 2-3-bracteate. *Sepals* 6, in two series. *Petals* 6, also in two series. *Stamens* 6, free; anthers dehiscing by two recurved valves. *Ovary* simple; stigma sessile or on a short style. *Fruit* a berry.

Analysis of the Species.

Leaves imparipinnate . . . . . . 1. *B. nepalensis.*
Leaves simple.
  Flowers umbellate. . . . . . . 3. *B. umbellata.*
  Flowers racemed.
    Leaves membranous, closely serrate; stigma sessile. . . . . 2. *B. vulgaris.*
    Leaves coriaceous, reticulate, entire or remotely toothed.
      Leaves obovate or broadly oblanceolate; stigma subsessile.
        Branches and pedicels red; racemes branched . . . . . . 4. *B. aristata.*
        Branches grey; pedicels pale-red or green; racemes not branched . . 5. *B. coriaria.*
      Leaves narrow-oblanceolate; stem white; style distinct . . . . . . 6. *B. Lycium.*
      Leaves broad-obovate, strongly reticulate; stem pale; style distinct . . . 7. *B. asiatica.*

1. **B. nepalensis,** Spreng.; Fl. Br. Ind. i. 109; Brandis For. Flora 12, Ind. Trees 28; Gamble Man. Ind. Timb. 28. Vern. *Khōru*, Jaunsar.

A small tree or large shrub with soft corky bark. *Leaves* coriaceous, shining, imparipinnate, with two recurved subulate spinescent stipules. *Leaflets* 2-12 pairs, 2-3·5 in. long, ovate or lanceolate, sessile, with 3-8 large spinous teeth on either side, shining above. *Bracts* 1-2 in. long, persistent, clothing the ends of the branches; bracteoles broad-ovate or oblong, deciduous. *Racemes* dense-flowered, 4-10 in. long, erect, in the axils of the bracts. *Flowers* yellow; pedicels ·3-·5 in. long. *Berries* ·3-·5 in. long, elliptic or globose, purple, glaucous.

JAUNSAR, 6,-8,000 ft. Common near Chakrata. Distrib. EUROPE.

The fruit is eaten.

Fl. Apr., May. Fr. May, June.

NOTE.—Like the English name *Barberry*, the Jaunsari names *Káshmoi* and *Káshmal* and the Garhwali name *Kingora* are applied indiscriminately to the following species, while their roots are sold by the dealers of country-drugs under the common name of *Rasaut* or *Dáruhald* (Sans. *Dáruharidrá*).

2. **B. vulgaris,** Linn.; Fl. Br. Ind. i. 109; Brandis For. Flora 11, Ind. Trees 28; Gamble Man. Ind. Timb. 29. Vern. *Chatrod*, Jaunsar.

A small shrub with soft brown bark. *Leaves* deciduous, 1-3 in. long, broadly obovate or spathulate, membranous, finely serrate, narrowed into a slender petiole which is ·1-1 in. long; spines 3-7-forked, rarely simple. *Flowers* pale-yellow, in simple racemes which are generally longer than the leaves. *Berries* oblong-ovoid, red, when ripe.

JAUNSAR and TEHRI-GARHWAL, 8,-12,000 ft.: Deoban; Rikhshin. Not very common.

The fruit is eaten.

Fl. Mar., Apr.

There are several varieties of this species, some of which seem almost specifically distinct, as they differ considerably in appearance and foliage from the type. One of these, which is found at Lokándi, Gidhi Khad and Rikhshin, is considered by Mr. Gamble to be var. *ætnensis*, sp. Presl.

3. **B. umbellata,** Wall.; Fl. Br. Ind. i. 110; Brandis Ind. Trees 30; Gamble Man. Ind. Timb. 28.

A small shrub, generally occurring in gregarious patches; branches slender. *Leaves* 1-2 in. long, obovate, rather membranous, sparingly serrulate. *Flowers* yellow, somewhat unevenly umbellate on a long peduncle; pedicels slender. *Berries* oblong.

JAUNSAR and TEHRI-GARHWAL, 9,-11,000 ft.: Gidhi Khad; Rikhshin, etc.

Fl. Apr., May.

4. **B. aristata,** Roxb.; Fl. Br. Ind. i. 110; Brandis For. Flora 12, Ind. Trees 29; Gamble Man. Ind. Timb. 29. Vern. *Káshmoi*, Jaunsar; *Kingorá*, Garhwal.

An evergreen shrub 10-12 ft. high; branches usually bright red. *Leaves* 2-3 in. long, obovate or oblanceolate, rather coriaceous, entire or with a few remote teeth, in the axil of a 3-fid or simple spine. *Flowers* bright-yellow, in cymosely branched racemes; peduncle 1-1·5 in. long, red; branches few-flowered; pedicels ·2-·3 in. long, also red. *Berries* tapering into a very short style, red.

JAUNSAR and TEHRI-GARHWAL, 6,-9,000 ft. Common.

An extract from the stem and roots is used in medicine.

Fl. Apr., May. Fr. June, July.

5. **B. coriaria,** Royle; Gamble Man. Ind. Timb. 29; Brandis Ind. Trees 30. Syn.—*B. aristata* var. *floribunda*, Wall.; Fl. Br. Ind. i. 110. Vern. *Káshmoi*, Jaunsar; *Kingorá*, Garhwal.

A large thorny shrub with grey bark; branches grey, rarely reddish, rather stouter than those of *B. aristata*. *Leaves* 3-4 in. long, obovate, entire or distantly sharp-toothed, green beneath; veins very fine or indistinct. *Flowers* usually in simple racemes which are 2-3 in. long; peduncle slightly angled; pedicels ·2-·3 in. long; bracts persistent. *Berries* ovoid, purple, covered with a glaucous bloom.

HIGHER HILLS, 7,-9,000 ft. Common at Bodyár, Konáin, Deoban and Lambátách.

Economic use as of *B. aristata*.

Fl. May, June. Fr. July, Aug.

6. **B. Lycium,** Royle; Fl. Br. Ind. i. 110; Brandis For. Flora 12, Ind. Trees 29; Gamble Man. Ind. Timb. 30. Vern. *Chutroi*, *Káshmal*, Jaunsar.

A shrub usually much smaller than the last two species, and somewhat gregarious in habit; bark white. *Leaves* 1·5-2·5 in. long, oblanceolate, subsessile, mucronate, coriaceous, glaucous beneath, with prominent reticulate veins. *Racemes* simple or compound, generally exceeding the leaves; peduncle glaucous. *Flowers* dull-yellow. *Berries* ovoid, violet, with a distinct style at the apex.

JAUNSAR, TEHRI-GARHWAL, and OUTER HIMALAYA, 3,-7,000 ft. Quite abundant in certain localities.: Korwá, Chakrata, Málkōt, below Mussoorie, etc.

Economic use as of the last two species.

Fl. Apr. Fr. May.

7. **B. asiatica,** Roxb.; Fl. Br. Ind. i. 110; Brandis For. Flora 12, Ind. Trees 29; Gamble Man. Ind. Timb. 30. Vern. *Kingorá*, Dún and Garhwal.

A much-branched spreading shrub with pale bark. *Leaves* 2-3 in. long, broad-obovate, hard, coriaceous, strongly reticulate and grey beneath, usually with large distant spinous teeth. *Racemes* corymbose, dense-flowered, shorter than the leaves. *Flowers* ·2 in. diam., pale-yellow. *Berries* ·4-·5 in. long, ovoid, red or black, glaucous.

LOWER HILLS, generally between 3,000 and 5,000 ft., but along the OUTER HIMALAYAN STREAMS as low down as Tháno, 2,400 ft., the Bindál nadi near Dehra, 2,200 ft., and in the Suswa near Phándowála, 1,800 ft.

Berry edible.

Fl. Feb.-Apr. Fr. Apr.-June.

To this Family belongs the herbaceous plant *Podophyllum emodi*, Wall.; Fl. Br. Ind. i. 112. Vern. *Rikhpetá*, Jaunsar;—the rootstock of which yields the valuable medicine known as Podophylline. *Leaves* 2 or 3, 6-9 in. diam., 3- or more-lobed, margins laciniate and serrate. *Flowers* 1-1·5 in. diam., white or light-rose. *Fruit* ovoid, 1·5-2·5 in. long. Common in shady places above 7,000 ft. in JAUNSAR and TEHRI-GARHWAL.—*G. P. n. 18.*

Order 2.—PARIETALES.

FAM. 7. CAPPARIDACEÆ; G. P. N. 12.

Herbs or shrubs, rarely trees. *Leaves* alternate, simple or palmately 3-9-foliolate. *Flowers* usually bisexual, cruciform, regular or irregular. *Sepals* 4, free or connate. *Petals* generally 4, hypogynous or seated on a disk. *Stamens* 4-8, or indefinite, inserted at the base of a gynophore; filaments slender; anthers versatile. *Ovary* usually long-stipitate, 1-celled; style short or 0; ovules indefinite, on parietal placentas. *Fruit* a berry or a capsule. *Seeds* exalbuminous.

Analysis of the Genera.

Generally climbing or straggling shrubs.
  Leaves simple: petals sessile . . 1. CAPPARIS.
A tree. Leaves trifoliolate; petals clawed . 2. CRATÆVA.

1. Capparis, Linn.; G. P. n. 17.

Shrubs, rarely trees, usually with stipulary thorns. *Leaves* simple, sometimes caducous. *Sepals* 4, usually free. *Petals* 4, sessile, imbricate. *Stamens* indefinite; filaments filiform. *Ovary* on a long gynophore; stigma sessile. *Fruit* a fleshy berry; seeds many.

Analysis of the Species.

Flowers large, solitary, axillary . . . 1. *C. spinosa.*
Flowers small, umbelled . . . . . 2. *C. sepiaria.*
Flowers large, 2-4 in vertical lines, supra-axillary . . . . . . 3. *C. horrida.*

1. **C. spinosa,** Linn.; Fl. Br. Ind. i. 173; Brandis For. Flora 14, Ind. Trees 33; Gamble Man. Ind. Timb. 33. The Caper plant. Vern. *Kiári, Báuri,* Jaunsar.

A small trailing shrub; young parts covered with a white or yellowish caducous tomentum; thorns straight or recurved, rarely absent. *Leaves* 1·2 in. long, orbicular or broad-ovate, entire, thick, mucronate, nearly glabrous. *Flowers* 1·3 in. diam., white, fading into purplish red. *Sepals* unequal, concave. *Petals* 1 in. long, clawed, obovate, undulate. *Stamens* numerous, purple, longer than the petals. *Gynophore* as long as the stamens, with glands at the base. *Fruit* 1·3 in. long, red inside when ripe.

On dry hot rocks at low elevations in the HILLS.: Tons and Pábar valleys.

"The fruit is pickled, and the leaves and ripe fruit are a favourite food of goats and sheep."—*Sir D. Brandis.*

Fl. May-July. Fr. Cold season.

2. **C. sepiaria,** Linn.; Fl. Br. Ind. i 177; Brandis For. Flora 15, Ind. Trees 34. Gamble Man. Ind. Timb. 35.

A large climbing shrub with thorny stem and branches. *Leaves* green, very variable, usually 1·2 in. long and ovate. *Flowers* white, ·3-·5 in. diam., in sessile or shortly peduncled umbels; pedicels slender, ·5-·8 in. long. *Sepals* ovate. *Petals* narrow-oblong. *Ovary* ovoid. *Fruit* ·3 in. diam., black, on a short gynophore.

Scrub forests at the foot of the SAHÁRANPUR SIWALIKS, *e.g.*, Barkálá, Kasúmri, Kôtri, Ránipur, etc.

Fl. Rainy season.

3. **C. horrida,** Linn.; Fl. Br. Ind. i. 178; Brandis For. Flora 15, Ind. Trees 35; Gamble Man. Ind. Timb. 36. Vern. *His. Hins, Kalis, Kálhis, Kálhins, Khalis,* Dún; *Jhiri,* Hind.

A tall scrambling shrub, covered when young with ferruginous caducous tomentum; stem thickly beset with scattered thorns. *Leaves* 4 by 2-5 in. but often much smaller, oblong or ovate, mucronate. *Flowers* 1·5-2 in. diam., white, fading into dull-rose; pedicels ·5-1 in. long, 2-4 in a vertical line above the leaf. *Stamens* very numerous, purple. *Fruit* subglobose, 1-1·5 in. diam., on a gynophore 1·5-2 in. long.

Common in scrub forests in the DÚN, and at the base of the SAHÁRANPUR SIWALIKS: Kálsi; Ránipur, etc.

The leaves and twigs are eaten by goats, cattle and elephants.

Fl. Feb.-May. Fr. Aug., Sept.

2. Cratæva, Linn.; G. P. n. 21.

1. **C. religiosa,** Forst.; Fl. Br. Ind. i. 172; Brandis For. Flora 16; Gamble Man. Ind. Timb. 32. Vern. *Bárna*, Saháranpur.

A moderate-sized deciduous tree; bark grey, fairly smooth, with long horizontal wrinkles. *Leaves* 3-foliolate; petiole 4-6 in. long. *Leaflets* 3-6 by 1·3-3 in., ovate or ovate-lanceolate, acuminate, entire, glabrous, subcoriaceous, pale beneath; petiolules auriculate. *Flowers* 2-3 in. diam., white, pale-yellow or light-rose, in many-flowered lax terminal corymbs. *Sepals* 4, deciduous. *Petals* 4, long-clawed, oblong, ovate or spathulate, 1-1·5 in. long. *Stamens* numerous; filaments slender, free, exceeding the petals. *Ovary* on a long gynophore. *Stigma* sessile. *Fruit* a many-seeded ovoid berry, 1-2 in. diam., rough with white specks; seeds imbedded in a yellow pulp.

Foot of the SAHÁRANPUR SIWALIKS near Bádsháhibágh, Mohand, Beribára, Gaj-Ráu Block, etc. Also Pathri Forest. Rather scarce. Cultivated in gardens for the flowers.

Wood yellowish-white, moderately hard, even-grained; weight about 45 lbs. per c. ft. It is used for drums, models, writing boards, combs, and turnery. The leaves are lopped for cattle- and camel-fodder.

Fl. Apr., May.

FAM. 8. BIXACEÆ; G. P. N. 17.

Trees or shrubs. *Leaves* alternate, simple; stipules minute or 0. *Flowers* regular, 1-2-sexual. *Sepals* 4-5, imbricate, often deciduous. *Petals* 4-5 or 0, caducous. *Stamens* often numerous and hypogynous, opening by pores or slits. *Ovary* generally 1-celled; ovules parietal, usually numerous. *Fruit* either a dry capsule dehiscing by valves, or a fleshy indehiscent berry. *Seeds* arillate or with a pulpy testa; albumen copious.

Analysis of the Genera.

Leaves lobed; petals large; fruit a capsule . 1. COCHLOSPERMUM.
Leaves not lobed; petals none; fruit indehiscent.
  Styles 2 or more . . . . . . 2. FLACOURTIA.
  Style 1 . . . . 3. XYLOSMA.

1. Cochlospermum, Kunth.; G. P. n. 1.

1. **C. Gossypium,** DC.; Fl. Br. Ind. i. 190; Brandis For. Flora 17, Ind. Trees 38; Gamble Man. Ind. Timb. 37. Vern. *Gejrá, Arlú,* Sahâranpur.

A small deciduous tree with short branches and deeply cracked thick bark. *Leaves* palmately 5-lobed, 4-6 in. diam.; lobes acuminate, more or less tomentose beneath; petioles thick, 6-9 in. long. *Flowers* 2-sexual, 3-4 in. across, in terminal panicles, appearing before the leaves; peduncle and pedicles covered with grey tomentum. *Sepals* 5, ovate or elliptic, 5 in. long, silky. *Petals* 5, bright-yellow, obovate, 1-2 in. long, with numerous fine parallel veins. *Stamens* numerous, inserted on a disk; filaments ·5-·7 in. long, filiform; anthers opening by a slit at the top or by a pore. *Fruit* a pyriform capsule, 5-valved; valves 2-3 in. long. *Seeds* kidney-shaped, ·2 in. long, covered with soft silky wool.

Common on dry slopes of the OUTER SIWALIKS, especially towards Ránipur.

Wood very soft, light and spongy, of no use. A white gum exudes from the bark which is used in country medicine under the name *Katírá.* A very showy tree in the hot season.

Leafless Dec.-Apr. Fl. Mar., Apr. Fr. June, July.

2. Flacourtia, Commers.; G. P. n. 17.

Trees or shrubs, generally spinous. *Leaves* crenate. *Flowers* small, usually diœcious. *Sepals* 4-5, small, imbricate. *Petals* none. *Stamens* numerous; anthers versatile. *Ovary* on a glandular disk; styles 2 or more. *Fruit* a berry with many seeds.

Analysis of the Species.

Leaves long-acuminate, quite glabrous; fruit large . . . . . . 1. *F. Cataphracta.*
Leaves rounded or obtuse, tomentose beneath; fruit small . . . . 2. *F. Ramontchi.*

1. **F. Cataphracta,** Roxb.; Fl. Br. Ind. i. 193; Gamble Man. Ind. Timb. 39; Brandis Ind. Trees 39. Vern. *Pathnálá, Jamnuá,* Dún.

A small evergreen tree, bearing compound spines up to middle age; bark smooth. *Leaves* 3-5 in. long., ovate or ovate-lanceolate, long-acuminate, crenate, thin but tough, quite glabrous, shining above; base acute, rarely rounded; petiole ·1-·2 in. long. *Flowers* very small, in irregular racemes; stigmas 4-6. *Fruit* globose, ·5-·7 in. diam., crowned by the persistent stigmas, on peduncles ·3-·5 in. long, very acid, dark-purple when ripe.

Sál forests of the DÚN. Common along the banks of the Ré nadi, and in other low-lying shady places. Occasionally in the SAHÁRANPUR DISTRICT, *e.g.*, at Dholkhand.

The wood is hard and compact and is used for agricultural implements. The acid fruit is eaten.

Fl. July, Aug. Fr. Nov., Dec.

2. **F. Ramontchi,** L'Herit.; Fl. Br. Ind. i. 193; Brandis For. Flora 18, Ind. Trees 40; Gamble Man. Ind. Timb. 40. Vern. *Kandái, Kandei,* Hind.; *Kángo,* E. DÚN.

A small thorny deciduous tree with rough whitish-grey bark; young parts tomentose. *Leaves* 2-4 in. long, ovate obovate or suborbicular, obtusely serrate or crenate, glabrous or glabrescent above, usually tomentose beneath; petiole ·2-·3 in. long, tomentose. *Flowers* small, greenish-yellow, in short racemes. *Sepals* rusty-hairy.

Stigmas 5-11, free or connate. *Fruit* globose, ·3-·5 in. diam. subacid, red or dark-brown when ripe; seeds 8-16.

Throughout the FORESTS of the SIWALIK DIVISION. Also MUSSOORIE and MÁLKÔT HILLS; at Kálsi, Saiá and in the Tons valley in JAUNSAR,—up to about 4,000 ft.; most abundant in scrub forests.

The wood is hard and durable, and is used for agricultural implements. The leaves and twigs are lopped for fodder. The fruit is eaten.

Leafless Feb., Mar. Fl. Mar., Apr. Fr. May, June.

3. Xylosma, Forster; G. P. n. 19.

1. **X. longifolium,** Clos.; Fl. Br. Ind. i. 1904; Brandis For. Flora 19, Ind. Trees 40; Gamble Man. Ind. Timb. 18. Vern. *Siálu, Kátári, Kandhára,* Dún; *Phaláma,* Garhwal.

A moderate-sized evergreen tree thorny when young, propagated chiefly by rootsuckers. *Leaves* 3-6 by 1-2 in., oblong-lanceolate, obtusely serrate, coriaceous, glabrous, shining above when young, deeper green but dull when old; petiole ·2-·4 in. long. *Flowers* small, yellow, diœcious, in short dense-flowered axillary panicles; pedicels bracteate. *Petals* none. *Style* 1, short. *Fruit* a 2-8-seeded more or less dry berry, about ·2 in. diam.

Common in shady ravines throughout the DÚN, occasionally also in the SAHÁRANPUR-SIWALIKS. Also in valleys in the MUSSOORIE and MÁLKÔT HILLS and in JAUNSAR. Lachiwála, Mohkumpur, Karwápáni, Ámbári, Chilláwáli Ráu, etc.

The wood is pinkish, moderately hard and even-grained, used chiefly for fuel and charcoal; weight 55 lbs. per c. ft.

Fl. Nov.-Jan. Fr. Mar.-May.

Order 3.—POLYGALES.

FAM. 9. PITTOSPORACEÆ; G. P. N. 18.

Trees or shrubs, sometimes climbing. *Leaves* alternate, rarely subverticillate, usually entire, exstipulate. *Flowers* usually 2-sexual. *Sepals* and *petals* 5 each, imbricate. *Stamens* 5, hypogynous, alternating with the petals; anthers versatile. *Ovary* 1-celled with 2-5 parietal placentas; ovules many; style simple; stigma 2-5-lobed. *Fruit* capsular or indehiscent. *Seeds* usually many.

1. Pittosporum, Banks; G. P. n. 1.

Trees or shrubs. *Sepals* and *petals* free or connate at the base. *Stamens* erect; filaments subulate. *Ovary* usually 2-valved. *Fruit* a 1-celled 2-valved capsule. *Seeds* smooth, imbedded in a viscid pulp.

Analysis of the Species.

(Sir D. Brandis.)

Leaves, young branches and capsules glabrous	1. *P. floribundum.*
Leaves, young branches and capsules tomentose	2. *P. eriocarpum.*

1. **P. floribundum,** W. & A.; Fl. Br. Ind. i. 199; Brandis For. Flora 19, Ind. Trees 42; Gamble Man. Ind. Timb. 43.

A small handsome tree with a short trunk and spreading branches; bark ash-colour or yellowish-grey, rough with small white specks. *Leaves* 3-6 in. long, lanceolate or elliptic-oblong, acute or acuminate, thinly coriaceous, shining above; margins wavy or obscurely toothed; midrib prominent; lateral nerves faint; petiole ·5-·7 in. long. *Flowers* yellowish, numerous, about ·3 in. across, in corymbosely branched short terminal panicles. *Sepals* subciliate. *Petals* free, linear-oblong. *Style* persistent. *Capsule* the size of a pea, rugose, yellow when ripe; seeds about 6, in a red pulp.

OUTER HIMALAYA and the DÚN, in shady places or ravines.—Rámgarh, Mohkumpur, Lachiwála, Mothroṇwála, Karwápáni, Timli Pass, etc.

Wood light-grey, strong and tough, but used only for fuel.

Fl. Jan.-June. Fr. Apr.-Nov.

2. **P. eriocarpum,** Royle; Fl. Br. Ind. i. 199; Brandis For. Flora 19, Ind. Trees 43; Gamble Man. Ind. Timb. 44.

A small tree with spreading branches; young parts brown-tomentose. *Leaves* 4-8 in. long, obovate or broadly oblanceolate, glabrate above, yellowish-tomentose beneath; petiole ·7-1·2 in. long. *Flowers* pale-yellow, ·3 in. across, in many-flowered umbellate corymbs. *Sepals* lanceolate, tomentose. *Petals* free, linear. *Capsules* ·5 in. diam., felted-tomentose, tipped with the persistent style; valves woody; seeds many.

MUSSOORIE HILLS; above Rájpur in Kiárkuli Forest, also at Sahansra-dhárá, 3,-6,000 ft.: Ámláwa Valley in JAUNSAR.

Wood used only for fuel.

Fl. Mar., Apr. Fr. May-July.

Order 4.—CARYOPHYLLALES.

FAM. 10. TAMARICACEÆ; G. P. N. 24.

Shrubs or small trees. *Leaves* alternate, minute, often scale-like and adpressed on the branches, exstipulate. *Flowers* regular, usually 2-sexual, in simple or panicled spikes or racemes. *Sepals* and *petals* often 5 each, imbricate, free or connate below. *Stamens* as many or twice as many as the petals, inserted on a glandular disk; anthers versatile. *Ovary* with 3-5 carpels. *Fruit* a capsule dehiscing into 3-5 valves. *Seeds* hairy or winged.

1. Tamarix, Linn.; G. P. n. 1.

1. **T. dioica,** Roxb.; Fl. Br. Ind. i. 249; Brandis For. Flora 21, Ind. Trees 46; Gamble Man. Ind. Timb. 46. Vern. *Jháu Lál Jháu*, Hind.

A gregarious shrub; bark reticulately cracked. *Leaves* minute, sheathing, acuminate, green with white margins. *Flowers* usually diœcious, light rose-coloured. *Sepals* and *petals* free.; bracts acuminate, with a sheathing base, as long as the flowers. *Stamens* 5, about twice as long as the petals. *Capsules* oblong, ·2 in. long.

Along open streams in the DÚN, such as the Sông and Suswá rivers; also in the ráus of the SAHÁRANPUR SIWALIKS, and at Bishenpur and other places along the Ganges.

Wood red and moderately hard, but used chiefly for fuel. Weight about 50 lbs. per c. ft.

Fl. May-July. Fr. Cold season.

Order 5.—GUTTIFERALES.

FAM. 11. HYPERICACEÆ; G. P. N. 26.

Herbs or shrubs. *Leaves* opposite, entire, gland-dotted, exstipulate. *Flowers* regular, 2-sexual, usually cymose, terminal or axillary, generally yellow. *Sepals* usually 5, imbricate. *Petals* as many as the sepals, contorted in bud. *Stamens* indefinite, 3-5-adelphous, rarely free or monadelphous; anthers versatile. *Ovary* 1-3-5-celled; ovules numerous, generally on axile placentas; styles 3-5, filiform, united. *Fruit* a septicidal capsule. *Seeds* numerous, exalbuminous.

1. Hypericum, Linn.; G. P. n. 2.

Herbs or shrubs. *Leaves* generally sessile. *Flowers* cymose. *Petals* yellow, usually oblique, sometimes gland-dotted.

Analysis of the Species.

Flowers large; styles twice the length of the ovary . . . . 1. *H. cernuum.*
Flowers small; styles as long as the ovary . 2. *H. patulum.*

1. **H. cernuum,** Roxb.; Fl. Br. Ind. i. 253; Brandis Ind. Trees 48; Gamble Man. Ind. Timb. 48. Vern. *Pingniárá, Phiuṇli*, Jaunsar; *Piuli*, Málkōt.

A glabrous shrub. *Leaves* 1-3 by ·5-1 in., decussate, sessile, elliptic or ovate-lanceolate, entire, minutely dotted, glaucous beneath; *tip acute or rounded. Flowers 2* in. diam., *bright golden-yellow, 3-5 in a short terminal cyme. Petals obovate, longer than the stamens. Styles* ·5-·8 in. long, spreading. *Capsules* conical, ·3-·5 in. long.

Throughout JAUNSAR and the OUTER HIMALAYA, 5,-8,000 ft., often on rocks.—Korwá, Kathián, Málkōt, etc.

Fl. Apr., May.

2. **H. patulum,** Thunb.; Fl. Br. Ind. i. 254; Brandis Ind. Trees 48; Gamble Man. Ind. Timb. 48.

A shrub. *Leaves* distichous, ·5-1·5 in. long, narrow-rhomboid or elliptical, very shortly petioled, black-dotted and rusty beneath; margins reflexed. *Flowers* 1 in. diam. *Sepals* ·2 in. *Petals* yellow, orbicular or elliptical, longer than the stamens. *Styles* equalling the ovary but exceeding the stamens. *Capsules* obtusely conical, ·2-·3 in. long.

HILLS of MUSSOORIE and JAUNSAR at 5,-7,000 ft. in shady ravines, sometimes on rocks.

Fl. Apr., May.

FAM. 12. TERNSTRŒMIACEÆ; G. P. N. 28.

Shrubs or trees. *Leaves* alternate, simple, exstipulate, usually coriaceous. *Flowers* regular, generally showy and 2-sexual, usually subtended by a pair of bracts. *Sepals* and *petals* 5 each, imbricate, the latter sometimes connate below. *Stamens* numerous, hypogynous, free or connate at the base, often adnate to the petals. *Ovary* syncarpous, usually 3-5-celled, rarely many-celled; ovules 2 or many in each cell, on axile placentas; styles as many as the cells, free or connate. *Fruit* a berry or a capsule. *Seeds* few or many; albumen scanty or 0.

Analysis of the Genera.

Erect shrubs or trees.
Leaves smooth, evergreen; flowers white, on simple pedicels.
Flowers small, diœcious; fruit a berry . . 1. EURYA.
Flowers large, 2-sexual; fruit a capsule . 4. CAMELLIA.
Leaves rough, deciduous; flowers usually pink, panicled. . . . . 3. SAURAUJA.
Climbing shrubs. Flowers white, cymose; fruit a fleshy berry . . . . 2. ACTINIDIA.

1. Eurya, Thunb.; G. P. n. 12.

1. **E. acuminata,** DC.; Fl. Br. Ind. i. 285; Gamble Man. Ind. Timb. 64. Brandis Ind. Trees 58. Syn.—*E. japonica*, Thunb. (partly); Brandis For. Flora 24.

An evergreen shrub with brown smooth bark; branchlets terete; young parts generally hairy. *Leaves* 2-4 by ·5-·8 in., oblong-lanceolate, acuminate, closely crenate-serrulate, coriaceous, usually glabrous above; midrib depressed above, hairy beneath; lateral nerves indistinct; petiole very short. *Flowers* white, small, diœcious, about 5 together in the axils of the leaves; pedicels short, 2-bracteolate. *Sepals* 5, concave, pubescent outside. *Petals* 5, white, alternating with and exceeding the sepals, ·1 in. long, more or less united below. *Stamens* 12-15, shorter than the petals. *Fruit* globose, of the size of a peppercorn, crowned by the remains of the styles.

OUTER HIMALAYA, 3,-7,000 ft.: Málkōt Hills; Mussoorie. Also low valleys in the HILLS, *e.g.*, Bámsu, Kulni, etc.

Wood reddish-brown, close-grained, moderately hard.

Fl. Nov., Dec.

2. Actinidia, Lindl.; G. P. n. 14.

1. **A. callosa,** Lindl.; Fl. Br. Ind. i. 286; Brandis Ind. Trees 62.

A climbing shrub; stems brown, white-warted. *Leaves* 3-5 by 2-3 in., broadly elliptic, acuminate, serrulate; lateral nerves 6-8 pairs; petiole 1-2·5 in. *Flowers* white, ·5 in. diam., polygamous or diœcious in lax umbellate axillary cymes. *Sepals* 5, oblong, obtuse, tomentose. *Petals* 5, contorted-imbricate. *Stamens* many. *Ovary* hairy, many-celled; styles numerous, elongated after flowering. *Fruit* a fleshy ovoid berry, ·8 in. long, edible.

Valleys below MUSSOORIE and in DEHRA DÚN (*Mr. P. W. Mackinnon*). Very scarce.

Fl. June. Fr. Sept.

3. Saurauja, Willd.; G. P. n. 15.

1. **S. napaulensis,** DC.; Fl. Br. Ind. i. 286; Brandis For. Flora 25, Ind. Trees 62; Gamble Man. Ind. Timb. 65. Vern. *Ratendú*, Jaunsar; *Goginá*, Hind.

A small tree sparingly branched; bark reddish-brown; young parts and inflorescence covered with long tapering stiff brown hairs. *Leaves* approximate at the ends of the branches, 7-14 by 2·5-4 in., oblong or oblanceolate, acute or short-acuminate, acutely serrate, rusty-tomentose beneath, especially when young; lateral nerves numerous, parallel, prominent; petiole 1-1·5 in., rough. *Flowers* pink, ·5 in. diam., in lax drooping axillary panicles; bracts imbricate. *Sepals* small, fleshy. *Petals* pink, usually connate at the base; margins fimbriate. *Stamens* many; anthers dehiscing by pores. *Fruit* fleshy, green, 5-lobed, with a mealy sweet pulp. *Seeds* reddish-brown, small.

Damp valleys in the HILLS, 3,-5,000 ft.: Mayargádh below Jádi, Garugádh in the Tons Valley, Sansáru Khálá, etc.

Wood light-pink, soft, spongy. The ripe fruit is eaten.

Fl. Apr., May. Fr. May, June.

4. Camellia, Linn.; G. P. n. 24.

1. **C. theifera,** Griff.; Fl. Br. Ind. i. 292. Syn.—*C. Thea*, Link; Brandis For. Flora 25, Ind. Trees 61; Gamble Man. Ind. Timb. 68. The Tea plant. Vern. *Chá* or *Cháh*, Hind.

A large evergreen shrub. *Leaves* 3-6 by 1-2·5 in., elliptic-oblong, acute or acuminate, serrate, usually coriaceous, glabrous above, slightly pubescent along the nerves beneath; petiole ·15 in. *Flowers* 1-1·5 in. diam., axillary, solitary or a few together on short peduncles; bracts 2-3, sepal-like. *Sepals* 5, leathery, concave, more or less pubescent, edges ciliate. *Petals* white, ·5-·7 in. long, broadly obovate, slightly coherent at the base. *Stamens* numerous, cohering at the base, adherent to the base of the petals. *Ovary* 3-5-celled. *Fruit* a loculicidal capsule, ·7-·9 in. diam., leathery; seeds few, pale-brown.

Largely cultivated in plantations in the DÚN. The wood is moderately hard and close- and even-grained. Straight branches of unpruned shrubs make very good walking sticks.

Fl. Dec.-Mar. Fr. Sept.-Dec.

FAM. 13. DIPTEROCARPACEÆ; G. P. N. 29.

Usually resinous trees. *Leaves* alternate, simple, entire, penninerved; stipules usually small and early deciduous. *Flowers* regular, 2-sexual, in panicles. *Calyx* gamosepalous, campanulate, free or adnate to the ovary, 5-lobed; 2 or more of the lobes usually accrescent in fruit forming wings. *Petals* 5, twisted. *Stamens* 5-15 or indefinite, hypo- or perigynous, free, connate or adnate to the petals; anthers with an aristate connective. *Ovary* slightly immersed in the torus, usually 3-celled. *Fruit* capsular or nut-like, usually winged with the variously enlarged calyx-lobes. *Seed* usually exalbuminous; cotyledons fleshy.

1. Shorea, Roxb.; G. P. n. 8.

1. **S. robusta,** Gærtn.; Fl. Br. Ind. i. 306; Brandis For. Flora 26, Ind. Trees 69; Gamble Man. Ind. Timb. 77. The Sál tree. Vern. *Sál*, Hind.

A large tree, deciduous but seldom quite leafless; bark of young trees blackish-brown, smooth or with a few longitudinal cracks, marked with minute grey specks; of old trees very thick, dark-grey, rough with irregular furrows. *Leaves* 4-12 by 2-7 in., ovate-oblong, acuminate, tough, thinly coriaceous, glabrous and shining when fully mature; lateral nerves 12-15 pairs, those near the apex very slender; base cordate or rounded; petiole terete, ·5-·8 in. long; stipules ·3 in. long, pubescent, caducous. *Flowers* subsessile, in large lax terminal or axillary racemose panicles, covered with white pubescence. *Calyx-tube* short, adnate to the torus; segments ovate, all accrescent in fruit. *Petals* pale-yellow, about ·5 in. long, narrow-oblong or lanceolate, much exceeding the calyx-segments in flower. *Stamens* up to 50, many times shorter than the petals; connective subulate, bearded, minutely trifid at the apex. *Ovary* 3-celled; style subulate. *Fruit* ·5 in. long, ovoid, acute, rather fleshy, indehiscent, white-pubescent; wings 5, 2-3 in. long, spathulate, narrowed at the base, brown when dry, somewhat unequal, with 10-12 straight parallel nerves.

The principal tree of the SIWALIK DIVISION ascending to 4,000 ft. in the OUTER HILLS OF MÁLKÔT, MUSSOORIE and JAUNSAR, everywhere most remarkably gregarious. "In the NEPAL TERAI, the sál tree attains 100-150 ft. with a clear stem to the first branch of 60-80 ft., and a girth of 20-25 ft."—*Sir D. Brandis.* Within the limits of this Flora, however, it is seldom more than 80 ft. in height and 6 ft. in girth, unless hollow inside. The sapwood is whitish, not durable. The heartwood is brown, cross-grained, hard, and very durable; weight when fully seasoned 50-60 lbs. per c. ft. It seasons very badly and warps and splits in drying. For building purposes, however, it is the strongest and most important timber of Northern India. The tree yields, when tapped, a large quantity of a white opaline resin which is burnt as an incense, being considered indispensable as such in certain Hindu religious ceremonies, and is also used to caulk boats and ships. An oil is extracted from the fruit, which is used for burning and to adulterate ghee. The fruit is also ground into flour and eaten by the poorer classes during times of scarcity.

New leaves and Fl. Mar., Apr. Fr. May-July.

Order 6.—MALVALES.

FAM. 14. MALVACEÆ; G. P. N. 31.

Herbs, shrubs or soft-wooded trees; bark with mucilaginous juice and tenacious fibre; young parts mostly covered with stellate hairs. *Leaves* alternate, stipulate, simple lobed or degitately compound, usually palminerved. *Bracteoles* 3 or more, often forming an epicalyx. *Flowers* regular, generally 2-sexual, axillary or terminal, solitary fascicled or cymosely panicled. *Sepals* 5, more or less connate, valvate in bud. *Petals* 5, hypogynous, twistedly imbricate. *Stamens* generally indefinite, monadelphous, rarely pentadelphous; anthers 1-celled, bursting longitudinally. *Ovary* syncarpous; carpels generally numerous; ovules attached to the inner angle of each carpel. *Styles* more or less connate; stigma various. *Fruit* a loculicidal capsule, or of dry cocci. *Seeds* sometimes with silky tubular hairs well-known as cotton; albumen scanty or 0.

Analysis of the Genera.

Leaves simple; bracteoles 4-6; seeds naked . 1. KYDIA.
Leaves digitate; bracteoles 0; seeds woolly . 2. BOMBAX.

1. Kydia, Roxb.; G. P. n. 19.

1. **K. calycina,** Roxb.; Fl. Br. Ind. i. 348; Brandis For. Flora 29. Ind. Trees 78; Gamble Man. Ind. Timb. 89. Vern. *Púlá, Fúlú, Púli,* Hind.

A moderate-sized deciduous tree; bark grey, exfoliating in long strips, rough with large white specks on branches; young parts covered with grey stellate hairs. *Leaves* 4-6 in. diam., rounded, cordate, palmately 5-7 nerved, generally with as many lobes or angles as nerves, glabrate or with scattered hairs above, downy and pale beneath; petiole about half the length of the blade. *Flowers* ·5-·7 in. across, polygamous, generally diœcious, in much-branched axillary or terminal panicles. *Bracteoles* 4-6, accrescent and spreading in fruit. *Calyx* campanulate, 5-lobed, accrescent. *Petals* white, clawed, adnate to the staminal tube, longer than the calyx. *Stamens* monadelphous; the tube shorter than the petals and split half way into 5 segments, each bearing at the apex 3-5 sessile anthers. *Carpels* 3; style 3-cleft. *Capsule* subglobose, 3-valved; seeds reniform, furrowed.

Very common in the DÚN and SAHÁRANPUR FORESTS, also in valleys in the HILLS at low elevations.

Wood white, soft, used only for fuel; weight 40-45 lbs. per c.ft. The tree is of little value except as a help to reproduction in blanks and glades. The bark is often used for tying up bundles of faggot in the forest. "In North India it is employed for the clarification of sugar."—*Sir D. Brandis.*

Leafless Feb.-Apr. Fl. July-Oct. Fr. Dec.-Feb.

2. Bombax, Linn.; G. P. n. 42.

1. **B. malabaricum,** DC.; Fl. Br. Ind. i. 349; Brandis For. Flora 30, Ind. Trees 77; Gamble Man. Ind. Timb. 90. The Silk-cotton tree. Vern. *Simal, Semal,* Hind.

A large deciduous tree. *Stem* straight, more or less buttressed at the base when old, covered with large conical prickles when young; branches whorled, horizontally spreading. *Leaves* digitate; common petiole 6-12 in. long. *Leaflets* 5-7, 6-9 by 3-5 in., lanceolate oblanceolate or obovate, acuminate, entire, more or less coriaceous, glabrous; petiolule 1 in. long; stipules small, caducous. *Flowers* 4-5 in. across, fleshy. *Calyx* very fleshy, cup-shaped, bright silky-hairy inside. *Petals* crimson or orange, 3-6 in. long, oblong, white-tomentose outside. *Stamens* usually 5-adelphous; filaments numerous, the innermost forked. *Ovary* 5-celled; style 5-lobed at the apex. *Capsule* 5-7 in. long, oblong-ovoid, 5-angled. *Seeds* obovate, smooth, surrounded by long white silky hairs.

Common in the DÚN and SAHÁRANPUR DISTRICTS ascending to 4,000 ft. in the OUTER HIMALAYA and in valleys in the HILLS, generally affecting water-logged places, *e.g.*, the Pathri Forest, SAHÁRANPUR DISTRICT, and Nakraunda, Jogiwála, and dry beds of the Sông in the DÚN.

The wood is very soft and perishable, but durable under water; weight 17-32 lbs. per c. ft. It is used for planking, packing cases, toys, well-curbs and water-shoots. The calyx of flowers not yet fully open is eaten cooked as a vegetable. The cotton is used to stuff pillows and cushions. The seed is valued as a nourishing food for cattle which also greedily devour the flowers. The roots of saplings are used as a nervine tonic in Indian medical practice.

Fl. Jan.-Mar. Fr. Apr., May.

There are several shrubs or undershrubs belonging to this Family, either wild or cultivated in the SIWALIK

DIVISION, which deserve mention. Among these are—

i. Cultivated plants.—

1. *Gossypium herbaceum*, Linn.
2. „ *barbadense*, Linn.

} Fl. Br. Ind. i. 346, 347. The cotton plants,—which are easily recognized by the large leafy bracteoles and the white cotton surrounding the seeds. Vern. *Kapás*, Hind.—*G. P. n. 39.*

3. *Hibiscus esculentus*, Linn.; Fl. Br. Ind. i. 343. The Okra or Ladies' finger. Vern. *Bhindi*. The tender fruit is used as a vegetable.—*G P. n. 34.*

4. *Hibiscus Rosa-sinensis*, Linn. Vern. *Jaiá*, Hind.
5. „ *mutabilis*, Linn. Vern. *Gul-i-ajáib*, Hind.
6. „ *syriacus*, Linn. Vern. *Gur-hal*, Hind.

} Fl. Br. Ind. i. 344. These are common garden plants in the DÚN with large showy flowers.

ii. Wild plants.—

1. *Sida carpinifolia*, Linn.
2. „ *rhombifolia*, Linn. Vern. *Kharenti*, Dún.
3. „ *cordifolia*, Linn.

} Fl. Br. Ind. i. 323, 324. *Leaves* narrow, not lobed. *Flowers* yellow.—*G. P. n. 16.*

4. *Abutilon indicum*, G. Don.
5. „ *ramosum*, Guill. & Perr.

} Fl. Br. Ind. i. 326 and 328; Vern. *Tepári*, Hind. *Leaves* cordate, hairy. *Flowers* yellow, opening in the evening.—*G. P. n. 21.*

These are all weeds of roadside, forest-glades or waste places, but yield fibres which will probably be found of value in the future.

5. *Urena lobata*, Linn., Fl. Br. Ind. i. 329. Vern. *Úngá*, Dún. Noticeable for its pink flowers and barbed capsules which attach themselves on to clothes. The stem gives a useful fibre. *Leaves* about 3 in. across, 5-7-lobed. Common in coppice areas and road-sides—*G. P. n. 25.*

6. *Thespesia Lampas*, Dalz. & Gibs.; Fl. Br. Ind. i. 345 Vern. *Ban Kapási*, Dún. A common undershrub in glades in Sál forests and also on fire-traces, easily recognized by its large bright-yellow flowers with a crimson centre which appear during the rains. *Leaves* 4-6 in. diam., 3-lobed, cordate; petiole 2-3 in. long. *Capsule* ovoid, 1 in. long, erect, generally infested with a bug of the Lygæidæ family. The plant yields a strong white fibre, and the flower is likely to give a useful dye.—*G. P. n. 37.*

FAM. 15. STERCULIACEÆ; G. P. N. 32.

Herbs, shrubs or trees, usually with soft wood; young parts generally tomentose; bark mucilaginous and with strong fibres. *Leaves* alternate, simple and lobed, or digitate, usually stipulate. *Flowers* generally regular, 1- or 2-sexual or polygamous, often bracteate, in axillary or terminal cymes or panicles, rarely solitary or fascicled. *Calyx* usually gamosepalous; segments 5. *Petals* 5 or none. *Stamens* usually monadelphous, with 5, 10, or 15 2-celled extrorse anthers. *Ovary* stipitate or sessile, free, 2-5-celled, apocarpous or syncarpous. *Fruit* a loculicidal capsule, or of distinct follicular carpels. *Seeds* attached to the inner angle of the carpels, sometimes arillate.

Analysis of the Genera.

Flowers 1-sexual or polygamous; petals none;
  (fruit of distinct carpels) . . . . 1. STERCULIA.
Flowers 2-sexual; petals 5, deciduous.
  Ovary long-stipitate; fruit of distinct
    twisted carpels . . . . . 2. HELICTERES.
  Ovary on a short gynophore; fruit a
    5-valved capsule . . . . . 3. PTEROSPERMUM.

1. Sterculia, Linn.; G. P. n. 1.

Trees or shrubs. *Leaves* simple and lobed, or digitate. *Flowers* polygamous. *Calyx* tubular, often coloured. *Staminal column* bearing a ring of sessile anthers. *Carpels* 5, more or less distinct and follicular, usually on a long gynophore, opening long before ripening. *Seeds* one or more in each carpel, often winged or arillate.

Analysis of the Species.

Lvs. sharply lobed ; follicles woody. . . 1. *S. villosa.*
Lvs. obscurely lobed ; follicles membranous . 2. *S. pallens.*

1. **S. villosa,** Roxb. ; Fl. Br. Ind. i. 355 ; Brandis For. Flora 32, Ind. Trees 80 ; Gamble Man. Ind. Timb. 94. Vern. *Godgudála*, Hind.

A moderate-sized deciduous tree with grey bark ; branches few, spreading ; branchlets stout. *Leaves* approximate at the ends of the branches, 9-18 in. diam., cordate, nearly glabrous above, tomentose beneath, deeply 5-7-lobed ; lobes ovate-oblong, acuminate, entire toothed or cleft ; petiole 12-24 in. long, hollow, downy outside ; stipules lanceolate, deciduous. *Flowers* yellow, in much-branched rusty-pubescent drooping panicles which are crowded at the ends of the leafless branches ; male flowers the most numerous ; bracts linear, caducous. *Calyx* campanulate, pinkish within, downy outside. *Anthers* inserted on a membranous ring which is adnate to the short gynophore. *Ovary* globose. *Fruit* follicular ; follicles 1·5-2·5 in. long, oblong, spreading, coriaceous, rusty-villous, red within ; seeds black.

Fairly common in the DÚN and SAHÁRANPUR FORÉSTS, also at Kálsi, generally on sandy or gravelly soil.

Wood very soft and light, about 20 lbs. per c. ft., of no use. The inner bark yields a coarse strong fibre which is made into ropes and is used, either twisted or in broad bands, in dragging timber. A white clear gum exudes from cuts made in the bark which is used medicinally, and is sold in the bazaar under the name of *katíla.*

Leafless Jan.-May. Fl. Mar., Apr. Fr. June, July.

2. **S. pallens,** Wall. ; Sir G. King's Flora of the Malayan Peninsula 182 ; Brandis Ind. Trees 84 ; Gamble Man. Ind. Timb. 96. Syn.—*S. fulgens*, Wall. (partly), Fl. Br. Ind. i. 360 ; Vern. *Khardála*, Málkōt,

A middle-sized tree with yellowish-grey smooth bark. *Leaves* 8-12 in. diam., obscurely lobed, coriaceous, scabrid above, covered with dense pale-yellow stellate tomentum beneath ; petiole 8-15 in. long, pubescent. *Flowers* ·5-·7 in., in erect panicles, pale-yellow, very downy all over, caducous. *Calyx* tubular, curved ; teeth ovate, acute. *Follicles* membranous, stipitate, opening long before maturity, rather scarce.

MÁLKŌT HILLS, below MUSSOORIE. Tháno Forest in the DÚN, and Saiá in JAUNSAR ;—2,200 to 5,000 ft. Also in shady ravince in the SIWALIKS, *e.g.*, Timli and Mohand Passes.

Economic uses similar to those of *S. villosa.*

Fl. Mar., Apr. Fr. May, June.

2. Helicteres, Linn.; G. P. n. 10.

1. **H. Isora,** Linn.; Fl. Br. Ind. i. 365; Brandis For. Flora 34, Ind. Trees 88; Gamble Man. Ind. Timb. 99. Vern. *Maror-phal*, Hind.; *Kapási*, Sahắranpur.

A shrub with thin spreading branhces and grey bark; young parts covered with stellate hairs. *Leaves* 3-6 by 2-4 in., bifarious. broad-obovate or orbicular, often lobed, obliquely cordate or rounded at the base, short-acuminate, irregularly toothed, scabrous above, pubescent beneath; petiole ·2-·4 in. *Flowers* 1-2 in. long, axillary, usually 2 or 4 together, bracteate; pedicels ·2-·5 in. *Calyx* tubular, ·6-·8 in. long, indistinctly 2-lipped, brown-floccose outside. *Petals* 5, scarlet, clawed, twice the length of the calyx, reflexed, the two lower ones much larger than the rest; claws winged. *Staminal column* adnate to the gynophore; anthers 10, on short filaments; staminodes 5, scale-like. *Ovary* 5-celled, on a gynophore which is elongated in fruit; styles 5, much exserted, more or less connate. *Fruit* 1·5-·2 in. long, cylindrical, pubescent, composed of 5 spirally twisted carpels; seeds tuberclcd.

A very common shrub in the DÚN and SAHÁRANPUR FORESTS, especially in coppice areas, generally gregarious; rather scarce in Sál forests.

The branches are used for fencing and thatch-frames, and the bark yields a strong white fibre. The fruit and leaves are used in Indian medicine.

Fl. Apr.-Aug. Fr. Cold season.

3. Pterospermum, Schreb.; G. P. n. 11

1. **P. acerifolium,** Willd.; Fl. Br. Ind. i. 368; Brandis For. Flora 35, Ind. Trees 91; Gamble Man. Ind. Timb. 100. Vern. *Máyeng*, Jaunsar.

A large tree with thin grey smooth bark; young branches covered with ferruginous tomentum. *Leaves* 6-12 by 5-10 in., roundish or oblong, often lobed, entire or remotely toothed, deeply cordate or peltate, coriaceous, glabrous and deep-green above, grey-tomentose and strongly reticulate beneath, palmately 8-10-nerved from the tip of the petiole; lateral nerves 4-6 pairs; petiole 3-6 in. long, striate; stipules multifid, caducous. *Flowers* axillary, solitary or in 2-3-flowered cymes, 5-6 in. diam., fragrant, bracteate; pedicels 5 in. long. *Calyx* 5-cleft; segments valvate, 3-5 by ·3-·5 in., linear, very fleshy, floccosely brown-tomentose outside, villous within. *Petals* twistedly imbricate, linear, pure white, slightly shorter than the calyx, membranous, deciduous. *Filaments* 15, 1-1·5 in. long, filiform, in threes opposite to each sepal, with a staminode 2-3 in. long between; the whole staminal whorl forming a tube about 1 in. long below the ovary and adnate to the short gynophore; anthers 15; cells linear, ·5 in. long. *Ovary* oblong, 5-angled, inserted on the top of the staminal column; style undivided, club-shaped. *Fruit* a capsule, 4-6 in. long, 5-celled, 5-angled, woody, dark-brown, tomentose. *Seeds* compressed, with large brown membranous wings.

Banks of the Jumná from below Mussoorie to its junction with the Tons, and the Ámláwa valley up to near Saiá. Very common in the swampy forests of the EASTERN DÚN about Khairi and Sidhárwála. Frequently cultivated in DEHRA.

Growth quick. Sapwood white; heartwood soft or moderately hard, red; weight about 48 lbs. per c. ft. The leaves are lopped for cattle-fodder, and are laid on roofs underneath thatch or slate in Jaunsar; the down of the leaves is used for tinder and to stop bleeding from wounds. A plaster made of the calyx is considered infallible in glandular swellings about the neck and ears.

Fl. Mar.-June. Fr. Cold season.

P. lanceæfolium, Roxb.; Fl. Br. Ind. i. 368; is a handsome tree cultivated in gardens at DEHRA, and is found wild in the hills of KUMAON. *Leaves* lanceolate. *Flowers* 1·5 in. long. *Fruit* 2-3 in. long, woody.

FAM. 16. TILIACEÆ; G. P. N. 33.

Trees, shrubs, or herbs; bark usually mucilaginous and with strong fibres. *Leaves* usually alternate, simple or lobed; stipules free. *Flowers* regular, generally bisexual. *Sepals* 3-5, free or connate, valvate. *Petals* as many as the sepals, free, rarely absent. *Stamens* usually indefinite, free or connate, frequently inserted on a gonophore; anthers introrse. *Ovary* free, 2-10-

celled; styles columnar, or parted into as many divisions as there are cells in the ovary; placentation axile. *Fruit* a drupe or a capsule.

1. Grewia, Linn ; G. P. n. 8.

Trees or shrubs, more or less stellate-pubescent. *Leaves* alternate, usually distichous, often inequilateral, variously toothed, with 3-7 basal nerves. *Flowers* usually 2-sexual, axillary, solitary cymose or panicled. *Sepals* 5, distinct, coriaceous, coloured inside. *Petals* 5, usually glandular at the base, sometimes wanting. *Stamens* indefinite, free, all fertile, inserted on a gonophore when the petals are glandular. *Ovary* 2-4-celled. *Fruit* a drupe, more or less fleshy, entire or lobed; lobes 1-or more-seeded.

Analysis of the Species.

Peduncles generally solitary, leaf-opposed; leaves scaberulous . . . . . 1. *G. oppositifolia.*
Peduncles generally fascicled, axillary.
  Leaves oblong or ovate, more or less cordate.
    Drupe fleshy, under ·5 in. diam.; leaves softly hairy beneath.
      Trees Peduncles scarcely exceeding the petioles.
        Buds ovoid, not ribbed . . . 2. *G. vestita.*
        Buds cylindrical or clavate, ribbed . . . . . . 3. *G. asiatica.*
      An undershrub. Peduncles many times longer than the petioles 4. *G. sapida.*
    Drupe crustaceous, about 1 in. diam.; leaves scabrous . . . . 5. *G. scabrophylla.*
  Leaves lanceolate, never cordate.
    Leaves glabrescent; drupe rugose, 2-lobed, black when ripe . . . 6. *G. lævigata.*
    Leaves velvety beneath; drupe shining, smooth, 4-lobed, whitish when ripe . . . . . . 7. *G. polygama.*

1. **G. oppositifolia**, Roxb. ; Fl. Br. Ind. i. 384 ; Brandis For. Flora 37, Ind. Trees 95 ; Gamble Man. Ind. Timb. 109. Vern. *Biul, Biur*, Jaunsar ; *Bewal, Bhimal*, Dún ; *Behel*, Sahàranpur.

A moderate-sized tree with whitish bark. *Leaves* 3-6 by 1·5-3 in., broadly ovate-lanceolate, acuminate, obtusely but closely serrate, scabrous above, pubescent beneath ; base unequally rounded, usually 3-nerved (occasionally 3-6-nerved) ; cross-veins transverse and straight ; petiole ·2-·5 in. ; stipules subulate, caducous. *Flowers* in leaf-opposed umbellate cymes, rarely axillary or terminal ; buds cylindrical, pilose. *Sepals* linear, ·6-1 in. long, 3-ribbed, red and smooth inside. *Petals* linear, shorter than the sepals, white or yellow. *Drupe* 1-4-lobed, fleshy, dark-green, black when ripe, rough with scattered stiff white hairs.

Fairly common in the DÚN, *e.g.*, Tháno, Lachiwála, Phándowála, Ámbári, etc. ; more so along the foot of the SAHÁRANPUR SIWALIKS and in the Pathri Forest. Also found in JAUNSAR up to 6,000 ft., often cultivated about villages : Saiá, Dálmigádh, Tons Valley, etc.

It reaches about 40 ft. in height, with a short trunk and a spreading crown. Wood white, weighing 45-50 lbs. per c. ft. It is unpleasantly scented, and is therefore seldom used for fuel. Being tough and elastic, it is used for oar-shafts, axe-handles, banghy-poles, bows, etc. The inner bark yields a fibre which is used for rope and paper-making, and the leaves are much valued for fodder, especially in the Hills. The ripe fruit is eaten.

Fl. Apr.-June, and occasionally in winter in the Sahàranpur Forests. Fr. Oct.-Dec.

There seem to be two forms, if not two varieties, grouped under this—one represented by the SAHÁRANPUR tree with white petals, and the other by the HILL one which has yellow petals.

2. **G. vestita**, Wall. ; Brandis For. Flora 40, Ind. Trees 98 ; Gamble Man. Ind. Timb. 110. Syn.—*G. asiatica*, var. *vestita*, Wall.; Fl. Br. Ind. i. 387. Vern. *Dháman*, Hind.

A tree with grey bark ; branches and young plants with large white blotches. *Leaves* 3-5 by 2-3·5 in., obliquely ovate, generally not cordate, acuminate, minutely serrate, sometimes obscurely 3-lobed, pale and softly downy beneath, especially when young ; basal nerves 5-6 ; petiole generally not exceeding ·5 in. ; stipules linear. *Flowers* in densely crowded (rarely solitary) axillary cymes ; peduncles ·3-·4 in. long, hairy, bearing 2-3 bracteolate pedicels ; buds ovoid, ·15-·2 in. long, not ribbed. *Sepals* slightly pubescent and yellow inside. *Petals* yellow, much shorter than the sepals. *Drupe* globose, ·2-·3 in. diam., sometimes indistinctly 2-4-lobed, dark-brown or black when ripe.

A very common tree in both Sál and mixed forests of the SIWALIK DIVISION, extending to the SIWALIKS and to the OUTER HIMALAYAN slopes and low-level valleys in JAUNSAR.

Wood grey, tough, elastic, hard and close-grained, used for banghy-poles, bows, spear-handles, etc. Weight about 50 lbs. per c. ft. The branches are lopped for fodder, and the fruit is eaten. The bark yields strong white fibres.

Fl. Apr.-June. Fr. Aug.-Nov.

On comparing a series of specimens collected by me, Mr. Duthie was satisfied that *G. elastica*, Royle, was quite distinct from *G. vestita*, Wall., on the grounds that in the former the innovations were dark rusty-tomentose, the petals not glandular at the base, and the leaves very frequently lobed. It occurs only in the HILLS; *e.g.*, above Thadiár. Mr. Haines' investigations, however, went to show that the foregoing characters were by no means constant. It would, therefore, appear to be only a local form of Wallich's *G. vestita*.

3. **G. asiatica**, Linn.; Fl. Br. Ind. i. 386; Brandis For. Flora 40, Ind. Trees 98; Gamble Man. Ind. Timb. 111. Vern. *Phálsá*, *Phálsá-Dháman*, Hind.

A small or moderate-sized tree; bark dark-grey or greenish-white, longitudinally wrinkled; young parts brown-pubescent. *Leaves* 4-6 by 3-5 in., obliquely ovate or orbicular, closely and irregularly serrate, densely brown-tomentose beneath; base 5-7 nerved, more or less cordate; petiole ·5-1 in., densely rusty-tomentose, thickened at the top, rather stout; stipules, linear or subulate. *Peduncles* generally 2-3, rarely more or solitary, usually shorter than or as long as the petioles; pedicels 2-3, somewhat shorter than the peduncles; buds cylindrical or clavate, generally distinctly ribbed, softly woolly. *Sepals* ·3-·4 in. long, oblong-lanceolate, rusty-floccose outside, orange and glabrous inside. *Petals* oblong, yellow, half the length of the sepals. *Drupe* globose, about ·4 in. diam., not or indistinctly 2-lobed, pilose, dark-brown when ripe.

Two distinct forms of this plant are met with:—**1.** a stunted tree with a short trunk, straggling branches and short-petioled more or less orbicular hard leaves, more common about Rámgarh in the DÚN; and **2.** a middle-sized tree with a large spreading crown and long-petioled somewhat soft ovate leaves, found along the foot of the SAHÁRANPUR SIWALIKS, especially at Beribárá, and in the Tons and Ámláwa valleys in JAUNSAR.

Wood similar to that of *G. vestita*, and is used for the same purposes. The sweetmeat-makers of Sahâranpur use the mucilaginous bark to clarify sugar. The fruit is eaten, and the tree is often cultivated for its sake.

Fl. Apr., May. Fr. June-Aug.

4. **G. sapida,** Roxb.; Fl. Br. Ind. i. 387; Brandis For. Flora 41, Ind. Trees 98; Gamble Man. Ind. Timb. 108. Vern. *Bistú*, Jaunsar; *Phálsá*, Hind.

A prostrate undershrub with a perennial woody rootstock throwing out annually a number of switchy shoots, which, after bearing leaves, flowers and fruit, are burnt or browsed down to be renewed next year. *Leaves* 2-4 by 1·5-3 in., ovate obovate or orbicular, usually doubly serrate, sometimes obscurely lobed, pilose or scabrid above, pubescent beneath; petiole ·2-·3 in. long; stipules linear. *Flowers* axillary; peduncles 2-5 together, ·7-1·2 in. long, slender, each 2-5-flowered; buds oblong. *Sepals* oblong, ·2-·3 in. long, reddish brown inside. *Petals* yellow, half the length of the sepals, elliptic, entire. *Drupe* the size of a pea, slightly lobed.

Open grass-lands up to 3,500 ft. Common in fire-traces and forest paths in the SIWALIK DIVISION, also in low valleys in the HILLS, *e.g.* at Thadiár, Bámsu, etc.

A favourite fodder plant. Fruit edible.

Fl. Apr., May. Fr. Oct., Nov.

5. **G. scabrophylla,** Roxb.; Fl. Br. Ind. i. 387; Brandis Ind. Trees 99. Syn.—*G. sclerophylla*, Roxb.; Brandis For. Flora 39, Vern. *Gúrbheli*, Dún.

A small shrub 5 to 6 ft. high, apt to be mistaken for a young *Helicteres Isora*, which it somewhat resembles in foliage. *Leaves* 4-7 by 3-4 in., ovate or obovate, acuminate, irregularly serrate, coriaceous, scabrous above, pubescent beneath; basal nerves 3-5; petiole ·5-·7 in. long; stipules subulate. *Flowers* ·7 in. long, white; buds ribbed. *Sepals* pubescent, more than twice the length of the petals. *Petals* white, notched. *Drupe* about ·8 in. diam., globose, slightly depressed, with a brown crustaceous and scabrous rind and a scanty pale-yellow viscid sweetish pulp; stones 4.

Common in open grass lands in the DÚN and SAHÁRANPUR FORESTS. The stem yields a strong white fibre which can be made into ropes. Fruit edible but not very tasty.

Fl. Apr.-Sept. Fr. Nov.-Mar.

6. **G. lævigata**, Vahl; Fl. Br. Ind. i. 389; Brandis For. Flora 42, Ind. Trees 96; Gamble Man. Ind. Timb. 111. Vern. *Kath Bhemal, Phirsau,* Dún.

A small tree; bark dark-brown. *Leaves* 3-5 by 1·3-2 in. tapering at both ends, acuminate, serrate, glabrescent or with a few scattered hairs, 3-nerved; transverse veins fine; petiole ·5 in. long; stipules linear, caducous. *Flowers* axillary; peduncles 2-3 together, longer than the petiole, each 2-3-flowered. *Sepals* about 1 in. long, 3-ribbed. *Petals* white, about one-fourth the length of the sepals, entire. *Style* longer than the stamens. *Drupe* ·3 in. diam., 1-4-lobed, rugose, black when ripe.

Throughout the DÚN in shady localities and in ravines; also in the western half of the SAHÁRANPUR FORESTS, and valleys in the HILLS.

The leaves are lopped for fodder.

Fl. June-Sept. Fr. Cold season.

7. **G. polygama**, Roxb.; Fl. Br. Ind. i. 391; Brandis For. Flora 42, Ind. Trees 100.

An undershrub with a short trunk and bifarious spreading branches. *Leaves* 2-3 in. long, narrow-lanceolate, sharply serrate, nearly glabrous above, white-tomentose beneath. *Flowers* polygamous, mostly 1-sexual, on slender axillary peduncles. *Stigma* stellate. *Drupe* ·5 in. diam., whitish-brown, shining, sometimes with a few scattered hairs.

In blanks throughout the DÚN and SAHÁRANPUR FORESTS, chiefly with sál; also in grass-lands. Pathri Forest. Particularly common in the SIWALIK TRACTS.

The leaves are browsed by cattle.

Fl. July, Aug. Fr. Nov., Dec.

To this Family belongs *Corchorus olitorius*, Linn.; *Fl. Br.* Ind. i. 397;—which is one of several annual plants of the same Genus, from which the 'jute' fibre is obtained. *Stem* 8-12 ft. high. *Leaves* 3-4 in. long, ovate-lanceolate, long-petioled. *Flowers* yellow. *Fruit* an elongated capsule, 2 in. long, 10-ribbed. It is found in DEHRA, and also in large quantities in the Pathri Forest, SAHÁRANPUR DISTRICT. The very light soft wood is used for country-made sulphur matches—*G. P. n. 18.*

DISCIFLORÆ.

Order 1.—GERANIALES.

FAM. 17. LINACEÆ; G. P. N. 34.

HERBS or shrubs. *Leaves* usually alternate, simple, entire, rarely crenate. *Flowers* regular, 2-sexual, usually 5-merous. *Sepals* quite entire. *Petals* contorted in bud, fugacious, each with a gland inside near the base, adnate to the staminal ring. *Stamens* 5, often alternating with minute staminodes, or 10, connate at the base into a tube or ring; anthers versatile. *Ovary* 3-5-celled; styles 3-5, more or less free. *Fruit* a capsule, splitting into 3-6 cocci.

1. Reinwardtia, Dumort.; G. P. n. 3.

1. **R. trigyna,** Planch.; Fl. Br. Ind. i. 412; Brandis Ind. Trees 107; Gamble Man. Ind. Timb. 116. Vern. *Basant,* Dún; *Pengúṇ,* Jaunsar.

A glabrous undershrub, 2 to 3 ft. high or occasionally higher. *Leaves* 1-4 in. long, narrow-oblong or oblanceolate, narrowed into a slender petiole, usually entire and mucronate, membranous. *Flowers* about 1 in. long, in axillary or terminal cymes or panicles, sometimes solitary. *Sepals* 5, green, lanceolate, acuminate. *Petals* 5, bright-yellow, obovate, about 1 in. long. *Styles* usually 3, more or less connate below. *Capsule* the size of a pea, papery.

Very common in the DÚN and the HILLS up to 6,000 ft., growing fairly large if not too much browsed.

Fl. Feb.-Apr. Fr. Apr.-June.

FAM. 18. MALPIGHIACEÆ; G. P. N. 36.

Climbing or suberect shrubs. *Leaves* opposite, simple, entire, usually exstipulate. *Flowers* regular or irregular, bisexual, pentamerous, white or yellow, in axillary or terminal panicles. *Calyx* deeply 5-partite, usually with a large gland outside. *Petals* free. *Disk* obscure. *Stamens* 10, hypogynous, equal or unequal; filaments free or connate below. *Ovary* free, 3-celled, 3-lobed; cells 1-ovuled; styles 1-3. *Fruit* of 1-3 samaras. *Seeds* exalbuminous.

Analysis of the Genera.

Calyx glandular; style 1; carpels winged only at the end . . . . . 1. HIPTAGE.
Calyx eglandular; styles 3; carpels winged all round . . . . . . 2. ASPIDOPTERYS.

1. Hiptage, Gærtn.; G. P. n. 34.

1. **H. Madablota,** Gærtn.; Fl. Br. Ind. 148; Brandis For. Flora 44, Ind. Trees, 108; Gamble Man. Ind. Timb. 118. Vern. *Anetá*, Dún; *Madh Málti*, Hind; *Mádhavilatá*, Sans.

A large evergreen climbing shrub. *Leaves* 4-6 by 1·5-2·5 in., oblong or ovate-lanceolate, acuminate, entire, coriaceous, glabrous; main lateral nerves 4-6 pairs, arcuate, base acute, rarely rounded; petiole ·2-·5 in. long; stipule 0. *Flowers* showy, fragrant, in large terminal and smaller axillary panicles. *Calyx* with a large oblong gland outside; segments ·2 in. long, imbricate, pubescent. *Petals* ·5-·7 in. long, unequal, silky, clawed, fimbriate, 4 white, 1 yellow. *Stamens* 10, one much larger than the rest. *Style* 1, filiform. *Fruit* of 1-3 samaras; wings 3, obovate or oblanceolate, one large about 2 by ·5 in., two small about 1 by ·2 in.

Common in ravines and moist places in the DÚN, *e.g.*, the Bindál nálá, Kuáwála, Nakraunda, Nágsidh, Karwápáni, etc.; also at Kálsi.

The woody stem is used for fuel.

Fl. Feb.-Apr. Fr. May, June.

2. Aspidopterys, A. Juss.: G. P. n. 37.

1. **A. Wallichii,** Hook. f.; Fl. Br. Ind. i. 421; Brandis Ind. Trees 110; Gamble Man. Ind. Timb. 118. Syn.—*A. nutans.* A. Juss.; Brandis For. Flora 45. Vern. *Jugtér*, Málkōt.

A climbing shrub; branches slender, white-pubescent. *Leaves* usually opposite,* sometimes in whorls of three, 3·5 by 2·5-3·5 in., ovate oblong or orbicular, acuminate, glabrescent above, white-tomentose beneath; main lateral nerves 4-5, arcuate; base sub-cordate or rounded; petiole ·5-·7 in. long. *Panicles* large, pendulous, terminal but running down among the leaves below so as to appear partly axillary; pedicels rather stout, with very minute bracteoles. *Flowers* white or cream-colour, about ·2 in. across. *Calyx* glandular, minute. *Petals* 5, equal, entire, not clawed, 3 or 4 times the length of the calyx. *Stamens* 10, all fertile. *Ovary* white-tomentose; styles 3, glabrous. *Fruit* of 1-3 samaras; wings variable, usually orbicular-oblong, 1-1·5 in. long; nucleus without crest or wing.

Hedges and open forest lands throughout the SIWALIK DIVISION, and the OUTER HIMALAYA;—very conspicuous in fruit.

Fl. Aug., Sept. Fr. Nov., Dec.

Very similar in appearance, but with larger and less tomentose leaves which are not cordate, larger panicles and somewhat larger flowers—is *Aspidopterys nutans*, Hook. f.; Fl. Br. Ind. i. 421, Syn.—*A. lanuginosa.* A. Juss.; Brandis For. Flora 44,—occurring in much the same localities. Common towards Ráipur in the DÚN.

FAM. 19. RUTACEÆ; G. P. N. 39.

Trees or shrubs, rarely herbs, usually aromatic. *Leaves* alternate, compound, rarely opposite or simple, exstipulate, usually with translucent glandular dots. *Flowers* regular, in cymes corymbs or panicles, rarely solitary. *Calyx* of 4-5 small imbricate lobes. *Petals* as many as the calyx-lobes, usually hypogynous. *Stamens* as many or twice as many as the petals, rarely more, with an annular or cylindrical disk within; anthers 2-celled, often versatile. *Ovary* of 4-5 free or connate carpels; styles 1-5, usually free. *Fruit* a berry, less frequently capsular or drupaceous.

---

* There is a specimen in the College Herbarium with leaves distinctly alternate, which is quite exceptional in the Family.

Analysis of the Genera.

Armed.
  Scandent shrubs. Fls. polygamous; style 1 . . . 2. TODDALIA.
  Erect shrubs or trees.*
    Flowers 1-sexual; styles 2-5; fruit of capsular carpels . . . . 1. ZANTHOXYLUM.
    Flowers 2-sexual; style 1; fruit a berry.
      Leaves 3-foliolate or imparipinnate; pericarp pulpy. . . . . 6. LIMONIA.
      Leaves 1-foliolate; pericarp leathery . 9. CITRUS.
      Leaves 3-foliolate; pericarp woody . 10. ÆGLE.
Unarmed.
  Flowers polygamous; petals valvate.
    Trees. Leaves 1-(rarely 3-) foliolate, thin; stamens 8 . . . . . 3. ACRONYCHIA.
    A small shrub. Leaves simple, fleshy; stamens never more than 5 . . 4. SKIMMIA.
  Flowers 2-sexual; petals imbricate.
    Leaves 1-5-foliolate; style persistent. (Flowers panicled; filaments subulate) . . . . 5. GLYCOSMIS.
    Leaves imparipinnate; style deciduous.
      Flowers corymbose or solitary; ovary usually 2-celled . . . . 7. MURRAYA.
      Flowers usually in terminal panicles; ovary 4-5-celled . . . . 8. CLAUSENA.

1. Zanthoxylum, Linn.; G. P. n. 51.

1. **Z. alatum**, Roxb.; Fl. Br. Ind. i. 493; Brandis For. Flora 47, Ind. Trees 116; Gamble Man. Ind. Timb. 121. Vern. *Timbúr, Timrú, Temrú*, Jaunsar; *Tejbal*, Hind.

A shrub or small tree with corky bark, and strong prickles on the branches, petioles and midrib of the leaflets; branchlets often rough with raised grey specks. *Leaves* alternate, imparipinnate, common petiole and rachis narrowly winged. *Leaflets* 2-6 pairs, opposite, sessile, 1-3 by ·3-·8 in., elliptic-lanceolate, more or less serrate, obtusely acuminate, pellucid-punctate. *Flowers* small, yellow, usually 1-sexual, in dense lateral panicles. *Calyx* 6-8-fid. *Petals* none. *Stamens* 6-8, much exceeding the calyx; anthers large. *Fruit* usually of a solitary carpel which dehisces ventrally, of the size of a peppercorn, tubercled, strongly aromatic.

---

* Some species of Zanthoxylum, not found within the limits of this Flora are scandent.

Hot valleys and in forest undergrowth up to 6,000 ft. in JAUNSAR, TEHRI-GARHWAL and the OUTER-HIMALAYA. Above Rájpur; Dhármigádh, Tons and Bámsu Valleys; Korwá, Koti Forest, etc.

Wood close-grained, heavy, hard, and of a yellow colour (whence the generic name), used for walking-sticks. Tooth-brushes are made of the branchlets, which and also the aromatic fruit are good for toothache. The fruit is also used as a condiment and to purify water. The bark is used to intoxicate fish.

Fl. Apr.-June. Fr. Aug.-Oct.

2. Toddalia, Juss.; G. P. n. 62.

1. **T. aculeata,** Pers.; Fl. Br. Ind. i. 497; Brandis Ind. Tree 119; Gamble Man. Ind. Timb. 123. Vern. *Kánj*, Hind.

A large prickly scandent shrub, even old stems bearing curved prickles with a large conical corky base. *Leaves* alternate, usually 3-foliolate. *Leaflets* sessile, 2-4 by ·7-1·5 in., obovate elliptic or oblanceolate, crenulate, glabrous, more or less coriaceous, with many straight lateral nerves. *Flowers* polygamous, in axillary cymes or less frequently in terminal panicles, ·2 in. diam., pale-yellow. *Calyx* usually 5-lobed, pubescent outside. *Petals* 5, imbricate. *Stamens* generally 5, longer than the petals in the male flowers, imperfect or 0 in the female flowers; anthers round. *Ovary* 5-celled. *Fruit* globose, the size of a large pea, shallowly 5-grooved or -lobed; seeds reniform.

In swampy places or deep open ravines in the DÚN, *e.g.*, Káluwála, Nakraunda, Mothronwálá, Bindál nálá, etc.

The bark of the roots gives a yellow dye, and a bitter aromatic tonic which is used as a remedy for fever.

Fl. Feb.-Apr. Fr. July-Sept.

3. Acronychia, Forst.; G. T. n. 67.

1. **A. laurifolia,** Bl.; Fl. Br. Ind. i. 498; Brandis Ind. Trees 116; Gamble Man. Ind. Timb. 124.

A tree. *Leaves* usually 1-foliolate, subopposite or crowded at the ends of the branches. *Leaflets* variable, 3-6 by 1·5-3 in., elliptic-oblong obovate or oblanceolate, quite entire, glabrous, sometimes obtusely acuminate, more or less aromatic; base acute; lateral nerves 12-15 pairs; petiolule ·5-1 in. long. *Cymes* axillary, trichotomous corymbose; peduncles 3-4 in. long, slender. *Flowers* whitish, fragrant; buds oblong. *Calyx* 4-lobed; lobes small, rounded. *Petals* 4, valvate, ·2 in. long, oblong, with a broad base, more or less villous inside. *Stamens* 8, alternately longer; filaments subulate, bearded below. *Ovary* 4-celled, hairy, sunk in the disk. *Fruit* a drupe, ·3-·4 in. diam., slightly lobed or grooved; seeds black.

Occurs but rarely in the DÚN.—Mothroṇwála swamp.

Wood white, fine- and close-grained, but liable to crack; weight about 42 lbs. per c. ft. Old stems sometimes with irregular patches of brown mottled harder wood inside, which however is not the true heartwood.

Fl. May-July. Fr. Nov.-Jan.

4. Skimmia, Thunb.; G. P. n. 68.

1. **S. Laureola,** Hook. f.; Fl. Br. Ind. i. 499; Brandis For. Flora 50, Ind. Trees 116; Gamble Man. Ind. Timb. 124. Vern. *Kathúr-chará, Gurlpatá*, Jaunsar.

A strongly aromatic small evergreen shrub; bark white. *Leaves* 4-6 by ·8-1·5 in., alternate, simple, oblong oblanceolate or obovate, acute or acuminate, coriaceous, rather succulent, quite entire, glabrous, gland-dotted, crowded at the ends of the branches; midrib stout; nerves indistinct; petiole ·1-·3 in., flattened above. *Flowers* polygamous, yellow, ·3-·5 in. diam., in compact terminal panicles. *Calyx* 4-5-lobed, imbricate. *Petals* 4-5, oblong, valvate. *Stamens* 4-5, hypogynous; filaments stout, subulate. *Ovary* 2-5-celled; style 1. *Fruit* an ovoid or subglobose fleshy drupe, ·5-·7 in. long, red when ripe, with 2-5 1-seeded stones.

A common undershrub in shady localities in the HILLS 6,-10,000 ft., generally in dense gregarious patches. "The odour of the musk-deer *Kastúrá* is popularly supposed to be derived from it." —*Mr. A. Smythies.*

Fl. Apr., May. Fr. July-Sept.

5. Glycosmis, Correa; G. P. n. 71.

1. **G. pentaphylla,** Correa; Fl. Br. Ind. i. 499; Brandis For. Flora 49, Ind. Trees 112; Gamble Man. Ind. Timb. 125. Vern. *Ban Nimbú*, Hind.

A small evergreen shrub. *Leaves* alternate, usually 1-5-foliolate; petiole and rachis stout. *Leaflets* very variable in size and shape, usually 4-6 by 1·5-2 in., ovate lanceolate or obovate, entire or obscurely crenulate, dark-green, quite glabrous. *Flowers* white, fragrant, in axillary or terminal panicles. *Calyx* 4-5-fid; segments broad. *Petals* 4-5, white, imbricate. *Stamens* 8-10, free; filaments dilated below. *Ovary* 2-5-celled; style short, persistent. *Fruit* a globose or depressed berry, pink or bluish-white when ripe, with an aromatic sweetish pulp.

Forms a thick undergowth in shady moist evergreen forests in the DÚN, *e.g.*, Khairi, Kánsráo, Nakraunda and Káluwála; also at Kálsi.

The wood is tough and hard, but is seldom found of a utilizable size. It makes a good hedge-plant, for which purpose it is often planted. The twigs are used as tooth-sticks. The ripe fruit is eaten, and the roots are used in country medicine.

Fl. and Fr. throughout the year.

6. Limonia, Linn.; G. P. n. 75.

1. **L. acidissima,** Linn.; Fl. Br. Ind. i. 507; Brandis For. Flora 47, Ind. Trees 118; Gamble Man. Ind. Timb. 127.—Syn. *L. crenulata*, Roxb.; Duthie Fl. Up. Gang. Pl. i. 39. Vern. *Beli*, Hind.

A large spinous shrub or small tree with white or ash-coloured corky bark. *Leaves* alternate, imparipinnate, 3-6 in. long; petiole and the rachis between each two pairs of leaflets winged to the size and shape of leaflets. *Leaflets* 5-9, ·5-1·5 in. long, quite sessile, ovate-rhomboid or ovate-lanceolate, acuminate, crenulate, gland-dotted; base cuneate. *Flowers* 4-merous, white, fragrant, in short axillary often leaf-bearing racemes. *Calyx* 4-partite, small. *Petals* 4, elliptic or oblong, much larger than the calyx-segments. *Stamens* 8, inserted round an annular or columnar disk. *Ovary* 4-celled; cells 1-ovuled; style short, deciduous. *Fruit* a globose berry, ·3-·4 in. diam., fleshy, black when ripe, exceedingly acid (whence the specific name).

Common in the EASTERN DÚN and western half of the SAHÁRANPUR SIWALIKS: Tháno, Lachiwála, Barkálá, etc.

Wood cream-coloured, hard and close-grained, capable of employment as a substitute for box-wood, but chiefly used for fuel; walking-sticks are made of the branches. "The pulp of the fruit is considered protective against contagion, and an antidote to venomous poisons"—*Sir D. Brandis.*

Fl. Apr., May. Fr. Cold season.

7. Murraya, Linn.; G. P. n. 76.

Unarmed shrubs or small trees. *Leaves* alternate, imparipinnate. *Leaflets* alternate, petioluled. *Flowers* 2-sexual, cymose or corymbose. *Calyx* 5-fid. *Petals* 5, imbricate. *Stamens* 10, the alternate shorter; filaments, subulate; anthers short. *Ovary* usually 2-celled; style simple, long, articulated, deciduous. *Fruit* a berry.

Analysis of the Species.

An evergreen shrub. Leaflets 3-9; fruit red when ripe . . . . . . 1. *M. exotica.*
A deciduous shrub. Leaflets 9-25; fruit black when ripe. . . . . . 2. *M. Kœnigii.*

1. **M. exotica,** Linn.; Fl. Br. Ind. i. 502; Brandis For. Flora 48, Ind. Trees 113; Gamble Man. Ind. Timb. 125. Vern. *Bilgár*, Dún; *Márchulá*, Garhwal.

An evergreen shrub or small tree with thin grey corky bark. *Leaves* dark-green, glabrous, 3-8-foliolate. *Leaflets* 1-3 by ·5-1 in., obliquely rhomboid, more or less acuminate, entire, shining above, coriaceous when mature; petiolule ·1 in. long. *Flowers* 1 in. long, white, very fragrant, in terminal or axillary corymbs, sometimes solitary. *Sepals* minute, acute, dotted. *Petals* oblong-lanceolate. *Ovary* linear, 2-celled. *Berries* ·5-·7 in. long, narrowed at both ends, 2-seeded, rugose, red or deep orange when ripe.

Cool shady ravines in the DÚN and OUTER HILLS, and along ráus in the SAHÁRANPUR SIWALIKS.

Wood close-grained, hard, light-yellow, capable of being used for wood-engraving; weight 62 lbs. per c. ft. Handles of implements and walking-sticks are made of it, and the twigs are used for tooth-brushes. It is often planted as an ornamental shrub.

Fl. Mar.-Sept. but often throughout the year. Fr. Oct.-Feb.

2. **M. Kœnigii,** Spreng.; Fl. Br. Ind. i. 503; Brandis For. Flora 48, Ind. Trees 113; Gamble Man. Ind. Timb. 126. Vern. *Gandhelá*, Dún; *Káth Ním*, Hind.

A deciduous shrub with thin dark-brown bark. *Leaves* 6-12 in. long; rachis terete, pubescent. *Leaflets* 10-25, 1-2 in. long, ovate or lanceolate, oblique at the base, obtusely acuminate or retuse, subentire or irregularly crenulate; petiolule ·1 in. *Flowers*

·3-·5 in. long, white, in terminal corymbose panicles. *Sepals* small, acute. *Petals* oblong, dotted. *Ovary* 2-celled. *Fruit* subglobose, ·3 in. diam., rugose, black when ripe.

A common undershrub in the DÚN and SAHÁRANPUR FORESTS, generally in ravines and on waste lands. Often gregarious under Khair and Sissu in dry beds of streams in the DÚN, *e. g.*, near Kánsráu.

Wood even-grained, hard and durable, capable of being used for agricultural implements. The fresh leaves have a fetid smell, but give an agreeable flavour to curries, and are much used for this purpose in Southern India where it is known as the Curry-plant.

New leaves Mar., Apr. Fl. Apr., May. Fr. Cold season.

8. Clausena, Burm.; G. P. n. 77.

1. **C. Wampi,** Blanco; Fl. Br. Ind. i. 505; Brandis Ind. Trees 114; Gamble Man. Ind. Timb. 127. Vern. *Am-pich*, Dún.

A sweet-scented evergreen tree. *Leaves* alternate, imparipinnate; petiole and rachis terete. *Leaflets* 5-9, 3-5 by 1·7-3 in., ovate elliptic or lanceolate, oblique, shining above, margins wavy or crenulate; petiolule ·2-·3 in. long. *Flowers* 2-sexual, small, white, 4-5-merous, in large compound terminal panicles; inflorescence rusty-tomentose. *Calyx* 4-5-fid. *Petals* 4-5, imbricate, concave. *Fruit* a 1-seeded globose drupe, ·6-·8 in. diam., with a tough glandular rind.

Cultivated in the DÚN for its fruit and as an ornamental plant.

Fl. Mar., Apr. Fr. June, July.

C. pentaphylla, DC.; Fl. Br. Ind. i. 503. Vern. *Ratanjōt*, Hind.—has been found in the neighbourhood of Beribára and Dholkhand in the SIWALIK DIVISION. It is a small undershrub with rough coriaceous pinnate leaves and large aromatic leaflets.

9. Citrus, Linn.; G. P. n. 81.

1. **C. medica,** Linn.; Fl. Br. Ind. i. 514; Brandis For. Flora 51, Ind. Trees 123; Gamble Man. Ind. Timb. 130. The Lemon or Lime. Vern. *Nimbú*, Hind.

A shrub or small tree with strong axillary spines; **bark** greenish-grey, smooth. *Leaves* 1-foliolate; petiole ·3-·5 in. long, often winged. *Leaflets* 3-6 by 1-2·5 in., elliptic or ovate-lanceolate, entire or more or less serrate, coriaceous, glabrous. *Flowers* often 1-sexual ·5-1 in. long, white, sweet-scented, in axillary cymes or solitary; pedicels ·3-·5 in. long, stout. *Calyx* cup-shaped, 3-5-toothed or entire. *Petals* 4-8, imbricate, ·6-·8 in. long, oblong, fleshy, with large glandular dots, often tinged pink outside. *Stamens* 20-40, round a large disk; filaments variously connate. *Ovary* many-celled; ovules 4-6 in each cell; style deciduous; stigma lobed. *Fruit* 2-4in. long, ovoid oblong or globose, with a thick or thin rind which is generally yellow when ripe; pulp cellular and juicy, usually acid.

Indigenous in damp localities in the DÚN, *e.g.*, Nakraunda, Káluwála, Jogiwála, etc. Several varieties with acid or sweet juice are cultivated in gardens. The wood is tough and close-grained, and makes good walking-sticks.

Fl. Apr., May. Fr. Nov., Dec.

The following species are also cultivated in gardens in the DÚN:—

1. *C. Aurantium*, Linn.; Fl. Br. Ind. i. 515; Brandis Ind. Trees 123.—The Orange. Vern. *Nárengi*, Hind., of which there are several varieties, distinguishable from *C. medica* by pure-white 2-sexual flowers, and the characteristic colour and shape of the fruit.

2. *C. decumana*, Linn.; Fl. Br. Ind. i. 516; Brandis Ind. Trees 123. The Shaddock or Pumelo. Vern. *Chakutará*, Hind., a tree with large leaves, pubescent beneath; petiole broadly winged. *Flowers* large, white, strongly scented. *Fruit* 6-8 in. diam., globose or pyriform, with a thick spongy rind.

10. Ægle, Correa; G. P. n. 83.

1. **Æ. Marmelos**, Correa; Fl. Br. Ind. i. 516; Brandis For. Flora 57, Ind. Trees, 119; Gamble Man. Ind. Timb. 131. The Bael tree. Vern. *Bel, Bill, Bael*, Hind.; *Vilva*, Sans.

A glabrous deciduous tree with grey corky bark and sharp straight axillary spines about 1 in. long. *Leaves* alternate, 3-foliolate, with a resinous odour; common petiole 1-2·5 in. long, terete. *Leaflets* 2-4 by 1-2·5 in., ovate-lanceolate or rhomboidal, acuminate, crenate, gland-dotted, the lateral sessile or with a petiolule about ·1 in. long; terminal petiolule ·5-1 in. long, flattened above. *Flowers* greenish-white, about 1 in. diam., sweet-scented, in short lateral panicles. *Calyx* small, obscurely 4-5-toothed, pubescent, deciduous. *Petals* 4-5, imbricate, oblong, gland-dotted. *Stamens* numerous; filaments short, subulate, often fascicled; anthers long, narrow. *Ovary* 8-20-celled; ovules many in each cell; style short; stigma deciduous. *Fruit* 2·7 in. diam., with a smooth grey or yellow woody shell, and a mass of sweet yellow aromatic mealy pulp.

Common in the EASTERN DÚN and SAHÁRANPUR SIWALIKS, *e. g.*, Rikhikesh; Laohiwála; Ránipur, etc. Often cultivated for its fruit, and as a sacred tree.

Wood even- and close-grained, tough and strong, but liable to split badly in seasoning; weight 50-60 lbs. per c. ft. It is used in construction. The pulp of the ripe fruit is a laxative, and mixed with a little milk and sugar makes a very agreeable cooling sherbet. The unripe fruit, either boiled or roasted, is used as a specific for diarrhœa and dysentery. The pulp is also used to strengthen mortar. The mucus with which the cells of the fruit are filled is used for adhesive purposes, and is often mixed with water-paints to add to their strength and brilliancy. Snuff-boxes are made of the shell of the fruit. The leaves are very bitter and are used as a febrifuge; they are also lopped for cattle fodder. They are considered indispensable for the worship of the god *Shiva*, and the wood is one of the few that are prescribed by the Hindu scriptures for sacrificial fires.

Fl. Mar.-May. Fr. Mar.-June (next year).

FAM. 20. SIMARUBACEÆ; G. P. N. 40.

Trees or shrubs with bitter bark. *Leaves* alternate, pinnate, usually exstipulate. *Flowers* in axillary panicled cymes, small, regular, generally unisexual. *Calyx* 3-5-lobed, valvate or imbricate. *Petals* 3-5. *Disk* entire or lobed, rarely 0. *Stamens* as many or twice as many as the petals, hypogynous, inserted at the base of the disk; filaments free. *Ovary* 1-6-celled, usually deeply lobed or with distinct carpels. *Fruit* drupacious or samaroid, rarely baccate or capsular. *Seeds* usually albuminous.

1. Picrasma, Bl. ; G. P. n. 12.

1. **P. quassioides,** Bennett ; Fl. Br. Ind. i. 520 ; Brandis For. Flora 59, Ind. Trees 127 ; Gamble Man. Ind. Timb. 133. Vern. *Karúi, Tithái*, Jaunsar.

A large shrub with bitter bark ; branches few, stout, usually with white specks. *Leaves* lyrately imparipinnate, 9-15 in. long, rusty-tomentose. *Leaflets* 9-15, generally 3-4 by 1-1·5 in., the lowest pair smallest and the penultimate pair largest, sub-opposite, ovate or oblong-lanceolate, long-acuminate, serrate, membranous, nearly glabrous when mature ; petiolule of lateral leaflets ·05-·08 in., of the terminal leaflet, ·5-1 in. long. *Flowers* 1-sexual or polygamous, ·2 in. across, pale-green, in axillary panicles. *Calyx* 4-5-lobed. *Petals* 4-5, valvate, enlarged and coriaceous in fruit. *Stamens* 4-5 ; filaments with a thick hairy base ; anthers versatile. *Fruit* a drupe, ·2-·3 in. diam., black when ripe. *Seeds* albuminous.

OUTER HIMALAYA above Rájpur, also in shady ravines in JAUNSAR and TEHRI-GARHWAL, 5,-8,000 ft. : Deoban, Bámnáigádh, Mundáli ; Deotá ; banks of the Rúpin, etc. Not very abundant.

Wood cream-colour, light, fine- and close-grained. The bark has the same properties as quassia, and is used as a tonic in Indian medical practice.

Fl. Apr.-June. Fr. July-Sept.

FAM. 21. BURSERACEÆ ; G. P. N. 42.

Resinous trees or erect shrubs. *Leaves* alternate, imparipinnate, usually exstipulate. *Flowers* regular, small, 2-sexual or polygamous. *Calyx* free, 3-7-lobed, often minute. *Petals* 3-7, usually distinct. *Disk* annular or cup-shaped, free or adnate to the base of the calyx. *Stamens* as many or twice as many as the petals ; filaments free. *Ovary* 2-5-celled ; ovules axile, 2-5 in each cell ; style single. *Fruit* usually a drupe, rarely dehiscent. *Seeds* exalbuminous.

Analysis of the Genera.

Leaflets sessile; fruit 3-gonous, pericarp woody . . . . 1. BOSWELLIA.
Leaflets petioluled; fruit globose, pericarp fleshy . . . . 2. GARUGA.

1. Boswellia, Roxb.; G. P. n. 1.

1. **B. serrata,** Roxb.; Fl. Br. Ind. i. 528; Brandis Ind. Trees 129; Gamble Man. Ind. Timb. 137. Syn. *B. thurifera,* Coleb.; Brandis For. Flora 61. Vern. *Salái, Salár,* Hind.

A gregarious deciduous tree; bark reddish-yellow or greenish-grey, smooth, peeling off in thin papery flakes; young parts pubescent. *Leaves* exstipulate, pubescent, crowded at the ends of the branches; rachis stout, 10-15 in. long. *Leaflets* 8-15 pairs (besides the odd one), sub-opposite, sessile or less frequently minutely petioluled, 2-3 by ·3-·6 in., lanceolate or linear, coarsely serrate, unequal-sided; tip rounded, sometimes mucronate. *Flowers* small, white, in axillary or sub-terminal fascicled racemes. *Calyx* 5-7-cleft, persistent. *Disk* annular, red, crenate. *Petals* 5-7, imbricate, broad-ovate. *Stamens* 10; anthers hairy. *Ovary* 3-celled. *Drupe* ·5-·7 in. long, 3-gonous; carpels 1-seeded, at length separating septifragally; endocarp heart-shaped, bony, beaked, surrounded by a membranous wing.

Throughout the SAHÁRANPUR SIWALIKS, all by itself on steep sandy slopes, but in a mixed state on gentler slopes.

Sapwood large, rough-grained, soft and perishable, weight 20-35 lbs. per c. ft. An irregular-shaped mass of dark-brown mottled heavy wood is often found in the centre of large trees, which may be the heart-wood or perhaps a kind of ebony, quite capable of being used for ornamental purposes. The charcoal is used for iron smelting in the Central Provinces. A transparent gum-resin exudes from wounds and cracks in the bark, which is used in medicine, and also burnt as an incense.

Leafless Mar.-June. Fl. Apr., May. Fr. July, Aug.

2. Garuga, Roxb.; G. P. n. 3.

1. **G. pinnata,** Roxb.; Fl. Br. Ind. i. 528; Brandis For. Flora 62, Ind. Trees 131; Gamble Man. Ind. Timb. 138. Vern. *Kharpát,* Hind.

A large deciduous tree; bark grey or brown, exfoliating in hard round flakes, red inside. *Leaves* exstipulate, 9-15 in. long. *Leaflets* 5-9 pairs besides the terminal one, opposite, 2-4 by 1-1·5 in., oblong-or ovate-lanceolate, crenate, caudate-acuminate, more or less pubescent; petiolule ·1-·2 in. long. *Flowers* polygamous, yellow, in large terminal panicles; panicles 8-10 at the end of each branch, tomentose. *Calyx* campanulate, green; segments 5, valvate. *Petals* 5, linear, induplicate-valvate, alternating with the calyx-segments. *Disk* large, clothing the calyx-tube. *Stamens* 10; filaments hairy. *Ovary* 4-5-celled, hairy. *Drupe* globose, ·5-·7 in. diam.

A very common tree in the DÚN and SAHÁRANPUR FORESTS generally with Sál, but not uncommon in scrub forests and glades.

Wood soft and light and is chiefly used for fuel, but is much prized for house-posts in Eastern Bengal for its durability. The leaves are lopped for camel-fodder. The tree can be easily propagated by cuttings, and is occasionally thus planted in hedgerows.

Leafless Dec.-Apr. Fl. Apr., May. Fr. Oct., Nov.

FAM. 22. MELIACEÆ; G. P. N. 43.

Trees or shrubs with bitter bark and leaves. *Leaves* alternate, exstipulate, usually pinnate, rarely 2- or 3-pinnate or simple; leaflets more or less oblique at the base. *Flowers* 2-sexual, regular, generally a large proportion sterile. *Calyx* 3-6-lobed. *Petals* 3-6, usually free. *Stamens* as many as the petals, or more frequently twice as many; filaments usually connate into a tube; anthers often sessile on the tube. *Disk* hypogynous, often forming a second tube inside the staminal tube. *Ovary* free, 3-5-celled; style simple. *Fruit* a drupe or a capsule. *Seeds* albuminous in the local species.

Analysis of the Genera.

Stamens united into a tube; fruit a drupe; seeds not winged.
 Leaves only once pinnate; drupe 1-celled . 1. AZADIRACHTA.
 Leaves 2- or 3-pinnate; drupe 5-celled . 2. MELIA.
Stamens free; fruit a capsule; seeds winged . 3. CEDRELA.

1. Azadirachta, A. Juss., G. P. n. 7.

1. **A. indica,** A. Jussieu; Brandis Ind. Trees 139.—Syn: *Melia indica,* Juss.; Brandis For. Flora 67; Gamble Man. Ind. Timb. 143. *M. Azadirachta,* Linn., Fl. Br. Ind. i. 544. The Neem tree. Vern *Ním,* Hind.

A large handsome tree. *Leaves* imparipinnate, 9-15 in. long, glabrous. *Leaflets* 9-15, subopposite, 2-4 by ·5-1 in., lanceolate or ovate-lanceolate, very unequal-sided, often falcate, deeply serrate, very gradually acuminate, bright-green and shining above, subsessile or with a minute petiolule. *Flowers* white, scented, in numerous axillary panicles which are shorter than the leaves; branches of panicles and pedicels very slender. *Calyx* small, flat; segments 5, rounded. *Petals* about ·2 in. long, spathulate, ciliate. *Anthers* 10, inserted inside the staminal tube. *Ovary* 3-celled. *Drupe* ·5-·7 in. long, ovoid-oblong, 1-celled, smooth, greenish-yellow when ripe.

Fairly common along the foot of the SAHÁRANPUR SIWALIKS and some distance in the interior, especially from Kasúmri to Hardwar, unmistakably wild, if not indigenous. Cultivated for shade and ornament in the DÚN and SAHÁRANPUR DISTRICTS, as also throughout the greater part of India.

Sapwood grey; heartwood dark-red, very hard; weight about 50 lbs. per c. ft. It is used in construction and for furniture, and makes good sonorous drums. It is one of the woods held sacred by the Hindus, and idols are made of it. The bark, leaves and fruit are used in medicine. The fruit gives an oil which is considered very good for small-pox sores and is also used for burning. The leaves are much lopped for goat and camel fodder.

Fl. Mar., Apr. Fr. July, Aug.

2. Melia, Linn.; G. P. n. 7.

1. **M. Azedarach,** Linn.; Fl. Br. Ind. i. 544; Brandis For. Flora 68, Ind. Trees 140; Gamble Man. Ind. Timb. 144. The Persian Lilac. Vern. *Bakáin, Dék,* Dún; *Deknoi,* Jaunsar.

A moderate-sized tree with smooth dark-grey bark. *Leaves* bipinnate, sometimes tripinnate, 9-18 in. long; pinnæ usually opposite. *Leaflets* 3-7 in each pinna or pinnule, ·5-1·5 in. long, ovate-lanceolate, serrate, acuminate, the lateral more or less oblique; petiolule 0-·2 in. *Flowers* lilac-blue, in numerous axillary cyme-bearing panicles; peduncles 3-4 in. long. *Calyx* deeply 5-lobed. *Petals* 5, ·2-·3 in. long, linear-oblanceolate. *Staminal tube* purple, ·2 in. long, cylindrical, with 20-30 linear teeth; anthers at the mouth of the tube. *Ovary* 5-celled. *Drupe* about ·5 in. diam., globose, generally 5-celled and 5-seeded, more or less dry, yellow when ripe, at first quite smooth, afterwards wrinkled, remaining on the tree long after ripening.

Very common in cultivation in DEHRA DÚN and SAHÁRANPUR; also in hot valleys in JAUNSAR,— doubtfully wild.

The tree grows very fast and coppices extremely well. Heartwood reddish-brown, takes a good polish, and is sometimes used for furniture. "The bark is extremely bitter, and is employed as an anthelmintic. The fruit yields an oil, and the nuts are frequently strung as beads. The leaves and pulp of the fruit are used in native medicine."—*Mr. J.S. Gamble.* The leaves are also lopped for fodder.

Leafless Dec.-Mar. Fl. Mar.-May. Fr. Cold season.

3. Cedrela, Linn.; G. P. n. 35.

Deciduous trees. *Leaves* pinnate; leaflets opposite or subopposite. *Flowers* small, in large axillary and terminal panicles. *Calyx* small, 5-fid. *Petals* 5, imbricate, keeled inside at the base. *Disk* thick, 4-6-lobed. *Stamens* 4-6, free, inserted on the top of the disk; filaments subulate; anthers oblong, versatile. *Ovary* 5-celled; style simple; ovules 8-12 in each cell, in two series. *Fruit* an oblong or ovoid capsule, septifragally 5-valved. *Seeds* numerous, flat, winged.

Analysis of the Species.

Leaflets entire; panicles scarcely exceeding the leaves; seeds winged at both ends . 1. *C. Toona.*

Leaflets serrate; panicles much exceeding the leaves; seeds winged only at the apex 2. *C. serrata.*

1. **C. Toona**, Roxb.; Fl. Br. Ind. i. 568; Brandis For. Flora 72, Ind. Trees 145; Gamble Man. Ind. Timb. 157. The Toon tree. Vern. *Tún*, Hind.

A large tree with a dense spreading crown and thin dark-grey bark which is smooth up to middle age. *Leaves* paripinnate, 1-2 ft. long, generally glabrous. *Leaflets* 8-30, usually opposite, 2-6 by ·7-2·5 in., lanceolate or ovate-lanceolate, acuminate, sometimes pubescent beneath; margins entire, usually wavy; base acute, somewhat oblique; petiolule ·3-·7 in. long, slender. *Flowers* cream-coloured, scented like honey, in ample drooping panicles. *Calyx* short; lobes ciliate. *Petals* ·15-·2 in. long, free, oblong or ovate, ciliate. *Disk* hairy at the orange-coloured lobes. *Stamens* 5, inserted on the lobes of the disk. *Stigma* capitate, with a large depression at the apex. *Capsule* septifragally dehiscent, ·7-1 in. long by ·2-·3 in. diam., oblong or oblanceoloid, dark-brown. *Seeds* reddish-brown, light, with a membranous wing at either end, about ·5 in. long including the wings.

DÚN and SAHÁRANPUR FORESTS and valleys in the HILLS up to 3,500 ft., generally along the banks of streams or in marshy localities, *e.g.*, Káluwála, Rámgarh, Jogiwála; scarce with Sál. Largely planted in avenues, along canals, and in gardens.

Toon is a fast-growing species, attaining a girth of 60 inches in little more than 30 years. Trees 70-80 ft. in height and 8-10 ft. in girth are not at all uncommon. The heartwood is red, seasons well, takes a fine polish, and is easy to work. It is durable and is not eaten by white ants. Weight about 40 lbs. per c. ft. It is the chief furniture-wood of Dehra Dun and the adjoining districts. The leaves are sometimes lopped for fodder. A sulphur-coloured dye, *Basanti*, is extracted from the flowers. The bark has astringent properties and is used in medicine.

Leafless Jan., Feb. Fl. Mar. Apr. Fr. June, July.

2. **C. serrata**, Royle; Brandis For. Flora 73, Ind. Trees 145; Gamble Man. Ind. Timb. 160. The Hill Toon. Vern. *Darlú, Darli, Darloi*, Jaunsar.

A moderate-sized tree; bark with regular longitudinal fissures from very early age. *Leaves* usually imparipinnate, 2-3 ft. long. *Leaflets* 12-24 pairs, 3-8 by 1-2·5 in., ovate-lanceolate, acuminate, serrate, glaucous beneath when mature, very unequal-sided at the base; lateral nerves more or less straight; petiolule ·1-·2 in. long; rachis and midrib of leaflets red until fully mature; base of petiole much flattened. *Flowers* pink, often 6-merous, in lax drooping stringy panicles 3-5 ft. long (one of the largest inflorescences among Dicotyledons); pedicels rusty-tomentose. *Calyx* cup-shaped; lobes obtuse

Petals about ·2 in. long, oblong, glabrous. *Disk* glabrous. *Stamens* alternating with sterile filaments. *Capsule* about 1 in. long by ·5 in. diam., ovoid, acute, dark-grey. *Seeds* winged only at the upper end.

Valleys in JAUNSAR and TEHRI-GARHWAL ascending to about 8,000 ft.: Korwá, Binálgádh below Konáin, Dhárágádh, Tons Valley; Morágádh, etc.

Wood light-red or flesh-colour. It is lighter (about 31 lbs. per c. ft.), coarser and more open-grained than that of Toon, from which it is further recognized by its fetid smell. It is used for bridges, for hoops of sieves, for sleepers of sledge-roads, for jhampán-poles and such other purposes. The leaves and young shoots are lopped for cattle-fodder.

Leafless Feb., Mar. Fl. May, June. Fr. July, Aug.

Order 2.—OLACALES.

FAM. 23. OLACACEÆ; G. P. N. 45.

Trees or shrubs, sometimes climbing, often parasitic upon the roots of other plants. *Leaves* usually alternate, simple, exstipulate. *Flowers* regular, small, 4-5-merous, 1- or 2-sexual, in cymes or racemes, rarely solitary. *Calyx* small, sometimes accrescent; lobes 0 or tooth-like and small, valvate or imbricate. *Petals* free or more or less coherent, usually valvate. *Stamens* 3-15, free or more or less monadelphous, all fertile or some reduced to staminodes; anthers 2-celled, splitting longitudinally. *Disk* usually hypogynous, cup-shaped. *Ovary* always 1-celled above, imperfectly 3-5-celled below, ovules pendulous from the apex of the central placenta; funicle dilated. *Style* simple or 0. *Fruit* drupaceous, 1-celled, 1-seeded; seed pendulous, albuminous.

1. Olax, Linn.; G. P. n. 5.

1. **O. nana,** Wall.; Fl. Br. Ind. i. 576; Brandis For. Flora 75, Ind. Trees 148; Gamble Man. Ind. Timb. 163.

An undershrub with a woody rootstock from which annual shoots about 2 ft. high spring up during the rains; stems ribbed. *Leaves* alternate, 1·5-2·5 by ·3-·6 in, oblong-lanceolate, subsessile, glabrous and light-green above, glaucous beneath; margins recurved; midrib prominent beneath, straight; lateral nerves indistinct. *Flowers* solitary, ·4 in. across; buds ovoid. *Calyx* minute, accrescent. *Petals* 3, oblong-lanceolate. *Fertile stamens* 3, opposite to the petals; staminodes 5-6, bifid, longer than the fertile stamens. *Ovary* 1-celled; style simple, terminal. *Fruit* the size of a pea, globular.

On crests of the SAHÁRANPUR SIWALIKS behind Ránipur; rather scarce.

Fl. Apr., May.

FAM. 24. AQUIFOLIACEÆ (*ILICINEÆ*); G. P. N. 46.

Trees or shrubs, generally evergreen. *Leaves* alternate, simple, glabrous, usually coriaceous. *Flowers* small, unisexual and often diœcious, in axillary fascicles or congested cymes. *Calyx* 3-6-cleft, persistent, imbricate in bud. *Petals* 4-5, white, imbricate, deciduous. *Stamens* 4-5, hypogynous, free or adnate to the petals. *Disk* 0. *Ovary* 3-16-celled; style short. *Fruit* a drupe with 2 or more 1-seeded stones. *Seeds* with a membranous testa.

1. Ilex, Linn.; G. P. n. 1.

Leaves coriaceous, serrate; midrib depressed above, prominent beneath. *Flowers* 4-5-merous. *Calyx* small. *Corolla* rotate; petals free or connate at the base. *Stamens* adhering to the base of the corolla. *Ovary* 2-12-celled; style very short or wanting. *Drupe* globose or ovoid, with 2-12 stones.

Analysis of the Species.

Leaves coriaceous, serrate.
 Petiole not exceeding ·3 in. ; drupe with 2 stones . . . . . . 1. *I. dipyrena.*
 Petiole up to ·7 in. ; drupe with 4 stones 2. *I. odorata.*
Leaves membranous, entire.
 (Petiole ·5-1 in. long ; drupe with 5 stones) . . . . . . 3. *I. excelsa.*

1. **I. dipyrena,** Wall. ; Fl. Br. Ind. i. 599 ; Brandis For. Flora 76, Ind. Trees 154 ; Gamble Man. Ind. Timb. 168. The Himalayan Holly. Vern. *Kanderú*, Jaunsar.

A small evergreen tree with rough dark-grey bark. *Leaves* 3-5 by 1-1·7 in., elliptic, ovate on ovate-lanceolate, acute or acuminate, spinous-serrate on young plants, nearly entire on old trees, very coriaceous when fully grown ; lateral nerves indistinct ; petiole ·2-·3 in. long, channelled. *Flowers* ·25 in. diam., whitish-green, tetramerous, in round axillary clusters, 2-bracteolate. *Calyx-lobes* broad-ovate, ciliate. *Petals* obovate, connate below in the male, free in the female flowers. *Ovary* small ; stigma sessile. *Drupe* ·3-·5 in. diam., globose or ellipsoid, red when ripe ; stones usually 2, longitudinally grooved.

JAUNSAR and TEHRI-GARHWAL, 5-9,000 ft. Common about Chakrata and Deoban and elsewhere on limestone soils.

Wood white, hard and close-grained, but cracks in drying and is chiefly used for fuel.

Fl. Apr.-June. Fr. Aug.-Oct.

2. **I. odorata,** Ham. ; Fl. Br. Ind. i. 599 ; Brandis For. Flora 77, Ind. Trees 155 ; Gamble Man. Ind. Timb. 168.

An evergreen tree ; branches rather slender. *Leaves* 4-7 by 1·5-2·5 in., oblong oblong-lanceolate or oblanceolate, acute or acuminate, very regularly and minutely serrate, thinly coriaceous ; lateral nerves somewhat more distinct than in the last species ; petiole ·3-·7 in. long, channelled. *Flowers* small, white, 4-merous, bracteolate, in short axillary panicles. *Petals* of male flowers connate below, of female flowers free. *Stamens* much longer than the petals. *Ovary* globose, 4-celled ; stigma sessile. *Drupe* ·2 in. diam., globose, black ; stones 4, trigonous.

OUTER HIMALAYA, *e. g.*, below Mussoorie and the Málkōt hills ; also in the Valley of the Tons in JAUNSAR and TEHRI-GARHWAL, 3,000-4,500 ft. Bháshla Block, Khunigádh, etc.

Fl. Apr. Fr. June.

3. **I. excelsa** (exsulca), Wall.; Fl. Br. Ind. i. 603; Brandis For. Flora 76, Ind. Trees 156; Gamble Man. Ind. Timb. 167. Vern. *Túmari*, U. P.

A middle-sized graceful evergreen tree; bark moderately smooth, silvery-white outside, yellowish and soft inside, with long horizontal wrinkles; young shoots pubescent. *Leaves* 2-4 by 1·25-2 in., elliptic oblong or ovate, finely acuminate, entire, rather membranous, glabrous and dark-green above, finely grey-pubescent beneath when young, afterwards quite glabrous; lateral nerves about 8 pairs, arcuate; base acute; petiole ·5-1 in. long, channelled; stipules minute, caducous. *Flowers* 2-sexual, about ·15 in. across, greenish-white, usually 5-merous, in 8-12-flowered axillary pubescent umbels; peduncles ·3-·7 in. long, compressed; pedicels about ·1 in. long. *Calyx-lobes* ovate, ciliate. *Petals* ovate-orbicular, recurved, united at the base. *Stamens* dilated at the base, as long as the petals, inserted on and alternating with them; anther-lobes ovate. *Stigma* sessile. *Drupe* globose, about ·2 in. diam., with 5 3-sided stones.

JAUNSAR and TEHRI-GARHWAL, 4,-6,000 ft.: Kiárigádh below Kathián, Mautárgádh, Lúnágádh, etc. Rather scarce.

Fl. May, June. Fr. Oct., Nov.

Order 3.—CELASTRALES.

FAM. 25. CELASTRACEÆ; G. P. N. 47.

Trees or shrubs, the latter erect or scandent. *Leaves* opposite or alternate, simple, usually coriaceous; stipules minute and caducous, or 0. *Flowers* 2-sexual or polygamous, generally cymose. *Calyx* small, 4-5-lobed, imbricate, persistent. *Disk* conspicuous, sometimes lobed. *Petals* 0 or 4-5, imbricate, inserted on the disk. *Stamens* 3-5, inserted on the disk, alternating with the petals or, when the petals are absent, opposite to the calyx-lobes. *Ovary* 3-5-celled, surrounded by the disk; ovules erect, usually 2 in each cell; style none or short. *Fruit* various. *Seeds* mostly arillate, sometimes winged.

Analysis of the Genera.

Fruit a capsule; seeds arillate.
 Fruit lobed winged or echinate; leaves opposite . . . . 1. EUONYMUS.
 Fruit never winged or echinate, rarely lobed; leaves alternate . . . . . . 2. CELASTRUS.
Fruit a drupe; seeds exarillate; (leaves subopposite) . . . . 3. ELÆODENDRON.

1. Euonymus, Linn.; G. P. n. 1.

Trees or shrubs, the latter rarely scandent. *Leaves* opposite; stipules caducous. *Flowers* 2-sexual, 4-5-merous. *Calyx* flat or recurved. *Disk* broad, fleshy, 4-5-lobed. *Petals* often with coloured veins. *Stamens* inserted on the disk. *Ovary* sunk in the disk; style short. *Fruit* a capsule, 3-5-lobed -angled or -winged, rarely echinate; dehiscence loculicidal. *Seeds* enclosed in a fleshy arillode.

Analysis of the Species.

Erect shrubs or trees. Capsules without prickles.
 Flowers (usually) 5-merous.
  (Leaves coriaceous; capsules not winged) 1. *E. tingens.*
 Flowers 4-merous.
  Leaves membranous.
   Capsules 4-winged . . . . . 2. *E. fimbriatus.*
   Capsules 4-lobed . . . . . 5. *E. Hamiltonianus.*
  Leaves coriaceous; (capsules 4 winged). 4. *E. pendulus.*
Scandent shrub. Capsules covered with prickles; leaves subcoriaceous . . 3. *E. echinatus.*

1. **E. tingens,** Wall.; Fl. Br. Ind. i. 610; Brandis For. Flora 79, Ind. Trees 158; Gamble Man. Ind. Timb. 172. Vern. *Bhambeli, Roini,* Jaunsar.

An evergreen shrub; bark dark ash-coloured, tubercled or corky, bright-yellow inside. *Leaves* 1·5-3 by ·7-1·3 in., elliptic oblong or ovate-lanceolate, acute or acuminate, closely serrate or crenate, glabrous, rugose and dark-green above, pale beneath; lateral nerves faint; stipules brown, fimbriate; petiole ·2-·3 in. long. *Cymes* dichotomous, axillary or sub-terminal; peduncles ·5-2 in. long, compressed. *Flowers* usually 5-merous, about ·5 in. diam. *Calyx-lobes* irregularly divided or fimbriate. *Petals* orbicular, dull-white, crenulate, marked with brown or purple veins. *Stamens* shorter than the petals. *Style* subulate. *Capsule* ·5 in. long, globose, 3-5-angled, not winged. *Seeds* enclosed in an orange-coloured arillode.

JAUNSAR and TEHRI-GARHWAL, 6,-10,000 ft. Common at Chakrata, Bodyár, Deoban, Konáin; Deotá, etc.

The wood is fine-grained, compact and hard, but is seldom used except for fuel; weight 47 lbs. per c. ft. The corky outer bark of old stems gives a yellow dye.

Fl. Apr.-June. Fr. Aug., Sept.

2. **E. fimbriatus,** Wall.; Fl. Br. Ind. i. 611. Syn.—*E. lacerus*, Ham.; Brandis For. Flora 78, Ind. Trees 158; Gamble Man. Ind. Timb. 171. Vern. *Lichhoi*, *Angáo* or *Angáu*, Jaunsar.

A small deciduous tree with smooth grey bark; branchlets reddish-brown, compressed. *Leaves* 1·5-3 by ·8-1·3 in., ovate, acuminate, finely doubly-serrate, membranous, glabrous; lateral nerves 4-6, very slender; margins reddish-brown when young; petiole ·2-·3 in. long; stipules linear, deciduous. *Cymes* umbelliform, mostly from the base of current year's shoots; peduncles 1-3 in. long, with 3-7 very slender branches; pedicels capillary. *Flowers* ·15 in. diam., tetramerous. *Petals* cream-colour, ovate, entire. *Anthers* on short filaments. *Capsule* ·3-·5 in. diam., globose; wings usually 4, ·3 in. long, tapering. *Seeds* ovoid, enclosed in a red arillode.

Fairly common in JAUNSAR and TEHRI-GARHWAL, 6,-10,000 ft., generally affecting shady aspects.—Deoban, Konáin, Mundáli, etc.

Wood white, compact, tough, close- and even-grained; weight about 48 lbs. per c. ft. It is carved into spoons. The leaves and branches are lopped for fodder. The seeds are often strung up as beads.

Fl. Apr., May. Fr. Augt. Oct.

According to Rai Bahadur Keshavánand, *E. frigidus*, Wall.—Fl. Br. Ind. i. 611. Vern. *Angáu*, Jaunsar,—occurs in moist places in the Deoban Range, JAUNSAR. It very closely resembles *E. fimbriatus* differing only in having succulent young shoots, longer and narrower *leaves* with simple serratures, and much smaller *flowers* on weak succulent peduncles and pedicels.

3. **E. echinatus,** Wall.; Fl. Br. Ind i. 611; Brandis For. Flora 80, Ind. Trees 158; Gamble Man. Ind. Timb. 170. Vern. *Láduli*, Garhwal.

A climbing shrub adhering to rocks and trees by dense tufts of adventitious roots; shoots quadrangular. *Leaves* variable, ·5-3 by ·2-1 in., ovate- or oblong-lanceolate, acute, crenate or obtusely serrate, subcoriaceous, glabrous; main lateral nerves 8-10 pairs, prominent beneath, joining into an intramarginal vein; petiole margined, of the largest leaves ·3 in. long. *Flowers* about ·2 in. diam., greenish, in short axillary cymes. *Capsule* ·3 in. diam., globose, covered with dark-coloured spines.

Fairly common in JAUNSAR and TEHRI-GARHWAL, 7,-10,000 ft. Deoban, Bhújkōti, Mundáli; Deotá, etc.

Fl. Mar., Apr. Fr. Aug., Sept.

4. **E. pendulus,** Wall.; Fl. Br. Ind. i. 612; Brandis For. Flora 79, Ind. Trees 159; Gamble Man. Ind. Timb. 172. Vern. *Bhambélá*, Jaunsar.

A small evergreen tree or large shrub with a short trunk, numerous spreading branches and pendulous branchlets; bark grey, corky. *Leaves* 3-5 by 1-1·5 in., oblong-lanceolate, equally acute at both ends, sharply serrate, coriaceous, glabrous, shining above; lateral nerves indistinct; midrib pale, prominent; petiole ·3-·4 in. long, channelled; stipules minute. *Cymes* axillary or supra-axillary; peduncles 1-2 in. long, much compressed. *Flowers* ·3-·5 in. diam., 4-merous. *Calyx-lobes* obtuse, fimbriate. *Petals* about ·2 in. long, oblong, whitish, fimbriate. *Stamens* short; anthers ovate. *Style* short, filiform. *Capsule* ·5 in. diam., 3-4-lobed and sharply angled, more or less winged; arillode reddish-orange.

Open shady aspects and ravines in JAUNSAR and TEHRI-GARHWAL, ascending to 8,500 ft.—Korwá forest, Tutuá and Bámnái Gádhs, Konáin; Lambátách, etc. Very common about Mussoorie.

Wood close- and even-grained; weight 35-40 lbs. per c. ft. It is, however, rarely used except for fuel.

Fl. Apr., May. Fr. June, July.

5. **E. Hamiltonianus,** Wall.; Fl. Br. Ind. i. 612; Brandis For. Flora 78, Ind. Trees 159; Gamble Man. Ind. Timb. 171. Vern. *Dádúl*, *Dhárué*. Jaunsar.

A large deciduous shrub with a thick corky ashy-grey bark. *Leaves* variable, 2-6 by ·7 1·7 n., oblong or ovate-lanceolate, acuminate, finely serrate, membranous, glabrous, dull-green, not shining; petiole ·3-·5 in. long. *Cymes* dichotomous, axillary or intra-axillary; peduncles about 7-flowered. *Flowers* about ·3 in. diam., greenish-white. *Petals* ·2-·3 in. long, lanceolate or strap-shaped, margins revolute. *Stamens* and *style* ·1 in. long. *Capsule* ·2-·4 in. diam., turbinate, deeply 3-4-lobed, yellow when ripe. *Seeds* enclosed in a scarlet arillode.

TEHRI-GARHWAL, 8,-9,000 ft., generally in shady localities; Kotigádh, Bálchá, etc. Rather scarce in JAUNSAR; Agragádh near Deoban; also Bodyár.

Wood white, soft and close-grained, used for carving into ladles. Weight about 40 lbs. per c. ft. The branches are lopped for fodder.

Fl. Mar.-May. Fr. Aug.-Nov.

2. **Celastrus**, Linn.; G. P. n. 16.

Erect or climbing shrubs. *Leaves* alternate; stipules minute, deciduous, sometimes 0. *Flowers* small, 4-5-merous, 1-sexual or polygamous. *Disk* broad. *Petals* usually spreading. *Stamens* inserted on the margins of the disk. *Ovary* 2-4-celled, free or immersed in the disk, with 2 ovules in each cell; style short; stigma simple or 3-lobed. *Fruit* a globose or obovoid loculicidal capsule, 1-3-celled. *Seeds* 1-2 in each cell, more or less enveloped in an aril.

Analysis of the Species.

An unarmed climbing shrub. Flowers in large terminal panicles . . . . . 1. *C. paniculata.*
Armed erect shrubs or trees. Flowers in small axillary cymes.
  A shrub; leaves ovate or obovate . . . 2. *C. Royleana.*
  A tree; leaves lanceolate . . . . . 3. *C. rufa.*

1. **C. paniculata,** Willd.; Fl. Br. Ind. i. 617; Brandis For. Flora 82, Ind. Trees 162; Gamble Man. Ind. Timb. 175. Vern. *Málkángni, Málkákni,* Hind.

A large woody climber with corky bark; young shoots marked with lenticels. *Leaves* very variable in size and shape, generally 2-4 by 1·5-3 in., obovate orbicular elliptic or oblong-lanceolate, short-acuminate, crenate, more or less coriaceous, glabrous; base acute;

lateral nerves 4-6 pairs, parallel to the margins; petiole ·4-·6 in. long. *Panicles* terminal, large, drooping, pubescent, branching into compound cymes. *Flowers* ·15 in. across, pale-green. *Calyx-lobes* rounded, toothed. *Petals* oblong. *Anthers* large, about the size of the petals. *Ovary* free; stigma simple. *Capsule* ·4-·5 in. diam., globose, usually 3-celled, bright-yellow when ripe. *Seeds* 1-2 in each cell, black, enclosed in a red arillus.

Common in the DÚN and SAHÁRANPUR FORESTS, also at low elevations in JAUNSAR and the OUTER HIMALAYA. It has a striking appearance when in fruit, which hangs gracefully like bunches of yellow beads.

The leaves and seeds are used in country medicine. An oil is extracted from the seeds which is believed to have great medicinal virtue, and is also used for burning.

Fl. Apr.-June. Fr. Cold season.

2. **C. Royleana,** Wall.: Syn.—*Gymnosporia Royleana*, Wall.; Fl. Br. Ind. *i.* 620; Brandis Ind. Trees 163. *Celastrus spinosa*, Royle; Brandis For. Flora 80; Gamble Man. Ind. Timb. 176. Vern. *Gwála Dárim*, Hind.

A thorny shrub 8-10 ft. high; bark thin, grey, corky; spines ·5-1 in. long, axillary, straight, slender. *Leaves* ·5-2 by ·3-1·2 in., obovate or ovate, serrate crenate or subentire, coriaceous, very slightly pubescent when young, lateral nerves faint; tip acute rounded or emarginate; petiole ·1-·2 in. long. *Cymes* axillary, shorter than the leaves; pedicels slender. *Calyx-lobes* ciliate. *Petals* ·1 in. long, whitish, ovate-oblong. *Ovary* sunk in the fleshy disk. *Capsule* ·2-·3 in. diam., turbinate, 3-cornered; seeds partially covered with a white aril.

Banks of the Jumná near Dákhpathár, also Ámbári, in the DÚN; and Bádsháhibágh and Khárá in the SAHÁRANPUR DISTRICT. It is likely to be mistaken for *Flacourtia Ramontchi*, which it closely resembles in foliage and general appearance.

Fl. and Fr. almost throughout the year, but more generally in the cold season.

3. **C. rufa,** Wall.; Brandis For. Flora 80; Gamble Man. Ind. Timb. 176. Syn.—*Gymnosporia rufa*, Wall., Fl. Br. Ind. i. 620.

A tree armed with short axillary spines; very young leaves and inflorescence slightly rusty-pubescent (whence the specific name), otherwise glabrous. *Leaves* 2-4 by ·7-1·3 in., oblong-lanceolate, acuminate, spinous-serrate, subcoriaceous, pale beneath; midrib stout, prominent beneath; lateral nerves much branched, faint; petiole ·2-·3 in. long. *Cymes* axillary, fascicled, ·2-·5 in. long; branches and pedicels reddish, capillary. *Flowers* whitish, very small. *Petals* ·1 in. long. *Stigma* lobed, spreading. *Capsule* ·2-·3 in. diam., turbinate, 3-lobed, 3-celled, 3-seeded; seeds black, enclosed in a yellow arillus.

Very scarce. Has been only once found by Mr. J. F. Duthie in the khud below Zabarkhet at MUSSOORIE.

Fl. Mar., Apr. Fr. May, June.

The following species are also likely to occur in the region of this Flora :—

C. acuminata, Hook. f. Syn.—*Gymnosporia acuminata*, Hook f.; Fl. Br. Ind. i. 619. *Leaves* 2-3 in. long, narrowly ovate-oblong serrate, acute at both ends, membranous. *Capsule* about ·5 in. diam., 2-celled, 2-seeded.

C. montana, Roxb. Syn.—*Gymnosporia montana*, Roxb., Fl. Br. Ind. i. 621. *Celastrus senegalensis*, Lam.; Brandis For. Flora 81, Ind. Trees 163. *Leaves* subsessile, 1-2 by ·3-·8 in., oblanceolate or obovate, crenulate, coriaceous. *Capsules* ·15 in. diam., 1-3-celled, black.

3. Elæodendron, Jacq. fil.; G. P. n. 28.

1. **E. glaucum,** Pers.; Fl. Br. Ind. i. 623; Brandis Ind. Trees 164. Syn.—*E. Roxburghii*, W. & A.; Brandis For. Flora 82; Gamble Man. Ind. Timb. 178. Vern. *Dhebri*, Hind.; *Jangéla*, *Jangél*, E. Dún; *Pániála*, W. Dún.

A moderate-sized or large tree, often with reddish branchlets; bark dark-grey, smooth, blood-red inside, exuding when cut a profuse watery sap from the cambium-layer. *Leaves* opposite or sub-opposite; less frequently alternate, 2-6 by 1-3 in., elliptic ovate oblong or obovate, acuminate, crenate sub-coriaceous, glabrous, dark-green and shining above, glaucous, beneath (whence the specific name); main lateral nerves about 10 pairs, slender; petiole ·4-1 in. long, channelled. *Cymes* axillary, dichotomous, 3-5 in. long; peduncle 1-2·5 in. long, often red. *Flowers* ·2 in. diam., whitish. *Calyx* 4-5-cleft; segments obtuse. *Disk* fleshy. *Petals* 4-5, about ·1 in. long, oblong. *Stamens* 4-5, short, inserted under the edge of the disk; filaments recurved. *Ovary* adnate to the disk; style very short. *Fruit* a dry obovoid drupe, ·4-·6 in. long, 1-celled, 1-seeded, tipped with the persistent style, mostly sterile (reproduction chiefly by root-suckers).

SIWALIK DIVISION also in valleys in the HILLS, generally affecting a clayey binding soil, and consequently with Sáin in Sál forests.—Tháno, Lachiwála, Karwápáni, Timli Pass, Dholkhand, Ránipur, Ká'si, etc.

Wood moderately hard, even- and close-grained, deep-red when fresh-cut, turning light-brown in seasoning; weight 40-50 lbs. per c. ft. It takes a fine polish, and is used for cabinet-work and picture-frames. Forest contractors in the Dún generally convert it into karries, which are exported into the plains districts and sold there as Sál. "The root is believed to be a specific for snake-bites, and the bark is used in native medicine."—*Sir D. Brandis.*

Leafless in Apr. Fl. Feb.-June. Fr. Jan.-June of the next year.

FAM. 26. RHAMNACEÆ G. P. N. 49.

Trees or shrubs, often armed. *Leaves* simple, generally alternate; stipules small, sometimes changed into prickles. *Flowers* 1-sexual or polygamous, green or yellow, small, usually in axillary cymes. *Calyx* 4-5-cleft, sometimes superior; lobes triangular, valvate in bud. *Petals* 4-5 or 0, involute, inserted on the throat of the calyx-tube, alternating with and generally shorter than the calyx-segments. *Disk* various. *Stamens* 4-5, opposite to the petals and often enclosed within their folds; anthers versatile. *Ovary* free or more or less immersed in the disk, usually 3-celled, with one erect ovule in each cell.; styles united. *Fruit* various, generally indehiscent; seeds 1-4.

Analysis of the Genera.

Ovary superior or half-superior.
  Scandent shrubs. Fruit terminating in a long wing . . . . 1. VENTILAGO.
  Generally erect shrubs. Fruit not winged.
    Disk thick, filling the calyx-tube.
      Leaves more or less oblique, 3-5-nerved at the base.
        Armed. Fruit with a 1-4-celled stone; peduncle not thickened . . . 2. ZIZYPHUS.
        Unarmed. Fruit 3-seeded; peduncle thickened in fruit . . . . 5. HOVENIA.
      Leaves symmetrical, penninerved.
        Leaves alternate; drupe 2-celled, 2-seeded 3. BERCHEMIA.
        Leaves opposite or sub-opposite; fruit 3-celled, 3-seeded . . . . . 6. SAGERETIA.
    Disk thin, lining the calyx-tube.
      (Leaves symmetrical, alternate; fruit 2-4-seeded) . . . . 4. RHAMNUS.
Ovary inferior. Cirrhose climbing shrubs.
  Flowers racemed; fruit winged . . . . 7. GOUANIA.
  Flowers umbelled; fruit not winged . . . 8. HELINUS.

1. Ventilago, Gærtn.; G. P. n. 1.

1. **V. calyculata,** Tulasne; Fl. Br. Ind. i. 631; Brandis For. Flora 96, Ind. Trees 168; Gamble Man. Ind. Timb. 180. Vern. *Káli-bel*, Dún.

A large woody climber generally with strong tendrils; branchlets pubescent; bark dark-grey. *Leaves* 2-4 by 1-2·5 in., ovate- or oblong-elliptic, more or less acute, crenate or entire, subcoriaceous, pubescent when young; lateral nerves 6-8 pairs, arcuate; base unequal; petiole ·2-·4 in., pubescent. *Flowers* numerous, small, greenish, in large terminal panicles. *Calyx* pubescent; lobes 5, keeled inside. *Petals* 5, deflexed. *Disk* 5-lobed, filling the calyx-tube. *Ovary* 2-celled, sunk in the disk; style short, prolonged and winged on both sides in fruit. *Fruit* a sub-globose nut, about ·2 in. diam., girt about the middle by the rim of the adherent calyx-tube and prolonged into a wing which is 1-1·5 by ·3-·4 in., linear, strongly reticulate and with a prominent straight midrib.

Shady mixed forests and ravines in SAHÁRANPUR and the DÚN; — Kasúmri, Chilláwála; Tháno, Káluwála, Nakraunda, Laohiwála, Dúdhli, Ráiwála, Khairi, etc.

Wood pale-yellow, tough, capable of being used for fuel.

Fl. Feb., Mar. Fr. May, June.

2. Zizyphus, Juss.; G. P. n. 4.

Trees or shrubs, sometimes sarmentose, usually armed with stipulary prickles. *Leaves* alternate, more or less distichous, subcoriaceous, 3-5-nerved at the base. *Flowers* small, in axillary fascicles or cymes. *Calyx* 5-fid; lobes keeled within. *Petals* 5 or 0, deflexed. *Disk* 5-10-lobed, coating the calyx-tube; edges free. *Stamens* 5. *Ovary* immersed in the disk and adnate to it at the base, 2-4-celled; styles 2-4, free or partly connate. *Fruit* a fleshy or dry drupe with a hard 1-4-celled and 1-4-seeded stone.

Analysis of the Species.

Flowers fascicled or in sessile cymes.
 Leaves broad-ovate or suborbicular, glabrous above, felted beneath; drupe over ·5 in. long. 1. *Z. Jujuba.*
 Leaves ovate-lanceolate, acuminate; drupe about ·3 in. diam.
  An erect shrub. Leaves wholly glabrous; prickles usually in pairs . . . 2. *Z. oxyphylla.*
  A straggling shrub. Leaves hairy on both surfaces; prickles solitary . . . 3. *Z. Œnoplia.*
Flowers in peduncled cymes; leaves generally obtuse, glabrous above.
 Cymes short, simple; drupe 1 in. diam., dry, tomentose, 3-celled . . . . . 4. *Z. xylopyra.*
 Cymes long, panicled; drupe ·3 in. diam., fleshy, glabrous, 1-celled . . . . . . 5. *Z. rugosa.*

1. Z. Jujuba, Lam.; Fl. Br. Ind. i. 632; Brandis For. Flora 86, Ind. Trees 170; Gamble Man. Ind. Timb. 181. Vern. *Ber, Beri,* Hind. The cultivated variety is called *Pewandi* or *Pemdi Ber,* and the degraded form *Jhár Beri,* Hind.

A moderate-sized tree, almost evergreen; bark dark-grey or nearly black, with long deep vertical cracks, reddish and fibrous inside; young parts rusty-tomentose. *Leaves* very variable, 1·4 by ·6-3 in., suborbicular, elliptic or ovate, closely serrulate or entire, rounded at both ends, dark-green glabrous and often shining above, densely woolly-tomentose beneath; base more or less oblique, strongly 3-nerved, nerves closely penniveined; petiole ·1-·6 in. long; prickles solitary or in twos. *Flowers* greenish-yellow, in short axillary cymes or fascicles, scarcely exceeding the petioles. *Calyx* glabrous within. *Petals* concave, reflexed. *Disk* 10-lobed. *Ovary* 2-celled; styles 2. *Drupe* 2-celled, very variable in size and shape, ·5-1·5 in. long, globose to ellipsoidal or obovoid-acuminate, red or orange when ripe.

Extremely common and gregarious along the foot of the SAHÁRANPUR SIWALIKS, especially at Beribára. Represented in the DÚN by what appears to be a degraded form, which is common as a bush in grass-lands. The *Pewandi Ber* is cultivated in gardens, especially in SAHÁRANPUR.

Wood hard, compact, tough, reddish; annual rings not distinct; weight 43-52 lbs. per c. ft. It is used for agricultural implements, and is very good for fuel and charcoal. The fruit is eaten. Lac is produced on its branches. The branches and leaves are lopped for fodder.

Fl. Sept.-Nov. Fr. Dec.-Feb.

2. **Z. oxyphylla,** Edgew.; Fl. Br. Ind. i. 634; Brandis For. Flora 85, Ind. Trees 171; Gamble Man. Ind. Timb. 183. Vern. *Beri*, Jaunsar.

A thorny shrub, usually with a few scattered hairs on young parts, otherwise quite glabrous; bark thin, brown. *Leaves* 1-2 by ·7-1·3 in., ovate-lanceolate, gradually acuminate, mucronate, finely serrate, rather membranous, glabrous; base subcordate, oblique, 3-nerved; petiole 2-4 in. long, slender; prickles weak, usually in twos, one of which points upward. *Flowers* pale, in axillary fascicles, about ·15 in. diam.; pedicels slender, ·2-·3 in. long. *Calyx-lobes* triangular, acute. *Petals* clawed. *Disk* thin, 5-lobed. *Ovary* 2-celled; styles 2, united to beyond the middle. *Drupe* about ·3 in. long, ovoid, fleshy, 2-celled and 2-seeded, less frequently 1-celled and 1-seeded, orange-red when ripe but drying black; seeds brown plano-convex.

Up to 6,000 ft. in JAUNSAR and TEHRI-GARHWAL, generally round villages and in open valleys: Binálgádh, Dhármigádh, Siligádh, etc.

Wood white, moderately hard. It is often planted in hedges and also for its acid fruit which tastes like tamarind.

Fl. May, June. Fr. Oct., Nov.

3. **Z. Œnoplia,** Mill.; Fl. Br. Ind. i. 634; Brandis For. Flora 86, Ind. Trees 170; Gamble Man. Ind. Timb. 183. Vern. *Makōh*, Sahāranpur.

A thorny shrub with long sarmentose branches; bark rough, dark-grey. *Leaves* 1·2 by ·7-1 in., very obliquely ovate-lanceolate, mucronate, obscurely crenate-serrate or subentire, more or less pubescent above, softly rusty-tomentose beneath; base 3-4-nerved; petiole ·1-·3 in. long, pubescent, rather stout; prickles small, recurved, generally solitary. *Cymes* dichotomous, compressed. *Calyx* tomentose outside. *Petals* obtriangular. *Ovary* 2-celled: styles 2, united to above the middle. *Drupe* about ·25 in. diam., sub-globose or ovoid, black when fully ripe, with a scanty mealy acid pulp, 2-celled, 2-seeded, but generally 1-celled and 1-seeded by abortion.

Common along the foot of the SAHÁRANPUR SIWALIKS. Somewhat rare in the DÚN being found only about Pardúni.

The long branches are much in demand for fencing round fields, and the plant is often grown in hedges. The fruit is eaten.

Fl. Apr., May. Fr. Cold season.

4. **Z. xylopyra,** Willd.; Fl. Br. Ind. i. 634; Brandis For. Flora 90, Ind. Trees 171; Gamble Man. Ind. Timb. 183. Vern. *Bhander*, *Kath Ber*, Dún and Sahāranpur.

A large erect shrub; branches more or less straggling; young shoots rusty-tomentose; bark thin, brownish-grey, smooth or rough with small exfoliating scales. *Leaves* 1-3·5 by ·7-2·5 in., orbicular, broadly elliptic or obovate, serrulate, obliquely sub-cordate or rounded at the base, tip rounded or acute, slightly pubescent along the nerves, otherwise glabrous above, brown-pubescent beneath; petiole ·1-·3 in., tomentose; prickles usually in twos, one straight, the other recurved, often wanting. *Cymes* axillary, peduncled. *Flowers* scarcely ·1 in. diam. *Calyx-lobes* keeled only at the apex. *Petals* reflexed. *Disk* thin, 5-angled. *Ovary* usually 3-celled; styles 3, almost free. *Drupe* about 1 in. diam., globose, often depressed at the ends, more or less white-tomentose, 3-celled, dry, not edible.

Common in the DÚN and SAHÁRANPUR DISTRICTS, generally in scrub forests, but is sometimes also found with Sál.

Wood yellowish-brown, hard and durable, also easy to work, but is seldom used except for fuel; weight about 50 lbs. per c. ft. The bark is used for tanning, and the leaves for fodder. The fruit is used to give a black dye to leather.

Leafless Mar., Apr. Fl. Apr., May. Fr. Cold season.

5. **Z. rugosa,** Lam.; Fl. Br. Ind. i. 636; Brandis For. Flora 89, Ind. Trees 171; Gamble Man. Ind. Timb. 184. Vern. *Bhand Ber*, Dún.

A small evergreen tree; branches few, somewhat straggling; young parts generally rusty-tomentose, bark dark-grey or nearly black, deeply cracked into thick rectangular scales. *Leaves* 2-4 by 1·7-3·5 in., sub-orbicular ovate or elliptic, closely serrulate, sub-acute, obliquely rounded or sub-cordate at the base, dark-green and glabrous above, thickly grey- or rusty-felted beneath; basal nerves 3, each closely penniveined; petiole ·2-·3 in. long, stout; prickles few, usually solitary, recurved. *Cymes* arranged in long axillary or terminal panicles which are often 1 ft. long, rusty-tomentose throughout. *Calyx-lobes* not keeled. *Petals* 0. *Disk* 5-angled, hairy. *Ovary* 2-celled; styles 2, united below the middle. *Drupe* about ·3 in. long, globose or pyriform, 1-celled, 1-seeded.

Along the foot of the Nágsidh Hill and at Rámgarh in the DÚN, also in valleys in the HILLS up to 3,000 ft.; not very common.

Wood reddish, moderately hard, but warps and is liable to be attacked by insects. It is used chiefly for fuel. The fruit is eaten and the leaves are lopped for fodder.

Fl. Mar., Apr. Fr. Rainy season.

3. Berchemia, Neck.; G. P. n. 8.

Unarmed erect or climbing shrubs. *Leaves* alternate, closely penninerved. *Flowers* usually 5-merous and 2-sexual. *Calyx* persistent. *Petals* usually obovate or oblanceolate. *Disk* lining the calyx-tube. *Ovary* 2-celled, sunk in the calyx-tube, but not adnate to it. *Fruit* a drupe or a berry, usually tipped with the remains of the style; kernel 2-celled, 2-seeded.

Analysis of the Species.

A climbing shrub. Leaves 2-4 in. long . 1. *B. floribunda.*
An erect undershrub. Leaves about ·5 in. long . 2. *B. lineata.*

1. **B. floribunda,** Brongn.; Fl. Br. Ind. i. 637; Brandis For. Flora 91, Ind. Trees 169; Gamble Man. Ind. Timb. 184. Vern. *Kouloi* or *Káuloi*, Jaunsar; *Amili*, Garhwal.

A large climbing shrub; bark thin, whitish outside, inner layer purple. *Leaves* 2-4 by 1-2 in., ovate or oblong, acuminate, thinly sub-coriaceous, glabrous, rounded or sub-cordate at the base; lateral nerves 10-12 pairs, straight, parallel, slender but distinct; petiole ·5-·7 in. long, terete; stipules 2-fid. *Flowers* minute, "3-10 in cymose clusters, arranged in racemes 2-3 in. long, which again form large terminal panicles."—*Sir D. Brandis.* *Fruit* ·3-·5 in. long, ovate-oblong or cylindrical, fleshy.

Swampy localities in the DÚN, *e.g.*, Káluwála, Nakraunda Jogiwála, etc., and in shady ravines up to 4,500 ft. in the HILLS, *e.g.*, Binálgádh, Chátrágádh, etc.

Fl. May-July. Fr. Feb.-Apr.

2. **B. lineata,** DC.; Fl. Br. Ind. i. 638; Brandis For. Flora 91, Ind. Trees 169; Gamble Man. Ind. Timb. 184. Vern. *Angári*, Jaunsar.

An undershrub 3-5 ft. high, with smooth shining bark; young shoots puberulous. *Leaves* variable, generally about ·5 in. long, oblong or ovate, elegantly marked underneath with 6-8 pairs of fine straight nerves; petiole ·1-·2 in. long, slender; stipules bristle-like. *Flowers* minute, in axillary or terminal clusters. *Calyx-lobes* linear. *Petals* linear-lanceolate. *Berry* ·25-·4 in. long, cylindrical, blue when ripe.

JAUNSAR and TEHRI-GARHWAL, 8-9,000 ft.; not very common. Bájámára; below "Snow View" and at Kanjátra, Deoban, etc.

Fl. May-July. Fr. Sept.

B. Edgeworthii, Lawson; Fl. Br. Ind. i. 638; Brandis Ind. Trees 169; a shrub closely resembling the above, but with glabrous branches, 6-merous flowers, and somewhat larger leaves and fruit, has also been found in JAUNSAR and TEHRI-GARHWAL, *e. g.*, Durani Dhár, Oshlá, Kanjátra, etc.—*Mr. J. S. Gamble.*

4. Rhamnus, Linn.; G. P. n. 10.

Shrubs or trees, sometimes with spinescent branchlets. *Leaves* alternate or fascicled (by the arrest of the growth of the branchlets), penninerved. *Flowers* unisexual or polygamous, in axillary fascicles or cymes.

Calyx 4-5-fid; lobes keeled within. *Disk* thin, lining the calyx-tube. *Petals* 4-5 or 0. *Stamens* 4-5, inserted with the petals on the edge of the disk; filaments short. *Ovary* free, 3-4-celled, narrowed into a 3-4-celled style; stigma papillose. *Fruit* a berry-like drupe, 2-4-celled, 2-4-seeded, seated on the persistent calyx-tube.

Analysis of the Species.

Erect shrubs or trees.
  Spinescent shrubs. Leaves mostly fascicled; flowers 4-merous.
    Leaves sub-coriaceous, alternate on growing shoots; stem ash-coloured . . . 1. *R. persicus.*
    Leaves membranous, sub-opposite on growing shoots; stem shining dark-grey . 2. *R. dahuricus.*
  Unarmed, shrubs. Leaves not fascicled; flowers 5-merous.
    Leaves membranous; branchlets purple; cymes sessile . . . . . . 3. *R. purpureus.*
    Leaves sub-coriaceous; branchlets green; cymes racemed . . . . . 4. *R. triqueter.*
A prostrate shrub, not armed.
  (Leaves coriaceous; flowers 5-merous) . . 5. *R. procumbens.*

1. **R. persicus,** Boiss.; Fl. Br. Ind. i. 638; Brandis For. Flora 93; Gamble Man. Ind. Timb. 185. Vern. *Chirla*, Dún.

A deciduous shrub with a short erect trunk and stiff branches, often armed; bark smooth, ash-coloured; epidermis peeling off generally in vertical strips. *Leaves* alternate on growing shoots, fascicled on arrested branchlets, ·5-2 in. long, ovate elliptic lanceolate or obovate, acute acuminate or rounded at the tip, minutely serrulate or entire, sub-coriaceous, slightly tomentose beneath; petiole minute to ·3 in. long. *Flowers* 4-merous, short-pedicelled, diœcious, in axillary fascicles. *Petals* small, linear. *Fruit* about ·2 in. diam., obovoid or turbinate.

In the DÚN at Mothronwála, and near the Harbanswála Chauki; also in JAUNSAR up to 6,000 ft., *e. g.*, Saiá, the slopes below Konain village, etc.

The fruit is eaten, and the leaves are browsed by goats.

Fl. Mar.-May, before the new leaves, but generally throughout the year. Fr. Chiefly Nov., Dec.

✓ 2. **R. dahuricus,** Pall.; Fl. Br. Ind. i. 639. Syn.—*R. virgatus*, Roxb.; Brandis For. Flora 92, Ind. Trees 172; Gamble Man. Ind. Timb. 185. The Himalayan Buckthorn. Vern. *Thanthár*, Jaunsar; *Chaurdhá*, Garhwal.

A deciduous shrub or small tree, generally with a stout spine at the forks of the branches; bark dark-grey, thin, smooth, shining, peeling off in horizontal rolls. *Leaves* generally sub-opposite on growing shoots, fascicled on arrested branchlets, ·5-2 by ·2-1 in., rhomboidal ovate or ovate-lanceolate, acuminate, minutely serrulate or entire, membranous, slightly pubescent beneath when young; lateral nerves 3-5 pairs, slender; base acute; petiole ·1-·4 in. long. *Flowers* 4-merous, in dense axillary fascicles; buds pointed; pedicels long or short, filiform. *Calyx-tube* campanulate. *Petals* minute. *Fruit* about ·15-·25 in. diam., globose.

Common in JAUNSAR and TEHRI-GARHWAL between 3,000 and 9,000 ft., also along the Bindál nálá, DEHRA DÚN.

The wood is hard and close-grained; weight 56 lbs. per c. ft. Capable of being used for agricultural implements. "The fruit is bitter, emetic and purgative, and is given in affections of the spleen."—*Mr. J. S. Gamble.*

Fl. Apr.-June. Fr. Cold season. Often fl. and fr. throughout the year.

3. **R. purpureus,** Edgew.; Fl. Br. Ind. i. 639; Brandis For. Flora 91, Ind. Trees 173; Gamble Man. Ind. Timb. 186. Vern. *Luhish, Lhish*, Jaunsar.

An unarmed deciduous shrub; bark thin, smooth. *Leaves* alternate, 2-4 by 1-2 in., elliptic or ovate-lanceolate, acuminate, serrate or crenate, membranous, pubescent beneath when young; lateral nerves 6-10 pairs, somewhat arcuate, prominent. *Flowers* 2-sexual, 5-merous, in short axillary cymes; buds ovoid. *Calyx* cup-shaped; segments acute. *Petals* usually 0. *Style* short, 3-cleft, *Drupe* about ·2-·3 in. diam., sub-globose or pyriform.

JAUNSAR and TEHRI-GARHWAL, between 4,500 and 9,500 ft. Common at Deoban, Mundáli; Deotá, etc., generally on open shady aspects.

Wood brownish-grey, close-grained; weight 41 lbs. per c. ft. The fruit is used as a purgative.

Fl. May, June. Fr. July-Oct.

4. **R. triqueter,** Wall.; Fl. Br. Ind. i. 639; Brandis For. Flora 92, Ind. Trees 173; Gamble Man. Ind. Timb. 186. Vern. *Katherú*, Jaunsar; *Gaunt*, Dún and Garhwal.

An unarmed deciduous shrub; bark dark-grey, thin. *Leaves* 2-6 by 1-2 in., ovate-oblong, acuminate, closely serrate, glabrescent above, finely pubescent beneath, somewhat brittle, drying yellowish-green, often mixed with smaller leaves which are ·5-1 in. long; lateral nerves 8-10 pairs, arcuate; base rounded or acute; petiole ·3-1 in. long. *Racemes* of cymes 2-4 in. long, axillary, sometimes with a few leaf-like small bracts. *Flowers* puberulous. *Calyx-lobes* acute. *Petals* clawed, emarginate, sheathing the stamens. *Drupe* 3-lobed.

OUTER HIMALAYA and JAUNSAR, 3,-6,000 ft. Common below Mussoorie and also about Tiuni in the Tons Valley. MÁLKÔT HILLS down to Tháno in the DÚN; also near Ambári. Also found in the SIWALIKS, *e.g.*, in the Timli Pass.

Wood yellowish-brown, hard and close-grained, capable of being used for agricultural implements.

Fl. July, Aug. Fr. Oct.-Dec.

5. **R. procumbens,** Edgew.; Fl. Br. Ind. i. 640; Brandis For. Flora 93, Ind. Trees 173; Gamble Man Ind. Timb. 187.

A small procumbent shrub, usually trailing on rocks; young branches pubescent. *Leaves* ·3-1 in., elliptic or lanceolate, acute or acuminate, serrulate, coriaceous, dark-green; midrib prominent beneath, depressed above; lateral nerves faint; petiole of the largest leaf about ·1 in. long; stipules setaceous, persistent. *Flowers* axillary, often solitary, on slender pedicels which are ·2-·5 in. long. *Fruit* about ·15 in. diam., globose, fleshy.

JAUNSAR, 7,000 to 8,500 ft. Common on rocks at Matkángrá and in the Mohná Block, Deoban; Tutuá Block, Mundáli, etc.

Wood yellowish, hard, close-grained and tough.

Fl. July, Aug. Fr. May, June (next year ?).

5. Hovenia, Thunb.; G. P. n. 12.

1. **H. dulcis,** Thunb.; Fl. Br. Ind. i. 640; Brandis For. Flora 94, Ind. Trees 174; Gamble Man. Ind. Timb. 187.

A small deciduous tree with a straight trunk. *Leaves* alternate, 4-6 by 2-3·5 in., ovate, long-acuminate, often inequilateral, serrate, membranous, glabrescent above, more or less tomentose beneath, 3-nerved at the base; lateral nerves 3-5 pairs above the basal; petiole ·5-·7 in. long. *Flowers* 2-sexual, white, in axillary and terminal dichotomous cymes; peduncle 1-2 in. long. *Calyx* 5-fid; tube conical, deciduous. *Petals* 5, clawed. *Disk* fleshy, woolly. *Stamens* 5, longer than the petals, inserted on the edge of the disk. *Ovary* 3-celled, sunk in the disk; styles 3. *Fruit* a 3-celled 3-seeded indehiscent drupe, about ·3 in. diam.; the peduncle and part of the inflorescence thicken into a fleshy mass when the fruit ripens.

JAUNSAR and TEHRI-GARHWAL, 3,000 to 6,500 ft.: Thadiár, Bámsu, Dárnagádh, etc.

The fleshy peduncle is sweet and aromatic, and is eaten. The leaves are eaten by cattle.

Fl. Apr.-June. Fr. July-Sept.

6. Sageretia, Brongn.; G. P. n. 15.

1. **S. oppositifolia**, Brongn.; Fl. Br. Ind. i. 641; Brandis For. Flora 95, Ind. Trees 173; Gamble Man. Ind. Timb. 188. Vern. *Gonta*, E. Dún.

A shrub or small tree with long subscandent spinous branches; branchlets tomentose when young. *Leaves* usually opposite, 2-4 by 1-1·5 in., those towards the end of the branches usually much smaller, ovate-lanceolate, acute or acuminate, serrate or sub-entire, sub-coriaceous, glabrescent above, pubescent (at least along the nerves) beneath; lateral nerves 5-8 pairs, impressed above, prominent beneath; base rounded, rarely subcordate; petiole ·5 in. *Flowers* very small, in large terminal panicles with opposite racemose ramifications, often mixed with small membranous leaves. *Calyx* flat, 5-toothed. *Petals* 5, clawed, hooded. *Disk* cup-shaped, lining the calyx-tube. *Stamens* 5, as long as the petals. *Ovary* 3-celled, narrowed into three coherent styles. *Fruit* berry-like, turbinate, ·2-·3 in. diam., black when ripe.

Throughout the OUTER HIMALAYA, 3,-6,000 ft.: Málkōt, Jákhan Canal, below Mussoorie, Sahanara-dhárá, Saiá, Korwá, etc.

The wood is tough and is sometimes used for axe-handles. The fruit is edible.

Fl. July-Sept. Fr. Apr.-June.

7. Gouania, Linn.; G. P. n. 35.

1. **G. leptostachya**, DC.; Fl. Br. Ind. i. 643; Brandis For. Flora 574, Ind. Trees 175; Gamble Man. Ind. Timb. 189.

An unarmed climbing shrub bearing tendrils at the ends of the branchlets. *Leaves* alternate, 2-4 by 1·5-2·5 in., ovate, acuminate, crenate, sub-coriaceous, more or less rusty-pubescent beneath when young; lateral nerves 5-6 pairs, often opposite, arcuate, the lowest pair from near the base; base rounded or sub-cordate; petiole ·3-·6 in. long. *Flowers* white, about ·15 in. diam., in axillary or terminal often leaf-bearing racemes which are 6-10 in. long and generally simple. *Calyx* superior, 5-fid. *Disk* filling the calyx-tube, 5-lobed. *Petals* 5, inserted below the margin of the disk. *Stamens* 5, enfolded by the petals. *Ovary* 3-celled, sunk in the disk. *Fruit* ·5 in. long, 3-winged, 3-celled, 3-seeded, crowned by the remains of the calyx.

Common almost throughout the DÚN.: Barotiwála, Ambári, Robbers' Cave, Bindál nálá, Lachiwála, Káluwála, Tháno, Khairi, etc., spreading on trees, with a graceful appearance when in flower.

Fl. Aug., Sept. Fr. Nov., Dec.

8. Helinus, E. Meyer; G. P. n. 36.

1. **H. lanceolatus**, Brandis For. Flora 574; Gamble Man. Ind. Timb. 189; Fl. Br. Ind. i. 644.

An unarmed twining shrub; branches slender, branchlets angular, usually with a tendril near the end. *Leaves* 1-3 by ·5-1 in., lanceolate, very gradually acute, rather membranous, wholly glabrous or slightly canescent beneath; lateral nerves 3-4 pairs, slender; base rounded or sub-cordate, 3-nerved. *Flowers* about ·2 in. diam., pale-yellow, umbelled on short lateral branchlets, each umbel subtended by a bract or rudimentary leaf ·3-·7 in. long; peduncles ·51 in. long, slender. *Calyx* superior, cup-shaped. *Disk* filling the calyx-tube. *Petals* 5, hooded, inserted on the margin of the disk. *Stamens* 5, equalling the petals. *Ovary* 3-celled; stigmas recurved. *Fruit* ·2-·3 in. diam., broadly turbinate or globose, 3-celled, 3-seeded, tardily dehiscent.

Ravines, banks of streams and shady places in the DÚN, and n the SAHÁRANPUR SIWALIKS, also occasionally in valleys in JAUNSAR: Tapkeshwar, Lachiwála; Sháhjahánpur, Ránipur, etc.,

Fl. and fr. almost throughout the year.

FAM. 27. VITACEÆ (*AMPELIDEÆ*); G. P. N. 50.

Erect or climbing shrubs usually with copious watery juice. *Leaves* alternate, stipulate, simple or compound.

Flowers regular, cymose, usually 2-sexual. *Calyx* entire, or 4-5-toothed or -lobed. *Petals* 4-5, free or cohering at the base or apex, valvate, caducous. *Disk* fleshy. *Stamens* as many as the petals and opposite to them; filaments subulate, sometimes monadelphous. *Ovary* 2-6-celled; style short or none. *Fruit* a berry with 1-6 bony seeds.

Analysis of the Genera.

Climbing shrubs. Stamens free; ovary 2-celled	1. VITIS.
Erect shrubs or herbs: Stamens monadelphous; ovary 3-6-celled .	2. LEEA.

1. Vitis, Linn.; G. P. n. 1.

Climbing shrubs, sinistrorse if twining, usually with leaf-opposed tendrils. *Leaves* simple or 3-9-foliolate. *Flowers* variously cymose, 2-sexual or polygamous. *Calyx* 4-5-lobed. *Petals* 4-5, free or cohering at the apex. *Stamens* free, inserted below the margins of the disk. *Ovary* usually 2-celled, with 2 ovules in each cell; style short or 0. *Fruit* a 1-4-seeded berry.

Analysis of the Species.

Leaves simple.	
Flowers tetramerous	1. *V. repanda.*
Flowers pentamerous.	
Branches and under surface of leaves densely tomentose	2. *V. rugosa.*
Branches and leaves glabrous, or the latter slightly pubescent.	
Stem soft. Leaves broader than long	3. *V. latifolia.*
Stem woody. Leaves longer than broad	4. *V. parvifolia.*
Leaves 3-foliolate; flowers pentamerous .	5. *V. semicordata.*
Leaves pedately 5-foliolate; flowers tetramerous	6. *V. capriolata.*

1. **V. repanda,** W. & A. ; Fl. Br. Ind. i. 648. Gamble Man. Ind. Timb. 190.

A large climber ; branches ribbed, brittle, woolly when young ; old stem with wrinkled bark. *Leaves* simple, 3-5 by 2·5-4 in., ovate, cordate, acuminate, crenate with sharp points, rusty-tomentose beneath when young, glabrescent when old ; petiole 1-3 in. long ; tendril forked. *Flowers* in slender umbel-bearing cymes ; peduncle 1-4 in. long. *Petals* cream-coloured, connate at the apex. *Fruit* ·3-·4 in. long, pyriform, tipped with the persistent style.

The DÚN, and at low elevations in JAUNSAR and TEHRI-GARHWAL ; not common. Phándowála.

Fl. May, June. Fr. Rainy season.

2. **V. rugosa,** Wall. ; Sir G. King in Journ. As. Soc. Beng. lxv, Part ii, No. 2, p. 111. Syn.—*V. lanata*, Roxb. ; Fl. Br. Ind. i. 651 ; Brandis For. Flora 99, Ind. Trees 177 ; Vern. *Bhinána*, Jaunsar.

A large woody climber ; branches inflorescence and leaves covered with reddish or brown-felted tomentum. *Leaves* simple, 3-4 in. diam., ovate or suborbicular, cordate, acuminate, dentate, more densely tomentose beneath than above, sometimes obscurely 3-lobed, 3-7-nerved at the base ; petiole 1-2·5 in. long ; tendrils simple or forked. *Flowers* greenish, very sweet-scented, in large leaf-opposed compound panicles ; peduncle 1-3 in. long, generally with a tendril at the apex. *Petals* pale-green, connate above. *Stamens* long ; filaments very slender. *Fruit* about ·2 in. diam., globose, usually 1-seeded.

Common throughout the HILLS up to 5,000 ft. : Málkōt, Rájpur, Dhárágádh and other valleys, Thadiár, etc.

The stem yields an abundance of watery sap which can be drunk.

Fl. Apr.-June. Fr. July-Sept.

3. **V. latifolia,** Roxb. ; Fl. Br. Ind. i. 652 ; Brandis For. Flora 99, Ind. Trees 177 ; Gamble Man. Ind. Timb. 190. Vern. *Páni-bel*, Hind.

A large climber ; stem soft, very porous, furrowed and corky outside when old ; branches glabrous. *Leaves* simple, 3-7 by 4-8 in., suborbicular, cordate, 5-angled or 5-lobed, dentate, membranous, tomentose beneath when young, 5-nerved at the base ; lateral nerves 3-7 pairs above the base ; nerves and veins always more or less pubescent beneath ; petiole 2-4 in. long ; tendril slender, forked, one of the forks developing into inflorescence. *Flowers* reddish-brown, in compound pyramidal panicles. *Petals* distinct. *Stigma* sessile

Berry ·3-·4 in. diam. black, 2-seeded; seeds elliptic, rugose on the margins.

Common in the DÚN and SAHÁRANPUR FORESTS, generally climbing on Sál and other tall trees.

The stem yields when cut a large quantity of good potable water, which is a great relief to coolies working in dry waterless forests.

Leaflets Nov.-Mar. Fl. May-July. Fr. Oct.-Dec.

4. **V. parvifolia**, Roxb.; Fl. Br. Ind. i. 652; Brandis For. Flora 99, Ind. Trees 177.

A slender woody climber, wholly glabrous. *Leaves* simple, 1-2·5 by ·7-2 in., triangular-ovate, acuminate, dentate or very distantly serrate, sometimes lobed, membranous but tough, quite glabrous; lateral nerves 3-5 pairs above the cordate and 5-nerved base; tendrils 2-fid. *Flowers* minute, green, on slender umbellately-clustered pedicels; clusters arranged on simple or divided erect leaf-opposed racemes; peduncle ·5-·7 in. long; pedicels ·2 in. long, filiform, much thickened in fruit. *Petals* cohering at the apex. *Style* distinct, short. *Fruit* about ·3 in. diam., 1-seeded, globose, black when ripe.

Fairly common in JAUNSAR and TEHRI-GARHWAL and the OUTER HIMALAYA, 3,-6,000 ft.: Málkót; below Mussoorie; Saiá, Korwá, Dhárágádh; Thadiár, Bámsu, etc.

Fl. Apr., May. Fr. June, July.

Closely allied to the last two species is the European Grape Vine, *V. vinifera*, Linn.; Fl. Br. Ind. i. 652. Vern. *Angúr-ki Bél*, Hind.—which is cultivated to some extent in the Dún and at Sahāranpur, but does not bear good fruit, as the time for it to ripen comes in the rainy season, when there is not sufficient sunshine.

5. **V. semicordata**, Wall., var. **Roylei**, King Journ. As. Soc. Beng. lxv. Part ii. p. 113; Brandis Ind. Trees 178; Gamble Man. Ind. Timb. 190; Fl. Br. Ind. i. 655. Syn.—*V. himalayana*, Brandis For. Flora 100. Vern. *Kandár* (*Báli*), *Pánlu-ki Bál*, Jaunsar.

A large woody climber with smooth bark, generally not twining. *Leaves* 3-foliolate. *Leaflets* 2-4 by 1·5-2 in., the lateral very obliquely ovate, the terminal rhomboidal or elliptic, acuminate, serrate or dentate, pilose along the nerves beneath; lateral nerves about 8 pairs; common petiole 1-3 in.; petiolule ·1-·2 in.; tendril 0. *Flowers* yellowish-green, in compound trichotomous leaf-opposed cymes. *Style* short, stout. *Fruit* ·3-·4 in. diam., 4-sided, black when ripe.

JAUNSAR and TEHRI-GARHWAL, 3,-9,000 ft.; common.

Wood brown, hard, mottled with a pretty silver-grain, capable of being used for picture-frames.

Fl. Apr., May. Fr. Aug., Sept.

6. **V. capriolata** Don; Fl. Br. Ind. i. 659; Brandis For. Flora 101; Ind. Trees 178.

A slender wiry climber. *Leaves* pedately quinquefoliolate. *Leaflets* very variable, ·5-4 by ·3-1·3 in., obovate to narrow-lanceolate, acute or acuminate, the lateral more or less oblique, cuspidately serrate, membranous, glabrous; petiole 1-3 in.; secondary petiolule ·1-·15 in.; ultimate petiolule minute or 0; tendrils slender, smooth, generally forked near the end. *Inflorescence* a compound umbel, or simple umbels cymosely arranged; peduncle 1·5-2 in. long, usually with several conspicuous bracts; ultimate pedicels about ·2 in. long. *Flowers* 4-merous. *Stigma* sessile, flat. *Fruit* about ·4 in. long, globose, 2-4-seeded, black when ripe.

Valleys in JAUNSAR and TEHRI-GARHWAL, and the OUTER HIMALAYA near Mussoorie, 3,-7,000 ft., usually on trees or rocks in shady places. Also at Robber's Cave and elsewhere in the DÚN.

Fl. Aug., Sept. Fr. Oct., Nov.

2. Leea, Linn.; G. P. n. 3.

Erect shrubs or herbs. *Leaves* usually alternate, simple or 1-3-pinnate, dilated at the base into a sheath. *Flowers* in leaf-opposed compound corymbose cymes. *Calyx* 5-toothed. *Petals* 5, more or less connate at the base and adhering to the staminal tube. *Stamens* 5, united at the base into a tube; free end of filaments short, reflexed. *Ovary* 3-6-celled, inserted on the disk; ovules solitary in each cell; style short.

Analysis of the Species.

Leaflets acute, glabrous; flowers red . 1. *L. alata.*
Leaflets abruptly long-acuminate, scabrous; flowers green . . 2. *L. aspera.*

1. **L. alata,** Edgew.; Fl. Br. Ind. i. 665; Brandis For. Flora 102, Ind. Trees 179; Gamble Man. Ind. Timb. 191; Revision by Mr. C. B. Clarke in Trimen's Journal of Botany, x. 101.

A large perennial herb. *Leaves* imparipinnate; petiole grooved, winged. *Leaflets* 5-7, 6-12 by 1-2·5 in., oblong, acute, serrate, glabrous but rough with minute elevated dots, sessile or the lowest pair shortly petioluled; lateral nerves 8-12 pairs; base acute or rounded. *Cymes* compact, corymbosely branched, 2-3 in. across; peduncle 2-6 in. long, furrowed, rough with elevated glandular dots. *Flowers* small, red. *Anthers* united. *Fruit* ·3-·4 in. diam., reddish-purple, succulent.

Fairly common in the DÚN; Dehra, Lachiwála, etc.

Fl. June, July. Fr. Sept., Oct.

2. **L. aspera**, Edgew.; Fl. Br. Ind. i. 665; Brandis For. Flora 102, Ind. Trees 180; Gamble Man. Ind. Timb. 191; Revision by Mr. C. B. Clarke in Trimen's Journal of Botany, x. 136. Vern. *Kawá Okhár*, Jaunsar.

A large perennial herb. *Leaves* simply imparipinnate, or the lower often bipinnate. *Leaflets* (or pinnæ) 2-3 pairs, 3-6 by 2-3 in., ovate or ovate-oblong, abruptly long-acuminate, obtusely crenate, scabrous; lateral nerves 12-16 pairs, straight; base rounded or subcordate; common petiole not winged, of variable length; ultimate petiolule slender, ·2-·7 in. long. *Corymbs* sessile (so as to appear clustered) or shortly peduncled. *Flowers* small, green. *Anthers* not united. *Fruit* ·3-·4 in. diam., succulent, black when fully ripe.

Common in ravines in the DÚN. Also in JAUNSAR up to 6,000 ft.

The ripe fruit is eaten.

Fl. June, July. Fr. Oct., Nov.

Order 4.—SAPINDALES.

FAM. 28. SAPINDACEÆ; G. P. N. 51.

Trees or shrubs. *Leaves* various. *Flowers* usually polygamous. *Calyx* 4-5-lobed; lobes more or less connate. *Petals* 4-5 or 0, imbricate, often hairly at the base within. *Stamens* hypogynous, 5-10, generally 8;

filaments often pubescent. *Disk* complete or one-sided. *Ovary* sometimes eccentric, 1-4, generally 3-celled; ovules 1-2 in each cell, ascending; style simple or divided, usually terminal. *Fruit* various. *Seeds* generally exalbuminous, sometimes arillate, usually with a large hilum.

Analysis of the Genera.

Flowers irregular.	
(Leaves opposite, exstipulate, digitate; fruit a leathery capsule) . . .	1. ÆSCULUS.
Flowers regular.	
Leaves alternate, exstipulate.	
Leaves paripinnate; fruit indehiscent.	
Fruit dry; seeds in a fleshy arillus. .	2. SCHLEICHERA.
Fruit fleshy or coriaceous; seeds not arillate	3. SAPINDUS.
Leaves simple; fruit a membranous capsule.	5. DODONÆA.
Leaves opposite, exstipulate, palmately lobed or undivided; fruit a double samara.	4. ACER.
Leaves opposite, stipulate, trifoliolate or pinnate; fruit an inflated membranous capsule.	6. STAPHYLEA.

1. Æsculus, Linn.; G. P. n. 21.

1. **Æ. indica**, Colebr.; Fl. Br. Ind. i. 675; Brandis For. Flora 103, t. 19, Ind. Trees 185; Gamble Man. Ind. Timb. 193. The Horse-chestnut tree. Vern. *Pangár, Bankhór, Kándur, Kandár*, Jaunsar.

A large tree with scaly buds; the old bark peeling off upwards in long thick bands. *Leaves* opposite, digitate, exstipulate, deciduous; common petiole 4-6 in. long. *Leaflets* 5-9, 6-10 by 2-3·5 in., the centre ones largest, oblanceolate or oblong, acuminate, sharply serrate, glabrous; lateral nerves 15-22 pairs, arcuate; base acute; petiolules ·2-1 in. long; bud scales about 1·5 in. long, oblong, membranous, caducous. *Flowers* white, horizontal, in large thyrsoid cyme-bearing terminal panicles. *Calyx* ·2-·3 in. long, tubular, with

5 short rounded lobes, often split longitudinally in open flowers. *Petals* 4, the place of the 5th usually vacant, white and yellow, ·6-·8 in. long, clawed, unequal in breadth. *Stamens* 7, filiform, curved upward, longer than the petals; anthers versatile. *Disk* one-sided. *Ovary* sessile, 3-celled; style simple, slender. *Fruit* a 1-3-celled capsule, 1·52 in. long, ovoid, rough outside. *Seeds* exalbuminous, about 1·25 in. diam., dark-brown, smooth, shining; hilum about ·5 in. diam.

Shady ravines in JAUNSAR and TEHRI-GARHWAL, 5,-10,000 ft. Fairly common; abundant about Lokhár.

Wood of a cream-colour, soft and close-grained; pores small; medullary rays very fine and numerous; weight about 35 lbs. per c. ft. It is turned into cups, dishes and platters which are used to hold milk, ghee, etc., and are in common use in the HILLS. The fruit is given to cattle and goats, and the embroyo is eaten by the hill people ground and mixed with flour.

Fl. Apr.-June. Fr. July-Oct.

2. Schleichera, Willd.; G. P. n. 41.

1. **S. trijuga**, Willd.; Fl. Br. Ind. i. 681; Brandis For. Flora 105, t. 20, Ind. Trees 189; Gamble Man. Ind. Timb. 194. Vern. *Gausam, Gosúm, Kusam*, Hind.

A large umbrageous tree; bark grey, exfoliating in plates of irregular shape, red inside. *Leaves* paripinnate, thin and of a pink colour when very young, coriaceous and dark-green when old; rachis 3-5 in. long. *Leaflets* 2-4 pairs, opposite, 2·9 by 1·5-3·5 in., oblong elliptic ovate or obovate, subsessile, quite entire, glabrescent, the terminal pair much the largest; main lateral nerves 12-20 pairs. *Flowers* yellowish-green polygamous, fascicled on simple or compound interrupted drooping racemes which are 3-5 in. long and crowded near the ends of the branches; some trees produce only male flowers. *Calyx* cup-shaped, about ·1 in. across. *Petals* 0. *Disk* complete, wavy. *Stamens* 5-8, inserted within the disk, much exceeding the calyx. *Ovary* 3-4-celled; ovules solitary in each cell; style simple; stigma 3-4-cleft. *Fruit* ·6-·8 in. diam., 1-celled, globose, abruptly tapering to a point, dry, indehiscent. *Seeds* in a pulpy aril having an acid taste.

Somewhat scarce in the DÚN Forests, except at Tháno, Sainkōt, Khairi, etc., but very common along the foot of the SAHÁRANPUR SIWALIKS, and in the LOWER HIMALAYA and HIMALAYAN VALLEYS, *e.g.*, Kálsi, Málkōt, etc.

The wood is reddish-brown, very hard, and marked with white wavy concentric lines; weight about 70 lbs. per c. ft. It is used for oil and sugar mills, naves of carts, and such other purposes. The lac produced on this tree is considered to be of the finest quality. The young fruit is pickled and the acid pulp of the ripe fruit is eaten. The seed yields a fat oil which is used to burn. The tree is lopped for fodder.

New leaves and fl. Mar., Apr. Fr. Aug.-Oct.

3. Sapindus, Linn.; G. P. n. 43.

1. **S. detergens**, Roxb.; Brandis For. Flora 107; Gamble Man. Ind. Timb. 196. Syn.—*S. Mukorossi*, Gærtn.; Fl. Br. Ind. i. 683; Brandis Ind. Trees 191. The Soap-nut tree. Vern. *Ríthá*, Hind.

A handsome tree, somewhat resembling the *Tún*; bark grey. *Leaves* alternate, paripinnate, 12-20 in. long. *Leaflets* 5-10 pairs, opposite or alternate, 3·5-6 by 1-2 in., gradually smaller towards the apex of the rachis, lanceolate, acuminate, entire, coriaceous, glabrous; lateral nerves numerous; petiolule ·1-·2 in. long. *Inflorescence* a terminal thyrsus or a compound cymose panicle. *Flowers* small, regular, polygamous. *Calyx-lobes* somewhat unequal, ciliate. *Petals* white or purplish, alternating with the calyx-lobes, ciliate. *Stamens* 8, inserted in the centre of the disk; filaments white-woolly; anthers versatile. *Ovary* usually 3-celled. *Fruit* a fleshy globose 1-seeded drupe, ·7-1 in. diam.; seed smooth, black, loose inside when dry; the saponaceous pericarp wrinkled and somewhat translucent in the dry fruit.

Cultivated in the DÚN, as well as in JAUNSAR, *e.g.*, near Thádiar, Lokhár, etc.,—possibly, but somewhat doubtfully, indigenous.

Wood light-yellow, moderately hard, compact and close-grained, weighing about 44 lbs. per c. ft. It is not used. The tree is much valued for the fruit, which is a good substitute for washing-soaps, to which it is considered even superior in the case of woollen or silk fabrics. The leaves are given as fodder to cattle.

Fl. May, June. Fr. Oct.-Jan.

4. Acer, Linn.: G. P. n. 60.

The Maples.

Trees with scaly buds. *Leaves* opposite, palmately lobed or undivided. *Flowers* regular, usually polygamous. *Calyx* usually 5-parted, deciduous. *Petals* as many as the calyx-lobes, sometimes absent. *Disk* thick, annular, glabrous; margin lobed. *Stamens* generally 8, inserted on the disk; filaments usually longer in the male than in the hermaphrodite flowers. *Ovary* 2-lobed, laterally compressed, usually 2-celled; style deeply 2-fid. *Fruit* a double samara with membranous reticulate wings, indehiscent; seeds usually solitary.

Analysis of the Species.

Leaves undivided, margins entire.
 Leaves white beneath; petiole ·7-4 in. long. 1. *A. oblongum.*
 Leaves green beneath; petiole ·2-·5 in. long . . . . . 2. *A. lævigatum.*
Leaves 5-lobed, margins serrate.
 Leaves pale beneath.
  (Serratures large and obtuse) . . 3. *A. cæsium.*
 Leaves green beneath (sometimes 3-lobed).
  Serratures distant, acumen short . . 4. *A. villosum.*
  Serratures close, acumen long . . 5. *A. caudatum.*
Leaves 5-7-lobed, margins entire . . 6. *A. pictum.*

1. **A. oblongum,** Wall.; Fl. Br. Ind. i. 693; Brandis For. Flora 110, Ind. Trees 181; Gamble Man. Ind. Timb. 199. Vern. *Pångoi, Parángá,* Jaunsar; *Kirmolá, Kirmoli,* Garhwal.

A middle-sized tree; bark grey, smooth, with horizontal wrinkles; stem often irregularly buttressed at the base. *Leaves* 2·5-6 by ·7-2·5 in., oblong or ovate-lanceolate, acuminate, entire, glaucous beneath; lateral nerves 6-8 pairs; base rounded, rarely subacute, 3-nerved; petiole ·7-4 in. long, terete, flexuose, coral-red. *Flowers* pentamerous, in terminal or leaf-bearing lateral corymbose panicles; pedicels and calyx hairy. *Sepals* and *petals* ·1 in. long, linear-oblong. *Stamens* 8, exserted, glabrous. *Ovary* hairy. *Fruit* glabrous; nuts more or less angular; wings 1 in. long, contracted at the base, divergent, almost straight at the back.

OUTER HIMALAYA and HIMALAYAN VALLEYS up to 6,500 ft., *e.g.*, Málkōt Hills, Tons Valley, ravines below Mohná, etc. Also in marshy localities in the DŪN such as Nakraunda, Lachiwála, Mothronwála, etc.

Wood light reddish-brown, moderately hard, close-grained, weighing about 45 lbs. per c. ft. It is used for agricultural implements and made into drinking cups.

Fl. Feb.-Apr. Fr. Rainy season.

2. **A. lævigatum,** Wall.; Fl. Br. Ind. i. 693; Brandis For. Flora 110, Ind. Trees 181; Gamble Man. Ind. Timb. 200.

A fairly large tree with yellowish or ash-coloured smooth bark; stem often irregularly buttressed. *Leaves* 2·5-5 by 1-2 in., oblong, acuminate, entire or obscurely sinuate, coriaceous, glabrous, strongly reticulate, green beneath; main lateral nerves about 6 pairs, the basal pair faint and intramarginal; base rounded or more or less acute; petiole ·2-·5 in. long, channelled. *Flowers* in lax terminal panicles. *Sepals* 5, ovate, smaller than the petals. *Petals* white, about ·1 in long, obovate, clawed. *Stamens* 5-8, exserted, glabrous. *Ovary* hairy. *Fruit* glabrous; nuts ovoid, not angular; wings ·66-1 in. long, divergent, tinged with red until mature, back straight.

MUSSOORIE, in valleys at 6,-7,000 ft.; scarce.

Wood white, shining, hard and close-grained, weighing 43 lbs. per c. ft. It is used for building in Nepal and for tea-boxes in Assam.

Fl. Mar., Apr. Fr. July, Aug.

3. **A. cæsium,** Wall.; Fl. Br. Ind. i. 695; Brandis For. Flora 111, t. 21, Ind. Trees 183; Gamble Man. Ind. Timb. 201. Vern. *Kainju, Bara Kainju, Kainjal,* Jaunsar.

A large handsome deciduous tree; stem generally rough with knotty excrescences known as burrs; bark grey, exfoliating in thin, vertical strips. *Bud-scales* 1·5-2 by ·3-·5 in., reddish, white-pubescent. *Leaves* 3-6 in. diam., rather broader than long, 5-lobed, cordate, serrate, pale beneath, generally bright-red, especially when young; petiole 3-5 in. long, rather stout, flattened at the base. *Flowers* yellowish, in cymosely branched terminal corymbs, appearing with the leaves. *Petals* small, cream-coloured. *Stamens* short, longer on male trees. *Fruit* glabrate; nuts gibbous; wings 1·5-2 in. long, slightly divergent, or in some forms erect and overlapping at the inner edges; back somewhat curved.

HIMALAYAN FORESTS from 6,-10,000 ft., fairly common, generally in open places like grazing grounds.

Wood whitish, close-grained, soft or moderately hard; weight 40 lbs. per c. ft. It is scarcely used excepting that the burrs are sometimes made into cups.

New leaves and fls. Apr., May. Fr. July-Oct.

4. **A. villosum,** Wall.; Fl. Br. Ind. i. 695; Brandis For. Flora 111, Ind. Trees 182; Gamble Man. Ind. Timb. 201. Vern. *Kainju,* Jaunsar.

A fairly large deciduous tree with thin grey bark which is scarcely rough. *Leaves* 4-6 in. diam., generally as long as broad, 5-lobed or by suppression 3-lobed, cordate, irregularly dentate, deep-green, young with silky hairs beneath; petiole 2-5·5 in. long, rather stout. *Flowers* 5-merous, in compound lateral racemes, appearing before the leaves; peduncles and pedicels stout, hairy. *Sepals* about ·1 in. long, oblong, ciliate, 3-nerved. *Petals* about as long as the sepals but narrower, also ciliate. *Stamens* 5-8, exserted, glabrous. *Fruit* generally rusty villous; nuts quadrant-shaped, ·3-·4 in. long; wings 2 by ·8 in., divergent, incurved at the back, membranous at the inner edge.

JAUNSAR and TEHRI-GARHWAL, 7,-9,000 ft.: Deoban, Konáin, Mundáli; Deotá, etc.

Wood white, moderately hard, close-grained, beautifully mottled; weight 38 lbs. per c. ft. It is seldom used except for fuel. The leaves are lopped for fodder.

Fl. Feb., Mar. Fr. June-Aug.

5. **A. caudatum,** Wall.; Fl. Br. Ind. i. 695; Brandis For. Flora 112, Ind. Trees 183; Gamble Man. Ind. Timb. 201. Vern. *Kainjli, Kanjlá,* Jaunsar.

A sparingly branched moderate-sized deciduous tree; bark dark-grey, on young stems and branches dark-green or greenish-red, quite smooth. *Leaves* 2·5-5 by 2-3·5 in., 5-lobed, the two outer lobes smaller than the rest or absent; lobes caudate-acuminate, pointedly serrate to within ·5 in. of the tip of the narrow acumen which is 1·5-2·5 in. long; petiole 2-4 in. long, flattened and subamplexicaul at the base. *Flowers* in terminal and lateral racemes, appearing shortly after the leaves; pedicels 1-2 in. long, very slender. *Sepals* ·2 in. long, oblong, whitish-green. *Petals* somewhat shorter than the sepals, white, obovate, clawed. *Stamens* generally 4-6, exserted. *Fruit* glabrous; nuts irregularly grooved or pitted; wings about 1 in. long, erect or divergent, membranous except at the outer edge, undulate at the inner edge.

JAUNSAR and TEHRI-GARHWAL, 8,-11,000 ft.: Deoban, Konáin; Deotá, etc.; generally affecting open ravines on shady aspects.

Wood whitish, compact and moderately hard, seldom used; weight 43 lbs. per c. ft.

Fl. Mar., Apr. Fr. July-Sept.

6. **A. pictum,** Thunb.; Fl. Br. Ind. i. 696; Brandis For. Flora 112, Ind. Trees 183; Gamble Man. Ind. Timb. 202. Vern. *Kainchli, Kabási, Dúdh Kainju*, Jaunsar.

A moderate-sized handsome tree with thin grey bark. *Leaves* 2-5 by 2·5-7 in., broader than long, 5-7-lobed, rather membranous, glabrous, turning red before falling; margins quite entire; base usually deeply cordate, rarely truncate; petiole 1-6 in. long, slender, flexuous. *Flowers* glabrous, on slender pedicels arranged in terminal or lateral corymbs. *Sepals* about ·1 in. long, oblong. *Petals* as long as the sepals, spathulate. *Stamens* 8, shorter than the petals. *Fruit* glabrous; nuts thin; wings 1-1·3 in. long, very divergent, with the back sigmoidly curved.

JAUNSAR and TEHRI-GARHWAL, 5,-9,000 ft., the most common of all high-level maples.

Wood white, moderately hard and close-grained, used for ploughs, bedsteads, etc. Tibetan drinking-cups are made of the knotty excrescences (burrs).

Fl. Apr., May. Fr. June, July.

5. Dodonæa, Linn.; G. P. n. 63.

1. **D. viscosa,** Linn.; Fl. Br. Ind. i. 697; Brandis For. Flora, 113, Ind. Trees 186; Gamble Man. Ind. Timb. 202. Vern. *Sonátta, Waláyti Mehndi*, Hind.

An evergreen shrub with glabrous red branchlets. *Leaves* alternate, simple, exstipulate, subsessile, 1·5-3 by ·2-1 in., oblanceolate to linear-cuneate, coriaceous, glabrous, shining above, more or less viscid with a yellow resin (whence the specific name); lateral nerves numerous, not very prominent. *Inflorescence* a short terminal panicle with racemose branches. *Flowers* polygamous, about ·2 in. across. *Sepals* usually 5, about ·1 in. long, oblong, greenish-yellow. *Petals* 0. *Stamens* generally 8; filaments short; anther-cells comparatively large. *Disk* obsolete in the male flowers, small in the female. *Ovary* 3-4-celled, with 2 ovules in each cell; style 3-4-cleft at the apex. *Fruit* a compressed capsule, septicidally 2-4-valved, each valve with an oblong membranous wing which is about ·5 by ·3 in.

LOWER HIMALAYA, about 4,500 ft. Cultivated in the DÚN and SAHÁRANPUR DISTRICTS in hedges round gardens and railway-platforms.

Wood hard, compact and close-grained, capable of being used for engraving. The branches are used to support the earth of flat roofs. "The shrub grows readily from seed without much water in arid places"—*Sir D. Brandis*; and "is likely to be important in reclothing denuded tracts."—*Mr. J. S. Gamble.* It makes an excellent hedge.

Fl. Aug.-Feb. Fr. Jan.-June.

6. Staphylea, Linn.; G. P. n. 71.

1. **S. Emodi,** Wall.; Fl. Br. Ind. i. 698; Brandis For. Flora 114, Ind. Trees 181; Gamble Man. Ind. Timb. 203. Vern. *Chitrá, Márchhob,* Jaunsar; *Nágdaun,* Hind.

A large shrub; bark with grey and dark-brown reticulate streaks. *Leaves* 3-foliolate; stipules linear, about 1 in. long. *Leaflets* 3-6 by 1·5-3 in., ovate or elliptic, acuminate, closely serrate, membranous, white-pubescent beneath when young, the lateral very shortly petioluled or sessile, often somewhat oblique; main lateral nerves 6-8 pairs; common petiole 3-6 in., petiolule of the terminal leaflet ·5-2 in. long; stipules and stipels caducous. *Flowers* 2-sexual, regular, 5-merous, ·5 in. long, in dense pendulous cymes. *Sepals* and *petals* similar, white, erect. *Disk* 5-lobed. *Stamens* 5, inserted between the lobes of the disk. *Ovary* 2-3-celled; styles 2-3, more or less connate. *Fruit* an inflated membranous capsule, 2-3 in. long, 3-lobed, 3-celled; cells tapering to a tail and dehiscing from the apex.

Shady ravines in the HIMALAYA, 5,000 to 9,000 ft.: Jhálkúri Mundáli, Kathián, Deotá, Lambátach, etc.

Wood white, soft, weighing about 44 lbs. per c. ft. Walking-sticks are made of the long straight branches with the bark unstripped, which, if cut on a Sunday and not shod with iron, are believed to have the property of keeping off snakes.

Fl. Apr., May. Fr. July, Aug.

To this Family belongs the Lichi. *Nephelium Litchi,* Camb.; Fl. Br. Ind. i. 687; which is commonly cultivated in the DÚN and yields an excellent fruit, the edible part being the fleshy aril. Vern. *Lichi,* Hind.—*G. P. n. 47.*

FAM. 29. SABIACEÆ; G. P. N. 52.

Climbing or erect shrubs, or trees. *Leaves* alternate, exstipulate, usually simple. *Flowers* small, 1-2-sexual, generally in panicles. *Calyx* 4-5-cleft; lobes imbricate. *Petals* 4-5, imbricate, sometimes unequal. *Stamens* 4-5, inserted below the ovary and opposite to the petals. *Disk* small, annular. *Ovary* 2-3-celled, compressed or lobed; ovules 1-2 in each cell; styles 2-3, free or connate. *Fruit* a drupe or of 1 or 2 dry carpels; seeds with a broad hilum.

Analysis of the Genera.

Climbers. Petals and stamens equal, the latter all fertile . . . . . 1. SABIA.
Trees. Petals and stamens unequal, only 2 stamens fertile . . . . . . 2. MELIOSMA.

1. Sabia, Colebr.; G. P. n. 1.

Scandent shrubs. *Leaves* simple, entire. *Flowers* usually 2-sexual, solitary or in cymes or panicles, each subtended by a pair of opposite bracts. *Calyx-lobes* and *petals* 4-5, equal. *Stamens* 4-5, all fertile. *Disk* 4-5-lobed. *Ovary* 2-lobed; styles 2, more or less cohering. *Fruit* of 1 or 2 dry carpels.

Analysis of the Species.

Flowers large, solitary or fascicled . . . 1. *S. campanulata.*
Flowers small, in large panicles . . . . 2. *S. paniculata.*

1. **S. campanulata,** Wall.; Fl. Br. Ind. ii. 1; Brandis For. Flora 116, Ind. Trees 193; Gamble Man. Ind. Timb. 204.

A climber with woody branches. *Leaves* 1-3·5 by ·4-1·3 in., oblong-lanceolate, acuminate, membranous, soft, puberulous, pale beneath; nerves reticulate; petiole ·2-·6 in. long, channelled, ciliate, *Flowers* ·5 in. across, green or pale-yellow with a dash of purple, usually solitary in the axils of the leaves; peduncle 1-2 in. long. *Sepals* minute. *Petals* ·2-·3 in. long, orbicular, enlarging in fruit. *Stamens* included. *Fruit* ·3-·4 in. diam., of two distinct turquoise-blue compressed reniform carpels; seeds rugose.

JAUNSAR and TEHRI-GARHWAL, 5,-10,000 ft. in shady places; common, though not prevalent.

Fl. Apr., May. Fr. Rainy season.

2. **S. paniculata,** Edgew.; Fl. Br. Ind. ii. 3; Brandis For. Flora 117, Ind. Trees 194; Gamble Man. Ind. Timb. 204.

A large climber with a dark-grey stem. *Leaves* 3-8 by 1·3-3 in., oblong-lanceolate, acuminate, tough, coriaceous, dark-green and shining above, pale and strongly reticulate beneath main lateral nerves 6-8 pairs; base rounded; petiole ·4-·7 in. long. *Flowers* yellowish, ·15-·2 in. across, in large lateral often leaf-bearing panicles; pedicels hairy. *Drupe* ·3 in. diam., orbicular, compressed.

Shady swampy places in the DÚN such as Mothronwála, Gulargháti, Káluwála, Nakraunda, etc.

Fl. Feb., Mar. Fr. June-Aug.

2. Meliosma, Bl.; G. P. n. 2.

Trees or erect shrubs usually with hairy extremities. *Leaves* simple, rarely pinnate. *Flowers* minute, in large thyrsoid panicles. *Sepals* and *petals* 4-5, unequal. *Stamens* generally 5, two fertile and adnate to the smaller petals, the rest without anthers. *Disk* 4-5-toothed. *Ovary* sessile, usually 2-celled. *Fruit* a drupe, obliquely globose, with a hard kernel; seed solitary.

Analysis of the Species.

Leaves soft, lateral nerves close and straight;
flowers pedicellate . . . . . 1. *M. dilleniæfolia.*
Leaves hard, lateral nerves distant and
arcuate; flowers sessile . . . 2. *M. pungens.*

1. **M. dilleniæfolia,** Bl.; Fl. Br. Ind. ii. 4; Brandis For. Flora 115; Ind. Trees 195; Gamble Man. Ind. Timb. 205. Vern. *Goi*, Jaunsar.

A small deciduous tree; young parts covered with rusty pubescence; bark ashy-grey. *Leaves* 4-12 by 2-5 in., obovate or elliptic, abruptly acuminate, cuspidate-serrate, membranous, rough with minute raised dots above, rusty-pubescent beneath; lateral nerves 15-20 pairs, straight and parallel; base acute; petiole ·5-1 in. long. *Flowers* 2-sexual, bracteate, in large lax terminal panicles, which extend downward with branches at the axils of the upper leaves. *Sepals* 5, ciliate, the two outer smaller. *Petals* 5, orbicular, white, the two attached to the stamens smaller. *Drupe* ·1 in. diam., globose, black when ripe.

JAUNSAR and TEHRI-GARHWAL, up to 10,000 ft., in shady ravines; common in the Bájámárá and Kcnáin Blocks.

Wood dull-white, soft, coarse-grained, used only for fuel.

Fl. May-July. Fr. Aug.-Oct.

2. **M. pungens,** Wall.; Fl. Br. Ind. ii. 4; Brandis For. Flora 116, Ind. Trees 194; Gamble Man. Ind. Timb. 205. Vern. *Búshkuá, Bushá*, Jaunsar; *Kharás*, Garhwal.

A small tree with grey bark; young parts covered with rusty pubescence. *Leaves* 5-10 by 1-3 in., oblanceolate, abruptly long-acuminate, very distantly cuspidate-serrate, hard, coriaceous, pubescent beneath along the midrib and nerves; lateral nerves 8-10 pairs, arcuate, prominent beneath; base very gradually narrowed; petiole ·2-·7 in. long. *Flowers* small, sessile, in large compact panicles, supported by 1 or 2 bracteoles which resemble the sepals. *Sepals* round, ciliate. *Petals* membranous, whitish, three large and entire supporting as many staminodes, and two smaller and bilobed supporting 2 fertile stamens. *Drupe* ·3 in. diam., globose.

JAUNSAR and TEHRI-GARHWAL, 4-8,000 ft., generally in ravines and along streams; Lokhár, the Ámláwa and Tons Valleys, etc.

Wood soft, of no special value.

Fl. May, June. Fr. July, Aug.

FAM. 30. ANACARDIACEÆ; G. P. N. 53.

Trees or shrubs, generally with milky or resinous juice. *Leaves* usually alternate, simple trifoliolate or pinnate, exstipulate. *Inflorescence* generally a terminal panicle, less frequently lateral or axillary. *Flowers* small, mostly regular, unisexual or bisexual. *Calyx* 3-5-cleft. *Petals* free, as many as the calyx-divisions and alternating with them, sometimes absent. *Disk* usually annular. *Stamens* generally as many or twice as many as the petals, inserted under (rarely on) the disk, sometimes not all perfect. *Ovary* superior or half-inferior, usually 1-celled and 1-seeded. *Fruit* a drupe. *Seed* exalbuminous.

Analysis of the Genera.

Fruit 1-celled, 1-seeded.
  Pericarp dry.
    (Leaves simple or compound, petals 4-5) . . 1. RHUS.
  Pericarp more or less fleshy.
    Leaves simple.
      Receptacle of fruit enlarged and fleshy . . 6. SEMECARPUS.
      Receptacle of fruit not enlarged or fleshy.
        Stamens 1-5, generally only 1 perfect . 3. MANGIFERA.
        Stamens 8-10, all perfect . . . 4. BUCHANANIA.
    Leaves pinnate.
      Petals none . . . . 2. PISTACIA.
      Petals 4-5 . . . . 5. ODINA.
Fruit 2-5-celled, 2-5-seeded; pericarp fleshy; leaves imparipinnate . . . . . . 7. SPONDIAS.

1. Rhus, Linn.; G. P. n. 1.

Trees or shrubs with a resinous or acrid juice. *Leaves* 3-foliolate or pinnate, rarely simple. *Flowers* small, polygamous, panicled. *Calyx-limbs* 4-6. *Petals* 4-6, imbricate. *Disk* fleshy, annular. *Stamens* 4-10, inserted at the base of the disk. *Ovary* sessile, 1-celled; styles 3. *Drupe* dry, with a pendulous seed.

Analysis of the Species.

Leaves simple	1. *R. Cotinus.*
Leaves 3-foliolate	2. *R. parviflora.*
Leaves imparipinnate.	
Petiole winged; (leaflets sessile) . . .	3. *R. semi-alata.*
Petiole not winged.	
Leaflets sessile; inflorescence terminal	4. *R. punjabensis.*
Leaflets short-petiolulate; inflor, axillary.	
Innovations densely tomentose . .	5. *R. Wallichii.*
Wholly glabrous	6. *R. succedanea.*

1. **R. Cotinus,** Linn.; Fl. Br. Ind. ii. 9; Brandis For. Flora 118, Ind. Trees 196; Gamble Man. Ind. Timb. 207. The Wig tree. Vern. *Túng, Túngoi,* Jaunsar; *Túngá,* Garhwal.

A shrub or small tree with thin reddish-brown bark; branchlets red; young parts grey-tomentose. *Leaves* simple, 2-4 by 1·5-3 in., ovate elliptic obovate or orbicular, entire, usually tomentose beneath, less frequently so above; main lateral nerves 10-15 pairs; base more or less acute; petole 1·5-3 in. long. *Flowers* about ·15 in. diam., on very slender pedicels which are arranged in lax terminal panicles, pedicels of sterile flowers elongated and feathery. *Sepals* ovate-oblong. *Petals* elliptic, pale-yellow, much exceeding the sepals. *Filaments* short; anthers comparatively large. *Disk* broad, 4-angled. *Drupe* ·2 in. long, compressed, oblique, reddish, covered with white hairs.

Common in JAUNSAR, TEHRI-GARHWAL and OUTER HIMALAYAN slopes, 3,-6,000 ft., generally in open sunny places.

Heartwood of a dark yellow colour and mottled, weighing 56 lbs. to the c. ft. It makes very pretty picture-frames and might be used for cabinet-work. The twigs are used for basket-making, and the bark and leaves for tanning. The leaves and flowers emit the characteristic resinous odour of mango when bruised.

New leaves and fls. Apr., May. Fr. Autumn.

2. **R. parviflora,** Roxb.; Fl. Br. Ind. ii. 9; Brandis For. Flora 119, Ind. Trees 196; Gamble Man. Ind. Timb. 208. Vern. *Ninás, Ninάwa,* Jaunsar; *Túnglá,* Hind.

A shrub; young parts densely covered with rusty tomentum; bark grey, smooth. *Leaves* 3-foliolate; common petiole 1-2 in. *Leaflets* 1-3 by ·6-2 in., the terminal much larger than the other two, obovate, crenate, sparsely hairy above, pubescent beneath; the terminal leaflet often narrowed into a marginate petiolule, the others sessile; lateral nerves 8-12 pairs, straight, prominent. *Inflorescence* a terminal panicle with racemose branchlets, some of which rise from the axils of the upper leaves. *Flowers* ·1 in. across. *Sepals* ovate. *Petals* oblong, longer than the sepals. *Drupe* ·2 in. diam., ovoid, glabrous, brown, shining.

JAUNSAR, TEHRI-GARHWAL and the OUTER HIMALAYA, 2,-5,000 ft.: Dhárágádh, Tons (Tiuni, Morá Depôt, etc.) and Jumna Valleys; Málkōt, etc.

Wood hard and close-grained. The fruit is eaten, and is used in Hindu medicine.

Fl. May, June. Fr. July, Aug.

3. **R. semi-alata,** Murray; Fl. Br. Ind. ii. 10; Brandis For. Flora 119, Ind. Trees 197; Gamble Man. Ind. Timb. 208. Vern. *Tibri, Árkhoi*, Jaunsar.

A small decidous tree; young parts covered with dark-grey pubescence. *Leaves* imparipinnate, over a foot long turning red before falling; common petiole usually winged. *Leaflets* 4-6 pairs, opposite, sessile, 2-4 by 1-2 in., elliptic, acuminate, deeply crenate or dentate, glabrous above, soft-tomentose beneath; lateral nerves 10-15 pairs, parallel; base rounded, somewhat oblique. *Panicles* terminal, 6-8 in. long, conical, dense-flowered. *Flowers* ·1 in. diam., pale-green. *Sepals* ovate. *Petals* oblong, ciliate, much exceeding the sepals. *Drupe* ·2 in. diam., subglobose, compressed.

JAUNSAR and TEHRI-GARHWAL, 3,-7,000 ft.: Dhárágádh and Tons Valleys.

Wood soft, shining, white but with darker streaks, weighing about 27 lbs. per c. ft., not used. The fruit is often eaten by the hill people, and is used medicinally.

New leaves and fls. Apr., May. Fr. Aug.-Oct.

4. **R. punjabensis,** Stewart; Fl. Br. Ind. ii. 10; Brandis For. Flora 120, Ind. Trees 197; Gamble Man. Ind. Timb. 209. Vern. *Titri, Titroi*, Jaunsar.

A small deciduous tree with rough dark-grey bark and aromatic leaves; young parts covered with short pubescence. *Leaves* imparipinnate, over a foot long; petiole and rachis slender, not winged. *Leaflets* 5-6 pairs, opposite or subopposite, sessile, 3-6 by 1-2·5 in., ovate-oblong or lanceolate, acuminate, entire or serrate near the apex, membranous, pubescent beneath, with scattered hairs above; lateral nerves about 20 pairs, very slender; base rounded. *Panicles* terminal, compact, much shorter than the leaves. *Flowers* less than ·1 in. diam., yellowish-green. *Drupe* about ·2 in. diam., on short pedicels, compressed, covered with a dense purplish tomentum.

JAUNSAR and TEHRI-GARHWAL, 3,-8,500 ft., towards the interior; *e.g.*, Lokhár, Kathián; Deotá, etc.

Fl. Apr., May. Fr. Aug., Sept.

5. **R. Wallichii,** Hook. f.; Fl. Br. Ind. ii. 11; Gamble Man. Ind. Timb. 209; Brandis Ind. Trees 198. Syn.—*R. vernicifera,* DC.; Brandis For. Flora 120, Vern. *Árkhoi, Árchoi,* Jaunsar.

A small deciduous tree somewhat resembling the walnut, with smooth grey bark which exudes a black acrid varnish; young parts covered with rusty-brown or ash-coloured tomentum. *Leaves* imparipinnate, approximate near the ends of the branches; common petiole terete, stout. *Leaflets* 3-5 pairs, opposite, subsessile, 4-6 by 2-3·5 in., oblong-elliptic, acuminate, entire, grey-tomentose beneath, more or less pubescent above; lateral nerves 20-25 pairs; base rounded, oblique. *Panicles* short, compact, from the axils of the lower or last year's leaves. *Flowers* subsessile, ·1 in. diam. *Sepals* obtuse. *Petals* much larger than the sepals, obovate, greenish-white, with dark veins. *Drupes* ·3 in. diam., much crowded together; pericarp dry, splitting irregularly to form a stellate receptacle for the kernel which is long-persistent and covered with a vegetable wax.

JAUNSAR and TEHRI-GARHWAL, 4,-7,000 ft.; Binálgádh, Dharágádh, Kathián, Tons Valley, etc.

Sapwood white, soft; heartwood reddish-brown. It is used for saw-frames and axe-handles. The juice of the leaves is corrosive. "In Jaunsar Bawar it is rubbed on thread to strengthen it"—(*Sir D. Brandis*)—but the Junsaris have a superstition against the tree which is said to be inhabited by an evil spirit, and consequently they most scrupulously avoid touching it or even going near it.

Fl. May, June. Fr. July-Sept.

6. **R. succedanea,** Linn.; Fl. Br. Ind. ii. 13; Brandis For. Flora 121, Ind. Trees 199; Gamble Man. Ind. Timb. 210. Vern. *Arkhol,* U. P.

A middle-sized deciduous tree with dark-grey thin bark, somewhat resembling the *Tún. Leaves* imparipinnate, approximate near the ends of the branches. *Leaflets* 3-6 pairs, opposite, 3-6 by 1·5-3 in., ovate-lanceolate, long-acuminate, entire, thinly coriaceous, usually quite glabrous; lateral nerves 8-15 pairs, alternating with shorter intermediate ones; base rounded acute or oblique; petiolules slender, ·2-·4 in. long. *Panicles* axillary, with slender and drooping ramifications, much shorter than the leaves. *Flowers* pedicelled, scarcely ·1 in. diam., greenish-yellow. *Sepals* ovate, obtuse. *Petals* much larger, oblong or obtuse. *Disk* 5-lobed. *Drupes* ·25 in. diam., compressed, glabrous, rugose, yellow or light-brown; epicarp thin, bursting irregularly; mesocarp fibrous; kernel compressed, hard, surrounded by a vegetable wax.

TEHRI-GARHWAL, 4,-7,000 ft.; Lambatách, Pájidhár, above Naintwár, etc.

Sapwood white, turning brown, soft; heartwood scanty, yellow; not much used. The juice is acrid, but the snow-white wax is much appreciated in Japan where the tree is planted along road sides for its sake. The wax is made into candles. Lacquer varnish is also obtained by tapping the bark. The acid pulp of the fruit is eaten in Sikkim and Nepal.

Fl. May-Aug. Fr. Aug.-Oct.

2. Pistacia, Linn.; G. P. n. 53.

1. **P. integerrima,** Stewart; Fl. Br. Ind. ii. 13; Brandis For. Flora 122, Ind. Trees 190; Gamble Man. Ind. Timb. 210. Vern. *Kakkar, Kákroi,* Jaunsar.

A middle-sized deciduous tree with rough grey bark. *Leaves* alternate, pari- or imparipinnate, 6-9 in. long. *Leaflets* 4-6 pairs, subopposite, minutely petioluled, 3-6 by 1-1·7 in., lanceolate, long-acuminate, entire, hard, coriaceous, glabrous; main lateral nerves about 20 pairs, slender; base oblique. *Inflorescence* a lateral panicle. *Flowers* small, apetalous, diœcious. MALE FLS.: *panicles* 2-4 in. long, compact, pubescent; *calyx* gamosepalous, 3-5-fid; *stamens* 5-7 on a small disk; *anthers* large, red. FEM. FLS.: *panicles* 6-10 in. long, lax, thyrsoid; *sepals* 4, free, linear, deciduous; *ovary* sessile, 1-celled; *styles* 3, cohering only near the base. *Drupe* ·25 in. diam., oblique, broader than long, glabrous, rugose.

JAUNSAR and TEHRI-GARHWAL, also the MÁLKŌT HILLS, 3-6,000 ft. Ámláwa nálá, Binálgádh, Tons Valley, etc.

Sapwood white; heartwood mottled with yellow and green streaks, very hard and durable, valued as an ornamental timber; weight 54 lbs. per c. ft. "The leaves are lopped for fodder for buffaloes and camels, and the galls (*Kákrasingi*) are used in native medicine."—*Mr. J. S. Gamble.* The latter are in the shape of a horn, attaining 3-6 in. in length, and are dull-red in colour. They are produced by a Hemipterous insect.

New leaves and fls. Mar.-May. Fr. June-Oct.

3. Mangifera, Linn.; G. P. n. 7.

1. **M. indica,** Linn.; Fl. Br. Ind. ii. 13; Brandis For. Flora 125, Ind. Trees 206; Gamble Man. Ind. Timb. 211. The Mango tree. Vern. *Ám.* Hind. *Ámbī*, Dún and Sahâranpur (vulgar).

A large evergreen tree with rough thick dark-grey bark. *Leaves* alternate, simple, crowded at the ends of the branches, 6-12 by 1·5-4 in., oblong or obovate-lanceolate, entire, coriaceous, dark-green, glabrous; margins often wavy; lateral nerves numerous, arcuate; base acute; petiole 1·2·5 in. long, swollen at the base. *Inflorescence* a terminal panicle about 1 ft. long; bracts elliptic, concave. *Flowers* about ·15 in. across, yellowish-green, scented, male and 2-sexual on the same panicle. *Calyx* 4-5-partite; segments imbricate, ovate, concave, deciduous. *Petals* 4-5, imbricate, much longer than the calyx-segments, ovate, yellow, with 3-5 longitudinal ridges. *Disk* fleshy. *Stamens* 4-5, inserted on the disk, only one perfect and longer than the rest; filaments subulate. *Ovary* sessile, obliquely ovoid, glabrous; ovule solitary; style lateral. *Drupe* 2-6 in. long, ovoid, laterally compressed, with a protuberance on one side near the tip indicating the position of the style; putamen fibrous.

Cultivated and almost wild in SAHÁRANPÚR and the DÚN. Several varieties are recognized under cultivation which differ chiefly in the quality of the fruit.

No distinct heartwood and sapwood. Wood grey, coarse-grained, soft, liable to attacks of insects; weight 41 lbs. per c. ft. It is made into planks, and is as yet the only wood used for tea-boxes in the Dún. Doors and windows and sometimes cheap furniture are made of it. The tree is, however, valued chiefly for its fruit. The green fruit is pickled, and is dried in slices as an article of trade in Bengal and elsewhere. The pulp of the ripe fruit is dried in thin plates, which can then be kept for months without losing flavour. Throughout the United Provinces the kernel of the fruit is dried and pounded into a meal, which is used by the poorer classes during famine as a substitute for wheat-flour.

Fl. Mar., Apr. Fr. June, July.

4. Buchanania, Roxb.; G. P. n. 11.

1. **B. latifolia,** Roxb.; Fl. Br. Ind. ii. 23; Brandis For. Flora 127, Ind. Trees 205; Gamble Man. Ind. Timb. 216. Vern. *Piyál* or *Piál*, Hind.; *Kath Bhiláwa*, Dún,

A moderate-sized tree, almost evergreen; bark dark-grey or black, furrowed into thick small quadrangular plates, reddish inside. *Leaves* alternate, simple, 6-10 by 2-3·5 in., oblong or elliptic, entire, obtuse at both ends, coriaceous, hard, generally pubescent beneath, closely reticulate; lateral nerves 15-20 pairs, stout, nearly straight; petiole ·2-·3 in. long, pubscent. *Flowers* 2-sexual, sessile, ·15-·2 in. diam., greenish-white, in terminal and axillary pyramidal panicles. *Calyx* 5-toothed, persistent. *Petals* 5, oblong. *Disk* fleshy, 5-lobed. *Stamens* 10, as long as the petals. *Carpels* 5, hairy, inserted at the base of the disk, 1 perfect, 4 reduced to thread-like processes. *Drupe* ·5 in. long, ovoid-oblong, black when ripe; stone hard, 2-valved; seeds oily.

Common in the Sál forests of the SIWALIK DIVISION, where the soil is at all clayey. Scarce in the E. DÚN beyond the Sông river.

Wood greyish-brown, moderately hard, with a small dark-coloured heartwood, fairly durable if kept dry and free from white-ants. Weight 33 lbs. per c. ft. It seasons well, and is used for boxes, bedsteads, yokes, doors, furniture, and the like. The poles are made into *tōrs* in the Sahāranpur Division, which are used to support light roofs. The bark is used for tanning. The ripe fruit has a pleasant sweetish-acid flavour, and the kernel, which resembles the pistachio-nuts, is an important article of trade in the Central Provinces, where it is called *chironji*. The leaves are sometimes used as a substitute for plates.

Fl. Feb., Mar. Fr. May, June.

5. Odina, Roxb.; G. P. n. 22.

1. **O. Wodier,** Roxb.; Fl. Br. Ind. ii. 29; Brandis For. Flora 123, Ind. Trees 200; Gamble Man. Ind. Timb. 218. Vern. *Jhinghan*, Hind.: *Jinghinī*, Sans.

A moderate-sized deciduous tree with thick soft branchlets; bark grey, smooth up to middle age, afterwards exfoliating in thin round plates, red inside. *Leaves* alternate, few at the ends of the branches, imparipinnate, 12-18 in. long, turning yellow before falling. *Leaflets* 7-11, shortly petiolulate, 3-6 by 2-3·5 in., ovate, long-acuminate, quite entire, rather membranous, glabrous when old; lateral nerves 4-6 pairs, arcuate; base rounded. *Flowers* 1-sexual, 4-merous, ·1-·15 in. diam., fascicled on simple and compound racemes which are crowded at the extremities of the still leafless branches; male and female usually on different branches. *Bracts* numerous, ciliate. *Calyx* 4-lobed, persistent; lobes obtuse, ciliate, about ·05 in.

long. *Petals* longer than the sepals, oblong, spreading, greenish-yellow. *Disk* annular, 4-lobed. MALE FLS.: *racemes* panicled; *stamens* twice as many but as long as the petals, inserted within the *disk*; *anthers* versatile. FEM. FLS.: *racemes* simple; *disk* surrounded by *sterile stamens*; *ovary* sessile, 1-celled, with 3-4 distinct *styles*. *Drupe* ·6 in. long, oblong, compressed.

Extremely common in the DÚN and SAHÁRANPUR FORESTS. Also found at low elevations in the HILLS, *e.g.*, near Thadiár.

Sapwood white and soft; heartwood scanty, red when fresh-cut, afterwards reddish-brown, moderately hard and close-grained, but not durable; weight 50-60 lbs. per c. ft. A useful gum exudes from wounds made in the wood, for which the tree is tapped in April and May on a regular rotation in the Sahâranpur half of the SIWALIK DIVISION. The leaves are greedily eaten by cattle, and elephants are fond of the young shoots. The tree can be most easily propagated by cuttings.

Fl. Mar., Apr. Fr. June, July.

6. Semecarpus, Linn. fil.; G. P. n. 25.

1. **S. Anacardium,** Linn. fil.; Fl. Br. Ind. ii. 30; Brandis For. Flora 124; Gamble Man. Ind. Timb. 220. The Marking-nut tree. Vern. *Bhiláwa*, Hind.

A moderate-sized decidous tree with rough dark-brown bark which yields an acrid juice; young parts, leaves beneath, and inflorescence pale-tomentose. *Leaves* crowded at the extremities of the branches, alternate, simple, 9-24 by 5-14 in., obovate-oblong, often pandurate, entire, rather coriaceous, more or less hispidly pubescent, pale beneath; tip and also the base rounded, or the latter sometimes cordate; lateral nerves 16-24 pairs, stout, slightly arched. *Flowers* polygamous or diœcious, ·2-·3 in. diam., in fascicles on large terminal panicles; bracts lanceolate. *Calyx* 5-cleft; segments deciduous. *Petals* 5, oblong, glabrous, greenish-yellow, much longer than the sepals. *Disk* broad, annular. *Filaments* subulate. *Styles* 3. *Drupe* 1 in. long, the shape of a mango, compressed, shining, black when ripe, seated on an orange-coloured fleshy recepticle formed of the disk, the base of the calyx and the extremity of the peduncle.

Fairly common in the Sál forests of the SIWALIK DIVISION, generally on clayey soil and in the moister localites.

Sapwood and heartwood not distinct. The wood is soft and light, weighing about 35 lbs. per c. ft.; not used. The cup of the ripe fruit is eaten raw, dried or roasted. The pericarp contains an acrid juice which is used as marking-ink and in medicine.

Leafless Feb.-Apr. New leaves May. Fl. May, June. Fr. Nov.-Feb.

7. Spondias, Linn.; G. P. n. 36.

1. **S. mangifera,** Willd.; Fl. Br. Ind. ii. 42; Brandis For. Flora 128, Ind. Trees 201; Gamble Man. Ind. Timb. 223. The Hog-plum tree. Vern. *Ambára,* Hind.

A deciduous tree with smooth grey bark, every part of which has a characteristic aromatic smell. *Leaves* alternate, imparipinnate, 12-18 in. long. *Leaflets* 9-11, opposite, short-petiolulate, 3-9 by 1·5-4 in., oblong-elliptic, acuminate, entire, soft, rather membranous, quite glabrous, turning bright-yellow before falling; lateral nerves 10-30 pairs, straight, parallel, nearly transverse, joined by a strong intramarginal nerve. *Flowers* ·2 in. diam, polygamous, nearly sessile, in spreading terminal panicles. *Clayx* 5-toothed, deciduous. *Petals* 5, about ·1 in. long, oblong, greenish-white, spreading. *Disk* cupular, crenate. *Stamens* 10, inserted below the disk; filaments subulate, shorter than the petals; anthers versatile. *Ovary* sessile, free; carpels 4-5, distinct in flower, coalescing into a single stone in fruit; ovules solitary, pendulous; styles as many as the carpels. *Drupe* 1·5-2 in. long, ovoid or oblong, fleshy, smooth, yellow when ripe; putamen fibrous and pitted with cavities outside, with 2-5 seeds, of which, however, usually only one is perfect.

Fairly common in the DÚN and SAHÁRANPUR FORESTS. Also found in the Tons Valley, JAUNSAR and TEHRI-GARHWAL.

Wood soft, light grey, with large pores, weighing about 26 lbs. per c. ft.; useless even as fuel. The tree is often attacked by insects, and the holes made by them exude a gum which is insoluble in water. The fruit is eaten when ripe, or pickled or made into curries when green and tender. The flower-buds also make a very agreeable curry. The tree can be most easily propagated by cuttings, and is invariably thus planted in hedgerows.

Leafless Dec.-Apr. Fl. Mar.-May. Fr. Cold seasons.

FAM. 31. CORIARIACEÆ; G. P. N. 54.

Glabrous erect shrubs with quadrangular branches. *Leaves* opposite or in whorls of three, simple, more or less entire, exstipulate. *Flowers* small, green, 2-sexual or polygamous, usually in axillary racemes. *Sepals* 5, spreading. *Petals* smaller than the sepals, fleshy, keeled within, sometimes adnate to every second stamen, accrescent in fruit. *Disk* none. *Stamens* 10, hypogynous ; filaments short. *Carpels* usually 5, free, 1-celled ; ovule solitary, pendulous ; styles fleshy, feathered. *Fruit* of 5-10 compressed nuts, encircled by the fleshy petals ; seeds compressed.

1. Coriaria, Linn. ; G. P. n. 1.

1. **C. nepalensis,** Wall. ; Fl. Br. Ind. ii. 44 ; Brandis For. Flora 128, Ind., Trees 200. Gamble Man. Ind. Timb. 224. The Mussoorie-berry. Vern. *Mansúri, Masúri,* Mussoorie ; *Mosroi,* Jaunsar ; *Gangeru, Gangára,* Tons Valley.

A large shrub with long spreading branches ; bark reddish-brown, rough ; branchlets quadrangular. *Leaves* 2-4 by 1-2·5 in., ovate-oblong, cordate, acuminate, obscurely serrulate, 3-7 nerved at the base, sometimes puberulous beneath ; petiole 0-·1 in. long. *Racemes* 2-6 in. long, usually clustered. *Flowers* ·3 in. diam., greenish-yellow. *Fruit* ·2-·3 in. diam., dark-brown or black.

JAUNSAR and TEHRI-GARHWAL, 4,-8,000 ft., fairly common among shrubby vegetation on hill-sides and in ravines. Occasionally in the SAHÁRANPUR SIWALIKS, *e.g.*, Chilláwáli Ráu.

Wood grey, hard, beautifully mottled, and takes a good polish ; weight 47 lbs. per c. ft. It is fit to be used for picture-frames and other small articles. The branches are browsed by sheep and goats.

Fl. Apr., May. Fr. June, July.

FAM. 32. MORINGACEÆ ; G. P. N. 55.

Deciduous trees with corky bark and soft spongy wood. *Leaves* alternate, imparipinnately twice or thrice compound ; leaflets opposite, entire, caducous. *Inflorescence* an axillary panicle. *Flowers* 2-sexual, irregular, white or pink. *Calyx* cup-shaped, with 5 deciduous petaloid segments. *Petals* unequal, erect, spreading. *Disk* lining the calyx-tube. *Perfect stamens* 5, opposite the petals, alternating with 5 antherless filaments, all inserted on the edge of the disk and all declinate; anthers 1-celled. *Ovary* stipitate, lanceolate, 1-celled; ovules numerous, on parietal placentas; style slender, tubular. *Fruit* a pod-like capsule, rostrate, 3-angled, 3-valved. *Seeds* many; testa corky, usually winged.

1. Moringa, Lamk.; G. P. n. 1.

1. **M. pterygosperma,** Gærtn.; Fl. Br. Ind. ii. 45; Brandis For. Flora 129, Ind. Trees 209; Gamble Man. Ind. Timb. 224. The Horse-radish tree. Vern. *Sanjná, Sainjná, Sohjná, Sondná,* Hind; *Shobhánjana,* Sans.

A fairly large tree with thick corky bark; roots pungent. *Leaves* 1-2·5 ft. long, usually 3-pinnate; petiole sheathing at the base; pinnæ opposite, 4-6 pairs; pinnulæ opposite, 6-9 pairs, the uppermost pair 1-foliolulate; a hairy gland between each pair of pinnæ and pinnulæ. *Ultimate leaflets* opposite, ·4-·8 in. long, obovate or elliptic, entire, membranous, pale beneath. *Flowers* 1 in. diam., strongly honey-scented. *Sepals* linear lanceolate, reflexed. *Petals* ·7-·9 in. long, linear-spathulate, white, with yellow dots near the base *Filaments* villous at the base. *Ovary* hairy. *Capsule* 9-20 by ·6-·8 in., 3-gonous, linear, pendulous, longitudinally ribbed, slightly constricted between the seeds. *Seeds* 3-cornered, winged at the angles, about 1 in. long including the wings.

Common in the DÚN along the banks of the Jumná, Sông and Suswá rivers; also found in the SAHÁRANPUR SIWALIKS, along the ráus and in the Tons valley in JAUNSAR and TEHRI-GARHWAL. Cultivated at DEHRA for the fruit.

The wood is absolutely useless, rotting away in a few months. The leaves, flowers, and fruits are eaten as vegetables. The tender fruit is sometimes pickled. Most wild trees, however, produce bitter flowers and fruits which are therefore not edible. The leaves are also lopped for fodder, especially for camels. A gum, obtained by making incisions in the bark, as well as the pungent roots, are used in medicine. The tree is most easily propagated by cuttings.

Fl. Feb.-Apr. Fr. May, June.

CALYCIFLORÆ.

Order 1.—ROSALES.

FAM. 33. LEGUMINOSÆ; G. P. N. 57.

TREES, shrubs or herbs. *Leaves* alternate, usually compound, stipulate. *Inflorescence* an axillary or terminal simple raceme or panicle. *Flowers* 2-sexual, regular or irregular, bracteate. *Sepals* 5, connate or free, in the former case often 2-lipped. *Petals* free, usually 5, equal or unequal. *Stamens* normally 10, sometimes fewer by suppression or indefinite; filaments free or variously combined; anthers usually dehiscing longitudinally. *Ovary* free, often stipitate; carpel solitary; ovules one or more on the ventral suture of the carpel; style simple. *Fruit* a pod (*legume*), usually dehiscent along one or both sutures. *Seeds* flat or more or less compressed, with a horny or coriaceous testa, very rarely albuminous.

This large and most important Family is divided into three Sub-Families :—

Analysis of the Sub-Families

Petals unequal, free, imbricate; stamens up to 10.
  Stamens diadelphous, less frequently monadelphous, rarely free; calyx gamosepalous . I. PAPILIONEÆ.
  Stamens free; calyx divided to or nearly to the base . . . . II. CÆSAPINIEÆ.
Petals equal, more or less connate, valvate; stamens usually indefinite . . . III. MIMOSEÆ.

SUB-FAMILY I. *PAPILIONEÆ.*

Mostly herbs, less frequently shrubs or trees. *Leaves* pinnate or digitate; leaflets often stipellate. *Flowers* 2-sexual, irregular. *Calyx* gamosepalous, 2-lipped. *Corolla* of 5 imbricate petals which are more or less clawed, the 2 innermost (which are also anterior) similar, free or connate into a sheath next to the ovary, and are called the *keel* petals; the next two are immediately outside the keel, also similar, and are called the *wings*; and the fifth is the outermost or odd petal, called the *standard*, which is posterior in position and is generally broad and reflexed. This type of corolla is known as *papilionaceous*, whence the name of the Sub-Order. *Stamens* generally 10, diadelphous, sometimes monadelphous, rarely free, inserted with the petals on the calyx-tube; anthers often versatile. *Pod* dry, generally dehiscent. *Seeds* exalbuminous.

Analysis of the Genera.

Leaves digitately 3-foliolate; pod compressed; stamens free . . . . 1. PIPTANTHUS.
Leaves digitately 3-foliolate or simple; pod inflated.
  Leaves not gland-dotted; stamens monadelphous . . . . 2. CROTALARIA.
  Leaves gland-dotted; stamens diadelphous . 18. FLEMINGIA.
Leaves imparipinnate.
  Stamens free; (pod moniliform, indehiscent) . 20. SOPHORA.
  Stamens equally or unequally diadelphous.
    Leaflets alternate; pod indehiscent . . 19. DALBERGIA.
    Leaflets opposite; pod dehiscing sooner or later.
      Pod cylindrical; stamens apiculate . . 3. INDIGOFERA.
      Pod compressed; stamens obtuse.
        Pod few-seeded, tardily dehiscent . . 4. MILLETTIA.
        Pod many-seeded, soon dehiscent . . 5. TEPHROSIA.

Leaves paripinnate; stamens diadelphous.
Unarmed. Pod septate; calyx not oblique.
Pod long, many-seeded. Erect plants . 6. SESBANIA.
Pod short, few-seeded. Climbing shrubs . 11. ABRUS.
Armed. Pod not septate; calyx very oblique 7. CARAGANA.
Leaves pinnately 3-foliolate.
Stamens diadelphous.
Pod indehiscent, (1-seeded) . . . . 8. LESPEDEZA.
Pod dehiscent.
Pod with articulate joints.
Trees. Racemes fascicled, on old wood 9. OUGEINIA.
Shrubs. Racemes simple or panicled, on current year's shoots (leaves often 1-foliolate) . . . 10. DESMODIUM.
Pod without articulate joints.
Nodes of racemes tumid; leaves not gland-dotted.
Petals very unequal; pod few-seeded.
Keel exceeding the wings and standard. Climbing shrubs . 12. MUCUNA.
Standard exceeding the keel and wings. Trees . . . 13. ERYTHRINA.
Petals equal; pod 1-seeded.
Flowers small, panicled . . 14. SPATHOLOBUS.
Flowers large, racemed. . . 15. BUTEA.
Nodes of racemes not tumid; leaves gland-dotted . . . . . 17. RHYNCHOSIA.
Stamens monadelphous (pod dehiscent, not jointed, few-seeded) . . . . . 16. PUERARIA.

1. Piptanthus, D. Don; G. P. n. 2.

1. **P. nepalensis,** D. Don; Fl. Br. Ind. ii. 62; Brandis For. Flora 132, Ind. Trees 216; Gamble Man. Ind. Timb. 229. Vern. *Chamba, Chamboá,* Jaunsar.

A shrub 8 to 12 ft. high, with green bark. *Leaves* digitately 3-foliolate; common petiole ·7-1·5 in.; stipules connate, opposite to the petiole, ·2-·3 in. long, broadly triangular, drying brownish-grey, pubescent, deciduous. *Leaflets* sessile, 2-4 by ·5-1 in., lanceolate or narrow-elliptic, acuminate, entire, dark-green above, pale beneath, grey-pubescent when young, afterwards glabrous and shining; midrib prominent beneath; main lateral nerves about 12 pairs, faint. *Flowers* yellow, about 1·25 in. long, in short compact hairy racemes

4-5 in. long; peduncle triquetrous; pedicels ·5-·7 in. long; bracts ternate, tomentose. *Calyx* about ·5 in. long, campanulate, densely white-pubescent, deciduous from the base. *Petals* bright-yellow, all clawed, 1 in. long including the claw which is about ·5 in. long. *Stamens* 10, free, equal or frequently alternately long and short; anthers uniform. *Ovary* linear, stipitate, hairy. *Pod* 3-5 by ·4-·5 in., flat, narrowed at both ends, on a stipe ·8-1 in. long; seeds 3-10.

JAUNSAR and TEHRI-GARHWAL, 7,-9,000 ft. Deoban near "Chakrata View" and below "Snow View"; on the slopes of the Karámbá peak and elsewhere about Mundáli. Common about the temple in the Temple Block, Deotá Forest.

Planted for ornament in the hills on account of its handsome yellow flower.

Fl. Apr.-June. Fr. Aug., Sept.

2. Crotalaria, Linn.; G. P. n. 53.

The Kidney Beans.

Herbs or shrubs. *Leaves* simple or 3-foliolate, rarely imparipinnate. *Flowers* yellow blue or purplish, in terminal or leaf-opposed lax racemes. *Calyx-tube* short; teeth almost equal, or connate and 2-lipped. *Corolla* generally showy; standard shortly clawed, round; wings and keel of the same length; the latter broader, beaked. *Stamens* monadelphous, forming an open sheath; anthers alternately versatile and basifixed. *Ovary* linear; style incurved at the base, bearded. *Pod* inflated.

This large Genus is noted for strong fibre.

Analysis of the Species.

Corolla much exserted; pod glabrous . . 1. *C. sericea.*
Corolla little exserted; pod densely velvety . 2. *C. tetragona.*

1. C. sericea, Retz.; Fl. Br. Ind. ii. 75. Vern. *Chhûnmuna*, Hind.; *Sanni*, E. Dún.

An undershrub 4-6 ft. high with stout but fleshy striated branches. *Leaves* simple, 3-6 by 2-3·5 in., oblanceolate-oblong, tapering into a short petiole, subcoriaceous but soft, glabrous above, finely silky beneath; stipules leafy, persistent. *Racemes* terminal, about a foot long. *Calyx* ·5 in.; teeth lanceolate. *Corolla* ·7-·8 in. long, golden-yellow. *Pod* 1-2 by ·7-·8 in., smooth; seeds kidney-shaped, many, imbricating in two rows, on long funicles.

Common in fallow lands and forest-glades in the DÚN and in the SAHÁRANPUR SIWALIKS; Doiwála, Phándowála, Karwápáni, Dholkhand, etc.

The stem yields a fairly strong fibre.

F. & Fr. Nov.-Mar.

2. **C. tetragona,** Roxb.; Fl. Br. Ind. ii. 78 Gamble Man. Ind. Timb. 230.

A stiff shrub, 4-6 ft. high; branches quadrangular, silky. *Leaves* 6-12 by ·5-1·5 in., linear or lanceolate, acuminate, membranous, thinly silky or glabrescent; stipules usually 0. *Racemes* 6-8 in. long, few-flowered. *Flowers* 1-1·5 in. long. *Calyx* ·7-1 in. long, brown-velvety. *Corolla* yellow, very slightly exserted. *Pod* 1·5-2 in. long, densely dark-brown-velvety, 12-20-seeded.

Ráu-beds in the SAHÁRANPUR SIWALIKS; Timli Pass. Also in the DÚN; Nakraunda, Lachiwála, etc.

Fl. Sept.-Nov. Fr. Mar.-June.

The cultivated *Sann* or *Sun*, *C. juncea*, Linn.; Fl. Br. Ind. ii. 79, closely resembles the last species, but has smaller leaves, and pods clothed with persistent silky hairs. It yields the *sun* fibre. Many other species occur in our region, but they are mostly herbaceous or inconspicuous.

3. Indigofera, Linn.; G. P. n. 91.

Herbs or shrubs clothed with adpressed white hairs. *Leaves* usually imparipinnate; leaflets entire. *Inflorescence* a copious axillary raceme. *Calyx* small, campanulate, 5-toothed. *Standard* ovate; *keel* at first held in a bent position by spurs on either side which catch on the wings, but straightens afterwards with a sudden jerk—a contrivance in nature for the dissemination of pollen. *Stamens* diadelphous; anthers apiculate. *Ovary* sessile, many-ovuled; style glabrous, stigma capitate. *Pod* usually linear-cylindrical and straight.

Analysis of the Species.

Branchlets white-canescent; bracts minute; (leaves subcoriaceous) . . . . 1. *I. heterantha.*
Branchlets glabrescent; bracts exceeding the buds.
  Leaves membranous.
    Stipels minute; corolla dark-purple . 2. *I. atropurpurea.*
    Stipels distinct; corolla crimson-red . 3. *I. hebepetala.*
  Leaves subcoriaceous; (corolla rose-coloured) 4. *I. pulchella.*

1. **I. heterantha,** Wall.; Brandis For. Flora 135, Ind. Trees 218; Gamble Man. Ind. Timb. 230. Syn.—*I. Gerardiana*, Wall., var. *heterantha*; Fl. Br. Ind. ii. 100. Vern. *Káthi, Káthoi*, Jaunsar; *Sákiná*, Garhwal.

A shrub with brown bark; branchlets white-canescent. *Leaves* 1·5-2·5 in. long, short-petioled. *Leaflets* 17-31, opposite, ·3-·5 in. long, obovate, mucronate, subcoriaceous, pale-grey beneath, clothed with short white hairs above; stipels and bracts minute. *Racemes* 1-2·5 in. long, peduncled. *Flowers* about ·5 in. long. *Calyx* campanulate, hairy outside. *Corolla* ·2-·4 in. long, red. *Pod* 1-1·5 in. long, spreading, cylindrical, glabrous.

JAUNSAR and TEHRI-GARHWAL, 3,-8,500 ft., from Saiá all the way to Deotá, Lam bátách, etc.

The twigs are used for basket-work. The shrub is gregarious and has some value as fuel near hill-stations like Chakrata.

Fl. May, June. Fr. Sept.-Nov.

I. *Gerardiana*, Wall., or the type of this species according to the Fl. Br. Ind., is a smaller plant with fewer leaflets, but larger pod. It is less common; Koti-Kanásar, Deotá, etc.

2. **I. atropurpurea,** Hamilt.; Fl. Br. Ind. ii. 101. Brandis For. Flora 136; Ind. Trees 217; Gamble Man. Ind. Timb. 230. Vern. ***Káthi, Káthoi, Dande-ká Kátha***, Jaunsar; ***Kálá Sákiná***, Garhwal.

A tall shrub; branchlets glabrescent. *Leaves* imparipinnate, 4-8 in. long; petiole 1-3 in. long. *Leaflets* 5-13, opposite, ·8-2 by ·6-1 in., ovate obovate or elliptic, membranous, glabrescent, dark-green; stipels minute. *Racemes* 4-6 in. long; peduncle 1-2 in.; bracts lanceolate, exceeding the buds. *Flowers* ·3-·4 in. long. *Calyx* about ·1 in. long, obliquely campanulate, with scattered white hairs outside. *Corolla* deep-pink or dark-purple. *Pod* linear, turgid, glabrous, not narrowed into a beak.

JAUNSAR and TEHRI-GARHWAL, up to 8-500 ft.; Deoban Mundáli, Kathián, etc.

Economic use as of the foregoing species.

Fl. Mar.-June, according to elevation.

3. **I. hebepetala,** Benth.; Fl. Br. Ind. ii. 101; Brandis Ind. Trees 217; Gamble Man. Ind. Timb. 231.

A tall shrub; branchlets glabrescent. *Leaves* imparipinnate, 4-6 in. long. *Leaflets* 13-17, opposite, usually 1-1·5 in. long, ovate, obtuse, membranous, dull-green above, pale beneath; stipels distinct. *Racemes* 2-4 in. long, few-flowered, peduncled; bracts boat-shaped, bristly at the tip, exceeding the buds. *Calyx* ·1 in. long, obliquely campanulate. *Corolla* ·5 in. long, deep-red. *Pod* glabrous, 1·5-2 in. long, 8-10-seeded.

JAUNSAR, 7,-10,000 ft., generally in shady places: Jhálkúri, Konáin, etc.

The stems and branches are used for fuel.

Fl. May, June.

4. **I. pulchella,** Roxb.; Fl. Br. Ind. ii. 101; Brandis For. Flora 136, Ind. Trees 217; Gamble Man. Ind. Timb. 231. Vern. *Nil*, Hind.; *Sákiná*, Dún and Garhwal.

A shrub 10-12 ft. high; branchlets glabrescent. *Leaves* imparipinnate, 3-6 in. long. *Leaflets* 13-21, opposite, ·6-·8 by ·3-·4 in., obovate-oblong, subcoriaceous, pale-green above, glaucous beneath, with adpressed grey hairs on both surfaces; stipels minute or 0. *Racemes* 1-4 in. long, moderately compact, short-peduncled; bracts boat-shaped, exceeding the buds. *Calyx* about ·1 in. long, white-canescent; teeth short. *Corolla* about ·8 in. long, bright-red or rose-coloured; standard reflexed. *Pod* 1·2-1·7 in. long, straight, turgid, glabrous, 8-12 seeded; sutures broad.

Sál forests of the DÚN and the SIWALIKS, and the HILLS up to 9,000 ft., very common in some localities, *e.g.*, Karwápáni; Konáin, Mundáli, etc.

The branches are often used for fences, and also for fuel.

Fl. Nov.-Mar., according to elevation. Fr. Rainy season.

I. hirsuta, Linn.; Fl. Br. Ind. ii. 98; —is a short suberect herbaceous plant with stems densely clothed with brown pubescence. *Racemes* 2-4 in. long, very dense. *Flowers* red. *Pod* ·7-1 in. long, densely pubescent. Found in grass-lands and ráu-beds in the SIWALIK TRACTS. Phándowála, Ránipur, etc.

I. Dosua, Ham.; Fl. Br. Ind. ii. 102; Brandis Ind. Trees 218—is a low shrub densely pubescent like the above. *Flowers* bright-red. *Pod* about 1 in. long, glabrescent. Common in grass-lands and fire-traces in the HILLS: Lokhár, Ringáli, Bháshlá, etc.

4. Millettia, W. & A.; G. P. n. 104.

1. **M. auriculata,** Baker; Fl. Br. Ind. ii. 108; Brandis For. Flora 138; Ind. Trees 219; Gamble Man. Ind. Timb. 232. Vern. *Gauj*, Hind.

A large woody gregarious climber. *Leaves* 1-2 ft. long, crowded at the ends of the branches; petiole with a swollen base. *Leaflets* 7-9, lateral opposite, 3-8 by 2-5 in., obovate elliptic or oblong, abruptly acuminate, entire, subcoriaceous, densely grey-silky when young, afterwards glabrescent above, pale beneath; stipels minute. *Racemes* 4-10 in. long, axillary; rachis downy. *Flowers* ·3-·4 in. long, dull-white, fascicled on the rachis. *Calyx* about ·1 in. long, shortly toothed, densely silky. *Corolla* ·3-·4 in. long, silky all over; standard auriculate above the claw (whence the specific name); wings falcate; keel-petals incurved. *Stamens* monadelphous (though generally diadelphous in the Genus). *Style* filiform, incurved, glabrous; stigma capitate. *Pod* 4-7 by 1-1·5 in., hard, brown-velvety, with very thick sutures.

Extremely common and a pest in the DÚN and SAHÁRANPUR FORESTS; also found in the Tons Valley and elsewhere in JAUNSAR and TEHRI-GARHWAL, up to 3,000 ft.

The branches when beaten give a coarse fibre which is used for rough cordage. They are also made into brushes for daubing trees with paint. The leaves and twigs are lopped for cattle-fodder and eaten by elephants.

Fl. May, June. Fr. Cold season.

5. Tephrosia, Pers.; G. P. n. 100.

1. **T. candida,** DC.; Fl. Br. Ind. ii. 111; Brandis For. Flora 138; Gamble Man. Ind. Timb. 234. Vern. *Kulthi, Loshtia,* DÚN; *Masethi,* Málkōt.

A low shrub; branches grooved, clothed with brown or grey velvety pubescence. *Leaves* imparipinnate, 5-9 in. long, short-petioled; stipules setaceous. *Leaflets* 19-25, opposite, 2-3 by ·3-·7 in., narrow-elliptic, acute at both ends, entire, coriaceous, dark-green and glabrous above, pale and silky beneath; lateral nerves numerous, straight, very fine; midrib prominent. *Racemes* 6-9 in long, terminal and lateral, often fascicled; pedicels ·3-·5 in. long, silky. *Calyx* campanulate, ·15-·2 in. long, short-toothed, silky. *Corolla* ·7-1 in. long, white with a shade of red; petals clawed; standard suborbicular, densely silky. *Stamens* diadelphous. *Pod* 3-4 by ·3 in., 10-12 seeded, continuous, slightly recurved, clothed with adpressed brown silky hairs, generally tipped with the persistent style.

Common in some parts of the DÚN, *e.g.*, Chandrabani, Rámgarh, Bindál-nálá, Bidhalna Block, etc.

Much planted as a fertiliser in tea-gardens in Assam. The leaves and bark are used to intoxicate fish.

Fl. Aug., Sept. Fr. Nov., Dec.

6. Sesbania, Pers.; G. P. n. 118.

1. **S. ægyptiaca,** Pers.; Fl. Br. Ind. ii. 114; Brandis For. Flora 137, Ind. Trees 219; Gamble Man. Ind. Timb. 235. Vern. *Jaent,* Hind.

A soft-wooded shrub 10-15 ft. high, of brief duration. *Leaves* paripinnate, 3-6 in. long. *Leaflets* 9-20 pairs, ·6-1 by ·1-·2 in., linear-oblong, minutely petioluled, membranous, glabrous, pale-green. *Racemes* 3-6 in. long, axillary, few-flowered; pedicels about ·2 in. long. *Flowers* pale-yellow. *Calyx* campanulate, ·2 in. long, short-toothed, membranous, glabrous. *Petals* ·5-·7 in. long, yellow, often with purple spots. *Stamens* diadelphous. *Pod* 6-9 by ·15 in., torulose, flexible, twisted, 20-30 seeded, septate between the seeds.

Cultivated throughout the plains of India for its very rapid growth and shade-yielding capacity.

Wood white, extremely soft, weighing about 27 lbs, per c. ft. It is said to give the best gunpowder charcoal. The fibre of the bark is used for rope, and the leaves and tender branches for cattle-fodder.

Fl. Aug., Sept. Fr. Dec.-Feb.

7. Caragana, Lam.; G. P. n. 130.

1. **C. brevispina,** Royle; Fl. Br. Ind. ii. 116; Brandis For. Flora 133, Ind. Trees 216; Gamble Man. Ind. Timb. 236. Vern. *Ári, Kathúr-kantá,* Jaunsar.

An erect spinescent shrub, 6-8 ft. high; young branches finely downy. *Leaves* paripinnate, 2-4 in. long; rachis finally spinescent. *Leaflets* 8-16, variable, ·3-·6 by ·2-·5 in., obovate, pubsecent beneath, minutely petioluled. *Racemes* 2-3 in. long, unbellately 1-3-flowered; pedicels downy, bracteate. *Calyx* campanulate, placed very obliquely on the pedicel, ·3-·4 in. long, pubescent; teeth acute. *Petals* yellow, ·6-1 in. long, all of nearly the same length; standard broad, reflexed, much thicker and firmer than the other petals. *Stamens* diadelphous. *Style* incurved, glabrous. *Pod* 2-3 in. long, straight, cylindrical, turgid, glabrous outside, woolly inside.

JAUNSAR and TEHRI-GARHWAL, 6,-9,000 ft. Common at Konáin, Mundáli and Deotá.

Fl. Apr.-June. Fr. Aug.-Oct.

C. Gerardiana, Royle; Fl. Br. Ind. ii. 116; Brandis Ind. Trees 216—has also been found in TEHRI-GARHWAL, *e.g.,* in the Jaurási and Morirú Blocks. It is a diffuse undershrub differing from the above in having smaller leaves and leaflets, subsessile flowers, and shorter pods which are hirsute outside.

Fl. May-Aug.

8. Lespedeza, Mich.; G. P. n. 182.

Herbs or undershrubs. *Lcaves* pinnately 3-foliolate, without stipels. *Flowers* axillary, fascicled or racemed. *Calyx-tube* campanulate; teeth long. *Corolla* exserted; standard broad. *Stamens* diadelphous. *Ovary* sessile or stipitate, 1-ovuled; style long, incurved, often persistent; stigma minute. *Pod* 1-seeded, small, oblong, compressed, reticulate, indehiscent.

Analysis of the Species.

Keel obtuse, not much incurved; flowers fascicled in leaf-axils . . . . 1. *L. sericea.*

Keel acute, much incurved; flowers racemed.

Pod about 1 in. long, densely grey-silky . . 2. *L. stenocarpa.*

Pod ·2 in. long, clothed with adpressed hairs . 3. *L. eriocarpa.*

1. **L. sericea,** Miq.; Fl. Br. Ind. ii. 142. Vern. *Khúnjú*. Dún.

An erect undershrub, 2-4 ft. high, with long slender branches. *Leaves* ascending; petiole short. *Leaflets* ·3-·6 by about ·1 in., linear-cuneate, emarginate, minutely petioluled, rigidly coriaceous, usually glabrous above, adpressedly silky-hairy beneath. *Flowers* 2-4 together in the axils of the leaves; pedicels short; bracteoles minute. *Calyx* ·1 in. long, canescent, teeth very long. *Corolla* about ·2 in. long, white but tipped with purple. *Pod* ·1 in. long, thinly silky; style ·2 in. long, persistent.

JAUNSAR and the DÚN. Lachiwála, Rámgarh; Chakrata.

Fl. May, June. Fr. Oct., Nov.

2. **L. stenocarpa,** Maxim.; Prain's Additional Leguminosæ in Journ. As. Soc. Beng. lxvi, Part II, No. 2, 376; Gamble Man. Ind. Timb. 236. Syn.—*L. macrostyla*, Baker (in part); Fl. Br. Ind. ii. 143.

An undershrub, 3-5 ft. high; branches densely white-pubescent. *Petiole* ·5-·7 in. long. *Leaflets* ·5-·8 by ·4-·6 in., obovate-cuneate, often emarginate, rigidly subcoriaceous, white-silky beneath. *Racemes* short, dense, silky; buds hidden by ovate silky bracts; pedicels ·1-·2 in. long. *Calyx* ·1 in.; teeth longer than the tube. *Corolla* ·4-·6 in. long, red. *Pod* about 1 in. long, shortly stalked, narrow-oblong, densely grey-silky, gradually tapering to the base of the persistent hairy style.

Common in the SIWALIK TRACT, on steep sandy hill-slopes and banks of ráus. Mohand Pass, Dholkhand, Ránipur, etc. Also low elevations in the HILLS.

Fl. Aug., Sept. Fr. Dec.-Feb.

3. **L. eriocarpa,** DC.; Fl. Br. Ind. ii. 144; Gamble Man. Ind. Timb. 236.

A much-branched erect shrub, 3-4 ft. high; branchlets slender, angular, furrowed, silky. *Petiole* (except in var. *Falconeri*, Prain) longer than in the other two species, sometimes up to 1·5 in.; stipules setaceous, ·2-·3 in. long. *Leaflets* ·3-1 in. long, obovate cuneate, adpressedly silky-hairy beneath. *Racemes* 2-3 in. long, rather lax, peduncled; bracts not exceeding the buds; pedicels ·15-·2 in. *Calyx* ·15 in. long; teeth much longer than the tube. *Corolla* ·4-·5 in. long, bright-pink. *Pod* ·2-·3 in. long, coriaceous; style as long as the pod, pubescent near the base.

Fairly common in JAUNSAR and TEHRI-GARHWAL, 4,-8,000 ft. Lúrli, Missáu, Kathián, Tons Valley, etc.

Fl. May-Sept. Fr. Cold season.

9. Ougeinia, Benth.; G. P. n. 169.

1. **O. dalbergioides,** Benth.; Fl. Br. Ind. ii. 161. Brandis For. Flora 146, Ind. Trees 224; Gamble Man. Ind. Timb. 237. Vern. *Sáṇdan*, Hind.

A middle-sized tree with a thin ashy-grey or light-brown bark which exudes beads of red gum when cut. *Leaves* pinnately 3-foliolate, stipellate; rachis 3-6 in. long, channelled above. *Lateral leaflets* opposite, 2·5-4·5 by 1·5-3 in., obliquely elliptical; *terminal* 3-6 by 2-3·5 in., broad-ovate; all entire or obscurely crenate, coriaceous, glabrous above, more or less downy or glabrescent beneath; lateral nerves about 6 pairs; petiolules ·1-·2 in. long. *Flowers* light-pink or white, in fascicled racemes generally from the old wood; pedicels ·5-·8 in. long, very slender, clustered on short branches of the raceme; bracts small, scaly. *Calyx* ·1-·15 in. long, pubescent; teeth obtuse. *Corolla* ·3-·4 in. long; standard nearly orbicular, shortly clawed; keel obtuse. *Pod* very distinctly jointed, 2-4 by ·3 in., flat; joints ·6-·8 in. long. *Seeds* about ·2 in. long, smooth, brown when mature.

A common tree in Sál forests in the DÚN and SAHÁRANPUR SIWALIKS and in the OUTER HIMALAYA; also found in the chir forests of JAUNSAR and TEHRI-GARHWAL, up to 4,000 ft., *e.g.*, Khunigádh, Moltá, etc.

Heartwood pale or deep reddish-brown, hard, close-grained, strong, tough and durable, and takes a beautiful polish; weight 55-65 lbs. per c. ft. It is much used for agricultural implements, furniture, building, and the like. The bark yields an astringent red gum, and is pounded and used to intoxicate fish. The twigs are lopped for cattle-fodder. The tree can be most easily propagated by root-suckers.

Leafless Feb., Mar. Fl. Mar., Apr. Fr. May, June.

10. Desmodium, Desv.; G. P. n. 170.

Shrubs or herbs. *Leaves* pinnately 3-foliolate or 1-foliolate, stipellate. *Flowers* small, red or whitish, in axillary and terminal simple or panicled racemes, rarely umbelled. *Calyx* campanulate or turbinate. *Corolla* exserted; standard broad; wings more or less attached to the keel, which is usually obtuse. *Stamens* diadelphous, sometimes the upper stamen only partially free.

Style incurved; stigma minute, capitate. *Pod* compressed, usually with articulate joints; joints 1-seeded, generally indehiscent, rarely splitting open in a continuous line along the ventral suture.

Anaylsis of the Species.

Flowers umbelled; leaves 3-foliolate.
  Umbels axillary, naked . . . . . 1. *D. Cephalotes.*
  Umbels arranged in plicate racemes, hidden by a pair of persistent foliaceous bracts. 2. *D. pulchellum.*
Flowers in axillary and terminal, simple or panicled racemes.
  Pod distinctly jointed and articulate; joints generally indehiscent.
   Leaves 1-foliolate.
    Petiole winged . . . . . 4. *D. triquetrum.*
    Petiole not winged . . . . . 6. *D. latifolium.*
   Leaves 3-foliolate.
    Leaflets dark-green, narrow; pod beset with hooked hairs. . . . 3. *D. laburnifolium.*
    Leaflets pale-green, broad; pod thinly silky-hairy . . . . . 5 *D. tiliæfolium.*
  Pod indistinctly jointed and not articulate, dehiscing in a continuous line along the ventral suture; (leaves normally 3-foliolate). . . . . . . 7. *D. gyrans.*

1. **D. Cephalotes,** Wall.: Fl. Br. Ind. ii. 161; Gamble Man. Ind. Timb. 238; Brandis Ind. Trees 222; Vern. *Bhattá,* Garhwal.

A shrub 4-6 ft. high, with grey bark; branches triquetrous. *Leaves* 3-foliolate; petiole 1-2 in. long, deeply furrowed, grey-downy. *Leaflets* 3·5-6 by 1·5-2·5 in., oblong or elliptic, subcoriaceous, grey-silky beneath; lateral nerves and midrib prominent and brightly silky beneath, the former 10-16 pairs. *Flowers* about ·3 in. long, 20 or more in dense axillary umbels; pedicels silvery, jointed at the apex. *Calyx* ·15 in. long; teeth lanceolate. *Corolla* red, ·25 in. long. *Pod* about 1 in. long, 4-5-jointed, indented more or less along both sutures, densely grey-silky.

Common in the Sál forests of the DÚN, especially at Lachiwála and Tháno.

The pods are said to be poisonous for cattle.

Fl. July, Aug. Fr. Nov., Dec.

2. **D. pulchellum,** Benth.; Fl. Br. Ind. ii. 162; Brandis For. Flora 145, Ind. Trees 223: Gamble Man. Ind. Timb. 239. Vern. *Thápi,* Garhwal; *Jatá Sálpán,* Hind.

An erect shrub, 4-6 ft. high; branches ribbed, grey-downy. *Leaves* 3-foliolate; petiole ·3-·5 in. long. *Lateral leaflets* 1·5-2·5 by ·6-1 in., ·5-·8 in. below the *terminal* which is 2·5-4 by 1·2-1·5 in., both elliptic or oblong-lanceolate, generally acute, rounded at the base, pubescent beneath; lateral nerves 8 pairs. *Flowers* ·2-·3 in. long, in 2-6-flowered umbels, each umbel subtended by a pair of persistent orbicular foliaceous bracts about ·5 in. diam., the umbels themselves in axillary and terminal plicate racemes, 4-10 in. long. *Calyx* ·1 in. long; teeth shorter than the tube. *Corolla* ·25 in., white with a shade of red. *Pod* ·25 in. long, generally with 2 joints, constricted at both sutures.

Common in the DÚN in the same localities as the preceding species.

Fl. July-Sept. Fr. Cold season.

3. **D. laburnifolium,** DC.; Fl. Br. Ind. ii. 163.

A shrub 6-8 ft. high; branches few, slender, glabrescent; bark dark-grey. *Leaves* 3-foliolate; petiole 1-1·5 in., thickened, grooved; stipules free, minute. *Leaflets* 2-4 by 1-1·5 in., oblong-lanceolate, acute at both ends, dark-green, glabrous and shining above, hairy on the nerves beneath. *Racemes* about 6 in. long; pedicels ·2-3 in. *Flowers* whitish, ·3-·4 in. long. *Calyx* about a third of the flower, hairy; teeth narrow, as long as the tube. *Corolla* ·2-·3 in. *Pod* 2-4 in. by ·3 in., beset with short hooked hairs; joints 6-8, rectangular, twice as long as broad, easily breaking off.

In damp shady localities in the DÚN, such as Mothronwála, Nakraunda, Jōgiwála, Khairi, Robbers' Cave, etc.

The leaves are eaten by buffaloes.

Fl. July, Aug. Fr. Dec., Jan.

4. **D. triquetrum,** DC.; Fl. Br. Ind. ii. 163; Brandis For. Flora 146, Ind. Trees 224.

A sub-procumbent shrub, 3-4 ft. long; branches triquetrous, glabrescent. *Leaves* 1-foliolate. *Leaflet* 3-6 by 1·2-2·2 in., oblong, lanceolate, acute, subcoriaceous, scaberulous above, hairy on the nerves beneath; petiole ·7-1·3 in. long, winged to an oblanceolate shape, ·2-·4 in. broad; main lateral nerves 12-15 pairs. *Racemes* 6-12 in. long, axillary and terminal; pedicels ·1-·2 in. *Calyx* about

·1 in., campanulate. *Pod* 1-2 by ·2 in., 6-8-jointed, glabrous or pubescent, indented between the joints at the ventral suture.

Common about Lachiwála on forest-paths, in grass-lands, and along the banks of the Ré-nadi in the DÚN.

Fl. July, Aug. Fr. Sept.-Dec.

5. **D. tiliæfolium,** D. Don; Fl. Br. Ind. ii. 168; Brandis For. Flora 145, Ind. Trees 223; Gamble Man. Ind. Timb. 239. Vern. *Mártoi, Mátoi,* Jaunsar.

A somewhat diffuse shrub, 4-10 ft. high; branchlets pubescent. *Leaves* 3-foliolate; rachis 1·5-3·5 in. long, pubescent. *Leaflets* 1-3 by ·7-2·2 in., broad-ovate or rhomboid, often mucronate at the apex, subcoriaceous, glabrescent above, silky-pubescent beneath, margins entire or wavy; main lateral nerves about 6 pairs, the lowest pair from near the base. *Flowers* red, in terminal panicles and axillary racemes; pedicels ·3-·4 in. long, filiform, finely downy. *Calyx* ·1 in., downy; teeth shorter than the tube. *Corolla* ·3-·5 in. long. *Pod* 2-3 by ·25 in., slightly falcate, compressed, indented between the joints at the inner edge, thinly silky-hairy; joints 6-9, longer than broad.

Common and somewhat gregarious in JAUNSAR and TEHRI-GARHWAL, between 4,000 and 8,500 ft.

The thin grey bark is used for rope and paper-making. The twigs are browsed by cattle, and the branches are cut up into faggots and used for fuel in Chakrata.

Fl. June, July. Fr. Oct., Nov.

6. **D. latifolium,** DC.; Fl. Br. Ind. ii. 168; Brandis For. Flora 145, Ind. Trees 224.

An erect undershrub, 4-6 ft. high. *Leaves* 1-foliolate. *Leaflet* 2-5 by 1·5-3·5 in., broad-ovate, truncate or cordate and 3-nerved at the base, hispid above, densely soft-pubescent beneath; tip rounded or acute, mucronate; lateral nerves 7-8 pairs including the basal; petiole ·4-·7 in. long; stipules semicordate, cuspidate. *Flowers* ·2 in. long, bright-purple, clustered on axillary and terminal racemes which are 4-8 in. long. *Calyx* minute; teeth linear. *Pod* ·6-1 by about ·1 in., 4-6-jointed, much constricted between the joints, densely clothed with minute hooked hairs; joints 4-6, rather longer than broad, readily separating.

The DÚN and the OUTER HIMALAYA, up to 3,500 ft.

Fl. Aug., Sept. Fr. Nov., Dec.

7. **D. gyrans,** DC.; Fl. Br. Ind. ii. 174; Brandis For. Flora 146; Gamble Man. Ind. Timb. 238. The Telegraph plant. Vern. *Khúni,* Garhwal.

An erect shrub, 4-8 ft. high, with glabrous green branches. *Leaves* normally 3-foliolate, but often 1-foliolate by the abortion or early fall of the small lateral leaflets; petiole 1-1·5 in. *Terminal leaflet* 3-4 by 1-1·7 in., oblong-lanceolate, quite entire, rather membranous, glaucous beneath, often with irregular-shaped glaucous blotches above; main lateral nerves about 10 pairs. *Lateral leaflets* absent or rudimentary, ·5-·7 by ·1-·12 in., rotating by jerks. *Flowers* ·5 in. long, in axillary racemes and terminal panicles, at first hidden by large ovate bracts; pedicels ·25 in. long, downy. *Calyx* ·1 in. long, campanulate; teeth short. *Corolla* ·2-·3 in. long. *Pod* ·1-1·5 by ·2 in., falcate, 6-10-jointed, not articulate, slightly indented along the lower, and dehiscing in a continuous line along the upper, suture.

Common in the DÚN and in Chir forests along the TONS VALLEY, usually with grass.

Fl. Aug., Sept. Fr. Nov.-Jan.

Two forms of this plant are noticeable;—one scarcely exceeding 4 ft. in height, with narrow-lanceolate, somewhat coriaceous terminal leaflet, petiole less than 1 in. long, and scaberulous pods,—and the other about twice as tall, with broader oblong-elliptic rather membranous terminal leaflet, much longer petiole, and glabrous or glabrescent pods. Is the latter var. *Roylei,* W. & A.?

This large Genus comprises several other shrubs and undershrubs occurring in the region of this Flora, of which the following deserve brief notice:—

1. *D. laxiflorum,* DC.; Fl. Br. Ind. ii. 164; Brandis Ind. Trees 223. A weak suberect plant with 3-foliolate leaves. *Leaflets* 3-6 in. long, elliptic, membranous. *Racemes* 8-15 in. long, slender, drooping. *Pod* 1·5-2 by ·08 in., somewhat constricted and easily breaking off between the joints, catching on clothes by hooked hairs. Common in the DÚN. Fl. Aug., Sept. Fr. Nov., Dec.

2. *D. sambuense,* DC.; Prain's Additional Leguminosæ in Journ. As. Soc. Beng., lxvi, Part ii., No. 2, 394; Brandis Ind. Trees 223. Syn.—*D. floribundum,* G. Don.; Fl. Br. Ind. ii. 167. Vern. *Gor Mártoi,* Jaunsar. *Stem* angular. *Leaves* 3-foliolate. *Leaflets* 1·5-2 by 1-1·5 in., rhomboid or elliptic; common petiole 2-3 in.; stipules prominent. *Racemes* 3-6 in. long. *Flowers* ·5 in. long.

Pod ·7-1 by ·1 in., 6-8-jointed. JAUNSAR about Chakrata, Dhármigádh, etc.; also Sainjni, Kúlni, etc., in TEHRI-GARHWAL.

3. *D gangeticum*, DC.; Fl. Br. Ind. ii. 168; Brandis Ind. Trees 224. *Stem* 2-3 ft. high. *Leaves* 1-foliolate; petiole ·7-1·2 in. *Leaflet* 2-4 in. long, variable in width, ovate to narrow-lanceolate, membranous. *Racemes* 6-12 in. long, mostly terminal; pedicels ascending. *Flowers* about ·2 in. long. *Pod* ·5-·7 by ·1 in., 6-8-jointed, common in blanks in Sál forests in the DÚN. Fl. July, Aug. Fr. Cold season.

4. *D. concinnum*, DC.; Fl. Br. Ind. ii. 170; Brandis Ind. Trees 223. A tall undershrub with slender drooping branches. *Leaves* 3-foliolate; petiole ·5-1 in. *Leaflets* oblong, obtuse, 1·5-3 in. long, lateral ones smaller. *Racemes* terminal and lateral, 6-12 in. long; bracts conspicuous. *Flowers* ·2-·3 in. long. *Pod* 1 by ·12 in., 4-6-jointed. Robbers' Cave near DEHRA DÚN.

5. *D. parvifolium*, Baker; Fl. Br. Ind. ii. 172. A diffuse undershrub with 1-3-foliolate leaves. *Leaflets* very variable in size, ·2-1·5 in. long, oblong, subcordate, membranous. *Flowers* ·15 in. long; corolla included in the calyx. *Pod* about ·5 in. long, falcate, 4-6-jointed. Rámgarh and Karwápáni in the DÚN. Fl. Aug., Sept. Fr. Nov., Dec.

11. Abrus, Linn.; G. P. n. 188.

1. **A. precatorius**, Linn.; Fl. Br. Ind. ii. 175; Brandis For. Flora 139, Ind. Trees 225; Gamble Man. Ind. Timb. 240. Vern. *Chúṇtli, Ratgiri*, Dún; *Gúnjá, Gúnchi*, Hind.

A much-branched climber with a woody stem. *Leaves* paripinnate, 2-3 in. long. *Leaflets* 20-40, opposite, deciduous, ·4-1 by ·2-·3 in., oblong-ligulate, membranous, glabrous or thinly silky beneath. *Flowers* reddish or white, in dense pedunculate racemes which are shorter than, or as long as, the leaves; peduncles often leaf-bearing. *Calyx* ·1-·15 in. long, campanulate, truncate, thinly silky. *Corolla* ·3-·5 in. long; standard ovate, acute; wings narrow; keel larger than the wings, arcuate. *Stamens* 9, united in a sheath which is slit above; the tenth absent. *Ovary* many-ovuled; style short, incurved, not bearded; stigma capitate. *Pod* 1-1·7 by ·4-·5 in., oblong, turgid, 3-5-seeded. *Seeds* about ·2 in. long, ovoid or subglobose, generally two-thirds scarlet or white and the rest jet-black, with a large white hilum in the black part, sometimes wholly black or white, smooth, shining.

Very common along the foot of the SAHÁRANPUR SIWALIKS, especially near Khárá, Ránipur and Kasúmri; also on hedges in the DÚN. Amláwa Valley, JAUNSAR.

The seeds are recognized by Indian jewellers as the minimum unit of weight, and are used for weighing gold and precious stones. The root resembles liquorice in medicinal property.

Fl. Aug., Sept. Fr. Cold season.

A. pulchellus, Wall., Fl. Br. Ind. ii. 175—differs from the above in having larger leaflets, racemes exceeding the leaves, larger but thinner-valved pod and greyish-brown compressed seeds. Found in the DÚN (Lachiwála, Tháno, Ráipur, etc.) and the OUTER HIMALAYA. Fl. Aug., Sept.

12. Mucuna, Adans.; G. P. n. 205.

Climbers, generally herbaceous. *Leaves* large, pinnately 3-foliolate, stipellate. *Flowers* large, usually dark-purple, in few-flowered racemes or corymbs. *Calyx* campanulate, the two upper teeth connate. *Corolla* much exserted; keel rostrate, much exceeding the standard and usually slightly exceeding the wings. *Stamens* 2-adelphous; anthers alternately versatile and basifixed. *Ovary* sessile, many-ovuled; style incurved, beardless; stigma capitate. *Pod* hard, usually covered with irritating bristles.

Analysis of the Species.

Leaves glabrous; pod obliquely plaited on the faces . . . . . . 1. *M. atropurpurea.*

Leaves silky beneath; pod not plaited on the faces . . . . . . 2. *M. pruriens.*

1. **M. atropurpurea,** DC.; Fl. Br. Ind. ii. 186; Brandis Ind. Trees 226; Gamble Man. Ind. Timb. 240. Vern. *Bhainswalibel*, Dún.

A climber with soft porous wood. *Leaflets* 5-8 by 3·5-5 in., ovate or elliptic, 3-5-nerved at the base, membranous, shining above, lateral very oblique, the end one cuspidate; rachis 5-8 in. long.

Racemes 6-12 in. long, long-peduncled, drooping, 12-30 flowered, often forked; bracts small, deciduous; bracteoles ·2-·3 in. long. *Calyx* ·5-·6 in. long, 2-lipped, grey-pubescent and also with scattered irritating brown bristles. *Corolla* 2-2·5 in. long, dark-purple; standard about half the length of the keel; wings about half the length of the standard. *Pod* 3-4 by 1-1·3 in., with close oblique plaits on the faces, covered with brownish-yellow irritating bristles.

Found in the DÚN about Dehra, and also in the Dhármigádh valley, JAUNSAR. Not common.

Fl. Aug., Sept. Fr. Cold season.

2. **M. pruriens,** DC.; Fl. Br. Ind. ii. 187; Gamble Man. Ind. Timb. 240; Brandis Ind. Trees 226. The Cowitch or Cowhage plant. Vern. *Káunch, Gáunch,* Dún.

An annual twining herb. *Leaflets* 3-8 in. long, ovate or rhomboid, membranous, glabrescent above, adpressedly silky pubescent beneath, mucronate; rachis 6-10 in. long. *Racemes* 4-8 in. long, short-peduncled, drooping, 10-20-flowered. *Calyx* ·25-·4 in. long, 2-lipped, with a few irritating bristles. *Corolla* 1·3-1·6 in. long, purplish. *Pod* 2-3 by ·6-·8 in., 5-6-seeded, turgid, turned up at the end, longitudinally ribbed, covered with dense pale-brown bristles.

On hedges in the outskirts of villages and in abandoned village sites in SAHÁRANPUR and the DÚN. Fairly common.

The seeds and roots are used in medicine and the irritating hairs as a vermifuge.

Fl. Feb., Mar.

M. capitata, W. & A., Fl. Br. Ind. ii 187,—is closely allied to the last species, but the flowers are corymbose, and the pod about twice as long and covered with deciduous bristles. Found in the SAHÁRANPUR SIWALIKS.

Fl. Rainy season. Fr. Cold season.

M. imbricata, DC., Fl. Br. Ind. ii. 185 Brandis Ind. Trees 225, resembles *M. atropurpurea,* but the pod, besides being plaited, is broadly winged at both sutures. It is found in the DÚN. (*Mr. J. F. Duthie.*)

13. Erythrina, Linn.; G. P. n. 01.

1. **E. suberosa,** Roxb.; Fl. Br. Ind. ii. 189; Brandis For. Flora 140, Ind. Trees 227; Gamble Man. Ind. Timb. 241. Vern. *Dhaul Dhák, Madár,* Hind.

A moderate-sized deciduous tree; outer bark corky, light-grey, 1-2 in. thick, with deep irregular vertical cracks; branches armed with straight whitish conical prickles; young parts, leaves beneath and inflorescence usually covered with soft tomentum. *Leaves*

ends of the branches. *Flowers* bright scarlet, 1·5-2 in. long, in fascicles of 2-3; pedicels ·3-·5 in. long. *Calyx* campanulate, obsoletely 2-lipped in flower. *Corolla* much exserted, straight; standard 1·5-2 in. long, ·5-7 in. broad, narrowed into a short claw; wings ·2-·3 in. long, falcate; keel-petals ·6-·8 in. long, connate. *Stamens* 2-adelphous; upper stamen free nearly to the base. *Ovary* stipitate, many-ovuled; style incurved, beardless; stigma capitate. *Pod* stipitate, 3-4 by ·3-·4 in., tapering at both ends, torulose, 4-6-seeded; seeds black.

Var. *glabrescens*, Prain, Journ. As. Soc. Beng. lxvi, Part ii. No. 2. 410—differs from the type in that the leaflets are glabrescent beneath at an early age, afterwards glaucous.

The type is occasionally met with along ráus in the SIWALIKS, but the above variety is common in the Sál forests of the SIWALIK DIVISION, and also in the Tons and Jumna Valleys in JAUNSAR and TEHRI-GARHWAL, up to 4,000 ft.

Wood soft, white, spongy, but fibrous and tough, very light, weighing 13-20 lbs. per c. ft. It is used for scabbards, ladles, sieve-frames, and butter and ghí-pots. The tree is easily propagated by cuttings.

Leafless Jan., Feb. Fl. Mar., Apr. Fr. June.

14. Spatholobus, Hassk.; G. P. n. 208.

1. **S. Roxburghii,** Benth.; Fl. Br. Ind. ii. 193; Brandis For. Flora 143, Ind. Trees 229; Gamble Man. Ind. Timb. 243. Vern. *Maulá* or *Maulá-bel*, Dún.

A large sinistrorse climber; branches grey-pubescent; stem with concentric layers of bast inside, which exude a red gum when cut. *Leaves* pinnately 3-foliolate, stipellate; rachis 3-4 in. long. *Leaflets* 4-9 by 3-5 in., ovate or elliptic, acuminate, subcoriaceous, pubescent beneath, the lateral oblique; lateral nerves 6-8 pairs, irregularly branched; petiolules ·1-·3 in. long. *Flowers* ·3-·4 in. long, white or reddish, in fascicles of 3 on large terminal panicles which are often 2-3 ft. long; pedicles very short. *Calyx* campanulate, grey-velvety, half the length of the flower; teeth acute, the two upper connate. *Standard* emarginate, longer than the keel, which is obtuse and nearly straight; wings free. *Stamens* diadelphous. *Ovary* shortly stipitate, 2-ovuled; style incurved, beardless; stigma capitate. *Pod* 3-5·5 by 1-1·3 in., suddenly narrowed into a stalk ·4-·6 in. long, softly brown-velvety, with only one seed near the end, dehiscing from the apex only down to the seed.

Common in the Sál forests of the SIWALIK DIVISION, especially in the Siwalik Range, where it does considerable harm to all trees by bending and distorting their stems, round which it twines with a very tight grip. In this respect it is the worst of all harmful climbers.

Wood soft and porous, but burns slowly and keeps on fire for a long time, for which purpose it is often used by people living near forests.

Fl. Sept.-Dec. Fr. Feb.-Apr.

15. Butea, Roxb.; G. P. n. 207.

1. **B. frondosa,** Roxb.; Fl. Br. Ind. ii. 194; Brandis For. Flora 142, Ind. Trees 230; Gamble Man. Ind. Timb. 243. Vern. *Dhák, Palás,* Hind.

A moderate-sized deciduous tree; bark fibrous, bluish-grey or light-brown outside, exuding a red juice when cut. *Leaves* pinnately 3-foliolate, stipellate; rachis 5-9 in. long; stipules and stipels tomentose, deciduous. *Leaflets* hard, rigidly coriaceous, glabrescent above, silky-tomentose beneath; lateral leaflets 6-8 by 5-7·5 in., obliquely ovate or broad elliptic; petiolules ·3-·4 in. long, stout; terminal 5-8 by 4·5-7 in., rhomboid or broadly obovate from a cuneate base; lateral nerves 4-6 pairs, prominent. *Flowers* 2-3·5 in. long, fascicled on rigid axillary and terminal racemes which are 4-7 in. long; inflorescence bracts and calyx dark brown-velvety. *Calyx* ·5 in. long, fleshy, grey-silky inside. *Petals* bright orange-red, equal, silvery-tomentose outside; standard 1 in. broad, recurved; keel incurved, beaked; wings falcate, adhering to the keel. *Stamens* 2-adelphous. *Ovary* shortly stalked, 2-ovuled; style filiform, curved, not bearded; stigma capitate. *Pod* 4-6 by 1·5-2 in., ligulate, firm, pendulous, silky-tomentose, abruptly narrowed to a stalk ·5-·7 in. long, with only one seed near the apex, indehiscent below the seed.

Common in the DÚN and SAHÁRANPUR FORESTS in blanks and open places, especially on water-logged soils as at Pathri. It is the most common indigenous tree of the UPPER GANGETIC PLAIN.

Wood dirty-white, porous, soft; annual rings indistinct; weight about 36 lbs. per c. ft. It is durable under water, and is used for well-curbs and piles. The bark of the roots yields a coarse brown fibre used for rough cordage and for caulking boats on the Ganges. The red juice exuded by the bark hardens into beads of ruby-coloured gum similar to kino, and is used as a substitute for it. The flowers give an orange dye, and a decoction of them is used to keep out white-ants from fields. The seeds have a medicinal use. Lac is often collected on the branches. The leaves are used as plates and to wrap up parcels, and are also lopped for buffalo-fodder.

Leafless in March. New leaves and fl. Apr., May. Fr. June, July.

16. Pueraria, DC.; G. P. n. 218.

1. **P. tuberosa,** DC.; Fl. Br. Ind. ii. 197; Brandis For. Flora 141, Ind. Trées 228; Gamble Man. Ind. Timb. 245. Vern. *Surál, Sirál, Sarúr,* Dún and Sahåranpur.

A twining shrub with stringy grey bark; young branches grey-pubescent; stem porous, producing large globose underground tubers which are often of immense size,—whence the specific name. *Leaves* pinnately 3-foliolate, stipellate; rachis 5-8 in. long. *Leaflets* 4-6 by 3-4 in., broad-ovate, acuminate, silky-pubescent when young, glabrescent above and thinly pubescent beneath when mature, the lateral oblique; main lateral nerves 6-8 pairs including the stronger basal pair; base truncate or subacute, 3-5-nerved; lateral petiolules ·2-·3 in. long. *Flowers* bright blue, in simple or panicled terminal racemes, 6-12 in. long; bracts minute. *Calyx* about ·2 in. long, densely silky; teeth shorter than the tube. *Corolla* about ·4 in. long; standard spurred at the base; wings oblong-falcate; keel obtuse, nearly straight. *Stamens* usually monadelphous. *Ovary* sessile, many-ovuled; style filiform, much incurved, beardless; stigma capitate. *Pod* 2-3 in. long, flat, flexible, 3-6-seeded, contracted between the joints, clothed with long bristle-like brown hairs.

Remarkably common about Kálsi; also found throughout the DÚN and SAHÁRANPUR FORESTS, especially on *Zizyphus Jujuba* near Sháhjahánpur.

The large tubers which are sometimes up to 18 in. in length and 12 in. in diameter, have a liquorice taste, and are eaten and used in medicine.

Leafless Nov.-May. Fl. Mar., Apr. Fr. Nov., Dec.

17. Rhynchosia, Lour.; G. P. n. 233.

1. **R. pseudo-cajan,** Camb.; Fl. Br. Ind. ii. 223; Brandis Ind. Trees 707; Gamble Man. Ind. Timb. 264.

An erect shrub, 4-6 ft. high; branches longitudinally ribbed; grey-tomentose. *Leaves* pinnately 3-foliolate, gland-dotted beneath; rachis ·5-1 in.; stipules minute. *Leaflets* ·5-2 by ·3-1·5 in., ovate to rhomboid, very softly woolly-tomentose and reticulate beneath, strongly 3-nerved at the base; stipels 0. *Flowers* in short-peduncled compact corymbs; pedicels short. *Calyx* ·2 in. long; teeth narrow-acuminate, densely woolly. *Corolla* ·4-·6 in. long, pale-yellow; keel incurved. *Stamens* 2-adelphous. *Ovary* subsessile, usually 2-ovuled; style long, much incurved; stigma capitate. *Pod* 1 by ·4 in., oblong, straight, slightly compressed, 1-2-seeded, persistently grey woolly.

Fairly common in fire-traces and grass-lands in the Tons Valley and elsewhere in JAUNSAR and TEHRI-GARHWAL, up to 7,000 ft. Also at higher elevations in the SIWALIKS.

Fl. and fr. Apr.-June.

18. Flemingia, Roxb.; G. P. n. 235.

Generally moderate-sized shrubs. *Leaves* digitately 3-foliolate or simple, gland-dotted beneath. *Flowers* generally in cymes. *Calyx-tube* short; teeth narrow, the lowest often the longest. *Corolla* scarcely exserted; petals equal. *Stamens* 2-adelphous. *Ovary* subsessile, 2-ovuled; style filiform, beardless; stigma capitate. *Pod* small, inflated, usually 2-seeded.

Analysis of the Species.

A. Leaves simple; bracts persistent, folding, (hiding the flowers).
  - Leaves oblong-lanceolate, rounded at the base; axis of raceme zigzag . 1. *F. strobilifera.*
  - Leaves orbicular, cordate; axis of raceme straight . . . . 2. *F. Chappar.*

B. Leaves digitately 3-foliolate; bracts caducous, not folding.
Branches triquetrous; bracts linear, exceeding the flowers . . . . 3. *F. stricta.*
Branches scarcely angled; bracts lanceolate, shorter than the flowers.
Racemes condensed, shorter than the petioles . . . . . . 4. *F. congesta.*
Racemes elongated, exceeding the petioles . . . . . 5. *F. semialata.*

1. **F. strobilifera,** R. Br.; Fl. Br. Ind. ii. 227; Brandis For. Flora 143, Ind. Trees 231; Gamble Man. Ind. Timb. 246.

An undershrub, usually about 5 ft. high; branches terete, velvety. *Leaves* simple, 3-6 by 1-1·8 in., oblong-lanceolate, subacute, rounded at the base, subcoriaceous, glabrescent above, thinly silky-pubescent beneath; petiole ·2-·7 in. long; stipules linear, scarious, ·2-·4 in. long. *Racemes* 3-6 in. long; rachis zigzag, downy; bracts ·5-1 in. long, rather broader than long, deeply cordate, membranous, reticulate, downy, folded. *Flowers* ·2-·3 in. long; calyx hairy; corolla purple, little exserted. *Pod* ·3-·4 in. long, 2-seeded, downy.

Very common in blanks in Sál forests in the SIWALIK DIVISION, also in the HILLS, up to 3,000 ft.

The leaves are used for thatching.

Fl. Aug.-Nov. Fr. Cold season.

Very similar in appearance is *F. paniculata* Wall.; Fl. Br. Ind. ii. 227, but with panicled racemes, naked flowers and larger pods. Common near Lachiwála in the DÚN. Fl. and fr. Mar. May.

2. **F. Chappar,** Ham.; Fl. Br. Ind. ii. 227; Brandis For. Flora 143, Ind. Trees 231; Gamble Man. Ind. Timb. 246. Vern. *Sálṛán*, Hind.; *Chhánchra*, E. Dún.

A gregarious undershurb often up to 7 ft. in height. *Leaves* simple, 2·5-4 in. diam., orbicular, cordate, acuminate, glabrescent above, more or less pubescent beneath, especially along the nerves, 3-nerved at the base; lateral nerves 6-8 pairs above the basal; petiole ·6-1·5 in. long. *Racemes* often panicled; rachis woody, pubescent; bracts 1 by 1·5 in., cordate, deeply emarginate, membranous, reticulate, folded, salmon-brown when mature. *Flowers* ·3-·4 in.; corolla about half-exserted. *Pod* ·3-·4 in. long, 2-seeded, downy.

Characteristic of the moister localities in the DÚN, *e.g.*, Káluwála, Lachiwála, Tirsál, Kánsrao, Motichúr, etc.

The roots are used in Hindu medicine.

Fl. Aug.-Oct. Fr. Cold season.

3. **F. stricta,** Roxb. Fl. Br. Ind. ii. 228; Brandis Ind. Trees 232; Gamble Man. Ind. Timb. 246. Vern. *Bebar*, Garh.

A tall shrub, 6-10 ft. high; branches triquetrous, hairy. *Leaves* digitately 3-foliolate; petiole 4-5·5 in. long, 3-quetrous, furrowed; stipules 2 in. long, striate, caducous. *Leaflets* 6-12 by 2·5-4 in., oblong, narrowed at both ends, quite glabrous above, thinly hairy along the nerves beneath, very shortly petioluled, 3-5-nerved at the base; lateral nerves 12-16 pairs; glandular dots few, minute, black. *Racemes* 3-4 in. long, dense-flowered; bracts ·6-1 in., linear subulate, scariose, rigid; pedicels very short. *Flowers* ·5 in. long.; calyx-teeth linear, the lowest much longer than the others; corolla as long as the lowest tooth. *Pod* ·5 in. long, glabrescent.

Common at Karwápáni in the DÚN, and also in low valleys in the HILLS.

Fl. Mar., Apr. Fr. Aug., Sept.

4. **F. congesta,** Roxb.; Fl. Br. Ind. ii. 228; Brandis For. Flora 143, Ind. Trees 232; Gamble Man. Ind. Timb. 246. Vern. *Banchhúi*, Dún.

An erect undershrub, 4-6 ft. high; branches slightly ribbed. *Leaves* digitately 3-foliolate; petiole 2·5-4 in. long, flattened; stipules ·5 in. long, linear, caducous. *Leaflets* 4-6 by 2-3 in., ovate- or oblong-lanceolate, glabrous above but pubescent and with brown or ruby-coloured glandular dots and hairy along the nerves beneath; the lateral oblique; base strongly 3-nerved; main lateral nerves about 6 pairs above the basal. *Racemes* dense, 1-2 in. long, sessile; bracts ·12-·25 in. long, lanceolate, membranous, not rigid, grey-silky outside, deciduous; pedicels very short. *Flowers* about ·5 in. long; calyx densely silky, teeth lanceolate; corolla scarcely exserted. *Pod* ·3-·5 in. long, turgid, 2-seeded, obscurely downy; seeds ·1 in. diam., shining, brown or blue-black.

Very common in the DÚN, especially in Sal forests.—Lachiwála, Karwápáni, etc.

A dye may be obtained from the hairs of the pod.

Fl. Apr.-Aug. Fr. Cold season.

5. **F. semialata,** Roxb.; Prain in Journ. As. Soc. Beng. lxvi, Part ii, No. 2, 439-441; Brandis For. Flora 143, Ind. Trees 232; Gamble Man. Ind. Timb. 246. Syn.—*F. congesta*, var. *semialata*, Fl. Br. Ind. ii. 229. Vern. *Bará Sálpán*, Hind.

A shrub closely resembling the last, but generally much taller, the *petiole* is shorter and narrowly winged towards the upper end, glandular dots often absent, the *racemes* longer (3-6 in.) and laxer and the *calyx-teeth* narrower.

As common as the last species, in much the same localities.

Fl. Apr.-Aug. Fr. Cold season.

F. prostrata, Roxb.; Prain in Journ. As. Soc. Beng. xvi, Part ii, No. 2, 440;—is simply a prostrate form of *F. congesta* with tawney pubescent inflorescence. Found near Lachiwála, Hardwar, etc.

19. Dalbergia, Linn. fil.; G. P. n. 236.

Trees, rarely climbing shrubs. *Leaves* imparipinnate; leaflets alternate, subcoriaceous, without stipels. *Flowers* small, in terminal or lateral panicles; bracts and bracteoles small. *Calyx* campanulate; teeth 5, short. *Corolla* exserted; standard broad; wings oblong; keel-petals shorter than the standard, connate at the tip. *Stamens* 9-10, diadelphous or monadelphous; anthers minute. *Ovary* stipitate, few-ovuled; style short, incurved, glabrous; stigma capitate. *Pod* thin, flat, coriaceous, 1-4-seeded, indehiscent.

Analysis of the Species.

Leaflets acuminate; stamens monadelphous . 1. *D. Sissoo.*
Leaflets obtuse; stamens diadelphous.
  Leaflets 11-15; panicles large, lax . 2. *D. lanceolaria.*
  Leaflets 17-25; panicles small, compact . 3. *D. sericea.*

1. **D. Sissoo,** Roxb.; Fl. Br. Ind. ii. 231; Brandis For. Flora 149, Ind. Trees 233; Gamble Man. Ind. Timb. 247. Vern. *Shisham, Sissú*, Hind.; *Táli*, Punjab.

A fairly large tree; bark grey, somewhat reticulately longitudinally furrowed, exfoliating in narrow strips; young parts grey-downy. *Leaflets* 3-5, distinctly alternate, 1-2·5 in. diam., broad-ovate or rhomboid, tough, acuminate, glabrescent; lateral nerves very slender; rachis 2-4 in. long, zigzag, pubescent when young; petiolules ·1-·2 in. long. *Flowers* ·2-·3 in. long, pale-white, in racemes

1-1·5 in. long, which are arranged in short axillary panicles. *Calyx* downy, about half the length of the flower. *Standard* with a long claw. *Stamens* 9, united in a sheath which is slit along the top. *Ovary* pubescent; style much shorter than the ovary; stigma large. *Pod* 2-3 by ·3-·5 in., strap-shaped, glabrous, pale-brown, a large proportion 1-seeded, narrowed at the base to a stipe ·3-·4 in. long. *Seeds* ·25 in. long, kidney-shaped, flat.

Indigenous in the banks and beds of streams and on sandy soils in the SIWALIK DIVISION, also in the Tons Valley, JAUNSAR. Extensively planted in avenues and as a nurse and a fertiliser in tea-gardens in the DÚN.

The heartwood is brown, mottled with darker longitudinal veins, hard and close-grained; annual rings not distinctly marked; medullary rays very fine; pores uniformly distributed, joined by wavy white concentric bands; weight 45-55lbs. per c. ft. "It is very elastic, seasons well, does not warp or split, and takes a fine polish."—*Sir D. Brandis.* It is highly esteemed for all purposes where strength and elasticity are required, its use being limited only by the supply. The twigs and leaves are lopped for fodder.

The tree can be easily raised from seed, *e.g.*, Sháhdera and Changá Mangá plantations in the PUNJAB, and also from root-cuttings, *e.g.*, at Jeypore in RAJPUTÁNA.

Leafless Jan., Feb. New leaves Feb., Mar. Fl. Mar.-May; Fr. Nov.-Feb., remaining long on the tree.

Allied to the Sissu is *D. latifolia*, Roxb., Fl. Br. Ind. ii 231; Brandis Ind. Trees 233, the Blackwood or Rosewood tree of S. India. Vern. *Waláyti Shisham*, Hind. The bark is of a lighter colour and less furrowed, the leaflets thicker and emarginate, and the pod larger and firmer. The wood is even more valued than that of Sissu. It has a spreading crown with thick boughs and is often planted in avenues, *e.g.*, at Máyápur near Hardwar.

2. **D. lanceolaria,** Linn.; Fl. Br. Ind. ii. 235; Brandis, For. Flora 151, Ind. Trees 236; Gamble Man. Ind. Timb. 253.

A large deciduous tree with glabrous branches; bark smooth, greenish-grey, yellow inside but instantly turning brown on exposure. *Leaflets* 11-15, 1-2 by ·6-1·2 in., elliptic or oblong, acute or emarginate, subcoriaceous, pale beneath. *Flowers* ·2-·4 in. long, dull-white, in large lax terminal and axillary panicles. *Calyx* about ·1 in. long, silky outside. *Standard* obovate, ·25 in. broad, clawed, keel short. *Stamens* 10, equally diadelphous. *Ovary* 3-ovuled, hairy at the base. *Pod* 2-3 by ·5-·7 in., narrowed at both ends, on a stipe ·3-·5 in. long, glabrous, flexible, bright-brown, generally 1-seeded, reticulate over the seed.

Occasionally met with in the SIWALIK TRACTS and in valleys in the OUTER HILLS. Very scarce. Chirak Block, along the Jhábri Sōt in the Máyápur Block. Also found by Mr. A. Smythies at Ráiwála in the DÚN.

Wood white or yellow, moderately hard, not durable, no heartwood; weight 33-44 lbs. per c. ft.

Fl. May, June. Fr. Sept., Oct.

3. **D. sericea,** G. Don; Prain in Journ. As. Soc. Beng. Vol. 70, 51; Brandis Ind. Trees 237.—Syn. *D. hircina,* Ham.; Fl. Br. Ind. ii. 236; Brandis For. Flora 151, ; Gamble Man. Ind. Timb. 255.

A small tree; young parts ferruginous-tomentose. *Leaves* 6-10 in. long. *Leaflets* 17-25, 1-1·5 by ·6-·9 in., ovate or elliptic, emarginate or rounded at the tip, rather membranous, clothed with very minute grey hairs. *Flowers* about ·25 in. long, in short congested axillary corymbose panicles, 1-2 in. long. *Calyx* about ·1 in. long, densely pubescent. *Standard* obovate, ·12 in. broad, gradually narrowed into a claw. *Stamens* 10, equally 2-adelphous. *Ovary* hairy. *Pod* 1-1·5 by ·2-·3 in., 1-3-seeded, but less frequently 1-seeded than in the last two species.

OUTER HIMALAYA, *e.g.*, Málkōt, Sahansra-dhárá, below Mussoorie, etc.; also in TEHRI-GARHWAL, up to 5,500 ft.

Fl. Apr., May. Fr. July, Aug.

D. paniculata, Roxb., Fl. Br. Ind. ii, 236, is a tree which has leaves and pods exactly like those of *D. lanceolaria,* but the panicles are much smaller. The wood is of a curious structure, consisting of thin layers of fibrous tissue, resembling the inner bark, alternating with masses of white wood. The tree is very scarce in our region having been only once found in the E. SAHÁRANPUR SIWALIKS by the late Mr. N. Hearle.

20. Sophora, Linn.; G. P. n. 273.

1. **S. mollis,** Grah.; Fl. Br. Ind. ii. 251; Brandis For. Flora 132, Ind. Trees 244; Gamble Man. Ind. Timb. 264. Vern. *Sákiná,* Garhwal,—a name also applied to all shrubby *Indigoferas,* which it somewhat resembles in foliage.

A low shrub with grey-downy branches; bark dark-grey. *Leaves* imparipinnate, 4-6 in. long. *Leaflets* 21-35, ·5-1 in. long, elliptic, obtuse, emarginate, subcoriaceous, grey-green, finely grey-downy, prominently veined. *Racemes* 2-4 in. long, axillary, ascending. *Flowers* about 1 in. long, yellow, developed before the leaves.

Calyx ·15-·2 in. long, oblique, grey-downy. *Corolla* ·6-·8 in. long; petals equal in length, clawed; standard broad. *Stamens* free; anthers versatile. *Ovary* stalked, many-ovuled; style incurved. *Pod* 3-4 in. long, 4-6 seeded, slightly pubescent when young, glabrous when mature, distantly moniliform; joints with 4 crustaceous wings, two along each suture; seeds brown, hard, shining.

Sahansra-dhárá and probably also in similar other localities in the OUTER HIMALAYA.

The wood is used for fuel, and the leaves and twigs for fodder.

Fl. Mar., Apr. when leafless. Fr. Rainy season.

The following plants of this SUB-ORDER deserve mention :—

1. *Æschynomene aspera*, Linn.; Fl. Br. Ind. ii. 152; Brandis Ind. Trees 224. The Sola plant. Vern. *Sola*, Hind. *Stem* erect, full of white pith-like light wood, 5-6 ft. high, 1-1·5 in. diam. *Leaves* imparipinnate; leaflets very small, numerous. *Flowers* yellow, about ·7 in. long. *Pod* 2-2·5 by ·3 in., long-stalked, with 3-6 separating joints. Found in swamps in the Pathri Forest. The so-called pith is made into hats and is used as floats by fishermen. Fl. Rainy season. Fr. Nov., Dec.—*G. P. n.* 159.

2. *Uraria picta*, Desv.; Fl. Br. Ind. ii. 155. A little-branched erect perennial, 3-6 ft. high. *Leaves* paripinnate; leaflets 4-8 by ·2-1 in., strongly net-veined beneath. *Flowers* small, in a dense cylindrical terminal raceme about a foot long. *Pod* twisted, of 3-6 white polished indehiscent but separating joints. Found about DEHRA DÚN and the OUTER HIMALAYA.—*G. P. n. 174.*

3. *Uraria lagopus*, DC.; Fl. Br. Ind. ii. 156;—has also been found in the same localities. *Leaves* 1- and 3-foliolate; leaflets 2-4 by 1·5-2 in., oblong, subcoriaceous, strongly net-veined. *Racemes* long, both axillary and terminal; pedicels woolly. *Joints* 2-6, dark or pale.

4. *Uraria hamosa*. Wall.; Fl. Br. Ind. ii. 156;—is an undershrub somewhat resembling a *Desmodium*. *Leaves* 1-3-foliolate; leaflets 3-5 by 2-3 in., oblong. *Racemes* 6-12 in. long, lax; bracts cuspidate. *Corolla* about ·4 in. long, much exceeding the calyx. *Joints* 4-6, opaque. Found in swampy places in the DÚN, *e.g.*, Nakraunda.

5. *Alysicarpus vaginalis*, DC.; Fl. Br. Ind. ii. 158. A little-branched erect undershrub, 1-4 ft. high. *Leaves* simple or 3-foliolate; leaflets ·5-2 in. long, broad or very narrow. *Calyx* about ·12

in. long; corolla included. *Pod* ·5-·7 in. long, terete; joints indehiscent. Found at Lachiwála in the DÚN.—*G. P. n. 176.*

6. *Shuteria vestita*, W. &, A.; Fl. Br. Ind. ii. 181. A slender climber with pinnately 3-foliolate leaves; leaflets 1-2 in. long, obovate-oblong, glabrescent. *Flowers* reddish, ·3-·4 in. long, in axillary racemes, 1-4 in. long. *Pod* 1-1·5 in., linear, flat, recurved, 5-6-seeded. Found in the HILLS, up to 6,000 ft.; Málkōt, Korwá Forest, etc.—*G. P. n. 195.*

7. *Atylosia mollis*, Benth.; Fl. Br. Ind. ii. 213. Vern. *Ban Sem*, Garhwal. A middle-sized twining shrub; young parts inflorescence and leaves beneath densely grey- or rusty-tomentose. *Leaves* 3-foliolate; leaflets 1·5-3·5 in. long, roundish-obovate, cuspidate, stipellate. *Flowers* ·6-·8 in. long, yellow, in lax racemes; calyx grey-downy, half the length of the flower. *Pod* 1-2 by ·4 in., 4-9-seeded, with transverse lines between the seeds. Common throughout the DÚN and OUTER HIMALAYA, and also along the foot of the SAHÁRANPUR SIWALIKS. Fl. Dec., Jan, Fr. Mar., Apr.—*G. P. n. 231.*

8. *Atylosia scarabæoides*. Benth.; Fl. Br. Ind. ii. 215;—is a twining biennial found in ráu-beds in the SIWALIK TRACT. *Leaves* 3-foliolate; leaflets 1·5 in. long, obovate-oblong, subcoriaceous, densely grey-downy beneath. *Flowers* 2-6 on a short peduncle, about ·5 in. long, yellow; corolla about 3-times the length of the calyx. *Pod* about 1 by ·25 in., 4-6-seeded, densely grey-silky.

SUB-FAMILY II. *CÆSALPINIEÆ.*

Mostly trees or shrubs. *Leaves* abruptly pinnate or bipinnate, sometimes 2-foliolate or simple and 2-lobed; leaflets rarely stipellate. *Flowers* 2-sexual, generally irregular. *Calyx* divided to or nearly to the base; lobes usually 5, rarely valvate, generally concave. *Petals* 5, imbricate, quite free, slightly unequal, the upper or odd petal innermost. *Stamens* normally 10, usually free, often declinate; anthers large. *Pod* often indehiscent. *Seeds* sometimes albuminous.

Analysis of the Genera.

Leaves bipinnate; petals 5 . . . . . 1. CÆSALPINIA.
Leaves pinnate.
  Petals 5; stamens free, generally all perfect 2. CASSIA.
  Petals 3; stamens monadelphous, only 3 perfect . . . . 3. TAMARINDUS.
Leaves simple, 2-lobed; petals 5 . . . 4. BAUHINIA.

1. Cæsalpinia, Linn.; G. P. n. 308.

Trees, erect shrubs, or prickly climbers. *Leaves* abruptly bipinnate. *Flowers* showy, yellow, in axillary or terminal racemes, the latter often corymbose. *Calyx-lobes* 5, imbricate, hood-shaped, many times larger than the tube, the lowest largest. *Petals* 5, usually clawed, the uppermost smaller than the others. *Stamens* 10, free, declinate; anthers versatile. *Ovary* sessile few-ovuled; style filiform. *Pod* various.

Analysis of the Species.

Pod armed with wiry prickles . . 1. *C. Bonducella.*
Pod not armed, quite smooth . . 2. *C. sepiaria.*

1. **C. Bonducella,** Fleming; Fl. Br. Ind. ii. 254; Brandis For. Flora 156, Ind. Trees 246; Gamble Man. Ind. Timb. 267. Vern. *Káth Karanj,* Hind.

A scandent prickly shurb. *Leaves* over a foot long; pinnæ 6-8 pairs, 3-8 in. long; stipules large, 2-fid; rachis and its branches armed with recurved prickles. *Leaflets* 6-10 pairs on each pinna, opposite, ·7-1 by ·4-·6 in., oblong or elliptic, obtuse, mucronate, membranous, downy beneath, minutely petioluled. *Racemes* 6-12 in. long, gradually denser towards the top; pedicels ·2-·3 in., downy; bracts ·5 in. long, linear-lanceolate, generally recurved at the tip, exceeding the flower-buds. *Calyx* ·2-·3 in. long, finely rusty-tomentose. *Petals* ·4-·5 in. long, oblanceolate, yellow, the smallest sometimes spotted with red. *Pod* 2-3 by 1·5-2 in., coriaceous, dehiscent, thickly beset with sharp wiry prickles ·2-·3 in. long. *Seeds* 2-3, ·7 in. long, globose or ovoid, shining, lead-coloured, with numerous very fine horizontal cracks when dry.

SAHÁRANPUR and the DÚN, generally in abandoned village sites or in hedges; Sháhjahánpur; Dúdhli, Tháno, Khairi, etc. Also at Kálsi in JAUNSAR.

The tender shoots and seeds which are known as fever-nuts in some parts are used medicinally, the farina of the cotyledons, which is white and very bitter, being considered a good substitute for quinine. It makes an effective hedge-plant.

Fl. Aug., Sept. Fr. Cold season.

2. **C. sepiaria,** Roxb.; Fl. Br. Ind. ii. 256; Brandis For. Flora 156, Ind. Trees 246; Gamble Man. Ind. Timb. 267, The Mysore-thorn. Vern. *Álai*, Dún; *Ári*, Jaunsar; *Karanj*, Hind.

A large prickly climber, pubescent or downy; prickles strong, recurved or less frequently curved upwards. *Leaves* 9-16 in. long; pinnæ 6-10 pairs, 2-4 in. long; stipules semisagittate, deciduous. *Leaflets* 8-12 pairs on each pinna, opposite, ·6-·8 by ·2-·4 in., oblong, very obtuse, green and glabrous above, glaucous beneath, minutely petioluled. *Racemes* simple, about 1 ft. long; pedicels ·7-1 in. long, jointed at the top; bracts lanceolate, rusty-tomentose. *Calyx* pale-yellow, about ·5 in. long, deeply 5-lobed, pubescent or tomentose. *Petals* ·5-·7 in. long, bright-yellow. *Stamens* ·5 in. long, exserted; filaments thickened and woolly at the base. *Pod* 2·5-4 by about 1 in., somewhat woody, glabrous, obliquely cuspidate, tardily dehiscent. *Seeds* 4-8, ovoid, ·4 in. long, rather compressed, smooth, mottled brown and black.

Common in swampy localities in the DÚN, and also in ravines in JAUNSAR and TEHRI-GARHWAL, ascending to 6,000 ft.—Nakraunda, Jogiwála, Bagúr Block near Kathián, Tons Valley, etc.

It is an excellent hedge-plant. The bark is astringent and may be used for tanning.

Fl. Mar.-June. Fr. Rainy season.

2. Cassia, Linn.; G. P. n. 326.

1. **C. Fistula,** Linn.; Fl. Br. Ind. ii. 261; Brandis For. Flora. 164, Ind. Trees 253; Gamble Man. Ind. Timb. 271. Vern. *Ámaltás* Hind.; *Királa*, Dún; *Sinára*, Garhwal.

A moderate-sized tree, wholly glabrous; bark greenish-grey, smooth up to middle age. *Leaves* paripinnate, 1-2 ft. long; rachis terete. *Leaflets* 4-8 pairs, 3-6 by 2-3 in., ovate or ovate-oblong, subcoriaceous, acuminate, entire; lateral nerves parallel, numerous.

Flowers bright-yellow, in thyrsoid pendulous axillary racemes 12-18 in. long; pedicels ·3-1 in., gradually longer towards the base of the raceme. *Calyx* ·2-·4 in. long, glabrous, caducous. *Petals* ·8-1 in. long, shortly clawed, nearly equal. *Stamens* of 3 kinds,—3 about 1 in. long behind the ovary with large oblong anthers, 4-6 about ·4 in. long in front of the ovary with diverging anther cells, the remaining 3-1 shorter and more slender being staminodes with indehiscent anthers; anthers of fertile stamens open by terminal pores. *Ovary* shortly stipitate; style incurved; stigma terminal. *Pod* up to 2 ft. long, 1 in. diam., cylindrical, smooth, hard, indehiscent, dark-brown when fully ripe, obscurely transversely ribbed and transversely fragile, septate into numerous 1-seeded cells. *Seeds* about ·4 in. diam., compressed, albuminous, parallel with the septa.

Common throughout the DÚN and SAHÁRANPUR FORESTS; also found in low valleys up to 4,000 ft. in JAUNSAR and TEHRI-GARHWAL, *e.g.*, Ámláwa Valley up to Saiá.

The heartwood is yellowish or brick-red, tough, very hard and extremely durable, excellent for posts, carts and agricultural implements; weight about 60 lbs. per c. ft. The dark-brown sweetish pulp of the ripe fruit is a strong purgative, and is an ingredient of spiced native tobacco. The gum exuded by the bark is astringent. The bark is used for tanning and dyeing. The twigs are often lopped for cattle fodder. It is a very handsome tree, and is often cultivated for ornament.

Scarcely ever wholly leafless. New leaves and fl. Apr.-July. Fr. Cold season.

The following smaller plants belong to this Genus :—

1. *C. occidentalis*, Linn.; Fl. Br. Ind. ii. 262. Vern. *Chakunda*, Hind. A diffuse undershrub. *Leaflets* 2-4 by ·6-1·3 in., elliptic-lanceolate, acuminate. *Flowers* ·5-·7 in. diam.; petals yellow with reddish veins. *Pod* 3 by ·4 in., compressed, glabrous. A weed common in blanks and along forest roads, especially in the DÚN.

2. *C. Tora*, Linn.; Fl. Br. Ind. ii. 263. Vern. *Panwár*, Dún. A gregarious annual with a whitish stem. *Leaflets* about 3 pairs, 1-1·7 by ·7-1·3 in., obovate, mucronate. *Flowers* ·4 in. diam., orange-yellow; sepals concave. *Pod* 6-9 by ·15 in., tapering, curved, flexuose; seeds truncately cylindrical, about ·2 in. long, length parallel to the sutures. A common weed in blanks and about villages in the DÚN and in SAHÁRANPUR. Fl. July, Aug. Fr. Oct.-Dec.

3. *C. mimosoides*, Linn.; Fl. Br. Ind. ii. 266. A diffuse perennial. *Leaflets* very numerous, ·5 by ·1 in., linear-oblong, acuminate. *Flowers* yellow, ·3 in. long, in 2-3-flowered axillary racemes. *Pod* flat, 2-2·5 by ·2 in., 10-14-seeded. DÚN,—Ráipur, Rámgarh, Lachiwála, etc. Fl. July, Aug. Fr. Sept.-Nov.

3. Tamarindus, Linn.; G. P. n. 348.

1. **T. indica,** Linn.; Fl. Br. Ind. ii. 273; Brandis For. Flora 163, Ind. Trees 252; Gamble Man. Ind. Timb. 278. The Tamarind tree. Vern. *Imli*, *Ámli*, Hind.

A large unarmed tree; bark dark-grey, with longitudinal fissures. *Leaves* abruptly pinnate; rachis 2-5 in. long; stipules small, caducous. *Leaflets* 10-20 pairs, opposite, ·5-·7 by ·15-·2 in., linear-oblong, obtuse, often emarginate, subcoriaceous, glabrescent, very minutely petioluled, with intramarginal nerves. *Flowers* in few-flowered lax sub-terminal racemes. *Calyx-tube* turbinate; teeth lanceolate, the two lowest connate. *Petals* only the 3 upper developed which are ·4-·6 in. long, pale-white, variegated with red stripes, the middle one hooded, the two lower reduced to scales. *Stamens* only 3 perfect, monadelphous, the others reduced to bristles: anthers versatile. *Ovary* stipitate, the stalk adnate to the calyx-tube; ovules many; stigma capitate. *Pod* 3-8 by ·8-1 in., oblong, slightly compressed, usually falcate, many-seeded, indehiscent, with a crustaceous brittle epicarp which ultimately cracks irregularly; sutures indistinct. *Seeds* ·5 in. diam., compressed, with a dark-brown or black hard shining smooth testa, embedded in a brown pulpy mesocarp.

Cultivated throughout the DÚN and SAHÁRANPUR DISTRICTS for its fruit; almost wild towards Hardwar.

Sapwood yellowish-white, hard and close-grained. Very old trees produce a scanty ebony-like dark purplish-brown heartwood which is very durable; annual rings indistinct; weight about 75 lbs. per c. ft. Wood highly prized though extremely difficult to work. "It is used for wheels, mallets, planes, rice-pounders, oil and sugar mills and is an excellent wood for turning."—*Sir D. Brandis.* The fruit is an article of food and is also used in medicine. The leaves make an agreeable curry, and the inner substance of the seeds ground into paste gives a strong cement which is much used by book-binders.

Fl. May, June. Fr. Mar., Apr., *i.e.*, 10-11 months after flowering.

4. Bauhinia, Linn.; G. P. n. 333.

Trees, shrubs or climbers. *Leaves* simple, more or less distinctly 2-lobed, palmately nerved. *Flowers* white pink or purple, in simple or panicled racemes. *Calyx* gamosepalous, turbinate or tubular; limb 5-cleft, or split on one side (spathaceous) and minutely 5-toothed at the apex. *Petals* 5, sub-equal, usually clawed. *Stamens* 10, free, all or 3-5 perfect, the others rudimentary or absent; anthers versatile. *Ovary* stalked, many-ovuled. *Pod* linear or oblong, flat, dehiscent or indehiscent. *Seeds* albuminous.

Analysis of the Species.

Fertile stamens 10; pod indehiscent.
  Leaves not acid; calyx spathaceous; pod rigid, falcate . . . . . . 1. *B. racemosa.*
  Leaves acid; calyx 5-cleft; pod flexible, straight . . . . 2. *B. malabarica.*
Fertile stamens 3-4, rarely 5; pod dehiscent.
  Lvs. cleft only at the tip or not cleft at all 3. *B. retusa.*
  Lvs. deeply cleft.
    A climber. Lvs. often broader than long 4. *B. Vahlii.*
    Trees. Leaves as long as broad.
      Leaves cleft nearly half way down; calyx-tube shorter than the limb. 5. *B. purpurea.*
      Leaves cleft scarcely through a third of their length; calyx-tube as long as the limb . . . . 6. *B. variegata.*

1. **B. racemosa,** Lam.; Fl. Br. Ind. ii. 276; Brandis For. Flora 159, Ind. Trees 256; Gamble Man. Ind. Timb. 281. Vern. *Jhanjhorá, Jhinjhorá,* Dún and Sahháranpur; *Pápri,* Saháranpur.

A small deciduous tree; bark dark bluish-brown, rough, with numerous deep vertical cracks. *Leaves* broader than long, ·8-2 by 1·3 in., cleft nearly half way down, 7-9-nerved, slightly cordate, coriaceous, grey-pubescent beneath; petiole ·5-·7 in. long. *Raceme* 3-5 in. long, terminal and leaf-opposed; rachis downy. *Flowers* pale-white, about ·5 in. long, on short pedicels; buds oblanceolate, pointed at the tip; bracts subulate, deciduous. *Calyx-tube* about ·1 in. long; limb about three times as long, entire, 5-toothed, at length reflexed. *Petals* oblanceolate, as long as the calyx-limb. *Stamens* 10, all perfect, united at the base. *Stigma* sessile. *Pod* 5-8 by ·7-1 in., sometimes longer, turgid, rigid, falcate, 12-20-seeded, glabrous, irregularly reticulate outside.

Common in blanks and the drier parts of forests in SAHÁRANPUR and the DÚN.

Wood light-brown, hard, weighing 50 lbs. per c. ft. It is fairly good, but not used except for fuel. The fibre of the bark is used to make ropes.

Fl. Mar.-June. Fr. Cold season.

2. **B. malabarica,** Roxb.; Fl. Br. Ind. ii. 277; Brandis For. Flora 159, Ind. Trees 256; Gamble Man. Ind. Timb. 282. Vern. *Ámli*, Hind.; *Khat Pápri*, Saháranpur; *Khatta Jhanjhorá* or *Jhinjhorá, Imli*, Dún; *Khatuá*, Garhwal.

A moderate-sized deciduous tree; bark dark-brown, exfóliating in thin long strips, fibrous, red inside. *Leaves* acid, broader than long, 1·5-4 by 2-5 in., cleft through about a third of the length, 7-9-nerved, slightly cordate, coriaceous, glabrate and glaucous beneath; petiole ·8-1·2 in. long, rusty-pubescent. *Racemes* axillary, sessile, 1·5-2 in. long, often 2-3 together. *Flowers* ·5 in. long, dull-white, on very slender pedicels which are 1 in. long; buds obovoid, rounded at the tip. *Calyx* brown-tomentose; tube ·15 in. long; limb slightly longer, 5-cleft. *Petals* equal, spathulate, ·4-·5 in. long. *Stamens* 10, all perfect, alternately longer and shorter, slightly united at the base. *Style* produced. *Pod* 7-12 by ·7-1 in., on a stalk 1 in. long, flat, flexible, many-seeded, more or less straight, gradually tapering to the tip, marked with regular reticulate veins which, starting diagonally from both sutures, meet in the middle.

Common in the DÚN and SAHÁRANPUR FORESTS, especially in the Sál areas.

Wood light reddish-brown, coarse-grained; weight 48 lbs. per c. ft. It is never used, except for fuel. The acid leaves are eaten.

Fl. Aug.-Oct. Fr. Jan.-May.

3. **B. retusa,** Ham.; Fl. Br. Ind. ii. 279; Brandis For. Flora 161, Ind. Trees 257; Gamble Man. Ind. Timb. 282. Vern. *Semla*, Hind.

A moderate-sized tree; individuals that escape tapping attaining a fairly large size; bark dark-brown, with a few shallow vertical cracks, but usually much disfigured by the diagonal cuts that are made to tap its gum. *Leaves* 4-6 in. diam., rather broader than long, entire or cleft only at the tip, cordate or truncate, 9-11-nerved, coriaceous, more or less pubescent beneath; petiole 1·5-3·5 in. long. *Flowers* ·5 in. long, in large corymbosely branched terminal panicles; buds ovoid-globose. *Calyx* ·2-·3 in. long, split into 2-3 sections nearly to the base. *Petals* ·3-·4 in. long, obovate, yellow, with red spots and purple veins, clawed, pubescent. *Stamens* only 3 perfect. *Ovary* hairy below; stipe adnate to the calyx-tube; style produced; stigma large. *Pod* 4-7 by 1·2-1·5 in., flat, oblanceolate, deep-red until ripe, glabrous, hard, tardily dehiscent; seeds flat, about ·5 in. diam., dark-brown, smooth.

Fairly common in the SIWALIK TRACT and in places in the OUTER HIMALAYA: Málkōt, Paléd, Bindál-nálá near Dehra, Timli Pass, Sháhjahánpur Ráu, etc.

Wood reddish-white, hard, close-grained; weight 58 lbs. per c. ft. It is not used. A clear gum resembling gum-arabic is collected by making cuts in the bark, and is largely exported from the Dún. It is used in medicine, and in the manufacture of sweetmeats.

Fl. Sept.-Nov. *Fr.* Feb., Mar.

4. **B. Vahlii,** W. & A.; *Fl. Br. Ind.* ii. 279; Brandis For. Flora 161, Ind. Trees 258; Gamble Man. Ind. Timb. 283. Vern. *Máljhan*, *Málo*, Hind.

A gigantic evergreen climber; branchlets often terminating in a pair of revolute tendrils; young branches, petioles and leaves beneath, especially along the nerves, densely rusty- or grey-velvety. *Leaves* very variable in size, often up to 18 in. across, as broad as long or broader, deeply cordate, 11-15-nerved, cleft through about a third of the length, sub-coriaceous, drak-green and glabrescent above, more or less downy beneath; lobes obtuse, rounded; petiole 3-6 in. long, stout. *Flowers* white, in terminal corymbs or corymbose racemes; pedicels 1-2·5 in. long, slender, with a lanceolate caducous bract at the base and a pair of small bracteoles above the middle, all densely woolly. *Calyx-tube* ·2-·3 in. long; limb ·6-1 in. long, splitting into two lobes, densely rusty-tomentose. *Petals* 1-1·7 in. long, obovate, shortly clawed, white-canescent outside along the middle. *Stamens* 3. *Ovary* hairy, adnate to the calyx-tube. *Pod* 9-12 by 2-3 in., flat, woody, rusty-velvety. *Seeds* 8-12, about 1 in. diam., flat.

Common in the DÚN and SAHÁRANPUR FORESTS, especially in moist localities and shady hill-slopes; also in the OUTER HIMALAYA, up to 3,000 ft.

It often attains an enormous size, stems 4-5 ft. in girth not being uncommon. There is a famous climber on the left bank of the Kasumri Ráu above the temples which measured 6 ft. 7 in. in girth in January 1899. The stem consists of a mass of phloëm tissue which is traversed by strands of xylem of various thicknesses round the pith, together presenting a beautiful floral design on a transverse section. "Its large flat leaves are sewn together and used as plates, cups, rough table-cloths, umbrellas and rain caps; its pod is roasted and the seeds eaten; its bark is made into rough ropes."—*Mr. J. S. Gamble.* It is, however, one of the greatest enemies of forest trees, and every attempt is made to exterminate it where possible.

Fl. Apr.-June. Fr. Cold season.

5. **B. purpurea,** Linn.; Fl. Br. Ind. ii. 284; Brandis For. Flora. 160, Ind. Trees 258; Gamble Man. Ind. Timb. 283. Vern. *Khairwál*, Dún; *Khairwál Pápri*, Sahàranpur; *Guirál*, Garhwal.

A moderate-sized tree; bark ash-coloured or dark-brown; young parts covered with brown pubescence. *Leaves* 3-6 in. long, rather longer than broad, 9-11-nerved, cordate, less frequently truncate, coriaceous, cleft about half-way down; lobes usually subacute, sometimes overlapping at the inner margins; petiole 1-1·5 in. long. *Flowers* deep-rose, in paniculate or corymbose recemes; pedicles ·2-·5 in. long, tomentose; buds obovoid or oblong, acute, strongly 5-ribbed. *Calyx-tube* ·3-·4 in. long; limb nearly twice as long, slit on one side, 5-toothed at the apex. *Petals* reddish, 1·5-2 in. long, oblanceolate, clawed, with a distinct midrib and fine straight lateral veins. *Stamens* usually 3 fertile, slightly shorter than the petals; staminodes filiform, of varying lengths. *Ovary* long-stalked; style long; stigma large, oblique. *Pod* 6-10 by ·6-·8 in., on a tomentose stipe ·6-1 in. long, thick, pointed, slightly falcate, greenish-purple, pubescent along the sutures, late in dehiscing; seeds 12-15.

Common in the SAHÁRANPUR SIWALIKS; also found in the DÚN and in the Tons Valley in JAUNSAR.

The heartwood is of a reddish-brown colour, moderately hard, fairly close-grained; weight about 50 lbs. per c. ft. It is used for agricultural implements and in construction. The bark is used for tanning, the leaves are lopped for cattle and camel fodder, and the flower-buds are eaten cooked or pickled. Often cultivated for its flower.

Fl. Sept.-Nov. Fr. Jan.-Mar.

6. **B. variegata,** Linn.; Fl. Br. Ind. ii. 284; Brandis For. Flora 160, Ind. Trees 258; Gamble Man. Ind. Timb. 284. Vern. *Kachnár*, Dún; *Goriáo*, Jaunsar.

A fairly large tree, closely resembling the last species. *Leaves* 4-6 in. long, as broad as long or sometimes broader, usually deeply cordate, 11-15-nerved, sub-coriaceous, cleft through about a quarter; lobes obtuse; petiole 1-1·5 in. *Flowers* large, fragrant, sessile or shortly pedicelled, in few flowered lateral corymbs. *Calyx-tube* ·5-1·2 in. long, slender; limb spathaceous, as long as the tube, 5-toothed at the apex, pubescent outside. *Petals* about 2 in. long, obovate or oblong, generally four white and one red, with a strong midrib and red or purple lateral veins radiating from near the base. *Fertile stamens* 5, rarely 3 or 4. *Ovary* long-stalked; style long; stigma minute. *Pod* 6-10 by ·7-·9 in., hard, flat, glabrous, slightly falcate, dehiscent; seeds 10-15.

Occurring in the same localities as the last species, but is more common in the DÚN and in valleys in the HILLS, *e.g.*, Amláwa and Tons Valleys.

Wood grey, moderately hard; weight 42 lbs. per c. ft. Economic uses as of the last species.

Fl. Feb.-Apr. when leafless. Fr. Rainy season.

SUB-FAMILY III. *MIMOSEÆ.*

Usually trees or shrubs. *Leaves* abruptly bipinnate. *Flowers* regular, minute, in heads or spikes. *Sepals* 5, usually combined, valvate. *Petals* 5, equal, more or less connate, valvate. *Stamens* definite or indefinite, hypogynous, generally much exserted; anthers small. *Pod* various. *Seeds* without albumen.

Analysis of the Genera.

Joints of pod separating; stamens 8-10, free . 1. MIMOSA.
Joints of pod not separating; stamens indefinite.
 Armed.* Stamens free . . . . . 2. ACACIA.
 Unarmed. Stamens more or less connate . 3. ALBIZZIA.

---

* Some Australian Acacias are not armed.

Mimosa, Linn.; G. P. n. 387.

1. **M. rubicaulis,** Lam.; Fl. Br. Ind. ii. 291; Brandis For. Flora 172, Ind. Trees, 263; Gamble Man. Ind. Timb. 290. Vern. *Áláy,* Dún; *Ál,* Sahāranpur.

A straggling prickly shrub; young branches red (whence the specific name), closely ribbed, thickly beset with short recurved prickles. *Leaves* 4-6 in. long, with prickly rachis; pinnæ usually opposite, 4-10 pairs, 1-1·5 in. long, not armed. *Leaflets* 12-28 on each pinna, ·15-·3 in. long, oblong, unequal-sided, caducous. *Flowers* tetramerous, red to white, in globose heads which are ·4-·6 in. across; peduncles 1-2 in. long. *Calyx* campanulate, shortly toothed. *Petals* ·04 in. long, connate at the base. *Stamens* usually 10, exserted. *Pod* 3-4 by ·4 in., linear-oblong, 5-10-seeded, slightly falcate, glabrous; joints square, separating from the sutures before dehiscing.

Common in grass-lands and fallows in the DÚN and in ráu-beds in the SAHÁRANPUR SIWALIKS. Also found in valleys in the HILLS up to 5,000 ft.

Heartwood red, hard; weight 40-50 lbs. per c. ft. It can be used for tent-pegs and such other purposes.

Fl. July-Sept. Fr. Nov.-Jan.

M. pudica, Linn.; Fl. Br. Ind. ii. 291,—the well known Sensitive plant, Vern. *Lájwanti,* Hind.;—is cultivated and also found wild in waste lands in the DÚN. *Rachis* 1-1·5 in. long. *Pinnæ* 1·5-2 in. long, approximate at the end of the rachis and spreading to look like digitate, very sensitive. *Leaflets* ·2-·3 in. long, sensitive. *Flower-heads* long-peduncled. *Pod* ·5-·8 in. long, with densely-prickly sutures. Fl. Aug., Sept. Fr. Nov., Dec.

2. Acacia, Willd.; G. P. n. 391.

Erect or climbing shrubs or trees, armed with stipular spines and prickles (in India). *Leaves* bipinnate; leaflets minute. *Flowers* yellow or white, hermaphrodite or polygamous, in globose heads or cylindrical spikes. *Calyx* campanulate, short-toothed. *Petals* valvate, more or less connate towards the base. *Stamens* indefinite, free, much exserted; anthers minute. *Pod* dry or fleshy, dehiscent or indehiscent; seeds compressed.

Analysis of the Species.

Trees or erect shrubs.
- Flowers in axillary globose heads; spines straight.
  - Pod short, cylindrical; seeds in two rows. 1. *A. Farnesiana.*
  - Pod long, not cylindrical; seeds in one row.
    - Pod convex, downy, deeply indented between the seeds . . . 2. *A. arabica.*
    - Pod flat, glabrous, slightly contracted between the seeds . . . 3. *A. eburnea.*
- Flowers in axillary cylindrical spikes; spines recurved . . . . . 4. *A. Catechu.*

Climbing shrubs. (Flowers in copiously panicled globose heads).
- Pod succulent, thick . . . . . 5. *A. concinna.*
- Pod dry, thin.
  - Leaflets ·5 by ·15 in., few; stem fluted . 6. *A. Intsia.*
  - Leaflets ·3 by ·05 in., numerous; stem not fluted . . . . . . 7. *A. pennata.*

1. **A. Farnesiana,** Willd.; Fl. Br. Ind. ii.; 292 Brandis For. Flora 180, Ind. Trees 263; Gamble Man. Ind. Timb. 292. Vern. *Waláyti Kikar,* Hind.

A thorny shrub, 12-15 ft. high, with dark-brown smooth bark; branches marked with grey dots and armed with stipular spines ·3-·5 in. long. *Leaf-rachises* 1·5-2 in. long, downy; pinnæ 4-8 pairs, 1-1·5 in. long. *Leaflets* 20-40 on each pinna, very small, rigid. *Flowers* bright-yellow, exceedingly sweet-scented, in globose heads which are ·4-·6 in. diam.; peduncles ·5-·8 in. long, slender, crowded in the axils of the leaves, with a whorl of bracts at the apex. *Calyx* and *corolla* 5-toothed. *Pod* 2-3 by ·5 in., cylindrical, turgid, dark-brown, with a double row of seeds.

It is a native of tropical America and is, no doubt, introduced, but is quite wild now in the DÚN and SAHÁRANPUR DISTRICTS, *e.g.*, beds of the Suswá river; Pathri Forest; Barkalá, etc. Also cultivated in gardens for its flower.

Wood white, hard, close-grained; weight about 50 lbs. per c. ft. An excellent perfume is extracted from the flower.

Fl. Jan.-Mar. Fr. June, July, but remains long on the plant.

2. **A. arabica,** Willd.; Fl. Br. Ind. ii. 293; Brandis For. Flora 180, Ind. Trees 264; Gamble Man. Ind. Timb. 292. Vern. *Babul,* Hind.; *Kikar,* Sahéranpur and the Punjab.

A moderate-sized tree with a large spreading crown; bark dark-brown, almost black, much fissured; spines ·5-2 in. long, straight, white, sharply pointed. *Leaves* 1-2 in. long; rachis and pinnæ downy; pinnæ 3-6 pairs, ·5-1·2 in. long, with several glands at their insertions. *Leaflets* 10-20 pairs. ·1-·2 in. long, linear, glabrous. *Flowers* yellow, fragrant, in axillary globose heads which are about ·5 in. diam.; peduncles in fasciles of 3-5, short, slender, grey-downy, with a whorl of bracts above the middle. *Calyx* cup-shaped, ·04 in. long. *Corolla* twice the length of the calyx. *Pod* generally solitary, 4-6 by ·5-·6 in., 8-12-seeded, stalked, convex, rather fleshy, deeply indented between the seeds, densely grey-downy, tardily dehiscent.

Cultivated in the SAHÁRANPUR DISTRICT, and apparently self-sown in many places, *e.g.*, at Ránipur, Jawálapur, Tirá, etc.

Sapwood large, whitish; heartwood becoming reddish or dark brown on exposure; weight about 55 lbs. per c. ft. The latter is hard and very durable, and is used for wheels, well-curbs, sugar- and oil-presses, rice-pounders and for ploughs and other agricultural implements. The gum is readily soluble in water and is largely collected and used for various purposes. The pod is a favourite food for cattle, sheep and goats, and is very rich in tannin before ripening.

Fl. Rainy season. Fr. Cold season.

3. **A. eburnea,** Willd.; Fl. Br. Ind. ii. 293; Brandis For. Flora 183, Ind. Trees 264; Gamble Man. Ind. Timb. 294. Vern. *Pahári Kikar*, Sahâranpur; *Kikar*, Dún.

A small deciduous tree with rough dark-grey bark; spines straight, generally dark-brown and about ·5 in. long, the larger ones white and up to 2 in. long. *Leaves* 1-1·5 in. long; pinnæ usually 4 pairs, ·3-·5 in. long, the uppermost pair with a large gland at the insertion besides often a second one below the lowest pair. *Leaflets* 8-12 pairs, about ·1 in. long, oblong. *Flowers* pale-yellow, in axillary globose heads about ·5 in. diam.; peduncles 1 in. long, filiform, with an involucre of connate bracts about ·3 in. from the base. *Calyx* funnel-shaped, ·04 in. long. *Corolla* about twice the length of the calyx. *Pod* 2-4 on the same peduncle, 3-6 by ·25 in., narrow-linear, flat, stalked, rigidly coriaceous, glabrous, shining, slightly contracted between the seeds.

Common in the SAHÁRANPUR SIWALIKS, generally in beds of ráus, where it is associated with Khair. Also found in the DÚN, *e.g.*, at Sáhanspur and Dharmawála.

Wood yellowish-white, extremely hard, splitting in drying; weight 52 lbs. per c. ft. It is used chiefly as fuel, especially for lime-burning.

Fl. Cold season, rarely Mar., Apr. Fr. about 4 months after flowering, generally Apr., May.

4. **A. Catechu,** Willd.; Fl. Br. Ind. ii. 295; Brandis For. Flora 186; Gamble Man. Ind. Timb. 292. Vern. *Khair*, Hind.

A moderate-sized tree with thorny branches; stipular spines in pairs, short and recurved, shining-brown or nearly black; bark rough, dark-grey or ash-coloured, exfoliating in long narrow rectangular flakes. *Leaves* 4-7 in. long; rachis prickly and with 4-5 glands; pinnæ 20-60, 1-1·3 in. long. *Leaflets* 60-100 on each pinna, about ·15 in. long, ligulate. *Flowers* pale-yellow or cream-coloured, in lax axillary cylindrical spikes which are 3-4 by ·4 in.; peduncle ·5-·7 in. *Calyx* about ·04 in. long, grey-tomentose. *Corolla* two to three times longer than the calyx. *Stamens* numerous, much exserted. *Pod* 2-3·5 by ·5-·6 in., on a stalk ·2-·3 in. long, straight, flat, dry, dark-brown, shining, 5-6-seeded. *Seeds* ·2 in. diam., orbicular, flat, dark-brown.

Common in the DÚN and the SAHÁRANPUR SIWALIKS, generally in ráu-beds, either pure or mixed with Sissu; occasionally also in mixed scrub forests and on hill-sides away from the ráus.

Sapwood comparatively large, yellowish-white, not durable. Heartwood dark-red, so hard as to be proof against white-ants, hence very durable, seasons well and takes a fine polish. The weight varies between wide limits, the average being about 60 lbs. per c. ft. Pores distinct, being usually filled with a white substance which is in fact the *kathá* or catechin. This substance, as well as the cutch—products of great commercial value,—are obtained by boiling chips of heartwood in earthern pots. The wood is used for rice-pestles, sugarcane- and oilseed-crushers, ploughs, sword-handles and various other purposes. There is, however, a local superstition against it, in common with other thorny trees, owing to which it is never used in house-building in this part of the United Provinces. It yields the best charcoal for blacksmith's work. The astringent bark is sometimes used for tanning.

Fl. May-July. Fr. Nov.-Jan., but remains long on the tree after ripening.

5. **A. concinna,** DC.; Fl. Br. Ind. ii. 297; Brandis For. Flora 188, Ind. Trees 269; Gamble Man. Ind. Timb. 291. Vern. *Álláh*, Hind.

A large climbing shrub, suberect up to about middle age; stem terete, greyish-brown, with 5 vertical lines of strong conical prickles; branches grey-canescent. *Leaf-rachises* 4-8 in. long downy, with a large gland about ·5 in. above the base and a smaller one between the uppermost pinnæ; pinnæ 3-6 pairs, 2-3·5 in. long; stipules ·25-·3 in. long, lanceolate. *Leaflets* acid, 6-20 but generally 10-14 pairs on each pinna with a small odd one near the base, ·5-·6 by ·1-·25 in., linear, oblique at the base, quite rounded at the tip, membranous, pale-green above, glaucous beneath; midrib somewhat diagonal. *Panicles* 3-4 ft. long, interrupted with leaves at the base of the ramifications; peduncles 1-1·5 in. long, slender, downy, in fascicles of 2-4, lower in the axils of the leaves, upper bracteate; bracts ·15-·25 in. long, obliquely obovate-cordate, deciduous. *Heads* ·4-·5 in. diam., 55-60-flowered, brick-red in bud. *Flowers* ·2 in. long. *Calyx* deep-crimson, about ·1 in. long, tubular, deeply 5-toothed; teeth subacute. *Petals* acute, white with a reddish median line, slightly exserted. *Stamens* numerous, much exserted, at first white, withering yellow; filaments very slender. *Pod* 3-4 by ·7-1 in., straight, thick, fleshy, 6-10-seeded, slightly indented between the seeds; sutures broad.

Nawáda in the DÚN, and in the Amláwa valley near Tilwári in JAUNSAR; rather rare, but remarkably gregarious where it occurs.

The pods are used for washing the hair, and the acid leaves are eaten.

Fl. Apr., May. Fr. Cold season.

6. **A. Intsia,** Willd.; Fl. Br. Ind. ii. 297; Brandis For. Flora 189, Ind. Trees 268; Gamble Man. Ind. Timb. 300. Vern. *Áláy*, Hind.

A large prickly climber, at first with 5 vertical lines of hooked prickles, afterwards deeply 5-fluted along those lines, suberect and bushy in early youth; bark grey. *Leaf-rachises* 5-7 in. long, angled; with a gland near the base, and 0 or 2-3 below the upper pinnæ; pinnæ 6-8 pairs, 2-3 in. long. *Leaflets* 8-12 pairs, ·3-·5 by ·15-·2 in., ligulate, dark-green, nearly glabrous and shining above, pale beneath. *Panicles* large, leafless. *Heads* pale-yellow, peduncled, ·4-·5 in. diam., brown in buds, generally 1-4 together. *Pod* 4-6 by ·7-1·2 in., strap-shaped, dark-brown, finely pubescent, hardly stalked.

Fairly common in the vicinity of the Jumna, both in SAHÁRANPUR and the DÚN, *e.g.*, Khárá, Bádsháhibágh; Dákhpathar, etc. Also Khairi swamp, E. DÚN.

The bark is said to be used as a substitute for soap in washing the hair.

Fl. Apr.-Aug. Fr. Dec.-Mar.

A. cæsia, W. & A.; Prain in Journ. As. Soc. Beng. lxvi. Part ii, No. 2, 510. Syn.—*A. Intsia*, var. *cæsia*, W. & A.; Fl. Br. Ind.

ii. 297,—is the form occasionally met with in the DÚN and SAHÁRANPUR FORESTS, *e.g.*, at Khairi, Tháno; Barkálá, etc. *Stems* fluted like the above, but always climbing, usually on tall trees. *Pinnæ* and *leaflets* nearly twice as many, the former (and the rachis) pubescent, the latter firm, ciliate, glabrate above, hairy beneath, tip acute. *Pod* somewhat smaller, reddish-brown, glabrous, dehiscent, narrowed to a short stalk.

Fl. Rainy season. Fr. Nov.-Jan.

6. **A. pennata,** Willd.; Fl. Br. Ind. ii. 297; Brandis For. Flora 189; Gamble Man. Ind. Timb. 300. Vern *Ágiá-bel, Áglá, Áláy,* Dún.

A prickly climber, attaining a larger size than any other climbing Acacia; bark reddish-brown, with horizontal cracks. *Leaf-rachises* 6-10 in. long, not angled, downy, with a large dark-brown gland near the base of the petiole, and several between the upper pinnæ, closely prickly; pinnæ 10-15 pairs, 2-3 in. long. *Leaflets* 80-100 on each pinna, ·2-·3 by ·03-·05 in., firm, quite glabrous, dark-green and shining above. *Panicles* 1·5-2 ft. long; peduncles 1-4 together, ·6-·9 in. long, finely downy. *Heads* ·5 in. diam. *Flowers* pale, smaller than in the last three species. *Pod* 4-6 by ·6-1 in., straight, strap-shaped, reddish-brown, glabrous, 8-12-seeded; stalk ·25 in. long; sutures raised.

Very common in the DÚN and SAHÁRANPUR FORESTS, especially in the moister parts, spreading over the tallest trees.

Wood yellowish-white, porous, moderately hard.

Fl. June-Aug. Fr. Nov.-Jan.

3. Albizzia, Durazz.; G. P. n. 394.

Unarmed trees. *Leaves* bipinnate; leaflets opposite. *Flowers* 2-sexual, in large globose heads, usually white or rose-coloured. *Calyx* tubular or campanulate, distinctly toothed. *Petals* 4-5, valvate, united below the middle. *Stamens* indefinite, many times the length of the corolla; filaments united at the base, sometimes forming a long sheath. *Ovary* sessile or shortly stalked; style filiform; stigma minute. *Pod* large, thin, flat, strap-shaped, straight, sub-indehiscent; seeds compressed.

Analysis of the Species.

Flower-heads on corymbosely arranged simple peduncles; flowers shortly pedicelled.
Leaflets few, oblong, more than ·5 in. broad . . . . 1. *A. Lebbek.*
Leaflets many, falcate and tapering, scarcely ·2 in. broad . . . 4. *A. mollis.*
Flower-heads in panicles; flowers sessile.
Leaflets ovate-oblong, more than ·5 in. broad . . . . 3. *A. procera.*
Leaflets linear-oblong, about ·2-·3 in. broad . . . . 2. *A. odoratissima.*
Leaflets falcate and tapering, scarcely ·1 in. broad . . . . . 5. *A. stipulata.*

1. **A. Lebbek,** Benth.; Fl. Br. Ind. ii. 298; Brandis For. Flora 176; Ind. Trees 271; Gamble Man. Ind. Timb. 303. Vern. *Siris, Sirs, Sirás* or *Sirsá*, Hind.

A large deciduous tree with a spreading crown; bark dark-grey, irregularly cracked. *Leaf-rachises* 5-6 in. long, stout, with a large oblong gland near the base, and 1 or more smaller ones between the upper pinnæ; pinnæ 2-6 pairs, 4-6 in. long. *Leaflets* 4-9 pairs, 1·3-2 by ·7-1 in., shortly petioluled, oblong, oblique, obtuse, glabrous or glabrescent; midrib nearly paralled to the upper edge; lateral nerves not very prominent. *Peduncles* 2-4 in. long, downy, in fascicles of 2-4 from the upper axils, forming short corymbose racemes; heads many-flowered. *Flowers* greenish-white, shortly pedicelled, fragrant, about 1·5 in. long to the extremities of the stamens. *Calyx* funnel-shaped, ·15 in. long, short-toothed. *Corolla* twice the length of the calyx; segments lanceolate. *Filaments* 1-1·5 in. long, rose-tinted, united inside the calyx-tube. *Pod* 8-12 by 1·2-1·7 in., flat, thin, firm, straw-coloured, 6-10-seeded, with brown spots and depressions alternately on either side over the seeds.

Common, though not numerous, in the DÚN and SAHÁRANPUR FORESTS, and also in low valleys in JAUNSAR, generally along banks of streams.

Sapwood large, white; heartwood dark-brown, mottled and streaked with a darker colour, tough, hard, fairly durable, seasons well, and takes a fine polish; weight 50-55 lbs. per c. ft. It is used for sugarcane-crushers, oil-mills, well-curbs, wheel-work and furniture. The leaves and twigs are lopped for camel-fodder. The tree is often planted in avenues. It is a rapid grower and can be easily propagated by cuttings.

New leaves Mar., Apr. Fl. Apr., May. Fr. Oct., Nov. but remains long on the tree.

2. **A. odoratissima,** Benth.; Fl. Br. Ind. ii. 299; Brandis For. Flora 175, Ind. Trees 271; Gamble Man. Ind. Timb. 304. Vern. *Káli Siris*, Hind.

A fairly large tree having a general dark appearance; bark dark-grey with patches of darker colour; extremities grey-tomentose. *Leaf-rachises* 4-7 in. long, downy, with a gland near the base and 1-2 more at the points of insertion of the upper pinnæ; pinnæ 3-8 pairs, 3-5 in. long. *Leaflets* 8-20 pairs, generally about 1 by ·2 in., sometimes much broader, linear-oblong, unequal-sided, acute, minutely mucronate, dark-green, glaucous beneath; midrib paralled to the upper edge and close to it. *Inflorescence* a terminal (rarely axillary) panicle, 10-15 in. long, with corymbose branches on which the peduncles are disposed in fascicles. *Heads* few-flowered; peduncles ·5-·8 in. long. *Flowers* sessile, pale-white, fragrant. *Calyx* about ·04 in. long, hairy. *Corolla* silky; segments ·1 in. long, lanceolate. *Stamens* about 1 in. long. *Pod* 6-12 by 1-1·2 in., 8-12-seeded, flexible, reddish-brown or dusky-green, with darker blotches indicating the position of the seeds.

Occurs sporadically in SAHÁRANPUR and the DÚN. Also in JAUNSAR up to 5,000 ft.

Sapwood rather large, white; heartwood dark-brown with darker streaks, very hard, fairly durable, seasons well, and takes a fine poilsh; weight 54 lbs. per c. ft. It is used for wheels, oil-mills and furniture. The leaves and twigs are lopped for cattle-fodder.

Scarcely ever quite leafless. New leaves Mar., Apr. Fl. Apr.-June. Fr. Jan., Feb., but remains long on the tree.

A tree much resembling this species but differing from it in having fewer and larger leaflets and smaller panicles was considered, but not described, by Sir D. Brandis as a separate species under the name of *A. Thomsonii*. There are a few fruiting specimens in the College Herbarium from the SAHÁRANPUR SIWALIKS, but none with flowers. The pod does not show any marked difference. Is it var. *mollis*, Benth.?

3. **A. procera,** Benth.; Fl. Br. Ind. ii. 299; Brandis For. Flora 175, Ind. Trees 271; Gamble Man. Ind. Timb. 305. Vern. *Karha, Karhár, Karhái*, Dún; *Safed Siris* or *Siras*, Hind.

A very large graceful tree with a deep oval crown when growing in the open; bark yellowish- or greenish-white, smooth, peeling off in thin flakes, often with horizontal lines. *Leaf-rachises* 10-15 in. long, glabrous or pubescent, with a large gland near the base;

pinnæ 3-5 pairs, 6-9 in. long. *Leaflets* 12-24 on each pinna, 1-2 by ·6-·9 in., shortly petioluled, obliquely oblong-ovate, glabrous; midrib diagonal and nearer the lower edge; lateral nerves rather prominent. *Heads* about ·5 in. diam., 15-20-flowered, in fascicles of 2-5, arranged on large lax corymbosely branched terminal panicles which are 1-2 ft. long; peduncles ·5-1 in., the lower from the axils of the upper leaves. *Flowers* yellowish-white, sessile, about ·3 in. long. *Calyx* about ·1 in. long, tubular, shortly toothed. *Corolla* ·15 in. long, deeply cleft; segments oblong. *Stamens* a little more than twice the length of the corolla. *Pod* 4-6 by ·6-·9 in., glabrous, brown, 8-12-seeded with darker blotches over the seeds.

SAHÁRANPUR and the DÚN in mixed forests and generally in moist localities, *e.g.*, Káluwála, banks of the Ré nadi, Khairi swamp, etc. Planted in avenues in Dehra.

Sapwood large, of a white colour, not durable. Heartwood light- or dark-brown, straight and even-grained, hard though rather porous, takes a fairly good polish, seasons well and is durable; weight 46 lbs. per c. ft. "It is largely used for sugarcane-crushers, rice-pounders, wheels, agricultural implements, bridges, and house-posts."—*Sir D. Brandis.* Its charcoal is considered very good. The bark is used for tanning, and is eaten mixed with flour in times of scarcity.

Fl. June-Aug. Fr. Cold season.

4. **A. mollis,** Boivin; Prain in Journ. As. Soc. Beng. lxvi, Part ii, No. 2, 514. Gamble Man. Ind. Timb. 306. Syn.—*A. Julibrissin,* Boivin; Fl. Br. Ind. ii. 300; Brandis For. Flora 177, Ind. Trees 272. Vern. *Bhondir, Kurmurá,* Jaunsar.

A sparingly-branched moderate-sized deciduous tree; bark dark-grey, smooth, with long horizontal wrinkles. *Leaf-rachises* 6-12 in. long, bearing glands at the base and also between the upper pinnæ; pinnæ 6-12 pairs, 3-5 in. long. *Leaflets* 10-25 pairs, ·5-·7 in. long by ·15-·2 in. at the base, falcate, acute, very oblique, sensitive; midrib very close and paralled to the upper edge, which is quite straight. *Peduncles* 2-3 in. long, fascicled, corymbosely disposed at the axils of the fallen upper leaves. *Flowers* rose-coloured, 1-1·5 in. long, very shortly pedicelled. *Calyx* and *corolla* tubular, pubescent, the former ·1 in., the latter ·3 in. long and with lanceolate segments. *Filaments* 1 in. long, very slender, rose-coloured. *Pod* 3-5 by ·6-·9 in., linear, thin, rather membranous, uniformly pale-brown or yellow, softly tomentose until mature, afterwards glabrous, 8-12-seeded.

JAUNSAR and TEHRI-GARHWAL, up to 5,000 ft. usually in open sunny ravines — Dhárágádh; Mautárgádh, etc.

Sapwood large; heartwood dark, almost black in old trees, hard, strong, and takes a good polish; weight about 47 lbs. per c. ft. It is used for furniture.

Fl. Apr.-June. Fr. Sept.-Nov., but remaining long on the tree.

5 **A. stipulata,** Boivin; Fl. Br. Ind. ii. 300; Brandis For. Folra 178, Ind. Trees 272, 709; Gamble Man. Ind. Timb. 306. Vern. *Siran,* Hind.

A large flat-topped tree of very rapid growth, remarkable for its large semi-cordate acute membranous pubescent *stipules,* whence the specific name; bark grey, with short vertical wrinkles crossed by deeper horizontal furrows. *Leaf-rachises* 7-12 in. long, bearing many glands; pinnæ 6-16 pairs, 4-6 in. long. *Leaflets* 20-40 pairs, ·3-·5 in. long by about ·1 in. at the base, falcate, tapering to a sharp point from a broad base; midrib so close to the straight upper edge as to be hardly distinguishable from it. *Heads* in axillary panicled racemes. *Flowers* yellowish-white, slightly tinged with red. *Calyx* funnel-shaped, about ·1 in. long, short-toothed, pubescent. *Corolla* twice the length of the calyx; segments ovate, pubescent. *Stamens* 1-1·3 in. long, very slender, red-tinged. *Pod* 4-5 by ·5-·7 in., thin, of a uniform light-brown colour, 8-10-seeded, often rugose over the seeds.

I quite follow Col. Prain in thinking that there are two distinct varieties of this species. The type with large stipules is found in JAUNSAR and TEHRI-GARHWAL up to 4,000 ft., *e.g.,* at Thadiár; and the other,—var. *Smithiana,* Roxb.,—with smaller stipules, is what is found near swamps in the DÚN, *e.g.,* Kálimatti, Káluwála, banks of the Ré nadi, Sidharwála, etc. Vern. *Kauneră,* Garhwal; *Bhandir,* Hind.

Sapwood large, white; heartwood reddish-brown; weight varying from 25 to 45 lbs. per c. ft., the typical variety being probably the heavier of the two. The wood is likely to be found suitable for tea-boxes. The tree yields a gum which "is used by the Nepalese for sizing their Daphne paper."—*Mr. J. S. Gamble.* The branches are lopped for fodder.

New leaves Feb., Mar. Fl. Apr.-June. Fr. Autumn.

A. lucida, Benth., Fl. Br. Ind. ii. 299, is a graceful tree with dark-green foliage. It is not indigenous within the range of this flora, but deserves mention as it grows well under cultivation at DEHRA, and is a good tree for avenues. It differs from all other species by having large penninerved acuminate *leaflets,* 3-5 in. long and 2-3 in. broad. *Flowers* sessile. *Pod* about 6 by 1 in., thin, flexible.

FAM. 34. ROSACEÆ; G. P. N. 58.

Herbs, shrubs or trees. *Leaves* stipulate, usually alternate, simple or compound. *Flowers* regular, 2-sexual. *Calyx* gamosepalous, superior or inferior. *Disk* annular or lining the base of the calyx-tube. *Petals* usually 5, imbricate. *Stamens* perigynous, usually indefinite, in one or many series, incurved in bud; anthers small. *Ovary* superior or inferior, of one or more free or connate carpels; styles as many as the carpels, free or connate. *Fruit* a pome, a drupe, or an aggregate of drupes achenes or follicles, rarely baccate or capsular. *Seeds* erect or pendulous, without albumen.

Analysis of the Genera.

Ripe carpels not enclosed within the calyx-tube, *i.e.*, calyx always inferior.
  Leaves simple; carpel solitary; fruit a simple drupe.
    Style terminal; branches unarmed . 1. PRUNUS.
    Style basal; branches spinous . . 2. PRINSEPIA.
  Leaves generally simple; carpels few; fruit an aggregate of follicles . . 3. SPIRÆA.
  Leaves generally compound; carpels many; fruit an aggregate of drupes 4. RUBUS.
Ripe carpels more or less enclosed within the calyx-tube, *i.e.*, calyx at least ultimately superior.
  Stipules adnate to the petiole.
    (Fruit an aggregate of achenes enclosed in a fleshy calyx) . . . 5. ROSA.
  Stipules free, deciduous.
    Fruit a pome; leaves simple, rarely pinnate . . . . . . 6. PYRUS.
    Fruit a drupe with 1-5 bony stones; leaves always simple.
      Leaves toothed or serrate . . 7. CRATÆGUS.
      Leaves quite entire . . . . 8. COTONEASTER.

1. Prunus, Linn.; G. P. n. 13.

Shrubs or trees. *Leaves* alternate, simple, usually serrate or crenate, convolute or conduplicate in bud; petiole often with 2 glands. *Flowers* white or red, solitary fascicled corymbose or racemed. *Petals* 5. *Stamens* many, perigynous, free. *Carpel* 1; style terminal; ovules 2, pendulous. *Fruit* a drupe, with a smooth or rugged 1-seeded stone.

Analysis of the species.

Flowers long-pedicelled in umbellate fascicles, appearing before the leaves .	1. *P. Puddum.*
Flowers short-pedicelled in long nodding racemes, appearing after the leaves .	2. *P. Padus.*

1. **P. Puddum,** Roxb.; Fl. Br. Ind. ii. 314; Brandis For. Flora 194, Ind. Trees 279; Gamble Man. Ind. Timb. 313. Vern. *Phájá*, Jaunsar; *Padam*, Hind.

A moderate-sized tree; bark brownish-grey, smooth, peeling off in thin shining horizontal strips. *Leaves* 3-5 by 1-1·5 in., ovate-lanceolate, long-acuminate, closely doubly-serrate, glabrous, shining, conduplicate in bud, appearing after the leaves; petiole about ·5 in. long, with 2-4 glands at the base; stipules ·6-·8 in. long, feathery and glandular. *Flowers* about ·8 in. across, at first rose-coloured, fading to nearly white; peduncles ·5-1·5 in., in umbellate fascicles. *Calyx* glabrous; tube ·3-·4 in. long, funnel-shaped; lobes acute, entire. *Petals* about ·5 in. long, obovate or oblong. *Stigma* 3-lobed. *Fruit* ·5-·7 in., ovoid, obtuse at both ends, acid, yellow or red; stone rugose and furrowed.

JAUNSAR, TEHRI-GARHWAL and the OUTER HIMALAYA up to 8,000 ft., mostly in the outskirts of villages, apparently cultivated or run wild.—Korwá, Koti-Báwar, Bodyár; Málkōt Forest, etc. Also cultivated in DEHRA.

Heartwood reddish, moderately hard, strong, durable, with a pleasant smell; weight 40-45 lbs. per c. ft. The branches with the shining bark on are used for walking-sticks. The fruit is eaten, and the stones are strung up in rosaries and necklaces used by faqirs.

New leaves May, June. Fl. Apr., May, and sometimes also in autumn. Fr. Two months after flowering.

2. **P. Padus,** Linn.; Fl. Br. Ind. ii. 315; Brandis For. Flora 194, Ind. Trees 280; Gamble Man. Ind. Timb. 314. The Bird Cherry. Vern. *Jámoi, Jámroi, Jámnoi,* Jaunsar.

A moderate-sized tree; bark rough, dark-grey or brown; young parts and inflorescence softly pubescent. *Leaves* 4-6 by 1-2·5 in., oblong elliptic or lanceolate, acuminate, closely serrate, often slightly cordate, conduplicate in bud, turning red before falling; lateral nerves 12-15 pairs, red and hairy at the axils underneath; midrib and petiole red, stout, the latter 1-1·5 in. long, with a pair of glands near the apex; bud-scales 1·5 by ·25 in., reddish brown. *Flowers* ·2-·3 in. diam., white, in many-flowered nodding axillary and terminal racemes which are 4-6 in long; pedicels ·25 in. *Calyx* turbinate, about ·1 in. long. *Petals* white, ·15 in. long, round, concave. *Drupe* acid, about ·4 in. diam., globose, somewhat compressed, red when half ripe, almost black when fully ripe; stone rugged.

Common in JAUNSAR and TEHRI-GARHWAL, 6,-9,000 ft.—Deoban, Konáin, Bhujkōti, Mundáli; Deotá, etc., characteristic of grazing grounds. Scarce in the outer ranges.

Wood brownish-white, close and even-grained; weight about 40 lbs. per c. ft. It takes a fine polish, but is seldom used. The acid fruit is eaten by the hill people. The leaves are lopped for fodder.

New leaves Apr. Fl. Apr.-June. Fr. July-Oct.

To this Genus belong the following well-known fruit-trees, the cultivation of which is gradually extending in the HILLS :—

1. *P. persica,* Benth. & Hook. f.; Fl. Br. Ind. ii. 313. The Peach. Vern. *Árú,* Hind. *Leaves* 3-5 by ·7-1·3 in., oblong-lanceolate, serrate. *Flowers* about 1 in. across, pink, sessile. *Fruit* about 1·5 in. long; stone deeply furrowed. Now found in a semi-wild state in most parts of the DÚN. Cultivated throughout the HILLS.

2. *P. armeniaca,* Linn.: Fl. Br. Ind. ii. 313. The Apricot. Vern. *Chúlú, Chilu,* Hills; *Zardálu,* Hind. *Leaves* 2-3·5 in. diam., broad-ovate, acuminate, crenate; petiole 1-1·5 in. long, flexible, glandular. *Flowers* about ·8 in. across, white or pinkish. *Fruit* about 1 in. long; stone smooth. Cultivated in the HILLS and also in DEHRA.

3. *P. Cerasus*, Linn.; Fl. Br. Ind. ii. 313.—The Cherry. *Leaves* 2-3 by 1-1·2 in., ovate, elliptic, abruptly acuminate, crenate, serrate. *Flowers* white, on long slender peduncles, in fascicles of 2-5. *Drupe* ·4-·5 in. diam., globose, smooth and shining; stone round, smooth. Cultivated in the HILLS.

4. *P. communis*, Hudson; var. *insititia*; Fl. Br. Ind. ii. 315. The Plum. Vern. *Álúcha, Álú-bukhára*, Hind. *Leaves* 3-4 in. long, ovate-lanceolate, serrate; nerves pubescent beneath. *Flowers* white or pink, on long slender peduncles. *Drupe* smooth, globose or oblong. Cultivated in the HILLS, and some varieties are grown in DEHRA and also in the PLAINS.

2. Prinsepia, Royle; G. P. n. 16.

1. **P. utilis**, Royle; Fl. Br. Ind. ii. 323; Brandis For. Flora 196, Ind. Trees 281; Gamble Man. Ind. Timb. 316. Vern. *Bhekoi, Bhek*, Jaunsar; *Bhekal, Bhekar*, Garhwal.

A dark-green spinous shrub; bark green on branches, brownish-white and peeling off in vertical strips on the main stem; spines often leaf-bearing. *Leaves* alternate, simple, 1·5-5 by ·5-1·2 in., elliptic or narrow-lanceolate, acuminate, entire or sharply serrate, coriaceous, dark-green, glabrous; petiole ·2-·5 in. long. *Flowers* white, ·3-·4 in. across, in short axillary racemes. *Calyx* cup-shaped, persistent. *Petals* 5, shortly clawed. *Stamens* numerous, in many series; filaments short; anther-cells separating by a broad connective. *Carpel* 1; style basal; ovules 2, pendulous. *Drupe* ·5-·7 in. long, obliquely obovate or oblong, with the remains of the style near the base, deep-purple and pruinose when ripe; kernel coriaceous, 1-seeded, smooth; cotyledons oily.

JAUNSAR 4,-8,000 ft.; common in sunny open places.—Saiá, Korwá, Matkángrá, Konáin, Koti-Báwar, etc.

Heartwood red, very hard, compact, but much liable to split; weight 69 lbs. per c. ft. An oil is expressed from the seeds, which is used chiefly for burning.

Fl. Apr. May. Fr. Rainy season.

3. Spiræa, Linn.; G. P. n. 8.

Perennial herbs or shrubs. *Leaves* alternate, simple or compound. *Flowers* white or red, in axillary or terminal cymes. *Calyx* persistent; lobes 4-5. *Petals* as many as the calyx-lobes. *Stamens* many ; filaments free or connate below. *Disk* fleshy. *Carpels* 5 or more, free or connate below ; ovules 2 or more, pendulous. *Fruit* an aggregate of 5 or more follicular carpels.

Analysis of the Species.

Leaves pinnate ; carpels connate below . 1. *S. sorbifolia.*
Leaves simple ; carpels quite free.
  Branches slender ; leaves glaucous beneath ; flowers dimorphous . . 2. *S. bella.*
  Branches stout ; leaves pale beneath ; flowers not dimorphous , . . 3. *S. canescens.*

1. **S. sorbifolia,** Linn. ; Fl. Br. Ind. ii. 324 ; Brandis Ind. Trees 283 ; Gamble Man. Ind. Timb. 316. Vern. *Latkár, Lotkár* ; Jaunsar.

A tall shrub ; bark reddish-grey. *Leaves* imparipinnate, less frequently paripinnate, 8-12 in. long ; rachis terete. *Leaflets* 6-10 pairs, sessile, 3-5 by ·7-1 in., linear-lanceolate, rounded at the base, long acuminate, doubly serrate, glabrous or hairy beneath ; midrib stout ; lateral nerves numerous, straight ; stipules linear-subulate, ·25 in. long. *Flowers* white, ·25 in. diam., in many-flowered cymes which are disposed in large thyrsoid much-branched terminal panicles 1-1·5 ft. long. *Calyx-tube* hemispherical ; lobes rounded. *Petals* orbicular. *Carpels* 5, connate below, separating and dehiscing dorsally in fruit.

JAUNSAR and TEHRI-GARHWAL, 7,-9,000 ft. ; common at Konáin. Also found at Mundáli ; Deotá, etc.

Wood hard, compact, even-grained ; weight 49 lbs. per c. ft.

Fl. May, June. Fr. June, July.

2. **S. bella,** Sims. ; Fl. Br. Ind. ii. 324 ; Brandis Ind. Trees 283.

A small shrub 2-6 ft. high. *Leaves* simple, very variable in size and shape, ·5-2 in. long, broadly oblong ovate or ovate-lanceolate, obtusely inciso-serrate throughout or towards the apex only, membranous, dark-green above, glaucous beneath. *Flowers* generally pink, dimorphous and subdiœcious, in corymbosely much-branched cymes. *Calyx-tube* villous within ; lobes acute. *Petals* orbicular.

Stamens deformed in the female flowers, long in the male. *Style* long in the female flowers, short in the male. *Ripe carpels* dark-brown, shining.

TEHRI-GARHWAL, *e.g.*, Deotá, etc.; not very common.

Fl. Apr., May. Fr. Oct., Nov.

3. **S. canescens,** Don; Fl. Br. Ind. ii. 325; Brandis Ind. Trees 283; Gamble Man. Ind. Timb. 317. Vern. *Tákoi*, *Chakroi*, Jaunsar.

A stiff small shrub; branches striate, grey-canescent, arching. *Leaves* simple, ·4-·8 by ·3-·5 in., obovate, entire or toothed towards the apex on luxuriant shoots, subcoriaceous, pale-green beneath; lateral nerves 2-4 pairs; petiole up to ·15 in. *Flowers* hermaphrodite, bracteate, white or pale-pink, ·2 in. diam., in small dense compound corymbs at the ends of all the branches and branchlets. *Stamens* not longer than the petals. *Ripe carpels* villous, partially sunk in the calyx-tube.

JAUNSAR and TEHRI-GARHWAL, above 7,000 ft., chiefly on open hill-sides. Quite common.

Wood fairly hard, even- and close-grained; weight 47 lbs. per c. ft. Light walking-sticks are made of the branches.

Fl. May-July. Fr. Autumn.

S. vaccinifolia, Don.; Fl. Br. Ind. ii. 325; occurs in the HILLS below 7,000 ft.—Bámsu Valley, valleys below Konáin, Málkōt, etc. It is very similar in appearance to *S. bella*, but is more gregarious in habit, and the flowers are hermaphrodite and white.

4. Rubus, Linn.; G. P. n. 36.

The Brambles.

ly trailing shrubs, almost always prickly. *Leaves* (on the local species) generally compound; stipules more or less adnate to the petiole. *Flowers* white or red, in terminal or axillary corymbose panicles, rarely solitary. *Calyx* 5-lobed, persistent. *Petals* 5. *Stamens* numerous. Carpels many, distinct, on a convex receptacle; style subterminal. *Fruit* of many 1-seeded drupes crowded on the receptacle which becomes conical in the fruit.

Analysis of the Species.

Leaves simple ; petals white ; fruit black . 1. *R. paniculatus.*
Leaves pinnately 3- rarely 5-foliolate.
Petals pink ; fruit red, generally dry . 2. *R. niveus.*
Petals white ; fruit yellow, succulent.
Leaflets grabrous . . . . . 3. *R. macilentus.*
Leaflets tomentose or pubescent beneath.
Stem bristly ; flowers in dense-flowered terminal panicles . 4. *R. ellipticus.*
Stem quite glabrous, pruinose ; flowers in 1-3-flowered axillary peduncles . . . . 5. *R. biflorus.*
Leaves pinnately 5-11-foliolate ; petals pink ; fruit black . . . . 6. *R. lasiocarpus.*

1. **R. paniculatus,** Smith ; Fl. Br. Ind. ii. 329 ; Brandis For. Flora 196, Ind. Trees 283 ; Gamble Man. Ind. Timb. 318. Vern. *Pándroi, Kálá Ánchhu,* Jaunsar.

A large rambling shrub ; all parts except the upper surface of the leaves clothed with soft white cottony tomentum ; prickles few, minute. *Leaves* 3-6 by 2·5-3·5 in., ovate, cordate, long-acuminate, obscurely lobed, irregularly serrate, 3-5-nerved at the base ; lateral nerves about 8 pairs ; petiole 1-2 in. long. *Flowers* ·7-1 in. diam., in much-branched lax terminal panicles which are 4-12 in. long ; pedicels ·5-1 in. long. *Calyx-lobes* ovate-lanceolate, often caudate-acuminate, erect in fruit. *Petals* ·2-·3 in. long, much shorter than the calyx-lobes. *Carpels* glabrous. Fruit ·5-·7 long, conical, black ; drupes large ; receptacle villous.

JAUNSAR and TEHRI-GARHWAL, up to 6,000 ft. Generally in damp shady ravines : Korwá, Dhárágádh, Bagúr Block, Kōti, Tons Valley, etc.

The fruit is good to eat.

Fl. Apr.-June. Fr. June, July.

2. **R. niveus,** Wall. ; Fl. Br. Ind. ii. 335 ; Brandis For. Flora 199 ; Gamble Man. Ind. Timb. 317. Vern. *Bheré, Bherá, Bheáré,* Jaunsar.

A very variable shrub, rambling or suberect ; branches usually glabrous. *Leaves* pinnately 3-foliolate, rarely 5-foliolate, 3-6 in. long ; petiole with several prickles beneath. *Leaflets* 1-4 by ·8-3 in., ovate or elliptic, often cordate, lobed or incised, generally doubly serrate, membranous. *Flowers* ·3-·7 in. diam., axillary or in few-flowered corymbose terminal cymes; pedicels ·2-·8 in. long. *Calyx-segments* ·3-·4 in. long, ovate-lanceolate, pubescent, spreading or reflexed in fruit. *Petals* pink, ·2-·3 in diam., broad-ovate, much smaller than the calyx-lobes, erect, concealing the stamens. *Stamens* very numerous. *Fruit* globose; drupes many, dry, not edible,—less frequently few, fleshy, very acid.

Gregarious in JAUNSAR and TEHRI-GARHWAL, 7,-10,000 ft.; extremely common.

It interferes with the reproduction of tree species on shady northern aspects as in the Mundáli Forest, but in other places is useful as a shade-giver to young plants of delicate species.

Fl. Apr, May. Fr. May, June.

3. **R. macilentus,** Camb.; Fl. Br. Ind. ii. 336; Brandis For. Flora 190, Ind. Trees 286.

A trailing shrub, deep-green all over; stem nearly glabrous, shining; prickles flattened. *Leaves* pinnately 3-foliolate; rachis 3-4 in. long. *Leaflets* ·5-2·5 in. long, ovate or ovate-lanceolate, doubly crenate-toothed, subcoriaceous, glabrous, prickly along the midrib, —the lateral very variable in size and shape. *Flowers* ·3-·6 in. across; peduncles ·2-·8 in. long, pubescent, generally 1-flowered, axillary and terminal. *Calyx-lobes* caudate, erect in fruit, silky outside, tomentose within. *Petals* white, broad-obovate, clawed, exceeding the sepals. *Fruit* globose, yellow or deep-orange; drupes few, glabrous, juicy; receptac leelongated, pubescent.

Common in JAUNSAR and TEHRI-GARHWAL, up to 8,000 ft.—Chakrata, Jádi, Konáin, Mundáli; Deota, etc.

The fruit is eaten.

Fl. Apr., May. Fr. June, July.

4. **R. ellipticus,** Sm.; Fl. Br. Ind. ii. 336. Brandis Ind. Trees 286; Gamble Man. Ind. Timb. 317. Syn.—*R. flavus,* Ham.; Brandis For. Flora 197, Vern. *Hinsáu,* Jaunsar; *Hinsar,* Garhwal; *Ánchhu, LálÁnchhu,* Hind.

A large shrub; branches stout, shaggy with long reddish bristles, often also with glandular hairs; prickles sharp. *Leaves* pinnately 3-foliolate, the lower ones sometimes 1-foliolate; rachis 1-3 in. long. *Leaflets* 2-4 in. long, obovate elliptic or orbicular, closely serrate, dark-green above, pale-green and usually tomentose beneath. *Flowers* ·3-·6 in. across. *Calyx-segments* ovate, erect in fruit. *Petals* white, obovate, exceeding the calyx-segments. *Fruit* ·4-·6 in. diam., yellow; drupes small, crowded; receptacle cylindrical, hairy.

JAUNSAR and TEHRI-GARHWAL, 3,-5,000 ft.; common on open hill-sides and round villages: Saiá, Binálgádh, Dhárágádh, Kōti Báwar, Tons Valley, etc. Also OUTER HAIMLAYA and the DÚN; —Málkōt, Tháno, Ráipur, etc.

The fruit has an agreeable flavour, and is greedily eaten wherever the plant grows.

Fl. Feb., Mar. Fr. Apr., May.

5. **R. biflorus**, Ham.; Fl. Br. Ind. ii. 338, *R. biflorus*, Buch.; Brandis For. Flora 198, Ind. Trees 286; Gamble Man. Ind. Timb. 317. Vern *Áchhoi*, Jaunsar.

A large spreading shrub; branches glabrous, white with a glaucous bloom; prickles sharp and strong. *Leaves* usually 3-foliolate, sometimes 5-foliolate, rarely 1-foliolate and 3-lobed; petiole 1-2 in., pubescent, prickly. *Leaflets* 2-3·5 in. long, ovate-lanceolate, often obscurely lobed, irregularly doubly-serrate or toothed, hairy above, white and densely tomentose beneath. *Flowers* ·5-·7 in. diam.; peduncles axillary, slender, drooping, ·5-1·5 in. long, 1-3-flowered. *Calyx-lobes* ovate-lanceolate, mucronate. *Petals* white, orbicular, equal to, or exceeding, the calyx-lobes. *Fruit* ·6-·7 in. diam., globose, yellow; drupes 20-30, juicy; receptacle elongated, villous.

JAUNSAR, up to 8,000 ft.: Bodyár, Kathián, Dhárágádh, etc. Less common than any of the preceding species.

The fruit has a sweetish taste and is eaten.

Fl. Apr., May. Fr. May, June.

6. **R. lasiocarpus**, Sm.; Fl. Br. Ind. ii. 339; Brandis For. Flora 198, Ind. Trees 286; Gamble Man. Ind. Timb. 317. Vern. *Bheré, Kálá Hinsálu*, Jaunsar; *Káli Ánchhi*, Dún.

A spreading shrub, often gregarious; branches long, thickly pruinose, purple below the bloom, quite glabrous. *Leaves* 5-7-9-11-foliolate, 3-10 in. long. *Leaflets* 1-3 in. long, ovate elliptic or ovate-lanceolate, acutely toothed or serrate, subcoriaceous, glabrous or silky above, thickly white-tomentose beneath, terminal often lobed; lateral nerves close, straight, very strong beneath. *Flowers* ·3-·7 in. diam., in terminal and axillary simple or panicled lax corymbs; peduncles 1-2 in. long; pedicels of various lengths. *Calyx* densely woolly; lobes ovate or ovate-lanceolate. *Petals* red, round or obovate, usually shorter than the calyx-lobes. *Fruit* ·3-·5 in. diam., black when fully ripe, dry or fleshy; drupes numerous; receptacle villous.

Fairly common in the DÚN and the OUTER HIMALAYA: Karwápáni, Rámgarh, Tháno, Málkōt, etc. Also found in JAUNSAR up to 7,000 ft., *e.g.*, Lúrli forest, Kathián, etc.

The fruit has a good flavour and is eaten.

Fl. Apr., May in the Hills; Feb., Mar. in the Dúṇ. Fr. About two months after flowering.

5. Rosa, Linn.; G. P. n. 60.

Erect scrambling or climbing shrubs, more or less prickly. *Leaves* alternate, imparipinnate; leaflets serrate; stipules more or less adnate to the petiole. *Inflorescence* various. *Flowers* white yellow or pink. *Calyx-tube* globose ovoid or pitcher-shaped; mouth contracted; segments foliaceous. *Disk* coating the calyx-tube, silky. *Petals* 5, rarely 4. *Stamens* numerous, inserted on the edge of the disk. *Carpels* 1-ovuled, hairy, usually many, enclosed in the calyx-tube; styles free or connate above the neck of the calyx-tube; stigma thickened; ovule pendulous. *Fruit* an aggregate of 1-seeded dry hairy achenes enclosed in the fleshy calyx-tube.

Analysis of the Species.

Suberect shrubs. Styles distinct; sepals persistent in fruit.
  Leaflets serrate nearly down to the base; flowers bracteate; petals 5 . . 1. *R. macrophylla.*
  Leaflets toothed only in the upper half; flowers ebracteate; petals usually 4. 2. *R. sericea.*
A large climber. Styles united into an exserted column; sepals deciduous in fruit 3. *R. moschata.*

1. **R. macrophylla,** Lindl.; Fl. Br. Ind. ii. 366; Brandis For. Flora 203, Ind. Trees 288; Gamble Man. Ind. Timb. 319. Vern. *Bháuṇrá Kujoi*, Jaunsar.

An erect shrub, 6-10 ft. high, with smooth green branches; bark of stem dark-brown, peeling off in thick flakes; prickles more or less straight, often 0. *Leaves* 3-8 in. long; petiole pubescent, slightly channelled above; stipules ·4-·6 in. long, spreading, ciliate with glands. *Leaflets* 7-11, ·5-2·5 by ·3-1·3 in., gradually smaller from the terminal downwards, elliptic, usually grey-pubescent beneath, minutely petioluled. *Flowers* 1-2·5 in. diam., bright-red or pink, solitary or in few-flowered subterminal corymbs; pedicels ·5-1·5 in. long, studded with glandular bristles. *Bracts* 1-1·5 in. long, lanceolate, leaf-like, glandular on the margins. *Calyx* with glandular bristles outside; lobes much elongated, filiform in the middle, dilated and leafy above, persistent in fruit. *Petals* 5, broadly obcordate. *Styles* hairy, exserted. *Fruit* 1-2 in. long, turbinate.

Common in the HILLS, 7,-10,000 ft.; almost gregarious in some forests, *e.g.*, Mohná Block, Mundáli, Konáin, Deotá, etc., where it often interferes with the natural reproduction of tree species.

Wood hard, compact, weighing 55-60 lbs. per c. ft. It makes good hedges. The fruit is eaten when ripe.

Fl. May, June. Fr. July, Aug.

Var. *minor*, Lindl.—has leaflets up to ·5 in. long and somewhat smaller flowers.

2. **R. sericea,** Lindl.; Fl. Br. Ind. ii. 367; Brandis For. Flora 202, Ind. Trees 288; Gamble Man. Ind. Timb. 319.

A suberect thorny shrub, 4-8 ft. high; bark greyish brown, peeling off in papery flakes; prickles nearly straight, brown. *Leaves* 1-3 in. long; stipules oblong, spreading, membranous. *Leaflets* 7-11, ·25-1 in. long, oblong or obovate-oblong, dentate or coarsely serrate in the upper half, glabrous above, silky along the nerves beneath. *Flowers* 1·5-2·5 in. diam., solitary, white or pink; peduncle and calyx-tube glabrous; bracts 0. *Calyx-lobes* lanceolate, pubescent, persistent in fruit. *Petals* usually 4, ·6-1·2 in. long, obcordate, pure white or with a shade of pink. *Fruit* pyriform, scarlet.

TEHRI-GARHWAL, above 9,000 ft.: Deotá (Rikshin), Bálchá, Harki-Dún, etc. Likely also to occur at higher elevations in JAUNSAR.

Fl. May-July.

3. **R. moschata,** Mill.; Fl. Br. Ind. ii. 367; Brandis For. Flora 201, Ind. Trees 288; Gamble Man. Ind. Timb. 318. Vern. *Kújoi*, Jaunsar; *Kúnjo*, Garhwal.

A large thorny climbing shrub; bark greyish-brown; prickles stout, recurved. *Leaves* 2-6 in. long; petiole pubescent, slightly channelled, with scattered prickles beneath; stipules about 1 in. long, membranous, with a spreading tip and a few glandular hairs along the margins. *Leaflets* 5-9, 1-3 by ·4-1·3 in., ovate ovate-lanceolate or elliptic, acuminate, very regularly closely serrate, finely grey-pubescent beneath, lateral subsessile. *Flowers* sweet-scented, 1·5-2 in. diam., in large terminal corymbose racemes; pedicels 1-1·5 in. long, slender, grey-pubescent and also with a few scattered red glands. *Calyx-lobes* about 1 in. long, narrow-lanceolate, often with 1-2 pairs of foliaceous appendages at the margins, deciduous in fruit. *Petals* 5, pure white, obovate, generally with a distinct tip. *Stamens* yellow, much shorter than the petals. *Styles* exserted, united into a hairy column above the neck of the calyx-tube. *Fruit* ·3-·4 in. long, obovoid, dark-brown.

Common in JAUNSAR and TEHRI-GARHWAL, 3,000 to 8,000 ft.; also in the OUTER HIMALAYA, generally along streams or in open ravines: Korwá, Konáin, Dhárágádh, Kathián, Tons Valley; Láduakōt, etc.

Often injures forest trees by spreading over their crowns. An excellent otto is extracted from the flowers at Náhan in SIRMOOR.

Fl. May, June. Fr. June, July.

6. Pyrus, Linn.; G. P. n. 63.

Trees or shrubs. *Leaves* alternate, generally simple, rarely pinnate; stipules deciduous. *Flowers* white or pink, in terminal corymbs. *Calyx-tube* urceolate or turbinate; lobes erect or reflexed, persistent or deciduous. *Petals* 5. *Stamens* many; filaments sometimes connate at the base. *Carpels* 2-5, adnate to the calyx-tube; ovules usually 2 in each carpel; styles 2-5. free or connate below. *Fruit* a pome, 2-5-celled, more or less fleshy.

Analysis of the Species.

Leaves simple.
  Leaves glabrous, green beneath . 1. *P. Pashia.*
  Leaves always white-woolly beneath 2. *P. lanata.*
Leaves pinnate, (rusty-tomentose beneath) . . . . . . 3. *P. foliolosa.*

1. **P. Pashia,** Ham.; Fl. Br. Ind. ii. 374; Brandis For. Flora 575, Ind. Trees 291; Gamble Man. Ind Timb. 322. Syn.—*P. variolosa,* Wall. Brandis For. Flora 204. Vern. *Káint, Káenth,* Jaunsar; *Mohál, Mehál, Meyel, Mahol,* Dún and Garhwal.

A moderate-sized deciduous tree; bark on old stems almost black, both longitudinally and transversely split into small thick rectangular scales, on branches dark-brown smooth and with small white lenticel-dots. *Leaves* simple, very variable in size and shape, generally 2-4 by ·7-1·5 in., ovate or ovate-lanceolate, long-acuminate, closely serrate or crenate, glabrous, shining, lobed and often woolly beneath on young plants; lateral nerves 8-10 pairs, very slender, more prominent above than beneath; petiole ·3-1·5 in long, slender, often reddish; stipules ·5 in. long, setaceous, early deciduous. *Inflorescence* a corymb or an umbel,—or the flowers are fascicled at the ends of short branchlets,—appearing shortly before the leaves; pedicels ·5-2 in. long, thickened in fruit. *Flowers* white, about 1 in. across. *Calyx-tube* urceolate; lobes spreading, white-woolly. *Petals* obovate, with dark radiating veins. *Stamens* 25-30. *Styles* 3-5, woolly. *Fruit* globose, ·7-1·5 in. diam., dark-brown, covered with raised white dots.

Common in JAUNSAR and TEHRI-GARHWAL up to 7,500 ft.: Chakrata, Koti-Kanásar, Konáin, Dhárágádh, Kathián, etc. Also found in the OUTER HIMALAYA and in certain localities in the Dún: Málkōt, Paléd, Ṭháno, Mothroṇwála, Bindál-nálá near Dehra, etc.

Wood brown, compact, fine-grained, hard and durable, but liable to split and warp in seasoning; weight 47 lbs. per c. ft. It is used for walking-sticks, combs, tobacco-pipes and such other purposes. The fruit is eaten when half-rotten. The leaves and twigs are lopped for fodder.

New leaves and flowers Mar., Apr. in the hills, and about a month earlier in the Dún. Fr. Sept.-Dec.

2. **P. lanata,** Don; Fl. Br. Ind. ii. 375; Gamble Man. Ind. Timb. 323; Brandis Ind. Trees 291; Syn.—*P. Aria*, Ehrh.; Brandis For. Flora 206. Vern. *Pái*, *Páhi*, Jaunsar.

A moderate-sized deciduous tree; bark dark-brown with shallow longitudinal furrows. *Leaves* simple, 5-8 by 2-4 in., broadly oblong or obovate, acute, lobulate, finely serrate, white-woolly beneath, glabrescent above; lateral nerves 8-12 pairs, nearly straight, very prominent beneath; base rounded or acute; petiole ·5-1 in. long. *Flowers* white, ·4-·6 in. diam., in short hemispherical corymbs, 3-5 in. across; pedicels short, woolly. *Calyx* turbinate; lobes ovate, acute. *Petals* obovate-oblanceolate, shortly clawed. *Stamens* 20. *Styles* 2-3, villous. *Fruit* ·5-1 in. long, pyriform and 1-2 seeded (in the region of this Flora).

JAUNSAR and TEHRI-GARHWAL, above 8,000 ft., characteristic of the high-level grazing grounds. Konáin, Mundáli; Deotá, Bálchá, etc.

Wood close- and even-grained, "might be used for boxes and other purposes."—*Mr. J. S. Gamble.* Weight 40-47 lbs. per c. ft. The fruit is eaten when half-rotten.

Fl. Apr., May. Fr. Aug.-Oct.

3. **P. foliolosa,** Wall.; Fl. Br. Ind. ii. 376; Gamble Man. Ind. Timb. 323; Brandis Ind. Trees 292. Syn.—*P. ursina,* Wall.; Brandis For. Flora 206.

A shrub or small tree; bark reddish-grey, peeling off in horizontal papery strips. *Leaves* imparipinnate, 4-6 in. long, rusty-tomentose at first, glabrate afterwards. *Leaflets* 9-15 pairs, opposite, sessile, 1-1·5 in. long, the middle ones longer than the others, linear-oblong, acute or obtuse, cuspidate-serrate. *Flowers* greenish-white, ·3-·5 in. diam., in compound terminal and axillary corymbs; pedicels short, glabrous; bracts rusty-hairy. *Calyx* cup-shaped, glabrous; segments triangular. *Petals* orbicular-ovate, rusty-villous. *Styles* thick, short. *Fruit* ·3-·5 in. diam., ovoid or globose, bluish-red when ripe.

JAUNSAR and TEHRI-GARHWAL, above 7,000 ft.

Fl. June, July. Fr. Sept., Oct.

Two well-known fruit trees belong to this Genus :—

1. *P. Malus,* Linn.; Fl. Br. Ind. ii. 373. The Apple tree. Vern. *Sew,* Hind. *Leaves* 2-3 in. long, ovate, glabrous above, tomentose beneath, acuminate, crenate, long-petioled. *Flowers* pink-tinged, 1 in. diam. *Calyx-lobes* persistent. *Petals* clawed. *Pome* 2-3 in. diam., globose, intruded at both ends; seeds brown, lenticular. Cultivated at Chakrata. Fl. Mar.-May. Fr. Dec., Jan.

2. *P. communis,* Linn.; Fl. Br. Ind. ii. 374. The Pear tree. Vern. *Náshpáti,* Hind. *Leaves* variable in size, oblong or ovate, acute, entire or slightly crenulate; petiole slender, very long. *Flowers* white, 1 in. diam. *Calyx-lobes* persistent. *Petals* obovate. *Pome* 1-2 in. diam. pyriform or sub-globose, intruded at the apex. Much cultivated in DEHRA. Fl. Mar., Apr. Fr. July-Sept.

7. Cratægus, Linn.; G. P. n. 64.

1. **C. crenulata,** Roxb.; Fl. Br. Ind. ii. 384; Gamble Man. Ind. Timb. 325; Brandis Ind. Trees 294. Syn.—*C. Pyracantha,* Pers.; Brandis For. Flora 208. Vern. *Gingáru,* Jaunsar.

A large rigid spinescent evergreen shrub. *Leaves* alternate, simple, generally crowded on short lateral branchlets, 1-2·5 by ·2-·5 in., linear-oblong or oblanceolate, obtuse, very coriaceous, crenulate, glabrous, shining above; lateral nerves close, parallel, indistinct; petiole very short, margined; stipules deciduous. *Flowers* white, ·2-·3 in. diam., in terminal corymbose cymes; pedicels slender; bracts caducous. *Calyx-tube* hemispherical; lobes obtuse. *Petals* orbicular, very shortly clawed, inserted at the mouth of the calyx-tube. *Stamens* many. *Carpels* 5, connate below; ovules 2 in each cell, ascending. *Fruit* a dry globose drupe, ·2-·3 in. diam., orange or red when ripe.

JAUNSAR and TEHRI-GARHWAL, ascending to 6,500 ft. generally along streams in open valleys: Korwá Forest, Binalgádh, Dhárágádh, Tons Valley, etc. Also along Sub-Himalayan mountain streams in the DÚN, *e.g.*, Bidhálna Ráu and Birdál-nálá.

Wood white, hard, very close- and even-grained; weight 48 lbs. per c.ft. The branches are made into walking-sticks and khud-sticks in the hills.

Fl. Apr., May. Fr. July, Aug.

8. Cotoneaster, Linn.; G. P. n. 65.

Shrubs or small trees. *Leaves* alternate, simple, entire, usually downy beneath; stipules deciduous. *Flowers* middle-sized, white or pink, solitary or in axillary or terminal corymbose cymes. *Calyx-tube* turbinate; segments 5, short, persistent. *Petals* 5. *Stamens* many, inserted at the mouth of the calyx-tube. *Carpels* 2-5, more or less adnate to the calyx-tube; ovules 2 in each cell, erect; styles 2-5, free. *Fruit* small, with 2-5 bony 1-seeded stones.

Analysis of the Species.

Erect shrubs. Leaves deciduous.
  Flowers in many-flowered terminal cymes . . . . . . 1. *C. bacillaris.*
  Flowers in few-flowered axillary cymes or solitary . . . . . 2. *C. acuminata.*
A prostrate shrub. Leaves persistent . 3. *C. microphylla.*

1. **C. bacillaris,** Wall.; Fl. Br. Ind. ii. 384; Brandis For. Flora 208, Ind. Trees 294; Gamble Man. Ind. Timb. 326. Vern. *Ráunsh, Ruinsh, Leonsh,* Jaunsar.

A very variable shrub, usually 10-18 ft. high, but under favourable circumstances a small tree attaining a considerable girth (*e. g.*, 9 ft. 6 in. at Bálchá)*; crown spreading; bark bluish-grey, almost smooth, marked with short transverse white bars. *Leaves* 1-3·5 by ·7-1·7 in., ovate ovate-oblong obovate or lanceolate, rather membranous, finely pubescent or glabrescent and pale beneath, often minutely mucronate; midrib very prominent beneath, depressed above; main lateral nerves 6-10 pairs; base acute; petiole ·2-·4 in.; stipules ·2-·3 in. long, subulate, early caducous. *Flowers* white, ·25-·3 in. across, in spreading compound cymes at the end of short leaf-bearing branchlets; minute or 0. *Fruit* ·2-·5 in. diam., globose, 2-celled, in spreading bunches, dark-brown when ripe.

JAUNSAR and TEHRI-GARHWAL, 4,-8,500 ft.: Deothát, Bodyár, Konáin, Mundáli; Deotá, Lambátách, Bálchá, etc. Generally in open ravines and on grassy hill-sides.

Wood brownish-white, very hard, tough, close and even-grained; annual rings distinct; weight 57 lbs. per c. ft. The branches are much sought after for making walking-sticks; indeed no tree of any size is ever found which has not been repeatedly mutilated.

C. rosea, Edgew. is relegated under var. *affinis* of the above species in the Fl. Br. Ind. It is a much smaller shrub, and the smaller pink flowers open later. Found by Mr. Duthie near the Deotá temple, TEHRI-GARHWAL, and by myself at Bájámárá, JAUNSAR, and at Kulni, TEHRI-GARHWAL.

Fl. Apr.-June. Fr. June, July.

2. **C. acuminata,** Lindl.; Fl. Br. Ind. ii. 385; Brandis For. Flora 209, Ind. Trees 295; Gamble Man. Ind. Timb. 326. Vern. *Leonshi, Ráunshi, Ruinshi,* Jaunsar.

A shrub smaller than the last, never with a spreading crown; bark dark bluish-grey, shining. *Leaves* 1-2·5 by ·4-·8 in., ovate-lanceolate or elliptic, acuminate, silky-pubescent beneath; margins usually ciliate with silky hairs. *Flowers* white, ·3-·4 in. diam., solitary or in few-flowered axillary and subterminal cymes. *Calyx* turbinate, reddish-brown inside. *Fruit* ·3 in. long, turbinate, red when ripe.

---

* Measured 3rd June 1900.

JAUNSAR, 8,-10,000 ft.; common at Deoban, less so at Konáin and Mundáli.

Wood as of the last species. The branches are made into walking-sticks, but pieces of sufficient thickness are rather rare.

Fl. May, June. Fr. June, July.

3. **C. microphylla,** Wall.; Fl. Br. Ind. ii. 387; Brandis For. Flora 209, Ind. Trees 295; Gamble Man. Ind. Timb. 327. Vern. *Bheddá*, Jaunsar.

A small much-branched prostrate evergreen shrub; bark dark-grey, almost black. *Leaves* ·3-·5 by ·2-·35 in., ovate obovate or elliptic, acute obtuse or retuse, coriaceous, dark-green and glossy above, pubescent or pilose beneath, minutely petioled; margins recurved, more or less ciliate when young. *Flowers* white, ·4-·5 in. diam., axillary, solitary. *Fruit* ·3-·4 in. long, globose or obovoid, finely pubescent, scarlet when ripe.

Common in JAUNSAR and TEHRI-GARHWAL, between 6,500 and 10,000 ft., trailing on rocks or spreading on grassy hill-sides. The branches are used in Kashmir for making baskets. The ripe fruit is sweet.

Fl. Apr.-June. Fr. July, Aug.

Very similar in appearance are *C. thymifolia*, Hort., and *C. buxifolia*, Wall., Fl. Br. Ind. ii. 387, differing chiefly in the flowers being generally cymose. Both are likely to occur in the same localities, especially in the inner ranges.

Mr. Gamble thinks that *C. multiflora*, Bunge, and *C. nummularia*, Fisch., Fl. Br. Ind. ii. 386, also occur above 10,000 ft. These are bushy plants generally with small leaves. The former is somewhat larger than the other, and has, as the specific name implies, more-flowered cymes. The latter has orbicular leaves, whence its specific name.

Potentilla fruticosa, Linn., Fl. Br. Ind. ii. 347,—is a low undershrub found near Pandáwa in JAUNSAR and at Rikhshin and Moriru in TEHRI-GARHWAL. *Leaves* usually 3-foliolate; leaflets ·4-·7 in. long, lanceolate. *Flowers* solitary, diœcious. *Fruit* of hairy achenes.—*G. P. n. 48.*

Eriobotrya japonica, Lindl., Fl. Br. Ind. ii 372; the Loquat. Vern. *Loká'*, *Lukát*, Hind.—is another well-known fruit tree of this Family. *Leaves* subsessile, 6-10 in. long, oblanceolate, acuminate, distantly serrate, hard, coriaceous, densely woolly and strongly nerved beneath. *Flowers* dull-white, fragrant, in terminal panicles. *Fruit* pyriform or globose, baccate, 1·5-2 in. long, yellow or orange when ripe; seeds 2-5, dark-brown, smooth. Much cultivated at DEHRA and SAHÁRANPUR. Fl. Nov., Dec. Fr. Mar., Apr.—*G. P. n. 66.*

FAM. 35. SAXIFRAGACEÆ; G. P. N. 59.

Herbs, less frequently shrubs or trees. *Leaves* opposite or alternate, simple, usually exstipulate. *Flowers* regular, generally 2-sexual. *Calyx* more or less adnate to the ovary, rarely quite free. *Petals* 5, sometimes o, rarely 0. *Stamens* free, as many as the petals or twice their number, exceptionally numerous. *Disk* annular or glandular. *Ovary* of 2 or 3-5 carpels and as many cells, rarely 1-celled; styles as many as the carpels, free or united; ovules many; placentation axile (parietal in 1-celled 4varies). *Fruit* a berry or capsule, or composed of follicles. *Seeds* usually many, albuminous.

Analysis of the Genera.

Leaves opposite; stamens not fewer than 8.
 Stamens 8 or 10.
  Flowers polygamous; stamens linear 1. HYDRANGEA.
  Flowers 2-sexual; stamens winged . 2. DEUTZIA.
 Stamens 20-40 . . . . . . 3. PHILADELPHUS.
Lvs. alternate; stamens not more than 5.
 Ovary almost wholly superior; fruit a capsule . . . . . . 4. ITEA.
 Ovary wholly inferior; fruit a berry . 5. RIBES.

1. Hydrangea, Linn.; G. P. n. 22.

1. **H. altissima,** Wall.; Fl. Br. Ind. ii. 404; Brandis For. Flora 211, Ind. Trees 297; Gamble Man. Ind. Timb. 328. Vern. *Kathmorá,* Garhwal.

A large climbing shrub; bark cinnamon-colour, shining, membranous, loose, peeling off in long papery rolls. *Leaves* 3-6 in. long, ovate- or ovate-lanceolate, acuminate, sometimes cordate, entire or more or less dentate, membranous; main lateral nerves 6-8 pairs; petiole 1-2 in. long. *Flowers* cream-colour, polygamous, very small if fertile, enlarged to about 1 in. diam., and apetalous if sterile. *Calyx-tube* adnate to the ovary; limb 4-5-fid; segments of sterile flowers, ·2-·5 in. long, spreading. *Petals* (if present) 4-5, valvate, falling off in a cap. *Stamens* 10; filaments filiform. *Ovary* inferior, styles 2-4. *Fruit* a membranous capsule.

JAUNSAR and TEHRI-GARHWAL, in shady ravines up to 7,000 ft.: Bámsu, Lambátách, Kulni, etc.; Bear Garden, Chakrata.

The bark is used as a substitute for paper.

2. Deutzia, Thunb.; G. P. n. 27.

Shrubs with opposite branches. *Leaves* opposite, stellate-pubescent, exstipulate, serrate. *Flowers* white, more or less corymbose. *Calyx* adnate to the ovary; teeth 5, small. *Petals* 5. *Stamens* 10, alternately longer; filaments winged. *Ovary* 3-5-celled; styles 3-5. *Fruit* a 3-5-celled capsule, dehiscing septicidally.

Analysis of the Species.

Bark peeling off in papery rolls; leaves green beneath; petals imbricate . . 1. *D. corymbosa.*

Bark peeling off in thin longitudinal strips; leaves pale beneath; petals induplicate-valvate . . . . 2. *D. staminea.*

1. **D. corymbosa,** Br.; Fl. Br. Ind. ii. 406; Brandis For. Flora 212, Ind. Trees 296; Gamble Man. Ind. Timb. 329. Vern. *Bhújroi*, Jaunsar.

A shrub, 4-8 ft. high; bark light cinnamon-colour, peeling off in thin papery rolls, inner layer white. *Leaves* 1·5-3·5 by ·7-1·5 in., ovate-lanceolate, long-acuminate, closely serrate, membranous, with scattered stellate hairs beneath; petiole short. *Flowers* white, fragrant, ·5-·7 in. diam., in trichotomously corymbose terminal panicles; bracts small, deciduous; pedicels ·2-·3 in. long. *Calyx-teeth* shorter than the tube, spreading. *Petals* obovate or rounded, generally glabrous. *Styles* usually 3. *Capsule* ·2 in. diam., hemispherical, truncate.

Common in JAUNSAR and TEHRI-GARHWAL, above 6,000 ft., usually affecting shady ravines.

Wood white, soft, even-grained; weight 46 lbs. per c. ft.

Fl. May, June.

2. **D. staminea,** Br.; Fl. Br. Ind. ii. 407; Brandis For. Flora 212, Ind. Trees 296; Gamble Man. Ind. Timb. 329. Vern. *Ghúgtai, Dáhlochi,* Jaunsar.

A shrub, smaller than the above; bark dark-grey, peeling off in thin longitudinal strips, inner layer lighter coloured; branchlets scabrous with stellate pubescence. *Leaves* 1-2·5 by ·4-1·3 in., lanceolate, minutely serrulate, rough with stellate pubescence, grey beneath; petiole short. *Flowers* white, fragrant, ·3-·4 in. diam., in short trichotomous terminal panicles. *Calyx* stellate-hairy outside; teeth triangular, erect. *Petals* oblong, induplicate-valvate, pubescent outside. *Styles* usually 4. *Capsule* smaller than of the other species.

Very common in JAUNSAR and TEHRI-GARHWAL, 5,-9,000 ft., usually associated with the last, but sometimes also found on sunny hill-sides which that species avoids.

Wood similar to that of *D. corymbosa*, but somewhat lighter.

Fl. Apr.-June.

3. Philadelphus, Linn.; G. P. n. 29.

1. **P. coronarius,** Linn.; Fl. Br. Ind. ii. 407; Brandis For. Flora 212, Ind. Trees 296; Gamble Man. Ind. Timb. 329. The Mock Orange.

A shrub with light-grey bark, somewhat resembling *Deutzia corymbosa*. *Leaves* opposite, 1·5-4 by ·7-2·5 in., ovate-lanceolate, long-acuminate, finely hairy and rather glossy beneath; lateral nerves 3 pairs, sub-basal, prominent beneath, very arcuate; petiole ·25-·5 in. long. *Flowers* white, ·6-·8 in. diam., solitary or in few-flowered axillary cymes; pedicels ·3-·5 in. long. *Calyx-tube* adnate to the ovary; lobes 4, rarely 5, valvate, pubescent within. *Petals* 4, rarely 5, convolute in bud, ·3-·5 in. long. *Stamens* 20-40; filaments subulate. *Ovary* inferior, 3-5-celled; styles 3-5, more or less combined at the base. *Fruit* a capsule, ·5 in. long, 3-5-celled, turbinate or obovoid, subtruncate, dehiscing loculicidally.

Common in TEHRI-GARHWAL beyond the Tons, above 6,000 ft.; Lambátách, Deotá, etc. Rather scarce in JAUNSAR: Konáin.

Wood soft, white, with a large pith; weight 44 lbs. per c. ft.

Fl. May-July.

4. Itea, Linn.; G. P. n. 47.

1. **I. nutans**, Royle; Fl. Br. Ind. ii. 408; Brandis For. Flora 213; Ind. Trees 299; Gamble Man. Ind. Timb. 329.

A small tree with dark-grey bark. *Leaves* alternate, 4-6 by 1·5-2·5 in., ovate or elliptic-oblong, acuminate, glandular-serrate or denticulate, subcoriaceous, glabrous, dark-green and shining above; lateral nerves 5-7 pairs, joined by distinct intramarginal veins. *Flowers* white, small, in fascicles of 2-5, in simple terminal and axillary racemes which are much longer than the leaves. *Calyx* adnate to the ovary at the base; teeth 5, erect, persistent. *Petals* 5, valvate, erect. *Stamens* 5. *Ovary* oblong, 2-celled; styles simple, furrowed, persistent. *Capsule* ·2 in. long, septicidally 2-valved.

OUTER HIMALAYA and the DÚN, also TEHRI-GARHWAL; above Rájpur; banks of the Ré-nadi near Lachiwála and at Nakraunda and Mothroowála (1,800 ft.); Thadiár, 3,000 ft.

Wood brownish-white, moderately hard.

Fl. Apr.-July. Fr. Oct., Nov.

5. Ribes, Linn.; G. P. n. 71.

Usually unarmed shrubs. *Leaves* alternate, generally palmately lobed. *Flowers* middle-sized, often 1-sexual, racemed or solitary; pedicels bracteate. *Calyx* superior; tube as long as, or longer than, the ovary. *Petals* 4-5, epigynous, white yellow red or dark-purple. *Stamens* 4-5, epigynous. *Ovary* inferior, 1-celled; ovules numerous, on 2 perietal placentas; styles 2, free or connate. *Fruit* an oblong or globose berry.

Analysis of the Species.

Racemes erect in flower; calyx-tube hardly exceeding the fruit . . . 1. *R. glaciale.*
Racemes drooping; calyx-tube produced above the fruit . . . 2. *R. rubrum.*

1. **R. glaciale**, Wall.; Fl. Br. Ind. ii. 410; Brandis For. Flora 14, Ind. Trees 299; Gamble Man. Ind. Timb. 330.

A shrub, 5-8 ft. high, with shining brown stems; cuticle peeling off in long strips or rolls. *Leaves* 1-2·5 in. long, cordate, 3-5-lobed with the middle lobe often elongated, or not lobed and ovate, 3-5-nerved at the base, with 2-4 pairs of lateral nerves in the middle lobe, glabrous or pubescent along the nerves beneath, sometimes with scattered hairs above; margins crenate-serrate. *Flowers* about ·25 in. diam., greenish (drying brownish or pink), in pubescent racemes 2-3 in. long which are erect in flower but drooping in fruit; bract much longer than the pedicels. *Berries* acid, ·25 in. long, globose, smooth, glabrous or minutely pubescent.

TEHRI-GARHWAL, above 9,000 ft.: Rikhshin. Rare, if it occurs at all, in JAUNSAR.

Fl. May. Fr. July.

2. **R. rubrum,** Linn.; Fl. Br. Ind. ii. 411; Brandis For. Flora 215, Ind. Trees 299; Gamble Man. Ind. Timb. 330. The Red Currant. Vern. *Karan,* Jaunsar, probably from *currant.*

A shrub 6-10 ft. high with dark-brown shining stems marked with horizontal lenticel-bars; cuticle peeling off in long strips or rolls; young shoots red, glabrate. *Leaves* (closely resembling those of *Acer cæsium*) 3-5 in. diam., as broad as long or broader, cordate, 3-5-lobed, crenate-serrate, 3-5-nerved at the base, membranous, glabrescent, somewhat shining beneath; lateral nerves 3-5 pairs on the 3 larger lobes, depressed above, very prominent beneath; petiole red, 3-4 in. long, flattened and with a few scattered grey hairs along the margins near the base. *Racemes* 4-6 in. long, pubescent, many-flowered, from the nodes of last year's shoots with a few small leaves near the base; bracts not exceeding the pedicels. *Flowers* greenish-yellow, ·3-·4 in. diam.; pedicels about 1 in. long. *Berries* ·3-·4 in. long, globose, smooth, red.

Common in JAUNSAR and TEHRI-GARHWAL, above 7,500 ft. —Deoban to Mundáli; also at Deotá.

Fl. Apr., May. Fr. May, June.

Saxifraga ligulata, Wall., Fl. Br. Ind. ii. 398. The Wax Flower. Vern. *Shilphára* (the *rock-splitter,* which curiously corresponds to the meaning of the generic name), *Dhonk-phúlúté,* Jaunsar, —is an herbaceous plant common and conspicuous enough to deserve mention. *Leaves* 3-5 in. diam., suborbicular, fleshy, glabrous, strongly ciliate, often pinkish beneath. *Flowers* pinkish-white, waxy, ·6-·8 in. diam. *Petals* clawed. *Carpels* and *styles* 2, the latter very long. Fl. Apr., May.—*G. P. n. 6.*

Order 2—MYRTALES.

FAM. 36. RHIZOPHORACEÆ; G. P. N. 65.

Trees or shrubs. *Leaves* opposite, entire, coriaceous, generally glabrous; stipules interpetiolar, early caducous. *Flowers* regular, axillary, usually bisexual. *Calyx* more or less adnate to the ovary or free, 4-14-toothed or lobed, persistent. *Petals* as many as the calyx-lobes. *Stamens* 2-4 times the number of petals; filaments free. *Ovary* 5-1-celled by the absence of the septa; styles usually connate; ovules pendulous. *Fruit* 1-celled, 1-seeded, coriaceous, indehiscent. *Seeds* exalbuminous.

1. Carallia, Roxb.; G. P. n. 5.

1. **C. integerrima,** DC.; Fl. Br. Ind. ii. 439; Brandis For. Flora 219; Gamble Man. Ind. Timb. 335. Syn.—*C. lucida*, Roxb.; Brandis Ind. Trees 305, 709.

An evergreen tree; bark dark-grey and smooth on old stems, lighter-grey and corky on young poles, often developing bunches of fleshy adventitious roots on the trunk. *Leaves* 3-5 by 1·5-3 in., elliptic-obovate, entire or minutely serrulate above the middle, coriaceous, glabrous, shining; margins usually recurved; main lateral nerves 8-10 pairs, indistinct until dry; petiole ·2-·4 in. long, stout, margined; stipules ·5-1·2 in. long, interpetiolar, lanceolate, convolute, terminating the branchlets. *Flowers* sessile, 6-8-merous, ·2 in. across, in short axillary trichotomous cymes; peduncles and pedicels stout. *Calyx-lobes* 5-8, erect, valvate. *Petals* 5-8, white, orbicular, serrate at the apex. *Stamens* twice as many as the petals and opposite to them; filaments filiform. *Fruit* about ·2 in. across, globose, 1-celled, usually 1-seeded.

Only a few trees have been found in the Nakraunda swamp and along the banks of the Ré-nadi near Lachiwála, 1,800 ft.; also on the Táwá nálá near Khairi, 1,200 ft.

The heartwood is red, hard and durable, and works and polishes well. It has a very pretty silver-grain resembling that of the oaks. "It is used in South Kanara for furniture and cabinetmaking and in Burma for planking, furniture and rice-pounders."—*Mr. J. S. Gamble.* The leaves are lopped for cattle-fodder.

Fl. Dec.-Apr.

FAM. 37. COMBRETACEÆ; G. P. N. 66.

Trees or shrubs. *Leaves* usually simple, petiolate, entire, opposite or alternate, exstipulate. *Flowers* bracteate, usually bisexual. *Calyx-tube* adnate to the ovary; lobes 4-5, valvate. *Petals* 4-5, or none. *Stamens* 4-5, or twice as many, inserted on the calyx. *Ovary* inferior, 1-celled; style simple; ovules 1-7, pendulous from the apex of the cell. *Fruit* usually a coriaceous drupe, 1-celled, 1-seeded, winged or angular; seed exalbuminous; cotyledons convolute or plano-convex, often fleshy and oily.

Analysis of the Genera.

Flowers in spikes or racemes.
  Large trees with alternate or sub-opposite leaves.
    Petals none . . . . 1. TERMINALIA.
  Climbing shrubs with opposite leaves. Petals
    generally present . . . . . 3. COMBRETUM.
Flowers in heads; leaves alternate or inconstantly
  opposite; petals none . . . . . 2. ANOGEISSUS.

1. Terminalia, Linn.; G. P. n. 1.

Large trees. *Leaves* alternate or sub-opposite, entire or slightly crenulate, exstipulate, often with glands on the petiole. *Flowers* small, sessile, usually bisexual; bracts deciduous. *Calyx-tube* produced over the ovary with a constricted mouth; lobes 4-5, valvate. *Petals* 0. *Stamens* 8-10, inserted on the calyx-tube in two rows. *Ovary* 1-celled; ovules 2-3, pendulous. *Fruit* oblong ovoid ellipsoidal or globose, winged or angular, with a coriaceous or bony kernel; cotyledons convolute.

Analysis of the Species.

Fruit fleshy, not winged.

Petiole long; fruit velvety, not ribbed . . 1. *T. belerica.*

Petiole short; fruit glabrous, more or less ribbed 2. *T. Chebula.*

Fruit coriaceous, with 5 broad wings . . . 3. *T. tomentosa.*

1. **T. belerica,** Roxb.; Fl. Br. Ind. ii. 445; Brandis For. Flora 222, Ind. Trees 307, 709; Gamble Man. Ind. Timb. 337. Vern. *Baherá*, Hind.

A large deciduous tree with bluish or ashy-grey bark uneven with longitudinal furrows. *Leaves* alternate, crowded towards the ends of the branches, 3-8 in. long, obovate-elliptic, coriaceous, pale beneath, subacute or acuminate; lateral nerves 5-8 on either side of the thick midrib; base often unequal; petiole 1-3 in., usually glandular. *Spikes* 3-6 in. long, simple, slender, interrupted. *Flowers* about ·2 in. across, pale-white or greenish-yellow, with an offensive smell, the upper often male; bracts early caducous. *Calyx-lobes* triangular, woolly inside. *Ovary* tomentose. *Fruit* 1 in. long, ovoid ellipsoidal or globose, grey-velvety; nut thick-walled and hard.

It is a constant companion of Sál and is found almost everywhere in the DÚN and SAHÁRANPUR FORESTS; also in JAUNSAR in the Ámláwa and Tons Valleys.

It grows to a height of 80-100 ft. with a girth of 8-10 ft., and is easily recognized from a distance by its characteristic bark and broad massive crown. The wood is light-grey or yellowish, hard and coarse-grained, not durable; heartwood and annual rings not distinct; weight about 50 lbs. per c. ft. It is used for various purposes, from house-building to packing-cases, and sells readily in the region of this Flora. The fruit is very valuable, being one of the myrobolans of commerce. "It is a favourite food of monkeys, deer, sheep, goat and cattle,"—*Sir D. Brandis*, and is used in dyeing and making ink. The kernel is edible, and gives an oil which is used for the hair.

Fl. Apr.-June, after the new leaves. Fr. Dec.-Feb.

2. **T. Chebula,** Retz.; Hook. Fl. Br. Ind. ii. 446; Brandis For. Flora 223, Ind. Trees 308; Gamble Man. Ind. Timb. 338. Vern. *Har*, *Harr*, *Harh*, or *Hararh*, Hind.

A large deciduous tree with dark-brown bark; young parts covered with rusty hairs. *Leaves* **mostly sub-opposite, 3-6 in. long, ovate or oblong-ovate, acuminate; lateral nerves arcuate, prominent, 6-12 on either side of the midrib; base acute or rounded; petiole hardly exceeding 1 inch, often with 2 or more glands on the upper**

side. *Flowers* about ·1 in. across, all bisexual, sessile, dull-white, in panicled or clustered usually-terminal spikes; bracts subulate. *Calyx-lobes* acutely triangular, covered inside with brown hairs; limb cup-shaped. *Stamens* 8-10; filaments long, spreading. *Fruit* 1-2 in. long, obovoid, ellipsoidal or ovoid, more or less distinctly ribbed; nut hard, with a rough grooved surface.

Found in the same localities as the last, but is generally less common. It is, however, fairly common in certain limited areas, *e.g.*, along the Lambi Ráu, Thäno; south of the Sample area, Lachiwála; forests near Timli, etc.

In the region of this Flora it is a smaller tree than the last. The heartwood is pale or dark-brown with a greenish tinge, finely mottled, hard, close-grained, fairly durable, and is used for house-building, agricultural implements and furniture; weight about 60 lbs. per c. ft. The bark, the galls formed on young twigs, and the fruit are used for tanning and dyeing. Indeed the last is the most important part of the tree, being the black myrobolan of commerce and is largely exported to Europe from Bombay. The unripe fruit is a favourite drug in Hindu medical practice.

New leaves in April. Fl. Apr.-June. Fr. Jan.-Mar.

3. **T. tomentosa**, W. & A.; Fl. Br. Ind. ii. 447; Brandis For. Flora 225, Ind. Trees 310; Gamble Man. Ind. Timb. 341. Vern. *Sáin*, Dún and Sahàranpur; *Asainá*, Hind.

A large deciduous tree; bark dark-grey or black much furrowed, exfoliating in thick rectangular plates; inner bark reddish-brown; young parts rusty-pubescent. *Leaves* alternate or sub-opposite, 5-9 by 2·5-4 in., oblong elliptic or obovate, coriaceous, glabrescent above, tomentose beneath; lateral nerves 10-20 pairs, parallel, slightly arcuate; base often unequal sided, acute or rounded; petiole ·3-·4 in., often with a gland or two on the sides. *Flowers* bisexual, dull-yellow, ·1-·15 in. across, sessile, in large erect panicled spikes. *Calyx-lobes* ovate, broad-acute, often hairy; free part of the tube salver-shaped. *Fruit* 1·5-2·5 in. long, with 5 broad transversely-striated coriaceous wings having a crenulate edge.

Associated with Sál in the SIWALIK DIVISION, especially in clayey localities; also found in the OUTER HIMALAYAN VALLEYS, up to 4,000 ft.

It grows to a height of 80-100 ft. with a girth of 8-10 ft. Sapwood reddish or yellowish-white; heartwood dark-brown, with darker streaks, very hard, seasons well, but is liable to split. It is used for house-building, agricultural implements and such other purposes. It is also an excellent fuel and gives very good charcoal.

The bark is much used for tanning and sometimes also for dyeing. The "Tassar" silkworm is fed on the leaves in the Central Provinces. Sáin coppices and pollards well, and is a good nurse for young Sál in frosty localities. The ovary is sometimes attacked by a gall-insect which prevents the fruit being formed.

New leaves May, June. Fl. June-Aug., and sometimes a second flush in the cold season (Dec. 1893 in the Dún). Fr. Feb.-Apr.

T. Arjuna, Bedd.; Fl. Br. Ind. ii. 447.; Vern. *Arjún*, Hind.;— is a tree closely resembling the last species in foliage and inflorescence, but differs in having smooth grey bark and smaller 5-7-winged fruit. It is an excellent avenue tree and has been planted as such near Fatehpur on the Sahāranpur-Chakrata road, and (but looking almost like self-sown) on the Dehra-Hardwar and Hardwar-Rikhikesh roads not far from Pardúni and in the swamp near that place. The wood is used for much the same purposes as that of *Sáin*.

Fl. Apr., May. Fr. Cold season.

2. Anogeissus, Wall.; G. P. n. 5.

1. **A. latifolia,** Wall.; Fl. Br. Ind. ii. 450; Brandis For. Flora 227, Ind. Trees 315; Gamble Man. Ind. Timb. 346. Vern. *Bákli*, *Báṇkli*, Hind.

A tall tree with smooth greenish-white bark. *Leaves* alternate or inconstantly opposite, 2-4 by 1-2·5 in., elliptic, ovate or ovate-lanceolate, acute obtuse or emarginate, subcoriaceous, glabrescent; petiole ·3-·5 in. long. *Flowers* small, in globose heads; heads about ·5 in. diam., in short axillary racemes. *Calyx-tube* compressed, laterally 2-winged, long and narrowed above the ovary. *Petals* 0. *Stamens* 10, in two series. *Ovary* 1-celled; ovules 2, pendulous. *Fruit* a dry drupe ·3 by ·2 in., compressed, narrowly 2-winged, imbricately arranged in the head, crowned with the remains of the calyx-tube which is now modified into a stiff beak.

Common in the DÚN and SAHÁRANPUR FORESTS and on the OUTER HIMALAYAN slopes ascending to 4,000 ft.; sometimes gregarious in small patches on alluvial banks of streams.

Wood grey, close- and even-grained, compact, hard, very tough and elastic, but splits in seasoning, and is not durable unless kept dry; weight 55-70 lbs. per c. ft. It is used extensively for construction, furniture, agricultural implements, house-posts, poles for carrying loads and such other purposes requiring toughness and elasticity. The tree yields a very clear gum which is soluble in water, and the leaves are much valued for tanning.

Fl. May, June. Fr. Cold season.

3. Combretum, Linn.; G. P. n. 10.

1. **C. decandrum,** Roxb.; Fl. Br. Ind. ii. 452; Brandis For. Flora 221, Ind. Trees 312; Gamble Man. Ind. Timb. 349. Vern. *Rúel* or *Roel*, Dún.

A large climbing shrub; young parts covered with silky pubescence. *Leaves* opposite, 4-5 by 1·5-2·3 in., elliptic-oblong, acuminate, glabrous, the floral ones or bracts 2-2·5 in. long, dull-white, villous; lateral nerves 6-8 on either side of the midrib, arcuate; petiole ·2-·4 in. long. *Flowers* greenish-white, about ·15 in. long, numerous, in dense villous cylindrical racemes about 1 in. long, which in their turn are arranged in large terminal panicles. *Calyx* hairy; lobes 5, valvate, deciduous. *Petals* 5, small, oblong, glabrous, inserted between the calyx-lobes. *Stamens* 10, in two series. *Ovary* 1-celled; ovules 2-5, pendulous. *Fruit* 1 in. long, oblong or elliptic, with 4-5 smooth papery wings.

Very common in the WESTERN DÚN, especially from Ámbári to Kálsi. All the hill-side round the latter town is clothed in white when this climber flowers with its characteristic petaloid bracts.

Fl. Feb., Mar. Fr. May, June.

C. nanum, Ham.; Fl. Br. Ind. ii. 457;—is a small procumbent undershrub found in grass lands near Maindrot in the Tons Valley, TEHRI-GARHWAL, and also occasionally in similar localities in the DÚN, *e.g.*, Sabháwála. *Leaves* opposite, 2-4 by 1·5-3·5 in., ovate or obovate, glabrous. *Flowers* in terminal and axillary racemes. *Fruit* 1·5 by 1 in., coriaceous, light, with 4-5 papery wings. It grows annually from a perennial rootstock down to which it is burnt by forest fires.

Quisqualis indica, Linn.; Fl. Br. Ind. ii. 459, the Rangoon-creeper,—is a climbing shrub cultivated in gardens in SAHÁRANPUR and the DÚN. *Leaves* opposite, about 4 in. long, obovate, acuminate, entire. *Calyx-tube* prolonged about 2 in. above the ovary; limb 5-fid. *Petals* red, oblong or round. *Fruit* extremely rare, about 1 in. long, sharply 5-angled, glabrous, black.—*G. P. n. 12.*

FAM. 38. MYRTACEÆ; G. P. N. 67.

Trees or shrubs, rarely herbs. *Leaves* opposite, exceptionally alternate, simple, usually entire and gland-dotted, exstipulate, mostly coriaceous. *Flowers* generally bisexual, solitary or in heads cymes or corymbs. *Calyx-tube* adnate to the ovary; limb 4-5-cleft, or entire, deciduous or persistent. *Disk* coating the calyx-tube. *Petals* inserted on the disk, as many as the calyx-lobes and alternating with them, rarely absent. *Stamens* usually indefinite, inserted with the petals in several rows; filaments free or connate at the base forming bundles or a short tube. *Ovary* syncarpous, inferior or half-inferior, 1-celled, 1-ovuled, or 2-many-celled with indefinite ovules on axile placentas. *Fruit* dehiscent or indehiscent, crowned with the remains of the calyx-limb; seeds compressed or angular, exalbuminous.

Analysis of the Genera.

Leaves opposite, entire, gland-dotted . . . . 1. EUGENIA.
Leaves alternate, crenate-serrate, not gland-dotted 2. CAREYA.

1. Eugenia, Linn.; G. P. n. 58.

Evergreen trees or shrubs. *Leaves* opposite, entire, penninerved. *Flowers* usually tetramerous, in lateral or terminal trichotomous cymes or panicles. *Bracts* small, deciduous. *Calyx-tube* globose or more or less elongate; lobes usually 4. *Petals* generally 4, free or united in a calyptra. *Stamens* indefinite, in several series, free or slightly combined into four bundles; anthers versatile. *Ovary* usually 2-celled, with several ovules in each cell. *Fruit* a drupe-like berry, crowned with the remains of the calyx-limb; seeds variously compressed.

Analysis of the Species.

Lvs. subcoriaceous, soft; lateral nerves distant 1. *E. operculata.*
Lvs. coriaceous, tough; lateral nerves very close 2. *E. Jambolana.*

1. **E. operculata,** Roxb.; Fl. Br. Ind. ii. 498; Brandis For. Flora, 234, Ind. Trees 322; Gamble Man. Ind. Timb. 360. Vern. *Piáman, Thúti,* Dún.

A moderate-sized evergreen tree; bark rough with irregular hard scales. *Leaves* 3-6 by 2-3·5 in., broad-ovate or elliptic, rounded at the apex or obtusely acuminate, very variable in shape and size, subcoriaceous, soft, turning red in the cold season; lateral nerves 8-12 pairs, prominent beneath, gradually fainter towards the margin; petiole ·7-1 in. long. *Flowers* tetramerous, small, greenish, sub-sessile, in 3-flowered cymes arranged in trichotomous lateral panicles below the current year's leaves. *Calyx* campanulate, with short obtuse lobes. *Petals* united and falling off in one piece (*operculum*). *Berry* globose or ovoid, ·3-·5 in. diam., juicy.

Common in the DÚN and SAHÁRANPUR FORESTS, especially in blanks inside Sál areas, where it is often the first tree to appear, under whose shelter seedlings of superior species have a better chance against frost and excessive heat.

Heartwood not distinct. Wood brown or reddish-grey, hard, close- and fine-grained; weight 45-50 lbs. per c. ft. It is used for building and agricultural implements. The fruit is edible.

Fl. Apr., May, sometimes also in autumn. Fr. three months after flowering.

2. **E. Jambolana,** Lam.; Fl. Br. Ind. ii. 499; Brandis For. Flora 233, Ind. Trees 323; Gamble Man. Ind. Timb. 361. Vern. *Jáman, Jámún,* Hind.

A large evergreen tree; bark light-grey, fairly smooth, with shallow depressions caused by exfoliation. *Leaves* 3-6 by 1·5-2·5 in., very variable in shape, ovate-oblong or oblong-lanceolate, acuminate, coriaceous, tough, smooth, shining above except when very old; lateral nerves numerous, almost straight, very fine, uniting within the margin to form intramarginal nerves; petiole ·3-1 in., channelled. *Flowers* tetramerous, small, greenish, subsessile, arranged in threes in lateral or terminal trichotomous panicles. *Calyx-tube* funnel-shaped; limb campanulate, subtruncate. *Petals* united into a calyptra and falling off in one piece. *Berry* ·5-1 in. long, oblong-obovoid or sub-globose, pink while ripening; black smooth shining and very juicy when fully ripe, deep-pink below the thin elastic black skin.

Very commonly associated with Sál in the DÚN, less so in the SAHÁRANPUR FORESTS. It is almost gregarious in damp and swampy localities, mixed with laurels and other evergreen trees. It is also found in the Tons Valley, JAUNSAR and TEHRI-GARHWAL, up to 4,000 ft., and along streams in the SAHÁRANPUR SIWALIKS.

The heartwood is reddish-brown, tough and hard, very durable under water but less so and liable to warp if kept dry; weight about 45 lbs. per c. ft. It is used for building, agricultural implements and well-work, being especially suitable for use under water. The bark is used for dyeing and tanning and also in medicine. The fruit is eaten, and is considered good for people suffering from want of appetite or enlargement of the spleen. The kernel of the fruit is a specific for diabetes.

E. Jambos, Linn., Fl. Br. Ind. ii. 474. Vern. *Guláb Jámún* or *Guláb Jám*, Hind., the Rose-apple,—is cultivated for its fruit and for ornament in gardens in the DÚN. It is an evergreen tree with narrow lanceolate acuminate shining *leaves*, and large white tassel-like tetramerous *flowers* in short cymose terminal *racemes*. *Berry* 1-2 in. long, obovoid or subglobose, crowned with the 4 persistent calyx-lobes, having a sweet taste and a delicate odour of rose when ripe,—whence the vernacular names.

2. Careya, Roxb.; G. P. n. 62.

1. **C. arborea,** Roxb.; Hook. Fl. Br. Ind. ii. 511; Brandis For. Flora 236, Ind. Trees 322; Gamble Man. Ind. Timb. 364. Vern. *Kúmbi*, *Kúmbhi*, Hind.

A fairly large deciduous tree; bark dark-grey, exfoliating in thin narrow strips, fibrous inside. *Leaves* alternate, 6-12 by 3-6 in., obovate oblanceolate or oblong, obtuse or shortly acuminate, sessile or narrowed into a very short marginate petiole, finely crenate or serrate, rather membranous, glabrous. *Flowers* sessile, 3-4 in. across, usually a few together in terminal spikes, 3-8 in. long. *Calyx-lobes* 4, ovate, obtuse, imbricate; tube almost wholly adnate to the ovary, funnel-shaped. *Petals* 4, about 2 in. long, elliptic, white, very tender, caducous. *Stamens* very numerous, in several series; filaments red, filiform, 2-3 in. long, connate into a short tube below, the innermost and outermost without anthers. *Ovary* 4- rarely 5-celled; style long, simple, erect; ovules many, on axile placentas. *Fruit* globose, about 3 in. diam., crowned with the calyx-segments and the remains of the long filiform style.

Found only sporadically in the DÚN and SAHÁRANPUR FORESTS, usually in shady places.

The heartwood is scanty, dull-red or reddish-brown, mottled, even-grained, hard, strong and elastic, takes a good polish, seasons well and is very durable; the weight varies between wide limits, being 38-60 lbs. per c. ft. It is used for agricultural implements and cart-building, and is much sought after by boatmen in Assam for oars and rudders on account of its elasticity and durability. The bark is used in medicine, and fuzes, coarse cordage and sacks are made from the inner substance.

Fl. and new leaves Mar., Apr. Fr. July.

C. herbacea, Roxb.; Fl. Br. Ind. ii. 510, is a small perennial undershrub having a woody rootstock, found on grassy slopes of the SIWALIKS, and in the Pathri forest, SAHÁRANPUR. *Leaves* 6-8 by 2-3 in., obovate, oblanceolate or spathulate. *Petals* about 1·5-2 in. long, greenish-purple, elliptic. *Fruit* 1·5 in. diam., much like that of *C. arborea*.

The following Genera need only be briefly noticed:—

1. PSIDIUM, Linn.; *G. P. n. 45. Leaves* opposite, aromatic but not dotted. *Flowers* large, white, on axillary peduncles. *Calyx-tube* obovate; lobes 4-5, valvate. *Petals* free. *Fruit* a many-seeded berry.

P. Guava, Raddi.; Fl. Br. Ind. ii. 468. Vern. *Ámrúd* Hind.,—is the Guava tree of gardens. The wood is hard and even-grained and is used for wood-engraving, instruments, and handles of spears.

2. EUCALYPTUS, L'Her.; *G. P. n. 30. Leaves* in saplings opposite, horizontal, cordate, sessile; in mature trees alternate, vertical, petiolate, ovate to lanceolate, acuminate, falcate. *Flowers* in umbels or heads. *Stamens* very numerous, capped in the bud with a caducous operculum. *Fruit* woody consisting of the enlarged calyx-tube; seeds often very minute.

Many species of this very large Australian Genus have been introduced in India, and plantations of one of them,—*E. globulus*, Labill, the Blue Gum,—successfully made in the Nilgiris. *E.*

tereticornes, Smith, and *E. citriodora*, Hooker, are growing fairly well in DEHRA and SAHÁRANPUR.

3. BARRINGTONIA, Forst.; *G. P. n. 61*. *Leaves* alternate, crowded at the ends of the branches, crenate-serrate, not dotted. *Flowers* in long terminal or lateral racemes. *Calyx-tube* ovoid. *Petals* 4-5, imbricate. *Stamens* indefinite; filaments very long. *Fruit* fibrous and berry-like.

B. acutangula, Gærtn.; Fl. Br. Ind. ii. 508. Vern. *Sanáffar, Injar*, Hind.,—cultivated in gardens in DEHRA for its red flowers in long pendulous racemes. *Leaves* obovate, usually serrulate, narrowed into a short petiole. *Ovary* 2-celled. *Fruit* oblong, 4-angled. The wood has a handsome silver-grain and can be used for furniture.

FAM. 39. MELASTOMACEÆ; G. P. N. 68.

Herbs or shrubs. *Leaves* opposite or whorled, simple, entire, 3-7-nerved from the base to the apex. *Flowers* usually terminal, regular, 2-sexual. *Calyx-tube* generally constricted above, more or less adnate to the ovary. *Petals* twisted in bud. *Stamens* 4-10, alternate ones being often rudimentary; anthers usually opening by pores at the apex, connective tubercled or spurred. *Ovary* 4-5-celled; style simple, filiform. *Fruit* usually a many-seeded capsule. *Seeds* exalbuminous.

This Order is of little interest in this part of the country although some Genera as *Memecylon*, are common and important in the forests of Southern and Eastern India. The following plants of Genus *Osbeckia*, Linn.; *G. P. n. 38*,—need only be briefly noticed:—

1. *O. stellata*, Wall.; Fl. Br. Ind. ii. 517. A hairy shrub, 4-6 ft. high, with tetragonal branches, found at Chakrata, Mussoorie, etc. *Leaves* 3 in. long, lanceolate, 5-nerved, with short hairs on both surfaces; petiole ·4 in. *Flowers* purple, about 1 in. across. *Calyx* densely woolly outside. *Fruit* ·5 in. long, ovoid, felted outside. Fl. Aug.-Oct.

2. *O. chinensis*, Linn.; Fl. Br. Ind. ii. 515. An undershrub about 2 ft. high, found in damp localities in the DÚN, *e.g.*, Rámgarh. *Leaves* 2-3 in. long, narrow-oblong, 3-5-nerved, hairy; petiole ·15 in. *Flowers* mauve. *Calyx* slightly pubescent outside, nearly glabrous in the fruit. *Fruit* ovoid, ·3 in. long. Fl. Sept., Oct.

FAM. 40. LYTHRACEÆ; G. P. N. 69.

Trees, shrubs, or herbs, often with quadrangular branches. *Leaves* entire, generally opposite; stipules none. *Flowers* bisexual, usually regular, solitary or in cymes or panicles. *Calyx-tube* free, persistent; lobes 3-6, valvate. *Petals* as many as the calyx-lobes, and alternating with them, rarely absent. *Stamens* definite or indefinite, inserted on the calyx-tube. *Ovary* 2-6-celled, usually free; style long, persistent; ovules many, attached to an axile placenta. *Fruit* a capsule, 1-4- or many-celled; seeds numerous, without albumen.

Analysis of the Genera.

Flowers irregular; ovary superior . 1. WOODFORDIA.
Flowers regular; ovary superior.
  Flowers 4-merous; stamens 8 . . 2. LAWSONIA.
  Flowers 6-merous; stamens indefinite 3. LAGERSTRŒMIA.
Flowers regular; ovary inferior . . 4. PUNICA.

1. Woodfordia, Salisb.; G. P. n. 8.

1. **W. floribunda**, Salisb.; Fl. Br. Ind. ii. 572; Brandis For. Flora 238, Ind. Trees 341; Gamble Man. Ind. Timb. 369. Vern. *Dháulá*, *Dháu*, Hind.; *Dháttri*, Sans.

A large shrub with long spreading branches; stem more or less fluted, often with 1 or 2 concentric bands of cortical tissue inside the wood; bark smooth, peeling off in thin scales; young shoots and leaves with numerous black glands. *Leaves* opposite or sub-opposite, sometimes in whorls of 3, distichous, subsessile, 2-4 by ·8-1·3 in., lanceolate or ovate-lanceolate, usually acuminate, rounded or cordate at the base, entire, pale and generally grey pubescent beneath; lateral nerves 6-12 pairs, prominent beneath and joined by intramarginal veins. *Flowers* in short panicled axillary cymes, rarely solitary. *Calyx* ·4-·6 in. long, tubular, bright-red, curved, oblique at the mouth; teeth 6, short, with as many minute accessory lobes outside. *Petals* 6, white, acute, inserted in the sinuses of the calyx-tube and scarcely exceeding the calyx-teeth. *Stamens* 12, much exserted, declinate, inserted near the base of the calyx; filaments red; anthers versatile. *Ovary* 2-celled; ovules many, on axile placentas. (The stamens and styles are of varying lengths, the flowers thus becoming dimorphic or trimorphic.) *Capsule* ellipsoid, included in the persistent calyx-tube; seeds many.

Very common in SAHÁRANPUR and the DÚN. Also in valleys up to 5,000 ft. in the HILLS, *e.g.*, Ámláwa, Binálgádh, Dhárágádh, Dhármigádh, Tons and Pábar Valleys, etc.

Wood reddish-white, close-grained, hard, weighing 46 lbs. per c. ft. It is suitable for axe-handles, but is used chiefly for fuel. The flowers give a red dye, which is used for dyeing silk. The bark is used in Hindu medicine.

Fl. Feb.-Apr. Fr. Apr.-June.

2. Lawsonia, Linn.; G. P. n. 19.

1. **L. alba,** Lamb.; Fl. Br. Ind. ii. 573; Brandis For. Flora 238, Ind. Trees 340; Gamble Man. Ind. Timb. 370. Vern. *Mehndi*, Hind.

A shrub with thin greyish-brown bark; branchlets angular, sometimes spinescent. *Leaves* opposite, ·7-1 in. long, elliptic, acute at both ends or the tip obtuse, minutely petioled, entire, coriaceous. *Flowers* ·2 in. diam., greenish-white, sweet-scented, in large cymosely-branched terminal panicles. *Calyx-tube* exceedingly short; lobes 4, ·1 in. long, ovate, persistent. *Petals* 4, wrinkled. *Stamens* usually 8, inserted in pairs between the petals. *Ovary* free, 4-celled; ovules many, on axile placentas; style long. *Capsule* ·2 in. diam., globose, ultimately 1-celled, irregularly breaking up; seeds angular, on a central placenta.

It is cultivated in SAHÁRANPUR and the DÚN, indeed throughout India, as a hedge-plant, and also for its leaves, which are used to dye the nails, skin and beard. A plaster of the green leaves is said to be good for itches and other skin-diseases. A delightful essence is extracted from the flowers, which passes by the name *Henna* in Upper India.

Fl. and fr. throughout the year.

3. Lagerstrœmia, Linn.; G. P. n. 24.

Trees or shrubs. *Leaves* opposite (or the uppermost alternate), entire, short-petiolate. *Flowers* bracteate in axillary or terminal panicles. *Calyx-tube* funnel-shaped, smooth or grooved; lobes usually 6, ovate, valvate. *Petals* 6, long-clawed, inserted between the calyx-lobes. *Stamens* numerous; filaments filiform exserted; anthers versatile. *Ovary* sessile, 3-6-celled; style filiform; ovules numerous on axile placentas. *Capsule* coriaceous, 3-6-celled, loculicidally dehiscent, strongly seated on the persistent calyx; seeds winged.

1. **L. parviflora,** Roxb.; Fl. Br. Ind. ii. 575; Brandis For. Flora 239, Ind. Trees 338; Gamble Man. Ind. Timb. 371. Vern. *Dhaurá, Dhauri,* Dún; *Adhuári,* Saháranpur.

A fairly large deciduous tree; bark light-brown or ash-coloured, even, smooth, exfoliating in dark-coloured scurfy pieces. *Leaves* 2·5-4 in. long, oblong, acute or acuminate, coriaceous, glabrous above, glaucous and very closely reticulate beneath; petiole about ·1 in. long. *Flowers* ·2-·3 in. across, white, fragrant, in lax axillary and terminal panicles. *Calyx* smooth, glabrous or pubescent. *Petals* very membranous, with a wavy margin. *Filaments* too weak to be straight, 6 of the outermost series longer than the rest. *Capsule* ovoid or cylindrical, ·6-1 by ·4-·6 in., a quarter immersed in the somewhat accrescent and woody calyx; seeds with a terminal wing having a thick curved back, ·5 in. long including the wing.

A constant companion of Sál and also one of the principal species in scrub jungles; hence very common in the DÚN and SAHÁRANPUR FORESTS.

Wood greyish-brown, often with a reddish tinge, smooth and even-grained, very hard, seasons well, takes a fine polish; fairly durable; weight 40-60 lbs. per c. ft. It is used for agricultural implements, for construction, buggy-shafts and axe-handles. The bark and the leaves are used for tanning.

New leaves in May. Fl. May-July. Fr. Autumn, but remains long on the tree.

L. indica, Linn.; Fl. Br. Ind. ii. 575. Vern. *Sáoni,* Hind.—a shrub with showy flowers, is cultivated in gardens throughout India and is conspicuous in DEHRA DÚN. *Leaves* 2 in. long, glabrous, oblong. *Calyx* not woody in the fruit. *Petals* bright-pink or milky-white, long-clawed, much curled.

L. Flos-Reginæ, Retz.; Fl. Br. Ind. ii. 577. Vern. *Járúl*, E. Beng., *Ajhár*, Assam—is a large tree cultivated in gardens at DEHRA for ornament. *Leaves* 5-10 in. long, elliptic or lanceolate, petiolate. *Flowers* 2-3 in. across, mauve, in large terminal panicles. *Calyx* woody and much grooved in the fruit. *Petals* clawed, margins very wavy. *Capsule* 1 in. long, globose. It is a well-known timber tree of Eastern Bengal, Assam and Burma.

4. Punica, Linn.; G. P. n. 27.

This is an anomalous Genus, being closely allied to MYRTACEÆ through *Psidium* and to ROSACEÆ through *Cydonia*.

1. **P. Granatum,** Linn.; Fl. Br. Ind. ii. 581; Brandis For. Flora 241, Ind. Trees 341; Gamble Man. Ind. Timb. 377. The Pomegranate. Vern. *Dánoi*, Jaunsar; *Ánár*, Hind.

A shrub or small tree with dark-grey bark; branchlets often spinescent. *Leaves* opposite sub-opposite or clustered, 1-2·5 by ·4-1 in., oblong, obovate or oblanceolate, obtuse, narrowed to a short marginate petiole, entire, rather membranous, quite glabrous, shining, lateral nerves indistinct. *Flowers* sessile, terminal, solitary or in short 3-flowered cymes. *Calyx* adnate to the ovary below, (in flower) about 1 by ·5-·6 in., tubular, greenish-red, fleshy; lobes 5-7, valvate, acute, sub-erect. *Petals* as many as the calyx-lobes, ·5-1 in. long, oblanceolate, very membranous, wrinkled, bright-red. *Stamens* numerous, inserted in the calyx-tube below the petals; filaments distinct. *Ovary* inferior, with many cells in two whorls; ovules numerous on axile placentas in the inner cells and parietal in the outer; style long; stigma capitate. *Fruit* (in the wild state) about 1·5 in. diam., globose, with a reddish-brown coriaceous rind which ultimately breaks up irregularly; seeds about ·2 in. long, angled, with a pellucid reddish-yellow or ruby-coloured aril filled with an acid or sweet juice. Under cultivation the fruit is about 3 in. in diam., and very much better in quality.

The Pomegranate is cultivated in SAHÁRANPUR and the DÚN, and is found wild in valleys below 6,000 ft. in JAUNSAR and TEHRI-GARHWAL; Dhármigádh, Maindrot, Binálgádh, Khúnigádh, etc.

Wood light-yellow, compact and close-grained; weight 57 lbs. per c. ft. The flowers give a light red dye. The fruit is eaten, the bark and the rind of the fruit are very astringent, and are used in medicine as well as for tanning.

Fl. Apr., May. Fr. July-Sept.

Order 3.—PASSIFLORALES.

FAM. 41. SAMYDACEÆ; G. P. N. 71.

Trees or shrubs. *Leaves* alternate, distichous, simple; stipules small, deciduous. *Flowers* regular, small, shortly pedicelled, often fascicled. *Calyx* coriaceous, persistent, free or adnate to the ovary; limb 3-7-fid. *Petals* imbricate, as many as, and alternating with, the calyx-lobes, or none. *Stamens* definite or indefinite, often with staminodes between. *Ovary* free or more or less adnate to the calyx-tube, 1-celled; style 1 or 2-5; ovules few or many, on usually 3 parietal placentas. *Fruit* a 1-celled, generally 2-5-valved, loculicidally-dehiscent capsule; seeds albuminous.

1. Casearia, Jacq.; G. P. n. 1.

Shrubs or small trees. *Leaves* entire or slightly serrate, often remotely punctate beneath; stipules small, caducous. *Flowers* greenish-yellow, small, fascicled. *Calyx-tube* short, with 4-5 imbricate lobes. *Petals* none. *Stamens* 6-15, alternating with as many staminodes or scales, usually united in a short hypogynous tube. *Ovary* superior, 1-celled, narrowed into a short style; stigma 3-fid; ovules many, attached to 3-4 parietal placentas. *Fruit* fleshy, ovoid, usually 3-valved; seeds with a fleshy aril.

Analysis of the Species.

Leaves and branchlets glabrescent, the former elliptic. 1.*C. graveolens.*
Leaves and branchlets tomentose, the former oblong. 2.*C. tomentosa.*

1. **C. graveolens,** Dalz.; Fl. Br. Ind. ii. 592; Brandis For. Flora 243, Ind. Trees 343; Gamble Man. Ind. Timb. 378. Vern. *Chilli*, Hind.; *Nará* or *Narhá*, Dún; *Phempri*, Garhwal.

A small deciduous tree with long horizontal branches; bark dark-grey, with white specks and a few longitudinal wrinkles. *Leaves* 4-8 by 2·5-4 in., elliptic, obtuse or shortly acute, more or less crenate, glabrous; lateral nerves 8-10 pairs; base rounded, sometimes acute; petiole ·2-·5 in. long; stipules ·5 in. long, deciduous. *Flowers* glabrous, numerous, clustered in the axils of the leaves; pedicels short, jointed, pubescent below the joint. *Calyx* 5-lobed, pubescent. *Stamens* 8, alternating with hairy staminodial scales. *Fruit* 3-valved, ·7-1 in. long, ellipsoid, glabrous.

Fairly common in certain parts of the DÚN FORESTS, less so on the other side of the SIWALIKS,—Tháno, Nágsidh, Ásárori, Karwápáni, Dharmáwála, Pardúni; Ránipur, Dholkhand, etc.

Wood light-yellow, even-grained and moderately hard, weighing 40-50 lbs. per c. ft., used only for fuel. The fruit is used to poison fish.

Fl. May, June. Fr. July, Aug.

2. **C. tomentosa,** Roxb.; Fl. Br. Ind. ii. 593; Brandis For. Flora. 243, Ind. Trees 343; Gamble Man. Ind. Timb. 379. Vern. *Chillá*, Hind.

A small deciduous tree with numerous horizontal branches; bark light-grey on branches but dark-brown on old stems, peeling off in square flakes; inner substance not fibrous. *Leaves* 3-7 by 1·7-3 in., oblong elliptic-oblong or lanceolate, serrate or crenate, sometimes nearly entire, sub-coriaceous, tomentose, remotely gland-dotted; base rounded or acute, often oblique; petiole very variable in length; stipules minute, caducous. *Flowers* tomentose, small, greenish-yellow, numerous, fascicled in the axils of leaves; pedicels ·2-·3 in. long, hairy. *Calyx* 4-5-cleft, hairy. *Stamens* 8, alternating with hairy scale-like staminodes. *Fruit* 3-valved, ·7-·8 in. long, obovoid, fleshy, yellow when ripe, 6-ribbed in dry specimens; seeds embedded in a red pulp.

Very common throughout the DÚN and SAHÁRANPUR FORESTS, especially in scrub-jungle and in the outskirts of Sál forests.

Wood dirty-white or yellowish, even-grained, compact, moderately hard, strong and elastic; medullary rays fine and wavy; heartwood not distinct; weight about 40 lbs. per c. ft. It is sometimes used for making combs. The pounded fruit is used to poison fish.

New leaves Mar., Apr. Fl. Mar.-May. Fr. June, July.

Order 4.—UMBELLALES.

FAM. 42. ARALIACEÆ; G. P. N. 81.

Soft-wooded trees or shrubs, sometimes scandent. *Leaves* alternate, simple or compound, long-petioled; stipules adnate to the petiole, or absent. *Flowers* regular, small, sometimes polygamous, in umbels racemes or panicled heads; bracts and bracteoles small or conspicuous. *Calyx-tube* adnate to the ovary; limb short, truncate or with small teeth. *Petals* usually 5, valvate or sub-imbricate, deciduous. *Stamens* as many as, and alternating with, the petals, inserted on an epigynous disk; filaments inflexed; anthers versatile. *Ovary* inferior, 2- or more-celled; styles as many as the cells; ovules solitary, pendulous. *Fruit* a drupe or a berry, sometimes 1-celled by suppression.

Analysis of the Genera.

Leaves simply or compoundly pinnate or digitate.
  Petals imbricate in bud.
    Styles free . . . . . 1. ARALIA.
    Styles combined . . . . . 2. PENTAPANAX.
  Petals valvate in bud.
    Leaves digitate; styles generally free . 3. HEPTAPLEURUM.
    Leaves tripinnate; styles always free . 4. HETEROPANAX.
Leaves simple (petals valvate; styles combined) . . . . 5. HEDERA.

1. Aralia, Linn.; G. P. n. 4.

1. **A. cachemirica,** Dcne.; Fl. Br. Ind. ii. 722; Brandis For. Flora 248, Ind. Trees 351; Gamble Man. Ind. Timb. 384. Vern. *Akhōti*, Jaunsar.

A large perennial herb, 5-10 ft. high. *Leaves* 2-pinnate, or 3-pinnate, 1·5-3 ft. long. *Leaflets* 3-9 on each pinna (secondary pinna if 3-pinnate), 3-5 by 1·5-2·5 in., ovate or oblong-lanceolate, long-acuminate, obliquely rounded or cordate at the base, unequal-sided, doubly serrate, with distant short hairs above, generally hispid on the nerves beneath; rachises hispid; petiolules 0-1·3 in.; stipules ·5-1 in. long, erect, fimbriate. *Flowers* in umbels, which are disposed in large terminal panicles often about a foot long. *Petals* 5, ovate, imbricate. *Stamens* 5. *Ovary* usually 5-celled; styles 5, free above the base. *Fruit* with 5 stones.

Extremely common in JAUNSAR and TEHRI-GARHWAL, above 6,000 ft., generally in shady ravines.

New shoots Apr. Fl. June-Oct.

2. Pentapanax, Seem.; G. P. n. 5.

1. **P. parasiticum,** Seem.; Fl. Br. Ind. ii. 724; Brandis Fr. Flora 248, Ind. Trees 349; Gamble Man. Ind. Timb. 384.

A scandent soft-wooded shrub with rootlets at the nodes. *Leaves* simply imparipinnate, 6-10 in. long. *Leaflets* 5, 2-3 by 1-1·7 in., ovate-lanceolate, entire, rounded or sub-acute at the base, coriaceous, glabrous, glaucous beneath; petiolules 0-·1 in. *Umbels* 2-8 in a short panicle; pedicels ·5-·7 in. long, jointed below the flowers, glabrous. *Flowers* pentamerous. *Petals* imbricate. *Styles* 5, long, combined to near the top. *Fruit* small, sub-globose, obscurely 5-angled.

MUSSOORIE HILLS (*Mr. P. W. Mackinnon*). Very scarce.

3. Heptapleurum, Gærtn.; G. P. n. 23.

1. **H. venulosum,** Seem.; Fl. Br. Ind. ii. 729; Brandis For. Flora 249, Ind. Trees 348; Gamble Man. Ind. Timb. 386. Vern. *Káth Semal, Kot Semal,* Dún.

A soft-wooded scandent shrub attaching itself to trees by adventitious rootlets. *Leaves* digitate; petiole 6-9 in. long; stipules ·3-·5 in. long, connate in the angle between the branch and the petiole, amplexicaul. *Leaflets* 5-7, 4-8 by 2-3·5 in., the middle one largest, elliptic-oblong or lanceolate, acuminate, entire, sub-acute or rounded at the base, coriaceous, glabrous, shining above; petiolules 1-2 in. long. *Flowers* about ·2 in. diam., cream-coloured, umbelled; umbels in large twice-compound terminal panicles; pedicels ·1-·3 in.; bracts woolly, caducous. *Petals* 5-6, valvate. *Stamens* as many as the petals. *Ovary* with as many cells as the stamens; styles small, free. *Berry* 5-celled, ·3-·4 in. diam., globose, smooth, yellow.

Fairly common in the DÚN: Lachiwála, Dúdhli, Mothronwála, Jhájrá, etc. Also found in the Tons Valley, JAUNSAR and TEHRI-GARHWAL.

Fl. Jan., Feb. Fr. Apr., May.

4. Heteropanax, Seem.; G. P. n. 31.

1. **H. fragrans**, Seem.; Fl. Br. Ind. ii. 734; Brandis For. Flora 249, Ind. Trees 352; Gamble Man. Ind. Timb. 386. **Vern.** *Tarlá*, Dún (*i.e.*, larger than *Tarlu—Oroxylum indicum*, Vent.).

A small soft-wooded tree; bark soft, even, dark brownish-grey. *Leaves* tripinnate, 2-4 ft. long; petiole with a swollen base; stipules minute. *Leaflets* 3-5 by 1·7-3 in., ovate or elliptic, shortly acuminate, narrowed at the base, entire, glabrous; petiolules 0-·4 in. long. *Panicles* about 3 ft. long, lowermost branches 1-1·5 ft., branchlets or umbel-bearing racemes 2-3 in., umbels sub-capitate. *Flowers* ·2-·3 in. diam., polygamous, small, yellow, fragrant. *Calyx* nearly truncate. *Petals* 5, valvate. *Stamens* 5. *Ovary* 2-celled; styles 2, distinct, filiform. *Fruit* compressed, ·2-·3 in. long, ·3-·4 in. broad, ·1 in. thick; seeds 2, flat, orbicular.

Fairly common in the DÚN and also in the SAHÁRANPUR SIWALIKS: Kánsráo Pass, Tháno, Lachiwála, Dúdhli, Phandowála, Karwápáni; Sháhjahánpur Ráu, etc. The tree is likely to be mistaken, when not in flower and fruit, for *Oroxylum indicum*, Vent., which, however, has opposite leaves.

The leaves are lopped for cattle-fodder, and the Eri silkworm of Assam is sometimes fed on them.

Fl. Jan., Feb. Fr. Feb., Mar.

5. Hedera, Linn.; G. P. n. 35.

1. **H. Helix**, Linn.; Fl. Br. Ind. ii. 739; Brandis For. Flora 248, Ind. Trees 349; Gamble Man. Ind. Timb. 387. The Ivy. Vern. *Mithiári*, Jaunsar.

A large evergreen woody climber adhering to trees, rocks or walls by numerous fine adventitious rootlets. *Leaves* simple, extremely variable in size and shape, generally 2-5 in. long, often variously lobed, leathery, dark-green and shining above; margins entire; base cordate rounded or cuneate; petiole slender, ·5-2·5 in. long. *Flowers* polygamous, yellowish-green, in pedunculate globose umbels, which again are arranged in sub-corymbose panicles; peduncles 1·2 in., pedicels ·5-·8 in. long, both clothed with minute stellate scales. *Calyx* 5-toothed or nearly entire. *Petals* 5, valvate. *Stamens* 5. *Ovary* 5-celled; styles connate in a short column. *Fruit* ·25-·3 in. diam., globose, yellow, turning black when fully ripe, shining; seeds 3-4, ovoid.

Common in JAUNSAR and TEHRI-GARHWAL, up to 9,500 ft. Also found in the Nakraunda, Mothroṇwála and Kánsráo swamps in the DÚN, 1,400-1,800 ft.

Wood light-grey or yellow, soft and porous; annual rings distinct; weight 35 lbs. per c. ft. The leaves are a favourite fodder for sheep.

Fl. Oct.-Apr. Fr. Jan.-June.

FAM. 43. CORNACEÆ; G. P. N. 82.

Shrubs or trees. *Leaves* simple, opposite or alternate, usually entire, frequently unequal at the base; stipules none. *Flowers* regular, in axillary or terminal heads cymes or panicles. *Calyx-tube* adnate to the ovary; limb truncate or 4-5-toothed, persistent. *Petals* 4-5, valvate, or none. *Stamens* inserted with the petals and generally equal to them in number. *Disk* epigynous. *Ovary* inferior, 1-4-celled; style single; ovules pendulous, usually solitary. *Fruit* usually a succulent drupe with a 1-4-celled kernel, less often with two distinct stones; seeds pendulous, oblong, albuminous.

Analysis of the Genera.

(Adopted from Brandis' For. Flora, p. 250.)

Leaves alternate; petals, anthers and style long.
  Flowers fasciculate; stamens numerous . . 1. ALANGIUM.
  Flowers paniculate; stamens as many as the petals . . . . 2. MARLEA.
Leaves generally opposite; petals, anthers and style short . . . . . . 3. CORNUS.

1. Alangium, Lamk. ; G. P. n. 1.

1. **A. Lamarckii,** Thwaites ; Fl. Br. Ind. ii. 741 ; Brandis For. Flora 250, Ind. Trees 354 ; Gamble Man. Ind. Timb. 389. Vern. *Akolá, Ankora,* Hind. ; *Bismár,* Sahåranpur.

A shrub or small tree, almost evergreen ; branchlets spinescent ; bark grey. *Leaves* alternate, simple, 3-6 in. long, membranous varying in shape from linear oblong to elliptic, obtuse acute or acuminate, glabrous or nearly so ; lateral nerves 5-8, fine ; base acute or rounded ; petiole ·2-·5 in. long, hairy. *Flowers* ·6-·8 in. long, white, fragrant, solitary or fascicled ; inflorescence and calyx woolly. *Calyx* minutely 6-10-toothed. *Petals* 5-10, nearly 1 in. long, silky outside. *Stamens* up to 30, short, hairy ; anthers very long. *Ovary* inferior, 1-celled ; style long, filiform. *Fruit* a berry, ·7 in. long, ellipsoidal, crowned with the enlarged calyx-limb, quite smooth, black outside when ripe, filled with a red pulp ; endocarp bony ; seeds oblong.

Occasionally met with along the foot of the SAHÁRANPUR SIWALIKS : Ráuṇli, Ránipur, Jawálápur, etc. Not found in the DÚN.

Wood light-brown, fine- and smooth-grained, very tough and strong ; weight 45-56 lbs. per c. ft. Used for pestles for oil-mills, wooden cattle-bells, carrying-poles and yokes. The bitter bark of the roots is used in country medicine, and the leaves often as poultice. The fruit is eaten, and an oil is extracted from the seeds which is used in medicine and also for burning.

New leaves Apr., May. Fl. Feb.-Apr. Fr. May-Aug.

2. Marlea, Roxb. ; G. P. n. 2.

1. **M. begoniæfolia,** Roxb. ; Fl. Br. Ind. ii. 743 ; Brandis For. Flora 251, Ind. Trees 355 ; Gamble Man. Ind. Timb. 389. Vern. *Bhút Kainju,* Jaunsar ; *Garh Kimu,* Dún.

A small tree with smooth grey bark ; branches horizontal ; young parts pubescent. *Leaves* alternate, simple, 3-10 in. long, varying from orbicular to broad-oblong, acuminate, distantly angular-lobed or quite entire, usually glabrous above when mature ; base unequal, from cuneate to deeply cordate, with 3-5 basal nerves ; petiole 1-1·5 in. long. *Flowers* bracteate, ·6-·9 in. long, 2-sexual, white, in axillary dichotomously-compound cymes. *Calyx* shortly toothed. *Petals* usually 6-8, strap-shaped, ·5-·7 in. long, white, slightly hairy.

Stamens 6-8; filaments short, hairy; anthers ·4 in. long, linear. *Ovary* usually 2-celled; ovules 2, pendulous; style long, glabrous; stigma capitate. *Fruit* a drupe, ·3-·5 in. long, ovoid, obscurely ribbed, glabrous, crowned with the presistent calyx-limb still encircling the disk; seeds oblong, compressed.

Valleys up to 5,000 ft. in JAUNSAR and TEHRI-GARHWAL, and in the OUTER HIMALAYAN HILLS: Binálgádh, Thádiár; Paléd, above Rájpur, etc. Also in the Nakraunda swamp in the DÚN, 1,900, ft.

The wood is even-grained, white and soft, used in building huts in Sylhet. The leaves are given as fodder to sheep and cattle. Lac is sometimes grown on it in Kámrúp, ASSAM.

Fl. Mar-May. Fr. July-Oct.

3. **Cornus,** Linn.; G. P. n. 5.

Trees or shrubs. *Leaves* entire, usually opposite. *Flowers* small, bisexual, in cymes or heads. *Calyx* 4-toothed; tube campanulate or urn-shaped. *Petals* 4. oblong, valvate. *Stamens* 4, alternating with the petals; anthers oblong, versatile. *Ovary* usually 2-lobed; ovules solitary, pendulous; style short, club-shaped. *Fruit* a 2-celled, 2-seeded drupe; endocarp bony.

Analysis of the Species.

Flowers in compound cymes, without bracts; drupes free.
- Leaves broad-ovate, glabrous and glaucous beneath . . . . . . 1. *C. macrophylla.*
- Leaves narrow-oblong, glabrous or minutely hairy and green beneath . . 2. *C. oblonga.*

Flowers in dense heads subtended by 4 large white bracts; drupes confluent . . 3. *C. capitata.*

1. **C. macrophylla,** Wall.; Fl. Br. Ind. ii. 744; Brandis For. Flora 252, Ind. Trees 355; Gamble Man. Ind. Timb. 390. Vern. *Kágshi, Khágsha, Khákshá,* Jaunsar.

A middle-sized tree with rough brown bark and horizontal branches. *Leaves* opposite, rarely a few alternate, 6 by 4 in., ovate, sometimes unequally divided by the midrib, acuminate, glabrescent above, glaucous beneath; lateral nerves 5-8 pairs, arcuate; base sub-acute rounded or rarely slightly cordate; petiole 1 in. *Panicles* terminal, with several pairs of usually-opposite branches and dichotomous branchlets bearing cymes. *Calyx-tube* urn-shaped, covered with white adpressed hairs. *Petals* ·2-·3 in. long, strap-shaped, valvate, hairy outside. *Drupe* globose, ·2 in. long, crowned with the remains of the calyx-tube and the disk.

Fairly common in JAUNSAR and TEHRI-GARHWAL, 4,-8,000 ft., especially in shady depressions: Chakrata, Lokhár, Kathián, Dhármigádh Valley; Deotá, Kúlni, etc.

Wood pinkish-white, hard, close-grained but warps badly, noted as yielding excellent charcoal for gun-powder; weight about 45 lbs. per c. ft. The leaves are lopped for goat-fodder and the fruit is eaten.

Fl. Apr., May. Fr. June, July.

2. **C. oblonga,** Wall.; Fl. Br. Ind. ii. 744; Brandis For. Flora 253, Ind. Trees 355; Gamble Man. Ind. Timb. 390. Vern. *Korh.i*, Jaunsar.

A small tree with reddish-brown rough bark. *Leaves* opposite, sometimes a few alternate, 2-6 by ·7-1·5 in., narrowly oblong or elliptic, narrowed at both ends, sub-coriaceous, glabrescent above; lateral nerves 3-7 pairs, arcuate, prominent below, often glandular at the axils; petiole ·2-·6 in. long. *Panicle* of cymes terminal, pubescent. *Calyx-tube* campanulate, slightly hairy. *Petals* about ·2 in. long, almost glabrous. *Drupe* ovoid, about ·3 in. long, crowned as in the last species.

OUTER HIMALAYAN HILLS, JAUNSAR and TEHRI-GARHWAL, 3,-7,000 ft.: Mussoorie, Láduakōt; Korwá, Kathián; Bámsu, etc.

Wood pinkish-white, hard and even-grained, warps in seasoning. Weight 46-50 lbs. per c. ft.

Fl. Sept.-Dec. Fr. Jan.-Apr.

3. **C. capitata,** Wall.; Fl. Br. Ind. ii. 745; Brandis For. Flora 253, Ind. Trees 356; Gamble Man. Ind. Timb. 391. Vern. *Thanboi*, Jaunsar; *Bhamorá*, Garhwal.

A small deciduous tree with greyish-brown bark; young branches and leaves rough with short adpressed hairs. *Leaves* opposite, approximate at the ends of the branchlets, 2-3·5 by 1·2-1·5 in., oblong or elliptic, coriaceous, pale beneath, lateral nerves usually 4 pairs, arcuate; petiole ·5 in. long, channelled, with a broad base. *Bracts* 4, 1 by ·8 in., white or yellowish. *Heads* hemispherical, ·5 in. diam. *Flowers* small, closely packed in the head. *Calyx-teeth* reflexed. *Fruits* coalesced in a fleshy strawberry-like head 1 in. diam.; endocarp solitary, about ·15 in. long, 1-seeded, bony, compressed, angular.

JAUNSAR and OUTER HIMALAYA, from 3,500 to 8,000 ft. Soitoli, Dhárágádh, Kathián, Nágthát; below Mussoorie, etc.

Wood very hard and close-grained, but warps in seasoning. Weight 45 lbs. per c. ft. Used chiefly for fuel. The fruit when ripe is red, and is eaten and made into preserves.

Fl. Apr.-Oct. Fr. Nov.-Jan.

GAMOPETALÆ.

Series I.—*Epigynæ.*

Order 1.—RUBIALES.

FAM. 44. CAPRIFOLIACEÆ; G. P. N. 83.

SHRUBS or small trees, rarely herbs. *Leaves* opposite or ternate; stipules generally absent. *Flowers* bisexual, regular or irregular. *Calyx-tube* adnate to the ovary; limbs 3-5-lobed. *Corolla* gamopetalous, often 2-lipped; lobes 5, imbricate in bud. *Stamens* 5, rarely fewer or more, inserted on the corolla-tube between the lobes; anthers versatile. *Ovary* inferior, 1-6-celled; ovules solitary and pendulous, or several on axile placentas. *Fruit* a berry or a drupe, rarely a capsule; seeds with copious fleshy albumen.

Analysis of the Genera.

Corolla-tube straight, limb not lipped.
  Fruit 1-seeded; stem solid.
    Leaves generally toothed or serrate; calyx-lobes not elongated . . . . . 1. VIBURNUM.
    Leaves entire; calyx-lobes elongated and feathery . . . . . . 2. ABELIA.
  Fruit many-seeded; stem hollow . . . 4. LEYCESTERIA.
Corolla-tube oblique, limb more or less lipped (fruit many-seeded; leaves entire) . . 3. LONICERA.

1. Viburnum, Linn.; G. P. n. 3.

Shrubs or small trees. *Leaves* simple, opposite, sometimes ternate, generally serrate or toothed. *Flowers* white or pink, in terminal or axillary corymbs or panicles. *Calyx-limbs* short, 5-toothed. *Corolla* 5-lobed. *Stamens* 5. *Ovary* 1-3-celled with 1 pendulous ovule in each cell; style short, or stigma sessile. *Fruit* a drupe, usually 1-celled, 1-seeded.

Analysis of the Species.

Flowers in corymbs, appearing with or after the leaves.
  Leaves serrate.
    Leaves obtuse, woolly beneath . 1. *V. cotinifolium.*
    Leaves acuminate, stellate-pubescent beneath . . . . 2. *V. stellulatum.*
  Leaves entire, glabrous . . . 3. *V. coriaceum.*
Flowers in panicles, appearing before the leaves.
  Corolla-tube less than half an inch long; adult leaves hairy beneath . . 4. *V. nervosum.*
  Corolla-tube half an inch or more; adult leaves glabrous. . . . 5. *V. fœtens.*

1. **V. cotinifolium,** Don; Fl. Br. Ind. iii. 3; Brandis For. Flora 358, Ind. Trees 361; Gamble Man. Ind. Timb. 393. Vern. *Bhutnoi*, Jaunsar.

A large deciduous shrub with greyish bark. *Leaves* 3-3·5 in. long, ovate elliptic or orbicular, obtuse, crenulate or nearly entire, rugose, woolly beneath; base obtuse or subcordate; lateral nerves 5-6 pairs, branching. *Flowers* generally in dense terminal corymbs which are 3-4 in. diam.; bracteoles linear. *Calyx-lobes* short. *Corolla-tube* ·2 in. long, turbinate, white tinged with pink; lobes round. *Style* very short, conical. *Drupe* ·3 in. long, oblong, compressed, ribbed, red.

Abundant in JAUNSAR and TEHRI-GARHWAL, above 4,000 ft., affecting open sunny aspects.

Wood white, hard and close-grained. The ripe fruit is eaten.

Fl. Apr.-June. Fr. July, Aug.

2. **V. stellulatum,** Wall.; Fl. Br. Ind. iii. 4; Brandis For. Flora 258, 576, Ind. Trees 361; Gamble Man. Ind. Timb. 394. Vern. *Richhoi*, Jaunsar.

A shrub with long branches, and dark-grey almost black bark. *Leaves* 3-4 by 1·5-2 in., ovate or ovate-lanceolate, long-acuminate, distantly sharp-toothed, membranous, glabrous above, sparingly stellulate-pubescent beneath; base rounded or subacute; petiole ·3-1 in. long. *Flowers* small, very numerous, in large bracteate umbellate cyme-bearing terminal corymbs. *Calyx-tube* stellately hairy. *Corolla* rotate, white, pubescent; lobes round. *Drupe* ·25 by ·2 in., broadly oblong, compressed, bright-red when ripe.

Fairly common in JAUNSAR and TEHRI-GARHWAL, above 6,000 ft., generally in cool shady localities: Deoban, Mundáli; Deotá, etc.

Walking-sticks are often made of the branches. The acid fruit is eaten.

Fl. July, Aug. Fr. Sept., Oct.

3. **V. coriaceum,** Bl.; Fl. Br. Ind. iii. 5; Brandis For. Flora 259, Ind. Trees 362; Gamble Man. Ind. Timb. 394. Vern. *Rashniá*, Jaunsar.

A shrub or small tree with grey bark. *Leaves* 4-9 by 1·5-2·5 in., oblong, acuminate, entire, thickly coriaceous, glabrous; lateral nerves 3-4 pairs, arcuate; petiole ·5-1 in. long. *Flowers* ·25 in. long, numerous, in terminal umbellate corymbs; bracts 0. *Calyx-tube* truncate, glabrous. *Corolla* white, tubular. *Drupe* ·2 in. long, 1-celled, black.

JAUNSAR and TEHRI-GARHWAL, 4,-7,000 ft.; also the OUTER HIMALAYA: Korwá forest, Kathián, Moltá; both slopes of the Mussoorie Hill, Málkōt Forest, etc.

Wood white, hard, close-grained, weighing 50 lbs. per c. ft. An oil is said to be extracted from the seeds in Nepal.

Fl. May, June. Fr. July, Aug.

4. **V. nervosum,** Don; Fl. Br. Ind. iii. 8; Brandis For. Flora 259, Ind. Trees 363; Gamble Man. Ind. Timb. 395. Vern. *Tirnoi*, Jaunsar.

A shrub with stout grey or brownish branches. *Leaves* 2·5-4 by 1·3-1·5 in., elliptic-oblong, acute, serrate, glabrous above, hairy on the nerves beneath; lateral nerves 8-10 pairs, prominent, closely parallel; base cuneate; petiole ·3-·6 in. long. *Panicles* compact, silky; branches short. *Calyx-tube* glabrous. *Corolla-tube* ·3-·5 in. long; lobes elliptic, light-rosy. *Stamens* in 2 series, 2 above and 3 below. *Drupe* ellipsoid, up to ·3 in. long.

TEHRI-GARHWAL FORESTS, above 9,000 ft.; Rikhshin. Rather scarce.

Fl. Apr., May. Fr. May, June.

5. **V. fœtens,** Dcne.; Fl. Br. Ind. iii. 8; Brandis For. Flora 259, Ind. Trees 364; Gamble Man. Ind. Timb. 395. Vern. *Tirnoi*, Jaunsar.

A shrub very closely resembling the last species. *Leaves* about 4 in. long, elliptic or oblong, serrate, glabrous, emitting a strong unpleasant smell; nerves 7-9 pairs, distantly parallel. *Panicles* lax; branches glabrous or nearly so. *Flowers* sweet-scented. *Corolla-tube* ·5-·7 in. long; lobes rosy. *Stamens* in two series. *Drupe* up to ·5 in. long, ellipsoid, red.

Fairly common in JAUNSAR and TEHRI-GARHWAL, above 8,000 ft.: Deoban, Mundáli; Deotá, etc.

The fruit is said to be edible.

Fl. May, June. Fr. July, Aug.

2. Abelia, R. Br.; G. P. n. 7.

1. **A. triflora,** R. Br.; Fl. Br. Ind. iii. 9; Brandis For. Flora 257, Ind. Trees 360; Gamble Man. Ind. Timb. 396. Vern. *Máli*, *Málé*, Jaunsar.

A large shrub; branches long, fluted; branchlets slender and often drooping; bark grey. *Leaves* 2-3 by ·7-1·3 in., ovate-lanceolate, hairy all over or only along the margins and the midrib, finely reticulate; petioles short, often connate at the base. *Flowers* scented, ·4-·6 in. long, usually 3 together in dense bracteate heads or cymes; bracts and bracteoles foliaceous. *Calyx-lobes* ·5-1 in. long in fruit, feathery, with a distinct midrib. *Corolla* tubular, funnel-shaped or with a wide mouth, pinkish-white. *Fruit* ·2-·3 in. long, 1-seeded, linear-oblong, dry.

Fairly common in JAUNSAR and TEHRI-GARHWAL, above 4,000 ft., frequently on calcareous soils: Deoban, Bodyár, Mundáli, Dhárágádh; Bámsu, Deotá, etc.

Wood bluish-white, hard, close- and even-grained; weight 65 lbs. per c. ft. Walking-sticks are often made of the branches, and the leaves are browsed by goats.

Fl. May-July. Fr. July-Oct.

3. Lonicera, Linn.; G. P. n. 9.

Shrubs, erect or scandent. *Leaves* opposite, entire. *Flowers* in peduncled pairs, often connate by their ovaries, supported by bracts and bracteoles; peduncles axillary or subterminal. *Calyx-tube* ovoid; limb short, 5-toothed. *Corolla* tubular, limb oblique or 2-lipped, 5-lobed. *Stamens* 5. *Ovary* 2-3-celled; ovules many in each cell, in double rows; style slender, stigma capitate. *Fruit* a fleshy berry, often two connate into one, 2-3-celled; seeds few in each cell; albumen fleshy.

Analysis of the Species.

Corolla not distinctly 2-lipped.
  Leaves oblong; fruit black . . 1. *L. purpurascens.*
  Leaves lanceolate; fruit red . . 2. *L. angustifolia.*
Corolla distinctly 2-lipped.
  Fruits free.
    Peduncles extremely short . . 3. *L. quinquelocularis.*
    Peduncles 1-2 in. long. . . 5. *L. alpigena.*
  Fruits confluent . . . . . 4. *L. orientalis.*

1. **L. purpurascens,** Hook. f. & T.; Fl. Br. Ind. iii. 12; Brandis For. Flora 255, Ind. Trees 359; Gamble Man. Ind. Timb. 396.

A small shrub; branches dark-grey; bark peeling off in thin shreds. *Leaves* 1·5 by ·5 in. or less, oblong or obovate-oblong, pilose or glabrescent above, usually villous beneath. *Bracts* linear. *Corolla* ·5-·7 in. long, hairy, purple, funnel-shaped. *Style* hairy. *Fruit* globose, black when ripe.

TEHRI-GARHWAL, above 10,000 ft.: Rikhshin, Chánsil, etc.

Fl. May, June.

2. **L. angustifolia,** Wall.; Fl. Br. Ind. iii. 13; Brandis For. Flora 255, Ind. Trees 359; Gamble Man. Ind. Timb. 397. Vern. *Geáng, Chalú, Pirlú, Banchulú,* Jaunsar.

A small shrub with smooth grey bark which exfoliates in long papery flakes. *Leaves* 1·5 by ·5 in., lanceolate or oblong-lanceolate, pale and nearly glabrous beneath. *Flowers* in pairs on slender axillary peduncles ·5-1 in. long; bracts linear; bracteoles connate, enclosing the confluent ovaries. *Corolla* white tinged with rose, ·2-·4 in. long, scented; lobes subequal. *Style* short, glabrous. *Fruit* confluent, globose, bright ruby-colour and translucent when ripe; seeds few.

Common in JAUNSAR and TEHRI-GARHWAL, above 6,000 ft.

Wood hard and very close-grained. Good walking-sticks can be made of the branches, if found long and thick enough. The fruit is sweetish and is greedily eaten by the hill people.

Fl. May, June. Fr. July, Aug.

3. **L. quinquelocularis,** Hardwick; Fl. Br. Ind. iii. 14; Brandis For. Flora 255, Ind. Trees 359; Gamble Man. Ind. Timb. 397. The Himalayan Honey-suckle. Vern. *Taknoi,* Jaunsar.

A large shrub, occasionally a small tree; bark grey, with longitudinal fissures, peeling off in long shreds; branchlets pubescent. *Leaves* 1·5-3 by 1-2 in., obovate or ovate-lanceolate, acute or obtuse at either end, glabrate above, pilose beneath. *Flowers* clustered, axillary; peduncles extremely short; bracts linear, ciliate; bracteoles obtuse, connate at the base. *Calyx-limb* cup-shaped, hairy. *Corolla* ·7-1·2 in. long, white, fading into pale-yellow, hairy. *Style* hairy, exserted. *Berries* not connate, brownish-black when ripe.

Fairly common throughout the OUTER HIMALAYA, JAUNSAR and TEHRI-GARHWAL, 2,500-9,000 ft.

Wood greyish-white, hard and close-grained; takes a fine polish, but is used chiefly for fuel; weight 52 lbs. per c. ft. Cattle are fed on the leaves. The branches are sometimes used for walking-sticks.

Fl. May, June. Fr. July, Aug.

4. **L. orientalis,** Lamk.; Fl. Br. Ind. iii. 15; Brandis For. Flora 256, Ind. Trees 359; Gamble Man. Ind. Timb. 398. Vern. *Taknoi,* Jaunsar.

A large shrub with compressed horizontal branches; bark peeling off in thin shreds. *Leaves* 2-4 by 1·5-2·5 in., ovate or ovate-lanceolate, acute at both ends, mucronate, more or less pubescent beneath; nerves 10-12 pairs, slender. *Peduncles* ·5-1 in. long, thickened upwards; bracts linear-lanceolate; bracteoles small and rounded, or none. *Calyx-lobes* linear-lanceolate. *Corolla* pink, nearly glabrous outside, deeply 2-lipped, gibbous at the base; tube very short. *Style* hairy. *Berries* confluent, black when ripe.

JAUNSAR and TEHRI-GARHWAL, above 6,000 ft.; Mundáli, Deoban, etc.

Fl. June. Fr. July, Aug.

5. **L. alpigena,** Linn.; Fl. Br. Ind. iii. 15; Brandis For. Flora 256, Ind. Trees 358; Gamble Man. Ind. Timb. 398. Vern. *Phulor,* Jaunsar.

A shrub with pubescent branchlets, and grey-brown bark which peels off in irregular papery flakes. *Leaves* 3-4 by 1-2 in.

elliptic-oblong or ovate-lanceolate, long-acuminate, glabrate above, pilose beneath; base rounded or cuneate; nerves 6-8 pairs, slanting. *Peduncles* 1·2 in. long, thickened upwards; bracts lanceolate or linear; bracteoles small. *Calyx-tube* pubescent; limb short. *Corolla* glandular-hairy, very gibbous at the base. *Fruit* not connate.

JAUNSAR and TEHRI-GARHWAL, above 8,000 ft., not common: Bájámárá, Mundáli; Deotá, Rikhshin, etc.

Fl. May, June. Fr. July, Aug.

4. Leycesteria, Wall.; G. P. n. 10.

1. **L. formosa,** Wall.; Fl. Br. Ind. iii. 16; Brandis For. Flora 56, Ind. Trees 360; Gamble Man. Ind. Timb. 398. Vern. *Bhúj-nali*, Jaunsar; *Dándá Bhekar*, Garhwal.

A bushy shrub (perennial herb ?) with grey stems and deep-green hollow branches, usually from near the base. *Leaves* opposite, 2-5 by 1-3 in., ovate or ovate-lanceolate, long-acuminate, entire or with the margins irregularly uneven, membranous, glaucous or puberulous beneath, glabrous or slightly scabrous above; base from subacute to cordate; petioles ·2-1 in. long, connate at the base. *Flowers* about 1 in. long, sessile, in axillary or terminal bracteate whorls; bracts sessile, greenish-purple, ovate or ovate-lanceolate, generally connate at the base; bracteoles very variable. *Calyx-lobes* 5, unequal, persistent. *Corolla* funnel-shaped, swollen at the base, red or white with a purplish tinge. *Fruit* a fleshy berry, ·5 in. long, subglobose, dark-purple when fully ripe, glandular-hairy, usually 5-celled, many-seeded. *Seeds* round and compressed.

Fairly common in cool shady forests in JAUNSAR: Deoban, Mundáli, etc.

The hollow stems are made into toy flutes and trumpets by Jaunsari shepherd boys.

Fl. June, July. Fr. July, Aug.

FAM. 45. RUBIACEÆ; G. P. N. 84.

Trees, shrubs or herbs. *Leaves* simple, opposite or whorled, entire, stipulate; stipules inter- or intra-petiolar, free or adnate to the petioles, or forming a sheath round the stem. *Inflorescence* various. *Calyx-tube* adnate to the ovary; limb entire or toothed. *Corolla* gamopetalous, regular; lobes usually 4-5, valvate imbricate or contorted in the bud. *Stamens* as many as the corolla-lobes and alternating with them, inserted on the corolla-tube. *Ovary* inferior, 2- or more-celled, rarely 1-celled; ovules 1 or more in each cell, anatropous. *Fruit* various; seeds usually with a fleshy or horny albumen.

Analysis of the Genera.

Fruit capsular.
  Ovary 2-celled, cells many-seeded.
    Corolla-lobes valvate in bud.
      Flowers in dense globose heads.
        Calyx 5-lobed; no bract-like leaves . 1. ADINA.
        Calyx truncate; inflorescence supported by bract-like leaves . 2. STEPHEGYNE.
      Flowers in panicled spikes supported by large leafy bracts . . . 3. HYMENODICTYON.
    Corolla-lobes imbricate in bud; flowers in large terminal panicles . . 4. WENDLANDIA.
  Ovary 5-celled, seeds solitary in each cell; corolla-lobes valvate in bud.
    Capsule 1-celled, 5-valved only at the top; bracteoles free . . . 9. HAMILTONIA.
    Capsule 5-celled to the base; bracteoles connate . . . . . 10. LEPTODERMIS.
Fruit indehiscent; ovary 2-celled; corolla lobes twisted in bud.
  Fruit with a pair of 1-seeded crustaceous pyrenes.
    Flowers in trichotomous corymbose panicles . . . . . . 7. PAVETTA.
    Flowers axillary, fascicled or solitary . 8. COFFEA.
  Fruit fleshy, seeds more than 1 in each cell (flowers axillary, fasciled or solitary).
    Ovary 2-celled; placentas on the septum 5. RANDIA.
    Ovary 1-celled; placentas parietal . 6. GARDENIA.

1. **Adina**, Salisb.; G. P. n. 4.

1. **A. cordifolia,** Hook. f.; Fl. Br. Ind. iii. 24; Brandis For. Flora 263, Ind. Trees 368; Gamble Man. Ind. Timb. 401. Vern. *Haldú*, Hind.

A large deciduous tree, often buttressed; bark grey or brownish-grey, rough, inner substance reddish-brown with streaks of white. *Leaves* opposite, 4-9 in. diam., orbicular, cordate, abruptly acuminate, coriaceous, glabrate above, pubescent beneath; petiole 3-4 in. long; stipules ·5-·8 in. long, triangular, elliptic or obovate, brown, concealing the uppermost pair of leaf-buds. *Flowers* yellow, downy, bracteolate, in globose peduncled heads which are ·7-1 in. diam.; receptacle hairy; peduncles axillary, 2-4 in. long, usually with one head. *Calyx-tube* 5-angled; limb 5-lobed. *Corolla* trumpet-shaped; tube long glabrous inside; lobes valvate. *Stamens* 5, inserted in the mouth of the corolla-tube; filaments short. *Ovary* 2-celled; ovules many in each cell; style filiform, long-exserted. *Capsules* 200-300 in each head, of 2 dehiscent cocci, dry, many-seeded; seeds oblong, winged, very minute.

A common tree throughout the DÚN and SAHÁRANPUR FORESTS and in the OUTER HIMALAYA, usually overtopping all other trees, and can be easily recognized from a distance by its dark-green umbrageous crown.

Wood yellow when fresh-cut, afterwards changing into reddish-brown, even-grained, compact, moderately hard; weight 40-50 lbs. per c. ft.; heartwood and annual rings not distinct. It seasons well, works easily, takes a good polish and is fairly durable. Used for construction, furniture and agricultural implements. In the SIWALIK DIVISION there is a special demand for good trees, which are carted down to Sahāranpur to be made into combs, writing-tablets and ornamental platters.

Leafless for a short time in May. Fl. June, July. Seeds ripen in the cold season.

2. Stephegyne, Korth.; G. P. n. 5.

1. **S. parvifolia,** Korth.; Fl. Br. Ind. iii. 25; Brandis For. Flora 262, Ind. Trees 369; Gamble Man. Ind. Timb. 403. Vern. *Káem,* Hind.; *Phaldú,* Garhwal.

A large deciduous tree; trunk irregularly shaped, often buttressed; bark brownish- or greenish-grey, smooth, with shallow depressions left by exfoliating scales. *Leaves* opposite, very variable, 2-6 in. long, orbicular oblong ovate or obovate, coriaceous, glabrous or pubescent; lateral nerves 6-8 pairs, oblique; base cuneate to subcordate; stipules obovate, pale, membranous. *Flowers* white or light-yellow, bracteolate, glabrous inside, in globose heads about 1 in. diam. *Peduncles* ·5-3 in. long, simple or trichotomously divided to form usually 3-headed panicles, supported by a pair of bract-like oblong leaves narrowed into a long slender petiole; bracteoles spathulate, minute. *Calyx-tube* short; limb truncate or minutely 5-toothed. *Corolla* trumpet-shaped; lobes 5, valvate. *Stamens* 5, inserted on the throat of the corolla-tube; filaments short. *Ovary* 2-celled; ovules many in each cell; style filiform, much exserted; stigma cylindrical, with a concave base. *Capsules* 100-150 in each head, dry, ·12 in. long, of 2 dehiscent cocci; seeds many, winged, minute.

Abundant in the SAHÁRANPUR FORESTS, and fairly common in the DÚN. Some individuals attain enormous sizes, *e.g.*, those in the camping-ground at Dholkhand.

Wood light pinkish-brown, close- and fine-grained, generally harder than that of *Adina cordifolia*; weight about 42 lbs. per c. ft. Heartwood not distinct; rings visible. Used generally for the same purposes as *Haldú*. The leaves are used for fodder.

Leafless Apr., May. Fl. June, July. Fr. Nov.-Jan.

Allied to the two preceding trees is *Anthocephalus Cadamba*, Miq.; Fl. Br. Ind. iii. 23. Vern. *Meo*, E. DÚN;—a large handsome tree, a few individuals of which, probably originally planted, are found near the old Khairi fort, E. DÚN. *Leaves* resembling those of *Holarrhena antidysenterica*. *Flower-heads* about 2 in. diam. The ripe fruit is acid and is eaten raw or cooked.—*G. P. n. 2.*

3. Hymenodictyon, Wall.; G. P. n. 19.

1. **H. excelsum,** Wall.; Fl. Br. Ind. iii. 35; Brandis For. Flora 267, Ind. Trees 371; Gamble Man. Ind. Timb. 406. Vern. *Bhaulan*, Dún; *Kúkurkát*, Hind.

A large deciduous tree; bark soft, brownish-grey, smooth on branches and poles, corky and furrowed on the stems of mature trees. *Leaves* opposite, 4-10 by 3-5 in., elliptic or obovate-oblong, acuminate, often obtuse or rounded, membranous, pubescent; lateral nerves 7-10 pairs; base acute; petiole 1-3 in.; stipules oblong with a broad base, caducous, usually glandular-serrate; floral leaves long-petioled, strongly nerved. *Flowers* about ·2 in. long, white, fragrant, in large terminal panicles with bracteate spicate branches; pedicels very short; bracts large, leafy, persistent. *Calyx-tube* short; lobes 5-6, deciduous. *Corolla* ·2 in. long, funnel-shaped, pilose outside; lobes 5, short, valvate. *Stamens* 5; filaments dilated upwards; anthers linear. *Ovary* 2-celled; ovules numerous; style long-exserted; stigma spindle-shaped. *Fruit* a loculicidally dehiscent capsule, ·5-·7 in. long, on short recurved pedicels, ellipsoid, 2-valved, many-seeded; seeds flat, lenticular, winged all round the margin, ·3 by ·1 in. including the wing.

Not uncommon in the Sál forests of the DÚN although rare in the WESTERN DÚN, and frequently met with in the better class of SAHÁRANPUR FORESTS: Phándowála, Lachiwála, Tháno; Mohand, etc.

Wood brownish-grey, close-grained but light and soft; heart-wood not distinct; weight about 30 lbs. per c. ft. Used for agricultural implements, palanquins, scabbards, toys and similar other articles. The bark is used for tanning and as a febrifuge, and the leaves as cattle-fodder.

Leafless Nov.-May. Fl. June-Aug. Fr. Cold season.

4. Wendlandia, Bartl.; G. P. n. 62.

Shrubs or small trees. *Leaves* opposite or ternately whorled. *Flowers* small, white or rosy, in terminal panicled cymes, 2-3-bracteolate. *Calyx-lobes* 4-5, sub-equal, persistent. *Corolla* tubular or funnel-shaped; lobes 4-5, imbricate in bud. *Stamens* 4-5, between the corolla-lobes; anthers exserted. *Ovary* usually 2-celled; cells many-seeded; style slender; stigma entire or bifid. *Capsule* globose, 2-valved, many-seeded; seeds very minute, obscurely winged.

Analysis of the Species.

Stipules recurved; leaves at least three times as long as broad; lateral nerves 12-20 pairs . 1. *W. exserta.*

Stipules erect; leaves about twice as long as broad: lateral nerves 10-12 pairs . . 2. *W. puberula.*

1. **W. exserta,** DC.; Fl. Br. Ind. iii. 37; Brandis For. Flora 268, Ind. Trees 373; Gamble Man. Ind. Timb. 408. Vern. *Bathúá*, E. Sahāranpur; *Chaulái*, W. Sahāranpur.

A small deciduous tree; bark rough, brown, longitudinally cracked and exfoliating in long strips; branchlets, leaves and inflorescene grey-tomentose. *Leaves* 4-9 by 1·3-5 in., ovate ovate-lanceolate or narrow-oblong, finely acuminate, coriaceous, sometimes glabrate above, often densely pubescent beneath; lateral nerves

12-20 pairs, parallel; petiole ·5-1 in. long; stipules interpetiolar, ovate, acute, recurved. *Flowers* sessile, ·15 in. diam., dull-white, fragrant, in cymes which again are disposed in large very dense conical terminal panicles much exceeding the leaves. *Calyx-lobes* 4-5, ovate or subulate, persistent. *Corolla* funnel-shaped; lobes imbricate in bud. *Anthers* versatile, exserted. *Ovary* 2-celled. *Capsules* ·1 in. long, white-tomentose.

Very common in the SIWALIK TRACTS, especially along the passes and on land-slips; also found in the TONS VALLEY; from Kálsi to Thadiár.

Wood reddish-brown, hard and close-grained; weight 47 lbs. per c. ft. It is used for building and agricultural implements.

Fl. Mar., Apr. Fr. Rainy season.

2. **W. puberula,** DC.; Fl. Br. Ind. iii. 37; Brandis For. Flora 576, Ind. Trees 373; Gamble Man. Ind. Timb. 408.

A small deciduous tree with rough brownish-grey bark; innovations puberulous. *Leaves* 4-8 by 2·5-4 in., elliptic or oblong, acute, less frequently acuminate, rather membranous, glabrous above except along the nerves, with brown pubescence along the midrib and nerves beneath; lateral nerves 10-12 pairs, less prominent than in the other species; base acute; petiole ·3-·7 in. long; stipules ·2-·3 in. long, usually caudate-acuminate, erect, persistent. *Flowers* sessile, very small, bluish-white, in terminal and axillary panicles which are generally shorter than the leaves. *Calyx* hairy; lobes triangular. *Corolla* funnel-shaped; lobes shorter than the tube. *Capsules* about ·1 in. long, nearly glabrous.

Fairly common along banks of streams in the TONS VALLEY, JAUNSAR and TEHRI-GARHWAL, up to 4,000 ft.: Dhármigádh; Thadiár, Sendrá, etc. Also Sansáru Khálá, MÁLKŌT.

Fl. May, June. Fr. Dec.-Jan.

5. Randia, Linn.; G. P. n. 166.

Shrubs or trees, often spinous. *Leaves* opposite or falsely alternate; stipules intrapetiolar, short. *Flowers* white, fading to yellow, solitary fascicled or corymbose, usually axillary. *Calyx-limb* tubular; lobes long or short. *Corolla-tube* usually cylindrical, long or short; lobes usually 5, twisted in bud. *Stamens* 5; anthers subsessile, narrow. *Ovary* generally 2-celled; ovules usually numerous, on fleshy placentas; style entire or bifid. *Fruit* a succulent berry, 2-celled, generally many-seeded; seeds angular.

Analysis of the Species.

A small shrub. Fruit ·3 in. long, 4-seeded . 1. *R. tetrasperma.*
Small trees. Fruit 1-2 in. long, many-seeded.
  Spines short, at the ends of the branchlets; corolla glabrous outside . . . . . 2. *R. uliginosa.*
  Spines long, axillary; corolla hairy outside . 3. *R. dumetorum.*

1. **R. tetrasperma,** Benth. & Hook. f.; Fl. Br. Ind. iii. 109; Brandis For. Flora 272, Ind. Trees 381; Gamble Man. Ind. Timb. 412. Vern. *Bhedrá, Dánwá, Chhotá Gingárú,* Jaunsar.

A small shrub with stiff grey branches and branchlets. *Leaves* crowded at the ends of the branchlets, ·5-2 in. long, obovate or oblanceolate, narrowed into a short petiole, glabrous; stipules small. *Flowers* sessile, ·4-·6 in. across, greenish-white, fragrant. *Calyx-lobes* subulate. *Corolla-tube* ·3 in. long; lobes oblong. *Anthers* exserted. *Stigma* long, spindle-shaped. *Berry* globose, ·3-·4 in. diam., 4-seeded,—whence the specific name.

JAUNSAR and TEHRI-GARHWAL, up to 5,000 feet: Tons Valley from Maindrot to Mautárgádh. Common at Korwá. Also OUTER HIMALAYA: Málkōt.

Wood white, very hard and tough; weight 56 lbs. per c. ft.; straight branches can be made into walking-sticks.

Fl. Apl., May. Fr. Cold season.

2. **R. uliginosa,** DC.; Fl. Br. Ind. iii. 110; Brandis For. Flora 273, Ind. Trees 381; Gamble Man. Ind. Timb. 412. Vern. *Pindálú, Pindár, Pindorá, Pendúá, Penáúrá,* Hind.; *Pandárá,* Saháranpur.

A rigid small tree with reddish-brown bark and quadrangular branches. *Leaves* approximate at the ends of the branchlets, 2-8 by 1-4 in., obovate or obovate-oblong from a cuneate base, shining above, often pubescent along the nerves beneath, the upper usually subtending a few ·5 in. long sharp decussate weak spines. *Flowers* white, solitary, sessile or peduncled. *Calyx-tube* over 1 in. long; lobes rounded. *Corolla* large, 1-2 in. diam., showy; limb spreading; mouth of the tube partially closed with a ring of white hairs in the sessile flowers. *Stigma* fusiform, often 2-lobed. *Fruit* ovoid, up to 2 in. long, with a thick hard pulp.

Likely to occur in swampy grass lands in the DÚN ; common in wet lands in LOWER SAHÁRANPUR as at Pathri.

Wood whitish-grey, close-grained and hard ; weight 48 lbs. per c. ft. The fruit is eaten, and the leaves are browsed by deer and cattle.

New leaves April. Fl. May, June. Fr. Cold season.

3. **R. dumetorum,** Lamk. ; Fl. Br. Ind. iii. 110 ; Brandis For. Flora 273, Ind. Trees 382 ; Gamble Man. Ind. Timb. 413. Vern. *Maindal, Mainphal,* Hind.

A large deciduous shrub or small tree with grey bark, and often long and stout axillary spines. *Leaves* 1-2 in. long, obovate, obtuse or acute, narrowed into the short marginate petiole, glabrous or pubescent or rough with stiff hairs ; stipules ovate, acuminate. *Flowers* greenish- or yellowish-white, fragrant, solitary or 2-3 together at the ends of short lateral branchlets, shortly pedunculate. *Calyx* strigose ; tube ·2-·3 in. long ; lobes ovate, foliaceous, as long as the tube. *Corolla-lobes* spreading, oval or oblong, ·5-·75 in., covered with adpressed white hairs ; tube up to the tips of the calyx-lobes. *Fruit* a soft fleshy berry, 1-1·5 in. long, globose or ovoid, yellow, glabrous or pubescent ; pericarp thick, leathery ; seeds compressed, imbedded in a gelatinous pulp.

Extremely common throughout the SIWALIK DIVISION, and also found in the Ámláwa and Tons Valleys in JAUNSAR. Affects the shade of Sál and other forest trees.

Wood light-brown or white, compact, hard,—used for agricultural implements, walking-sticks, fences and fuel. Weight 55-60 lbs. per c. ft. The leaves are lopped for fodder. The unripe fruit is used to poison fish, and is also eaten raw or roasted when ripe. The bark and the fruit are used in Indian medicine.

Fl. Apr.-June. Fr. Cold season.

6. Gardenia, Linn. ; G. P. n. 167

1. **G. turgida,** Roxb. ; Fl. Br. Ind. iii. 118 ; Brandis For. Flora 270, Ind. Trees 380 ; Gamble Man. Ind. Timb. 416. Vern. *Thanelá,* Hind.

A small deciduous tree, armed with strong axillary often leaf-bearing spines ; bark smooth, bluish-grey, mealy on branches. *Leaves* opposite, crowded at the ends of the branches, very variable in size, 1-4 in. long, obovate or elliptic, obtuse or short-acuminate, coriaceous, tomentose beneath, pubescent or glabrous and at length shining above, sessile or narrowed into a short marginate petiole; stipules triangular, distinct, caducous. *Flowers* 1-4, about 1 in. long, fragrant, axillary or at the ends of short lateral branchlets. *Calyx* ·15 in. long, sub-truncate in male flowers, with oblong foliaceous lobes in female flowers. *Corolla* white; tube ·3-·5 in. long, slightly dilated upwards; lobes oblong, longer than the tube. *Stamens* as many as the corolla-lobes; anthers sessile, linear, included with only the tips slightly exserted. *Ovary* 1-celled; ovules numerous, inserted in 2 series on 2-6 parietal placentas. *Fruit* 2-3 in. long, pyriform, obovoid or globose, grey-mealy outside, furrowed at the base; pericarp thick, leathery; endocarp woody; seeds numerous, compressed, immersed in pulp.

Common throughout the SAHÁRANPUR SIWALIKS, especially near Ranipur, Dholkhand and Sháhjahánpur. Also found in certain localites in the DÚN, *e.g.*, Lachiwála, Nágsidh, Timli, etc., but not quite so common.

Wood dirty-white, close-grained, fairly hard, weighing about 55 lbs. per c. ft. It splits and cracks in seasoning, and is scarcely used except for fuel. The fruit is eaten cooked in Central India, and is also used medicinally, especially in affections of the mammary glands,—whence the vernacular name.

According to Forest Ranger Pandit Nathu Singh, if one places one's hands on the stem of this tree in the summer so as to encircle it, the leaves begin to shake.

Fl. Mar., Apr. Fr. Cold season.

7. Pavetta, Linn.; G. P. n. 236.

1. **P. indica,** Linn.; Fl. Br. Ind. iii. 150; Brandis Ind. Trees 387; Gamble Man. Ind. Timb. 421. Syn.—*P. tomentosa,* Smith; Brandis For. Flora 275, Vern. *Angári*, Dún.

A large shrub with smooth brownish-grey bark. *Leaves* opposite, 3-9 by 1-3·5 in., elliptic obovate or oblanceolate, obtuse acute acuminate or caudate, subcoriaceous, glabrous or tomentose; lateral nerves 10-15; petiole ·5-1·5 in. long; stipules united into an intrapetiolar sheath, generally persistent. *Inflorescence* a terminal or sub-lateral, dense or lax, flat-topped corymb. *Flowers* white, fragrant; bracts broad, membranous. *Calyx* about ·08 in. long, shortly-toothed. *Corolla* about 1 in.; tube long, very slender; lobes 4, oblong, twisted in bud, afterwards spreading and recurved. *Stamens* 4, on the mouth of the corolla-tube; filaments short. *Ovary* 2-celled; ovule solitary, attached to a prominent placenta; style filiform, twice as long as the corolla-tube; stigma slender, fusiform. *Berry* the size of a pea, with 2 plano-convex pyrenes; seeds peltate.

Var. *tomentosa*, Roxb., is characterised by having the inflorescence and leaves beneath pubescent or villous, and the corymbs sublateral (at the extremities of lateral often leafless branchlets) and long peduncled.

Common in moister parts of forest in the DÚN and the SIWALIK TRACT: Tháno, Lachiwála, Mohkumpur, Rámgarh, Ásárori, etc.

Wood light-brown, hard and close-grained; weight 59 lbs. per c. ft.

Fl. Apr., May. Fr. Cold season.

8. Coffea, Linn.; G. P. n. 238.

1. **C. bengalensis,** Roxb.; Fl. Br. Ind. iii. 153; Brandis For. Flora 277, Ind. Trees 390; Gamble Man. Ind. Timb. 422.

A small deciduous shrub with slender spreading branches, and thin brownish-grey bark. *Leaves* opposite, about 5 by 3 in., ovate or elliptic, acuminate, membranous, glabrous, narrowed into a short petiole; stipules interpetiolar, broad, subulate, persistent. *Flowers* solitary or in pairs, axillary, white, fragrant, 1-1·5 in. across, appearing before or with the leaves. *Calyx-tube* short, many-toothed. *Corolla* funnel-shaped; tube ·5-·7 in. long; lobes ovate-oblong, slightly shorter than the tube, spreading or recurved, twisted in bud. *Stamens* inserted in the mouth of the corolla-tube; anthers subsessile, narrow. *Ovary* 2-celled; ovules solitary, peltately attached to the dissepiment; style bifid, filiform. *Fruit* a drupe, about ·5 in. long, oblong, black, with 2 plano-convex pyrenes; seeds plano-convex, with a ventral groove; albumen horny.

Fairly common in shady ravines in the DÚN, and along the foot of the OUTER HIMALAYA: Bindál-nálá, Lachiwála, Rámgarh, Tháno, Nálápáni, Robbers' Cave, Mothronwála, etc.

The seeds are used as coffee in the Eastern Duárs of Bengal.

Fl. Mar., Apl. Fr. June, July.

The real Coffee shrub, *C. arabica*, Linn.; Fl. Br. Ind. iii. 153—is cultivated as an ornamental garden plant in the Dún. It is usually of a larger size than the above. *Flowers* numerous, in axillary fascicles. *Fruit* fleshy, purple when ripe.

9. Hamiltonia, Roxb.; G. P. n. 289.

1. **H. suaveolens,** Roxb.; Fl. Br. Ind. iii. 197; Brandis For. Flora 278, Ind. Trees 390; Gamble Man. Ind. Timb. 425. Vern. *Páderá,* Málkōt; *Páderái,* Jaunsar.

A small shrub with divaricate branches. *Leaves* opposite, 6-9 by 2-4 in., elliptic oblong or ovate, acute or acuminate, glabrous or pubescent, coriaceous, tough; main lateral nerves 10-15 pairs, arcuate, very prominent beneath; base acute; petiole ·5-1 in.; stipules intrapetiolar, short, acute, persistent. *Flowers* sessile or shortly pedicelled, bluish-purple, sweet-scented but give an unpleasant smell when bruised, club-shaped in bud; fascicled in large lax trichotomous panicles; fascicles subumbellate; bracts subulate. *Calyx-segments* 4-5, longer than the ovary, persistent. *Corolla-tube* ·5 in. long, trumpet-shaped, pubescent; lobes valvate. *Stamens* and *style* more or less exserted according to sex. *Capsules* ellipsoid, ·1-·15 in. long, 1-celled, 5-seeded; seeds triquetrous.

OUTER HIMALAYA, the DÚN and the SIWALIKS, also low hot valleys in JAUNSAR; fairly common; a prevalent gregarious weed about Paléd, Málkōt and such other places.

The wood is used for making gun-powder charcaol in Chamba.

Fl. Oct.-Jan.

10. Leptodermis, Wall.; G. P. n. 290.

1. **L. lanceolata,** Wall.; Fl. Br. Ind. iii. 198; Brandis For. Flora 279, Ind. Trees 391; Gamble Man. Ind. Timb. 426. Vern. *Páderá,* Jaunsar; *Páderá* or *Jogiá Páderá,* Garhwal and Kumaon.

A small shrub, generally gregarious on rocks; bark thin, grey. *Leaves* opposite or whorled, very variable, ·5-4 by ·15-1·5 in.; ovate elliptic or elliptic-lanceolate, fetid when bruised; petiole ·1-·3 in. long. *Flowers* ·5-·7 in. long, white but fading to pale-yellow, 4-6-merous, in bracteate heads which are disposed in large terminal panicles; bracteoles cuspidate, connate to form an involucre. *Calyx-tube* obconic; lobes 5, valvate, persistent. *Corolla* funnel-shaped, hairy within; lobes 5, valvate. *Stamens* 5, exserted in the male flowers. *Ovary* 5-celled; ovule 1 in each cell; style filiform, with 5 linear arms, exserted in the female flowers. *Capsules* 5-valved, each valve terminating in a persistent ciliate calyx-tooth; seeds with a membranous testa.

OUTER HIMALAYA and JAUNSAR, 3,-9.000 ft.: Sahansra dhárá, Mussoorie; Konáin, etc. Wood hard, close-grained, white.

Fl. July-Sept. Fr. Nov.-Jan.

Order 2.—ASTERALES.

FAM. 46. COMPOSITÆ; G. P. N. 88.

Herbs or shrubs, rarely trees. *Leaves* exstipulate, alternate or opposite, simple or compound. *Inflorescence* a bracteate head. *Flowers* numerous, small, sessile, all tubular, or the outer or all ligulate; all bisexual, or the inner male and the outer female or neuter, sometimes diœcious. *Calyx* superior; limb none, or of hairs or scales. *Corolla* either tubular or campanulate with 4-5 valvate lobes, or ligulate with strap-shaped elongated connate lobes. *Disk* epigynous. *Stamens* 4-5, usually syngenesious, anthers basifixed; connective produced. *Ovary* inferior, 1-celled; ovule solitary, erect; style slender, 2-fid, arms linear, often hairy. *Fruit* a cypsela usually crowned with the hairy calyx (pappus); seed exalbuminous; testa membranous.

With very few exceptions, all the species in this largest of all Families are herbaceous, *Leucomeris*, described below, being the only tree Genus found within our limits.

1. Leucomeris, Don; G. P. n. 674.

1. **L. spectabilis,** Don; Fl. Br. Ind. iii. 386; Brandis Ind. Trees 400; Gamble Man. Ind. Timb. 428. Vern. *Phúsiári, Phúsára,* Hind.

A large shrub or small tree with white corky bark; branches stout, grooved. *Leaves* alternate, 4-14 by 1·5-4 in., narrow-oblong or oblanceolate, entire or minutely cuspidate-serrate, coriaceous, glabrous above, thickly white-felted beneath, narrowed into a marginate petiole ·5-1 in. long; lateral nerves about 16 pairs. *Heads.* ·7-1 in. long, in globose thickly white-tomentose bracteolate corymbs. *Flowers* 4-8 in each head, all similar and fertile, about 1 in. long; bracts in many series. *Involucre* much shorter than the flowers. *Corolla* ·5 in. long, tubular; segments narrow. *Style* 2-fid. *Cypsela* about ·2 in. long, 5-ribbed, slender, densely silky; pappus ·5 in. long, rather rigid.

Fairly common in the OUTER HIMALAYA from Sáiá to Rikhikesh, 3,-6,000 ft. Occasionally in the DÚN, *e.g.*, at Buláwála and Káluwála.

The wood is brownish-white, fairly compact and even-grained, but the tree is generally hollow in the centre, rendering the wood useless.

Fl. Cold season. Fr. Apr., May.

The following plants deserve notice :—

1. *Vernonia Roxburghii*, Less.; Fl. Br. Ind. iii. 232; Brandis Ind. Trees 399. An undershrub common in blanks and grass lands near Lachiwála and elsewhere in the DÚN. *Leaves* alternate, subsessile or shortly petiolate, scabrid, cuspidate-serrate. *Heads*, 30-flowered, sessile, in terminal corymbs. *Cypsela* hairy; pappus whitish.—*G. P. n. 16.*

2. *Inula Cappa*, DC.; Fl. Br. Ind. iii. 295; Brandis Ind. Trees 400. An undershrub common in the OUTER HIMALAYA. Branches, inflorescence and under-side of leaves silky-tomentose. *Leaves* alternate, oblong-lanceolate, shortly petiolate, distantly toothed, hairy or scabrid above. *Heads* small, very numerous, heterogamous. *Cypsela* ·05 in.; pappus ·15 in., dirty yellowish-white; hairs thickened at the end.—*G. P. n. 275.*

3. *Inula cuspidata*, Clarke; Fl. Br. Ind. iii. 296; Brandis Ind. Trees 401. A glabrous undershrub with slender branches. *Leaves* 3-5 in., elliptic-lanceolate, serrulate, acuminate, pubescent when young. *Heads* numerous, in terminal corymbs. *Cypsela* silky, ·06 in.; pappus yellowish, hairs thickened at the tip. JAUNSAR and OUTER HIMALAYA, up to 6,000 ft.

4. *Siegesbeckia orientalis*, Linn.; Fl. Br. Ind. iii. 304; Duthie Fl. Up. Gang. Pl. 467. Vern. *Lichkurá*, Garhwal. A large erect annual up to 6 or 7 ft. in height, common on damp fallow lands and coppice areas throughout the SIWALIK DIVISION and the HILLS up to 5,000 ft., conspicuous by the large spreading linear-spathulate outer

involucrate bracts which by means of their viscous glandular hairs catch on to clothes. *Leaves* opposite, 2-5 by 1-3·5 in., gradually smaller upwards, triangular-ovate, irregularly toothed, velvety-pubescent, gradually narrowing into a winged petiole. *Heads* small, peduncled, one at each node of the branches or branchlets. *Flowers* usually yellow. *Cypsela* curved, quadrangular, black, each enclosed in an inner bract. The leaves, which are very bitter, are used by the hill-people as a febrifuge, each being pounded and kneaded into a pill to be taken with a little water. Fl. Oct.-Dec.—*G. P. n. 361.*

5. *Artemisia vulgaris*, Linn.; Fl. Br. Ind. iii. 325; Brandis Ind. Trees 402. Vern. *Sámri*, Dún. A gregarious weed in gardens and camping grounds in the DÚN, and sunny slopes in the HILLS, aromatic and shrub-like. *Leaves* large, ovate, lobed or laciniate, tomentose beneath. *Heads* ·15-·2 in., in large panicled racemes.—*G. P. n. 551.*

6. *Echinops echinatus*, DC.; Fl. Br. Ind. iii. 358. Vern. *Gokhrú*, Hind. A thistle-like herb with white felt, common in fallow lands in the DÚN. *Leaves* alternate, pinnatifid, spinous, thickly white-felted beneath. *Heads* 1-flowered, crowded in a globose white ball 2-3 in. across. *Cypsela* obconic, silky.—*G. P. n. 621.*

7. *Catamixis baccharoides*, Thoms.; Fl. Br. Ind. iii. 389. An undershrub 3-5 ft. high, found in sandy cliffs in the SIWALIK-TRACT, *e. g.*, Timli Pass, Beribárá, etc. *Leaves* alternate, 2-3 by 1-1·5 in., obovate, distantly crenate above the middle, coriaceous; petiole very short, half-amplexicaul. *Heads* yellow, small, in broad terminal corymbs. *Corolla* ·2 in. long, ligulate. *Cypsela* turbinate, silky-villous; pappus ·3 in. long, white. Fl. Dec., Jan.—*G. P. n. 688.*

8. *Gerbera lanuginosa*, Benth.; Fl. Br. Ind. iii. 390. Vern. *Kúpherú*, Jaunsar; *Jhúlá*, *Jhúlú*, *Kapás*, Garh. JAUNSAR and TEHRI-GARHWAL up to 8,000 ft., also in shady places along the crest of the SIWALIKS, almost always on cliffs. A scape-bearing small herb with lyrately pinnatifid or lobed radical *leaves* thickly felted below. *Scape* 4-12 in. long, cottony. *Heads* 1-1·5 in. across, hemispherical. *Cypsela* ribbed. The cotton obtained from the leaves is used by the JAUNSARIS as tinder for their *chuck-muck*, and occasionally made into coarse cloth or bags.—*G. P. n. 695.*

Series ii.—*Hypogynæ.*

Order 3.—ERICALES.

FAM. 47. ERICACEÆ; G. P. N. 93.

Shrubs or trees, rarely herbs. *Leaves* usually alternate, simple, exstipulate. *Flowers* solitary fascicled or racemed, usually regular, sometimes dimorphous. *Calyx* usually free; lobes 5, rarely 4 or 6. *Corolla* hypogynous, campanulate or urceolate. *Stamens* generally twice as many as the corolla-lobes, hypogynous or epipetalous; filaments free; anthers 2-celled, opening at the top by pores or slits, rarely longitudinally. *Ovary* superior, 4-5-many-celled; ovules many in the inner angles of the cells; style cylindrical; stigma entire or obscurely lobed. *Fruit* a 5-valved capsule; seeds very small, albuminous.

Analysis of the Genera.

Flowers in racemes; capsules globose, loculicidally dehiscent . . . . . 1. PIERIS.
Flowers fascicled or subcorymbose; capsules elongate, septicidally dehiscent . . 2. RHODODENDRON.

1. Pieris, D. Don; G. P. n. 17.

1. **P. ovalifolia,** D. Don; Fl. Br. Ind. iii. 460; Gamble Man. Ind. Timb. 431; Brandis Ind. Trees 409. Syn. *Andromeda ovalifolia* Wall.; Brandis For. Flora 280. Vern. *Áyár, Ányár,* Jaunsar.

A small deciduous tree; bark brown, peeling off in narrow strips, often deeply furrowed with spiral clefts. *Leaves* 3-6 in. long, ovate or elliptic-oblong, acute or acuminate, entire, rounded at the base, coriaceous, glabrous, often pilose beneath when young; petiole ·2-·5 in. *Inflorescence* a simple raceme, rarely falsely panicled; bracts lanceolate or linear, deciduous. *Flowers* white. *Calyx-lobes* 5, triangular-lanceolate, ·10-·12 in., connate at the base. *Corolla* ·2-·4 in. long, elongate-ovoid, pubescent without; lobes 5, short, recurved. *Stamens* 10, hypogynous; filaments subulate, ciliate, with two filiform appendages at the apex; anthers open by terminal pores. *Ovary* 5-celled, ovules many in each cell. *Capsules* ·2 in. diam., globose, loculicidally 5-valved; seeds many, minute, linear-oblong.

Common in JAUNSAR, between 4,000 and 8,000 ft., always associated with *Quercus incana* and *Rhododendron arboreum*.

Wood light, reddish-brown, moderately compact and hard, but not durable and warps and shrinks badly in seasoning; weight 41 lbs. per c. ft. It is used only for fuel and charcoal, but even as fuel it is not considered good, as it does not burn well but only smoulders. The leaves are poisonous to goats and camels; they are used to kill insects, and an infusion of them is applied in skin diseases of parasitic origin.

Fl. Apr.-June according to elevation. Fr. July-Sept.

2. Rhododendron, Linn.; G. P. n. 46.

Trees or shrubs. *Leaves* alternate or falsely whorled, often clustered at the ends of the branches, entire, coriaceous, edges often slightly recurved. *Flowers* usually in compact terminal clusters or in umbelliform corymbs, rarely solitary; buds enclosed in scaly bracts. *Calyx* 5-lobed, sometimes obsolete. *Corolla* campanulate or funnel-shaped; lobes 5-10. *Stamens* usually 10, rarely 5 or 20; anthers dehiscing by terminal pores. *Ovary* 5-20-celled; ovules many in each cell. *Capsules* septicidally 4-20-valved from the apex; seeds very numerous, scale-like, albuminous.

Analysis of the Species.

Trees or large shrubs ; calyx small or obsolete (flowers in terminal corymbs).	
Leaves silvery- or rusty-tomentose beneath ; pedicels 0 or very short ; ovary woolly .	1. *R. arboreum.*
Leaves cinnamonous-tomentose beneath ; pedicels long ; ovary glabrate . .	2. *R. campanulatum.*
Small shrubs ; calyx prominently lobed, lobes long, foliaceous.	
Flowers solitary or 2-3 together ; peduncles long, scabrous ; leaves subsessile .	3. *R. lepidotum.*
Flowers in terminal corymbs ; pedicels short, glabrous ; leaves petiolate .	4. *R. Anthopogon.*

1. **R. arboreum,** Sm. ; Fl. Br. Ind. iii. 465 ; Brandis For. Flora 281, Ind. Trees 409 : Gamble Man. Ind. Timb. 433. The Tree-Rhododendron. Vern. *Búráns,* Jaunsar.

A small evergreen tree ; bark reddish-brown, peeling off in small flakes. *Leaves* crowded at the ends of the branches, 4-6 in. long, lanceolate or elliptic-oblong, acute at both ends, coriaceous, glabrous above, rusty-tomentose or covered with small silvery scales beneath ; nerves and midrib prominent beneath, depressed above ; buds viscous. *Flowers* large, very showy, commonly deep-crimson, rarely pink or nearly white, in corymbose fascicles at the ends of the branches ; pedicels 0 to one-third the length of the corolla-tube ; bracts hairy. *Calyx-lobes* ·1 in. wide, ovate, or very obscure. *Corolla* campanulate, 1-1·5 by ·8-1 in. ; lobes 5, often unequal. *Stamens* 10, alternately longer. *Ovary* woolly, 7-9-celled. *Capsules* 1 in. long, cylindrical, curved, longitudinally ribbed ; seeds ellipsoid.

Common in JAUNSAR and TEHRI-GARHWAL, between 4,000 and 8,000 ft., almost always associated with *Pieris ovalifolia* and *Quercus incana.*

Wood soft, brownish or reddish-white, close-and even-grained, seasons badly, and is apt to warp and shrink ; weight 40-45 lbs. per c. ft. It is chiefly used for fuel and charcoal, but is sometimes locally used for building, for making dishes, gun-stocks, tool-handles, etc. The flowers which are sour to the taste are eaten and are made into preserves. They are believed to be good for dysentery and are applied as a poultice in headaches, also offered in temples in the hills. The viscid tender leaves are eaten cooked as a vegetable.

Fl. Usually Mar.-May. Fr. Autumn and cold season.

2. **R. campanulatum,** Don; Fl. Br. Ind. iii. 466; Brandis For. Flora 281. Ind. Trees 410; Gamble Man. Ind. Timb. 434. Vern. *Simris,* T.-Garhwal.

A moderate-sized evergreen shrub with thin grey bark. *Leaves* 3-5 in. long, elliptic or elliptic-oblong, rounded at both ends, crowded at the ends of the branches, mucronate, coriaceous, glabrous and finely reticulate above, with a dense cinnamon-colour tomentum concealing the nerves beneath; midrib prominent. *Flowers* large and showy, whitish-pink purple or lilac, in lax terminal corymbs; pedicels as long as the corolla-tube; bracts silky. *Calyx-teeth* broadly triangular, very small. *Corolla* campanulate, 1-1·5 by ·8-1 in.; lobes 5. *Stamens* 10. *Ovary* 5-9-celled, glabrous; style persistent. *Capsules* cylindrical, about 1 in. long, more or less curved; seeds linear-oblong, compressed.

TEHRI-GARHWAL, above 10,000 ft.: Rikhshin, Kedár Kántá Chánsil, etc.

Wood light pinkish-red, close-grained and moderately hard; weight about 40 lbs. per c. ft. "The leaves are brought to the plains and used as snuff."—*Sir D. Brandis.*

Fl. May-July. Fr. Oct.-Dec.

3. **R. lepidotum,** Wall.; Fl. Br. Ind. iii. 471; Brandis For. Flora 282, Ind. Trees 412; Gamble Man. Ind. Timb. 432. Vern. *Simris,* T.-Garhwal.

A small aromatic shrub; young parts covered with glandular scales. *Leaves* ·7-1 in. long, approximate at the ends of the branches, sessile or subsessile, obovate and obtuse, or lanceolate and subacute, glabrous above, silvery- or brown-tomentose beneath. *Flowers* red yellow or purple, solitary or 2-3 together; pedicels ·5-1·5 in. long, very scabrous. *Calyx-lobes* oval, not ciliate. *Corolla-tube* short; lobes round, spreading, ·2-·3 in. long. *Stamens* usually 8. *Ovary* 5-celled. *Capsules* 5-celled, ·3 by ·2 in.; seeds oblong, acute.

TEHRI-GARHWAL, 9,-11,000 ft., usually on rocks.: Chánsil, Gangottari, etc.

"The leaves of this and the preceding species are used as stimulants in native medicine" (*Sir D. Brandis*) under the name *Tálisfar* (?) or *Tálispát.*

Fl. June, July.

4. **R. Anthopogon,** Don; Fl. Br. Ind. iii. 472; Brandis For. Flora 282, Ind. Trees 412; Gamble Man. Ind. Timb. 432. Vern. *Tális, Tálisri,* Punjab Hills.

A small shrub with an aromatic odour; branchlets scabrous and scaly. *Leaves* 1-1·5 in. long, elliptic or broad-oblong, shining above, brown-tomentose beneath; petiole ·12-·25 in. long. *Flowers* yellow, in dense terminal corymbs. *Calyx-lobes* oblong or elliptic, membranous, ciliate. *Corolla* tubular with a dilated mouth; tube ·2 in. long; lobes obovate, entire, spreading. *Stamens* 6-8. *Ovary* scaly. *Capsules* ·2 in. long, ovoid; seeds oblong, subacute.

TEHRI-GARHWAL, above 11,000 ft.: Kedár Kánta, Harki Dún, etc. Also the Chur Mountain, JUBBAL. Gregarious and generally under the equally gregarious *Betula utilis.*

Fl. June, July.

Order 4.—PRIMULALES.

FAM. 48. MYRSINACEÆ; G. P. N. 100.

Shrubs or small trees. *Leaves* alternate, simple, exstipulate, generally gland-dotted. *Flowers* small, regular, in axillary clusters, racemes or panicles, rarely terminal. *Calyx* free, exceptionally adhering to the ovary; lobes persistent, sometimes accrescent in fruit. *Corolla* regular; petals connate or free, contorted or imbricate. *Stamens* epipetalous, as many as the petals or corolla-lobes and opposite to them; anthers oblong, free or united by their margins. *Ovary* 1-celled; ovules few or many, inserted on a free-central placenta; style filiform or columnar. *Fruit* a berry, often coloured; seeds excavate at the base.

Analysis of the Genera.

Calyx adnate to the ovary; fruit many-seeded . 1. MÆSA.
Calyx free; fruit 1-seeded.
  Petals free; flowers racemed or panicled . . 3. EMBELIA.
  Petals united into a short tube.
    Fls. in dense axillary clusters; corolla imbricate. 2. MYRSINE.
    Fls. in umbels racemes or corymbs; corolla twisted to the right . . . . . 4. ARDISIA.

1. Mæsa, Forsk.; G. P. n. 1.

1. **M. indica,** Wall.; Fl. Br. Ind. iii. 509; Brandis For. Flora 283, Ind. Trees 414; Gamble Man. Ind. Timb. 438.

A large shrub with long straggling branches. *Leaves* 3-5 by 1-1·5 in., lanceolate or elliptic-oblong, distantly sharp-toothed, subcoriaceous or membranous; primary nerves 5-9 pairs; petiole about ·5 in. *Flowers* white, small, in compound racemes; bracts minute. *Calyx-tube* more or less adnate to the ovary; lobes 5, obtuse, pubescent, persistent. *Corolla* gamopetalous, white, 5-lobed, twice the size of the calyx. *Stamens* 5; filaments short; anthers broad. *Fruit* a globose berry, about ·15 in. across, crowned with the persistent calyx-lobes and often tipped by the remains of the style, fleshy juicy and pinkish-white when ripe.

Common in the SUB-HIMALAYAN HILLS: Paléd, Sansárú Khálá, Mussoorie, etc.

The berries are eaten in Nepal, and the leaves are used to poison fish in Canara.

Fl. Dec.-Apr. and sometimes also in the rains. Fr. Cold season.

2. Myrsine, Linn.; G. P. n. 2.

Shrubs or small trees. *Leaves* entire or serrate, punctate, usually coriaceous. *Flowers* polygamous or diœcious, fascicled usually at the axils of fallen leaves; bracts densely imbricate. *Calyx* 4-5-lobed, persistent. *Corolla* 4-5-partite; segments imbricate, recurved. *Stamens* 4-5. *Ovary* superior, globose; ovules many; style short, cylindrical. *Fruit* a 1-seeded small globose berry, red or purple when ripe, seed excavate.

Analysis of the Species.

A small shrub with pubescent branchlets. Leaves small, subsessile . . . . 1. *M. africana.*

A small glabrous tree. Leaves usually large, petiolate . . . . 2. *M. semiserrata.*

1. **M. africana,** Linn.; Fl. Br. Ind. iii. 511; Brandis For. Flora 286, Ind. Trees 416; Gamble Man. Ind. Timb. 438. Vern. *Banwán*, Jaunsar; *Rikhdálmi*, Garhwal.

A small evergreen shrub; branchlets and petioles ferruginous-pubescent. *Leaves* ·5-1·5 by ·3-·5 in., lanceolate or obovate, sharply cuspidate-serrate; midrib prominent; petiole minute. *Flowers* small, subsessile, tetrandrous, in axillary fascicles of 4-6. *Anthers* exceeding the corolla. *Style* short; stigma flat. *Berry* usually solitary, red, smooth, ·1 in. diam., swelling to ·25 in. diam. and dark-purple or black when fully ripe.

Common in JAUNSAR and in the OUTER HIMALAYA, 3,-9,000 ft.

The fruit is used in Indian medicine as an anthelmintic under the name of *Bebrang*.

Fl. Mar.-May. Fr. Apr.-May to Nov.-Dec.

2. **M. semiserrata,** Wall.; Fl. Br. Ind. iii. 511. Brandis For. Flora 285, Ind. Trees 416; Gamble Man. Ind. Timb. 439. Vern. *Bains*, *Gaunta*, Garhwal.

A shrub or small tree with ash-coloured bark. *Leaves* 2-5 by ·5-1·2 in., lanceolate, acute, entire or sparingly cupsidate-serrate towards the apex, coriaceous, gland-dotted, glabrous; petiole ·1-·3 in. long. *Flowers* ·1 in. diam., in dense axillary fascicles; pedicels ·2-·3 in. long, glabrous. *Calyx* persistent, half the length of the corolla-lobes. *Style* short. *Berry* the size of a small pea, generally clustered, globose, red, shining; seed solitary, globose.

OUTER HIMALAYAN RANGES and valleys in JAUNSAR and TEHRI-GARHWAL up to 6,000 ft.: Sansárú Khálá, Mussoorie; Korwá Chakrata, Dhárágádh, etc.

Wood compact, heavy, hard and handsome, and said to be esteemed in Nepal for carpenter's work; weight 50 lbs. per c. ft.

Fl. and fr. Cold season.

3. Embelia, Burm.; G. P. n. 8 (Samara).

1. **E. robusta,** Roxb.; Fl. Br. Ind. iii. 515; Brandis For. Flora 284, Ind. Trees 416; Gamble Man. Ind. Timb. 440. Vern. *Gáiá*, Dún.

A large scrambling shrub; bark brown, with horizontal cracks and numerous lenticels on the branches. *Leaves* 5-7 by 2-3 in., obovate-oblong elliptic or oblanceolate, short-acuminate, undulate, sometimes obscurely serrulate, usually rusty-pubescent beneath; lateral nerves 6-12 pairs, prominent, arcuate; base cuneate; petiole glandular, usually channelled. *Flowers* small, mostly diœcious, in axillary and terminal simple or fascicled racemes. *Calyx* free, deeply 5-lobed, persistent. *Petals* 5, oblong, reflexed, puberulous. *Stamens* 5, adnate to the petals. *Ovary* superior, globose; ovules few, embedded in a fleshy placenta; style short, persistent. *Fruit* a dry berry, globose, red, more or less longitudinally ribbed, crowned with the remains of the style; seed usually solitary, globose, with a hollowed base.

Common in the DÚN and SAHÁRANPUR FORESTS: Lachiwála, Pardúni, Dharmáwála, Mohkumpur; Kasúmri, etc.

The fruit has the same vernacular name and economic use as those of *Myrsine africana*.

Fl. July-Sept. Fr. Cold season.

4. Ardisia, Swartz.; G. P. n. 12.

1. **A. humilis,** Vahl; Fl. Br. Ind. iii. 529; Brandis For. Flora 287, Ind. Trees 418; Gamble Man. Ind. Timb. 441.

A large glabrous shrub. *Leaves* 4-8 by 1·5-3·5 in., obovate-oblong or elliptic, acute or short-acuminate, entire, coriaceous, fleshy; lateral nerves not very conspicuous; base cuneate; petiole marginate. *Flowers* 2-sexual, rose-coloured or pinkish-white, about ·5 in. across, in axillary corymbose racemes; pedicels 1-2 in. long in the fruit, somewhat shorter in flower; bracts deciduous. *Calyx-lobes* 5, obtuse, oval or rounded, slightly enlarged in fruit. *Corolla* deeply 5-lobed; segments acute, twisted to the right in bud. *Stamens* 5; filaments short; anthers acute. *Ovary* free, 1-celled, tapering; style long, persistent. *Fruit* globose, the size of a large pea, black when fully ripe, full of a pink juice.

Fairly common in the damper parts of the DÚN FORESTS, especially along shady ravines.

Wood soft, used only for fuel.

Fl. in all seasons, but chiefly Mar., Apr. Fr. generally cold season.

Order 5.—EBENALES.

FAM. 49. SAPOTACEÆ; G. P. N. 101.

Trees or shrubs, often with milky juice. *Leaves* alternate, simple, entire, coriaceous, generally exstipulate. *Flowers* bisexual, axillary, solitary or clustered; bracts minute or none. *Calyx-lobes* 4-8 and imbricate, or multiseriate with the outer series valvate. *Corolla-tube* short; lobes as many, or 2-4 times as many, as the calyx-lobes. *Stamens* upon the corolla-tube, as many as the corolla-lobes or as the lobes of the inner series and opposite to them, or numerous in 1-3 series, sometimes alternating with staminodes; filaments short; connective, often produced. *Ovary* superior, 2-8-celled, with a solitary anatropous ovule in each cell. *Fruit* a berry. *Seeds* 1-8, ellipsoid, often compressed, exalbuminous and with large fleshy cotyledons, or albuminous and with flat cotyledons; testa usually crustaceous.

1. Bassia, Linn.; G. P. n. 14.

Trees with milky juice. *Leaves* stipulate; stipules caducous. *Flowers* on axillary, generally fasciculate, pedicels. *Calyx* deeply 4-8-lobed; lobes biseriate, the outer lobes valvate, the inner sub-imbricate, in bud. *Corolla-tube* ovoid or campanulate; lobes 5-14, contorted in bud. *Stamens* at least twice as many as the corolla-lobes, all fertile; anthers cordate, acute, with a mucronate connective. *Ovary* villous, usually 6-8-celled; style long-exserted, persistent. *Fruit* an oblong or globose berry, 1-3-seeded, exalbuminous; cotyledons fleshy, oily.

Analysis of the Species.

Corolla-tube fleshy, lobes erect anthers not exserted . . . . 1. *B. latifolia.*

Corolla-tube not fleshy, lobes spreading; anthers exserted . . . . 2. *B. butyracea.*

1. **B. latifolia,** Roxb.; Fl. Br. Ind. iii. 544; Brandis For. Flora 289, Ind. Trees 426; Gamble Man. Ind. Timb. 447. Vern. *Mauwá, Mahuá* or *Mohwá,* Hind.

A large deciduous tree; young parts pubescent; bark grey or blackish, with shallow wrinkles and vertical cracks. *Leaves* clustered at the ends of the branches, 5-7 by 3-4 in., elliptic or oblong-elliptic, short-acuminate or obtuse, coriaceous, densely woolly beneath when young, glabrescent afterwards; main lateral nerves 10-12 pairs; base cuneate; petiole 1-1·5 in.; stipules subulate. *Flowers* numerous at the ends of the branches, on drooping woolly pedicels 1-1·5 in. long. *Calyx* coriaceous, densely rusty-tomentose; lobes 4, rarely 5. *Corolla* ·6-·8 in. long, fleshy and juicy, cream-coloured, early caducous; tube ovoid; lobes 7-14, usually 8-9, short, erect. *Stamens* generally 24-26; anthers hairy at the back, subsessile, inserted in 3 series inside the corolla-tube. *Berry* ovoid, fleshy, green, 1-2 in. long, 1-4-seeded.

Not very common in the area covered by this Flora. Occurs sporadically at Kálsi in JAUNSAR, at Dúdhli, Phándowála and Sáinkōt in the DÚN, and about Beribára in the SAHÁRANPUR DISTRICT.

Heartwood scanty, reddish-brown, very hard, close- and even-grained, tough and durable, and seasons well; weight about 65 lbs. per c. ft. But the tree is so much prized for its flower and fruit that it is rarely felled. The flowers are eaten raw or cooked, or made into sweetmeats. A coarse and strong spirit is also distilled from them. The fruit is eaten and gives, when expressed, a thick oil which is eaten, burned in *chirághs,* and is also used to adulterate ghee. The oil-cake is used to poison fish.

Leafless Feb.-Apr. Fl. Mar., Apr. Fr. June, July.

2. **B. butyracea,** Roxb.; Fl. Br. Ind. iii. 546; Brandis For. Flora 290, Ind. Trees 427; Gamble Man. Ind. Timb. 448. Vern. *Chiura,* Dún; *Phalwárá, Phulel, Phuloá,* Hind.

A large deciduous tree with dark-grey bark. *Leaves* 6-12 by 4-7 in., obovate or obovate-oblong, coriaceous, soft-tomentose beneath, crowded near the ends of the branches; lateral nerves 15-20 pairs; base rhomboid; petiole 1-1·5 in. long; stipules minute, caducous. *Flowers* on drooping tomentose pedicels 1-1·3 in. long, crowded below the terminal leaves in the axils of the lower ones. *Calyx* coriaceous, rusty-tomentose, deeply 5-cleft: lobes ·3-·5 in. long. *Corolla* pale-yellow; tube ·7 in. long, cylindrical, not fleshy; lobes 8-10, spreading. *Stamens* 30-40; anthers exserted, not hairy. *Berry* ovoid, smooth, 1 in. long, 1-3-seeded.

It has only been found at Tapoban in the EASTERN DÚN, and may possibly be found in the inner hills of TEHRI-GARHWAL.

The tree is valued for its fruit, from the seeds of which a vegetable butter is extracted. It makes good soap, and made into candles is said to burn without smoke or unpleasant smell. It is used as an external application for headache and for rheumatism. The oil-cake, as also the pulp of the fruit, is eaten. The sweet juice of fresh corolla is expressed and boiled into *gúr* which is much prized in Kumaon.

Fl. Nov.-Jan. Fr. June, July.

To this Family belong the following which are cultivated in gardens in SAHÁRANPUR and the DÚN :—

Mimusops Elengi, Linn. ; Fl. Br. Ind. iii. 548. Vern. *Maulsári*, Hind.,—the fragrant flowers of which are used in Indian perfumery.—*G. P. n.* 22.

Also *Mimusops hexandra*, Roxb. ; Fl. Br. Ind. iii. 549, Vern. *Khirni*, Hind.—noted for its edible fruit and useful timber.

FAM. 50. EBENACEÆ; G. P. N. 102.

Trees or shrubs. *Leaves* alternate, entire, exstipulate. *Flowers* axillary, regular, usually diœcious, generally bracteate, solitary or in small cymes. *Calyx* inferior, gamosepalous, often accrescent in fruit. *Corolla* gamopetalous. *Stamens* as many, or 2-3 times as many, as the corolla-lobes, free or variously united, absent or rudimentary in the female flowers ; anthers linear, erect, introrse, with the connective usually prolonged beyond them. *Ovary* superior, 2 or more-celled, with usually one pendulous ovule in each cell ; styles 2-8, distinct or connate at the base. *Fruit* an indehiscent, coriaceous or fleshy berry ; seeds few, pendulous, albuminous ; cotyledons foliaceous.

1. Diospyros, Linn.; G. P. n. 4.

Trees, rarely shrubs. *Leaves* alternate, sometimes subopposite, entire. *Flowers* diœcious, rarely polygamous, the female often solitary. *Calyx* lobed; lobes often accrescent in fruit. *Corolla* tubular or urceolate, deeply lobed; lobes twisted to the right. MALE FLOWERS: *Stamens* 4-16 or more; ovary rudimentary. FEMALE FLOWERS: *Staminodes* 0-16. *Ovary* usually 4-5-celled; ovules solitary in each cell. *Fruit* generally pulpy, 1-10-seeded. *Seeds* usually compressed; albumen uniform or ruminated.

Analysis of the Species.

Leaves always alternate, oblong.
  Leaves glabrescent; fruit glabrous.
    Leaves light-green, usually membranous and cordate . . . . . 1. *D. cordifolia.*
    Leaves dark-green, coriaceous when mature, never cordate . . . 2. *D. Kanjilali.*
  Leaves quite glabrous; fruit densely rusty 3. *D. Embryopteris.*
Leaves alternate or subopposite, broad-ovate 4. *D. tomentosa.*

. **D. cordifolia,** Roxb. Cor. Pl. i 38, t. 50.—Syn. *D. montana,* Roxb.; Fl. Br. Ind. iii. 555; Brandis For. Flora 296, Ind. Trees 431; Gamble Man. Ind. Timb. 454. Vern. *Bis Tendú,* Hind.; *Chambér,* Sahâranpur.

A large shrub with a short trunk and a broad rounded dense crown, often spinescent. Bark thin smooth pinkish or bluish-grey on branches, dark-grey or almost black and deeply cracked on old stems. *Leaves* 2-4 by 1-1·5 in., ovate or oblong, soft, membranous or subcoriaceous, light-green, pubescent or glabrescent; nerves slender; base cordate rounded or cuneate; petiole ·2 in. or less. MALE FLOWERS in bracteate 3-flowered cymes. *Calyx* 4-cleft; lobes ovate. *Corolla* urceolate, with 4 short lobes. *Stamens* 16, in two series, glabrous; anthers not awned. FEMALE FLOWERS solitary, nodding, larger than the male flowers; pedicels with a pair of bracts at the apex. *Calyx* deeply 4-fid; lobes ovate. *Staminodes* 4-12 in one series. *Ovary* glabrous, 8-celled, 1 ovule in each cell. *Fruit* globose, ·5-1·2 in. diam., yellow when ripe, supported by the accrescent leathery calyx. *Seeds* compressed; albumen uniform.

Common in the lower SAHÁRANPUR FORESTS and also found occasionally in the DÚN, *e.g.*, Tháno, Lachiwála, etc.

The wood is hard and durable and is variegated with black and white streaks. It would perhaps be good for furniture, but at present there is no demand except for fuel. Heartwood not distinct, weight about 45 lbs. per c. ft. Every part of the tree, including the fruit, is bitter and has an unpleasant smell.

Fl. Mar.-May. Fr. Cold season.

Following the Flora of British India this tree was described as *D. montana* in the first edition of this book, but Roxburgh's distinction appears to be well founded and I have followed Col. Beddome and Mr. Duthie (*Ind. Forester* XXXI, 308) in keeping *D. cordifolia* distinct.

2. **D. Kanjilali,** Duthie in *Ind. For.* XXXI, 307; Brandis Ind. Trees 432, 713. Vern, *Pinná*, Málkōt.

A small or middle-sized tree with a fairly long trunk and greenish or ashy-grey smooth bark; branches forming a narrow and open crown, not spinescent. *Leaves* 1·5-5·5 by 1-2 in., generally elliptic or oblong, dark-green, densely velvety-tomentose when young, almost glabrous and rigidly coriaceous when mature; midrib impressed above but prominent beneath, lateral nerves faint, arcuate; petiole ·15-·4 in. long. MALE FLOWERS in short 3-flowered axillary cymes; pedicels ·06 in. long; bracts ovate, subacute, ciliate on the margins. *Calyx-lobes* broad and rounded, pubescent on both sides and with ciliate margins. *Corolla* ·2-·3 in. long, pale green, slightly pubescent outside, glabrous within. *Stamens* 16, in opposite pairs, united at the base; anthers awned, glabrous. FEMALE FLOWERS solitary, axillary, nodding, dark-green; pedicels ·1-·2 in. long. *Calyx* accrescent in fruit; lobes spreading, broader than in the preceding species. *Corolla* ·2 in. long, urceolate, dark-green. *Staminodes* 8, alternately longer, the longer ones often toothed at the apex, the shorter obtuse. *Fruit* up to 1 in. diam., subglobose. *Seeds* generally 8 in each fruit, about ·5 in. long, compressed, somewhat curved; albumen uniform.

Although not abundant, fairly common in certain localities, *e.g.*, below Sáiá and the Jumna Valley in JAUNSAR; Kálsi, Rájpur and Málkōt in the OUTER HILLS; Lachiwála and Tháno in the DÚN; and Ranipur, Dholkhand, Mohand and Bádsháhibágh along the foot of the SIWALIKS.

Wood brownish-grey with occasional iron-grey streaks, fine and close-grained, moderately hard; no distinct heartwood; weight 50 lbs. Used for agricultural implements in Málkōt.

Fl. Apr., May. Fr. Cold season.

3. **D. Embryopteris,** Pers.; Fl. Br. Ind. iii. 556; Brandis For. Flora 298, Ind. Trees 434; Gamble Man. Ind. Timb. 455. Vern. *Gáb, Kálá Tendú,* Hind.

A middle-sized evergreen tree, with dark-green shining foliage, and dark-grey or greenish-black bark. *Leaves* distichous, 5-8 by 1·5-2 in., oblong, subacute, coriaceous, smooth, shining; base obtuse; petiole wrinkled, ·5 in. long. *Flowers* tetramerous, scented, white or cream-coloured. MALE FLOWERS in short pedunculate cymes of 3-6 flowers. *Stamens* many, hairy. FEMALE FLOWERS 1-5 together, subsessile, larger than the male flowers. *Staminodes* up to 12. *Ovary* 8-celled; styles 4, lobed at the tips. *Fruit* subglobose, 1·5-2 in. diam., glandular or rusty, supported on the much-accrescent calyx, yellow when ripe. *Seeds* 5-8, compressed, embedded in a glutinous pulp, often rudimentary under cultivation.

Found in the DÚN in moist shady localities, *e. g.*, Khairi Forest, Jogiwála, Ámbári, Báronwála, etc. Also in ravines in the Kálsi Forest. Cultivated in DEHRA.

Wood white, moderately hard and close-grained, used for building. Heartwood not distinct, weight 52 lbs. per c. ft. Round the seeds of the ripe fruit, filling the cells, is a honey-like sweet substance which is eaten. The same substance in the unripe fruit is used as gum in book-binding, and in place of tar for paying the seams of country boats. An infusion of the pulp of unripe fruit is used to render fishing nets and lines durable. The extract of the fruit is used in medicine as an astringent. The oil extracted from the seeds is also used in country medicine.

Fl. June-Aug. Fr. Apr., May.

4. **D. tomentosa,** Roxb.; Fl. Br. Ind. iii. 564; Brandis Ind. Trees 433; Gamble Man. Ind. Timb. 460. Syn.—*D. Melanoxylon,* Roxb.; Brandis For. Flora 294. Vern. *Tendú,* Hind.

A moderate-sized tree with greyish-black bark, exfoliating in regular rectangular scales; young parts covered with grey or rusty tomentum. *Leaves* alternate and subopposite, 3-6 by 2-5 in., broad-ovate, very coriaceous, hairy when young, glabrous above when mature, ultimately glabrescent below; secondary nerves 6-10 pairs, impressed as broad furrows on the upper surface; base cordate or rounded, rarely cuneate; petiole ·3-·5 in. long. MALE FLOWERS subsessile in short drooping cymes. *Calyx* funnel-shaped. *Stamens* 12-16, free. FEMALE FLOWERS solitary, larger than the male flowers. *Calyx* 4-5-gonal. *Staminodes* 8-10 or fewer, sometimes connate in pairs. *Ovary* hairy, 4-8-celled; styles 2-3. *Fruit* globose, 1-1·5 in. diam., glabrous, smooth, yellow when ripe; pulp yellow, sweet, aromatic. *Seeds* 4-8, compressed, oblong; albumen ruminated.

Common in the western half of the SAHÁRANPUR SIWALIKS. Occasionally found in the W. DÚN SIWALIKS.

Wood hard, of a whitish-pink colour, tough and fairly durable, used for building, shoulder-poles, mine-props and shafts of carriages. In some trees irregular masses of black ebony is found, which is very heavy, weighing 75-80 lbs. per c. ft. and is used for carving and other ornamental work. The ripe fruit is edible. The tree coppices very well, and throws out vigorous root-suckers.

Fl. May, June. Fr. Apr. and May, next year.

FAM. 51. STYRACEÆ; G. P. N. 103.

Trees or shrubs. *Leaves* alternate, simple, exstipulate. *Flowers* hermaphrodite, regular, usually white. *Calyx-tube* more or less adnate to the ovary; limb 4-5-toothed or truncate, persistent. *Petals* 4-5, united into a short tube or almost free. *Stamens* usually indefinite, attached to the corolla-tube in one or more series. *Ovary* inferior or superior, 2-5-celled, with 2 or more ovules in each cell. *Style* undivided, filiform; stigma small or capitate. *Fruit* drupaceous, usually 1-seeded. *Seeds* albuminous.

1. Symplocos, Linn.; G. P. n. 1.

1. **S. cratægoides,** Ham.; Fl. Br. Ind. iii. 573; Brandis For. Flora 299, Ind. Trees 440; Gamble Man. Ind. Timb. 464. Vern. *Lōdh, Lōdra,* Jaunsar; *Lōdhra,* Sans.

A large shrub or small tree; bark light-grey, corky, with long vertical furrows. *Leaves* 2-4 by 1-1·5 in., broad-elliptic or ovate, acuminate, sharply glandular-serrulate towards the apex, membranous, pilose beneath or glabrescent. *Flowers* white, ·25 in. diam., fragrant, in cymose corymbs forming dense terminal or axillary panicles; bracts caducous. *Calyx* turbinate, lobes ciliate. *Corolla* 5-cleft nearly to the base. *Stamens* indefinite, connate in 5 bundles. *Ovary* inferior, 2-celled. *Fruit* ·12-·3 in. long, obliquely ovoid or obovoid, crowned with the remains of the calyx-limb, usually 1-seeded. *Embryo* curved, axile.

JAUNSAR, TEHRI-GARHWAL, and the OUTER HIMALAYA, 3,-9,000 ft., *e.g.*, Deoban, Lokhár, Bagur Block (Kathián), Tons Valley; Mautárgádh, Lúnágádh; Laduákōt, etc. Also Mothronwála swamp in the DÚN.

Wood white, hard and close-grained, but warps and splits in seasoning; weight 45-54 lbs. per c. ft. It is, however, fairly durable and has been recommended for turning, and would do even for carving if properly seasoned. The leaves and bark give a yellow dye, the former being also lopped for fodder.

Fl. and new leaves May, June. Fr. July-Oct.

Order 6.—GENTIANALES.

FAM. 52. OLEACEÆ; G. P. N. 104.

Erect or scandent shrubs, or trees. *Leaves* opposite (except in *Jasminum humile*), simple 3-foliolate or imparipinnate, exstipulate. *Flowers* regular, in axillary or terminal cymose panicles, rarely solitary. *Calyx* free; limb 4-5- or more-toothed or -lobed, sometimes truncate, rarely 0. *Corolla* gamopetalous; lobes 4-5 or more or none, imbricate or valvate in bud; tube narrow. *Stamens* 2, inserted on, and included in, the corolla-tube; filaments usually very short. *Ovary* free, 2-celled, with usually 1-2 ovules in each cell; style simple, long or short; stigma simple or 2-lobed. *Fruit* succulent or dry, berry-like capsular or drupaceous; seeds 1 or 2 in each cell, erect or pendulous; albumen fleshy or horny, or 0.

Analysis of the Genera.

Corolla-lobes much imbricate.
  Scandent shrubs. Fruit a berry . . . 1. JASMINUM.
  Erect small tree. Fruit a 2-valved capsule 2. NYCTANTHES.
Corolla-lobes induplicate-valvate or 0.
  Leaves imparipinnate; (fr. samaroid, indehiscent) . . . . 4. FRAXINUS.
  Leaves simple.
    Fruit a capsule . . . . . . 3. SYRINGA.
    Fruit a drupe.
      Inflorescence axillary; petals more or less connate in pairs or distinct . 5. LINOCIERA.
      Inflorescence axillary (except in *O. glandulifera*); corolla with a short tube . . . . . . 6. OLEA.
      Inflorescence terminal; corolla funnel-shaped . . . . . . 7. LIGUSTRUM.

1. Jasminum, Linn.; G. P. n. 1.

Shrubs, usually scandent. *Leaves* opposite (except in *J. humile*), simple 3-foliolate or imparipinnate; petiole usually articulated. *Flowers* fragrant, in axillary or terminal cymes; bracts sometimes petaloid. *Calyx* 5-9-fid; tube funnel-shaped; teeth long or short or 0. *Corolla* white pink or yellow; tube narrow; lobes spreading, imbricate in bud. *Stamens* 2, included in the tube; connective usually produced and triangular. *Ovary* 2-celled; ovules basal, usually 2 in each cell; style cylindrical; stigmas 2, linear. *Berry* 2-lobed, or entire by the failure of 1 carpel; seed usually 1 in each carpel, erect, exalbuminous.

Analysis of the Species.

Leaves opposite; flowers white.
  Leaves simple.
    Cymes dense; flowers sessile, calyx-teeth nearly as long as the corolla-tube . . . . 1. *J. pubescens.*
    Cymes lax; flowers pedicellate; calyx-teeth less than half the length of the corolla-tube . . . . . . 2. *J. arborescens.*
  Leaves imparipinnate.
    Calyx-teeth very short, triangular . 3. *J. dispermum.*
    Calyx teeth long, linear.
      Branches long and weak; corolla-lobes small . . . . . 5. *J. officinale.*
      Branches short and stiff; corolla-lobes large . . . . . 6. *J. grandiflorum.*
Leaves alternate, imparipinnate; flowers yellow (calyx-teeth very short) . . 4 *J. humile.*

1. **J. pubescens,** Willd.; Fl. Br. Ind. iii. 592; Brandis Ind. Trees 449; Gamble Man. Ind. Timb. 468. Syn.—*J. hirsutum,* Willd., Brandis For. Flora 312. Vern. *Chaméli,* Hind.

A scandent shrub; branches and young parts villous. *Leaves* opposite, simple, 1-3 by ·7-1·5 in., ovate, acuminate, entire, more or less pubescent beneath; base rounded or cordate, rarely slightly cuneate; petiole ·2-·4 in. long, pubescent. *Flowers* scented, white, subsessile, in compact short pedunculate cymes. *Calyx-teeth* usually 7-9, linear, hairy, nearly as long as the corolla-tube. *Corolla tube* ·7-·8 in. long; lobes oblong-lanceolate, shorter than the tube. *Fruit* of 1 or 2 carpels, globose or elliptic, surrounded by the calyx-teeth, black when ripe.

Common in the DÚN, especially in hedges outside villages, also along the foot of the SAHÁRANPUR SIWALIKS.

Fl. Dec.-Apr. and also during the rains.

2. **J. arborescens,** Willd.; Fl. Br. Ind. iii. 594; Brandis For. Flora 311, Ind. Trees 450; Gamble Man. Ind. Timb. 467. Vern. *Chaméli,* Hind.

A large shrub, usually suberect. *Leaves* opposite, simple, 3-5 by 2-3 in., ovate, acute or acuminate, entire, soft-tomentose when young, glabrate afterwards; base broadly rounded, sometimes cordate; petiole ·5-·8 in. long. *Flowers* white, fragrant, in lax terminal trichotomous cymes; pedicels ·2-·3 in. long; bracts ·2 in., linear,

Calyx-lobes 5-6, sometimes more, linear, ·1-·15 in. long. *Corolla-tube* ·5 in., lobes usually 9, ·7 in. long, lanceolate, acute. *Fruit* generally of 1 carpel, ·4-·6 in. long, ellipsoid, black when ripe.

Fairly common in the WESTERN DÚN, *e. g.*, Ámbári, Kálsi, etc.; also along the foot of the SAHÁRANPUR SIWALIKS: Ránipur, Bádsháhibágh, etc.

Fl. Apr., May. Fr. June, July.

Var. *latifolia*, Roxb. is scandent. Found about Ambári, W. DÚN.

3. **J. dispermum,** Wall.; Fl. Br. Ind. iii. 602. Brandis For. Flora 312, Ind. Trees, 452.

A glabrous scandent shrub; branches 4-sided. *Leaves* opposite, imparipinnate, upper often 1-foliate. *Leaflets* 3-5, cordate-lanceolate, acuminate, entire, coriaceous, glabrous, 3-5-nerved at the base, terminal 3-4 by 1·4-1·8 in., lateral smaller and very shortly petioluled. *Flowers* white, fragrant, both in few-flowered axillary cymes and many-flowered elongated terminal panicles; pedicels 0-·3 in. *Calyx-teeth* ·0-·4 in., triangular. *Corolla-tube* ·5-·7 in. long; lobes ·2-·3 in., elliptic or ovate. *Berries* ·5 in. long, ellipsoid, dark-purple when ripe.

Bindál-nálá and other ravines in the DÚN, less common than *J. pubescens.* Also Chatragádh in JAUNSAR.

Fl. May, June. Fr. Sept., Oct.

4. **J. humile,** Linn.; Fl. Br. Ind. iii. 602; Brandis Ind. Trees 452; Gamble Man. Ind. Timb. 468. Syn.—*J. revolutum*, Sims.; Brandis For. Flora 313. Vern. *Shanjoi, Shunjai*, Jaunsar.

An erect small shrub, wholly glabrous; branches angular, green; bark soft. *Leaves* alternate, imparipinnate. *Leaflets* 1-5 pairs, 2-3 by ·7-1·2 in., variable in size, ovate or ovate-lanceolate, the terminal usually the largest. *Flowers* dimorphic, yellow, fragrant, in short terminal compound corymbose cymes. *Calyx-teeth* 5, very short. *Corolla-tube* ·5-·8 in. long; lobes 5, ovate, obtuse. *Berries* ellipsoid, ·3-·4 in. long.

Common in the OUTER HIMALAYA, JAUNSAR, and TEHRI-GARHWAL, 4,000-9,500 ft.

Fl. Apr.-June. Fr. Sept.-Dec.

5. **J. officinale,** Linn.; Fl. Br. Ind. iii.603; Brandis For. Flora 313, Ind. Trees 452; Gamble Man. Ind. Timb. 467. Vern. *Hŏl-báli*, Jaunsar.

A large twining shrub, branches long, weak, dark-green, slightly ribbed. *Leaves* opposite, imparipinnate; rachis channelled. *Leaflets* 3-7, 2-3 in. long, rhomboid or lanceolate, the terminal largest. *Flowers* white, fragrant, about ·8 in. long, in few-flowered corymbose terminal cymes; pedicels 0-·7 in. *Calyx-teeth* linear, very variable in length. *Corolla-tube* ·6 in. long; lobes 5, ·3 by ·2 in., acute. *Berries* ·3 in. long, subglobose.

JAUNSAR and TEHRI-GARHWAL, 4-9,000ft.; Korwá, Deoban, Mundáli, etc.

Fl. May, June. Fr. Oct., Nov.

6. **J. grandiflorum,** Linn.; Fl. Br. Ind. iii. 603; Brandis For. Flora 313, Ind. Trees 452; Gamble Man. Ind. Timb. 469. Vern. *Chambéli*, Jaunsar; *Joi*, Garhwal.

A large glabrous scandent shrub, suberect in early life; branches ribbed. *Leaves* opposite, imparipinnate; leaflets 3-7, sessile, the upper pairs generally confluent with the terminal leaflet; petiole marginate. *Flowers* white, with faint pink streaks outside, delightfully fragrant, in lax terminal cymes, rarely solitary and axillary; pedicles slender, ·3-1 in. long. *Calyx-teeth* linear, half to two-thirds the length of the corolla-tube. *Corolla-tube* about 1 in.; lobes usually 5, about ·5 in. long, elliptic. *Berries* of 2 carpels, ellipsoid, ·3 in. long.

JAUNSAR and TEHRI-GARHWAL up to 8,500 ft., *e.g.*, Mundáli, Deotá, Lambátách, etc., especially conspicuous at Bodyár.

Fl. May-July.

2. Nyctanthes, Linn.; G. P. n. 3.

1. **N. Arbor-tristis,** Linn.; Fl. Br. Ind. iii. 603; Brandis For. Flora 314, Ind. Trees 442; Gamble Man. Ind. Timb. 469. Vern, *Kúrri*, Dún; *Harsingár*, Hind.

A small deciduous tree with quadrangular branches and grey or greenish-white rough bark. *Leaves* opposite, 4-5 by 2·5-3 in., ovate, acute, coriaceous, covered with stiff white hairs; base rounded or cuneate; petiole ·2-·5 in. long. *Flowers* sweet-scented, sessile, 3-7 together in pedunculate heads which are arranged in short trichotomous cymes; bracts elliptical. *Calyx-tube* 2 in., minutely 4-5-toothed. *Corolla-tube* ·3-·5 in. long, cylindrical, orange-red; limb white, spreading; lobes 5-8, ·2-·3 in. long, emarginate, contorted in bud. *Anthers* 2, subsessile, inserted near the mouth of the corolla-tube. *Ovary* 2-celled; ovule 1 in each cell, erect. *Capsule* ·3-·5 in. long, orbicular, compressed, chartaceous, 2-celled; seeds exalbuminous.

Extremely common in the forests of the SAHÁRANPUR SIWALIKS, and in some parts of the DÚN, as on the Nágsidh Hill and the southern slopes of the HIMALAYA, *e.g.*, at Málkōt, Rájpur, etc. Also at Kálsi in JAUNSAR. Cultivated in gardens for its flower.

The wood is used only for fuel. The leaves are used for polishing wood and also in country medicine as a febrifuge. The flowers are collected and dried to separate the white corolla-lobes which are then winnowed out, leaving the tubes, from which an orange dye is extracted.

Fl. Aug.-Oct. Fr. Cold season.

3. Syringa, Linn.; G. P. n. 6.

1. **S. Emodi,** Wall.; Fl. Br. Ind. iii. 605; Brandis For. Flora 306, Ind. Trees 445; Gamble Man. Ind. Timb. 470. Vern. *Shaphroi*, Jaunsar.

A large deciduous shrub; branches lenticellate. *Leaves* 3-4 by 1·5-2 in., elliptic-oblong, short-acuminate, entire, slightly pubescent beneath when young, glabrate and pale beneath when mature; base acute; petiole ·3-1 in. long. *Flowers* whitish or purple, scented, in dense-flowered thyrsoid panicles. *Calyx* subtruncate, about ·1 in. long, persistent, nearly glabrous. *Corolla* trumpet-shaped; tube ·2-·4 long; lobes 4, shorter than the tube, valvate, linear-oblong, tip generally inflexed. *Stamens* 2, near the top of the corolla-tube; anthers half-exserted. *Ovary* 2-celled; ovules 2 in each cell, pendulous; stigma bifid. *Fruit* a coriaceous capsule, ·5-·7 in. long, cylindrical, acute, slightly bent, loculicidally 2-valved; seeds pendulous, linear-oblong, flat, ridged along the middle, winged all round.

TEHRI-GARHWAL, JAUNSAR, and SIMLA HILL STATES, 8,-11,000 ft.: Jádi and Bájámárá Blocks, Cháchpur Range, etc.

Wood white, even and close-grained. The leaves are used as fodder for goats; cultivated in gardens for its flower.

Fl. May-July. Fr. Sept., Oct.

4. Fraxinus, Linn.; G. P. n. 7.

1. **F. floribunda,** Wall.; Fl. Br. Ind. iii. 605; Brandis For. Flora 302, Ind. Trees 443; Gamble Man. Ind. Timb. 471.

A large deciduous tree; bark ashy-grey; smooth on young poles, corky and deeply furrowed on mature trees. *Leaves* opposite, imparipinnate; rachis 5 8 in. long. *Leaflets* usually 7, less frequently 5 or 9, lateral opposite, 3-5 by 1-3 in., ovate oblong elliptic or lanceolate, usually long-acuminate, falcately serrate, membranous, glabrous above, pilose on the nerves beneath when young; main lateral nerves about 12 pairs, slender, joined by reticulated secondary nerves; petiolules ·2-·5 in. long. *Inflorescence* a large terminal panicle; pedicels fascicled on the branches of the panicle. *Flowers* about ·15 in. long, generally 2-sexual. *Calyx* minute, acutely 4-toothed, somewhat enlarged in fruit. *Corolla-lobes* ·12 in. long, linear-oblong, narrowed at both ends, induplicate-valvate in bud. *Stamens* near the base of the corolla tube; filaments about ·1 in. long. *Ovary* 2-celled: stigma 2-fid; ovules 2 in each cell, pendulous. *Fruit* an oblanceolate samara, 1-1·5 by ·2-·25 in., including the wing. *Seed* solitary.

Cultivated in JAUNSAR about Chakrata and in TEHRI-GARHWAL; also found indigenous in places *e. g.*, at Phaphrota below Deoban, Bear Garden near Chakrata, and at Kúlni; not very common.

Wood white, with a light reddish tinge, moderately hard and tough; no heartwood; annual rings distinct; weight 48 lbs. per c. ft. It is used for oars, ploughs, jhampan-poles, etc.

Fl. usually Apr., May. Fr. Aug., Sept.

5. Linociera, Swartz; G. P. n. 13.

1. **L. intermedia,** Wight: Fl. Br. Ind. iii. 609; Brandis Ind. Trees 448; Gamble Man. Ind. Timb. 473.

A small tree. *Leaves* 4-8 by 2-3 in., elliptic-oblong, acute at both ends, chartaceous, glabrous; main lateral nerves 10-14 pairs; reticulations prominent; petiole ·5 to 1·2 in. *Inflorescence* a dense glabrous compound trichotomous panicle, generally axillary, sometimes from the middle of the internodes; bracts lanceolate, generally minute. *Flowers* whitish, male or 2-sexual, sessile or nearly so. *Calyx-lobes* ·1 in., ovate, glabrous. *Petals* 4, ·12-·2 in. long, narrowly oblong, slightly connate in pairs. *Anthers* sessile or nearly so. *Ovary* glabrous. *Drupe* ·5-·7 by ·3 in.

Only found on the edges of the Mothronwála swamp and is likely to occur in similar other localities in the DÚN.

Wood white, moderately hard and close-grained.

Fl. Mar.-May. Fr. Rainy season.

6. Olea, Linn.; G. P. n. 16.

Trees or shrubs. *Leaves* opposite, simple, entire or toothed. *Flowers* often unisexual and diœcious, generally in terminal panicles. *Calyx* 4-toothed or-lobed, or truncate. *Corolla-tube* short, lobes 4 or 0. *Stamens* 2, epipetalous and exserted, or hypogynous (when the corolla is wanting); anthers oblong. *Ovary* 2-celled; ovules 2 in each cell; style short. *Fruit* a drupe, ellipsoid; endocarp hard; exocarp pulpy. *Seed* solitary, pendulous; albumen fleshy.

Analysis of the Species.

Lateral nerves indistinct, not glandular; under-surface of leaves clothed with reddish scales . . . . 1. *O. cuspidata.*
Lateral nerves distinct, glandular at the axils; leaves wholly glabrous . . . 2. *O. glandulifera.*

1. **O. cuspidata,** Wall.; Fl. Br. Ind. iii. 611; Brandis For. Flora 307, Ind. Trees 445. Syn.—*O. ferruginea,* Royle; Gamble Man. Ind. Timb. 474. Vern. *Káu,* Jaunsar; *Kahu,* Hind.

A middle-sized tree; bark thin, smooth when young, exfoliating in narrow strips when old. *Leaves* 2-4 in. long, oblong-lanceolate, cuspidate, entire, very coriaceous, dark-green and shining above, thickly clothed beneath with a dense film of minute red scales; margins slightly recurved; midrib prominent; petiole about ·2 in. *Flowers* bisexual, whitish, in axillary trichotomous cymes, 1-2 in. long. *Calyx* nearly truncate or with 4 short teeth. *Corolla* deeply divided; lobes ·1 in., elliptic, obtuse or acute with a ridge along the middle, induplicate-valvate in bud. *Anthers* oval, dehiscing laterally. *Style* short; stigma bifid. *Drupe* ·2-·3 in. long, ovoid, black when ripe, supported by the remains of the calyx; endocarp bony; pulp scanty, oily.

Fairly common in JAUNSAR and the OUTER HIMALAYA, 3,-6,000 ft.; cultivated in DEHRA.

Sapwood whitish; heartwood light-brown to nearly black, extremely hard, often beautifully mottled; weight 65-82 lbs. per c. ft. It polishes well and is much prized for turning, for combs and for agricultural implements. Fairly straight branches are in great demand for the purpose of making into walking sticks. The fruit is eaten, and oil can be extracted from it. The leaves are heavily lopped for fodder.

Fl. Apr., May, and sometimes in September. Fr. Aug.-Nov.

2. **O. glandulifera,** Wall. ; Fl. Br. Ind. iii. 612 ; Brandis For. Flora 309, Ind. Trees 446 ; Gamble Man. Ind. Timb. 474. Vern. *Gair, Gaild,* Málkōt.

A moderate-sized tree ; branches lenticellate ; bark of stem rough. *Leaves* 4 by 2 in., ovate-lanceolate, long-acuminate, entire, wholly glabrous ; margins slightly undulate ; base cuneate ; main lateral nerves 9-12 pairs, slender, with glands at their axils on either side of the midrib ; petiole ·5-1 in. long. *Flowers* cream-coloured, in terminal or lateral compound trichotomous cymes. *Calyx* 4-toothed. *Corolla* deeply divided ; lobes valvate, elliptic, ·1 in. long. *Anthers,* large. *Ovary* glabrate. *Drupe* ·5 in. long, ovoid, somewhat oblique, acute at the apex ; endocarp bony.

Fairly common along the OUTER HIMALAYAN TRACTS between 2,500 and 6,000 ft. : Málkōt Forest, Paléd, above Rajpur, Tons Valley near Kálsi, etc. . Also Mothroṇwála swamp in the DÚN, 1,900 ft.

The wood is reddish-grey, hard and durable, weighing 54 lbs. per c. ft. It takes a good polish and is avoided by insects. It is used in construction, turnery and agricultural implements. The bark is used in medicine, and the leaves are lopped for fodder.

Fl. Apr., May, occasionally during the rains. Fr. Cold season.

7. Ligustrum, Linn. ; G. P. n. 17.

1. **L. compactum,** Hook. f. & Th. ; Fl. Br. Ind. iii. 616 ; Brandis For. Flora 310, Ind. Trees 447 ; Gamble Man. Ind. Timb. 476. Vern. *Kakurchha,* Jaunsar.

A small tree with grey bark ; branches often lenticellate. *Leaves* 3-5 by 1-2 in., elliptic-lanceolate, coriaceous, glabrous, shining above ; petiole ·2-·3 in. long. *Flowers* white, subsessile, in compound racemes, which are arranged in terminal panicles. *Corolla-tube* short, funnel-shaped ; lobes oblong, induplicately valvate. *Anthers* half-exserted. *Ovary* 2-celled, with 2 ovules in each cell ; style of varying lengths, the longest reaching to the base of the anthers ; stigma nearly simple. *Fruit* numerous, ·2-·3 in. long, cylindrical, often slightly curved.

JAUNSAR and TEHRI-GARHWAL, 4,-9,000 ft. ; Karambá Peak (*Sir D. Brandis*), Lokhár, Kathián, Koti, Ghutugádh, Binálgádh, etc.; cultivated in DEHRA (Kowlágarh).

Wood white, moderately hard, close-grained and durable. The leaves are lopped for fodder.

Fl. Apr.-June. Fr. Nov.-Feb.

FAM. 53. APOCYNACEÆ; G. P. N. 106.

Erect or climbing shrubs, or trees, rarely herbs, usually with milky juice. *Leaves* entire, commonly opposite, sometimes whorled, very rarely alternate. *Flowers* regular, hermaphrodite, solitary or in cymes. *Calyx* inferior; sepals free or slightly connate at the base, generally imbricate in bud. *Corolla* hypogynous, gamopetalous, rotate or salver-shaped; lobes spreading, contorted or twisted (rarely valvate) in bud. *Stamens* 5, inserted on the tube, alternating with the corolla-lobes; anthers opening inward by longitudinal slits, sometimes spurred downwards; connective often adhering to the stigma; pollen granular. *Ovary* 1-celled, with 2 parietal placentas, or 2-celled with axile placentas, or of two distinct or more or less connate carpels; ovules 2 to many in each, rarely solitary; style simple or divided only at the base. *Fruit* a drupe or a berry, or of 2 drupes, berries or fallicles. *Seeds* pendulous, usually bearing a tuft of long silky hairs; albumen fleshy or scanty, rarely 0.

Analysis of the Genera.

A. Leaves in pairs, opposite.
  B. Seeds naked.
    Spinous shrubs, generally erect; fr. a 2-or few-seeded succulent berry . 1. CARISSA.
    Unarmed erect shrubs; fr. of two 1-many-seeded dry or fleshy follicles . 3. TABERNÆMONTANA.

B′. Seeds comose.
C. Trees or large erect shrubs.
Anthers included, free; mouth of the corolla-tube naked, white . 4. HOLARRHENA.
Anthers exserted, adherent to the stigma; mouth of the corolla-tube with scales, usually orange. 6. WRIGHTIA.
C′. Climbing shrubs.
Corolla-lobes narrow; carpels distinct.
Tips of corolla lobes deflected; seeds often beaked . . 8. ICHNOCARPUS.
Tips of corolla-lobes not deflected; seeds not beaked . 9. TRACHELOSPERMUM.
Corolla-lobes broad; carpels at first connate . . . 5. VALLARIS.
A′. Leaves whorled; seeds comose; anthers included.
Trees. Corona absent; carpels distinct 2. ALSTONIA.
Erect shrubs. Corona present; carpels at first connate . 7. NERIUM.

1. Carissa, Linn.; G. P. n. 17.

1. **C. spinarum,** A.DC.; Fl. Br. Ind. iii. 631; Brandis Ind. Trees 455; Gamble Man. Ind. Timb. 480. Syn.—*C. diffusa*, Roxb., Brandis For. Flora 321. Vern. *Karaunda*, Hind.

A small thorny evergreen shrub with light-grey bark and green branchlets; spines ·5-1 in. long, often forked, generally at the base of the branches. *Leaves* opposite, 1-1·5 by ·7-1 in., ovate, acute, mucronate, glabrate or pubescent beneath, coriaceous, dark-green and shining above. *Flowers* white, scented, in few-flowered corymbose cymes at the ends of the branches. *Calyx-teeth* 5, lanceolate, ciliate. *Corolla-tube* ·5 in. long, cylindrical; lobes 5, elliptic-lanceolate, slightly shorter than the tube. *Stamens* included in the corolla-tube. *Ovary* 2-celled, ovules 2 in each cell. *Berry* subglobose or elliptic, ·2-·3 in. long, shining or pruinose, dark-purple and juicy when ripe. *Seeds* 2, concavo-convex, not hairy.

Extremely common and gregarious in scrub jungles along the foot of the SAHÁRANPUR SIWALIKS and in open glades and stony soils (*e.g.*, Tháno) in the DÚN; also found in the lower valleys, up to 4,000 ft., in JAUNSAR and TEHRI-GARHWAL.

Wood hard, smooth and close-grained, and is used for turning and for making combs. It is an excellent fire-wood. The branches are in great demand for dry fences, and the leaves are greedily eaten by sheep and goats. The ripe berries have a sub-acid sweet taste, and are much eaten by men and birds.

Fl. Apr. June. Fr. Cold season.

C. Carandas, Linn.; Fl. Br. Ind. iii. 630. Vern. *Karaunda*, Hind.—is cultivated in gardens at DEHRA and SAHÁRANPUR. It resembles *C. spinarum* in habit, but is usually a taller shrub with larger leaves, and much larger and usually 4-seeded fruits.

2. Alstonia, Br.; G. P. n. 44.

1. **A. scholaris**, Br.; Fl. Br. Ind. iii. 642; Brandis For. Flora 325, Ind. Trees 459; Gamble Man. Ind. Timb. 483. Vern. *Sátián, Chhátián, Chhátwán, Sátni*, Hind.

A tall evergreen tree with grey bark and verticillate branches; stem often fluted or buttressed. *Leaves* in whorls of 4-7, 4-8 by 1-1·5 in., obovate elliptic-oblong or oblanceolate, subsessile or narrowed into a short petiole ·25-·5 in. long, coriaceous, glabrous and shining above, dull and pale-green beneath; lateral nerves numerous, straight, terminating in an intramarginal vein. *Flowers* greenish-white, in compact umbellately-corymbose cymes, the umbels whorled. *Calyx* small, 5-lobed. *Corolla* ·3-·5 in. diam., villous inside; lobes rounded, spreading, twisted in bud. *Stamens* above the middle of the corolla-tube, included; anthers acute. *Ovary* of two distinct carpels. *Fruit* of two long slender follicles over a foot long and ·2 in. diam., hanging in clusters. *Seeds* ·3 in. long, slender, flattened, peltately attached, densely ciliate with long hairs all round.

Not very common. Has been met with on the banks of the Bidhálná Ráu and at Kalimatti, Tháno, Rikhikesh, Gularparáo, Nakraunda and Kálsi.

Wood whitish, even-grained, porous, soft, light, but seasons badly; weight about 30 lbs. per c. ft. It is used in places for tea-boxes and other kinds of packing-cases, and for scabbards, coffins, blackboards, etc. The bark is bitter and possesses valuable medicinal properties.

Fl. Dec.-Mar. Fr. May, June.

3. Tabernæmontana, Linn. ; G. P. n. 46.

1. **T. coronaria,** Br. ; Fl. Br. Ind. iii. 646 ; Brandis For. Flora 322, Ind. Trees 460 ; Gamble Man. Ind. Timb. 485. Vern. *Chándni*, Dún.

An evergreen shrub, 10-15 ft. high, dichotomously branched, with silvery-grey bark. *Leaves* 4-6 by 1-1·5 in., elliptic-oblong, acuminate, rather coriaceous, shining-green above, pale beneath ; margins undulate, narrowed into a short petiole ·25-·5 in. long. *Flowers* pure white, fragrant, often (especially under cultivation) double. *Calyx-lobes* short, broad-ovate, acute, glandular within. *Corolla-tube* ·7-1 in. long, slightly inflated in the middle ; limb 1-1·5 in. diam., mouth glandular; lobes obtuse, margins overlapping, curled. *Stamens* inserted about the middle of the tube ; anthers acuminate. *Carpels* 2, distinct, glabrous ; stigma 2-lobed. *Fruit* of two 3-ribbed somewhat fleshy cylindrical follicles, 2-3 in. long, sessile or nearly so, recurved, deep-red or orange inside. *Seeds* 3-6, oblong, with a fleshy red aril.

Valleys in the OUTER HIMALAYA, *e.g.*, at Tháno and adjoining places, also about Rájpur. It is cultivated in gardens throughout India for its large fragrant flower.

Fl. May-Aug. Fr. Cold season.

4. Holarrhena, Br. ; G. P. n. 50.

1. **H. antidysenterica,** Wall. ; Fl. Br. Ind. iii. 644 ; Brandis For. Flora 326, Ind. Trees 459 ; Gamble Man. Ind. Timb. 484. Vern. *Kúra*, Hind.

A small deciduous tree with rough brown bark, exfoliating in irregular flakes. *Leaves* opposite, 6-12 by 2-5 in., elliptic-oblong, acute or acuminate, sub-coriaceous, glabrous ; lateral nerves 10-14 pairs ; base obtuse or cuneate ; petiole ·2 in. or less. *Flowers* white or cream-colour, slightly scented, 1-1·5 in. across, puberulous, in terminal corymbose cymes which are 3-6 in. in diam. *Calyx* deeply 5-partite ; lobes small, lanceolate, acuminate, with glands inside at their base. *Corolla-tube* ·3-·5 in. long, cylindrical, swollen at the base round the anthers, throat contracted, naked ; lobes as long as the tube, oblong, spreading, overlapping to the left. *Anthers* subsessile, inserted near the base of the corolla-tube ; cells rounded at the base. *Carpels* 2, distinct ; ovules numerous ; style short, filiform ; stigma oblong. *Fruit* of 2 distinct divaricate follicles, 8-16 by ·2-·4 in., spreading and incurved, smooth, usually with white specks. *Seeds* numerous, ·5 in. long, linear ; hairs silky, of a brownish-grey colour, 1·5 to 2 in. long.

Very common in the DÚN and SAHÁRANPUR FORESTS; also in valleys up to 4,000 ft. in JAUNSAR and TEHRI-GARHWAL.

The wood is white, soft and even-grained; weight about 40 lbs. per c. ft. It is said to be used at Sahâranpur for carving. It is also used for turning and furniture, and beads are made of it to be worn round the neck as a charm. The bark, leaves and seeds are used in medicine, especially the first for dysentery, whence the specific name.

New leaves Apr., May. Fl. May, June. Fr. Cold season.

5. Vallaris, Burm.; G. P. n. 56.

1. **V. Heynei,** Spreng.; Fl. Br. Ind. ii. 650; Brandis Ind. Trees 462; Gamble Man. Ind. Timb. 486. Syn.—*V. dichotoma,* Wall.; Brandis For. Flora 327. Vern. *Dudhi-bel, Safed-bel,* Dún.

A glabrous twining shrub; bark ash-coloured. *Leaves* opposite, 2-4 by 1-1·5 in., elliptic-oblong, acuminate, gland-dotted, glossy above; petiole ·3-·6 in., with glands at the axils. *Flowers* pure-white, ·7 in. across, fragrant, in lateral dichotomous cymes; pedicels slender. *Calyx* 5-partite; segments ovate-oblong, obtuse. *Corolla-limb* rotate, spreading; tube short, with a broad throat. *Stamens* woolly, inserted at the top of the corolla-tube; filaments short; anthers exserted, connivent, forming a cone with the stigma at the apex; cells rigidly spurred. *Carpels* 2, at first connate; style filiform. *Fruits* 4-6 by 1-1·5 in., tapering from a rounded base; pericarp thick. *Seeds* numerous, beaked, ·6 in. long, with a tuft of hairs three times their length at the hilum.

Common in the DÚN and SAHÁRANPUR FORESTS; also in low valleys in JAUNSAR and TEHRI-GARHWAL.

The switchy branches are used for baskets in the Sahâranpur District.

Fl. Dec.-Apr. Fr. Jan.-Apr., next year.

6. Wrightia, Br.; G. P. n. 61.

1. **W. tomentosa,** Roem. & Sch.; Fl. Br. Ind. iii. 653; Brandis For. Flora. 323, Ind. Trees 461; Gamble Man. Ind. Timb. 487. Vern. *Dúdhi,* Hind.

A small deciduous tree with grey corky bark; extremities tomentose. *Leaves* opposite, distichous, 3-6 by 1·5-3 in., elliptic, caudate-acuminate, rarely obscurely serrulate, rather membranous, velvety-tomentose often on both surfaces, always beneath, narrowed into a petiole ·2-·3 in. long; lateral nerves 10-16 pairs. *Flowers* 1 in across, in many-flowered corymbose terminal cymes; bracts deciduous. *Calyx* short, with 5-10 scales inside at the base; lobes rounded, half the length of the corolla-tube. *Corolla* pale-yellow with a fleshy orange-coloured corona of scales; lobes oblong, overlapping to the left. *Stamens* inserted at the top of the corolla-tube; filaments short and broad, continued into a broad tapering connective; anthers sagittate by the cells being spurred at the base, adherent to the stigma. *Ovary* of 2 connate carpels; style filiform; stigma ovoid. *Fruit* of 2 connate follicles, 8-12 by ·5-·7 in., straight, cylindrical, laterally compressed, rough with white specks; follicles separating before dehiscing. *Seeds* numerous, ·5-·7 in., slender, each with a tuft of pure-white silky hairs at the lower end.

Fairly common in the DÚN and SAHÁRANPUR FORESTS, and also found in the lower valleys (*e. g.*, Binálgádh,—*Sir. D. Brandis*, Dhárágádh, etc.) in JAUNSAR. Also in outer Himalayan open valleys up to 4,000 ft. in TEHRI-GARHWAL.

Wood yellowish-white, moderately hard, close-grained, easy to work; heartwood not distinct; weight about 40 lbs. per c. ft. Used in turning, and carved into bowls, plates, combs, picture-frames, etc., at Sahéranpur. The bark of the stem and the roots are given as an antidote to snake-bite and the sting of scorpions. The Nepalese are said to use the milky juice to stop bleeding.

New leaves Apr., May. Fl. May, June. Fr. Cold season.

7. Nerium, Linn.; G. P. n. 62.

1. **N. odorum,** Soland.; Fl. Br. Ind. iii. 655; Brandis For. Flora 328, Ind. Trees 462; Gamble Man. Ind. Timb. 487. Vern. *Kanér*, Hind.

An evergreen shrub with silvery-grey bark. *Leaves* usually in whorls of 3, 4-6 by ·5-1 in., linear-lanceolate or oblong, thickly coriaceous, acuminate, smooth dark-green and shining above, rough and dotted beneath; midrib stout; lateral nerves numerous, parallel and transverse; petiole short. *Flowers* 1·5 in. diam., red white or rose-coloured, generally sweet-scented, double under cultivation, in large terminal racemose cymes. *Sepals* broad-subulate. *Corolla* funnel-shaped; lobes spreading, overlapping to the right. *Corona-appendages* laciniate into numerous irregular segments. *Stamens* near the top of the tube; anthers sagittate, conniving around and adhering to the stigma; cells with long twisted appendages. *Fruit* 6-7 by ·3-·4 in., rigid. *Seeds* linear, ribbed, villous with, and having a coma of, greyish-brown hairs.

Found in dry Ráu beds in the SAHÁRANPUR SIWALIKS, *e.g.*, the Chápri and Ráni Ráus; not very common.

"The bark and root are poisonous, and the leaves are used in native medicine."—*Mr. J. S. Gamble.*

Fl. Apr.-June and often throughout the year. Fr. Cold season.

8. Ichnocarpus, Br.; G. P. n. 73.

1. **I. frutescens,** Br.; Fl. Br. Ind. iii. 669; Brandis For. Flora 327, Ind. Trees 464. Vern. *Bel Kámú,* Dún and Sahâranpur; *Kali Dúdhi,* Hind.

A twining shrub; extremities and under surface of leaves rusty-pubescent. *Leaves* 2-3 by 1·5-2 in., elliptic-oblong or ovate-lanceolate, acute or acuminate, glabrate and dark-green above, more or less pubescent beneath; petiole ·2 in. *Flowers* ·2-·3 in. diam., greenish-white, more or less scented, in axillary and terminal leafy cymose panicles. *Calyx* 5-cleft, with small glands inside; lobes ovate. *Corolla* hypo-crateriform, about ·2 in. diam., naked inside; tube swollen round the included anthers; throat contracted, villous; lobes narrowed, hairy inside, ciliate, overlapping to the right. *Anthers* sagittate. *Fruit* of two distinct slender cylindrical follicles, 3-6 by ·15 in. *Seeds* numerous, ·5 in. long, slender, pendulous, each with a tuft of scanty white hairs at the hilum.

Common in the DÚN and SAHÁRANPUR FORESTS.

The thin switchy branches are used for making baskets in the Sahâranpur District, and fishing-traps in Bengal. The root is often used as a substitute for Sarsaparilla.

Fl. Aug.-Nov. Fr. Feb.-Apr.

9. Trachelospermum, Lemaire; G. P. n. 82.

1. **T. fragrans,** Hook. f.; Fl. Br. Ind. iii. 667; Brandis Ind. Trees 464; Gamble Man. Ind. Timb. 489. Syn. *Ichnocarpus fragrans,* Wall.; Brandis For. Flora, 327.

A tall climber, young parts pilose; old stems strongly tubercled. *Leaves* 3-5 by 1-1·5 in., elliptic-oblong, acuminate, sub-coriaceous, shining above; petiole ·15-·3 in. long. *Flowers* white, fragrant, in compound trichotomous corymbose cymes. *Corolla* salver-shaped, with a campanulate mouth; tube ·3 in. long; lobes oblong, hairy near the base, tips not deflected, overlapping to the right, twisted to the left in bud. *Anthers* spurred at the base. *Follicles* 6-9 in. long, cylindrical, acuminate, incurved. *Seeds* ·7 in. long, compressed, smooth, having a coma of white hairs.

JAUNSAR and TEHRI-GARHWAL in moist shady ravines, 3,-6,000 ft.; Rámsu valley, Sendrá, Mautárgádh, etc. Also along the banks of the Ré-nadi and in the Mothronwála swamp in the DÚN.

Might possibly be used for the same purposes as *Ichnocarpus frutescens.*

Fl. Apr.-June. Fr. Oct.-Dec.

The following plants belonging to this Family deserve mention :—

1. *Rauwolfia serpentina.* Benth.; Fl. Br. Ind. iii. 632.—A small shrub about 2 ft. high. *Leaves* 3-7 in. long, elliptic or obovate-lanceolate, short-petioled, soft. *Flowers* pink, about ·5-·7 in. long., in long-peduncled many-flowered cymes which are 1-2 in. diam. *Fruit* an oblique drupe, about ·3 in. long, black when ripe. Found at Lachiwála in the DÚN. Fl. Nov., Dec.—*G. P. n. 20.*

2. *Thevetia neriifolia,* Juss.; Vern. *Pílá Kanér.*—An evergreen shrub with narrow-linear leaves resembling those of *Nerium odorum,* and large fragrant yellow flowers. *Fruit* a 2-celled drupe. Cultivated for its flower.—*G. P. n. 27.*

3. *Plumeria acutifolia,* Poiret; Fl. Br. Ind. iii. 641; Vern. *Gúláchin, Gúlchin,* Dún. A soft-wooded small deciduous tree with thick fleshy branches and scattered leaves. *Flowers* white, fragrant, yellow in the centre. *Fruit* follicular; seeds winged. It is a native of tropical America but has been naturalised in many parts of India, and is much planted about temples and Mahomedan burial grounds throughout N. India.—*G. P. n. 41.*

FAM. 54. ASCLEPIADACEÆ; G. P. N. 107.

Herbs or shrubs, often climbing, generally with milky juice and noted for strong fibre. *Leaves* opposite, simple, entire, exstipulate. *Flowers* regular, bisexual, 5-merous, usually in axillary cymes. *Calyx* inferior, deeply 5-lobed or divided; segments imbricate. *Corolla-tube* short; lobes valvate or twisted-imbricate, with a corona of scales at the throat called the *outer* or *corolline corona.* *Stamens* 5, rarely free, generally connate into a short fleshy column which usually bears a ring or series of processes that are attached to the filaments or to the back of the anthers : this is called the *inner* or *staminal corona.* (Only in rare cases are both coronas present or both absent.) *Anthers* adnate to the stigma by the connective; pollen in granular or waxy masses which are usually united in pairs (one belonging to each contiguous anther) to glands situated at the angles of the stigma. *Ovary* superior; carpels 2, distinct; ovules many, in 2 series in each carpel ; styles 2, uniting in the stigma which is 5-angled. *Fruit* of two follicles, or of only one by abortion ; seeds usually compressed or flat, with a tuft of silky hairs (coma) at the hilum ; albumen copious.

Analysis of the Genera.

Filaments free ; pollen-masses granular, in pairs in each cell.
  Coronal scales free, not aristate . . . 1. CRYPTOLEPIS.
  Coronal scales connate into a lobed ring ; lobes long-aristate . . . . . 2. PERIPLOCA.
Filaments connate into a staminal tube ; pol.-masses waxy, solitary in each cell.
  Anthers with a membranous tip.
    Stem erect. Corolla-lobes valvate ; follicles stout, oblique . . . 3. CALOTROPIS.
    Stem twining. Corolla-lobes valvate ; follicles slender, straight . . . 8. HETEROSTEMMA.
    Stem twining. Cor.-lobes overlapping.
      Follicles stout, straight.
        Corolla urceolate or campanulate.
          Corona on the corolla-tube . 4. GYMNEMA.
          Corona on the staminal column.
            Cymes axillary ; coronal scales simple . . . . . 6. MARSDENIA.
            Cymes generally interpetiolar ; coronal scales notched . 7. PERGULARIA.
        Corolla rotate ; corona of spreading scales . . . . . . 9. DREGEA.
      Follicles slender, straight. . . 5. GONGRONEMA.
  Anthers without a membranous tip.
    Leafy shrubs, more or less twining . 10. LEPTADENIA.
    A leafless erect shrub. . . . 11. ORTHANTHERA.

1. Cryptolepis, R. Br.; G. P. n. 6.

1. **C. Buchanani,** Roem. & Sch.; Fl. Br. Ind. iv. 5; Brandis For. Flora 330, Ind. Trees 467; Gamble Man. Ind. Timb. 490. Vern. *Dúdhi, Medhá-singhi*, Dún; *Karántá*, Hind.

A large climbing shrub with milky juice. *Leaves* 3-6 by 1-2·5 in., oblong or elliptic, acute or acuminate, coriaceous, glabrous and shining above, glaucous beneath; nerves many, slender, nearly horizontal, terminating in intramarginal veins; base acute; petiole ·3-·5 in. long. *Flowers* pale-white, in short peduncled lax dichotomous cymes. *Calyx* with 5 scales within, short, acute. *Corolla* ·6-·7 in. diam.; tube short, throat naked; lobes linear, twisted in bud. *Corona* of 5 fleshy clavate scales, included within the tube. *Stamens* free, included; filaments short, with a broad base; anthers sagittate, with a tuft of hairs at the back, tips acuminate, conniving. *Stigma* broadly conical. *Follicles* 2-4 by ·5-·7 in., in divaricate pairs, narrow-lanceolate, straight, somewhat compressed; seeds compressed, oblong-ovate, with a tuft of hairs at the hilum which are about 1 in. long.

Common in the SIWALIK DIVISION, and also met with up to 4,000 ft. in the HILLS, *e.g.*, Binálgádh, Thadiár, etc.

The milk of this climber quickly coagulates into a substance resembling caoutchouc and may be used for repairing punctures in bicycle tires.

Fl. May, June. Fr. Cold season.

2. Periploca, Linn.; G. P. n. 26.

2. **P. calophylla,** Falc.; Fl. Br. Ind. iv. 12; Brandis For. Flora 330, Ind. Trees 467. Vern. *Párh*, Jaunsar.

A glabrous shrub with slender branches. *Leaves* about 3 by ·5 in. or smaller, narrow-lanceolate, long-acuminate, coriaceous, shining; lateral nerves very numerous, parallel; petiole ·2-·3 in. *Flowers* in lax cymes. *Calyx* glandular within; lobes ovate, obtuse. *Corolla* ·3 in. diam., rotate, pinkish or pale-yellow; lobes ovate, longer than the tube, usually hairy on the upper surface, greenish below. *Corona* of 5 thick scales, connate into a 10-lobed ring, usually crowned with 5 filiform aristas. *Stamens* included, free; filaments short; anthers bearded at the back and cohering laterally; pollen granular. *Stigma* convex. *Follicles* about 6 by ·3 in., in divaricate pairs, cylindrical; seeds linear, ·5-·7 in. long; coma over 1 in. long.

In shady ravines in the OUTER HIMALAYA, *e.g.*, Sansárú Khálá. Also in the TONS VALLEY, *e. g.*, Khúnigádh.

Fl. Apr., May. Fr. Cold season.

3. Calotropis, R. Br.; G. P. n. 51.

Erect shrubs with milky juice. *Leaves* usually subsessile; rather fleshy. *Flowers* in umbelliform cymes. *Sepals* glandular within. *Corolla-tube* broad-can panulate; lobes ovate, valvate. *Corona* of 5 compressed fleshy appendages, adnate to and radiating from the staminal column, spurred at the back. *Anthers* with a broad membranous tip, inflexed on the stigma; pollen-masses waxy, stipitate, pendulous. *Stigma* depressed, pentagonous. *Follicles* single, thick, straight on the ventral and convex on the dorsal side, very oblique and sharply incurved near the base; seeds with a silky coma.

Analysis of the Species.

Coronal scales truncate; flower-buds ovoid; corolla-lobes spreading . . . . 1. *C. gigantea.*
Coronal scales acute; flower-buds hemispherical; corolla-lobes erect . . 2. *C. procera.*

1. **C. gigantea,** R. Br.; Fl. Br. Ind. iv. 17; Brandis For. Flora 331, Ind. Trees 471; Gamble Man. Ind. Timb. 491. Vern. *Madár, Safed Ák,* Hind.

A middle-sized shrub; young parts covered with adpressed white tomentum; bark pale. *Leaves* subsessile, 4-8 by 1-4 in., obovate or oblong, acute or acuminate, coriaceous, cottony beneath; base cordate. *Flowers* downy outside, on long pedicels arranged in axillary or subterminal pedunculate simple or compound umbels or corymbs; buds ovoid. *Corolla* dull-purple or white, ·5-1 in. diam.; lobes ovate-lanceolate, spreading. *Corona-scales* elongated but truncate at the apex, hairy. *Follicles* 3-4 in. long, recurved; seeds ovate, ·25 in. long, with a bright silky-white coma.

Believed to be found in the DÚN and possibly also in the SAHÁRANPUR DISTRICT, but is certainly very rare in our area.

The hair of the seeds makes a good stuffing material for pillows and cushions and mixed with a small proportion of ordinary cotton may be spun into thread. The fibre of the stems is used for bow-strings, fishing-lines and nets. The wood is made into gunpowder charcoal in the Deccan. The acrid juice and the roots are used in country medicine.

Fl. and fr. throughout the year.

2. **C. procera,** R. Br.; Fl. Br. Ind. iv. 18; Brandis For. Flora 331, Ind. Trees 472, Gamble Man. Ind. Timb. 491. Vern. *Ák, Madár*, Hind.

Habit, leaves and inflorescence as of the preceding species, excepting that the leaves, 8-9 by 4 in., are more gradually narrowed and somewhat less cottony beneath when mature, and the peduncles rather longer. *Flowers* purplish-red, silvery outside, odorous; buds hemispherical. *Corolla-lobes* erect. *Corona-scales* acute, nearly as broad as long, glabrous or pubescent. *Follicles* as of the last species.

Economic uses, as of *C. gigantea.*

Common throughout the SAHÁRANPUR and DÚN DISTRICTS, generally in fallow lands and ráu-beds, *e.g.*, Ránipur, Phándowála, etc. Also found in low valleys in the HILLS, *e.g.*, Binálgádh, Silgádh, etc.

Fl. and fr. throughout the year, but chiefly in the cold season.

C. Acia, Ham.; Fl. Br. Ind. iv. 18,—occurs in grass-lands about Lachiwála in the DÚN. It is an herbaceous plant with petiolate leaves, otherwise closely resembling *C. procera.*

4. Gymnema, R. Br.; G. P. n. 101.

1. **G. tingens,** W. & A.; Fl. Br. Ind. iv. 31; Brandis Ind. Trees 469.

A large twining shrub, almost wholly glabrous, old stems covered with reticulating ridges of white cork. *Leaves* 4-6 by 2-3·5 in., ovate, often cordate, membranous, acuminate or caudate; petiole 1-1·7 in. long. *Cymes* 4-6 in., corymbosely racemose, peduncle shorter than the petioles; bracts oblong. *Flowers* ·3 in. diam., pale-yellow. *Sepals* glabrate. *Corolla-lobes* broadly ovate or oblong, glabrous. *Corona* of double villous processes inside the corolla-tube and below the sinuses. *Filaments* connate into a short column; anther-tips small, membranous; pollen-masses one in each cell, waxy, stalked, erect. *Stigma* exserted. *Follicles* generally single, 3·5-4·5 by ·7-1·2 in., uniformly tapering and acute at both ends smooth and glabrous, slightly beaked. *Seeds* comose.

Nakraunda and Káluwála in the DÚN, not very common.

Fl. June-Aug. Fr. Nov.-Jan.

5. Gongronema, Dcne. ; G. P. n. 102.

1. **G. nepalense,** Dcne. ; Fl. Br. Ind. iv. 33 ; Brandis Ind. Trees 471.

A large twining shrub ; young shoots and inflorescence pubescent. *Leaves* 4-6 by 2-3·5 in., oblong elliptic or ovate, acuminate, membranous or subcoriaceous, glabrous above, puberulous along the nerves beneath ; main lateral nerves about 8 pairs, arcuate, the lowest pair from near the base ; base rounded, less frequently subcordate ; petiole ·8-1·7 in. long, rather slender. *Peduncles* 2-6 in. long, axillary, usually 1 to each pair of leaves, generally branching into 3 long divaricate umbel-bearing arms ; pedicels 2-·3 in., slender. *Flowers* yellow, ·25 in. across. *Calyx* small, 5-partite. *Corolla* campanulate ; tube and lobes of about the same length, the latter ovate, slightly overlapping to the right. *Coronal scales* generally absent. *Anther-tips* inflexed, concealing the stigma ; pollen-masses solitary in each cell, waxy, erect. *Stigma* clavate or conical. *Follicles* 2·5-3 by ·2-·3 in., acuminate, thin-walled ; seeds ·3 in. long, linear ; coma of very fine white silky hairs about 1 in. long.

Fairly common in the DÚN ;—Lachiwála, Ráipur, Bindál nálá, etc.

The strong fibre is used for the same purposes as that of *Marsdenia*.

Fl. Aug., Sept. Fr. Sept., Oct.

6. Marsdenia, R. Br. ; G. P. n. 108.

Twining shrubs. *Leaves* more or less membranous, often cordate. *Flowers* (in the species described below) in corymbosely branched compound cymes. *Calyx* 5-partite. *Corolla* usually campanulate, often with a brush of short hairs at the throat ; lobes spreading, overlapping to the right. *Coronal scales* 5, erect, adnate to the back of the anthers. *Anthers* with an inflexed tip ; pollen-masses waxy, stipitate, erect. *Stigma* truncate or beaked. *Follicles* usually in divaricate pairs, lanceolate ; seeds comose.

Analysis of the Species.

Coronal scales far exceeding the anther-tips; leaves cordate, velvety; follicles transversely rugose, beaked . . . . 1. *M. Roylei.*

Coronal scales not exceeding the anther-tips; leaves cordately 2-lobed, glabrescent; follicles longitudinally wrinkled, not beaked . . . . 2. *M. tenacissima.*

1. **M. Roylei,** Wight; Fl. Br. Ind. iv. 35; Brandis For. Flora 333, Ind. Trees 470; Gamble Man. Ind. Timb. 492. Vern. *Marua-bel* (?), Dún; *Khárchu,* Jaunsar.

A twining shrub; young parts soft-tomentose. *Leaves* 3-6 by 2-4·5 in., ovate, acuminate, often velvety beneath; base usually deeply cordate; petiole 1·5-2 in. *Cymes* 1-1·5 in. diam., much smaller and fewer-flowered than in *M. tenacissima. Flowers* somewhat larger. *Calyx* hairy outside. *Corolla-lobes* ·15-·25 in. long, hirsute inside. *Follicles* 3 by 1-1·5 in., with a beak-like tip, transversely rugose; pericarp thick; seeds ·5 in. long.

Outer slopes of the HIMALAYA; and also in JAUNSAR and TEHRI-GARHWAL, up to 7,000 ft. Common at Mussoorie.

It yields a silky-white strong fibre which is used for fishing-lines and similar other purposes.

Fl. May, June. Fr. Cold season.

2. **M. tenacissima,** W. & A.; Fl. Br. Ind. iv. 35; Brandis For. Flora 333, Ind. Trees 470; Gamble Man. Ind. Timb. 492 Vern. *Marua-bel,* Dún.

A large twining shrub; extremities soft-tomentose; bark grey, corky and deeply furrowed on old stems. *Leaves* 4-6 by 3-4 in., broad-ovate, cordately 2-lobed, acuminate, pubescent or tomentose when young; petiole 2-4 in. long. *Flowers* in corymbosely branched cymes. *Corolla* ·2 in. diam.; lobes oblong, ciliate. *Follicles* 4-6 by 1-·2 in., lanceolate, finely pubescent, longitudinally wrinkled; pericarp very thick; seeds ovate-oblong, ·5 in. long.

Occasionally in Khair forests of the DÚN and along the foot of the HIMALAYA. Less frequently in Sál areas.

The bark of young shoots yields a silky-white fibre of great strength, used for fishing-lines by the Goorkhas and for bow-strings by the "Mountaineers of Rajmahal."—*Sir D. Brandis.* The coagulated milky juice can be used as India-rubber.

Fl. Apr., May. Fr. Cold season.

7. Pergularia, Linn.; G. P. n. 110.

1. **P. pallida,** W. & A.; Fl. Br. Ind. iv. 38; Brandis For. Flora 334, Ind. Trees 470; Gamble Man. Ind. Timb. 493.

A large twining shrub with corky bark on old stems; young parts pubescent with soft curved hairs. *Leaves* 2-4 by 1·2-3 in., ovate, cordate, acute or acuminate, entire, rather membranous, tomentose or pubescent beneath until mature; lateral nerves up to 6 pairs; petiole ·8-1·3 in. long. *Cymes* very often interpetiolar, umbelliform, hairy; peduncle up to ·5 in. long; pedicels ·3-·7 in. long, slender, much crowded. *Flowers* ·5-·7 in. across, yellowish-white, inodorous; buds oblong or oblanceolate. *Calyx* ·15-·2 in. long, campanulate; segments subulate, ciliate at the edges. *Corolla-tube* as long as the calyx somewhat swollen at the base; lobes linear, ·2-·4 in. long, overlapping to the right. *Coronal scales* adnate to the back of the anthers ,erect, flattened, acute, membranous; pollen-masses erect, waxy. *Follicles* 3-4 by 1 in., lanceolate, longitudinally wrinkled; seeds ·4 in. long, broad-ovate, concave, comose.

Not uncommon in the DÚN, *e. g.*, at Karwápáni and Lachiwála.

The fibre of young shoots may be found useful.

Fl. May-July. Fr. Sept.-Nov.

8. Heterostemma, W. & A.; G. P. n. 114.

1. **H. alatum,** Wight; Fl. Br. Ind. iv. 47; Brandis Ind. Trees 473.

A twining shrub; branches with two lines of grey hairs. *Leaves* 3-6 by 2-4 in., ovate elliptic or oblong, entire, acute or acuminate; nerves 3-4 pairs, winged beneath, the first two pairs sub-basal; base rounded or cuneate; petiole 1-2 in. long. *Flowers* yellow, about ·5 in. diam., usually in racemose cymes; peduncles about ·5 in. long, stout; pedicels ·2·-5 in. long, slender. *Calyx* small, 5-partite. *Corolla* rotate; lobes triangular, valvate. *Corona* of 5 large spreading horizontal lobes; pollen-masses minute, erect, waxy. *Stigma* truncate, 5-angled. *Follicles* double, divaricate through nearly three right angles and therefore pointing obliquely upward, 3-5 by ·2-·3 in., straight, pointed; pericarp thin; seed about ·5 in. long, dark-brown, membranous; coma about 1 in. long, brownish-white.

Low valleys in JAUNSAR and TEHRI-GARHWAL, up to 5,000 ft.; rather scarce: Thadiár.—*Mr. J. S. Gamble.*

Fl. Rainy season. Ft. Cold season.

9. Dregea, E. Meyer; G. P. n. 117.

1. D. volubilis, Benth.; Fl. Br. Ind. iv. 46, Brandis Ind. Trees 468; Gamble Man. Ind. Timb. 493.

A stout twining shrub with a woody stem, and usually with rather stout and stiff branches; innovations generally hoary-tomentose. *Leaves* 3-5 by 2-3·5 in., ovate, entire, acute or acuminate, rather coriaceous, usually tomentose beneath when young; main lateral nerves up to 5 pairs; base rounded truncate or cuneate, less often cordate; petiole rather stout, ·8-2 in. long. *Cymes* axillary or interpetiolar, umbelliform; peduncles 1-3 in. long, slender, drooping; pedicels ·5-1·5 in., rusty-scaberulous. *Flowers* green, ·3-·5 in. diam. *Calyx* about ·1 in. across, stellate. *Corolla* dark-green, cup-shaped; lobes broadly triangular, overlapping to the right. *Coronal scales* 5, fleshy, hemispherical, adnate to the very short column, spreading, inner angle cuspidate; pollen-masses erect, waxy. *Stigma* dome-shaped. *Follicles* usually double, 3-4 by 1-1·2 in., lanceolate, longitudinally ribbed, velvety until mature, afterwards minutely tomentose; seeds ·3-·4 in. long, broad-elliptic, concave, shining, with sharp edges; coma of very fine white silky hairs about 1·5 in. long.

Very common in Khair forests in the SIWALIK DIVISION, especially in the Jumna and Sông Valleys, up to 5,000 ft. Also in low valleys in JAUNSAR, *e.g.*, Kándá, 4,500 ft.

Fl. Apr.-June. Fr. Cold season.

10. Leptadenia, Br.; G. P. n. 125.

1. L. reticulata, Wight; Fl. Br. Ind. iv. 63, Brandis Ind. Trees 472; Gamble Man. Ind. Timb. 493.

A diffuse twining shrub with corky bark on old stems; young parts hoary. *Leaves* 2-3 by 1-1·5 in., ovate oblong or elliptic, acute, entire, coriaceous, pale, glaucous beneath; lateral nerves 6-8 pairs but very faint; base rounded cuneate or acute, scarcely cordate; petiole ·3-1·3 in. *Cymes* axillary, umbelliform, ·5-1 in. diam., many-flowered; peduncle ·3-·6 in. long, rather stout; pedicels of varying lengths, but never exceeding the peduncle. *Flowers* dirty- or brownish-white, ·2 in. diam. *Calyx* half the length of the flower; lobes acute or obtuse. *Corolla* rather fleshy; lobes pubescent, with margins folded inward, hooked and bearded at the tip, valvate in bud. *Corona* double—corolline of 5 scales between the corolla-lobes, staminal of an undulate wing at the base of the anthers. *Stigma* included, 5-angled. *Follicles* generally solitary by abortion, 2-3 by ·5-·7 in., straight, turgid, very hard, smooth, with a thick curved beak; seeds ·5 in. long, narrow-ovoid, flat, winged, comose at the hilum.

Along the foot of the SAHÁRANPUR SIWALIKS: Khárá, Barkálá, Ránipur, etc. Also grass lands near Mothronwála, DEHRA DÚN.

Fl. May-July. Fr. cold season.

11. Orthanthera, Wight; G. P. n. 125.

(United with *Leptadenia* in the "Gen. Plantarum.")

1. **O. viminea,** Wight; Fl. Br. Ind. iv. 64; Brandis For. Flora 335, Ind. Trees 472; Gamble Man. Ind. Timb. 493. Vern. *Mahúr-ghás, Khip,* Hind.

A small erect twiggy leafless green shrub. *Flowers* about ·2 in. long, dirty-brown, in few-flowered woolly cymes; peduncles ·2-1 in. long. *Calyx* parted nearly to the base; sepals lanceolate, without glands. *Corolla* salver-shaped; tube cylindrical; lobes oblong, valvate in bud. *Corona* double, coralline of minute scales alternating with the corolla-lobes, staminal an undulating ring below the anthers; anthers without a tip; pollen-masses stipitate, erect. *Follicles* solitary, 4-6 in. long, linear, compressed, erect; pericarp thin, brown inside; seeds ·2 in. long, brown; coma of very fine silky hairs about ·5 in. long.

Found in the ráu-beds of the SAHÁRANPUR FORESTS; also in the Sông, Súswá and Ganges rivers in the DÚN.

The flower-buds are eaten as a vegetable in Oudh, and rope is made of the fibre.

Fl. Feb.-May. Fr. Sept.-Nov.

Tylophora tenuis, Bl.; Fl. Br. Ind. iv. 42,—is a very graceful slender little twiner found in grass lands near Nakraunda in the DÚN and towards Khárá in the SAHÁRANPUR DISTRICT. *Leaves* rather fleshy, 1-1·5 in. long, ovate-elliptic or oblong, acute or apiculate; base rounded or cordate; nerves indistinct; petiole ·1-·3 in. long. *Flowers* small, dark-purple, few together on a simple or branched filiform peduncle; pedicels ·3-·5 in. long. *Pollen-masses* suberect, waxy. *Follicles* 3 in. long, drooping; pericarp membranous. Fr. Oct.-Dec. —*G. P. n. 103.*

FAM. 55. LOGANIACEÆ; G. P. N. 108.

Trees, shrubs or herbs. *Leaves* opposite, simple, with interpetiolar stipules or a raised transverse line at the internodes. *Flowers* regular, in simple or compound axillary or terminal cymes. *Calyx* small, 4-5-toothed. *Corolla* 4-5-partite, imbricate or valvate. *Stamens* epipetalous, alternating with the corolla-lobes. *Ovary* free, 2-celled; ovules one or many in each cell; style simple; stigma simple or 2-lobed. *Fruit* a berry or a capsule, 1-many-seeded; albumen copious.

Analysis of the Genera.

Erect shrubs. Cor. imbricate; fruit a capsule . 1. BUDDLEIA.
Scandent shrubs. Cor. valvate; fruit a berry. 2. GARDNERIA.

1. Buddleia, Linn.; G. P. n. 14.

Trees, shrubs or herbs, usually mealy- or woolly-tomentose. *Leaves* united by a stipular line. *Flowers* tetramerous. *Corolla-lobes* imbricate in bud. *Stamens* 4; filaments very short. *Style* linear; ovules many in each cell; stigma obscurely 2-lobed. *Capsule* septicidally 2-valved; seeds small, many.

Analysis of the Species.

Flowers in interrupted panicles of heads; leaves broad and tomentose on both surfaces . . . . . . 1. *B. paniculata.*
Flowers in panicles of dense spikes; leaves narrow and glabrous above. . . 2. *B. asiatica.*

1. **B. paniculata,** Wall.; Fl. Br. Ind. iv. 81; Brandis For. Flora 318, Ind. Trees 475; Gamble Man. Ind. Timb. 495. Vern. *Sendroi*, Jaunsar.

An evergreen shrub with a crooked stem; bark thin, light-grey, peeling off in long strips; extremities rusty-tomentose. *Leaves* 4-6 by 2 in., variable from lanceolate to ovate-triangular, dentate crenate or sub-entire; petiole ·5-1·5 in. *Flowers* fragrant, subsessile in pedunculate heads or clusters forming an irregular panicle. *Calyx* ·15-·2 in., urceolate, woolly outside; teeth short. *Corolla* pink and white, tomentose outside, tubular; lobes rounded, obtuse. *Capsule* ellipsoid, ·2 in. long.

Fairly common in JAUNSAR and TEHRI-GARHWAL, 4,000-7,500 ft., especially on exposed sunny slopes; *e.g.*, Deoban, along the Lower Chakrata road; Luhásu Block, Lambátách; etc.

Wood moderately hard and close-grained, weighing 41 lbs. per c. ft., but is used only as fuel. Likely to be useful in re-stocking bare hillsides.

Fl. Apr., May.

2. **B. asiatica,** Lour.; Fl. Br. Ind. iv. 82; Brandis For. Flora 318, Ind. Trees 475; Gamble Man. Ind. Timb. 495. Vern. *Dúdhiá*, Dún.

A large evergreen shrub; bark thin, grey; extremities densely clothed with soft grey tomentum. *Leaves* 4-6 by 1-1·2 in., lanceolate, serrulate, glabrous and dark-green above, densely grey- or white-tomentose beneath; petiole ·2 in. or 0. *Flowers* odorous, sessile, in dense bracteate spikes arranged in large leafy terminal panicles. *Calyx* ·15-·2 in., campanulate; teeth triangular. *Corolla-tube* urceolate; lobes short, rounded, imbricate, at first white but fading into deep purple. *Capsule* 2-·3 in. long, ellipsoid; valves bifid.

Common in ravines and grass lands in the SIWALIK DIVISION, and is often planted in gardens for ornament.

Wood tough and moderately hard. The branches would probably make good walking-sticks. Weight 44 lbs. per c. ft.

Fl. Mar., Apr.

Gardneria, Wall.; G. P. n. 30.

1. **G. angustifola,** Wall.; Fl. Br. Ind. iv. 93; Brandis Ind. Trees 477; Gamble Man. Ind. Timb. 499.

A large scandent glabrous shrub. *Leaves* opposite, 3-4 by 1 in., lanceolate, acuminate, entire, glabrous, rounded or acute at the base; petiole ·2-·3 long. *Flowers* about ·5 in. across, solitary, on nodding filiform axillary peduncles ·4-1 in. long. *Calyx* small, deeply 4-5-lobed. *Corolla* rotate; lobes ·2 in. long, thick, valvate in bud. *Stamens* 4-5, on the corolla-tube; anthers subsessile; cells ovate, subconnate. *Ovary* 2-celled; ovule 1 in each cell; style cylindrical; stigma 2-lobed. *Fruit* a scarlet berry, ·3 in. diam.

Found at Mussoorie and in the Bear Garden below Chakrata. Very scarce.

Fl. June, July.

Order 7.—POLEMONIALES.

FAM. 56. BORAGINACEÆ; G. P. N. 112.

Herbs, shrubs or trees. *Leaves* simple, alternate, rarely subopposite or opposite. *Flowers* in simple or compound usually-terminal cymes, rarely solitary or axillary. *Calyx* persistent; lobes usually 5, valvate in bud. *Corolla* hypogynous, gamopetalous, often with scales in the throat; segments as many as those of the calyx, generally imbricate in bud. *Stamens* epipetalous, alternating with the corolla-lobes. *Ovary* superior, of two carpels, entire or 4-lobed; cells usually 2-ovuled; style simple or forked, terminal or gynobasic (from between the lobes of the ovary). *Fruit* a drupe with 1-4 kernels, or separating into 2-4 nutlets; seeds erect or oblique.

Analysis of the Genera.

Style twice forked; fruit at least ·5 in. diam., usually 1 celled, 1-seeded . . . 1. CORDIA.
Style 2-fid; fruit up to ·2 in. diam., with 1-4 kernels . . . . 2. EHRETIA.

1. Cordia, Linn.; G. P. n. 1.

Trees or shrubs. *Leaves* alternate, rarely subopposite, petioled, usually coriaceous. *Flowers* often polygamous, in terminal or leaf-opposed cymes. *Calyx* 4-5-toothed; teeth accrescent in fruit. *Corolla* funnel-shaped; lobes 4-8 *Stamens* 4-8; filaments hairy. *Ovary* entire, 4-celled. 1 ovule in each cell; style twice bipartite, terminal. *Drupe* ovoid; endocarp hard, usually 1-celled by abortion; albumen 0.

Analysis of the Species.

Leaves broad-ovate, glabrescent; calyx not ribbed 1. *C. Myxa.*
Leaves rotundate, scabrous above, tomentose beneath; calyx ribbed . . . . . 2. *C. vestita.*

1. **C. Myxa,** Linn.; Fl. Br. Ind. iv. 136; Brandis For. Flora 336, Ind. Trees 478; Gamble Man. Ind. Timb. 500. Vern. *Lassorá, Lassúrá, Lessorá,* Hind.

A middle-sized deciduous tree, usually with a long bole; bark grey or brown, with shallow longitudinal wrinkles. *Leaves* variable, 3-6 by 2-4 in., broad-ovate, crenate or wavy at the margins, coriaceous, obscurely hairy beneath when young, from slightly scabrous to glabrous above; base rounded or cuneate; lateral nerves 4-6 pairs, the first pair sub-basal; petiole ·5-2 in. *Flowers* white, polygamous, usually pentamerous, in loose ebracteate corymbose cymes. *Calyx* ·1-·15 in., irregularly toothed, not ribbed, accrescent in fruit. *Corolla-lobes* ·1-·12 in.; tube hairy within. *Drupe* yellow and glossy when ripe, usually 1-seeded, filled with a viscid sweetish pulp.

Common in the DÚN and SAHÁRANPUR FORESTS, affecting shady ravines. Also Tons and other low Valleys in JAUNSAR and TEHRI-GARHWAL.

Wood soft and porous, but seasons well and is fairly strong, used chiefly for fuel; weight 33 lbs. per c. ft. The fibre of the bark is made into ropes and is used to caulk boats. The fruit is eaten, both tender and ripe. The viscid pulp of the ripe fruit is used as bird-lime. The leaves are often used as plates.

Fl. Mar., Apr. Fr. May-July.

2. **C. vestita,** Hook. f. & Th.; Fl. Br. Ind. iv. 139; Brandis For. Flora 338, Ind. Trees 480; Gamble Man. Ind. Timb. 502. Vern. *Barolá, Bairolá,* E. Dún and Garhwal; *Kúm,* Sahåranpur; *Kúm-paiman,* Hind.

A small deciduous tree with a low rounded crown; bark greenish-grey, smooth, exfoliating in large woody scales; young parts covered with grey pubescence. *Leaves* 3-6 by 2·5-5 in., broad-elliptic or orbicular, acuminate, coriaceous, scabrous above, tomentose beneath until mature; lateral nerves 3-5 pairs, the lowest sub-basal; base cuneate rounded or shallow-cordate; petiole 1-1·5 in. *Flowers* yellowish-white, polygamous, in dense compound cymes. *Calyx* ·5 in. long, more or less ribbed outside. *Corolla-lobes* ·3 in., ovate-oblong, spreading; tube as long as the lobes. *Drupe* ·7 in. long, supported by the accrescent saucer-shaped calyx, and cuspidate with the remains of the style, filled inside with a gelatinous pulp.

Fairly common in the SAHÁRANPUR SIWALIKS and only occasionally met with in the DÚN, *e.g.* Tháno, Phándowála, Timli, Tirsál, etc. Also Kálsi.

Heartwood light-brown, beautifully mottled with darker veins, even-grained, hard, strong, tough and elastic, and is employed, where known, for wheel and well-work; weight 52-53 lbs. per c. ft. The pulp of the fruit is eaten.

Fl. and young leaves Mar., Apr. Fr. Oct., Nov.

2. Ehretia, Linn.; G. P. n. 6.

Trees or shrubs. *Leaves* alternate, entire or toothed. *Flowers* small, in axillary or terminal corymbs or panicles. *Calyx* deeply 5-partite. *Corolla* rotate; lobes 5, imbricate in bud. *Stamens* 5; anthers generally exserted. *Ovary* 2-celled; cells 2-ovuled; style terminal, bifid. *Fruit* a sub-globose drupe with 1-4 pyrenes; pyrenes solitary and 4-celled, or 2 and 2-celled, or 4 and 1-celled; cells 1-seeded; albumen scanty.

Analysis of the Species.

Leaves serrate; flowers in terminal panicles . 1. *E. acuminata.*
Leaves entire; flowers in terminal and axillary dichotomously compound corymbose cymes 2. *E. lævis.*

1. **E. acuminata,** R. Br.; Fl. Br. Ind. iv. 141; Brandis Ind. Trees 481; Gamble Man. Ind. Timb. 503. Syn.—*E. serrata,* Roxb.; Brandis For. Flora 339. Vern. *Pandáyan,* Dún; *Púna.* Jaunsar and Hind.

A middle-sized tree nearly glabrous; large stems more or less fluted; bark brown, or when old mostly dark-grey, with longitudinal furrows or cracks. *Leaves* 4-8 by 1·5-3 in., elliptic-oblong, acuminate, sharply serrate, glabrescent and shining above, tough but rather thin; lateral nerves 8-10 on either side; petiole ·5-1 in. *Flowers* numerous, white, fragrant, in large conical terminal panicles. *Corolla-lobes* ·12 in., reflexed. *Style* bifid for less than half its length. *Drupe* ·12-·16 in. diam., with two 2-celled and 2-seeded pyrenes.

Fairly common in grass-lands in the WESTERN DÚN, and also found at Kálsi and lower valleys in JAUNSAR up to 5,000 ft.: Binálgádh. Silgádh. Thadiár, etc. Also at Káluwála, Nakraunda, Gulátappar, etc., in the E. DÚN.

Wood light-brown, soft, light, fairly compact, easily worked; used for agricultural implements, scabbards, sword-hilts, etc.; weight 37 lbs. per c. ft. The fruit is eaten and the leaves are lopped for cattle-fodder.

Fl. Mar., Apr. Fr. Nov., Dec.

2. **E. lævis,** Roxb.; Fl. Br. Ind. iv. 141; Brandis For. Flora 340, Ind. Trees 481; Gamble Man. Ind. Timb. 503. Vern. *Chamror*, Hind.

A moderate-sized deciduous tree with an irregular-shaped trunk, and a spreading crown; bark smooth, mealy-grey outside, inner substance yellow, soft, not fibrous. *Leaves* 3-6 in. long, elliptic, obtuse or acuminate, entire, membranous while young, hard and fleshy when mature, glabrous or glabrescent, dark-green; nerves 6-10 on either side of the midrib; base cuneate, rarely rounded; petiole ·5-1 in. *Flowers* white, small, in terminal or axillary dichotomously-branched corymbose cymes. *Corolla-tube* ·1 in.; lobes ·12 in., spreading. *Drupe* ·2 in. diam., globose, depressed, 4-ribbed, with 1-4 one-seeded pyrenes.

Exceedingly common in the DÚN and SAHÁRANPUR FORESTS, generally in damp shady places, *e.g.*, Lachiwála Coppice, Kánsráo Pass, etc. Also in the Ámláwa and Tons Valleys in JAUNSAR.

Wood tough and fairly durable, and is sometimes used for agricultural implements, but in this part of the country chiefly as fuel; weight 33-38 lbs. per c. ft. "The leaves are given as cattle-fodder."—*Sir D. Brandis.*

Fl. Mar., Apr. Fr. Cold season.

FAM. 57. CONVOLVULACEÆ; G. P. N. 113.

Herbs or shrubs, usually twining, often with milky juice. *Leaves* alternate, simple, exstipulate. *Flowers* regular, bisexual, pentamerous, often showy. *Calyx* persistent, deeply 5-lobed; lobes imbricate, sometimes enlarged in fruit. *Corolla* campanulate or funnel-shaped often 5-plaited in bud. *Stamens* 5; anthers oblong *Ovary* superior, 2-carpelled and 2-celled, or by false dissepiments 4-celled; ovules 2 in each carpel. *Style* 1, rarely 2 ; stigma 2-lobed or branched. *Fruit* indehiscent, often breaking up irregularly ; albumen 0 or scanty ; cotyledons generally plaited (0 in *Cuscuta*).

A Family of very little forest interest.

1. Porana, Burm. ; G. P. n. 17.

1. **P. paniculata,** Roxb. ; Fl. Br. Ind. iv. 222 ; Brandis For. Flora 342, Ind. Trees 487 ; Gamble Man. Ind. Timb. 507. Vern. *Bel Kámú, Safed-bel,* Sahâranpur.

A large twining shrub ; branchlets, inflorescence and underside of leaves clothed with grey pubescence. *Leaves* very variable in size, 2-5 by 1·5-3 in. (those running into the inflorescence much smaller), ovate-cordate, acuminate, entire, membranous, pubescent, with 5-7 basal nerves ; petiole 1·5 in. long. *Flowers* very numerous, small, white, in large axillary and terminal leaf-bearing panicles. *Sepals* in flowers ·1 in. long, linear-oblong, at least 3 enlarged in fruit into ovate-oblong membranous strongly reticulate shortly-stalked wings, ·6-·9 in. long, with a prominent midrib. *Corolla* ·2 in. long ; limb 5-plaited. *Filaments* short. *Ovary* 2-celled, 4-ovuled ; style short ; stigma obscurely 2-lobed. *Capsule* ·2 in. diam., globose, hairy, membranous, fragile, 1-seeded by abortion ; seed glabrous.

Very common in the DÚN and SAHÁRANPUR FORESTS, generally in scrub jungles.

This climber is largely used in the Sahâranpur District for making into baskets, and is generally preferred to all other plants used for the same purpose. The baskets used in removing earth while the Ganges Canal was being excavated are said to have been chiefly made of this climber.

Fl. Oct.-Jan. Fr. Mar., Apr.

Several plants of this Family are cultivated for their showy flowers, notably the following :—

1. *Rivea ornata,* Chois. ; Fl. Br. Ind. iv. 183.—A climber with large white flowers about 2 in. across.—*G. P. n. 2.*

2. *Argyreia Roxburghii,* Chois. ; Fl. Br. Ind. iv. 185.—Flowers large, purple or rose.—*G. P. n. 3.*

3. *Ipomæa bona-nox*, Linn.; Fl. Br. Ind. iv. 197.—Flowers large, white, with greenish plaits.—*G. P. n. 9.*

The following indigenous plants deserve notice :—

1. *Lettsomia Thomsoni*, Clarke; Fl. Br. Ind. iv. 193.—is found on the dry bare hill-slopes above Moindrot, 3,000 ft., also in the SIWALIKS, 2,500 ft. Flowers rose-purple, May-Oct.—*G. P. n. 7.*

2. *Cuscuta reflexa*, Roxb.; Fl. Br. Ind. 225. The Dodder. Vern. *Akás-bel*, Hind.; *Surag-báli*, Jaunsar;—is the well-known leafless greenish-white or yellow flowering parasite very common in the scrub forests along the outer foot of the SIWALIKS and in similar localities in the DÚN, chiefly affecting all species of *Zizyphus* and also *Adhatoda Vasica*. The leafless character is carried even to the embryo which is destitute of cotyledons. The seed germinates on the ground, but the plant does not seem to derive much nourishment from it, its growth being sustained, for the little while it is obliged to shift for itself, by the fleshy albumen in which the germ-plant is imbedded in the seed. As soon as the seedling twines itself round a woody plant, it developes several thick sucker-like haustoria along the surface of contact, which, penetrating the bark of the host, begin to draw nourishment from the cambium-layer. Directly this is effected, it loses its attachment to the soil, and the portion of it below the lowest haustorium then dries and drops off. Henceforth the parasite goes on flourishing entirely at the expense of the host. It is used in veterinary practice for poultice on sprains. Fl. Sept.-Feb. *G. P. n. 32.* Fr. Feb.-Apr.

FAM. 58. SOLANACEÆ; G. P. N. 114.

Herbs or shrubs, rarely soft-wooded small trees. *Leaves* alternate, exstipulate. *Flowers* solitary or in clusters or cymes, axillary extra-axillary or terminal, regular, bisexual, usually pentamerous. *Calyx* inferior, free, usually persistent, sometimes enlarged in fruit. *Corolla* gamopetalous, rotate or campanulate, often plaited; limb 5- or more-lobed or entire. *Stamens* 5, epipetalous. *Ovary* superior, usually 2-celled; ovules many, on peltate placentas; style simple. *Fruit* a many-seeded berry or capsule; seeds generally compressed.

This Family is of no special forest interest, although plants of considerable economic importance, such as the potato, brinjal, chillie (*Capsicum*), tomato (*Lycopersicum*), tobacco (*Nicotiana*), and Cape-gooseberry (*Physalis*) belong to it. Some are poisonous, *e.g.*, *Datura*, while others are valuable in medicine.

1. Solanum, Linn.; G. P. n. 2.

1. **S. verbascifolium,** Linn.; Fl. Br. Ind. iv. 230; Gamble Man. Ind. Timb. 508. Brandis Ind. Trees 489. Vern. *Ban Tamákú*, Dún; *Asedú*, Garhwal.

A tall soft-wooded shrub, unarmed; bark light-grey; extremities and inflorescene stellate-woolly. *Leaves* alternate or falsely subopposite, 7-9 by 3-5 in., elliptic, acute at both ends or often rounded at the base, entire, subcoriaceous, stellately woolly, giving a fetid smell when bruised; petiole 1-2 in. *Flowers* in very woolly dichotomous cymes. *Calyx-lobes* enlarged in, but much shorter than, the fruit. *Corolla* ·7 in. diam., white, woolly outside; limb plaited in bud. *Stamens* 5, on the corolla-throat; anthers apicular and joined into a cone round the style, opening by terminal pores. *Ovary* usually 2-celled. *Berry* ·3-·5 in. diam., yellow when ripe.

Fairly common in moist shady places in the DÚN (*e.g.*, banks of the Song river), and in hedges round villages.

Wood very light, yellow, very soft, scarcely used even as fuel. The leaves and fruit are used in country medicine.

Fl. and fr. almost throughout the year.

S. indicum, Linn.; Fl. Br. Ind. iv. 234. Vern. *Bhút-katáiá* Hind.—is a common weed of waste lands, prickly all over, with blue flowers and yellow berries, the latter ·3-·5 in. diam. The fruit, leaves and roots are used in Hindu medicine.

S. Melongena, Linn.; Fl. Br. Ind. iv. 235. Vern. *Bhattá. Báigan*, *Báingan*, Hind. The Brinjal. Much cultivated throughout India, up to 3,000 ft.

S. tuberosum, Linn.; Fl. Br. Ind. iv. 229.—is the Potato, Vern. *Alú*, Hind., which is extensively cultivated throughout Upper India, up to 9,000 ft.

Order 8—PERSONALES.

FAM. 59. BIGNONIACEÆ; G. P. N. 120.

Usually trees, sometimes woody climbers, rarely herbs. *Leaves* usually opposite, pinnately compound, sometimes undivided; stipules none. *Flowers* bisexual, irregular, showy, generally in terminal panicles or racemes. *Calyx* free, 2-5-lobed, truncate or spathaceous; lobes valvate in bud. *Corolla* often 2-lipped; lobes 5, unequal, imbricate in bud. *Stamens* epipetalous, usually 4 and didynamous,—the fifth wholly absent or rudimentary, or rarely fertile and then nearly equalling the others. *Ovary* superior, free, 2-celled, more or less stipitate and supported by an annular disk; ovules numerous; style filiform; stigma 2-lobed. *Fruit* an elongated 2-valved capsule; seeds winged, exalbuminous.

Analysis of the Genera.

Perfect stamens 5; capsule flat, septicidally 2-valved; seeds discoid . . 1. OROXYLUM.

Perfect stamens 4; capsule terete, loculicidally 2-valved; seeds wedge-shaped . 2. STEREOSPERMUM.

1. Oroxylum, Vent.; G. P. n. 21.

O. indicum, Vent.; Fl. Br. Ind. iv. 378; Gamble Man. Ind. Timb. 510; Brandis Ind. Trees 496. Syn.—*Calosanthes indica,* Bl.; Brandis For. Flora 347. Vern. *Tarlú,* Dún; *Pharrái, Pharnát,* E. Dún; *Tantiá,* Garhwal.

A small tree with few branches and a small open crown; bark soft, light brownish-grey and corky outside. *Leaves* opposite, 3-pinnate near the base, 2-pinnate about the middle, and simply pinnate towards the apex, 4-6 ft. long; pinnæ 3-4 pairs; 2-3 lower pairs bipinnate at the base, the pinnules being 3-5 foliolate. *Ultimate leaflets* 3-5 by 2-3·5 in., broad-ovate, acuminate, entire, glabrous. *Flowers* large, fleshy, in lax terminal racemes; peduncle 2-3 ft., pedicels 1-1·5 in. long. *Calyx* 1 by ·6 in., leathery, thimble-shaped. *Corolla* campanulate; tube green outside; limb 2-3 in. across; lobes 5, dark-red. *Stamens* 5, all fertile and nearly equal. *Capsule* septicidally 2-valved; shortly stipitate, 18-30 by 2·5-3·5 in., scabbard-like; seeds surrounded by a broad transparent white papery wing, 2-2·5 in. across, including the wing.

Fairly common in the DÚN and SAHÁRANPUR FORESTS, and on the OUTER HIMALAYAN slopes up to 4,000 ft.

Wood yellowish-white, open-grained, very light and soft, scarcely used except for fuel. Weight 30 lbs. per c. ft.

"The bark and fruit are used in tanning and dyeing, and the seeds are used to line hats, and, placed between two layers of wicker-work to make umbrellas. Root, bark, leaves, and seeds are used in native medicine."—*Sir D. Brandis.*

Leafless Mar., Apr. Fl. June, July. Fr. Cold season.

2. Stereospermum, Chamisso ; G. P. n. 37.

1. **S. suaveolens,** DC.; Fl. Br. Ind. iv. 382; Brandis For. Flora 351, Ind. Trees 495; Gamble Man. Ind. Timb. 515. Vern. *Pádal*, Hind.

A large deciduous tree, young parts viscous hairy; bark grey, exfoliating in large flat scales. *Leaves* opposite, 12-24 in. long, imparipinnate. *Leaflets* 5-9, more commonly 7, 3-6 by 2-3·5 in., broad-elliptic, acute or acuminate, sharply serrate on young, entire on old trees, coriaceous, scabrous or velvety-tomentose; lateral nerves 6-8 pairs; petiolules about ·1 in. *Flowers* dark-purple, pubescent, fragrant, in viscid trichotomous panicles. *Calyx* ·2-·3 in., campanulate, shortly 3-5-lobed. *Corolla* 1-1·5 in. long, very soft; tube cylindrical, throat hairy; limb oblique, 2-labiate; lobes rounded, with curled edges. *Stamens* 4, didynamous, with a rudimentary fifth. *Disk* fleshy, annular. *Capsule* loculicidally 2-valved, 15-24 by ·6-·8 in., obscurely 4-ribbed, dark-grey with elevated white specks; dissepiment cylindrical, brown, corky; seeds 1·5 by ·3 in. including the two oblong wings which are lateral and set somewhat obliquely like those of an electric fan.

Fairly common in the DÚN and SAHÁRANPUR FORESTS, especially in Sál areas, with a tendency to become somewhat gregarious on clayey soils.

Sapwood white, fairly hard. Heartwood small, yellowish-brown, mottled with darker streaks, very hard, seasons and polishes well, and is fairly durable; weight 40-50 lbs. per c. ft. Sir D. Brandis says it is "much valued for building and generally commands a ready sale"; but it does not seem to be much cared for in the SIWALIK DIVISION. It yields excellent charcoal, and the root and bark are used in Hindu medicine.

New leaves and fl. May, June. Fr. Cold season, but remaining long on the tree.

1. *Millingtonia hortensis*, Linn.; Fl. Br. Ind. iv. 377. The Indian Cork-tree, Vern. *Akás Nim*, Hind.—is a handsome tall tree, with fragrant white flowers, cultivated in avenues and gardens in DEHRA and most places in the plains.—*G. P. n. 20.*

2. *Amphicome emodi*, Lindl.; Fl. Br. Ind. iv. 385;—is an herbaceous plant found in the crevices of limestone rocks in JAUNSAR, *e.g.*, Mátkángrá, and along the pipe-line between Chakrata and Deoban. *Leaves* alternate, imparipinnate; leaflets about 1 in. *Flowers* bright rose, about 2 in. long. *Capsule* terete, about 9 in. long.—*G. P. n. 42.*

FAM. 60. ACANTHACEÆ; G. P. n. 122.

Herbs or shrubs, rarely trees, usually with swollen joints. *Leaves* opposite, simple, exstipulate. *Flowers* with large persistent bracts and bracteoles. *Calyx* 5-partite. *Corolla* 2-lipped, or subequally 5-lobed; lobes imbricate or twisted in bud. *Stamens* 4 or 2, inserted on the corolla-tube. *Disk* often conspicuous. *Ovary* superior, 2-celled; ovules anatropous, 1 or more in each cell; style filiform, sometimes bifid. *Fruit* a loculicidal capsule, often elastically dehiscent. *Seeds* exalbuminous, ovoid or compressed, usually hard, seated on up-curved horny processes of the placenta, often clothed with white elastic hairs which are best seen when wetted.

Analysis of the Genera.

Corolla-lobes subequal, twisted to the left in bud ; fertile stamens usually 4.
- Capsule 6-8-seeded, seeds discoid . . 1. ÆCHMANTHERA.
- Capsule 2-4-seeded, seeds much compressed 2. STROBILANTHES.

Corolla 2-lipped, lobes imbricate in bud ; fertile stamens 2.
- Corolla tubular, slightly lipped ; capsule 12-14-seeded . . . . 3. PHLOGACANTHUS.
- Corolla broad-campanulate, deeply lipped ; capsule 4-seeded . . . . 4. ADHATODA.

1. Æchmanthera, Nees ; G. P. n. 38.

1. Æ. tomentosa, Nees ; Fl. Br. Ind. iv. 428 ; Brandis Ind. Trees 504 ; Gamble Man. Ind. Timb. 518.

A small shrub. *Leaves* 3-5 by 2 in., broad-lanceolate, acuminate, slightly crenate, coarsely pubescent ; base rounded ; petiole 1-1·5 in. *Flowers* in clusters of 3-8, arranged in axillary and terminal trichotomously-branched panicles. *Bracts* ·5 in. long ; bracteoles narrow. *Sepals* ·5 in. long, linear, usually viscous. *Corolla* purple, 1 in. long, tubular-ventricose, nearly straight, suddenly widening near the middle ; segments rounded, twisted in bud. *Stamens* 4, didynamous ; anthers obtuse. *Capsules* ·3-·5 in. long, narrow-oblong, 8-seeded. *Seeds* apparently glabrous, but are seen covered with white weak hairs when wetted.

Top of the SIWALIKS and OUTER HIMALAYAN slopes 3,-5,000 ft. : Málkōt, above Rájpur, etc. Also in inner valleys in JAUNSAR and TEHRI-GARHWAL, *e.g.*, Dhárágádh, Lunágádh, etc.

Fl. Dec. and Jan. at intervals of 5 (?) years when the plant dies in the same way as some Strobilanthes. It thus died over a large area in the Lúnágádh Valley in TEHRI-GARHWAL in the spring of 1900.

Var. *Wallichii,* Nees ; Vern. *Bair-ra, Bhardrá,* Málkōt ;—has stems covered with dense snow-white wool, and leaves with silky tomentum which is of a delicate purple colour, at least when young. It flowers gregariously after 4 or 5 years and dies as soon as the seeds are mature. Outer slopes of the HIMALAYA : Málkōt Forest. Also Ámláwa Valley in JAUNSAR and in the SIWALIKS, *e.g.*, behind Sháhjahánpur, and in the Timli and Mohand Passes.

2. Strobilanthes, Bl.; G. P. n. 59.

Small shrubs or herbs. *Leaves* frequently unequal, toothed or subentire, often with raphides. *Flowers* in axillary or terminal spikes or panicles. *Bracts* deciduous or persistent; bracteoles small or 0. *Calyx* usually deeply 5-fid, segments narrow, equal or unequal. *Corolla* tubular-ventricose, curved or straight; lobes 5, subequal, twisted in bud. *Stamens* 4 and didynamous, or 2. *Capsule* 4-2-seeded. *Seeds* compressed, hairy or glabrous; hairs, if present, elastic when wetted.

Analysis of the Species.

Fls. in spikes; (lvs. never quite glabrous.)
- Spikes with scale-like imbricate bracts; leaves sessile, auriculate . . . 1. *S. auriculatus.*
- Spikes without imbricate bracts.
  - Spikes 1-sided; leaves elliptic, the upper cordate.
    - Sepals linear, glabrous; corolla nearly straight . . . . 6. *S. Wallichii.*
    - Sepals obtuse, hairy; corolla much curved . . . . . . 7. *S. atropurpureus.*
  - Spikes symmetrical; leaves elliptic, none ever cordate . . . . 5. *S. angustifrons.*
  - Spikes panicled; leaves ovate, with usually a cordate or rounded base. 4. *S. alatus.*

Flowers in pedunculate heads (leaves narrowed at both ends).
- Leaves glabrous; calyx pubescent . . 2. *S. pentstemonoides.*
- Leaves hairy; calyx generally glabrous . 3. *S. Dalhousianus.*

1. **S. auriculatus,** Nees; Fl. Br. Ind. iv. 453; Brandis Ind. Trees 500; Gamble Man. Ind. Timb. 519.

A small shrub; branches quadrangular, often zigzag. *Leaves* variable and often very unequal in the same pair, from 10 by 2·25 in. to 3 by 1·5 in., sessile, auriculate, serrulate, sparsely hairy above. *Spikes* 3-4 by ·5 in., mostly terminal, solitary. *Bracts* broader than long, ·2-·3 in. long, persistent, with aromatic glandular hairs. *Calyx* velvety; segments ·2-·3 in., unequal. *Corolla* 1 in., bluish-purple, curved; tube short, narrow; limb slightly 2-lipped. *Capsule* glabrous, 4-seeded, ·3 in. long; seeds elastically hairy.

Throughout the DÚN and on the OUTER HIMALAYAN slopes up to 4,000 ft. Very common at Lachiwála.

Fl. Nov.-Mar.

2. **S. pentstemonoides,** T. Anders.; Fl. Br. Ind. iv. 460; Gamble Man. Ind. Timb. 519.

A much-branched glabrous shrub. *Leaves* 5-8 by 1·5-2·5 in., elliptic, acuminate at both ends, closely serrate; nerves 7 pairs; base decurrent into the petiole; petiole ·5-2 in. *Flowers* in buds in globose heads enclosed in white concave bracts ·25-·15 in. long, usually 3 heads to a peduncle. *Calyx* pubescent; lobes linear, ·2-·3 in. long. *Corolla* 1·5 in. long, curved, pale-purple. *Caspule* ·7 in., clavate, 4-seeded; seeds ovate, silky, ·1 in. long.

Banks of the Ré-nadi in the Dún; OUTER HIMALAYAN VALLEYS, *e.g.*, Mussoorie, and probably up to 6,000 ft. in JAUNSAR.

Fl. Rainy season.

3. **S. Dalhousianus,** Clarke; Fl. Br. Ind. iv. 460, Brandis Ind. Trees 501; Gamble Man. Ind. Timb. 519.

A suberect shrub, 2-3 ft. high; stems hairy. *Leaves* 4-6 by 1·3-2 in., elliptic, acuminate, hairy; petiole ·5-1·5 in. long. *Bracts* as in the last species but shorter than the heads. *Calyx* usually glabrous, subscarious; lobes linear-oblong. *Corolla-tube* yellow, 1-1·5 in. long, somewhat narrowed at the neck; limb oblique, purple; lobes rounded, emarginate, one much larger than the others. *Capsule* ·5-·6 in. long, 4-seeded.

HILLS, 6,-8,000 ft. Fairly common.

Fl. Rainy season.

4. **S. alatus,** Nees; Fl. Br. Ind. iv. 464; Brandis Ind. Trees 501; Gamble Man. Ind. Timb. 519. Vern. *Mashnoi, Lálor,* Jaunsar.

A small shrub; branches quadrangular. *Leaves* 4-6 by 2-3 in., ovate, acute or acuminate, crenate or serrate; nerves 7-9 pairs of which 4-5 pairs are crowded near the base; base cordate or rounded; petiole 1-3 in., often slightly winged; upper leaves sessile

Spikes forming terminal panicles. *Bracts* caducous. *Sepals* ·3-·4 in., ligulate, unequal. *Corolla* about 1 in. long, purple, campanulately ventricose, curved beyond the calyx, with 2 hairy lines within. *Capsule* narrow, ·75 in. long, elliptic, hairy, 4-seeded; seeds ovate, hairy, ·3 in. long.

JAUNSAR and TEHRI-GARHWAL, above 6,000 ft.: Deoban, Konáin, Mundáli; Deotá.

Fl. Rainy season.

5. **S. angustifrons,** Clarke; Fl. Br. Ind. iv. 466.

A small shrub with terete branches; old stems glabrous, young parts inflorescence and leaves white-tomentose. *Leaves* 3-4 by 1·5-2 in., elliptic, acuminate at both ends, glabrescent, pale beneath; nerves 6 pairs; petiole ·5-·7 in.; upper leaves never cordate. *Spikes* terminating in small heads and forming short irregular panicles. *Bracteoles* ·1 in., linear. *Calyx* linear, ·3-·5 in. long, pubescent. *Corolla* about 1 in. long, purple, nearly glabrous, narrow; mouth curved. *Capsule* ·3-·5 in. long, 4-seeded; seeds hairy, ·1 in. long.

Common in the DÚN and on the OUTER HIMALAYAN slopes, up to 6,000 ft.: Lachiwála, Rájpur; Málkōt.

Fl. Jan.-Mar.

6. **S. Wallichii,** Nees; Fl. Br. Ind. iv. 471; Brandis Ind. Trees 500; Gamble Man. Ind. Timb. 519. Vern. *Jánú*, or *Zánú*, Jaunsar.

A small shrub with quadrangular stems; upper portion herbaceous and renewed every year. *Leaves* 3-5 by 1-2 in., elliptic, acuminate, glabrescent, crenate-serrate; nerves 6-8 pairs; base acute, petiole 1-1·5 in.; upper leaves sessile, cordate. *Spikes* 1-6 in., one-sided. *Flowers* blue, usually in pairs. *Bracts* gradually smaller, persistent. *Sepals* ligulate, ·3 in. long., often with glandular hairs. *Corolla* 1-1·5 in. long, nearly straight, very gradually ventricose; segments round. *Capsule* linear, ·5-·7 in. long; seeds 4, ·1 in. long, suborbicular, brown-pubescent.

JAUNSAR and TEHRI-GARHWAL, 7-10,000 ft.: very common.

This plant is remarkable for its gregarious and exclusive habit, and is a pest in places where reproduction of tree species is needed. Its upper portion is herbaceous, and grows and dies every year, adding only one internode to the stumpy lower portion which thus goes on growing until there are about 12 internodes. It then flowers, and dies as soon as the seeds are mature. It is known to have flowered in Jaunsar in 1882, 1894 and 1906, giving a cycle of 12 years. On the second occasion, the seeds did not germinate until March 1896, but by the end of May all old *Strobilanthes* areas were seen thickly covered with a young crop of seedlings of its own and also of a species of *Impatiens*, which usurped the soil when the *Strobilanthes* had died. Being an annual, the former, however, was gradually ousted by the latter.

The leaves and young shoots are greedily browsed by sheep and goats.

Fl. Rainy season at intervals of 12 years. Fr. Sept., Oct.

7. **S. atropurpureus,** Nees; Fl. Br. Ind. iv. 472; Brandis Ind. Trees 501; Gamble Man. Ind. Timb. 519.

A perennial shrub often growing in swamps; stem 1-1·5 ft. high, succulent. *Leaves* 2·5-4 by 1-2 in., ovate, acuminate, crenate-serrate, the upper cuneate, petioled or decurrent to the base, very membranous. *Spikes* lax; flowers solitary or paired; lower bracts leaf-like. *Sepals* linear, subobtuse, hairy. *Corolla* 1·5-·2 in. long, much curved, blue; ventricle very broad. *Capsule* about 1 in. long; seeds ·2 in. long.

Fairly common in damp localities in the HILLS.

Fl. Aug.-Oct.

3. Phlogacanthus, Nees; G. P. n. 70.

1. **P. thyrsiflorus,** Nees; Fl. Br. Ind. iv. 512; Gamble Man. Ind. Timb. 523; Brandis Ind. Trees 501.

An evergreen shrub up to 8 ft. high; bark smooth, grey; branches 4-angled. *Leaves* 6-8 by 1·5-3 in., lanceolate or oblanceolate, tapering at both ends, subentire, glabrous, deep glossy-green, densely punctulate; petiole ·7-1 in. *Inflorescence* a thyrsoid terminal panicle up to 12 in. long. *Bracts* ·2 in., linear. *Calyx* deeply 5-fid; tube ·1 in. long; segments ·2-·3 in. long, bristle-like, pubescent. *Corolla* tubular, orange to brick-red, villous; tube ·7-1·2 in. long, curved upwards; upper lip sub-erect. *Fertile stamens* 2. *Capsule* 1-1·2 by ·1 in., 4-cornered, glabrous, 12-14-seeded; seeds compressed, covered with elastic hairs.

Common in the DÚN, on the OUTER HIMALAYAN slopes up to 4,000 ft., and also in ravines in the SAHÁRANPUR SIWALIKS, *e.g.*, Bádsháhibágh, Dholkhand and Ráni ráus. Always in shady moist localities.

Often cultivated in gardens for its flower and deep-green glossy foliage.

Fl. Feb.-Apr. Fr. Apr.-June.

4. Adhatoda, Nees ; G. P. n. 98.

1. **A. Vasica,** Nees ; Fl. Br. Ind. iv. 540 ; Gamble Man. Ind. Timb. 523 ; Brandis Ind. Trees 498. Vern. *Bánsá*, Dún ; *Arúsá*, Hind. ; *Vásiká*, Sans.

An evergreen and gregarious shrub with a fotid smell. *Leaves* 4-8 by 1·5-3 in., lanceolate or elliptic, acute at both ends, minutely pubescent especially when young ; lateral nerves 8-12 pairs ; petiole 1-1·5 in. *Inflorescence* a dense short-pedunculate bracteate spike, 2-4 in. long. *Bracts* ·7 by ·5 in., ovate or obovate, sessile ; bracteoles, ·7 by ·2 in. *Calyx* ·3-·5 in. long, deeply 5-lobed ; lobes equal, lanceolate. *Corolla-tube* ·3-·5 in. broad, white, lower portion short and barrel-shaped ; lower lip with two lines of oblique purple bars. *Stamens* 2 ; filaments dilated ; anther-cells acute at the apex, scarcely spurred at the base. *Capsule* ·7 in., clavate, longitudinally channelled, pubescent, 4-seeded ; seeds ·2 in. long, glabrous, tubercled.

Exceedingly common in the SIWALIK DIVISION and also found in JAUNSAR in valleys up to 4,000 ft.,—generally in moist or shady localities, and everywhere remarkably gregarious.

The leaves are considered valuable in Hindu medicine as a specific for cough and asthma. They are mixed with manure in the Punjab, presumably to keep off injurious insects. The flowers are used as a medicine for asthma and ophthalmia. The wood is white, moderately hard and very even-grained. It is used for gunpowder charcoal, and is turned into beads in Bengal. Every part of the plant is exceedingly bitter. Horses seem to be fond of the leaves.

Fl. Dec.-Apr. Fr. Feb.-May.

Among other plants of this large and widely diffused Family, the following deserve mention :—

1. *Petalidium barlerioides*, Nees ; Fl. Br. Ind. iv. 416 ;—is an undershrub, but occasionally fairly tall. *Leaves* 2-4 in. long, acuminate, crenate, grey-pubescent. *Flowers* subsessile, solitary or crowded, 1 in. long, yellowish-white. *Stamens* 4, didynamous

Capsule ·5 in. long, compressed. Not uncommon along the banks of the Jumná, *e.g.*, near Ambári. Fl. Mar.-May.—*G. P. n. 19.*

2. *Dædalacanthus nervosus*, T. Anders.; Fl. Br. Ind. iv. 418.—*Leaves* often 8 by 4 in., ovate acuminate, obscurely crenulate, glabrous. *Flowers* 1·5 in. long, blue, glabrous, in compound bracteate spikes; *corolla-tube* long and narrow; *stamens* 2. Common in the EASTERN DÚN and elsewhere, up to 3,000 ft. Fl. Feb., Mar.—*G. P. n. 23.*

3. *Barleria cristata*, Linn.; Fl. Br. Ind. iv. 488. A diffuse undershrub, yellow-hairy. *Leaves* 3-4 by 1 in., elliptic, entire, yellow-hairy beneath. *Flowers* 1·5 in. long, purple-blue or white. *Sepals* in 2 pairs, outer pair much the larger, toothed, spinescent. Fl. cold season. Common in shady places up to 3,000 ft.—*G. P. n. 84.*

4. *Barleria strigosa*, Willd.; Fl. Br. Ind. iv. 489.—*Leaves* larger than those of the preceding species, ovate, acute, long-decurrent. *Flowers* 1·5-2 in. long, blue; outer sepals 1 in., nervose, obscurely mucronate-serrulate. Fl. Cold season. Fairly common in the DÚN.

Order 9—LAMIALES.

FAM. 61. VERBENACEÆ; G. P. N. 125.

Herbs, shrubs or trees, with quadrangular stems. *Leaves* opposite or whorled, simple or digitate, very rarely pinnate; stipules none. *Flowers* irregular, rarely regular, usually bisexual, in bracteate simple or panicled cymes. *Calyx* 5-4-toothed, persistent, often enlarged in fruit, sometimes coloured. *Corolla* gamopetalous, more or less oblique, 2-lipped or subequally 4-5-lobed. *Stamens* usually 4, rarely more or fewer, didynamous or rarely equal. *Ovary* superior, 2-carpellary, 2-4-celled, with usually 1 ovule in each cell; style terminal; stigma usually 2-lobed. *Fruit* a dry or fleshy drupe with 1-4 one-seeded pyrenes or a 1-4-celled endocarp, rarely a 4-seeded capsule; seeds exalbuminous.

Analysis of the Genera.

Corolla regular, stamens equal;
- Calyx not accrescent; drupe with 4 one-celled pyrenes . . . . 1. CALLICARPA.
- Calyx much accrescent; drupe with a 4-celled endocarp . . . . 2. TECTONA.

Corolla 2-lipped, 5- or 4-lobed; stamens didynamous.
- Drupe with 1 pyrene.
  - Leaves simple.
    - Flowers very small, white. . . . 3. PREMNA.
    - Flowers large, yellow. . . . . 4. GMELINA.
  - Leaves digitate (flowers less than ·5 inch) . . . . 5. VITEX.
- Drupe with 4 pyrenes; leaves simple.
  - Drupe succulent; calyx usually coloured and enlarged in fruit . 6. CLERODENDRON.
  - Drupe dry; calyx not enlarged in fruit.
    - Calyx broadly salver-shaped, scarcely lobed, coloured. . . . . 7. HOLMSKIOLDIA.
    - Calyx small turbinate, deeply 5-lobed, not coloured . . . . . 8. CARYOPTERIS.

1. Callicarpa, Linn.; G. P. n. 37.

1. **C. macrophylla,** Vahl; Fl. Br. Ind. iv. 568; Brandis For. Flora 368, Brandis Ind. Trees 512; Gamble Man. Ind. Timb. 525. Vern. *Daiá*, Dún and Garhwal.

A shrub with straggling branches; extremities thickly woolly-tomentose. *Leaves* 6-10 in. long, ovate or ovate-lanceolate, acuminate, closely crenate, glabrescent above, thickly cottony-tomentose beneath; lateral nerves 12-15 pairs; petiole ·3-·5 in. *Inflorescence* a dense-flowered globose axillary compound cyme. *Flowers* small, pale rose-coloured. *Calyx* ·05 in., minutely 4-lobed. *Corolla* tubular, regular, 4-lobed, about ·1 in. long. *Stamens* 4, equal; anthers small, exserted. *Ovary* 4-celled. *Drupe* white, with 4 one-celled pyrenes, spongy-succulent outside when fully ripe.

Swampy localities in the DÚN, *e.g.*, Nakraunda, Misirwála, Káluwála, Khairi, and ravines along the base of the HIMALAYA.

Wood soft. The heated leaves are applied as a remedy or relief in rheumatism by villagers.

Fl. Rainy season. Fr. Cold season.

2. Tectona, Linn. f.; G. P. n. 40.

1. **T. grandis,** Linn. f.; Fl. Br. Ind. iv. 570; Brandis For. Flora 354, Ind. Trees 505; Gamble Man. Ind. Timb. 526. The Teak. Vern. *Sáigún*, Hind.

A large deciduous tree often fluted near the base; bark thin, fibrous, light-brown or grey, peeling off in long thin strips; branchlets quadrangular and deeply channelled, with a large white pith. *Leaves* opposite, simple, 12-24 by 10-12 in., gradually becoming smaller and bract-like in the inflorescence, ovate elliptic or obovate, acute or bluntly acuminate, rounded or shortly cuneate and sometimes decurrent at the base, entire, thickly coriaceous, glabrescent and rough above, stellately soft-tomentose beneath; lateral nerves 8-12 pairs, compound; secondary nerves transverse; petiole 1·5-2·5 in. long, stout, flattened above, sometimes narrowly margined. *Inflorescence* a large dicho- or trichotomously branched cyme-bearing bracteate terminal panicle 2-3 ft. long. *Flowers* regular, bracteolate, sweet-scented. *Calyx* 6-lobed, stellate-pubescent, globose in bud, salver-shaped and ·15 in. across in open flowers, much accrescent globose membranous and about 1 by ·8 in. in fruit. *Corolla* rotate, generally 6-lobed, slightly pubescent; tube very short, *Stamens* 6, inserted on the mouth of the corolla-tube; filaments ·1-·15 in. long, white. *Ovary* densely hairy; style slightly exceeding the stamens. *Drupe* ·5-·6 in. diam., globose, covered with a dense felt of branched hairs and enveloped by the inflated and loosely fitting enlarged calyx; endocarp very hard, 4-celled. *Seeds* 1-4, obovoid.

Indigenous in CENTRAL and SOUTHERN INDIA and in BURMA. Cultivated in DEHRA DÚN and SAHÁRANPUR, but young plants suffer much from frost in these parts.

Wood moderately hard, strongly scented, dark golden-yellow when freshly cut, turning dark-brown afterwards; annual rings distinct; medullary rays moderately broad, fairly numerous; weight 35 to 50 lbs. per c. ft. Taken all round teak is by far the best timber in India and perhaps also in the world, being capable of use for almost all conceivable purposes. It is in great demand for ship-building and railway-cars throughout the world, and consequently has a much larger export trade than any other Indian timber. An oil is extracted from the wood, which, rubbed on inferior timbers, increases their durability. The leaves are used for thatching and also for wrapping up parcels.

Leafless Dec.-Apr. Fl. Aug., Sept. Fr. Cold season, but remaining long on the tree.

3. Premna, Linn.; G. P. n. 42.

Trees or shrubs. *Leaves* opposite, simple, entire or toothed. *Cymes* terminal, panicled or corymbose; bracts small. *Flowers* often polygamous, greenish- or yellowish-white. *Calyx* 2-lipped or campanulately truncate or 2-5-toothed, often enlarged in fruit. *Corolla* short, tubular; limb 2-lipped. *Stamens* 4, more or less didynamous. *Ovary* 2- or 4-celled, 4-ovuled. *Drupe* small, globose or ovoid, supported by the persistent calyx; endocarp undivided, 1-4 celled, 1-4-seeded.

Analysis of the Species.

Leaves short-petioled; calyx 5-toothed, much enlarged in fruit. . . . . . 1. *P. latifolia.*
Leaves long-petioled; calyx-4-toothed, not enlarged in fruit. . . . . . 2. *P. barbata.*

1. **P. latifolia,** Roxb.; Fl. Br. Ind. iv. 577; Brandis For. Flora 266, Ind. trees 511; Gamble Man. Ind. Timb. 536. Vern. *Bakár,* Dún; *Bakárchá,* Garhwal.

A small tree with greyish-white bark. *Leaves* 3-5 by 2-3 in., ovate, cuneate or rounded, less frequently shallowly cordate and then slightly decurrent at the base, acuminate, undulate, usually entire, softly pubescent, ashy-grey beneath; lateral nerves 7 pairs; petiole ·3-·8 in. *Corymb* villous. *Calyx* ·08 in., in fruit up to ·2 in. *Corolla* about ·15 in., throat hairy. *Drupe* ·16 in., globose, black when dry.

Var. *mucronata,* Roxb.—differs from the type in having leaves with a cuneate base and longer acumen, corymbs rather flat-topped, and drupes more verrucose. It attains a considerable size in damp localities.

The type is not found in the region of this Flora, but the variety is fairly common in the outskirts of Sál forests in the DÚN, and also in the scrub forests of the SAHÁRANPUR DISTRICT, and low valleys in the HILLS: Phándowála, Lachiwála, Ambári; Ránipur; Bámsu Depôt, etc.

Wood moderately hard, light-purple or pink when freshly cut, considered a good fuel and is used to obtain fire by friction; weight 38-43 lbs. per c. ft.

Leafless Feb.-Apr. Fl. Apr.-June. Fr. Cold season.

2. **P. barbata,** Wall.; Fl. Br. Ind., iv. 579; Brandis For. Flora. 367, Ind. trees 511; Gamble Man. Ind. Timb. 535; Vern. *Bakár*, Dún; *Bakárchá*, Garhwal.

A small tree with grey bark. *Leaves* 5-6 by 2·5-3·5 in., oblong or ovate, acuminate, rounded or subcordate at the base, usually distinctly but very distantly toothed above the middle, softly pubescent when young, afterwards glabrescent; lateral nerves 6 pairs; petiole 1-2 in. long. *Corymbs* 1-2·5 in. diam., glabrate in fruit. *Calyx* ·08 in. long, 4-toothed; teeth obtuse, not enlarged in fruit. *Corolla* ·1-·2 in. long, 2-lipped, hairy in the throat. *Drupe* ·2 in., globose, obscurely verrucose.

OUTER HIMALAYA, up to 5,000 ft.: Jharipáni, Rájpur, Kálsi, etc. Also in the SIWALIK TRACT, *e.g.*, Timli Pass.

Fl. Apr., May. Fr. Cold season.

P. herbacea, Roxb.; Fl. Br. Ind. iv. 581, is a small inconspicuous undershrub, produced annually from woody rootstocks after the jungle fires. *Leaves* sessile, 4 by 2-3 in., cuneate or obovate, serrate- pubescent. *Flowers* greenish-white, 4-lobed. *Drupe* ·25 in. diam., globose. Grass-lands in the DÚN, *e.g.*, Sabháwála.

4. Gmelina, Linn.; G. P. n. 45.

1. **G. arborea,** Linn.; Fl. Br. Ind. iv. 581; Brandis For. Flora. 364, Ind. Trees 509; Gamble Man. Ind. Timb. 537. Vern. *Gamhár, Gumhár, Gambhár, Kumhár, Khamhár*, Hind.

A middle-sized or large deciduous tree; bark grey or greyish-brown, smooth, exfoliating in scurfy flakes; branchlets with white pecks. *Leaves* 4-8 by 3-6 in., broad-ovate, cordate with a shortly-cuneate glandular base, acute or acuminate, entire, finely tomentose and glaucous beneath; lateral nerves 6-10 pairs, straight, the lowest pair sub-basal and penniveined with 4-6 strong secondary nerves on either side; intermediate nerves straight, transverse with the main nerves; petiole 3-6 in., obscurely channelled above. (The leaves somewhat resemble those of *Trewia nudiflora*, Linn., which, however, are glabrous and have 5 arcuate basal nerves, besides other differences.) *Inflorescence* a terminal panicle with opposite decussate cymose branches. *Calyx* ·2 in. *Corolla* 1-1·5 in. long, 2-lipped oblique, brownish-yellow, densely soft-tomentose outside; lobes 5 or 4. *Stamens* 4, didynamous. *Ovary* 4-celled, 4-ovuled; style slender, unequally bifid. *Drupe* ovoid or oblong, ·7-1 in. long; pericarp leathery, shining, yellow outside when ripe; endocarp bony, embedded in an aromatic sweetish pulp; seeds usually 1 to 3, lenticular, ·2-·3 in. long.

Occasional in mixed forests in the DÚN, in shady localities in those of SAHÁRANPUR, and in the Lower HILLS and up to 4,000 ft. in valleys in the HIMALAYAS.

Wood yellowish- or greyish-white, close- and even-grained, soft, light, but strong and durable, does not warp or split, and takes a fine glossy polish; weight 30-40 lbs. per c. ft.; no distinct heart-wood. It is excellent for carpentry, but is little used in the DÚN. Valued for posts and boat-making in ASSAM and for drums in the CENTRAL PROVINCES. The fruit, root and bark are used in Hindu medicine, the former being also edible.

Fls. with new leaves in Mar., Apr. Fr. May, June.

5. Vitex, Linn.; G. P. n. 46.

1. **V. Negundo,** Linn.; Fl. Br. Ind. iv. 583; Brandis For. Flora. 369, Ind. Trees 503; Gamble Man. Ind. Timb. 539. Vern. *Shimálú, Sumálú, Chhátimal, Nishinda,* Dún; *Sonái,* Jaunsar; *Mallá,* Sahåranpur.

A deciduous shrub with thin grey bark and spreading branches. *Leaves* 3-5-foliolate (simple and more distinctly crenate on luxuriant young shoots), with a raised line across the stem at the base of the petioles. *Leaflets* lanceolate, 1-5 by ·3-1·3 in., the lowest pair smallest, sessile or subsessile, the middle pair, if present, more or less distinctly petiolulate, the odd leaflet largest and with a petiolule ·3-·6 in. long, entire or distantly crenate above the middle, glabrescent above, grey-pubescent beneath. *Panicles* up to 12 in. long. *Calyx* ·1-·15 in., 5-toothed. *Corolla* ·2-·5 in., bluish- or purplish-white; limb spreading, 2-lipped, 5-lobed, middle lobe of the lower lip the largest. *Stamens* 4, didynamous, exserted. *Ovary* 2-4-celled, 4-ovuled; style filiform, shortly 2-lobed. *Fruit* a succulent drupe supported by the more or less accrescent calyx, ·15-·25 in. diam., globose, black when ripe; endocarp normally 4-celled.

Common throughout the SIWALIK DIVISION, and planted in hedge-rows in villages. Also in valleys in the HILLS.

The roots and leaves are used in Hindu medicine, and the branches and twigs for basket-making.

Fl. June-Aug. Fr. Cold season.

There seem to be two distinct forms of this species,—one as described above, and the other a somewhat smaller shrub, with leaves more generally crenate, and panicles, flowers and drupes generally much smaller. This latter flowers later, and is perhaps more common about DEHRA. Is this var. *incisa*, Lam.?

6. Clerodendron, Linn.; G. P. n. 49.

Shrubs or small trees, rarely herbs. *Leaves* simple, opposite or whorled. *Calyx* 5-toothed or lobed, usually enlarged in fruit and coloured. *Corolla-tube* slender; limb spreading, 2-lipped or more or less obliquely 5-lobed. *Stamens* 4, often long-exserted. *Ovary* 4-celled, with 1 ovule in each cell; style filiform, bifid at the apex. *Fruit* a dry or succulent drupe, often lobed.

Analysis of the Species.

Corolla-tube less than 1 in. long.
  Leaves subsessile, narrow . . . . 1. *C. serratum.*
  Leaves long-petioled, broad . . . . 2. *C. infortunatum.*
Corolla-tube 3-4 in. long (leaves subsessile,
  very narrow) . . . . 3. *C. Siphonanthus.*

1. **C. serratum,** Spreng.; Fl. Br. Ind. iv. 592; Brandis For. Flora 364, Ind. Trees 508; Gamble Man. Ind. Timb. 543. Vern. *Baul ákri*, Jaunsar.

A shrub with annual shoots from a thick woody rootstock. *Leaves* opposite or in whorls of 3, 4-8 by 1·5-2·5 in., oblong elliptic-oblong or oblanceolate, serrate, smooth, puberulous or glabrate; base cuneate; petiole 0-·2 in. long. *Flowers* bluish-white, in terminal panicles; bracts ·5-1·5, obovate or lanceolate, often coloured; pedicels 0-·25 in. *Calyx* cup-shaped, ·2 in. long, shortly 5-lobed. *Corolla-tube* ·3-·5 in. long, narrow-cylindrical, slightly constricted at the neck; hairy within; mouth oblique, 2-lipped; lobes ·3-·5- in., oblong. *Stamens* hairy at the base. *Drupe* ·3 in. diam., black; pyrenes up to 4.

TEHRI-GARHWAL, 3,-5,000 ft., generally on grassy hill-sides and fire-traces: Thadiár, Bámsu, Moltá, Sendrá, etc.

Fl. May-Aug. Fr. Sept.-Nov.

2. **C. infortunatum,** Gærtn.; Fl. Br. Ind. iv. 594; Brandis For. Flora 363, Ind. Trees 507; Gamble Man. Ind. Timb. 543. Vern. *Karú*, Dún; *Bhant*, Hind.

A deciduous shrub up to 12 ft. high; bark with large grey raised corky lenticels; every part of the plant very bitter and with a fetid smell. *Leaves* opposite, 4-9 by 3-6 in., broad-ovate, acuminate, sometimes slightly cordate, entire or obscurely denticulate, roughly hairy above, tomentose or thinly hairy beneath; petiole 1-6 in. *Panicles* terminal, hairy; branches and calyx reddening in fruit. *Calyx* deeply 5-cleft; lobes lanceolate, ·3-·4 in. in flower but ·8-1 in. deep-red and leathery in fruit. *Corolla* white, tinged with red; tube cylindrical ·7-·9 in. long; lobes elliptic, acute, ·3-·5 in. long. *Stamens* exceeding the corolla-lobes. *Drupe* fleshy, somewhat tetragonal, rather depressed, bluish-black when ripe, enclosed in the accrescent leathery calyx.

Very common as an undershrub in Sál areas in the SIWALIK DIVISION, where the leaf-canopy is not open enough for grass.

The bitter leaves and bark are used in country medicine.

Fl. Jan.-Apr. Fr. Rainy season.

3. **C. Siphonanthus,** Br.; Fl. Br. Ind. iv. 595; Brandis For. Flora 364, Ind. Trees 508; Gamble Man. Ind. Timb. 543. Vern. *Chingári*, Dún.

A shrub 4-8 ft. high, with herbaceous fluted hollow stems. *Leaves* in whorls of 3-5, 6-9 by 1-1·5 in., narrow-lanceolate, sub-entire, glabrous, rather hard; petiole 0-·2 in. *Flowers* white fading into yellow, in rigid terminal panicles 9-18 in. long; pedicels ·5-1·5 in. *Calyx* ·5 in. long, dark-red and enlarged in fruit; segments oblong, acute. *Corolla-tube* 3-4 by ·2 in., drooping; lobes ·5-·7 in. long, obovate-oblong. *Drupe* ovoid, dark-blue, about ·5 in. long, supported by the spreading red calyx.

Fairly common in grass-lands in the DÚN: Ráipur, Lachiwála, Rámgarh, Dehra, etc. Often cultivated in gardens for its flower.

Sections of the hollow stem are tied round the neck in BENGAL as a charm against various ailments.

Fl. July, Aug. Fr. Cold season.

7. Holmskioldia, Retz.; G. P. n. 50.

1. **H. sanguinea,** Retz.; Fl. Br. Ind. iv. 596; Brandis For. Flora 370, Ind. Trees 506; Gamble Man. Ind. Timb. 544. Vern. *Rithout*, E. Dún; *Kápni*, Hind.

A large straggling shrub. *Leaves* opposite, 3-4 by 2-3 in., ovate, acuminate, generally crenate, pubescent; main lateral nerves about 6 pairs; base truncately cuneate; petiole ·5-1·2 in. long. *Calyx* ·7-1 in. across, salver-shaped, membranous, red-orange, entire or with a wavy margin. *Corolla-tube* ·6-1 in. long, cylindrical, curved, bright-red; limb unequally 5-lobed. *Stamens* 4, didynamous; filaments glabrous; anthers exserted. *Ovary* 4-celled, 4-ovuled;

style shortly bifid, glabrous. *Drupe* ·2-·3 in. long, obovoid, deeply 4-lobed at the apex; seeds 1-4, oblong.

Outer slopes and foot of the HIMALAYA and shady ravines in the DÚN: Tháno, Kálimatti, Ráipur, etc.; also passes in the DÚN side of the SIWALIKS. Cultivated in gardens at DEHRA.

Fl. Oct.-Dec.

8. Caryopteris, Bunge; G. P. n. 52.

Spreading shrubs; extremities pubescent or tomentose. *Leaves* opposite, simple, acuminate, minutely gland-dotted. *Cymes* small, dense, axillary or running into a terminal thyrsus; bracts small. *Flowers* light-mauve, generally pubescent. *Calyx* 5-fid; segments somewhat accrescent in fruit. *Corolla-tube* short; limb spreading, 2-lipped, middle lobe of the lower lip largest, much crisped. *Stamens* 4, didynamous; anthers exserted. *Ovary* 4-celled, 4-ovuled; style filiform, usually much exserted, shortly bifid. *Fruit* a small globose capsule; valves 4, induplicate, 1-seeded; seeds oblong, erect.

Analysis of the Species.

Cymes mostly in terminal thyrsus; calyx-segments in fruit lanceolate, erect, ribbed . 1. *C. Wallichiana.*

Cymes mostly axillary and corymbose; calyx-segments in fruit triangular, spreading, not ribbed . . . . 2. *C. grata.*

1. **C. Wallichiana,** Schauer; Fl. Br. Ind. iv. 597; Brandis For. Flora 370, Ind. Trees 512; Gamble Man. Ind. Timb. 544. Vern. *Chingári, Karui,* Dún.

A large shrub with quadrangular branches; bark peeling off in long papery strips; young shoots grey-pubescent. *Leaves* up to 4 by 1·5 in., narrow-elliptic or lanceolate, acuminate, toothed or nearly entire, puberulous; base cuneate; petiole ·3-·5 in. *Flowers* sweet-scented, light-mauve, in dense axillary cymes forming thyrsus at the ends of the branches. *Calyx* deeply 5-lobed; lobes in fruit erect, lanceolate, ribbed. *Corolla-tube* ·2-·3 in. long; lobes slightly larger than the tube, the lower middle one bluish, others white. *Style* more than twice the length of the corolla. *Fruit* ·2 in. long, globose, densely pubescent.

Common in ravines and on waste lands in the DÚN and LOWER HILLS; up to Saiá in JAUNSAR.

Fl. Mar., Apr. Fr. May, June.

2. **C. grata,** Benth.; Fl. Br. Ind. iv. 597. Brandis Ind. Trees 512; Gamble Man. Ind. Timb. 544.

A rambling shrub; branches brown-pubescent. *Leaves* 3-5 by 1-1·8 in., those near the cymes much smaller, elliptic, acuminate, crenate-serrate or subentire, pubescent; lateral nerves about 8 pairs in the larger leaves; base rhomboid or almost rounded; petiole ·3-·6 in. *Cymes* mostly axillary, densely rusty-pubescent, dichotomously corymbose, few-flowered. *Calyx* membranous, pubescent, triangular in fruit, not ribbed. *Corolla* about ·3 in. long, faintly bluish, pubescent, glandular. *Style* about twice the length of the corolla. *Capsule* ·15-·2 in. diam., globose, slightly ribbed, nearly glabrous.

JAUNSAR and TEHRI-GARHWAL, up to 5,000 ft.—Jharipáni below Mussoorie, Sáinji; Chátrágádh, Khúnigádh, etc.

Fl. Jan.-Apr. Fr. May-July.

The following plants belonging to this Family deserve notice :—

1. *Lantana Camara,* Linn.; Fl. Br. Ind. iv. 562;—is a small weedy shrub with recurved prickles on the branches, apparently wild and found in hedges in DEHRA. *Leaves* opposite, simple, up to 3 in. long, rugose. *Flowers* about ·5 in. long, sweet-scented, in peduncled capitate spikes which are 1-1·5 in. diam. *Corolla-tube* pink or red; lobes orange or yellow. *Drupe* purple when ripe. Fl. Rainy season. —*G. P. n. 18.*

2. *Lantana indica,* Roxb.; Fl. Br. Ind. iv. 562;—is very similar in appearance and found in the same places, but has no recurved prickles, and the flowers are smaller and not so strongly scented. *Corolla* pink, red, yellow or white. Fl. Rainy season.

3. *Verbena bonariensis,* Linn.; Fl. Br. Ind. iv. 565;—is another weed which is a native of Brazil, but is found near Mothronwala in the DÚN. *Leaves* sessile, 3-4 by ·5-·6 in., nervose, serrate. *Flower-spikes* in terminal corymbs. Fl. Aug., Sept.—*G. P. n. 26.*

FAM. 62. LABIATÆ; G. P. N. 126.

Herbs, rarely shrubs, usually with aromatic oil-glands; stem quadrangular. *Leaves* opposite or whorled; stipules none. *Flowers* irregular, in whorls which are either simple, or in simple or panicled spikes. *Calyx* persistent, sometimes enlarged in fruit, 4-5-lobed or 2-lipped. *Corolla* 4-5-lobed or 2-lipped; lobes imbricate in bud. *Stamens* 4, didynamous, the upper pair sometimes imperfect. *Disk* prominent. *Ovary* 4-lobed, 4-celled; ovules solitary in each cell, erect; style gynobasic, simple; stigma usually 2-fid. *Fruit* of 4 usually, dry 1-seeded nutlets included in the persistent calyx.

A family of very little forest importance in India, but containing many herbaceous plants of value for food, medicine, perfume, etc.

Analysis of the Genera.

Whorls of flowers in terminal panicled spikes; calyx not reticulate.
- Calyx-teeth long, feathery in fruit; nutlets hairy . . . . 1. COLEBROOKIA.
- Calyx-teeth short, naked; nutlets shining, tubercled . . . . . . 2. ELSHOLTZIA.

Whorls of flowers simple, axillary; calyx strongly reticulate; nutlets smooth . 3. ROYLEA.

1. Colebrookia, Smith; G. P. n. 25.

1. **C. oppositifolia,** Smith; Fl. Br. Ind. iv. 642; Brandis Ind. Trees 515; Gamble Man. Ind. Timb. 547. Vern. *Bindá, Bindú,* Dún and Garhwal; *Lúlri, Bambher,* Jaunsar; *Kálá Bánsá, Bintálakri,* Saháranpur.

A hoary shrub, under favourable circumstances up to 20 ft. high, with grey bark. *Leaves* opposite, 4-10 by 1·5-3 in., oblong-elliptic, acuminate, crenate, softly tomentose; lateral nerves 12-15 pairs, arcuate; petiole ·5-1 in., stout, white-felted. *Spikes* 2-4 in. long, in many-branched panicles, very numerous, hoary in fruit. *Flowers* about ·1 in. long, in congested clusters at varying distances on the rachis. *Calyx* very small, villous; tube much grooved; lobes elongated and feathery in fruit. *Corolla* white; lobes rounded. *Stamens* 4, usually exserted; anther-lobes round. *Style* 2-fid; lobes subulate. *Nutlets* usually only one, hairy, obovoid.

Common along ravines and raus in the SIWALIK DIVISION; also in low valleys in JAUNSAR and the OUTER HIMALAYA, up to 4,500 ft.: Silgádh, Binálgádh; Sansárú-Khálá; Bádsháhibágh, etc.

The wood weighs 46 lbs. per c. ft. It is used for gunpowder charcoal. The leaves are applied on wounds and sores.

Fl. Jan., Feb. The fruit-spikes remain long on the plants, almost throughout the year.

2. Elsholtzia, Willd.; G. P. n. 27.

1. **E. polystachya,** Benth.; Fl. Br. Ind. iv. 643; Brandis Ind. Trees 516; Gamble Man. Ind. Timb. 547. Vern. *Pathoi, Pothá*, Jaunsar.

A shrub up to 8 ft. in height, with grey fibrous bark which peels off in long strips. *Leaves* opposite, 3-6 in. long, elliptic-lanceolate, acuminate, serrate or crenate, pubescent, subsessile or minutely petioled. *Flowers* minute, spicate. *Spikes* 4-10 in. long, flowering ·3 in. diam., narrower in fruit, strongly aromatic. *Fruiting calyx* tubular, ribbed, ·1 in. long; teeth 5, erect, triangular. *Corolla* white, pubescent; limb 4-fid. *Stamens* 4, exserted, divergent. *Style* subequally 2-fid. *Nutlets* oblong.

Fairly common in JAUNSAR and TEHRI-GARHWAL, up to 9,500 ft., associated with *Indigoferas* in open grassy slopes.

Fl. Aug.-Oct. Fr. Cold season, but remains long on the plant.

3. Roylea, Wall.; G. P. n. 110.

1. **R. elegans,** Wall.; Fl. Br. Ind. iv. 679; Brandis Ind. Trees 515; Gamble Man. Ind. Timb. 548. Vern. *Karánoi*, Jaunsar; *Titpáti*, Garhwal.

A woody undershrub with grey bark. *Leaves* opposite, 1-2 in. long, ovate, crenately toothed, tomentose beneath; petiole about ·2 in. long. *Flowers* in 6-10-flowered axillary whorls. *Calyx* 5-lobed, 10-ribbed, rigid. *Fruiting calyx* ·5-·7 in. long; lobes as long as the tube. *Corolla* ·5 in., white with a touch of pink, 2-lipped; upper lip erect, lower spreading; tube narrow. *Stamens* 4, ascending. *Stigma* subequally 2-lipped. *Nutlets* ·1 in. long, obovoid-oblong, smooth.

OUTER HIMALAYA, JAUNSAR and TEHRI-GARHWAL, up to 5,000 ft.: Málkōt, Rájpur; Saiá, Dhárágádh; Thadiár, etc.

The leaves, which are extremely bitter, are used as a febrifuge by the Jaunsaris.

Fl. Mar., Apr. Fr. Apr., May.

The Túlsi plant (*Ocimum sanctum*, Linn.), the Common Mint. Vern. *Pudiná*, Hind. (*Mentha sativa*, Linn.), and Peppermint (*M. piperita*, Linn.) belong to this Family. They are cultivated in gardens in SAHÁRANPUR and the DÚN, and also found wild, probably as escapes, *e.g.*, *Pudiná* at Sahansra-dhárá, and *Túlsi* at Rikhikesh and Kasúmri.

The following plants also deserve mention :—

1. *Plectranthus rugosus*, Wall., Fl. Br. Ind. iv. 620 ; Vern. *Chichli*, Jaunsar ;—is a small shrub very common on bare hill-sides throughout the HILLS, about 4,-7,000 ft. *e.g.*, Bámsu, Dhárágádh, the Sacred Forest at Kōti, etc. *Leaves* ·5-1 in. long, ovate, crenate, rugose. *Flowers* bluish or purplish-white.—*G. P. n. 11.*

2. *Plectranthus ternifolius*, Don, Fl. Br. Ind. iv. 621 ;—is a rigid shrub 5-6 ft. high, found at Karwápáni, Lachiwála, etc., in the DÚN, also at Nonai in TEHRI-GARHWAL (*Mr. J. S. Gamble*). *Leaves* 4-6 by 1-1·3 in., lanceolate, densely tomentose ; regularly serrate ; petiole ·1-·2 in. *Flowers* white outside, sessile, in dense long white villous panicles.

3. *Pogostemon plectranthoides*, Desf.; Fl. Br. Ind. iv. 632 ;—is a gregarious bush having a strong mint-like smell ; stems dark purple, with a large pith. *Leaves* 3-7 by 1·5-3 in., ovate, acuminate, doubly serrate, membranous, pubescent ; lateral nerves very arching ; petiole 1-3 in. long. *Flowers* white or pink, in large terminal panicled bracteate spikes. Common in shady ravines in the DÚN, *e.g.*, Kánsráo, Thåno, etc. The smell of the bruised leaves is said to cure ague. Fl. Rainy season.—*G. P. n. 23.*

4. *Pogostemon parviflorus*, Benth. ; Fl. Br. Ind. iv. 632 ; closely resembles the above, but is usually a smaller plant, less hairy, with stems darker purple, and spikes shorter and more densely flowered. Common in ravines up to 4,000 ft. in the HILLS. The leaves are chewed and poulticed on snake-bites.—Fl. Cold season.

5. *Meriandra strobilifera*, Benth. ; Fl. Br. Ind. iv. 652 ; occurs in dry rocky places about Dúngri (6,-7,000 ft.) in JAUNSAR. *Leaves* 3-4 in. long, oblong, coriaceous, very rugose, usually with a sagittate base. *Spikes* with woody bracts in fruit.—*G. P. n. 67.*

APETALÆ.

Order 1.—CHENOPODIALES.

FAM. 63. AMARANTACEÆ; G. P. N. 130.

HERBS, rarely shrubs. *Leaves* generally alternate, exstipulate. *Flowers* small, occasionally unisexual, in spikes cymes or clusters, supported by scarious bracts and a pair of bracteoles. *Sepals* 5, scarious, persistent. *Petals* 0. *Stamens* 1-5, opposite the sepals. *Ovary* 1-celled. *Fruit* usually a utricle, rarely a berry or a capsule. *Seed* orbicular or ovate, compressed; testa crustaceous.

A weedy Family, not of much forest interest.

Analysis of the Genera.

Rambling shrubs; seeds few or many . . 1. DEERINGIA.
Erect shrubs; seed solitary . . . 2. BOSIA.

1. Deeringia, Br.; G. P. n. 1.

1. **D. celosioides,** Br.; Fl. Br. Ind. iv. 714; Brandis Ind. Trees 518; Gamble Man. Ind. Timb. 550. Vern. *Chúndri*, Dún; *Latman*, Hind.

A small shrub, very conspicuous when in fruit. *Leaves* alternate, up to 4 in. long, ovate or ovate-lanceolate, gradually diminishing in size towards the ends of the branches; base more or less rounded; petiole ·2-1 in. *Spikes* 6-12 in. long, terminal, panicled. *Flowers* ·2 in. diam., greenish-white, very shortly pedicellate. *Sepals* oblong, spreading in fruit. *Stamens* 4-5. *Fruit* a berry, ·2 in. diam., lobed, scarlet and filled with a frothy pink juice when ripe.

Common in hedges and scrub-forests in the DÚN. Young shoots and leaves are good for fodder, and are said to encourage the flow of milk in milch cows. The juice of the ripe fruit is used as a substitute for red ink.

Fl. Sept., Oct. Fr. Dec., Jan.

2. Bosia, Linn. ; G. P. n. 7.

1. **B. Amherstiana,** Hook. f.; Fl. Br. Ind. iv. 716; Brandis Ind. Trees 518; Gamble Man. Ind. Timb. 550. Vern. *Bhengoi*, Jaunsar.

A glabrous straggling shrub. *Leaves* alternate, 3-6 by 1-3 in., ovate, acute or acuminate, glabrous; base more or less acute; petiole ·2-·7 in. long. *Spikes* both axillary and terminal, never exceeding the leaves. *Flowers* ·2 in. diam., 5-merous, green, in compound racemes or spikes. *Sepals* concave. *Bracts* and *bracteoles* green, with white margins. *Stamens* 5. *Stigmas* sessile. *Fruit* a berry, ·15 in. diam., globose, crimson when ripe; seeds with a crustaceous testa.

Fairly common in the Tons Valley and other hot valleys in JAUNSAR.

The leaves dry black, and a black dye is obtained from them. The young shoots are eaten fried in ghee. The ripe berries are also eaten. Wood soft, very porous.

Fl. Apr., July. Fr. July, Oct.

Order 2.—PIPERALES.

FAM. 64. PIPERACEÆ; G. P. N. 139.

Aromatic herbs or shrubs, generally prostrate. *Leaves* alternate, simple, opposite or whorled, entire, often punctate, stipulate or exstipulate. *Flowers* in congested catkin-like spikes, supported by peltate bracts. *Perianth* 0. *Fruit* small; seeds with copious mealy albumen. *Embryo* minute.

This is a Family of no forest interest in North-Western India, but deserves mention as comprising such plants as *Piper longum*, Linn., Vern. *Pipúl*, and *P. Betle*, Linn., the well-known *Pán*. The following species are found in this part of the country:—

1. *Houttuynia cordata*, Thunb.; Fl. Br. Ind. v. 78.—A small plant with a creeping rootstock. *Leaves* broadly ovate, cordate; stipules membranous. *Bracts* over ·5 in. long, petaloid. Occasionally met with in hot damp localities in JAUNSAR and TEHRI-GARHWAL, *e.g.*, Dhármigádh, Khúnigádh, etc. Fl. Apr.-June.—*G.P. n. 3.*

2. *Piper brachystachyum*, Wall.; Fl. Br. Ind. v. 87.—A glabrous twiggy shrub with somewhat woody branches. *Leaves* 3-7 by 1-3·5 in., thin, elliptic- or ovate-lanceolate, 5-nerved; base acute; petiole ·2-·5 in. *Fruiting spikes* globose or slightly oblong, leaf-opposed; peduncles never exceeding the spikes. *Fruit* ·1 in. diam. Found in damp localities, *e.g.*, banks of the Ré-nadi, DEHRA DÚN, and Pámsu Valley in TEHRI-GARHWAL.—*G. P. n. 5.*

Order 3.—DAPHNALES.

FAM. 65. LAURACEÆ; G. P. N. 143.

Trees or shrubs, more or less aromatic. *Leaves* usually alternate, simple, exstipulate, generally entire, gland-dotted. *Flowers* 1-2-sexual, regular. *Perianth* inferior, 6-4-cleft; segments imbricate in bud; tube sometimes enlarged in fruit. *Stamens* up to 12, in 2-4 series, usually half or more wanting or reduced to staminodes; filaments flattened and often with 2 glands at the base; anthers 2-4-celled, cells opening by up-curved deciduous valves. *Ovary* superior, 1-celled; ovule solitary, pendulous. *Fruit* a 1-seeded berry or a drupe; peduncle often thickened; seed pendulous, exalbuminous.

Analysis of the Genera.

Flowers paniculate, usually bisexual; anthers of the inner stamens opening outwards.
  Fruit supported only by the base of the perianth 1. CINNAMOMUM.
  Fruit supported by the entire perianth.
    Perianth-segments spreading or reflexed, not stiffened . . . . 2. MACHILUS.
    Perianth-segments clasping the fruit and stiffened . . . . 3. PHŒBE.
Flowers umbellate, usually diœcious; anthers all opening inwards . . . . 4. LITSÆA.

1. Cinnamomum, Blume; G. P. n. 16.

1. **C. Tamala,** Fr. Nees; Fl. Br. Ind. v. 128; Brandis For. Flora 374, Ind. Trees 533; Gamble Man. Ind. Timb. 560. Vern. *Dálchini, Darchini*, Hind.; *Gúr-ándrá*, Jaunsar.

A moderate-sized tree, with thin dark-brown wrinkled bark. *Leaves* both alternate and opposite sometimes on the same twig, 4-6 by 1·5-2·5 in., ovate-oblong, acute or acuminate, 3-nerved, glabrous, shining above, pink when young. *Panicles* scarcely exceeding the leaves. *Perianth* of 6 unequal segments, silky-pubescent; lobes longitudinally ribbed, ovate-oblong, breaking off transversely about the middle in fruit. *Perfect stamens* 9, the 6 outer eglandular with 4-celled anthers opening inwards, the inner three with 2 glands at the base and 4-2-celled anthers opening outwards; innermost or fourth series of 3 short staminodes. *Ovary* free; style filiform. *Drupe* ·5 in. long, ovoid, succulent, supported by the thickened peduncle and the 6-toothed or truncate base of the perianth, black when ripe.

Occurs sporadically in damp ravines in JAUNSAR and TEHRI-GARHWAL, up to 6,000 ft.: Thadiár, Bagúr-nálá; Málkōt, etc. Very common and almost gregarious in the Mautárgádh.

The wood is moderately hard and close-grained, but is liable to split and warp; weight 39 lbs. per c. ft. The bark of the twigs is used as a substitute for the true cinnamon, which is obtained from a cogener of this tree (*C. zeylanicum*, Breyn.) and the leaves are the bay-leaves or *Tejpát* of Indian commerce.

New leaves Apr., May. Fl. Feb.-May. Fr. June-Oct., but remaining long on the tree.

The Camphor tree, *C. Camphora*, Linn.; Fl. Br. Ind. v. 134;—is cultivated for ornament in the DÚN, where it thrives well on good soil and is well worth cultivating in plantations on a commercial scale to produce camphor.

2. Machilus, Nees; G. P. n. 17.

Evergreen trees. *Leaves* alternate, penniveined. *Flowers* bisexual, in axillary and terminal panicles. *Perianth* divided to the base; segments 6, persistent but unchanged in fruit. *Stamens* as in *Cinnamomum Tamala*; anthers all 4-celled. *Berry* globose or oblong, seated on the spreading or reflexed perianth.

Analysis of the Species.

Leaves ovate-acuminate, short (fruit globose) . . . . 1. *M. Gamblei.*
Leaves ovate-lanceolate, long.
Fls. quite glabrous; fr. oblong or ellipsoid. 2. *M. odoratissima.*
Fls. silky-tomentose; fr. globose or nearly so . . . . 3. *M. Duthiei.*

1. **M. Gamblei,** King mss.; Fl. Br. Ind. v. 138, 860. Brandis Ind. Trees 531; Gamble Man. Ind. Timb. 566.

A moderate-sized tree; bark dark-grey, with even surface. *Leaves* 3-5 by 1-1·5 in., obovate to elliptic-lanceolate, acute or acuminate, entire, thinly coriaceous, glabrous and shining above, glaucous beneath; base cuneately acute; lateral nerves 8-10 pairs slender; petioles ·5 in. long, slender, glabrous or pubescent. *Panicles* terminal, lax, few-flowered. *Perianth-lobes* linear oblong, villous within. *Filaments* slender, almost glabrous; anther oblong. *Fruit* ·3 in. diam., globose, black when ripe.

Fairly common in shady and swampy localities in the DÚN: Káluwála, Rámgarh, Mothronwala, Karwápáni, etc.

Wood white, appears to be soft.

Fl. Mar., Apr. Fr. June, July.

2. **M. odoratissima,** Nees; Fl. Br. Ind. v. 139, 859; Brandis For. Flora. 378, Ind. Trees 530; Gamble Man. Ind. Timb. 565. Vern. *Káwalá,* Jaunsar; *Káulá, Kaulu,* Dún.

A middle-sized tree. *Leaves* 4-6 by 1·5-2 in., lanceolate or oblong, acuminate, dark-green and shining above, slightly glaucous beneath, impressed-punctate, lateral nerves 7-13 pairs; petiole ·5-·8 in. long. *Panicles* peduncled, shorter than the leaves. *Flowers* and *filaments* quite glabrous. *Fruit* ·5-·7 in. long, oblong or ellipsoid, purple and somewhat pruinose when ripe.

JAUNSAR, TEHRI-GARHWAL and OUTER HIMALAYAN VALLEYS, 3,000-6,500 ft.

Wood light, soft and even-grained, not much used. Weight 40 lbs. per c. ft.

Fl. Mar., Apr. Fr. May, June.

3. **M. Duthiei,** King mss.; Fl. Br. Ind. v. 861; Brandis Ind. Trees 531; Gamble Man. Ind. Timb. 567. Vern. *Káwalá, Bhojo,* Jaunsar.

A tree larger than the last species; young branches sometimes finely silky. *Leaves* 5-10 by 1·5-2·7 in., lanceolate, oblong or oblanceolate, very coriaceous, glaucous beneath; nerves 12-20 pairs, irregular; petiole ·5-1 in. *Flowers* larger than in the preceding species; perianth lobes linear-oblong, finely silky. *Filaments* glabrous. *Fruit* globose, ·5 in. diam., on thickened pedicels.

Common in shady ravines in the HILLS, 5,000-7,500 ft.

Fl. Apr., May. Fr. June, July.

In the description of the last two species I have followed the revised sketch given at the end of Vol. V of the "Flora of British India," but there are specimens in the College Herbarium which do not exactly fall under any of them. The fruit character, however, is the most reliable of all, and the trees can easily be distinguished in the forest from the colour of their foliage and the shape and general appearance of their crowns. Besides, they generally occur in somewhat different localities.

3. Phœbe, Nees; G. P. n. 18 (Persea).

1. **P. lanceolata,** Nees; Fl. Br. Ind. v. 141; Brandis For. Flora 377, Ind. Trees 532; Gamble Man. Ind. Timb. 568. Vern. *Bhadroi, Bhadeu,* Jaunsar; *Tumri,* Dún.

A small evergreen tree with yellowish-white bark. *Leaves* alternate, crowded at the ends of the branches, 5-8 by 1-2 in., narrow-lanceolate, finely or caudate-acuminate, glabrous; lateral nerves 6-10 pairs; petiole ·5-·8 in. *Flowers* 2-sexual or polygamous, in lax axillary panicles. *Perianth* cup-shaped; segments obovate, scarcely acute, pubescent within, enlarging hardening and imbricate in fruit. *Stamens* as in *Cinnamomum Tamala;* anthers all 4-celled. *Fruit* ·3-·4 in. long, narrow-ellipsoidal, black when ripe, half-buried in the enlarged calyx.

In shady damp valleys or near marshes in the DÚN: Karwápáni, Rámgarh, Kánsráo, Khairi; also up to 6,500 ft. in the HILLS, *e.g.*, Sainji, Korwá, Mussoorie, etc.

The wood is white, hard and close-grained, but does not seem to have ever been used for timber purposes. Growth fast. Weight 46-55 lbs. per c. ft.

Fl. Feb.-June. Fr. June-Sept.

4. Litsæa, Lamk.; G. P. n. 28.

Usually evergreen trees or shrubs. *Leaves* alternate, often crowded at the ends of the branches, generally penninerved. *Flowers* diœcious, in few-flowered umbels which are sessile or pedicellate, usually clustered and supported by 4-6 concave involucral bracts. *Perianth* tubular, 4-6-lobed. *Stamens* 6, less often 9 or 12, rarely more, those of the inner series with a pair of glands at the base; anthers 4-celled, all introrse. *Fruit* a drupe, seated on the much-enlarged perianth-tube, black when ripe.

Analysis of the Species.

Stamens 9 or more; lvs. penninerved throughout.
- Lvs. grey-tomentose beneath; fr. globose . 1. *L. sebifera.*
- Lvs. rusty-tomentose beneath; fr. ovoid or oblong.
  - Leaves broad; receptacle of fruit very small . 2. *L. polyantha.*
  - Leaves narrow; receptacle of fruit large . 3. *L. elongata.*

Stamens 6; lvs. 3-nerved at the base (Genus *Tetradenia*, Nees).
- Leaves 6-12 in. long, thickly coriaceous . . 4. *L. lanuginosa.*
- Leaves 3-6 in. long, thinly coriaceous . . 5. *L. umbrosa.*

1. **L. sebifera,*** Pers.; Fl. Br. Ind. v. 157; Brandis Ind. Trees 536; Gamble Man. Ind. Timb. 570. Syn.—*Tetranthera laurifolia*, Jacq.; Brandis For. Flora 379. Vern. *Chandná*, Dún; *Maidá-lakri*, Hind.

A moderate-sized evergreen tree with dark-grey soft corky bark; young parts grey-tomentose. *Leaves* 4-10 in. long, elliptic ovate oblong or lanceolate, acute or acuminate, pubescent or glabrescent above, grey-tomentose beneath, soft-coriaceous; lateral nerves 8-12 pairs; petiole ·5-1·5 in. *Umbels* ·3-·6 in. diam.; pedicels clustered on a common peduncle ·2-·3 in. long; bracts 4, rounded, tomentose. *Stamens* 9-20 or more; filaments hairy. *Fruit* about ·3 in. diam., globose, supported by the club-shaped pedicel.

Common in the DÚN and SAHÁRANPUR FORESTS, especially in shady ravines: Rámgarh, Karwápáni, Bádsháhibágh, Dholkhand, etc.

---

* According to Mr. Gamble this species ought to be called *L. chinensis*, Lamk.

Wood greyish-brown, close- and even-grained, durable, is not attacked by insects; heartwood not distinct; weight 46 lbs. per c. ft. "A fine wood worth notice."—*Mr. J. S. Gamble.* The inner bark, which is granular and viscid, is used as an external application for sprains and bruises.

Fl. Rainy season. Fr. Nov., Dec.

2. **L. polyantha,** Juss.; Fl. Br. Ind. v. 162; Brandis Ind. Trees 536; Gamble Man. Ind. Timb. 571. Syn.—*Tetranthera monopetala,* Roxb.; Brandis For. Flora 380. Vern. *Karkáwa* or *Karká,* Dún.

A moderate-sized evergreen tree with dark-grey smooth bark. *Leaves* 4-8 in. long, oblong ovate or obovate, tip acute or rounded, glabrous above, rusty-tomentose and strongly reticulate beneath; lateral nerves 5-10 pairs; petiole ·5-1 in. *Umbels* stoutly pedicelled, 5-6-flowered; bracts 5, membranous. *Stamens* 9-13; filaments hairy. *Fruit* ovoid; ·2-·3 in. long, on a small perianth-base.

Very common in scrub forests in the DEHRA DÚN and SAHÁRANPUR DISTRICTS, and in low valleys in the HILLS.

Wood of a dark-grey colour, not durable; weight 38 lbs. per c. ft. The bark is used in Indian medicine, and the leaves to feed cattle, and the Mugá silkworms in Assam.

Fl. Mar., Apr. and also irregularly throughout the year. Fr. four months after flowering.

3. **L. elongata,** Wall.; Fl. Br. Ind. v. 165; Brandis Ind. Trees 537; Gamble Man. Ind. Timb. 572.

A small tree with stout branches; branchlets rusty-tomentose. *Leaves* alternate, very variable, generally 4-5 by 1-1·5, but occasionally much longer and broader, oblong or elliptic-lanceolate, obtuse acute or acuminate, strongly reticulate and rusty-tomentose beneath; lateral nerves few or many; base generally acute; petiole stout, ·3-·5 in. long. *Umbels* 4-5-flowered, very rarely clustered; male larger than female; pedicels of varying lengths; flowers woolly. *Sepals* 4-6, obtuse. *Stamens* 8-12; filaments slender, villous. *Ovary* glabrous, rudimentary in the male fls.; style stout; stigma discoid. *Fruit* ·5 in. long, oblong, seated on a perianth-base which is ·3 in. in diam.

Shady ravines in the OUTER HIMALAYA,—along the 'Mall' at Mussoorie (*Mr. J. S. Gamble*), Sansárú Khálá in MÁLKÓT, etc. Rather rare.

Fl. Mar., Apr. Fr. June, July.

4. **L. lanuginosa,** Nees; Fl. Br. Ind. v. 178; Brandis For. Flora 382, Ind. Trees 540; Gamble Man. Ind. Timb. 573.

A moderate-sized tree with brown bark. *Leaves* crowded at the ends of the branches, 6-12 in. long, elliptic-lanceolate or oblanceolate, acute or acuminate, very tough and coriaceous, silky-hairy when young, afterwards glabrous above, glaucous beneath, strongly sub-triplinerved at the base; petiole ·3-·8 in. long. *Bracts* villous. *Umbels* in 4-fid sessile clusters nearly 1 in. in diam. *Stamens* 6; glands of inner stamens long-stalked. *Fruit* ·5 in. long, acute at both ends, seated at the thickened ends of the pedicels.

JAUNSAR and TEHRI-GARHWAL, up to 6,000 ft.; not common: Bámsu Valley, 4,000 ft. Tons Valley, 3,500 ft. Also in the Mothroṇwála swamp in the DÚN, 1,900 ft.

Wood yellow when fresh cut.

Fl. Feb., Mar. (?). Fr. Dec., Jan.

5. **L. umbrosa,** Nees; Fl. Br. Ind. v. 179; Brandis Ind. Trees 540; Gamble Man. Ind. Timb. 573. Syn.—*L. zeylanica*, Nees; Brandis For. Flora 382. Vern. *Shúrúr*, Jaunsar.

A moderate-sized evergreen tree with a spreading crown and dark-brown bark. *Leaves* alternate, 3-6 in. long, oblong elliptic or oblong-lanceolate, acute or acuminate, thinly coriaceous, glabrous above, glaucous beneath, usually sub-triplinerved at the base; petiole ·5-1·5 in. *Umbels* in small 4-5-fid sessile clusters, few-flowered. *Stamens* 6; glands sessile. *Fruit* ·3 in. diam., globose or oblong, on slender pedicels which are ·5 in. long.

Common in JAUNSAR and TEHRI-GARHWAL, 4,-7,000 ft., generally in shady forests or ravines.

Wood reddish-white, moderately hard; heartwood distinct with a darker colour; weight 36-38 lbs. per c. ft. Used for house-building in South India. An oil is extracted from the fruit, which is used for burning and is considered by the hill people as a specific for itches and other skin diseases.

Fl. Mar.-May. Fr. Sept., Oct.

FAM. 66. THYMELÆACEÆ; G. P. N. 145.

Small trees or shrubs. *Leaves* alternate or opposite, simple, entire, exstipulate. *Flowers* regular, usually 2-sexual; perianth tubular or campanulate; lobes 4-5, imbricate, sometimes with scales at the base. *Stamens* as many or twice as many as the perianth-lobes, in the latter case in two superposed series. *Ovary* superior, usually 1-celled; style long or short or 0; stigma capitate; ovule solitary, pendulous. *Fruit* indehiscent.

Analysis of the Genera.

Leaves alternate, subcoriaceous, persistent; scales and style 0 . . . . . 1. DAPHNE.
Leaves opposite and alternate, membranous, deciduous; scales and style present . 2. WIKSTRŒMIA.

1. Daphne, Linn.; G. P. n. 3.

1. **D. cannabina,** Wall.; Fl. Br. Ind. v. 193; Brandis Ind. Trees 544; Gamble Man. Ind. Timb. 577. Syn.—*D. papyracea,* Wall.; Brandis For. Flora 386. The Paper Daphne. Vern. *Dhák Chamboi, Chamua,* Jaunsar; *Satpurá,* Garhwal.

An evergreen shrub, 4-6 ft. high, with smooth grey bark. *Leaves* 2-4 in. long, oblanceolate or narrow-lanceolate, subcoriaceous, glabrous; nerves very slender, depressed above, just visible below; petiole short, marginate, channelled. *Flowers* scented, white, in sessile terminal heads, supported by oblong or lanceolate hairy bracts. *Perianth-tube* ·5-·7 in. long, slender, white-pubescent outside; lobes 4, short, acute. *Scales* 0. *Stamens* 8, in two series, one above the other. *Stigma* sessile or subsessile, capitate. *Fruit* a berry ·5-·7 in. long, ovoid, orange while ripening, deep-red or ruby when fully ripe, succulent, with a coriaceous rind.

JAUNSAR and TEHRI-GARHWAL, 4,000-9,500 ft. Very common in the Korwá and Lúrli Forests.

In Nepal and Kumaon paper is made out of the inner fibrous bark.

Fl. Mar., Apr., often also in autumn. Fr. Two months after fl.

2. Wikstrœmia, Endl.; G. P. n. 11.

1. **W. canescens,** Meissn.; Fl. Br. Ind. v. 195; Brandis Ind. Trees 545; Gamble Man. Ind. Timb. 578. Syn.—*W. virgata,* Meissn.; Brandis For. Flora 386. Vern. *Chamboi,* Jaunsar.

A small shrub with a few slender branches. *Leaves* 1-3 in., oblong-lanceolate, acute, membranous, often slightly pubescent; petiole ·1 in. long. *Flowers* white or yellowish, subsessile, in few-flowered heads, spikes or cymes. *Perianth* ·3 in. long, slender, silky outside; lobes 4. *Disk-scales* 1-4, linear. *Stamens* 8, in two series, one above the other *Style* short; stigma large. *Fruit* ·2 in. long, narrowly ovoid, silky.

JAUNSAR and TEHRI-GARHWAL, 5,-8,000 ft.: Deoban, Konáin, Mundáli, Kathián; Deotá, etc.

Fl. Apr.-June. Fr. Two months after fl.

FAM. 67. ELÆAGNACEÆ; G. P. N. 147.

Shrubs or trees with silvery or brown scales. *Leaves* usually alternate, entire, exstipulate. *Flowers* regular 1-2-sexual, in axillary fascicles or cymes. *Perianth* tubular; lobes valvate in bud. *Stamens* usually 4, epiphyllous, alternating with the perianth-lobes. *Ovary* superior, 1-celled, with a solitary erect ovule. *Fruit* indehiscent, enclosed in the accrescent perianth-tube.

Analysis of the Genera.

Fls. normally 2-sexual; perianth 4-fid . . 1. ELÆAGNUS.
Fls. 1-sexual, diœcious; perianth 2-partite or 2-fid. 2. HIPPOPHAË.

1. Elæagnus, Linn.; G. P. n. 1.

Shrubs or small trees, sometimes spinescent. *Leaves* alternate, covered with dense silvery scales beneath. *Flowers* 2-sexual or 1-sexual by abortion. *Perianth-tube* constricted above the ovary; lobes 4, valvate, deciduous. *Stamens* 4. *Fruit* with a bony or coriaceous endocarp.

Analysis of the Species.

An erect deciduous shrub ; leaves narrow ;
fruit ·3 in. long . . . . . 1. *E. umbellata.*
A straggling evergreen shrub ; leaves broad ;
fruit about 1 in. long . . . . . 2. *E. latifolia.*

1. **E. umbellata,** Thunb. ; Fl. Br. Ind. v. 201 ; Brandis For. Flora 390, Ind. Trees 547 ; Gamble Man. Ind. Timb. 580. Vern. *Giṇroi*, Jaunsar.

A thorny deciduous shrub with numerous branches, often forming a dense bush. *Leaves* 1-3 by ·3-·7 in., oblong or lanceolate, acute at both ends, clothed below with bright silvery scales, sparsely scaly or pubescent above ; nerves indistinct ; petiole ·2-·3 in. long. *Flowers* dull-white, silvery outside, appearing with the leaves, in small axillary clusters. *Perianth* ·2 in. ; lobes triangular-ovate. *Fruit* ·3 in. long, oblong-ovoid, succulent, ribbed outside.

JAUNSAR, TEHRI-GARHWAL and outer slopes of the HIMALAYA, usually 3,-7,000 ft. Between Saiá and Korwá ; below Konián ; Dhárágádh, etc.

The fruit is eaten.

Fl. Apr.-June. Fr. Rainy season.

2. **E. latifolia,** Linn. ; Fl. Br. Ind. v. 202 ; Brandis For. Flora 390, Ind. Trees 547 ; Gamble Man. Ind. Timb. 581. Vern. *Lcháru*, Garhwal.

A straggling shrub, often spiny. *Leaves* very variable, usually 3-6 by 1·5-2·5 in., ovate-oblong, acuminate, membranous, clothed beneath with silvery or ferruginous scales ; margins often slightly undulate ; lateral nerves 6-8 pairs ; petiole ·3-·4 in. long, channelled. *Flowers* few or numerous, in axillary clusters ; pedicels elongated in fruit. *Perianth-lobes* broad. *Fruit* about 1 in. long, sometimes longer, elliptic-oblong or pyriform, strongly 8-ribbed, red or yellow when ripe ; endocarp silky inside.

Mothroṇwála, Nakraunda and Lachiwála swamps, DEHRA DÚN, and possibly in similar places elsewhere.

The acid but somewhat astringent fruit is eaten by villagers.

Fl. Nov.-Feb. Fr. May, June.

2. Hippophaë, Linn. ; G. P. n. 2.

1. **H. rhamnoides,** Linn. ; Fl. Br. Ind. v. 203 ; Brandis For. Flora 388, Ind. Trees 547 ; Gamble Man. Ind. Timb. 581. Vern. *Dhurchuk, Tárwa, Chumá*, U. P.

A large thorny diœcious shrub, sometimes a small tree; bark dark-grey, rough with vertical furrows. *Leaves* alternate, ·5-2 by ·1-·3 in., subcoriaceous, glabrescent above, felted with grey or rust-coloured scales beneath. MALE FLS. in axillary clusters on the old wood; *perianth* with 2 opposite segments. FEM. FLS. axillary, solitary, pedicelled; *perianth* tubular, 2-denate. *Fruit* oblong or globose, orange or bright-scarlet when ripe, enclosed in the succulent perianth.

UPPER TONS VALLEY, TEHRI-GARHWAL: Dátmir and Oshlá; chiefly in moist gravelly stream-beds.

It is used for fuel and charcoal and the dry branches for hedges. The fruit is very acid, but boiled with sugar forms a palatable preserve.

Fl. Mar., Apr. Fr. July, Aug.

Very similar in appearance and hardly specifically different is *H. salicifolia*, Don. *Leaves* membranous, covered beneath with stellate hairs and scales. Gangottari and other places in TEHRI-GARHWAL.

Order 4.—SANTALALES.

FAM. 68. LORANTHACEÆ; G. P. N. 148.

Parasitic evergreen shrubs. *Leaves* generally opposite, exstipulate, entire, coriaceous. *Flowers* 1-2-sexual, usually bracteate. *Perianth* single or double; the outer (calyx) usually adnate to the ovary, limb truncate or 0; the inner (corolla) free or connate, valvate in bud. *Stamens* as many as, and opposite to, the lobes of the inner perianth. *Ovary* inferior, 1-celled, with usually one erect ovule. *Fruit* generally drupaceous, 1-seeded; albumen fleshy.

Analysis of the Genera.

Fls. 2-sexual, showy; style long . . . . 1. LORANTHUS.
Fls. 1-sexual, inconspicuous; style short or 0 . 2. VISCUM.

1. Loranthus, Linn.; G. P. n. 2.

Leaves generally opposite. *Flowers* 2-sexual, usually large, showy. *Calyx* adnate to the ovary; limb entire or minutely toothed. *Petals* free or more or less connate into a tube. *Stamens* epipetalous, subequal. *Style* long, stigma capitate. *Fruit* a fleshy drupe.

Analysis of the Species.

Flowers 4-merous.
  Petals free; (leaves glabrous) . . 1. *L. ligustrinus.*
  Petals connate into a tube.
    Leaves scurfy on both surfaces when young; peduncles many-flowered.
      Corolla buff or pink . . . . 2. *L. Scurrula.*
      Corolla green . . . . 3. *L. pulverulentus.*
    Leaves always glabrous above; peduncles few-flowered . . 4. *L. vestitus.*
Flowers 5-merous (leaves glabrous; petals red, connate into a tube) . . . 5. *L. longiflorus.*

1. **L. ligustrinus,** Wall.; Fl. Br. Ind. v. 207; Brandis For. Flora 395, Ind. Trees 549; Gamble Man. Ind. Timb. 582. Vern. *Bándá*, Hind.

A parasitic shrub, often apparently terrestrial. *Leaves* opposite, the upper sometimes alternate, 2-3·5 by ·6-1 in., lanceolate, thinly coriaceous, glabrous. *Flowers* ·3 in. long, rust-coloured or pale-pink outside, deep-red inside, in axillary panicles or racemes; bracts persistent. *Calyx-limb* entire. *Corolla-segments* linear, reflexed from the middle. *Ovary* rusty-tomentose. *Fruit* ovoid, ·2-·3 in. long, brown when ripe.

Occasionally met with in the DÚN FORESTS: Rámgarh, Karwárpáni, Mothronwála, etc.

Fl. May, June.

2. **L. Scurrula,** Linn.; Fl. Br. Ind. v. 208; Brandis Ind. Trees 549; Gamble Man. Ind. Timb. 582.

A very variable parasite with many distinct varieties. The following description refers to the variety found in the Siwalik Division. *Leaves* 2-4 in., opposite, ovate-oblong or obovate, young on both surfaces and old beneath scurfy or grey-tomentose; base rounded or cordate; petiole ·3-·6 in. *Flowers* ·2-1 in., very slender, usually buff outside, in axillary fascicles or short racemes; buds terete, with an acute tip. *Calyx-limb* wholly truncate. *Corolla* slightly curved, ·5-1 in. long; lobes 4, short. *Style* filiform, purple. *Fruit* ·2-·3 in., obconic.

Fairly common in the SIWALIK TRACTS.

Fl. Cold season.

Very closely allied to this is *L. cordifolius*, Wall.; Fl. Br. Ind. v. 209,—differing only in larger and more distinctly cordate leaves, and copious white tomentum; indeed some botanists suggest its being a variety of *L. Scurrula*. SUB-HIMALAYAN and SIWALIK (?) TRACTS.

3. **L. pulverulentus,** Wall.; Fl. Br. Ind. v. 211; Brandis For. Flora 396, Ind. Trees 549; Gamble Man. Ind. Timb. 582. Vern. *Parand*, Kumaon; *Bándá*, Hind.

A stout woody parasite with dark-grey bark. *Leaves* opposite, 4-6 in. long, broadly ovate or ovate-oblong, coriaceous, thickly mealy-tomentose when young; base acute or rounded; petiole ·5-·7 in. long. *Racemes* ·5-2·5 in. long, axillary, solitary or fascicled. *Flowers* 1 in. long. *Pedicels* ·2-·3 in. long, grey-scurfy outside. *Calyx-limb* 0. *Corolla* slender, tubular, curved; segments 4, linear, green. *Style* very slender. *Fruit* ·3 in. long, turbinate, grey-tomentose.

A common parasite in the DÚN and SAHÁRANPUR FORESTS. Has been found on *Butea frondosa*, *Dalbergia Sissoo* and many other trees.

Fl. Sept.-May, and probably throughout the year.

4. **L. vestitus,** Wall.; Fl. Br. Ind. v. 212; Brandis For. Flora 396, Ind. Trees 549; Gamble Man. Ind. Timb. 582. Vern., *Pand*, Hind.

A robust woody parasite. *Leaves* opposite, 2·3 by ·7-1·2 in., oblong ovate or elliptic, glabrous, deep-green and shining above; densely ferruginous-tomentose beneath; margins recurved; base acute; petiole ·2-·3 in. long. *Flowers* ·5-·7 in. long, rusty outside, in few-flowered clusters. *Calyx* distinctly toothed. *Corolla* tubular, lobes very short, obtuse; buds with a globose apex. *Fruit* ·3-·5 in. long, usually ovoid; seed imbedded in a viscid pulp.

Fairly common in JAUNSAR and TEHRI-GARHWAL and generally found on Oaks, especially *Quercus incana*; *e.g.*, at Kathián, where hardly any tree has escaped.

Fl. throughout the year, chiefly Oct.-Jan.

5. **L. longiflorus,** Desrouss.; Fl. Br. Ind. v. 214; Brandis For. Flora 397, Ind. Trees 549; Gamble Man. Ind. Timb. 583. Vern. *Pándá*, Hind.

A large woody parasite, with handsome flowers. *Leaves* opposite or alternate, 3-10 by ·5-5 in., very variable in shape, coriaceous, brittle when fresh, glabrous, young usually pink; nerves very faint; petiole ·3-·7 in. *Flowers* 1·5-2·5 in. long, scarlet or orange, sometimes tipped with green, in axillary or supra-axillary unilateral racemes which are 1-4 in. long. *Calyx-limb* truncate or with short sharp points. *Corolla* tubular, curved, somewhat swollen near the middle, split halfway down at the back; segments 5, linear. *Ovary* cylindrical or urceolate, glabrous. *Fruit* ·3-·5 in. long, oblong, black when ripe.

Extremely common, and has been found on most trees in the DÚN and SAHÁRANPUR FORESTS, ascending to 7,500 ft. in JAUNSAR and TEHRI-GARHWAL, where, however, the flowers are rather smaller and not quite so vividly coloured.

Fl. almost throughout the year but chiefly Nov.-June.

2. Viscum, Linn.; G. P. n. 3.

Parasitic shrubs with dicho- or trichotomous branches. *Leaves* opposite or wanting. *Flowers* unisexual, minute, solitary or fascicled in the axils of the leaves, or at the nodes of the branches. *Perianth-segments* 3-4, very thick, usually deciduous. *Anthers* sessile, epiphyllous, opening by many pores. *Stigma sessile*, large. *Fruit* succulent; embryos 1-2 in each seed in fleshy albumen.

Analysis of the Species.

Branches terete, leafy; flowers diœcious; berries white . . . . 1. *V. album.*
Branches flattened, leafless; flowers usually monœcious; berries pale-green or yellow.
Internodes 1-2 in., striate or furrowed; perianth-lobes deciduous . . . . 2. *V. articulatum.*
Internodes ·2-·6 in., with only a middle line or none; perianth-lobes persistent . 3. *V. japonicum.*

1. **V. album,** Linn.; Fl. Br. Ind. v. 223; Brandis For. Flora 392, Ind. Trees 552; Gamble Man. Ind. Timb. 583. The Mistletoe. Vern. *Chúlú-ká Bándá*, Jaunsar.

A large parasitic shrub, green all over; branches dichotomous or whorled. *Leaves* about 2 by ·4 in., sessile, cuneate-oblong or oblanceolate, with 3-5 longitudinal basal nerves. *Flowers* diœcious, sessile, in clusters of 3-5, supported by concave bracts. *Perianth-segments* 3-4, triangular, deciduous. *Fruit* ·2-·3 in. long, ellipsoid, white, smooth, almost transparent.

JAUNSAR and TEHRI-GARHWAL, up to 6,000 ft. (Lambátách), chiefly on Rosaceous shrubs, and on elm, walnut and willows.

It is used medicinally, and bird-lime is made of the viscid pulp of the fruit.

Fl. Mar.-May. Fr. Sept.-Nov.

2. **V. articulatum,** Burm.; Fl. Br. Ind. v. 226; Brandis Ind. Trees 552. Syn.—*V. attenuatum,* D.C.; Brandis For. Flora 394, Vern. *Budu, Pand,* Hind.

A much-branched, leafless, green parasite, greenish-yellow when dry. Main stem terete; branches flat, longitudinally striate and furrowed, contracted at the nodes, pendulous; internodes widening upwards, 1-2 in. long. *Flowers* sessile, in sessile 3-flowered spikes, two or several spikes at a joint. *Fruit* subglobose, ·15 in. long, yellow when ripe.

The SIWALIKS and OUTER HIMALAYA, up to 6,000 ft. Found on *Cordia vestita, Cornus capitata, Pyrus Pashia,* etc.

Fl. Rainy season.

3. **V. japonicum,** Thunb.; Fl. Br. Ind. v. 226; Brandis Ind. Trees 552. Syn.—*V. articulatum,* Burm.; Brandis For. Flora 393, Vern. *Pand, Báná, Bándá,* Hind.

A much-branched, small, tufted, leafless parasite. Main stem dark-grey, terete; branches flat and much contracted at the nodes, looking much like strings of beads; internodes ·2-·3 in. long, linear-cuneate, usually with a medial ridge. *Inflorescence* as in *V. articulatum. Flowers* very minute; perianth-segments 3-4, persistent. *Fruit* ·1 in. long, globose, greenish-yellow.

JAUNSAR and TEHRI-GARHWAL, up to 8,000 ft. Appears to be very partial to the Oaks, especially *Q. incana, e.g.,* at Kathián. *Rhus, Olea, Rhododendron* and Apricot trees have also been known to be attacked.

Fl. May-July. Fr. Oct., Nov.

FAM. 69. SANTALACEÆ; G. P. N. 149.

Trees, shrubs or herbs, generally parasitic on roots. *Leaves* alternate or opposite, simple, exstipulate, entire, sometimes wanting. *Flowers* regular, small, green, 1-2-sexual. *Perianth* generally superior, campanulate. *Stamens* opposite the perianth-lobes. *Ovary* usually inferior, 1-celled; placentation free-central. *Fruit* a nut or a drupe; seed globose, in copious fleshy albumen.

1. Osyris, Linn.; G. P. n. 17.

1. **O. arborea,** Wall.; Fl. Br. Ind. v. 232; Brandis For. Flora 399, Ind. Trees 554; Gamble Man. Ind. Timb. 588. Vern. *Dálmi, Dálimá,* Garhwal and Kumaon.

A fairly large twiggy shrub parasitic on roots; branchlets sharply 3-angled. *Leaves* alternate, 1-2 in. long, subsessile or with a short marginate petiole, obovate elliptic-oblong or lanceolate, mucronate. *Flowers* minute, polygamous. MALE FLS. in axillary long-peduncled clusters. FEMALE FLS. usually solitary, axillary, on slender drooping pedicels. *Perianth-lobes* conical, valvate. *Ovary* inferior; placenta very short. *Drupe* sub-globose, ·3 in. diam., glabrous, red when ripe.

Not uncommon in the OUTER HIMALAYA and in the SIWALIK TRACTS: Tháno, Málkōt, Rájpur, Saiá, near the watershed behind Ránipur, etc. Also found at Naintwár in TEHRI-GARHWAL.

Wood reddish-brown, hard, compact and close-grained.

Fl. Almost throughout the year. Fr. Chiefly cold season.

This small Family is remarkable as the one to which the Sandalwood, *Santalum album,* Linn.,—Fl. Br. Ind. v. 231, Vern. *Chandan,* Hind.,—belongs. *Leaves* opposite, 2-3 in. long, elliptic-ovate. *Flowers* small, inodorous. *Fruit* a globose drupe. This most valuable tree is indigenous in Southern India, particularly in Mysore. It has been successfully grown at DEHRA DÚN.—*G. P. n. 11.*

Order 5.—EUPHORBIALES.

FAM. 70. EUPHORBIACEÆ; G. P. N. 151.

Herbs, shrubs or trees, sometimes with milky juice. *Leaves* alternate or opposite, usually stipulate, rarely compound. *Inflorescence* various. *Flowers* generally small, always unisexual. *Perianth* usually single and calycine, rarely double or wholly wanting. *Stamens* various; anthers usually 2-celled. *Ovary* generally 3-celled, rarely 1-2- or more than 3-celled; styles as many as the carpels, free or connate, entire or divided; ovules 1 or 2 in each cell, pendulous from the inner angle of the cell. *Fruit* a capsule or a drupe, rarely a berry. *Seeds* oily, usually with a copious albumen; radicle superior; cotyledons flat.

Analysis of the Genera.

Fleshy plants with thick branches and milky juice . . . . . . 1. EUPHORBIA.
Trees or shrubs not fleshy.
  Leaves trifoliolate . . . . . . 10. BISCHOFIA.
  Leaves simple.
    a. Leaves large, usually over 4 in. long.
      Leaves more or less rounded at the

        Leaves fleshy, lobed. Plants with opaque juice . . . . 13. JATROPHA.
        Leaves tough, not lobed. Plants not juicy.
          Leaves opposite, cordate; fruit indehiscent . . . 14. TREWIA.
          Leaves alternate, punctate; fruit a capsule.
            Lvs. orbicular, usually peltate 16. MACARANGA.
            Lvs. ovate, not peltate . . . 15. MALLOTUS.
          Leaves alternate, not punctate, closely parallel veined; fruit a berry-like drupe . . . . 4. BRIDELIA.*
      Leaves narrow-lanceolate, base acute.
        Lvs. crenate. Plants with milky juice . . . . 17. SAPIUM (*insigne*).
        Lvs. entire. Plants without milky juice . . . . . . 11. DAPHNIPHYLLUM.

---

* Bridelia leaves are very variable, sometimes large, often quite small, according to locality and also position on the plant.

b. Leaves middle-sized, usually under 4 in. long and 1 in. broad.

Nerves many, closely parallel . . 4. BRIDELIA.

Nerves few, not closely parallel.

Leaves serrulate ; fruit a tomentose drupe . . . . 8. PUTRANJIVA.

Leaves entire.

Fruit a compressed drupe ; pericarp fleshy . . . 12. ANTIDESMA.

Fruit indehiscent, lobed ; pericarp hardened . . . 9. CYCLOSTEMON.

Fruit a capsule.

Calyx valvate ; cocci undivided . . . 17. SAPIUM(*sebiferum*).

Calyx imbricate ; cocci 2-valved

Styles recurved . . 7. FLUEGGEA.

Styles confluent . . 6. GLOCHIDION.

c. Leaves small and thick, usually not more than ·5 in. broad.

Leaves alternate ; fruit indehiscent . 2. SARCOCOCCA.

Leaves opposite ; fruit a capsule . 3. BUXUS.

d. Leaves very small, usually under 1 in. by ·2 in. . . . . . . 5. PHYLLANTHUS.

1. Euphorbia, Linn. ; G. P. n. 2.

Herbs or soft-wooded shrubs with copious milky juice. *Leaves* alternate, with or without strong stipular prickles, sometimes opposite or whorled especially on flowering branches. *Flowers* in heads resembling single flowers, consisting of a cup-shaped involucre which encloses many male flowers and one central female flower ; involucre-lobes 4-5 with thick horizontal glands at the sinuses ; glands sometimes winged and petaloid. MALE FL. consists of a pedicelled, articulated, often bracteolate stamen ; anther-cells usually globose. FEMALE FL. a pedicelled 3-celled ovary in the centre of the involucre, often protruding and recurved. *Styles* 3, free or connate, usually 2-fid. *Capsule* of three 2-valved cocci.

Analysis of the Species.

Branches sub-cylindrical . . . 1. *E. Nivulia.*
Branches with 5-7 prominent angles . 2. *E. Royleana.*

1. **E. Nivulia,** Ham.; Fl. Br. Ind. v. 255; Brandis For. Flora 439, Ind. Trees 558; Gamble Man. Ind. Timb. 590. Vern. *Thor, Thuor,* Dún; *Súrú,* Jaunsar; *Seṇhúr,* Hind.

A large shrub or small tree; branches in whorls of 4, fleshy, nearly cylindrical, with vertically or spirally arranged tubercles each supporting a pair of stipular prickles. *Leaves* alternate, 6-12 in. long, obovate-oblong or linear; tip rounded; midrib much elevated beneath; lateral nerves indistinct. *Involucres* 3 together, central sessile male, lateral pedunculate with only male or both male and female flowers; lobes fimbriate, erect, ovate; bracteoles many. *Capsule* ·3 in. diam.; seeds smooth.

Dry rocky hills in the OUTER HIMALAYA and TEHRI-GARHWAL; rather rare. Cultivated at DEHRA.

Leafless in cold and dry seasons. Fl. Mar., Apr. Fr. May.

2. **E. Royleana,** Boiss.; Fl. Br. Ind. v. 257; Brandis For. Flora 438, Ind. Trees 558; Gamble Man. Ind. Timb. 591. Vern. *Thor, Thuor,* Dún; *Súrú,* Jaunsar; *Seṇhúr,* Hind.

A large milky shrub with thick fleshy 5-7-gonous branches; ridges wavy with a pair of stipular prickles at the crest of each wave. *Leaves* alternate, sessile, 4-6 in. long, spatulate, very shortly mucronate, fleshy; lateral nerves 6-8 pairs, irregularly reticulate, quite indistinct until dry. *Involucres* hemispheric, about ·5 in. across, greenish-yellow, 3-4 together in axillary subsessile clusters; lobes fimbriate. *Styles* combined up to the middle. *Capsule* ·6 in. diam., 3-gonous; peduncles up to ·5 in. long.

OUTER HIMALAYA and valleys in JAUNSAR and TEHRI-GARHWAL, up to 5,000 ft.: Málkōt, Kálsi, Saiá, Tons Valley (Morágádh), etc.

It grows readily from cuttings and is often planted in hedges.

Leafless throughout the cold and hot seasons. Fls. and Fr. Mar.-May.

2. Sarcococca, Lindl.; G. P. n. 18.

1. **S. pruniformis,** Lindl.; Fl. Br. Ind. v. 266; Brandis Ind. Trees 565; Gamble Man. Ind. Timb. 592. Syn.—*S. saligna,* Muell. Arg.; Brandis For. Flora 448. Vern. *Tiliári,* Jaunsar.

A small evergreen shrub. *Leaves* variable, usually 1·3 in. long, elliptic or lanceolate, quite entire, coriaceous, glabrous, shining above, often 3-nerved at the base ; lateral nerves faint. *Flowers* ·3 in. diam., pale-yellow, monœcious, bracteate, in short axillary racemes. *Bracts* whitish, decussate. *Sepals* 4, imbricate, in two series, oblong, obtuse. *Stamens* 4, free, much longer than the sepals and opposite to them. *Ovary* 2-3-celled ; ovules 2 in each cell ; styles 2-3, at length recurved. *Fruit* a berry, ·3-·5 in. long, ovoid, purple when ripe.

JAUNSAR and TEHRI-GARHWAL, 5,-9,000 ft., generally gregarious in shady places.

Wood white, close-grained, moderately hard, sometimes used for walking sticks.

Fl. Mar.-May. Fr. June-Aug.

3. Buxus, Linn. ; G. P. n. 19.

1. **B. sempervirens,** Linn. ; Fl. Br. Ind. v. 267 ; Brandis For. Flora 447, Ind. Trees 559 ; Gamble Man. Ind. Timb. 592. The Box. Vern. *Pápri, Sansádu*, Jaunsar ; *Chikri*, Punjab.

A small or middle-sized tree with 4-sided branchlets ; bark yellowish-grey, soft, corky, fissured in crocodile-pattern on old stems. *Leaves* opposite, 1·3 by ·2-·4 in., linear-oblong or lanceolate, shining, glabrous ; tip acute obtuse or retuse ; petiole very short. *Flowers* apetalous, monœcious, sessile, bracteate, in short congested axillary spikes. *Disk* 0. MALE FLS. : *Sepals* 2 pairs, one inside the other and imbricating with it, yellowish. *Stamens* 4, free, opposite the sepals, exserted. FEMALE FLS. : *Sepals* 6, in two or three series, the outer smallest, all imbricate, yellowish. *Ovary* 3-celled, with 2 ovules in each cell ; styles 3, simple, short, thick, persistent ; stigma 2-lobed. *Capsule* ·5 in. long, ovoid, loculicidally 3-valved, wrinkled ; valves dehiscing through the styles, each valve having two halves. *Seeds* oblong, trigonous, with a black shining testa and a fleshy albumen.

Jádi and Mátkángrá Blocks in the Deoban Range, JAUNSAR, and in the Jumná Valley, TEHRI-GARHWAL, always in shady rocky ravines.

Boxwood is yellowish-white, hard, very close- and even-grained. Pores very small, medullary rays extremely fine, both very numerous. Annual rings distinct but narrow, the growth being very slow. Weight about 60 lbs. per c. ft. It is the nearest approach to ivory and is used for engraving, turning, carving and mathematical instruments. In India, however, it is chiefly carved into combs and various other articles, the principal market being Amritsar in the Punjab.

Fl. Mar.-May. Fr. June-Aug.

4. Bridelia,* Willd.; G. P. n. 22.

Trees or shrubs, sometimes climbing. *Leaves* alternate, entire, with prominent lateral nerves. *Flowers* monœcious or diœcious, small, bracteate, in axillary sessile (rarely spicate) clusters. *Calyx* 4-5-cleft; lobes valvate. *Petals* 5, alternating with, and smaller than, the calyx-lobes. MALE FLS.: *Stamens* 5, united below in a column in the centre of a flat sinuate disk. FEMALE FLS.: *Ovary* 2- rarely 3-celled, on a cup-shaped membranous disk which is variously lobed. *Styles* 2, bifid. *Fruit* a soft drupe with 2 (or 1) usually indehiscent 1-seeded pyrenes.

Analysis of the Species.

A large tree; leaves rigidly coriaceous, with straight nerves; bracteoles few, coriaceous; calyx enlarged in fruit . . . . . 1. *B. retusa.*

A small tree; leaves membranous, with more or less arcuate nerves; bracteoles numerous, membranous; calyx not enlarged in fruit . 2. *B. montana.*

1. **B. retusa,** Spreng.; Fl. Br. Ind. v. 268; Brandis For. Flora 449, Ind. Trees 560; Gamble Man. Ind. Timb. 595. Vern. *Ekdánid, Gopíni*, Sahâranpur; *Gáyá, Kháját*, Dún and Garhwal.

A large or middle-sized deciduous tree, with strong spines when young; bark thin, grey or brownish-black. *Leaves* very variable, 3-6 in. long, obovate elliptic oblong or ovate, rigidly coriaceous, glabrous above, glabrous or glaucous beneath; lateral nerves 15-22 pairs, strong, straight, parallel; petiole ·2-·5 in. long; stipules deciduous. *Flowers* diœcious, yellow, small, subsessile; bracts villous.

---

* Also written 'Briedelia.'

Calyx ·2 in. diam.; lobes ovate. *Petals* fleshy. Fruit ·3 in diam., globose, green, purplish-black when ripe, supported by the somewhat enlarged calyx; pyrene generally solitary.

Throughout the SIWALIK DIVISION, especially in the moister parts; often associated with Sál.

Sapwood yellowish-white; heartwood grey or olive-brown, hard, compact, even- and close-grained, seasons well; annual rings distinct; weight about 50 lbs. per c. ft. The wood is used for carts, agricultural implements and building, also for drums in the Kheri District. It stands well under water and might be used for well-curbs. The bark is used for tanning; the ripe fruit is sweetish and is eaten, and the leaves are used as cattle-fodder.

New leaves May, June. Fl. May-July. Fr. Oct.-Jan.

2. **B. montana,** Willd.; Fl. Br. Ind. v. 269; Brandis For. Flora 450, Ind. Trees 560; Gamble Man. Ind. Timb. 596. Vern. *Goṇdni*, Sahāranpur.

A small or moderate-sized deciduous tree, often only a shrub, with a short trunk and a low spreading crown; bark dark-grey; branchlets warted. *Leaves* very variable, 3-6 in. long, obovate or broad-elliptic, glabrous or shining above, paler beneath; lateral nerves 10-15 pairs, more or less arched; petiole ·1-·3 in. long; stipules deciduous. *Flowers* monœcious (?),* small, greenish-yellow, shortly pedicelled; bracts many and crowded, membranous, pubescent. *Calyx* ·1-·2 in. diam.; lobes triangular-ovate, unaltered in fruit. *Petals* oblanceolate. *Fruit* ovoid, ·2 in. long, black when ripe.

Fairly common in ravines or banks of ráus, up to 3,500 ft., especially in the SIWALIKS. Wood mottled, otherwise very similar to that of the last species, and might be used for the same purposes to the extent its smaller size would allow; weight 46-59 lbs. per c. ft. The leaves are lopped for fodder, but the fruits are not eaten.

Fl. Apr., May (*Sir D. Brandis*), but Oct., Nov. (a second flush ?) in the Dún. Fr. Nov.-Apr.

5. Phyllanthus, Linn.; G. P. n. 34.

1. **P. Emblica,** Linn.; Fl. Br. Ind. v. 289; Brandis For. Flora 454, Ind. Trees 570; Gamble Man. Ind. Timb. 599. Vern. *Aoṇlá, Amlá, Aolá*, Hind.

---

* *Fide* Fl. Br. Ind. and Brandis For. Flora; but I have seen several trees with only male, and several others with only female flowers, and, so far, none with both.

A moderate-sized deciduous tree; bark grey, exfoliating in irregular patches, red inside; branchlets finely pubescent. *Leaves* ·3-·5 in. long, subsessile, linear-oblong, acute or mucronate, distichously close-set on deciduous branchlets, together having the appearance of pinnate leaves; stipules minute. *Flowers* apetalous, monœcious, greenish-yellow, in axillary clusters. MALE FLS.: numerous and shortly pedicellate. *Stamens* 3, joined in a short column. *Disk* of distinct glands, alternating with the calyx-segments, rarely 0. FEMALE FLS.: *Sepals* as in the male flowers. *Ovary* 3-celled, with 2 ovules in each cell; styles 3, connate at the base, twice bifid. *Fruit* of three 2-valved cocci, ·5-·7 in. diam., obscurely 6-lobed, globose, fleshy, pale-yellow, dehiscent only when dry.

Throughout the SIWALIK DIVISION, and up to 4,500 ft. in JAUNSAR and TEHRI-GARHWAL; very common.

Wood red, hard and close-grained, but warps and splits in seasoning; it is, however, durable under water, and yields charcoal of excellent quality. Heartwood and annual rings not distinct; weight about 50 lbs. per c. ft. The bark and fruit are used in medicine and also for tanning. The fruit is eaten raw or pickled, and is believed to be good for chronic biliousness.

Leafless Feb.-Apr. Fl. Mar.-May. Fr. Cold season.

P. parvifolius, Ham.; Fl. Br. Ind. v. 294,—is a small prostrate shrub which has been found below MUSSOORIE, 5,-6,000 ft., by Rai Bahádur Keshavánand, too late to be described in full. *Leaves* ·15-·25 in. long, obovate. *Flowers* minute. *Fruit* a capsule, ·12 in. diam.

6. Glochidion, Forst.; G. P. n. 34.

(Placed under *Phyllanthus* in the "Genera Plantarum.")

Evergreen trees or shrubs. *Leaves* alternate, bifarious, entire. *Flowers* usually monœcious, apetalous, small. MALE FLS.: *Sepals* 6, imbricate, in two series. *Anthers* 3-8, connate into a column; connectives produced. *Disk* without glands. FEMALE FLS.: *Calyx* of 5-6 free or connate sepals. *Ovary* 3-15-celled; ovules two in each cell. *Styles* variously united in a column. *Fruit* of 3 or more 2-valved cocci, quite globular or depressed, generally more or less lobed. *Seeds* hemispherical, albuminous.

Analysis of the Species.

Lvs. glabrous ; anthers 4-6 ; branchlets angular 1. *G. lanceolarium.*
Lvs. velvety ; anthers 3 ; branchlets terete . 2. *G. velutinum.*

1. **G. lanceolarium,** Dalz. ; Fl. Br. Ind. v. 308 ; Brandis Ind. Trees 573 ; Gamble Man. Ind. Timb. 601. Syn.—*Phyllanthus lanceolarius,* Muell. Arg. ; Brandis For. Flora 453.

A glabrous tree about 25 ft. high ; bark grey, with longitudinal wrinkles. *Leaves* 4-6 in. long, elliptic-oblong or lanceolate, acuminate, coriaceous, glabrous, shining ; lateral nerves 6-10 pairs ; base acute ; petiole channelled, ·2-·4 in. long ; stipules triangular. *Flowers* pale-green, in axillary fascicles,—male numerous and long-pedicelled ; female few, sessile or shortly pedicelled. MALE FLS. : *Calyx* of 6 linear-oblong segments. *Anthers* 4-6, oblong, on a short column. FEMALE FLS. smaller ; *Calyx* of 6 acute, rigid, unequal segments. *Ovary* 6-8-celled, villous. *Styles* 6, connate into a glabrous conical column. *Capsule* 3-·5 in. diam., depressed, 8-lobed.

Fairly common in moist localities in the EASTERN DÚN : Nichlá Súswá Block, Kánsráú, Nakraunda, etc.

The wood is believed to be hard and durable.

Fl. Cold season. Fr. Mar.-May.

2. **G. velutinum,** Wight ; Fl. Br. Ind. v. 322. Brandis Ind. Trees 574 ; Gamble Man. Ind. Timb. 602. Syn.—*Phyllanthus nepalensis,* Muell. Arg. ; Brandis For. Flora 452. Vern. *Ánwin,* Jaunsar ; *Chamári,* Dún ; *Kath Mauwá,* Garhwal.

A small tree, tomentose throughout. *Leaves* 2-5 in. long, ovate elliptic or oblong, rather coriaceous, glabrate above ; lateral nerves 4-6 pairs ; base rounded or obtuse ; petiole ·1-·15 in. long ; stipules subulate. *Flowers* in axillary fascicles,—the male on long slender pedicels ; the female subsessile. *Calyx* of 6 segments, hairy outside. MALE FLS. : *Anthers* 3, oblong ; connective prolonged. FEMALE FLS. densely clustered. *Styles* connate into a cylindrical column. *Capsule* ·3-·5 in. diam., depressed, usually 4-celled and deeply 8-lobed.

Common in the DÚN and SAHÁRANPUR FORESTS, also in low valleys (Tons, etc.) in JAUNSAR and TEHRI-GARHWAL.

Wood brownish-white, compact. The bark is used for tanning.

Fl. Feb.-Apr. Fr. June-Aug.

7. Flueggea, Willd.; G. P. n. 38.

1. **F. microcarpa,** Bl.; Fl. Br. Ind. v. 328; Brandis Ind. Trees 609; Gamble Man. Ind. Timb. 603. Syn.—*Securinega obovata,* Muell. Arg.; Brandis For. Flora 455. Vern. *Rithoul,* Dún.

A small tree with rusty or reddish-brown thin bark and angular branchlets marked with small white specks; branches straight and regularly fluted. *Leaves* very variable, 1-4 in. long, elliptic ovate obovate or orbicular, membranous but tough, rather glaucous beneath; tip rounded obtuse or acute, rarely acuminate or retuse; lateral nerves 6-8 pairs, very slender; petiole ·1-·3 in. long, slender. *Flowers* diœcious, very small, pedicelled; usually in axillary fascicles. *Sepals* 5, imbricate. MALE FLS.: *Stamens* 5, alternating with disk-glands but opposite to the sepals; pistillode large, 3-fid. FEMALE FLS.: *Ovary* ovoid, on an annular disk; styles 3, 2-fid. *Fruit* of two sizes, mostly small and dry, about ·1-·15 in. diam., with a few larger ones, ·3 in. diam., which are white and fleshy; seeds 3-6, punctate.

Very common along the foot of the SIWALIKS in the SAHÁRANPUR DISTRICT, especially towards the west, and generally in scrub forests in the DÚN: Sháhjahánpur, Kasúmri, Barkálá, Lachiwála, Gularghàti, Káunli, etc.

Wood reddish-white, close-grained, strong and durable, used for agricultural implements; weight 52 lbs. per c. ft. The branches make handsome walking-sticks, and are much used for the framework of thatched roofs as a substitute for bamboos. The bark is astringent, and is used to intoxicate fish.

Fl. Apr., May. Fr. Sept.-Nov.

8. Putranjiva, Wall.; G. P. n. 41.

1. **P. Roxburghii,** Wall.; Fl. Br. Ind. v. 336; Brandis For. Flora 451, Ind. Trees 566; Gamble Man. Ind. Timb. 604. Vern. *Jiápútá, Pútijiá,* Hind.

A handsome evergreen tree generally with pendent branches; branchlets slender, pubescent; bark dark-grey, almost smooth, marked with horizontal lines of white specks. *Leaves* alternate, 2-4 in. long, elliptic-oblong, acute or acuminate, serrulate, rarely entire, glabrous, shining, dark-green; main lateral nerves 8-10 pairs besides secondary nerves and reticulate veins; petiole ·2-·3 in. long, pubescent; stipules subulate, deciduous. *Flowers* diœcious, small, yellow: MALE short-pedicelled in axillary clusters which are often spicate;

FEMALE long-pedicelled, axillary, solitary or in twos or threes. *Calyx* 3-5-cleft; segments imbricate. *Stamens* 3; filaments more or less connate. *Ovary* tomentose, 3-celled; styles 3; stigmas crescent-shaped. *Fruit* a drupe, ·5 in. long, obovoid or globose, white-tomentose; putamen very hard.

In moist shady mixed forests in the SIWALIK DIVISION, especially on the banks of the Suswá below Kánsráu; Khairi swamp, Rikhikesh, Gularparáo; Barkálá, Kasúmri, etc.

Wood light-grey, even-grained, shining, moderately hard, fairly durable; weight 50 lbs. per c. ft. Used for tools and turning. The leaves are used for cattle-fodder, and the nuts are strung up in rosaries and tied round children's neck to keep off disease, and also worn by women during pregnancy to prevent abortion.

New leaves in Apr. Fl. Apr., May. Fr. Cold season.

9. Cyclostemon, Bl.; G. P. n. 45.

1. **C. assamicus,** Hook. f.; Fl. Br. Ind. v. 342; Brandis Ind. Trees 567; Gamble Man. Ind. Timb. 607. Vern. *Chipla*, Dún; *Khadbehúlá*, Kumaun.

A very handsome small evergreen tree with smooth greenish-grey thin bark and slender branchlets. *Leaves* 3-5 in. long, ovate or elliptic-oblong, dark-green, quite glabrous and shining; margins entire but undulate; nerves 10-12 pairs, slender; petiole ·2-·3 in. *Flowers* axillary, diœcious, apetalous, shortly pedicellate. *Sepals* usually 4, imbricate. MALE FLS.: *Stamens* about 12; filaments free. FEM. FLS.: *Ovary* generally 2-celled; stigmas sessile, fleshy, spreading, light-brown, liable to get chipped off in drying. *Fruit* a drupe ·5 in. diam., brownish-grey-tomentose and chartaceous when young, but more or less distinctly lobed and bright scarlet when ripe; putamen hard, black; seeds albuminous.

Found in the Nakraunda and Mothronwála swamps, 1,900 ft., in the DÚN, and identified as the above by Col. Prain.

The wood is greyish-white, moderately heavy, hard, tough and even-grained, with distinct rings; no heartwood. The leaves are eaten by cattle. The ripe fruit has a sweet mesocarp and is much eaten in Assam.

Fl. Nov., Dec. Fr. From Jan., probably ripening, as in Assam, in April.

10. Bischofia,* Blume; G. P. n. 53.

1. **B. javanica,** Bl.; Fl.Br. Ind. v. 345; Brandis For. Flora 446, Ind. Trees 558; Gamble Man. Ind. Timb. 607. Vern. *Pániala,* Western Dún; *Bhillár,* Málkōt; *Kot Semlá, Káen,* Garhwal.

A large diœcious tree with a dark-brown bark exfoliating in angular scales. *Leaves* alternate, 3-foliolate, variable in size; common petiole 2-6 in. long. *Leaflets* 3-5, 1·5-3 in., ovate or ovate-oblong, acuminate, crenate; petiolule of lateral leaflets about ·5 in. long. *Inflorescence* a much-branched terminal panicle. MALE FLS. minute; *sepals* 5, concave, obtuse, enclosing the stamens and opposite to them. FEMALE FLS. ·2 in. diam.; *sepals* ovate, caducous. *Ovary* exserted, 3-celled, with two ovules in each cell; styles long, entire. *Fruit* a globose berry ·5 in. diam., brown when fully ripe, supported on the thickened pedicels.

Shady ravines and in swampy localities in the DÚN and OUTER HIMALAYA: Karwápáni, Lachiwála, Nakraunda, Khairi swamp, Káluwála, Sansáru khála, Málkōt Hills, etc.

Wood red, moderately hard, but rough-grained; heartwood of a darker colour, small. Weight 40-50 lbs. per c. ft. Little known in the Dún, but is used for all kinds of construction and for boat-building in other parts of India, notably in Eastern Bengal and Assam where it is also used for railway sleepers.

New leaves Feb., Mar. Fl. Apr., May. Fr. Cold season.

11. Daphniphyllum, Bl.; G. P. n. 57.

1. **D. himalayense,** Muell. Arg.; Fl. Br. Ind. v. 354; Brandis Ind. Trees 566; Gamble Man. Ind. Timb. 609. Vern. *Ratendú,* Jaunsar.

A small tree with stout trunk and branches. *Leaves* alternate, 6-8 in. long, linear-oblong or oblong-lanceolate, acute or acuminate, entire, glabrous and shining above, glaucous beneath; petiole 1·5-2 in. long. *Flowers* diœcious, apetalous, in 3-4 in. long axillary racemes. *Sepals* 3-8, small, deciduous in the female fl. *Stamens* 5; anthers apiculate. *Ovary* imperfectly 2-celled, cells 2-ovuled; styles short or stigmas sessile, distinct, recurved. *Fruit* an oblong drupe, ·5-·6 in. long; seed with a membranous testa, albuminous.

---

* Also written "Bischoffia."

Found in shady ravines at and near MUSSOORIE, and in the OUTER HIMALAYAS, *e.g.*, Málkōt. Also in JAUNSAR, 5,-7,000 ft.; Dárná, Mátkángrá, Bainání, etc.

Wood pale-brown, fine- and close-grained; pores minute; medullary rays numerous and fine; weight about 40 lbs. per c. ft.; wood of the roots is of a deep red colour and capable of being used for ornamental purposes.

Fl. Mar., Apr. Fr. June-Aug.

12. Antidesma, Linn.; G. P. n. 60.

1. **A. diandrum,** Roth; Fl. Br. Ind. v. 361; Brandis For. Flora 447, Ind. Trees 565; Gamble Man. Ind. Timb. 610. Vern. *Ámli, Imli, Káli Khatái,* Dún.

A low shrub (or small tree ?) with smooth grey bark and low spreading crown; branchlets rusty-tomentose. *Leaves* alternate, 2-5 by 1-2 in., ovate oblong or ovate-lanceolate, acute or acuminate, quite entire, glabrous and shining above, turning deep-red before falling; nerves faint, rusty-pubescent beneath; petiole 1 in., pubescent; stipules lanceolate. *Flowers* diœcious, apetalous, greenish-yellow, very small, in slender terminal racemes. *Calyx* cup-shaped, 5-toothed. *Stamens* generally two, filaments free, as long as the pedicels; disk lobed. *Ovary* 1-celled; stigma bifid. *Fruit* a compressed drupe, ·2 in. diam., of a pleasant acid taste and purplish-red when ripe.

Fairly common in Sál forests and on the outskirts of *tappars* in the DÚN, up to 2,500 ft.; less so in the SAHÁRANPUR DISTRICT.

Wood pinkish-grey, hard, close-grained, weighing 41 lbs. per c. ft. The acid leaves are greedily eaten by coolies when thirsty, and are made into *chutni.* The fruit also is eaten.

New leaves Apr., May. Fl. May, June. Fr. Dec., Jan.

13. Jatropha, Linn.; G. P. n. 79.

1. **J. Curcas,** Linn.; Fl. Br. Ind. v. 383; Brandis Ind. Trees 576; Gamble Man. Ind. Timb. 613. Vern. *Safed Arand,* Hind.

A shrub or small tree with a short irregular trunk; young shoots glandular-tomentose, with an opaque saponaceous juice; bark grey, smooth, peeling off in thin papery flakes. *Leaves* 4-6 by 3-5 in., broadly cordate, usually palmately 5-lobed; petiole 3-9 in. long.

Flowers yellowish, monœcious, in terminal or sub-terminal cymes. *Sepals* 5, imbricate, slightly puberulous, often coloured. *Corolla* tubular, pale-yellow, villous within; limb 5-lobed. *Stamens* 10, in two series; filaments of the inner series connate. *Ovary* 3-celled. *Styles* 3, glabrous. *Fruit* about 7 in. long, 3-lobed, oblong; seeds oblong, large, dark-brown, smooth; albumen oily.

Planted in hedge-rows in the DÚN and SAHÁRANPUR DISTRICTS and often growing wild as an escape. The juice of the twigs gives a soapy lather, believed to do good if applied on sores. The oil of the seeds is medicinal.

Fl. and Fr. throughout the year.

14. Trewia, Linn.; G. P. n. 144.

1. **T. nudiflora,** Linn.; Fl. Br. Ind. v 423; Brandis For. Flora 443, Ind. Trees 590; Gamble Man. Ind Timb. 617. Vern. *Gamhár* (which is also the name for *Gmelina arborea*), *Túmri*, Dún; *Dhaul-pedda* (white tree), Sáháranpur.

A middle-sized deciduous tree with smooth grey bark. *Leaves* 6-9 by 4·5-7 in., cordate or broad-ovate, glabrous, 3-5 nerved at the base; petiole 2-4 in. long, terete. *Flowers* pale-green, in axillary racemes, appearing before the leaves: MALE in fascicles of 3-4, each supported by a bract, in lax interrupted racemes 4-9 in. long; FEMALE long-pedicellate, solitary or in few-flowered racemes. *Calyx* in the MALE FLS. globose, splitting into 3-4 concave segments; in the FEMALE FLS. of 3-5 imbricate sepals. *Disk* 0. *Stamens* free, numerous. *Ovary* cottony, 3-4-celled, cells 1-ovuled; styles connate at the base, about 1 in. long, covered with papillose stigmas throughout. *Fruit* a berry, 1-1·3 in. diam., globose, depressed, smooth mesocarp not harder than potato.

Damp places and ravines in the SIWALIK DIVISION: Lachiwála, Nakraunda, Kálúwála, banks of the Jumná, Kánsráu and other Passes, etc.

Wood white, soft, fairly elastic, but not durable; weight 28-29 lbs. per c. ft. Used for country-made drums, and for yokes in Western Bengal.

Leafless Jan.-Mar. New leaves Mar., Apr. Fl. Feb.-Apr. Fr. Cold season.

15. Mallotus, Lour.; G. P. n. 146.

1. **M. philippinensis,** Muell. Arg.; Fl. Br. Ind. v. 442; Brandis For. Flora 444, Ind. Trees 590; Gamble Man. Ind.

Timb. 619. Vern. *Ráini*, Dún; *Kambel*, Jaunsar; *Rohni*, *Roini*, Garhwal.

Generally a small evergreen tree, but occasionally up to 50 ft. high and 5 ft. in girth; bark thin, dark-grey, somewhat rough; young branches rusty. *Leaves* alternate, simple, very variable both in size and shape, usually 3-9 in. long, ovate ovate-oblong or lanceolate, entire or, if of luxuriant coppice-shoots, closely toothed, glabrous above, pubescent and with close-set red glands beneath, 3-nerved at the base; petiole about half the length of the blade, rusty-pubescent. *Inflorescence* and *flowers* brown or brick-red. *Calyx* 3-cleft. *Petals* and *disk* none. MALE FLS. clustered, anther-cells distinct and globose. FEMALE FLS. solitary. *Ovary* 3-celled; cells 1-ovuled; styles 3, papillose inside. *Fruit* a 3-lobed capsule, ·3-·5 in. diam., covered with a crimson powder when ripe; seeds about ·1 in. diam., globose, smooth, black.

Extremely common in the DÚN and SAHÁRANPUR FORESTS and also up to 4,000 ft. in JAUNSAR and TEHRI-GARHWAL.

Wood smooth, hard and close-grained; sapwood white; heartwood light-red to darker red towards the centre in large stems; used chiefly, as fuel. Annual rings indistinct; weight 48 lbs. per c. ft. The bark is sometimes used for tanning. The crimson powder, *kamelá*. which covers the ripe fruit, is used for dyeing silk, and also in medicine and Hindu religious ceremonies. The tree coppices exceedingly well.

Fl. Sept.-Nov. Fr. Mar.-May.

16. Macaranga, Thouars; G. P. n. 148.

1. **M. indica,** Wight; Fl. Br. Ind. v. 446; Brandis Ind. Trees 592; Gamble Man. Ind. Timb. 621. Vern. *Pápri*, Málkōt; *Rámálo*, Kumaun.

A middle-sized tree with thick glaucous branches and grey smooth bark. *Leaves* alternate, 6-12 by 5-10 in., deltoid-ovate, peltate, acuminate, entire or very obscurely and distantly toothed, thinly coriaceous, glabrate and closely yellow-punctate beneath; base rounded or truncate with two glands above; lateral nerves about 10 pairs above the petiole, the basal pair penniveined; petiole 4-12 in. long, glaucous; stipules ·5 long, ovate, acuminate, recurved. *Flowers* diœcious, in axillary panicled racemes; bracts broad, concave. *Stamens* 6-8; anthers 4-celled. *Ovary* 1-celled. *Style* very short; stigma spurred. *Capsule* very small, covered with resinous points, crowned with the obliquely placed spurred stigma; seeds globose.

Only found in the Málkōt Hills, DEHRA DÚN, 4,-5,000 ft.: Sansárú and Láswáni Khálás.

Wood greyish-red, rather soft; pores large; medullary rays very fine, numerous; weight 33 lbs. per c. ft. Growth very fast.

Fl. Aug., Sept. Fr. Nov., Dec.

17. Sapium, P. Br.; G. P. n. 185.

Trees or shrubs. *Leaves* alternate, entire or toothed; petiole often with two glands at the top. *Flowers* in terminal racemes or spikes, monœcious, apetalous: MALES several in each bract; FEMALES at the base of the same racemes with male flowers, or in separate spikes, each in a bract. *Disk* none. *Calyx* 2-3-lobed or toothed or split to the base; sepals valvate. *Stamens* 2-3, filaments free; anther-cells distinct. *Ovary* 2-3-celled, with 1 ovule in each cell. *Styles* as many as the carpels, more or less connate at the base, undivided, spreading, stigmatose inside. *Fruit* a tardily dehiscent 3-valved capsule. *Seeds* globose; albumen fleshy.

Analysis of the Species.

Leaves rhomboid, entire; female flowers at the base of racemes of male flowers . 1. *S. sebiferum.*
Leaves oblong-lanceolate, crenate; female flowers in separate spikes . . . 2. *S. insigne.*

1. **S. sebiferum,** Roxb.; Fl. Br. Ind. v. 470; Brandis Ind. Trees 584; Gamble Man. Ind. Timb. 624. Syn.—*Excœcaria sebifera*, Muell. Arg.; Brandis For. Flora 441. The Chinese Tallow-tree. Vern. *Târ-charbi*, Dún; *Pahári Shisham*, Sahâranpur.

A small gnarled tree. *Leaves* 2-3 in. long, rhomboid or broad-ovate, sometimes broader than long, acuminate, entire, membranous, glaucous beneath, somewhat resembling the leaflets of *Sissu*; petiole flexible, nearly as long as the blade, with 2 glands at the top. *Flowers* greenish-yellow, monœcious, in terminal racemes 2-4 in. long: FEMALE FLOWERS few, stoutly pedicelled, at the base of racemes bearing male flowers above, the male portion being caducous; MALE

MALE FLOWERS at the end of racemes of the above kind, or forming racemes entirely of their own which appear generally before the female or androgynous racemes. *Calyx* truncate. *Anthers* 2-3, large, exserted. *Ovary* glabrous; styles 3, connate at the base; stigmas recurved. *Capsules* sub-globose, glaucous, ·4-·5 in. diam. *Seeds* 3, enclosed in a white fatty arillus.

Growing wild everywhere in the DÚN, but rather rare in the SAHÁRANPUR DISTRICT. It is generally planted in avenues.

The wood is even-grained, light, soft or moderately hard; weight 32 lbs. per c. ft. The tallow of the seeds is separated by boiling in water, and is made into candles in China and Japan, where the tree is indigenous. The seeds give an oil, and the leaves a black dye.

Leafless Feb.-Apr. Fl. June-Aug. Fr. Oct.-Dec.

2. **S. insigne,** Benth.; Fl. Br. Ind. v. 471; Brandis Ind. Trees 585; Gamble Man. Ind. Timb. 625. Syn.—*Excœcaria insignis,* Muell. Arg.; Brandis For. Flora 442. Vern. *Khinná, Khindrá, Khinni, Khirni,* Dún and Garhwal.

A middle-sized deciduous tree with grey corky bark and thick milky juice. *Leaves* 6-12 in. long, elliptic or oblong-lanceolate, acuminate, crenate-serrate, soft, glabrous; lateral nerves slender, 12-20 pairs; petiole 1-2 in. long, with a pair of glands near the apex. *Flowers* in long fleshy terminal spikes: MALE in circular clusters subtended by two fleshy ovate acute green bracts; *calyx* membranous, lobes 2, rounded; *stamens* 2: FEMALE shortly pedicelled; *sepals* ovate; *stigmas* short. *Fruit* an ovoid capsule ·3 in. long, closely packed on a fleshy spike; seeds with an oily albumen.

Foot of the HIMALAYA and hot valleys up to 4,000 ft. Common at Tháno, Kálimatti, Ráipur, Sahansra-dhárá, Saiá, etc.

Wood white, very soft, spongy and very light, weighing about 25 lbs. per c. ft. It is used for cylinders of Indian drums. The milk is acrid and is said to be poisonous. It is often planted in hedges.

Leafless Dec.-Apr. Fr. Cold season. Fr. May, June.

Other plants of the Family that may be mentioned are:—

1. *Andrachne cordifolia,* Muell. Arg.; Fl. Br. Ind. v. 283. Vern. *Bharti, Bhartoi,* Jaunsar. A small shrub with slender branches. *Leaves* 1-2 in. long, ovate-oblong, obtuse, hairy beneath;

petiole filiform, of various lengths. *Flowers* monœcious, on long filiform axillary pedicels. *Capsule* globose, ·3 in. diam. Wood white and close-grained. JAUNSAR and TEHRI-GARHWAL, up to 8,000 ft.; Mundáli, Konáin, etc. Fl. Rainy season.—*G. P. n. 30.*

2. *Ricinus communis*, Linn.; Fl. Br. Ind. v. 457. The Castor-oil plant. Vern. *Erandi, Arandi*, Hind.—An evergreen shrub; cultivated and run wild in villages. *Leaves* 1-2 ft. diam., palmately lobed, serrate, membranous, glaucous beneath, long-petiolate; stem and petiole hollow. *Flowers* monœcious, the male being above the female in the same panicle. *Stamens* numerous. *Ovary* 3-celled; styles spreading, feathery. *Fruit* a globose capsule, generally echinate, ·5-1 in. long; seeds oblong, mottled, with fleshy albumen. The Eri silkworm is reared on its leaves. Besides the well-known oil, many parts of the plant are used in medicine.—*G. P. n. 149.*

3. *Baliospermum axillare*, Bl.; Fl. Br. Ind. v. 461. A stout undershrub, fairly common in shady places in the DÚN: Lachiwála, Kálsi, etc. *Leaves* very variable, upper 2-3 in. long and lanceolate, lower 6-10 in. long, oblong or palmately lobed, 3-5-nerved at the base, rigidly coriaceous; petiole stout, of various lengths. *Flowers* small in interrupted racemes from the axils of the upper leaves. *Capsule* ·3-·5 in. long, 3-lobed. Fl. & fr. throughout the year.—*G. P. n. 160.*

Order 6.—URTICALES.

FAM. 71. URTICACEÆ G. P. N. 153.

Herbs, shrubs or trees, often with milky sap. *Leaves* usually alternate, simple, stipulate, generally stellately hirsute. *Flowers* mostly 1-sexual, monœcious or diœcious, small, in heads cymes or spikes or inside a hollow receptacle. *Perianth* simple, or of 3-5 free or connate segments. *Stamens* usually as many as perianth-segments and opposite to them, often inflexed in bud with reversed anthers. *Ovary* free, 1-celled, 1-ovuled; style simple or 2-fid, often eccentric; stigma armed or feathery. *Fruit* a samara, a drupe, a nut or an achene, the last often in variously shaped receptacles.

This Family may be divided into the following Tribes :—

I. ULMEÆ.—Flowers 2-sexual; stamens not inflected; style 2-fid; ovule suspended; fruit a samara.—*Ulmus, Holoptelea.*

II. CELTIDEÆ.—Flowers polygamous; stamens inflected in bud; style 2-fid; ovule suspended; fruit a drupe.—*Celtis, Trema.*

III. MOREÆ.—Flowers 1-sexual, in spikes or heads; stamens inflected; style generally 2-fid; ovule suspended; fruit usually compound.—*Streblus, Plecospermum, Morus, Broussonetia.*

IV. ARTOCARPEÆ.—Flowers 1-sexual, inside or around a fleshy receptacle; stamens not inflected; style simple; ovule suspended; sap milky.—*Ficus, Cudrania, Artocarpus.*

V. URTICEÆ.—Flowers 1-sexual, usually in heads or clusters stamens inflected; style simple; ovule erect; fruit a simple achene.—*Bœhmeria, Pouzolzia, Villebrunea, Debregeasia, Maoutia, Girardinia.*

Analysis of the Genera.

I. *ULMEÆ.*

Leaves serrate; lateral nerves many, straight; wing of samara continuous . . . 1. ULMUS.
Leaves entire; lateral nerves few, arcuate; wing of samara cleft at the tip . . 2. HOLOPTELEA.

II. *CELTIDEÆ.*

Lvs. 3-nerved, smooth; male sepals imbricate 3. CELTIS.
Lvs. 3-nerved, scabrous; male sepals valvate 4. TREMA.

III. *MOREÆ.*

Unarmed trees.
Flowers in spikes; fruit compound, fleshy 7. MORUS.
Flowers fascicled or solitary; fruit a 1-seeded berry . . . . 5. STREBLUS.
Armed shrubs (flowers in heads; fruit a 1-2-seeded compound berry) . . . 6. PLECOSPERMUM.

IV. *ARTOCARPEÆ.*

Leaves penni- or 3-nerved; fruit a hollow receptacle with free achenes inside .	8. FICUS.
Leaves penninerved; fruit a many-seeded compound berry	9. CUDRANIA.

V. *URTICEÆ.*

Fruiting perianth dry or membranous.	
Flower-heads in interrupted spikes . .	10. BŒHMERIA.
Flower-heads in sessile axillary clusters .	11. POUZOLZIA.
Fruiting perianth fleshy.	
Leaves broad	12. VILLEBRUNEA.
Leaves narrow	13. DEBREGEASIA.
Fruiting perianth none; flower-heads cymose	14. MAOUTIA.

I. ULMEÆ.

1. Ulmus, Linn.; G. P. n. 1.

1. **U. Wallichiana,** Planch.; Fl. Br. Ind. v. 480; Brandis For. Flora 432, Ind. Trees 594; Gamble Man. Ind. Timb. 627. The Himalayan Elm. Vern. *Emroi, Imroi,* Jaunsar.

A large deciduous tree with rough grey bark exfoliating in diamond-shaped scales; young branches pubescent. *Leaves* alternate, 2-6 in. long, elliptic-ovate or obovate, long-acuminate, doubly serrate, scabrous or smooth above, pubescent beneath; nerves 15-20 pairs, straight, each terminating in a large serrature, axils of nerves usually villous; base unequal; petiole ·3-·5 in. long; stipules subulate, membranous. *Flowers* 2-sexual, in dense lateral racemes, appearing before the leaves from the leaf-scars of last year's shoots; pedicels ·2 in., fascicled, jointed a little below the middle, pubescent below the joint. *Perianth* turbinate, glabrous, persistent; lobes 5-6, ciliate. *Stamens* as many as the perianth-lobes, not inflected in bud. *Ovary* compressed, stipitate; style 2-fid, inner side stigmatose to the base. *Fruit* a flat stipitate samara, ·6-·7 in. long, with an ovate or obovate membranous reticulate wing completely surrounding the seed.

JAUNSAR and TEHRI-GARHWAL, between 3,500 and 10,000 ft., generally in ravines, fairly common: Mohná Block, Konáin, Dhará-gádh, Bálohá, Kúlni, etc.

Heartwood greyish-brown, fine-grained, moderately hard, with a very beautiful silver-grain, capable of a fine polish. The bark contains a strong fibre which is made into cordage, sandals and slow matches. The leaves are much prized as cattle-fodder, for which reason the tree is planted about villages.

New leaves Apr., May. Fl. Mar., Apr. Fr. May, June.

2. Holoptelea, Planch.; G. P. n. 2.

1. **H. integrifolia,** Planch.; Fl.Br. Ind. v. 481; Brandis Ind. Trees 595, Gamble Man. Ind. Timb. 628. Syn.—*Ulmus integrifolia*, Roxb.; Brandis For. Flora 431. Vern. *Pápri, Káli Pápri, Bunchillá*, Sahâranpur.

A large deciduous tree; bark grey or light-brown, with an offensive smell when freshly cut, marked with tubercles on branches. *Leaves* alternate, 3-6 by 2-3 in., elliptic or broad-oblong, acuminate, entire, coriaceous, glabrous or pubescent beneath; nerves 5-8 pairs; arcuate; base rounded or acute, rarely cordate or oblique; petiole ·2-·3 in. long; stipules ovate, membranous. *Inflorescence* as in *Ulmus Wallichiana;* fascicles fewer-flowered. *Perianth* cleft to the base; segments pubescent. *Stamens* 8 in male fls., 5 in 2-sexual fls.; anthers hairy. *Ovary* long-stipitate. *Fruit* an oval or orbicular samara 1 in. long, generally chartaceous, cleft at the tip, often crowned with the remains of the style.

Common throughout the SAHÁRANPUR DISTRICT; also found in a few places in the DÚN, and at low elevations in JAUNSAR, *e.g.*, Khairi swamp, Barkōt, Thâno, Kâlimatti, Kâlsi, etc.

Wood yellowish-grey, moderately hard; pores small and uniformly distributed; heartwood and annual rings not distinct; weight 40 lbs. per c. ft. The wood is used for building, carts and carving. The leaves, which have an unpleasant smell, are lopped for cattle-fodder. An oil can be extracted from the seeds.

Leafless Feb., Mar. Fl. while leafless. Fr. May-Aug., remaining long on the tree.

II. CELTIDEÆ.

3. Celtis, Linn.; G. P. n. 7.

1. **C. australis,** Linn.; Fl. Br. Ind. v. 482; Brandis For. Flora 428, Ind. Trees 595; Gamble Man. Ind. Timb. 529. Vern. *Kharik, Kharak*, Jaunsar and Garhwal; *Kharak-chená*, Dún.

A middle-sized deciduous tree; bark bluish-grey or brown, often with whitish specks, larger trees with narrow horizontal wrinkles; branchlets drooping. *Leaves* alternate, 3-5 in. long, obliquely ovate or ovate-lanceolate, long-acuminate, entire towards the base, coriaceous and tough when full-grown, dark green and glabrous above, with 3 strong basal nerves, midrib penniveined; base acute or rounded, sometimes oblique; petiole ·3-·5 in. long; stipules subulate, caducous. *Flowers* polygamous, 4-5-merous, male and 2-sexual on short capillary pedicels at the base of the shoots; female long-pedicelled and axillary. *Sepals* 4-5, oblong, imbricate, deciduous, with woolly margins. *Stamens* 4-5, short. *Ovary* sessile, woolly. *Fruit* an ovoid drupe, ·3 in. long, more or less reticulately rugose; peduncle ·5-2 in. long.

Fairly common between 4,000 and 8,500 ft. in JAUNSAR and TEHRI-GARHWAL, especially about villages where it is planted for shade and fodder; very numerous at Bámsu and Kúlni. Also in many places in the DÚN, both planted and self-grown, *e.g.*, Nakraunda, Haráwála, Mothronwála, Karwápáni, etc.

Wood yellowish-grey with irregular streaks of darker colour; annual rings distinct; weight 47 lbs. per c. ft. It is tough and strong, and is used for oars, whip-handles, churn-sticks and other purposes. The leaves are lopped for fodder.

New leaves and fl. Mar.-May. Fr. June-Sept.

4. Trema, Lour.; G. P. n. 9.

Shrubs or trees. *Leaves* alternate, generally 3-nerved; stipules caducous. *Flowers* very small, monœcious, in axillary cymes. *Sepals* 4-5, induplicately valvate in the male fls., subimbricate in the female. *Stamens* 5, longer than the sepals. *Ovary* sessile; style 2-fid, arms linear. *Fruit* a small drupe, supported by the persistent perianth and crowned by the arms of the style.

Analysis of the Species.

Leaves broad, soft, tomentose beneath . 1. *T. orientalis.*
Leaves narrow, hard, rough on both surfaces 2. *T. politoria.*

1. **T. orientalis,** Bl.; Fl. Br. Ind. v. 484; Brandis Ind. Trees 597; Gamble Man. Ind. Timb. 630. Syn.—*Sponia orientalis*, Planch.; Brandis For. Flora 430, The Charcoal Tree. Vern. *Jiban*, Bengal.

A small rapidly-growing and short-lived tree; bark thin, greyish or bluish-green, smooth, but with numerous lenticels. *Leaves* 3-6 by 2-3·5 in., ovate or ovate-oblong, acuminate, crenate-serrulate, membranous, scabrid above, soft-tomentose beneath; base 3-7-nerved, cordate, lateral nerves 3-4 pairs above the basal; petiole ·3-·4 in. *Cymes* lax, spreading. *Drupes* ·15 in. long, ovoid, black when ripe.

Gularghâti, Nakraunda and other swampy places in the DÚN; fairly common, but is apt to be mistaken for *Grewia lævigata*.

Wood light-reddish-grey, light and soft; weight 28 lbs. per c. ft. The bark gives a strong fibre, and the leaves are lopped for fodder.

Fl. Feb.-Apr. Fr. June-Aug.

2. **T. politoria,** Planch.; Fl. Br. Ind. v. 484; Brandis Ind. Trees 597; Gamble Man. Ind. Timb. 631. Syn.—*Sponia politoria* Planch.; Brandis For. Flora 430. Vern. *Khágshi, Khákshi, Kúri*, Dún; *Khardál*, Sahâranpur.

A shrub or small tree with smooth bark and scabrid branches. *Leaves* 2-5 by ·3-2 in., oblong or ovate-lanceolate, acuminate, serrulate, subcoriaceous, very hard and scabrid on both surfaces, dark-green and shining above, paler beneath, trinerved at the base, lateral nerves 6-8 pairs, arcuate, depressed above; base nearly equal, rounded or cordate: petiole ·2-·4 in. *Cymes* compact, generally not exceeding the petiole. *Drupes* ·1-·15 in. diam., globose.

Common in the SIWALIK DIVISION, along **ráu** and river banks and in abandoned fields. Comes up freely on landslips as in the SAHÁRANPUR SIWALIKS, where it is very valuable for binding the soil.

Wood white, moderately hard. Growth very fast, only 2 rings per inch of radius. Weight 36 lbs. per c. ft. The bark gives a strong fibre used for making ropes. The leaves are lopped for fodder and are used like sandpaper to polish wood and horn.

New leaves Mar., Apr. Fl. Apr.-June. Fr. Oct., Nov.

III. MOREÆ.

5. Streblus, Lour.; G. P. n. 21.

1. **S. asper,** Lour.; Fl. Br. Ind. v. 489; Brandis For. Flora 410, Ind. Trees 615; Gamble Man. Ind. Timb. 632. Vern. *Dahiá Kurchná*, Sahâranpur.

A small evergreen tree with milky juice; bark light-grey, irregularly ribbed. *Leaves* alternate, 2-4 in. long, elliptic rhomboid or obovate, irregularly toothed, acute or obtuse, coriaceous, scabrid with minute raised dots; base cuneate; petiole ·08-·1 in. long, pubescent; stipules lanceolate. *Flowers* generally diœcious. MALE FLS. in short-peduncled heads or spikes; *sepals* 4, imbricate; *stamens* 4, inflexed in bud; *heads* sometimes androgynous. FEMALE FLS. pedunculate, solitary or a few together in the axils of leaves; peduncle slender, ·6-·8 in. long; *sepals* 4, concave, embracing the ovary, enlarged in fruit; *style* central, bifid, with long spreading arms. *Fruit* a 1-seeded globose berry, ·2 in. long, yellow when ripe.

Common in the SAHÁRANPUR DISTRICT, especially towards the Jumná; often planted in hedgerows: Roshanpur, Shúfipur, Kásimpur, Ránipur, etc.

Wood white, moderately hard, tough and elastic; weight 40 lbs. per c. ft.; no heartwood. It is much sought after in Bengal for making yokes. The twigs are used as tooth brushes, and the rough leaves to polish wood and ivory. The milky juice is medicinal. The fruit is eaten when ripe.

New leaves Mar. Fl. Jan.-Mar. Fr. May-July.

6. Plecospermum, Trecul; G. P. n. 26.

1. **P. spinosum,** Trecul; Fl. Br. Ind. v. 491; Brandis For. Flora 401, Ind. Trees 615, Gamble Man. Ind. Timb. 634.

A large thorny shrub, closely resembling *Cudrania javanensis* in habit and foliage; spines axillary, straight, stout; bark light-brown or orange. *Leaves* alternate, 2-3 in. long, elliptic-oblong or obovate, obtuse or acute, quite entire, glabrous, penniveined; petiole ·3-·5 in. long. *Flowers* diœcious, in axillary pedunculate heads: head solitary or 2-3 together. MALE HEADS ·2-·3 in. diam.; *sepals* 4, obtuse, imbricate, hairy outside, emarginate and ciliate at the tips; *stamens* 4, inflexed in bud, afterwards exserted. FEMALE HEADS smaller than male heads in flower, afterwards ·5 in. diam., pubescent; *perianth* gamophyllous, with a 4-toothed mouth, connate into a globose head; *style* simple, filiform, much exserted, hairy; stigma papillose. *Fruit* a 1-2-seeded irregularly shaped berry, ·5 in. diam., rather smooth, velvety outside.

Believed to occur in the DÚN, but has not yet (Sept. 1907) been satisfactorily localised.

Sapwood white; heartwood small, bright-orange, very hard, with a yellow resin; weight 50 lbs. per c. ft. A yellow dye is extracted from the wood in the Darjeeling Terai.

Fl. Feb.-Apr.

7. Morus, Linn.; G. P. n. 33.

The Mulberries.

Trees or shrubs. *Leaves* alternate, serrate; base 3-nerved; stipules small, caducous. *Flowers* unisexual, in spikes. MALE FLS.: *Sepals* 4, imbricate. *Stamens* 4, inflexed in bud, opposite to and longer than the sepals. *Pistillode* small. FEMALE FLS.: *Sepals* 4, imbricate, accrescent and succulent in fruit. *Ovary* 1-celled, straight; style central, 2-fid. *Fruit* a compound berry, the perianths coalescing to form a gelatinous pericarp.

Analysis of the Species.

Leaves shortly acuminate, glabrate; fruit whitish . . . . 1. *M. alba.*
Leaves short-tailed, soft-tomentose; fruit purple . . . . 2. *M. serrata.*
Leaves long-tailed, rough; fruit black . 3. *M. indica.*

1. **M. alba,** Linn.; Fl. Br. Ind. v. 492; Brandis For. Flora 407, Ind. Trees 61?; Gamble Man. Ind. Timb. 634. Vern. *Tútri, Túṇtri*, Dún; *Tút, Túṇt*, Hind.

A middle-sized deciduous tree with pubescent shoots. *Leaves* 2-3 in. long, ovate to lanceolate, acute or acuminate, dentate or serrate, sometimes lobed, membranous, glabrous above, slightly pubescent along the midrib and nerves beneath; base 3-nerved, rounded or truncate, sometimes cordate; petiole ·5-1·3 in. long, slender. *Flowers* monœcious. *Female spikes* short, ovoid, pedunculate; styles short. *Fruit* ·3-·5 in. long, white or tinged with pink; peduncle ·5-·7 in. long, slender.

Cultivated or run wild in the DÚN. Planted in avenues along the Dehra—Rámpur-Mandi Road.

The wood is fine and close-grained, and is used for building boats, furniture and agricultural implements; weight 36-56 lbs. per

c. ft. Silk-worms are fed on its leaves, and the fruit is eaten, that of some varieties being excellent.

New leaves and fl. Mar., Apr. Fr. May, June, or later.

2. **M. serrata,** Roxb.; Fl. Br. Ind. v. 492; Brandis For. Flora 409, Ind. Trees 612; Gamble Man. Ind. Timb. 635. Vern. *Kimú*, Jaunsar; *Himú*, also *Tút* or *Túṇt*, Dún.

A large deciduous tree with scaly buds; bark reddish- or greyish-brown, generally smooth and lenticellate on branches, exfoliating on old stems; young shoots pubescent. *Leaves* 2-8 by 1·5-6 in., broad-ovate, generally cordate, toothed or serrate (sometimes doubly), often 3-lobed, shortly caudate-acuminate, membranous, slightly pubescent or glabrous above, thickly grey-tomentose beneath, 3-nerved at the base; petiole 1-1·7 in., tomentose. *Flowers* diœcious. *Male spikes* 1-2 in. *Female spikes* ·5-·7 in. long; styles very hairy. *Fruit* ·7-1 in. long, mucilaginous, purple; peduncle ·1-·2 in. long, stout, hairy.

Cultivated and wild in JAUNSAR and TEHRI-GARHWAL, 4,-9,000 ft.; also in the DÚN, *e.g.*, at Kálúwála. Common at Mussoorie.

Sapwood small, white; heartwood yellow or brown, moderately hard, fine-grained; weight about 35 lbs. per c. ft. It works and seasons well and takes a fine polish. It is used for cabinet-work and agricultural implements. The leaves are used as cattle-fodder. The fruit is sweet, and is eaten.

New leaves and fl. in Apr., May. Fr. June-Aug.

3. **M. indica,** Linn.; Fl. Br. Ind. v. 492; Brandis For. Flora 408, Ind. Trees 612; Gamble Man. Ind. Timb. 635. Vern. *Siá Tút* or *Siá Túṇt*, Hind.

A moderate-sized deciduous tree with reddish- or yellowish-brown smooth bark marked with long horizontal lenticels. *Leaves* 2-5 by 1-3 in., ovate, caudate-acuminate, sharply serrate, often lobed, membranous, pubescent when young, scabrous when mature, 3-nerved at the base; petiole ·5 to 1·5 in. long, sparsely hairy. *Flowers* monœcious. *Female spikes* ·3-·5 in. long, ovoid; styles long, hairy. *Fruit* small, black when ripe; peduncle ·1-·2 in. long, very slender.

Some botanists consider this a form of *M. alba.*

Not uncommon in the DÚN and SAHÁRANPUR DISTRICTS and also in the PUNJAB (Sháhdará and Changá Mangá Plantations).

Wood yellow when fresh-cut, turning brown and mottled afterwards, rather hard; weight about 45 lbs. per c. ft.; growth very fast in favourable localities. Often cultivated for its leaves, which are used to feed silkworms.

New leaves and fl., Feb., Mar. Fr. May.

Broussonetia papyrifera, Vent. ; Fl. Br. Ind. v. 490 ; the Paper Mulberry,—was first introduced in the Kaunli garden at DEHRA, whence it has spread, and is now found self-grown in many places. *Leaves* 5-9 in. long, obliquely ovate, acuminate, often lobed, membranous, tomentose ; petiole 2-4 in. long. *Flowers* in heads. Wood very soft and light. The bark gives a fine fibre which is made into paper in Japan.—*G. P. n. 24.*

IV. ARTOCARPEÆ.

8. Ficus, Linn. ; G. P. n. 39.

The Figs.

Trees or shrubs with milky sap. *Leaves* alternate (opposite in *F. hispida* and *sæmocarpa*), entire toothed or lobed ; stipules deciduous. *Flowers* minute, unisexual, on the inner surface of a fleshy hollow receptacle which has an aperture at the apex partly closed by imbricate bracts, often mixed with bracteoles. MALE FLS.: *Perianth* thin, 2-6-partite, imbricate. *Stamens* 1-2 ; anthers of 2 distinct cells. FEMALE FLS. : *Perianth* as in the male, or none. *Style* eccentric ; ovule pendulous. *Achenes* crustaceous or fleshy. *Receptacles* bracteate, 1-sexual or androgynous, with the male flowers near the mouth.

NOTE.—Besides the male and female, two other kinds,—gall and neuter flowers,—are sometimes found in the receptacles. The gall flowers are females with shorter styles and with the ovary occupied by the pupa of a Hymenopterous insect (Gall-insect). The neuter flowers, which only occur in one or two species not found in India proper, have the perianth of the males, but no stamens. In the same receptacle there may be males and females, or males, females and galls, or males and galls, or females and neuters, or only females.

Analysis of the Species.

A. Epiphytic in early life. Receptacles axillary, in pairs, sessile except in 1 and 3.

- Petiole not jointed to the blade, and less than ⅓ its length.
  - Lvs. thinly coriaceous, often up to three times as long as broad.
    - Lvs. and branchlets scaberulous; stipules as long as the petiole . 1. *F. gibbosa.*
    - Lvs. and branchlets smooth; stipules scarcely ⅓ the length of the petiole . . . . . . 3. *F. glaberrima.*
  - Lvs. thickly coriaceous, scarcely twice as long as broad.
    - Lvs. large; nerves distinct, reticulate . . . . . . 2. *F. bengalensis.*
    - Lvs. small; nerves faint, parallel . 4. *F. retusa.*
- Petiole jointed to the blade, and usually equal to at least half its length.
  - Leaves broad, caudate acuminate; ripe fruit black.
    - Acumen short; petiole channelled or flattened above . . . . 5. *F. Rumphii.*
    - Acumen long; petiole quite terete . 6. *F. religiosa.*
  - Leaves narrow, abruptly acuminate; ripe fruit white . . . . . 7. *F. infectoria.*

B. Not epiphytic in early life. Receptacles axillary, solitary except in 16, peduncled.

- Erect shrubs or small trees.
  - Leaves narrow, abruptly long-acuminate, hard, distantly toothed . . 9. *F. clavata.*
  - Leaves narrow, gradually acuminate, soft, quite entire . . . . . 16. *F. nemoralis.*
  - Leaves broad, acute, closely dentate or crenate . . . . . . 15. *F. palmata.*
- Scandent or prostrate shrubs.
  - Leaves and fruit very rough . . . 8. *F. heterophylla.*
  - Leaves and fruit more or less smooth.
    - Leaves subacute, coriaceous; receptacles small . . . . . 13. *F. scandens.*
    - Leaves long-acuminate, membranous; receptacles large . . . . 14. *F. foveolata.*

C. Never epiphytic; receptacles generally on leafless racemose branches (axillary on young plants of 10 and 11).

Leaves opposite.
- A small tree; leaves broad . . . 10. *F. hispida.*
- A small prostrate shrub; leaves narrow 11. *F. sæmocarpa.*

Leaves alternate.
- Leaves unequal-sided; petiole very short . . . . 12. *F. Cunia.*
- Leaves symmetrical; petiole usually long.
  - A small tree; leaves large, hard, subcoriaceous . . . . 17. *F. Roxburghii.*
  - A large tree; leaves small, soft, membranous . . . 18. *F. glomerata.*

1. **F. gibbosa,** Bl.; Fl. Br. Ind. v. 496; King Fic. 4, t. 2; Brandis Ind. Trees 599; Gamble Man. Ind. Timb. 637. Syn.—*F. parasitica*, Kœnig; Brandis For. Flora 420. Vern. *Chhánchri*, Dún and Garhwal; *Dádu Bándá*, Dún.

A much-branched small evergreen tree, epiphytic in early life; bark thin, brownish-grey. *Leaves* alternate, 2·5-4·5 by 1-2 in., elliptic-oblong, acute at both ends, entire, subcoriaceous, generally smooth above, always more or less scaberulous beneath, somewhat oblique and 3-nerved at the base; lateral nerves 4-6 pairs, prominent beneath, arcuate, joining within the margins; petiole ·2-·4 in. long; stipules ovate-lanceolate, convolute, generally as long as the petiole. MALE FLS.: *sepals* 4-6, linear, fleshy, hairy; *stamen* 1; *pistil* abortive. GALL FLS.: *sepals* of the male; *style* short. FEM. FLS. in separate receptacles; *sepals* 4, hyaline; *style* elongate. *Receptacles* ·2-·3 in. across, solitary or in pairs, pyriform-globose, scabrid and mammillate, yellow when ripe; basal bracts 0; peduncle ·2-·3 in. long, bracteate at the base.

Very common in the DÚN as an epiphyte generally on large old trees, notably Pipal and Haldú: Káluwála, Lachiwála, Dúdhli, Phándowála, etc. Occasionally in the SAHÁRANPUR DISTRICT.

The leaves are very good for cattle-fodder, and are said to increase the flow of milk in milch cows.

Fr. ripens Jan.-Mar.

Two varieties of this species occur in the SIWALIK DIVISION.

1. Var. *parasitica*, sp. Kœnig. *Leaves* broad, nearly rhomboid, more or less scabrid on both surfaces.

2. Var. *tuberculata*, sp. Roxb. *Leaves* narrower and smaller, generally smooth above, sometimes (but not in the DÚN specimens) irregularly serrate.

2. **F. bengalensis,** Linn.; Fl. Br. Ind. v. 499; King Fic. 18, t. 13.; Brandis For. Flora 412, Ind. Trees 600; Gamble Man. Ind. Timb. 638. The Banyan tree. Vern. *Bar, Bargat,* Hind.

A large evergreen tree throwing down numerous aërial roots from the branches which are mostly horizontal; bark greyish-white, smooth, exfoliating in irregular flakes; young parts softly pubescent. *Leaves* alternate, 4-8 by 2-5 in., ovate or elliptic, entire, obtuse, subcordate or rounded at the base, thickly coriaceous, glabrescent above, with 3-7 basal nerves and 4-6 pairs of main lateral nerves; petiole 1-2 in. long, stout; stipules ·7-1 in. long, coriaceous, sheathing. MALE FLS. crowded near the mouth of the receptacle; *sepals* 4; *stamen* 1. FEMALE FLS. with a shorter *perianth*; *style* long; male and female in the same receptacle. *Receptacles* ·5 in. diam., in axillary pairs, sessile, globose, puberulous, red when ripe, supported on 3 broad coriaceous basal bracts.

Fairly common in the Sál forests of the DÚN and along the foot of the SIWALIKS in the SAHÁRANPUR DISTRICT. Much planted in villages and in avenues throughout India. Assisted by the aërial roots which serve as supports for the branches and also as feeders the crown spreads enormously when the tree grows out in the open. Trees with crowns 200 to 300 ft. in. diam. are not uncommon, while the girth often attains 25 to 30 ft., and the height 80 to 90 ft.

Wood grey, moderately hard, appearing as composed of thin plates on a cross section; no heartwood; weight about 40 lbs. per c. ft. It is durable under water, and is therefore used for well-curbs. The wood of the drops is tough and elastic, and is used for tent-poles, cart-yokes and carrying-poles. The milky juice is made into bird-lime. The leaves and twigs are a favourite fodder for cattle and elephants; the former are also used as plates. Lac is sometimes collected on the tree. The fruit is eaten in times of scarcity and is greedily devoured by birds and monkeys. The tree is easily propagated by cuttings. It is, however, a nuisance in forests where it takes too much space, and its dense shade makes it impossible for any other trees to grow under it. In the Dún Forests the Haldú seems to be the most favourite host for the epiphytic Banyan.

New leaves Mar., Apr. Fr. ripens Apr., May.

Allied to this is the India-rubber tree, *F. elastica*, Roxb.; Fl. Br. Ind. v. 508; King Fic. 45, t. 54;—a native of ASSAM and BURMA, successfully cultivated in DEHRA and SAHÁRANPUR. It is a handsome evergreen tree, exceedingly suitable for avenues. *Leaves* dark-green, glossy; lateral nerves numerous, straight and parallel; stipules long, lanceolate, coloured and amplexicaul. *Receptacles* ·5 in. long, ovate-oblong.

3. **F. glaberrima,** Bl.; Fl. Br. Ind. v. 506; King Fic. 37, t. 43; Brandis Ind. Trees 600; Gamble Man. Ind. Timb. 640. Vern. *Kákhri, Khánkri, Durlá,* Hind.

A tall tree, epiphytic in early life; bark thin, dark-grey, smooth. *Leaves* alternate, 4-6 by 1·5-2 in., oblong ovate-lanceolate or elliptic, shortly blunt-acuminate, entire, sub-coriaceous, glabrous and shining above, minutely pubescent or glabrescent beneath; main lateral nerves 8-10 pairs, rather horizontal, arcuate, joining within the margins; base subacute or slightly rounded, 3-nerved; petiole ·5-1·2 in. long; stipules linear-lanceolate, ·4-·75 in. long, glabrous. MALE FLS. few, near the mouth of the receptacle; *sepals* 4, lanceolate; *stamen* 1, filament short. GALL FLS.: *perianth* 4-cleft. FEM. FLS.: *perianth* 0. *Receptacles* ·2-·3 in. across, in axillary pairs, globose, slightly verrucose when young, smooth and orange-coloured when ripe; peduncle about half the length of the subtending petiole; basal bracts 3, broad, minute, deciduous.

Swampy localities in the DÚN, *e. g.*, Nakraunda and Mothronwála, and along streams in shady ravines at low elevations in the HILLS, *e. g.*, Tons bank near Kálsi. Also in the Sansárú Khálá, MÁLKŌT.

The leaves and tender young shoots are lopped for fodder.

Fr. ripens Feb., Mar.

4. **F. retusa,** Linn. var. **nitida,** Thunb.; Fl. Br. Ind. v. 511. King Fic. 50, t. 62; Brandis For. Flora 417, Ind. Trees 603; Gamble Man. Ind. Timb. 643. Of all the Figs described in this book, it resembles *F. elastica* most closely, from which, however, it differs in having smaller leaves and subglobose receptacles. The flowers also are different.

A large evergreen tree; bark dark-grey, smooth, with transverse lines of lenticel bars. Leaves alternate, 2-4 by 1·3-2·5 in., ovate elliptic or rhomboid, acute or short-acuminate, entire, coriaceous glabrous and shining; lateral nerves numerous, slender; base 3-nerved, narrowed into the petiole which is ·3-·5 in. long; stipules lanceolate, about ·5 in. long.: MALE FLS. numerous; *sepals* 3, oblanceolate; *stamen* 1. GALL FLS.: *sepals* 3, spathulate. FEM. FLS.: *perianth* very small; *ovary* smooth; *style* short. *Receptacles* about ·2 in. diam., in axillary pairs, sessile, subglobose, yellowish when ripe; basal bracts broad-ovate, persistent.

Only a few indigenous-looking trees in the Bulávála Pass in the SIWALIKS behind the crest; elevation 3,000 ft. Cultivated at DEHRA DÚN and SAHÁRANPUR.

Wood light reddish-grey, moderately hard, very prettily mottled, but used chiefly for fuel; weight about 40 lbs. per c. ft. The leaves are used for elephant-fodder. Evergreen and umbrageous, it makes an excellent avenue tree.

Fr. Feb., Apr.

5. **F. Rumphii,** Bl.; Fl. Br. Ind. v. 512; King Fic. 54, t. 67B; Brandis Ind. Trees 601; Gamble Man. Ind. Timb. 644. Syn.—*F. cordifolia*, Roxb.; Brandis For. Flora 416. Vern. *Pilkhan, Khabar*, Hind.; *Pilkhoi*, Jaunsar.

A large deciduous tree; bark yellowish-grey, smooth, on older stems exfoliating in hard scurfy scales. *Leaves* alternate, 4-6 in. long, broad-ovate or ovate-oblong, acuminate, quite glabrous, shining above; acumen never exceeding an inch, often quite short; margins entire, undulate; lateral nerves 3-6 pairs; base shallow-cordate, truncate, rounded or narrowed towards the petiole, 3-5-nerved; petiole 2-3·5 in., channelled or flattened above, jointed to the blade. MALE FLS. few near the mouth of the receptacles; *sepals* 3; *stamen* 1. FEMALE and GALL FLS.: *sepals* 3, lanceolate; *ovary* ovoid, smooth; *style* elongate. *Achenes* mucilaginous. *Receptacles* ·5 in. across, globose, sessile, in axillary pairs, black when ripe; basal bracts 3, orbicular.

Common in the DÚN and SAHÁRANPUR FORESTS, and also in the Tons and Jumná Valleys in JAUNSAR and TEHRI-GARHWAL.

Wood very soft, spongy, pinkish-white, mottled on a radial section; weight 27 lbs. per c. ft. Lac insects are reared on it in Assam. The leaves and branches are lopped for cattle- and elephant-fodder, and the fruit is eaten. Often planted in avenues, but is a destructive epiphyte in forests.

New leaves in Mar. Fr. ripens May, June.

Somewhat similar in appearance, though much smaller in size, is *F. Arnottiana*, Miq.; Fl. Br. Ind. v. 513; King Fic. 56, t. 68,—found by Mr. Gamble at Thadiár in TEHRI-GARHWAL. It is usually epiphytic, but is found more generally on rocks. *Leaves* resembling those of *F. Rumphii*, but the base is never narrowed to the petiole, and the stipules are larger. *Perianth* gamophyllous. *Receptacles* smaller, generally peduncled; basal bracts brown, membranous.

6. **F. religiosa,** Linn.; Fl. Br. Ind. v. 513; King Fic. 55, t. 67A; Brandis For. Flora 415, Ind. Trees 601; Gamble Man. Ind. Timb. 644. Vern. *Pípal, Pipli*, Hind.

A large deciduous tree; bark grey, with brownish specks, smooth, exfoliating in irregular flakes; trunk irregularly shaped.

Leaves alternate, 4·5-7 by 3-5 in., orbicular-ovate, thinly coriaceous but tough, shining above, reddish when young, white-tubercled when mature; acumen 1-3 in. long; margins entire, undulate; main lateral nerves 6-8 pairs, joined by prominent closely-reticulate veins; base shallow-cordate rounded or truncate, sometimes abruptly narrowed into the petiole, 5-7-nerved; petiole 3-4 in. long, terete, slender, nodding, jointed to the blade; stipules minute. MALE FLS. very few, often absent, sessile; *sepals* 3; *stamen* 1, filament short. GALL and FEMALE FLS.: *sepals* 5; *style* short, lateral. *Receptacles* ·5 in. across, sessile, in axillary pairs, sub-globose or somewhat depressed, dark-purple, when ripe; basal bracts 3, rounded, coriaceous, pubescent.

A well known and common tree throughout India, both in forests and about habitations, much planted by Hindus, especially near temples and wells, often up to as high as 5,000 ft. in the OUTER HIMALAYA. It is held in so much veneration by the Hindus that killing a Pipal tree is looked upon as a great sin, second only to that of killing a Bráhman.

Wood greyish-white, moderately hard, not so mottled as of the preceding species; weight 30-40 lbs. per c. ft. It is made into charcoal and used for packing cases. The leaves and branches are good for elephant-fodder. The milky juice hardens into a substance resembling guttapercha. It is a fast-growing tree and very suitable for avenues, for which purpose it can be propagated by cuttings. It is, however, an epiphyte destructive to forest trees, and often does great damage to buildings and walls on which it grows by sending down roots through their crevices.

New leaves Feb.-Apr. Fr. ripens Apr., May.

7. **F. infectoria,** Roxb.; Fl. Br. Ind. v. 515; King Fic. 60, t. 75-79; Brandis For. Flora 414, Ind. Trees 602; Gamble Man. Ind. Timb. 645. Vern. *Khabar*, Hind.; *Dúthli*, *Pilkhoi*, Jaunsar; *Pákhar*, Dún; *Kobrá*, *Pilkháru*, Garhwal. This tree is often mistaken for *F. Rumphii* and for *F. glaberrima*; consequently the same vernacular names are usually applied to all three of them indiscriminately.

A large tree with greenish-grey smooth bark, sometimes sending down a few aërial roots. *Leaves* alternate, 3-6 in. long, oblong-ovate or ovate, abruptly acuminate, glabrous and shining, rather membranous; margins entire, undulate; lateral nerves 6-8 pairs; base acute, rounded or cordate, 3-nerved; petiole 1·5-2 in. long, channelled. MALE FLS. few, sessile; *sepals* 4; *stamen* 1, anther broad-ovate. FEMALE and GALL FLS.: *sepals* 3 or 4; *stigma* elongate. *Receptacles* ·25 in. diam., sessile, globose, in axillary pairs, tubercled, white when ripe; basal bracts 3, ovate, minute.

Not uncommon in the DÚN, but abundant in the Pathri Forest and elsewhere in the SAHÁRANPUR DISTRICT, often as an epiphyte on other trees in early life; also found in the TONS VALLEY near Thadiár.

Wood grey, moderately hard, but not durable; weight 35 lbs. per c. ft. Medullary rays prominent on a radial section. The young shoots are eaten in curries; the leaves are a good elephant-fodder. The bark gives a fibre which can be used for rope.

Two varieties of this species occur in our area:—

1. The type: *leaves* rather narrow; petiole hardly exceeding 1·5 in.; *receptacles* sessile;—more common in the HILLS.

2. Var. *Lambertiana*, sp. Miq. *Leaves* broader, generally cordate or rounded at the base; petiole up to and even exceeding 2 in.; *receptacles* shortly peduncled, somewhat larger, sometimes white-felted:—found along the foot of the SIWALIKS, and also in the plains beyond.

New leaves Feb.-Apr. Fr. ripens May, June, but remains long on the tree.

8. **F. heterophylla,** Linn.; Fl. Br. Ind. v. 518; King Fic. 75, t. 94; Brandis For. Flora 424, Ind. Trees 606; Gamble Man. Ind. Timb. 646.

A straggling shrub. *Leaves* alternate, 2-6 in. long, very variable, from narrow-lanceolate to broad-ovate, entire or lobed, toothed or repand, scabrid, acuminate; petiole ·5-2 in. long; stipules ·5 in. long, ovate. *Receptacles* ·5-1 in. long, globose or pyriform, solitary, yellow and smooth when ripe, scabrid when young, mouth partially open; peduncle ·5-1 in. long; basal bracts minute.

Generally on banks of rivers and moist localities; *e.g.*, Robbers' Cave, Tapkeswar and such other places in the DÚN; rather rare.

9. **F. clavata,** Wall.; Fl. Br. Ind. v. 520; King Fic. 87, t. 111; Brandis Ind. Trees 604; Gamble Man. Ind. Timb. 646. Syn.—*F. trachycarpa*, Miq.; Brandis For. Flora 421. Vern. *Khánoi*, Jaunsar; *Sánsoi*, Kálsi.

A shrub or small tree with rough branchlets. *Leaves* alternate, 4-8 in. long, oblong-lanceolate, long-acuminate, distantly toothed; hard and rough; main lateral nerves 6-8 pairs, arcuate; petiole ·1-·2 in. *Receptacles* axillary, solitary, globose, ellipsoid or obovoid, ·5-·8 in. long, with a rough uneven surface, yellow when ripe; peduncle ·1-·2 in. long; basal bracts minute.

Shady valleys in the OUTER HIMALAYA and also in JAUNSAR and TEHRI-GARHWAL: Laduakōt, Kálsi, Thadiár, etc. Often cultivated round villages for fodder.

Fr. ripens in May and June.

10. **F. hispida,** Linn.; Fl. Br. Ind. v. 522; King Fic. 116, t. 154; Brandis For. Flora 423, Ind. Trees 606; Gamble Man. Ind. Timb. 647. Vern. *Káksá, Ghogshá, Gobhá,* Dún; *Goblá,* Hind.

A moderate-sized tree with hollow branches; bark thin, grey or greenish, warty on old stems, otherwise smooth, often with transverse wrinkles. *Leaves* opposite, 4-12 in. long, ovate or obovate-oblong, acute or shortly acuminate, serrate or dentate, rarely entire, coriaceous, scabrid above, tomentose beneath; lateral nerves 4-6 pairs, the lowest pair from the base; base rounded or subcordate, rarely cuneate; petiole ·5-4 in. long, hispid; stipules ·5 in. long, pubescent. MALE FLS.: *sepals* 3, broad. GALL and FEMALE FLS.: *perianth* tubular and short or none; *styles* short, lateral. *Achene* rhomboid. *Receptacles* obovate, 1 in. long, pale-green and faintly ribbed when ripe, hispid, usually clustered on leafless, often drooping, branchlets from the trunk or old wood, less frequently (generally on very young plants and shoots) in axillary pairs; peduncle ·2-·5 in. long; basal bracts 3, small, persistent.

Fairy common in the SIWALIK DIVISION, generally in shady places.

Wood dirty-grey, coarse-grained, soft, no heartwood, no annual rings; weight about 30 lbs. per c. ft. The leaves are lopped for cattle-fodder. The young fruit is made into curries. The bark of young shoots gives a strong fibre which is good for rope.

New leaves Feb., Mar. Fr. generally throughout the year.

11. **F. sæmocarpa,** Miq.; Fl. Br. Ind. v. 523; King Fic. 115, t. 152; Brandis Ind. Trees 606; Gamble Man, Ind. Timb. 647. Syn.—*F. tuberculáta,* Wall.; Brandis For. Flora 424.

A low spreading shrub; young shoots, petioles and nerves rusty hirsute. *Leaves* opposite, crowded at the ends of the branches, 3-9 by ·7-1·5 in., narrowly oblanceolate, less frequently lanceolate, acuminate, generally entire, often more or less scabrid; main lateral nerves 6-8 pairs, very arcuate; base 3-nerved, gradually narrowed to the petiole; petiole ·3-·9 in. long; stipules persistent, scarious, about as long as the petiole. MALE FLS. with 3-4 *sepals* and 1 *stamen.* GALL and FEM. FLS. without any *perianth.* *Receptacles* ·5-1 in. across, axillary and solitary on young plants, in short axillary panicles on old stems, pyriform-globose, verrucose, longitudinally 8-10-ribbed; peduncle ·3-·6 in. long, pubescent; basal bracts 3, triangular, deciduous.

Robbers' Cave in the DÚN; trailing on rocks near streams, Somewhat rare.

Fr. ripens Dec.-Feb.

12. **F. Cunia,** Ham.; Fl. Br. Ind. v. 523; King Fic. 101, t. 126; Brandis For. Flora 421, Ind. Trees. 606; Gamble Man. Ind. Timb. 648. Vern. *Khain, Kheiná,* Dún; *Jarhphali,* Hind.

A moderate-sized tree with dark-grey bark. *Leaves* alternate, 6-10 in. long, oblong-lanceolate, very unequal-sided, acuminate, serrate, rarely entire, scabrid on both surfaces or glabrate above and pubescent beneath, coriaceous; lateral nerves 8-12 pairs; base semi-cordate or semisagittate with a large round 3-nerved lobe on one side; petiole ·2-·6 in. long, scabrid; stipules ·7-1 in. long, linear-lanceolate. *Male sepals* 3. *Female* and gall *sepals* 4, united below; *style* lateral. *Achene* ovoid, mucilaginous. *Receptacles* globose or pyriform, ·5-·7 in. diam., hispid, reddish-brown and ribbed when ripe, on leafless panicled racemes which issue in great numbers from the trunk and the larger branches, and are often several feet long.

Along ravines and watercourses in the SIWALIK DIVISION, and also up to 4,000 feet in JAUNSAR and TEHRI-GARHWAL; fairly common.

Wood greyish-brown, rough, moderately hard; weight about 35 lbs. per c. ft. The fibres of the bark are made into coarse ropes. The fruit is eaten, though somewhat insipid. The leaves are good for fodder, and can be used for polishing wood.

Fr. ripens in Aug., Sept. or throughout the year.

13. **F. scandens,** Roxb.; Fl. Br. Ind. v. 526; King Fic. 129, t. 162; Brandis For. Flora 421, Ind. Trees 609; Gamble Man. Ind. Timb. 648. Vern. *Makhotá,* Jaunsar; *Chhánchri,* Dún and Garhwal.

A climbing shrub, stem often rooting; bark rather thick, horizontally wrinkled, tougher when dry than the porous wood inside. *Leaves* alternate, 2-4 in. long, ovate or elliptic, acute, entire, coriaceous, scabrid above, pubescent beneath; lateral nerves 3-6 pairs above the basal pair; base rounded; petiole ·3-·7 in., hairy; stipules ·2 in., acute. *Receptacles* solitary or in pairs, globose, ·3 in. diam., rough, often hairy outside, greenish-yellow when ripe; peduncle ·3-·6 in. long; basal bracts 3-4, ovate, persistent.

Common in the SIWALIK and JAUNSAR DIVISIONS, up to 5,000 ft., generally in damp places or not far from watercourses.

Fr. ripens rainy season.

14. **F. foveolata,** Wall.; Fl. Br. Ind. v. 528; King Fic. 133, t. 166-168; Brandis For. Flora 423, Ind. Trees 608; Gamble Man. Ind. Timb. 648.

An evergreen scandent shrub with pubescent shoots and rooting branches. *Leaves* alternate, 2-4 in. long, ovate elliptic oblong or lanceolate, usually acuminate (acumen ·5-·7 in. long), entire, membranous or thinly coriaceous, glabrous above, pubescent or glabrescent beneath; lateral nerves 3-6 pairs; base rounded or cuneate, 3-nerved; petiole ·5-·8 in., hairy. *Receptacles* ·3-·5 in. diam. if globose, twice as long if ovoid, hairy; peduncle ·1-·3 in. long; bracts 3, ovate, membranous, reflexed.

Generally in the same sort of localities as *F. heterophylla;* rather rare: Robbers' Cave, DEHRA DÚN, 2,500 ft.

15. **F. palmata,** Forsk.; Fl. Br. Ind. v. 530; King Fic. 146, t. 185; Brandis Ind. Trees 607; Gamble Man. Ind. Timb. 649. Syn.—*F. virgata,* Roxb.; Brandis For. Flora 419, Vern. *Phéru, Khemri,* Dún; *Anjiri,* U. P.; *Fagwára,* Punjab.

A bush or small tree with smooth grey bark. *Leaves* alternate, 3-5 in. long, orbicular-ovate, acute or apiculate, toothed or serrate, sometimes deeply palmately lobed with the lobes pinnatifid, scabrid above, tomentose beneath; lateral nerves 6-8 pairs, the lowest pair from the base; base truncate or abruptly narrowed to the petiole; petiole ·5-1 in. long, pubescent; stipules ovate, acute. MALE FLS. on hairy pedicels. GALL FLS.: *style* lateral, very short; stigma dilated. FEMALE FLS.: *style* subterminal, long, stigma 2-fid. *Receptacle* ·5-1 in. diam., usually solitary, subglobose or pyriform, generally pubescent, yellow when ripe; basal bracts 3, acute, deciduous; peduncle ·5-·7 in. long.

Common in JAUNSAR and TEHRI-GARHWAL, up to 5,000 ft., also along river banks a long way into the plains, no doubt from seeds deposited by flood-water, *e.g.,* the banks of the Jumná, Sông and Súswá: Ambári, Kánsráu; Khárá, etc.

Wood white, close- and even-grained, moderately hard; weight about 40 lbs. per c. ft. The leaves are lopped for cattle-fodder and the fruit is eaten.

New leaves Mar., Apr. Fr. ripens June-Oct.

Closely allied to this species is the Fig-tree, *F. Carica,* Linn., Vern. *Ánjir,* which is cultivated for its fruit in DEHRA and SAHÁRANPUR. Indigenous in Syria, Palestine and Southern Europe.

16. **F. nemoralis,** Wall.; Fl. Br. Ind. v. 534; King Fic. 161, t. 206; Brandis For. Flora 424, Ind. Trees 608; Gamble Man. Ind. Timb. 649. Vern *Dúdhlá, Dúdhoi,* Jaunsar; *Parphútá, Dúdhlá,* Garhwal. The type of this plant has not been found in the region of this Flora. The following description refers to var. **Fieldingii,** Miq.

A small handsome tree, not epiphytic; bark thin, greyish-brown, fairly smooth. *Leaves* alternate, 4-6 by 1-2 in., lanceolate or elliptic, sharply long-acuminate, quite entire, membranous, glabrous; main lateral nerves 8-12 pairs, rarely more, with regular reticulations between, which are very distinct and dark-coloured beneath, especially when young; base very acute, 3-nerved; petiole ·7-1·3 in. long, slender; stipules ·3-·5 in. long, convolute, glabrous. MALE FLS. pedicelled, few in the fem. receptacles, numerous in gall-receptacles; *sepals* (in all fls.) 3, lanceolate, fleshy; *stamens* 2-3. GALL FLS. many: *ovary* ovoid, crustaceous. FEM. FLS. few; *ovary* triangularly obovoid; *style* longer than in gall flowers. *Receptacles* ·2-·3 in. across, axillary, solitary or in pairs, subglobose, glabrous, reddish when ripe; peduncles as long as the receptacles; basal bracts 3, broad, united, persistent.

JAUNSAR and TEHRI-GARHWAL, 3,-7,000 ft., Chakrata, Gádi, Mautárgádh, Mussoorie, etc.; often planted about villages.

The leaves are lopped for cattle-fodder, and the ripe fruit is eaten.

Fr. ripens Oct., Nov.

17. **F. Roxburghii,** Wall.; Fl. Br. Ind. v. 534; King Fic. 168, t. 211; Brandis For. Flora 422, Ind. Trees 609; Gamble Man. Ind. Timb. 649. Vern. *Timlá, Timal, Tirmal,* Hind.; *Tirboi* Jaunsar.

A middle-sized tree with grey warty bark; young shoots hollow. *Leaves* alternate, 5-15 by 4-12 in., broad-ovate or rounded, acute or mucronate, entire or toothed, subcoriaceous, glabrous or glabrescent above, softly pubescent beneath; lateral nerves 3-6 pairs, joined by transverse veins; base generally deeply cordate, strongly 5-7-nerved; petiole 1-10 in.; stipules ·5-1 in., ovate-lanceolate, pubescent. MALE FLS.: *sepals* large, imbricate; *stamens* 2-3. GALL FLS.: *perianth* 2-3-lobed; *style* short, subterminal. FEMALE FLS.: *perianth* of gall fl.; *style* long, lateral. *Receptacles* turbinate, depressed, largest 2 in. long and 3 in. broad, tubercled, longitudinally ribbed, purple-orange when ripe, in clusters of 6 to 20 on short thick leafless branchlets from the trunk; peduncle ·7-1·5 in. long, pubescent; basal bracts 3, triangular. *Achene* viscid.

SIWALIK and OUTER HIMALAYA; also JAUNSAR and TEHRI-GARHWAL, ascending to 5,000 ft. Very common near Asárori in the DÚN and in the Mautargádh in TEHRI-GARHWAL. Often cultivated for its fruit.

Wood reddish-grey, moderately hard; medullary rays prominent on a radial section weight 34 lbs. per c. ft. The fruit is eaten.

The leaves make a good fodder for cattle and elephants, and are also used for plates.

Fr. ripens Apr.-June.

18. **F. glomerata,** Roxb. ; Fl. Br. Ind. v. 535 ; King Fic. 173, t. 218 ; Brandis For. Flora 422, Ind. Trees 609 ; Gamble Man. Ind. Timb. 650. Vern. *Gúlar*, Hind.

A middle-sized or large tree ; bark smooth, reddish-brown. *Leaves* alternate, 4-7 in. long, ovate- or obovate-oblong or oblong-lanceolate, subacute, entire, membranous, glabrous above when full-grown, generally somewhat pubescent beneath ; main lateral nerves 3-7 pairs ; base obtuse, rarely acute, 3-nerved ; petiole 1-2 in., stipules ·5-1 in., ovate-lanceolate. *Male sepals* inflated. *Gall* and *female perianths* toothed. *Receptacles* subglobose, 1-1·5 in. diam., downy, red or orange when ripe, in short thick paniculate clusters on the trunk and larger branches, rarely axillary ; peduncle ·3-1 in. long ; basal bracts 3, triangular-ovate, small.

Abundant throughout the SIWALIK DIVISION, especially in ravines, river banks and marshy places. Not uncommon in the Tons Valley, JAUNSAR.

Wood grey, soft, mottled on a radial section ; weight 25-36 lbs. per c. ft. It is used for making toys and effigies in Bengal, and is said to be durable in water. It is one of the few woods prescribed in Hindu scriptures for sacrificial fires. Bird-lime is made of the milky juice which is also good for gum-boils. The fruit is eaten raw or cooked. The leaves are used for cattle- and elephant-fodder. Several parts of the tree are used in Hindu medicine.

New leaves Jan.-Apr. Fr. ripens Apr.-July.

9. Cudrania, Trecul ; G. P. n. 53.

1. **C. javanensis,** Trecul ; Fl. Br. Ind. v. 538 ; Brandis For. Flora 424, Ind. Trees 614 ; Gamble Man. Ind. Timb. 651. Vern. *Mánda*, *Dammar*, Dún.

A straggling shrub, armed with axillary spines ; bark smooth, yellowish-brown, with white oblong lenticels, profusely exuding a pale milk when cut. *Leaves* alternate, 1-4 in. long, oblong elliptic obovate or oblanceolate, obtuse to acuminate, entire, penninerved ; nerves not prominent ; petiole ·2-·3 in. long. *Flowers* diœcious, in globose heads. MALE FLS. : *sepals* usually 4, oblong, imbricate. *Stamens* 4, erect, included. FEMALE FLS. : *sepals* broader than in the male. *Ovary* straight ; style terminal. simple but with a short rudimentary branch at the base. *Flower-heads* solitary or in pairs, pubescent ; male ·2-·3 in. diam. ; female smaller at first, ·7-1·2 in. diam.

in fruit. *Fruit* an irregularly shaped compound berry, marked outside in a regular pattern by the thickened tips of the perianth-lobes, pinkish-orange when ripe; peduncle ·2-·3 in. long; seeds nearly as many as the flowers in the female heads, elliptic, compressed; testa black, crustaceous.

Common in the EASTERN DÚN; also in shady ravines in the SIWALIKS.

Wood tough; heartwood scanty, deep-yellow. The ripe fruit, which has a mawkish sweet taste, is eaten. The leaves are often attacked by a fungus which converts the inner substance into a white brittle mass. This is called *mande-ki rōti* and is eaten by village boys.

Fl. Apr.-June. Fr. Aug.-Nov.

In the same Tribe, and allied to *Cudrania*, is the somewhat large Genus, *Artocarpus*, G. P. n. 56, noted for important timber trees, of which, however, none are indigenous in the region of this Flora. Only the following two trees are cultivated in gardens:—

1. *A. integrifolia*, Linn.; Fl. Br. Ind. v. 541. The Jack-tree; Vern. *Kanthál, Kathál, Kathár*, Hind. A large evergreen tree noted for its dark-green foliage, and huge echinate fruit, which is eaten when ripe or cooked while raw. The wood, which somewhat resembles mahogany, is used for carpentry, and is exported to Europe for various purposes. A yellow dye is extracted from it in Assam and Burma, which is used for dyeing silk.

2. *A. Lakoocha*, Roxb.; Fl. Br. Ind. v. 543. Vern. *Dheú*, Dún; *Barhál*, Hind.—A large evergreen tree. *Leaves* large, dark-green, tomentose beneath. *Fruit* 3-4 in. diam., velvety, yellow when ripe. The wood resembles that of the Jack-tree, though somewhat inferior. The male flower-heads are pickled, and the fruit is eaten both when ripe, and also cooked into a curry while raw. Occasionally wild in damp localities, *e.g.*, Nakraunda and Khairi swamps in the DÚN.

V. URTICEÆ.

10. Bœhmeria, Jacq.; G. P. n. 84.

Shrubs or small trees. *Leaves* opposite or alternate, toothed, 3-nerved; nerves penniveined. *Flowers* unisexual, in clusters which are axillary or arranged in interrupted axillary spikes racemes or panicles. MALE: *Perianth* 3-5-lobed, valvate; *stamens* 3-5, inflexed in bud; *pistillode* globose. FEMALE: *Perianth* tubular, narrowed to a 2-4-toothed mouth; *stigma* lateral, filiform, persistent. *Achenes* crustaceous, at length free and dry.

Analysis of the Species.

Leaves alternate. A tree . . 1. *B. rugulosa.*
Leaves opposite. Shrubs.
  Leaves lanceolate, petiole short . 2. *B. macrophylla.*
  Leaves broad-ovate, petiole long . 3. *B. platyphylla.*

1. **B. rugulosa,** Wedd.; Fl. Br. Ind. v. 577; Brandis For. Flora 403, Ind. Trees 617; Gamble Man. Ind. Timb. 657. Vern. *Genthi, Genti,* Dún and Garhwal.

A middle-sized or small tree. *Leaves* 3-6 by 1-2 in., alternate, elliptic-lanceoloate, closely crenulate or dentate, acuminate, glabrous and dark-green above, pale and velvety beneath, strongly 3-nerved at the base, the nervules anastomosing in an elegant pattern beneath, and forming an intramarginal vein; petiole ·7-1·5 in.; stipules connate. *Clusters* of flowers sessile in simple spikes, each in the axil of a cordate bract; spikes axillary, 3-8 in. long. *Perianth* compressed, ciliate. *Achenes* stipitate, acute at both ends.

Ravines in the OUTER HIMALAYA, up to 4,000 ft. and occasionally along Sub-Himalayan streams: Rájpur, Kálsi, Málkōt, banks of the Sông down to Misirwála, etc.

Wood reddish-brown, moderately hard, even-grained, seasons well, mottled on a radial section. It is easy to cut and work, and is used in the hills for making bowls and various kinds of dairy-utensils.

Fl. Rainy season. Fr. Cold season.

2. **B. macrophylla,** Don; Fl. Br. Ind. v. 577; Brandis For. Flora 403, Ind. Trees 617; Gamble Man. Ind. Timb. 658. Vern. *Bará Siáru,* Dún.

A large shrub or small tree with dark-brown bark; branchlets 4-sided, strigose. *Leaves* opposite, 6-12 by 2-3·5 in., lanceolate, very gradually tapering, caudate-acuminate, evenly serrulate, acute or rounded and 3-nerved at the base, hispid, rugulose and pustular above, pubescent beneath; petiole ·6-1 in. long, strigose; stipules lanceolate. *Flowers* monœcious, in long drooping simple axillary spikes often as long as the leaves; clusters ·2-·3 in. diam., subtended by lanceolate bracts. *Fruit* obovate-cuneate, compressed, ciliate.

OUTER HIMALAYAN slopes, *e.g.*, above Rájpur, and in ravines round the Nágsidh Hill in the DÚN; not very common.

The branches yield a strong fibre which is used for fishing lines, nets, and such other purposes.

Fl. Aug., Sept. Fr. Nov.-Jan.

3. **B. platyphylla,** Don; Fl. Br. Ind. v. 578; Brandis For. Flora 403, Ind. Trees 617; Gamble Man. Ind. Timb. 658. Vern. *Bimol*, Rájpur; *Siár*, Kálsi; *Khákshá*, Garhwal.

A shrub, often up to 10-12 ft. high, branches rough, dark-brown. *Leaves* usually opposite, 4-9 by 3-7 in., broad-ovate or orbicular, acuminate or caudate, closely dentate, scaberulous or glabrate, rather membranous; base cordate or rounded; margins and teeth strongly reticulate; petiole 1·5-8 in. long. *Flowers* whitish, monœcious or diœcious. *Male spikes* often branching, generally not exceeding the leaves. *Female spikes* (in the typical form) much exceeding the terminal leaves, brown when the achenes are dry. *Fruit* compressed or angled.

Common in the OUTER HIMALAYA, and in shady ravines and along streams throughout the DÚN.

Wood moderately hard, but hardly of any size to be of much use except for fuel. The bark yields a shining-white strong fibre, very good for rope, and probably also for textile purposes. The leaves make a good fodder for cattle.

Fl. Apr.-Aug. Fruiting spikes Oct.-Dec.

I have noticed two distinct varieties of this plant in the DÚN: one the typical form described above, with long slender flexuose fruiting spikes; and the other, a small undershrub, with rougher and thicker leaves, and shorter, stouter and erect fruiting spikes;—Var. *scabrella*, Wedd.?

11. Pouzolzia, Gaud.; G. P. n. 86.

1. **P. viminea,** Wedd.; Fl. Br. Ind. v. 581; Brandis For. Flora 405, Ind. Trees 617; Gamble Man. Ind. Timb 658.

A shrub with slender branches; bark thin, rough, grey. *Leaves* alternate, 1-6 by ·2-1·5 in., oblong or ovate-lanceolate dentate or serrate, acuminate, rather rough above, somewhat hirsutely grey-tomentose beneath; base rounded, strongly 3-nerved; nerves penniveined; petiole ·3-1·5 in. long. *Flowers* usually monœcious, bracteate, in sessile axillary clusters. MALE FLS.: *Perianth* 4-5-partite, segments valvate; stamens usually 4, inflexed in bud. FEMALE FLS.: *Perianth* tubular, narrowed and toothed above; stigma lateral, filiform, deciduous. *Achenes* enclosed in the persistent chaffy perianth.

Occasionally met with in moist shady ravines in the DÚN and in JAUNSAR. Nakraunda and Gángbhewa swamps; banks of the Tons near Kálsi, etc.

The wood is not of much use except for fuel. The leaves are eaten cooked in Sikkim, and the bark is used to make ropes.

Fl. Rainy season.

12. Villebrunea, Gaud.; G. P. n. 94.

1. **V. frutescens,** Bl.; Fl. Br. Ind. v. 590; Brandis For. Flora 406, Ind. Trees 618; Gamble Man. Ind. Timb. 659. Vern. *Gar-tushiárá, Poi-dhaulá,* Kumaun.

A shrub with slender pubescent branches; bark dark-grey, rough. *Leaves* alternate, 3-6 by 1·5-3·5 in., ovate or elliptic, acuminate, finely serrate or crenate, membranous, concolor or grey beneath, sparsely strigose or glabrate, penninerved in the upper half; base rounded or slightly sub-cordate, 3-nerved; petiole ·5-3 in. long, very slender; stipules lanceolate. *Flowers* usually diœcious, in subsessile clusters or short cymes in the axils of previous year's leaves. *Male perianth* valvate. *Female perianth* and bracteoles fleshy and juicy in the ripe fruit.

JAUNSAR and DEHRA DÚN, up to 5,000 ft., generally along watercourses; fairly common. Dhármigádh; Nakraunda, etc.

The bark gives a useful fibre.

Fl. and Fr. Apr. and May to Sept. and Oct.

13. Debregeasia, Gaud.; G. P. n. 95.

Shrubs or small trees. *Leaves* alternate, serrate, 3-nerved; stipules 2-fid. MALE FLS. clustered; *sepals* generally 4, valvate; *stamens* as many as the sepals, inflexed in bud; *ovary* rudimentary. FEMALE FLS. in small fleshy heads; *perianth* very minute, tubular, with a contracted mouth; *ovary* straight, included; *stigma* generally sessile, tufted. *Achenes* enclosed in the fleshy perianth; heads succulent when ripe.

Analysis of the Species.

Flower-heads in dichotomous cymes; leaves ashy beneath . . . . . 1. *D. velutina.*
Flower-heads sessile or subsessile; leaves white beneath . . . . . 2. *D. hypoleuca.*

1. **D. velutina,** Gaud.; Fl. Br. Ind. v. 590; Brandis Ind. Trees 618; Gamble Man. Ind. Timb. 660. Syn.—*D. longifolia,* Wedd.; Brandis For. Flora 405. Vern. *Túshiári,* Dún; *Sansárú,* E. Dún; *Siárú,* Mussoorie.

A moderate-sized shrub; bark thin, dark-brown. *Leaves* 3-5 by ·4-1 in., oblong or linear-elliptic, acute at the base, acuminate, serrulate, rugose, scabrid and dark-green above, ashy-tomentose beneath; petiole up to 1 in. long. *Flowers* monœcious (*Sir D. Brandis*), in small heads which are disposed in short sessile dichotomous cymes. *Male perianth* longer than the bracteoles. *Heads* yellow when ripe, with numerous minute nuts imbedded in it.

OUTER HIMALAYAN Valleys and the DÚN; also at low elevations in JAUNSAR and TEHRI-GARHWAL: Dúdhli, Sansárú Khálá, above Rájpur; Bámsu, etc.

The stem yields a strong fibre which is made into rope. The ripe fruit is eaten.

Fl. July, Aug. Fr. Nov.-Jan.

2. **D. hypoleuca,** Wedd.; Fl. Br. Ind. v. 591; Brandis Ind. Trees 618; Gamble Man. Ind. Timb. 660. Syn.—*D. bicolor,* Wedd.; Brandis For. Flora 405, Vern. *Túshiári,* Garhwal and the Dún; *Sansárú,* E. Dún; *Siár, Siṇár,* Jaunsar; *Siárú,* Mussoorie.

A large evergreen shrub with pubescent branches; bark thin, dark-grey. *Leaves* alternate, 3-6 by ·5-1·2 in., oblong- or linear-lanceolate, acuminate, serrulate, rather coriaceous, scabrous and with round elevated dots above, thickly white-felted beneath; base acute or rounded, 3-nerved, the midrib much stouter than the two side-nerves; lateral nerves 3-5 pairs above the basal; petiole ·1-1 in. *Flowers* generally diœcious, in sessile or subsessile axillary heads. *Female perianth* ovoid, succulent in fruit. *Stigma* sessile, tufted.

Fruit amber-coloured and berry-like, studded with the minute nuts (somewhat resembling strawberry), sweet, but insipid and mucilaginous.

Common along watercourses in the OUTER HIMALAYA and also in JAUNSAR and TEHRI-GARHWAL, generally between 2,000 and 5,000 ft., sometimes ascending to 6,500 ft. (*e. g.*, Lúrli Block, Chakratá ; also Mussoorie). Extremely abundant in the Sansárú Khálá, MÁLKÔT FOREST, 3,500 ft., which has been named after it.

The wood is grey, soft and light, not of much use. The fibre is made into twine and rope, and the ripe fruit is eaten.

Fl. Mar., Apr. Fr. June-Aug.

14. Maoutia, Wedd.; G. P. n. 97.

1. **M. Puya,** Wedd.; Fl. Br. Ind. v. 592; Brandis For. Flora 406, Ind. Trees 619; Gamble Man. Ind. Timb. 660. Vern. *Poi, Puá*, Hind. *Dhaul* (white) *Khágshi*, Dún; *Cháwṇá*, Kálsi.

A shrub with hairy shoots; bark dark-grey, with vertical lines of brown lenticels. *Leaves* alternate, 4-8 by 2-2·7 in., elliptic, caudate-acuminate, coarsely dentate or crenate with 15-20 teeth on either side, membranous, scabrid above, softly white-felted beneath; base rounded or sub-acute, 3-nerved; lateral nerves 3-4 pairs; veins transverse; petiole ·5-4 in. long, slender, pubescent. *Flowers* monœcious or diœcious, very minute, in small heads which are disposed in axillary dichotomous cymes or panicles; inflorescence generally with a small rudimentary branchlet bearing minute leaves at the same leaf-axil. *Male sepals* 5, valvate. *Stamens* 5, inflexed in bud. *male perianth* none. *Nuts* triquetrous.

Fairly common in the SUB-HIMALAYAN RAVINES: Banks of the Tons Ráu (DEHRA DÚN), Kálsi, Paléd, etc. Also in the SIWALIKS, *e.g.*, the Mohand Pass.

The plant gives a fine white strong fibre, which is used to make fishing-nets, twine and cloth.

Fl. and Fr. May-Nov.

In the same Tribe, URTICEÆ, are several Genera of annual or perennial herbs with stinging hairs commonly known as nettles; which are fairly well represented in the region of this Flora. The nettles are remarkable for strong fibres. The largest is *Girardinia heterophylla*, Dcne.; Fl. Br. Ind. v. 550. Vern. *Bichchhú*, Hind.;

Kúshki, Jaunsar. Common throughout the DÚN and in the HILLS, especially about Kulni in TEHRI-GARHWAL.—*G. P. n. 77.*

Belonging to quite a small Section of URTICACEÆ, which is destitute of woody plants, is the wild Hemp, *Cannabis sativa*, Linn., Fl. Br. Ind. v. 487. Vern. *Bháng*, Hind.,—an annual weed of camping grounds and roadsides in the DÚN, but is also found in all camping places throughout the HILLS. *Leaves* palmatipartite, lobes finely serrate. It gives a strong fibre, quite fit for rope.—*G. P. n. 15.*

Order 7.—AMENTALES.

FAM. 72. MYRICACEÆ; G. P. N. 157.

Aromatic trees or shrubs. *Leaves* alternate, simple, exstipulate. *Flowers* monœcious or diœcious, in bracteate catkin-like spikes. *Perianth* none. MALE FLS.: *Stamens* generally 3-6, on a torus adnate to the bract; filaments free or connate at the base. FEMALE FLS.: *Ovary* sessile, 1-celled, 1-ovuled; style 2-fid. *Fruit* a resinous drupe with a hard endocarp. *Ovule* erect, orthotropous, exalbuminous.

1. Myrica, Linn.; G. P. n. 1.

1. **M. Nagi,** Thunb.; Fl. Br. Ind. v. 597. Brandis Ind. Trees 620; Gamble Man. Ind. Timb. 664. Syn.—*M. sapida,* Wall.; Brandis For. Flora 495, Vern. *Káiphal,* Hind.; *Káphal,* Jaunsar.

A moderate-sized evergreen tree; bark brownish-grey, rough, vertically wrinkled. *Leaves* 3·7 by 1 2 in., lanceolate oblanceolate or obovate, obtuse or acute, serrate on young plants, entire on old trees, coriaceous, glabrous above, pale or rust-coloured and with resinous dots beneath; midrib stout; main lateral nerves 12-20 pairs, anastomosing at the ends to form an intramarginal vein; base very acute; petiole ·3-6 in. long. *Male spikes* solitary fascicled or panicled, sometimes with female flowers at the top. *Female spikes* axillary, slender. *Fruit* 5 in. long, ellipsoid or ovoid somewhat compressed, tubercled, reddish or yellowish-brown when ripe; pulp reddish, formed of radiating fleshy hairs; nut rugose.

JAUNSAR and TEHRI-GARHWAL, 3,-6,000 ft.: Korwá, 6,000 ft.; Gádhs in the Tons Valley; etc. Also MÁLKŌT HILLS, 4,-5,000 ft.

The wood is purplish-grey, hard and close-grained, but apt to split and warp; weight 58 lbs. per c. ft. It is good for fuel. The bark is used as an aromatic stimulant, and externally as a plaster for rheumatism. It is also used to poison fish. The fruit is eaten and makes a very refreshing sherbet in the hot weather when it ripens.

New leaves Apr., May. Fl. Oct.-Dec. Fr. May, June.

FAM. 73. SALICACEÆ; G. P. N. 160.

Deciduous trees or shrubs, generally fast-grown and soft-wooded. *Leaves* alternate, simple, stipulate; buds enclosed in scales. *Flowers* diœcious, both male and female in terminal catkins, each in the axil of a bract; bracteoles and perianth none. *Stamens* 2 or more, generally free, on a variously-shaped glandular disk. *Ovary* sessile or stipitate, 1-celled; style short or 0; ovules erect, anatropous, generally on 2-4 parietal or basal placentas. *Fruit* a 2-4-valved loculicidal capsule; seeds few or many, exalbuminous, each with a tuft of long silky hairs.

The plants of this Family can be easily propagated by cuttings, and being also fast-growing, might be useful in quickly filling up blanks.

Analysis of the Genera.

Lvs. short-petiolate; stamens generally 2; fr. 2-valved . . . 1. SALIX.

Lvs. long-petiolate; stamens 4 or more; fr. 2-4-valved . . . . 2. POPULUS.

1. Salix, Linn.; G. P. n. 1.

The Willows.

Trees or shrubs. *Leaves* ovate to narrow-lanceolate, short-petioled; stipules deciduous, larger and more persistent on luxuriant young shoots. *Catkins* usually on leaf-bearing peduncles. *Bracts* entire. *Disk* of 1-2 glands. *Stamens* generally 2, long-exserted; filaments usually free. *Stigma* 2-fid or lobed, rarely entire. *Capsule* conical or narrow-lanceolate, 2-valved, with placentas near the base of the valves.

Analysis of the Species.

Stamens 4 or more; flowers after the leaves.
- Leaves broadly lanceolate; capsules long-stipitate . . . . . . 1. *S. tetrasperma.*
- Leaves linear-lanceolate; capsules shortly stipitate . . . . . . 2. *S. acmophylla.*

Stamens 2.
- Fls. with or after the lvs.; peduncles long.
  - A large tree. Lvs. long, linear-lanceolate 3. *S. alba.*
  - A shrub. Lvs. short, elliptic or oblong . 4. *S. elegans.*
- Flowers before the leaves; peduncles short.
  - Leaves usually entire; style short . . 5. *S. Wallichiana.*
  - Leaves always serrate; style long . . 6. *S. daphnoides.*

1. **S. tetrasperma,** Roxb.; Fl. Br. Ind. v. 626. Brandis For. Flora 462, Ind. Trees 636; Gamble Man. Ind. Timb. 685. Vern. *Bed, Jalmálá,* Dún; *Lailá, Bhainsh,* Hind.

A moderate-sized tree; branchlets often tomentose; bark greyish-brown or blackish, rough with deep vertical furrows. *Leaves* 3-6 in. long, oblong or ovate-lanceolate, finely serrulate, rarely entire, glabrescent, glaucous beneath; lateral nerves numerous, prominent; petiole ·3-1 in. long; stipules ovate or orbicular. *Flowers* after the leaves, on leaf-bearing peduncles. *Male catkins* 2-4 in.; *female* 3-5 in. long. *Stamens* 5-10, free; anthers minute. *Stigmas* 2, subsessile, entire. *Capsules* ·1-·15 in. long, ovoid, on slender stipes of nearly the same length, in groups of 3-4, glabrous or puberulous; seeds 4-6.

Common on river-banks and moist or water-logged places in the SIWALIK DIVISION, and also up to 6,000 ft. in JAUNSAR and TEHRI-GARHWAL.

Heartwood red, soft, porous; annual rings not very distinct; weight about 33 lbs. per c. ft. It is used for gunpowder charcoal, and for posts and planks in Assam. The leaves are lopped for cattle-fodder, and the twigs are made into baskets.

New leaves Feb., Mar. Fl. generally Feb.-Apr., less frequently in autumn. Fr. two months after flowering.

2. **S. acmophylla,** Boiss.; Fl. Br. Ind. v. 628; Brandis For. Flora 463, Ind. Trees 636; Gamble Man. Ind. Timb. 686. Vern. *Bed*, *Bádá*, *Jalmálá*, Dún.

A middle-sized handsome tree with flexuose branches which break off easily from the stem; bark reddish-brown. *Leaves* 2-8 by ·3-·7 in., those near the catkins much smaller, linear-lanceolate, upper caudate-acuminate, typically quite entire, but glandular-serrulate in a local form, glabrate or with adpressed hairs when young, glabrous and glaucous beneath when mature; lateral nerves faint; petiole ·3-·5 in. *Flowers* after the leaves on leafy peduncles. *Male catkins* 1-2 in.; *female* 1 in. long, both nodding. *Bracts* long, hairy. *Stamens* 4-6 (always 6 in the local form alluded to above); anthers short, globose. *Stigmas* 2, sessile, entire, spreading. *Capsule* shortly stipitate, ovoid-oblong, glabrous.

SAHÁRANPUR-SIWALIKS and DEHRA DÚN; rather rare. Cultivated throughout N.-W. India for ornament, and very extensively in Baluchistan as a fodder-tree: Sháhjahánpur Ráu, Mohand Pass; Dúdhli, Khairi, etc.

Wood apparently of no great value. The leaves are lopped for fodder.

Fl. Feb., Mar. Fr. May, June.

The local form with reddish fragile branches, glandular-serrulate leaves, and 6-stamened flowers will probably be recognized as a distinct variety, if not a species.

3. **S. alba,** Linn.; Fl. Br. Ind. v. 629; Brandis For. Flora 466, Ind. Trees 637; Gamble Man. Ind. Timb. 687.

A fairly large tree; branchlets green, yellow, red or purple. *Leaves* 2-6 by ·5-1 in., narrow-lanceolate, very gradually acuminate, glandular denticulate, silky on both surfaces when young, dull-green above and white with adpressed silky hairs beneath when mature; lateral nerves numerous, fine; petiole ·2-·5 in.; stipules ·3-·6 in. long, falcately ovate, silky. *Flowers* after the leaves: peduncle leafy. *Male catkins* 1-1·5 in. long, compact, cylindrical, drooping; *female* 2-3 in. long, lax, hairy. *Bracts* yellow or brown. *Stamens* 2. *Style* very short, 2-fid; stigmas 2-fid. *Capsule* subsessile, ovoid, glabrous or pubescent.

JAUNSAR and TEHRI-GARHWAL, in the Tons, Jumná, and Ganges Valleys, ascending to 6,000 ft.; not very common, often cultivated near villages. Abundant in the SIMLA HILL STATES.

The wood is white near the circumference changing to pink or brown towards the centre; pores and madullary rays very fine, numerous and uniformly distributed; annual rings distinct. Weight about 30 lbs. per c. ft. This is the only wood which has so far been found fit for cricket-bats, and the demand for it has increased in the Punjab to such an extent of late years, that it is likely to be profitable to make plantations of it there.

Fl. Apr.

Allied to this is *S. babylonica*, Linn.; Fl. Br. Ind. v. 629;—the Weeping Willow, which is cultivated as an ornamental plant in gardens and cemeteries throughout India. Its long, slender, pendulous branches are quite characteristic. The leaves resemble those of *S. alba* in shape and size, but are not so white beneath.

4. **S. elegans,** Wall.; Fl. Br. Ind. v. 630; Brandis For. Flora 466, Ind. Trees 637; Gamble Man. Ind. Timb. 688. Vern. *Chhoti Báshroi*, Jaunsar; *Kadvi*, Garhwal.

A middle-sized shrub; branches dark-green, drying black; young parts often grey-pubescent. *Leaves* 1-3 in. long, elliptic, obovate or oblong, obtuse or rounded, rarely acute at the tip, serrulate or subentire, hairy along the midrib, otherwise glabrous above, glaucous beneath, subcoriaceous when mature; lateral nerves indistinct; petiole ·1-·2 in. long. *Flowers* after the leaves on leaf-bearing peduncles. *Male catkins* 1·5 in.; *fem.* 3-5 in. long. (Quite exceptionally some plants are not only monœcious but bear male and female flowers on the same catkins, the latter occupying the upper half.) *Bracts* yellow, pubescent. *Stamens* 2; anthers elliptic. *Stigmas* 2, subsessile, 2-partite. *Capsule* conical, under ·1 in. in length, but in some forms up to ·2 in., shortly stipitate, glabrous. "The leaves of this and *S. daphnoides* are often attacked by a brilliant orange-coloured fungus, which is *Lecythea salicina*, Lev."—*Mr. J. S. Gamble.*

An extremely common gregarious shrub in JAUNSAR and TEHRI-GARHWAL, 7,-10,000 ft., generally associated with brambles and roses.

Wood pinkish; annual rings distinct; weight 33 lbs. per c. ft. Chiefly used as fuel. The leaves are used as fodder for cattle and goats.

Fl. Mar., Apr. Fr. May., June.

5. **S. Wallichiana,** Anders.; Fl. Br. Ind. v. 628; Brandis For. Flora 468. Ind. Trees 637; Gamble Man. Ind. Timb. 687. Vern. *Bhainshrá*, Jaunsar.

A small tree; young parts silky; bark greenish-grey. *Leaves* 2-5 in. long, oblong or ovate-lanceolate, acuminate, usually quite entire, silvery-tomentose on both surfaces; lateral nerves numerous, not very distinct; petioles ·1-·3 in. long. *Flowers* before the leaves; peduncles very short, generally with 1-3 rudimentary leaves at the base. *Male catkins* erect, 1-1·5 in. long; *female* 3-4 in. long, drooping; rachis tomentose. *Bracts* black. *Stamens* 2; anthers elliptic-oblong. *Stigmas* 2, erect, subsessile. *Capsule* downy, slender, short-stipitate.

JAUNSAR and TEHRI-GARHWAL, ascending to 9,000 ft., but common between 7,000 and 8,000 ft.

Wood white or pinkish-white; weight 32 lbs. per c. ft. The branches are made into baskets, and the twigs are used as tooth-brushes.

Fl. Mar., Apr.

6. **S. daphnoides,** Villars; Fl. Br. Ind. v. 631; Brandis For. Flora 469, Ind. Trees 637; Gamble Man. Ind. Timb. 689. Vern. *Báshroi*, *Bhainshrá*, Jaunsar.

A small tree; branches dark-green or black, shining or with a glaucous bloom; bark smooth, greenish-grey. *Leaves* 3-5 in. long, elliptic-lanceolate (narrower in higher elevations), acuminate, serrate, glabrous above, glaucous beneath; lateral nerves numerous, prominent, silky beneath; petiole ·1-·4 in., pubescent or downy; stipules lanceolate. *Flowers* before the leaves; peduncle very short, with or without a few rudimentary leaves. *Male catkins* 1-2 in., erect; *female* 2-4 in., nodding or pendulous, both densely silky. *Bracts* black tipped, villous. *Stamens* 2; anthers oblong, yellow. *Style* filiform; stigmas diverging, entire. *Capsule* subsessile, glabrous

JAUNSAR and TEHRI-GARHWAL, 2,500 to 15,000 ft. Fairly common about Deoban, Koráin and Kathián.

Heartwood red, shining; annual rings distinct; weight about 34 lbs. per c. ft. In the arid tracts of the Himalaya the wood is used for building, and for pails, tubs and similar purposes. The twigs are made into baskets, and are used for wattle-and-daub walls. The leaves and twigs, and even the bark of branches, are used for cattle-fodder.

Fl. Mar., Apr. Fr. May, June.

S. flabellaris, Anders. and *S. Lindleyana*, Wall.; Fl. Br. Ind. v. 634, may be mentioned as examples of dwarf willows, similar in habit to *Cotoneaster microphylla*, Wall. *Leaves* and *catkins* up to 1 in. in length. *Capsules* ovoid, red, glabrous. Such willows are characteristic of the high arctic or alpine climates and are found about the heads of the Ganges, Jumná and Tons Rivers, 11,-15,000 ft., *e.g.*, Harki Dún.

2, Populus, Linn.; G. P. n. 2.

1. **P. ciliata,** Wall.; Fl. Br. Ind. v. 638; Brandis For. Flor. 475, Ind. Trees 640; Gamble Man. Ind. Timb. 690. The Himalayan Poplar. Vern. *Piplás* (corruption of Poplar), *Biáon, Sharphárú, Tilaunju, Kapási*, Jaunsar; *Pahári Pípal*, Hind.

A lofty tree; bark grey, smooth on young plants, with vertical wrinkles or fissures on old stems; buds viscid, lanceolate. *Leaves* 3-7 by 2·5-5 in., broad-ovate, acuminate, finely dentate, margins gland-ciliate, otherwise quite glabrous; base usually cordate, 3-5-nerved; lateral nerves 4-6 pairs above the basal, irregularly forked; petiole 2-5 in. long, compressed above. *Flowers* before the leaves in lateral catkins. *Male catkins* 2-4 in. long, somewhat interrupted; *female* 6-9 in. long, lax in fruit. *Disk* toothed, embracing half the ovary. *Bracts* ·3 in. long, early caducous. *Stamens* indefinite; filaments short, very slender. *Stigmas* 3-4, obcordate, subsessile. *Capsule* ·3-·5 in. long, ovoid, 3-4-valved; stipes and hairs of the seeds as long as the capsules.

JAUNSAR and TEHRI-GARHWAL, 4,-10,000 ft.; sometimes cultivated. Affects sunny blanks with a light soil. Male trees are very scarce.

Wood white or brownish-grey, shining, soft; annual rings distinct. Medullary rays fine, very numerous. Weight about 30 lbs. per c. ft. The wood is used for water-troughs, and the leaves are valued as fodder for goats.

Leafless Oct.-Feb. Fl. Mar., Apr.; the males much earlier than the females. Fr. May, June.

Order 8.—QUERNALES.

FAM. 74. JUGLANDACEÆ; G. P. N. 156.

Trees, often strongly aromatic. *Leaves* alternate, pinnate, exstipulate. *Flowers* monœcious, bracteate. MALE FLS. in lateral catkins. *Perianth* flat, 3-6-lobed, adnate to the supporting bract which is stipitate. *Stamens* 2-40, on lateral bracts; filaments short; anther-cells parallel. FEMALE FLS. subsolitary or spicate. *Calyx* adnate to the ovary; limb superior, 4-toothed. *Petals* minute or none. *Ovary* 1-celled, 1-ovuled; style 2-fid. *Fruit* a 1-seeded 2-valved nut or drupe; cotyledons contorted or corrugated.

Analysis of the Genera.

Fem. fl. subsolitary; bracts not enlarged in fr. 1. JUGLANS.
Fem. fl. spicate; bracts produced into a wing in fr. . . . . 2. ENGELHARDTIA.

1. Juglans, Linn.; G. P. n. 2.

1. **J. regia,** Linn.; Fl. Br. Ind. v. 595; Brandis For. Flora 497, Ind. Trees 619; Gamble Man. Ind. Timb. 662. The Walnut. Vern. *Ákhrōt*, Hind.; *Ákhōr*, *Okhár*, Jaunsar.

A large aromatic deciduous tree with velvety shoots; bark grey, longitudinally fissured. *Leaves* imparipinnate, 6-15 in. long, thickly tomentose while young. *Leaflets* 5-13, lateral subsessile, opposite or subopposite, 3-8 by 2-4 in., elliptic-oblong, generally entire, rather coriaceous, glabrescent or pubescent along the nerves beneath; lateral nerves 15-20 pairs. *Male catkins* green, 2-5 in. long, sometimes in pairs, in the axils of previous year's leaves; bracts stalked, oblong, lobed. *Stamens* 10-20 or more. FEMALE FLS. 1-3, opposite the terminal leaf. *Calyx* indistinctly 4-toothed. *Petals* 4, green, narrow-lanceolate, minute, in the sinuses between the calyx-teeth. *Stigmas* more or less fleshy. *Fruit* 2 in. long, ovoid, glabrous or pubescent, green, with yellow dots; pericarp leathery, very aromatic. *Nut* 1-1·5 in. long, ribbed, more or less thick-shelled. 2-valved; cotyledons irregularly corrugated, 2-lobed at the back, oily.

Wild throughout JAUNSAR and TEHRI-GARHWAL, between 4,000 and 10,000 ft., and generally cultivated about villages in the HILLS.

Heartwood greyish-brown with darker streaks, often mottled, even-grained, moderately hard, seasons and polishes well; weight 40-50 lbs. per c. ft. It is in great demand for gun-stocks and is used for ornamental furniture throughout the Himalaya. The bark is used as a dye and in medicine, and is exported to the plains for cleaning the teeth. The nut is a well-known article of commerce, and the rind of the unripe fruit is used to intoxicate fish, and for tanning and dyeing. The leaves are used for cattle-fodder. The tree attains an enormous size, as much as 100 to 120 feet in height and 28 feet in girth. The cultivated trees, however, have a low spreading crown not more than 50 feet high, and a short trunk about 8 or 10 ft. in girth.

Leafless in cold weather. New leaves and fl. Feb.-Apr. Fr. July-Sept.

2. Engelhardtia, Leschen.; G. P. n. 4.

1. **E. Colebrookiana,** Lindl.; Fl. Br. Ind. v. 596; Brandis For. Flora 499, Ind. Trees 620; Gamble Man. Ind. Timb. 664. Vern. *Mowá, Mauwá*, Jaunsar (Tons Valley).

A small deciduous tree with grey bark; young shoots tomentose. *Leaves* imparipinnate, 8-12 in. long. *Leaflets* 6-11, the terminal smallest, often absent (by abortion), the lateral sub-opposite, short-petioluled, 3-5 in. long, obovate or elliptic-oblong, obtuse or acute, entire, subcoriaceous, glabrescent above, densely tomentose beneath; main lateral nerves 8-12 pairs; base unequal-sided, sometimes half acute and half rounded. MALE FLS. in cylindrical lateral catkins, or exceptionally at the lower half of female spikes. *Perianth* 3-6-lobed, adnate to a 3-lobed stipitate bract. *Stamens* 4-12; filaments very short. FEMALE FLS. in drooping bracteate spikes 5-8 in. long. *Calyx* adnate to the ovary, 4-toothed. *Stigmas* 2, linear, papillose. *Fruit* a small globose nut, ·2-·3 in. diam., villous, adnate to the much enlarged 3-lobed bract; lobes of bract with a straight midrib and reticulate veins; middle lobe 1-1·3 in. long; lateral lobes ·7 in. long.

Common and often gregarious in the MÁLKÓT and MUSSOORIE HILLS and in the Tons Valley, JAUNSAR, and also, according to Sir D. Brandis, in the SIWALIK TRACT and N.-W. HIMALAYA, up to 6,500 ft., but has not, so far, been met with in the SAHÁRANPUR-SIWALIKS or anywhere above 5,000 ft. in the region of this Flora.

The wood is reddish-grey, even-grained, moderately hard, seasons and polishes well, but is not durable ; weight 33 lbs. per c. ft. The leaves and branches are burned for use as manure.

Leafless Dec.-Feb. New leaves and fl. Mar., Apr. Fr. May, June.

FAM. 75. FAGACEÆ (*CUPULIFERÆ*); G. P. N. 159.

Trees or shrubs. *Leaves* alternate, simple, stipulate. *Flowers* generally monœcious. MALE FLS. in catkin-like spikes ; *sepals* 1-5, or absent ; *stamens* 2-20, on a hairy torus. FEMALE FLS. solitary or in dense spikes or heads ; *perianth* adnate to the ovary, or absent ; *ovary* 2-3- rarely more-celled ; style-arms as many as cells in the ovary ; ovules 1 or 2, pendulous. *Fruit* included within, or in the axils of, enlarged bracts ; seed pendulous, exalbuminous.

This Family includes the following Tribes represented in the area covered by this Flora by the Genera analysed under them :—

I. BETULEÆ.*—*Male perianth* of 4 or fewer segments ; *fem. perianth* absent. *Female flowers* many in dense spikes. *Ovary* 2-celled ; cells 1-ovuled.

Scales of female spikes thin, deciduous . . . 1. BETULA.
Scales of female spikes woody, persistent . . . . . . 2. ALNUS.

II. CORYLEÆ.—*Male perianth* absent ; *female perianth* adnate to the ovary. *Female flowers* in pairs in the axils of bracts that are much accrescent in fruit. *Ovary* 2-celled ; cells 1-ovuled.

Bracts many, in long spikes, leafy and veined in fruit . . . . . 3. CARPINUS.
Bracts few, in very short spikes, coriaceous in fruit . . . . . 4. CORYLUS.

* This Tribe has affinities with those placed under Order *Amentales* and is for this reason treated as a separate Family by some authors.

III. QUERCINEÆ.—*Male perianth* 4-10-lobed; *female perianth* adnate to the ovary. *Female flowers* few in an involucre of bracts. *Ovary* 3-7-celled; cells 2-ovuled.

Bracts many, small, adpressed, usually imbricate . . . . . . 5. QUERCUS.

I. BETULEÆ.

1. Betula, Tourn.; G. P. n. 1.

Deciduous trees or shrubs; outer bark papery, peeling off in horizontal rolls. *Leaves* penninerved, toothed or serrate; stipules deciduous. *Flowers* monœcious, spicate. MALE SPIKES drooping; *bracts* stalked, peltate, bearing on the inner face 2-3 bracteolate flowers; *sepals* 2-4. *Stamens* 2; filaments forked, separating the anther-cells. FEMALE SPIKES erect or pendulous; *bracts* imbricate, each with two bracteoles on either side; *perianth* none. *Ovary* compressed; styles 2; stigmas terminal. *Fruit* a 1-seeded winged lenticular nut.

Analysis of the Species.

Female spikes sub-solitary, erect; bracts coriaceous, wider than the wings of the nut . . . . 1. *B. utilis.*

Female spikes usually panicled, sub-erect; bracts membranous, narrower than the wings of the nut . . . . . . 2. *B. alnoides.*

1. **B. utilis,** Don; Fl. Br. Ind. v. 599; Brandis Ind. Trees 622; Gamble Man. Ind. Timb. 668. Syn.—*B. Bhojpattra,* Wall.; Brandis For. Flora 457. Vern. *Bhújpattra,* Hind.; *Bhúj,* Jaunsar and Garhwal.

A moderate-sized tree; bark brownish-white, with numerous horizontal lenticels; extremities pubescent. *Leaves* 2-3 by 1·5-2·2 in., ovate, acuminate, irregularly serrate, pubescent when young, gland-dotted and hairy along the nerves beneath; lateral nerves 8-12 pairs; petiole ·3-·6 in.; stipules oblong, ·5 in. long. *Bracts* of male fls. ciliate, stalk scaly; anther-cells distinct. *Bracts* of female fls. pubescent, 3-lobed, hardened in fruit. *Male spikes* 4-5 in. long, ·2-·3 in. diam. *Female spikes* erect, 1·2 in. long, ·5-·6 in. diam. *Nut* with narrow wings.

TEHRI-GARHWAL, between 10,000 and 14,000 ft. and occasionally in JAUNSAR. Gregarious in higher elevations with *Rhododendron Anthopogon* as an undershrub, *e.g.*, at Cháchpur, Chánsil, Harki-Dún and Gangottari. Sporadic specimens occur at such places as Bhújkoti; Deotá, Lambátách Peak, etc.

The wood is pinkish-white, even-grained, tough and elastic; weight 44 lbs. per c. ft. It seasons well and does not warp, and is used for building in the inner arid Himalaya. The bark, however, is by far the most valuable part of the tree. It is used as paper for writing and packing, for umbrella covers, as a lining inside hooka-tubes, and for roofing houses. The leaves are lopped for cattle-fodder.

Leafless Oct.-Mar. New lvs. and fl. Apr., May. Fr. Aug.-Oct.

2. **B. alnoides,** Ham.; Fl. Br. Ind. v. 599; Brandis Ind. Trees 622; Gamble Man. Ind. Timb. 669. Syn.—*B. acuminata,* Wall.; Brandis For. Flora 458. Vern. *Kath Bhúj,* Jaunsar.

A moderate-sized tree; young shoots pubescent; rolls of bark thicker and lenticels shorter than in the last species. *Leaves* 3-6 by 2-3·5 in., ovate or ovate-lanceolate, sharply acuminate, very irregularly and doubly serrate, pubescent beneath when young, gland-dotted when old; lateral nerves 10-15 pairs; base from rounded to cordate; petiole ·5-·7 in. long, hairy; stipules lanceolate, ·3 in. long. *Bracts, stamens* and *ovary* hairy; male bracts sub-sessile. *Male* and *female spikes* fascicled or panicled or the latter sometimes solitary, of nearly the same size, 2-5 in. long, ·2-·3 in. diam. *Nut* with wings broader than itself.

Fairly common in JAUNSAR and TEHRI-GARHWAL, 5,-10,000 ft., with a somewhat gregarious tendency (*e.g.*, Tútuágádh, Mundáli).

The wood is white, fairly close-grained, but not very hard in Jaunsar, although esteemed for strength and durability in Nepal. Weight 41 lbs. per c. ft. The leaves are lopped for fodder. The bark, peeling off in somewhat stiff narrow bands, cannot be used in the same way as that of the preceding species.

Leafless in winter. Fl. Nov., Dec. Fr. Apr., May.

2. Alnus, Tourn.; G. P. n. 2.

The Alders.

Deciduous trees. *Leaves* alternate, penninerved, often with tufts of hairs beneath in the axils of the lateral nerves. *Flowers* monœcious. MALE FLS. in pendulous spikes, supported by bracts and bracteoles; *bracts* 3-fid; *sepals* 4. *Stamens* 4; anthers subsessile, cells connate. FEMALE FLS. 2 in the axil of each bract, in short erect spikes; *bracts* woody, persistent in fruit. *Styles* 2, stigmatose at the tips. *Fruit* a woody cone; nuts more or less winged.

Analysis of the Species.

Bark smooth, silvery-grey; fruiting spikes many, in large erect panicles . . 1. *A. nepalensis.*

Bark furrowed, brown; fruiting spikes solitary or 3-5 in short erect racemes . . 2. *A. nitida.*

1. **A. nepalensis,** Don; Fl. Br. Ind. v. 600; Brandis For. Flora 460, Ind. Trees 623; Gamble Man. Ind. Timb. 670. Vern. *Puzála,* Jaunsar; *Kúnis,* Tehri-Garhwal.

A large tree; branchlets glabrous; bark compact, silvery-grey. *Leaves* 3-7 by 2-3·5 in., elliptic or elliptic-lanceolate, acute, entire or denticulate, glabrous above, slightly glaucous beneath; nerves 10-18 pairs; base usually narrowed; petiole generally ·3-·5 in., sometimes much longer. *Male spikes* 4-10 in. long, short-peduncled, slender, in terminal drooping panicles. *Fem. spikes* ·2-·3 in., pendulous in flower. *Fruit spikes* ·5-1 by ·3 in., ovoid or cylindrical, short-peduncled, in lateral panicles. *Nuts* with a membranous wing.

JAUNSAR and TEHRI-GARHWAL, 3,900 ft.: Chakrata, Lambátách, Deotá, Tons Valley, etc. Generally in ravines or banks of streams.

Wood reddish-white, close- and even-grained, soft but tough. Medullary rays broad, with numerous fine ones between. Weight about 30 lbs. per c. ft. It is used for bedsteads and for the hooked sticks in rope bridges. The bark is used for dyeing and tanning.

Fl. Oct.-Dec. Fr. ripens in winter but remains long on the tree.

2. **A. nitida,** Endl.; Fl. Br. Ind. v. 600; Brandis For. Flora 460, 623; Gamble Man. Ind. Timb. 670. Vern. *Útis, Kúnis,* Jaunsar.

A large tree; new shoots and petioles pubescent; bark dark-brown, deeply furrowed. *Leaves* 4-5 by 2-3·5 in., elliptic or elliptic-ovate, acuminate, entire or obscurely crenate, glabrous; nerves 8-12 pairs; base generally cuneate; petiole 1-1·5 in. *Male spikes* 2-4 in. long, in erect terminal racemes; peduncle ·3-·6 in. *Female spikes* 1-2 by ·7 in. *Fruit spike* ·7-1·5 by ·5 in., ovoid, in erect racemes. *Nuts* with a thickened margin.

JAUNSAR and TEHRI-GARHWAL, usually at low elevations, generally fringing the banks of rivers and streams, *e.g.*, the Tons and Pábar Rivers; Thádiar, Morágádh, etc.

Wood similar to that of *A. nepalensis*, but somewhat lighter. The economic uses also are the same as of that species.

Fl. Sept., Oct. Fr. ripens in winter but remains long on the tree.

II. CORYLEÆ.

3. Carpinus, Tourn.; G. P. n. 3.

The Himalayan Hornbeams.

Deciduous trees with slender flexuose branchlets. *Leaves* alternate, membranous, serrate; lateral nerves many, straight, parallel, very regular; buds elongate. *Flowers* monœcious. MALE FLS. in drooping lateral spikes, ebracteolate; *perianth* none; *stamens* 3-4 on a hairy torus, filaments forked, separating the anther-cells. FEMALE FLS. in slender terminal spikes, in pairs at the base of a foliaceous bract; bracteoles 2; *perianth* superior; *ovary* 2-celled, 2-ovuled; *style-arms* 2, filiform. *Nut* ribbed, at the base of the much-enlarged leafy bract and bracteoles.

Analysis of the Species.

Leaves ovate-lanceolate, caudate; fruiting bracts lanceolate; branches verrucose . . . . . . 1. *C. viminea.*
Leaves ovate-oblong, acute; fruiting bracts triangular; branches soft-tomentose 2. *C. faginea.*

1. **C. viminea,** Wall.; Fl. Br. Ind. v. 626; Brandis For. Flora 492, Ind. Trees 623; Gamble Man. Ind. Timb. 684. Vern. *Shinroi, Shángri,* Jaunsar; *Chamkharik,* Hind.

A middle-sized tree; branches warted; stem irregularly fluted; bark compact, grey, with darker streaks. *Leaves* 3-4 in. long, ovate-lanceolate, caudate-acuminate, doubly serrate up to the tip, glabrous; base rounded or sub-cordate; petiole ·1-·5 in. long, hairy. *Male spikes* 1-2 in.; *female* 2-4 in. long. *Fruiting bracts* 1 in. long, lanceolate, unequal-sided, toothed on the broader side, often lobed at the base on the other side, 3-5-nerved. *Nut* ·1 in. long, glandular.

JAUNSAR and TEHRI-GARHWAL, 5,-7,000 ft., often in shady ravines and along watercourses.

Wood white, shining, moderately hard, warps in seasoning, believed to be durable; no heartwood; weight 50 lbs. per c.ft. It is used chiefly for fuel.

Fem. fl. and new leaves Mar., Apr.; male fl. shortly before the leaves.

2. **C. faginea,** Lindl.; Fl. Br. Ind. v. 626; Brandis For. Flora 492, Ind. Trees 623; Gamble Man. Ind. Timb. 684. Vern. *Gish,* Garhwal; also the names given to the last species.

A middle-sized tree; branches pubescent; bark dark-brown smooth, slightly wrinkled. *Leaves* 3-5 in. long, ovate-oblong, often falcate, acute, generally with simple serratures, glabrescent; base rounded or sub-cordate, sometimes oblique; petiole ·1-·3 in. long, hairy. *Male spikes* 1-2 in., *fem.* 2-3 in. long. *Fruiting bracts* ·6-·7 in. long, 4-6-nerved, pubescent along the nerves beneath, triangular-oblong, very unequal-sided, coarsely toothed and often also lobed on the broader side. *Nut* ·1 in. long.

Between 6,000 and 7,000 ft. in TEHRI-GARHWAL: Kulni, Sáhlrá, Upper Tons Valley. Rather rare in JAUNSAR.

Wood similar to that of the last species.

Fl. Mar., Apr. Fr. July, Aug.

4. Corylus, Linn.; G. P. n. 6.

1. **C. colurna,** Linn.; Fl. Br. Ind. v. 625; Brandis For. Flora 494, Ind. Trees 624; Gamble Man. Ind. Timb. 684. The Himalayan Hazel. Vern. *Kapási, Shárori,* Jaunsar; *Bhutiá Badám,* Hind.

A moderate-sized deciduous tree; bark dark-grey, thin, sometimes exfoliating upwards. *Leaves* 3-6 in. long, rather membranous, ovate or obovate, acuminate, often slightly lobed, unequally and doubly serrate, glabrous when mature; lateral nerves 10-12 pairs, straight, generally pubescent beneath, each terminating in a large tooth; base cordate; petiole ·7-1·5 in. long, glandular-pubescent; stipules ·6 in. long, lanceolate, hairy; leaf-buds rounded, in hairy ovate scales. *Flowers* monœcious. MALE FLS. 1 in each bract; *perianth* 0. *Stamens* usually 4; filaments forked, separating the anther-cells; spikes fascicled, 1-2 in. long, cylindrical, drooping. FEM. FLS. in pairs in the upper bracts of a small many-bracteate bud-like spike; *perianth* superior. *Ovary* 2-celled, 2-ovuled. *Nuts* 1-seeded, ·5-·7 in. long, globose, somewhat compressed, hard, deep-brown, 2-3 together in a ribbed coriaceous double-involucre.

JAUNSAR and TEHRI-GARHWAL, 5,500 to 10,000 ft., generally in shady places and northern aspects; not gregarious.

Wood pinkish-white, moderately hard; annual rings distinct; medullary rays fine, numerous; weight 35 lbs. per c. ft. It is used locally for various purposes. The fruit is as good as English Hazel-nut, and is an important article of food in the hills, where the tree is cultivated for its sake.

New leaves and fl. Mar., Apr. Fr. July, Aug.

III. QUERCINEÆ.

5. Quercus, Linn.; G. P. n. 7.

The Oaks.

Deciduous or evergreen trees. *Leaves* alternate, penninerved, generally serrate. *Flowers* monœcious. MALE FLS. usually in drooping spikes; *perianth* campanulate; *stamens* 6-12 or more; filaments slender, anther-cells connate. FEMALE FLS. solitary or in clusters or short spikes, each enclosed in an involucre of bracts; *perianth-tube* adnate to the ovary; limb minutely toothed; *ovary* 3-5-celled with 2 ovules in each cell; *styles* 3-5. *Nut* (usually called an *acorn*) 1-celled, seated in a cup of hardened bracts; seeds 1 or 2; cotyledons thick, fleshy.

Analysis of the Species.

Cupular bracts imbricate, tips free.
  Mature leaves rusty-tomentose beneath; fruit globose, less than half buried in the cup . . . . 1. *Q. semecarpifolia.*
  Mature leaves glabrous, green beneath; fruit ovoid, half buried in the cup. . 2. *Q. dilatata.*
  Mature leaves white-tomentose beneath; fruit conical, more than half buried in the cup . . . . 3. *Q. incana.*
Cupular bracts connate into concentric belts; leaves glaucous beneath . . . 4. *Q. glauca.*

1. **Q, semecarpifolia,** Smith; Fl. Br. Ind. v. 601; Brandis For. Flora 479, Ind. Trees 625; Gamble Man. Ind. Timb. 671. Vern. *Kharshu,* Jaunsar.

A middle-sized or large tree, generally evergreen; young parts clothed with soft hairs; bark dark-grey, cracked into more or less 4-sided scales. *Leaves* 2-5 by 1-3 in., elliptic or oblong, spinous-toothed on young trees, often entire on old individuals, coriaceous, glabrous and dark-green above, generally rusty-tomentose beneath; lateral nerves 6-12 pairs, bifurcating, impressed above; base cordate or rounded; petiole 0-·2 in. *Male spikes* crowded, 2-4 in. long and congested in seed-years, 4-8 in. long and interrupted in other years; *perianth-segments* obtuse, ciliate; *stamens* indefinite, anthers apiculate. *Fem. spikes* short, at the tip of the current year's shoots; *styles* long, recurved. *Acorn* solitary, on previous year's shoots, 1 in. diam., globose, black when ripe; cup ·5 in. diam., thin, enclosing about a third of the nut.

JAUNSAR and TEHRI-GARHWAL, 8,500 to 10,000 ft., generally gregarious, often mixed with spruce and silver firs, occupying a higher zone than any other oak found in the N. W. HIMALAYA. It is the most important fuel-tree in the Deoban Range, JAUNSAR DIVISION.

Heartwood reddish-grey, very hard. Annual rings not very distinct. Medullary rays of two kinds; a few broad rays with numerous very fine ones between. Weight 53 lbs. per c. ft. The wood splits in seasoning. It is used only locally for building, door-frames, bedsteads, ploughs, and mule-saddle, and is a good fuel. It might, as also the wood of *Mōru,* be useful in the plains, but they are too heavy to be floated. The leaves make a good cattle-fodder, and bears are extremely fond of the acorns. The tree coppices well. It seeds profusely every second or third year, but a few trees here and there produce acorns every year. Trees that bear acorns do not shed leaves that year, whereas those which produce male flowers are generally leafless by the middle of May.

New leaves and fl. May, June. The female flowers appear with the male flowers and become fertilized by their pollen, but the acorns begin to grow only in the next spring, often before the male flowers of the season have begun to open. By the first week of June the young acorns are about the size of a pea, while the female flowers (which will produce acorns next year) are then just visible. This peculiarity of fructification is, *mutatis mutandis*, common to all (?) the Oaks found in the N. W. HIMALAYA. Fr. Aug., Sept.,—15 months after flowering.

2. **Q. dilatata,** Lindl.; Fl. Br. Ind. v. 602; Brandis For. Flora 482, Ind Trees 627; Gamble Man. Ind. Timb. 673. Vern. *Mōru*, Jaunsar.

A large shade-enduring tree, almost evergreen; bark dark-grey or black, peeling off in longitudinal scales. *Leaves* 1·5-3·5 by ·5-1·7 in., oblong or oblong-lanceolate, acuminate, entire or spinous-serrate, coriaceous, quite glabrous when mature; lateral nerves 8-12 pairs, slender, forked and reticulate; base rounded or cordate; petiole ·2-·3 in. long. *Male spikes* crowded, drooping, lax, 1·5-3 in. long; bracts lanceolate. *Fem. spikes* short; *styles* 3-5, linear-clavate. *Acorn* solitary, on previous year's shoots, ·7-1·2 in. long, ·5-·7 in. diam., ovoid or oblong, glabrous, brown when ripe; scales of cup closely adpressed.

JAUNSAR and TEHRI-GARHWAL, 6,500 to 9,000 ft., occupying a zone intermediate between that of *Bán* and *Kharshu*, often gregarious, but generally associated with the firs and Deodar.

Heartwood reddish-grey, with darker streaks, very hard, seasons well. The broader medullary rays are more numerous but narrower than those of any other species described here; the others very fine, very numerous, and uniform; annual rings indistinct; weight 61 lbs. per c. ft. The wood is the most useful of all the Oaks in the region of this Flora. It is used for building, for agricultural implements, axe-handles, walking-sticks, jhampán-poles, soles of sledges and similar other purposes. The leaves are lopped for fodder. The tree reproduces itself freely both from seed and from coppice-stools. A kind of gall-insect produces galls on the leaves, which are sweet to the taste, and are eaten by the Jaunsaris, insects and all.

New leaves and fl. Apr., May. Fr. Cold season,—16-18 months after flowering.

3. **Q. incana,** Roxb.; Fl. Br. Ind. v. 603; Brandis For. Flora 482, Ind. Trees 626: Gamble Man. Ind. Timb. 675. Vern. *Bán*, Jaunsar; *Bánj*, Garhwal.

A large evergreen tree; bark dark-grey, rough with cracks and fissures. *Leaves* 3-6 by 1-2 in., oblong- or ovate-lanceolate, acuminate, mucronate-serrate, tough and coriaceous, young pinkish and woolly all over, mature dark-green and glabrous above, densely white- or grey- rarely brownish-tomentose beneath; lateral nerves 12-20 pairs, straight, parallel; base acute; petiole ·5-·7 in. long. *Male spikes* slender, drooping, 2-4 in. long, often much interrupted; *perianth* 4-5-lobed; anthers glabrous. *Fem. fls.* axillary, sessile, solitary or clustered, on current year's shoots; *styles* linear-clavate, spreading. *Acorn* generally solitary, usually on current year's shoots; cup at first enclosing the nut, glabrate, rough, woody; nut ·8 in. long, conico-ovoid, canescent, brown when ripe.

OUTER HIMALAYA, JAUNSAR and TEHRI-GARHWAL, between 4,000 and 8,000 ft., generally gregarious and associated with *Buráns* and *Ayár*. Also in the Mothroṇwála swamp in the DÚN, 1,900 ft.

Heartwood reddish-brown, very hard, warps and splits in seasoning. Annual rings indistinct. Medullary rays of two kinds; a few very broad rays with numerous fine ones between. Weight 64 lbs. per c. ft. The wood is used locally for building, and for ploughs, and is a good fuel. The acorns are greedily eaten by bears, monkeys and squirrels, which is a drawback to its reproduction by seed. It coppices well up to about 9 in. diam.

New leaves and fl. Apr., May. Fr. Aug.-Oct.,—15-17 (or 3-5?) months after flowering, but remains on the tree throughout the cold weather.

4. **Q. glauca,** Thunb.; Fl. Br. Ind. v. 604; Brandis Ind. Trees 627; Gamble Man. Ind. Timb. 677. Syn. *Q. annulata,* Sm.; Brandis. For. Flora 487. Vern. *Inái, Báni,* Jaunsar; *Phanát,* Garhwal.

A large evergreen tree; bark-grey, smooth up to pole stage, afterwards fissured and rough. *Leaves* 3-6 in. long, oblong or ovate-lanceolate, acuminate, cuspidate-serrate except near the base, coriaceous, glabrous and shining above, grey-pubescent when young, afterwards glaucous beneath; lateral nerves 12-14 pairs, straight, parallel; base acute; petiole ·5-1 in. long. *Male spikes* hairy, very slender, drooping, bracts lanceolate, hairy, much longer than the flowers; *perianth-segments* 5, lanceolate. *Female fls.* sessile, 2-3 together on stout axillary peduncles, on the current year's shoots. *Cup* ·5-·7 in. diam., of several thin concentric velvety belts of connate scales, sessile on last year's shoots; nut ·6-·7 in. long, sub-globose or ovoid, half-buried in the cup.

Shady valleys in JAUNSAR and TEHRI-GARHWAL, 3,-5,000 ft., not conspicuously gregarious, often associated with Laurels and other evergreen trees. Abundant in the Lúnágádh and Mautárgádh Valleys and their tributaries. Successfully cultivated in DEHRA.

The wood is grey or greyish-brown, tough and very hárd, handsomely mottled, takes a good polish, but warps and cracks in seasoning. Medullary rays in broad irregular plates. Weight 60 lbs. per c. ft. It is used for much the same purposes as *Q. dilatata*, notably for soles of sledges in the Tehri-Garhwal Leased Forests.

Fl. Mar.-June. Fr. Aug.-Oct., 15-17 months after flowering.

Q. serrata, Thunb.; Fl. Br. Ind. v. 601;—is a deciduous Oak of the N.-E. HIMALAYA and KHASIA HILLS which has been successfully cultivated at DEHRA DÚN. *Leaves* oblong-lanceolate, spinous-toothed, generally with tufts of hairs in the nerve-axils. *Fruiting bracts* imbricate, free, recurved, woody; nut at last half-exserted. Wood brown, compact, very hard, closely resembling that of English oak. It is used in Assam for building and various other purposes.

MONOCOTYLEDONS.

Sub-class i.—*Petaloideæ.*

Order 1.—AMOMALES.

FAM. 76. SCITAMINEÆ; G. P. N. 170.

HERBS, generally with a perennial rhizome and an unbranched stem, often aromatic. *Leaves* pinnately parallel-nerved from a stout midrib. *Flowers* irregular, usually 2-sexual, solitary or in spikes or panicles. *Calyx* superior, free, tubular or spathaceous. *Corolla* gamopetalous; limb 3-partite. *Stamens* usually only 1 fertile, the rest reduced to petaloid staminodes, rarely (in *Musa*) 5 fertile. *Ovary* 3-celled; ovules many, generally axile; style slender. *Fruit* a 3-valved capsule, sometimes indehiscent. *Seeds* often with an arillus.

This Family has great economic importance, but is not of much forest interest within the range of this Flora. The following are cultivated in these parts and are well-known throughout India:—

1. *Curcuma longa*, Linn.; Fl. Br. Ind. vi 214. The Turmeric plant. Vern. *Haldi*, Hind.—Remarkable for its bright-yellow tubers which are used as a condiment throughout India. *Leaves* 1-1·5 ft. by 4-8 in.; petiole as long as the blade. Peduncle about 6 in. long. *Flowers* yellowish. It is much cultivated near Kálsi and Saiá—*G. P. n. 9.*

2. *Zingiber officinale*, Rosc.; Fl. Br. Ind. vi. 246. The Ginger plant. Vern. *Ádrak*, Hind.—Well-known for its aromatic rootstock which is used as a condiment and also in medicine. *Leaves* distichous, 6-12 by 1-1·5 in., dark-green. Much cultivated in the DÚN and also above Kálsi.—*G. P. n. 15.*

3. *Musa sapientum*, Linn.; Fl. Br. Ind. vi. 262. The Banana or Plantain tree. Vern. *Kelá*, Hind.—This differs from the rest of the Family by having five perfect stamens, and unisexual flowers

arranged in a drooping spike. *Leaves* 4-8 ft. long, glabrous above, usually with a white bloom beneath. Two or three varieties are cultivated in the DÚN and OUTER HIMALAYA and also in the SAHÁRANPUR DISTRICT. A wild variety is found in ravines of the Nágsidh Hill and in the Khairi swamp in the DÚN, Sahansra-dhárá and similar other ravines in the OUTER HIMALAYA, and in the Ámláwa valley in JAUNSAR.—*G. P. n. 34.*

4. *Costus speciosus*, Smith ; Fl. Br. Ind. vi. 249 ;—is a common weed in Sál forests in the DÚN, characterised by large white flowers, pink bracts and bright-red capsules.—*G. P. n. 178.*

Order 2.—LILIALES.

FAM. 77. LILIACEÆ; G. P. N. 178.

Herbs or small shrubs with creeping root-stocks, bulbs or corms. *Flowers* usually 2-sexual. *Perianth* coloured, often herbaceous ; segments 6 or more in two series, usually imbricate in bud. *Stamens* 6, free or connate ; anthers often versatile. *Ovary* 3-celled ; ovules 1-2, axillary, style 1, often long. *Fruit* a 3-celled capsule, or a 1- or more-seeded berry ; seeds globose or flattened.

This large Family is well known for flowers of great beauty, some of them exquisitely fragrant. Of useful cultivated plants, the Onion, *Allium Cepa*, Linn., Vern. *Piáz*, Hind., and the Garlic, *Allium sativum*, Linn., Vern. *Lahsún*, Hind., Fl. Br. Ind. vi. 337,—deserve mention. Of forest Genera only the following two are briefly described.

Analysis of the Genera.

Lvs. normal, 3-5-nerved ; fls. 1-sexual, umbelled . 1. SMILAX.
Lvs. represented by cladodes ; fls. 2-sexual, solitary fascicled or racemed . . . . . . 2. ASPARAGUS.

1. Smilax, Linn.; G. P. n. 2.

Generally climbing shrubs. *Leaves* usually alternate, 3-5-nerved, net-veined; petiole often with tendrils near the base. *Flowers* diœcious, umbelled. *Perianth-segments* 6, free. MALE FLS.: *Stamens* 6, free, sometimes forked at the tip separating the anther-cells. FEM. FLS.: *Staminodes* 3 or 6. *Style* 0 or very short; stigmas 3. *Fruit* a globose berry; seeds 1-3, generally 2; albumen horny.

Analysis of the Species.

Petiole narrowly sheathing, without auricles;
umbels 2 or 3 . . . . . 1. *S. macrophylla.*
Sheath of petiole amplexicaul and auricled;
umbles 10 or more . . . . . 2. *S. prolifera.*

1. **S. macrophylla,** Roxb.; Fl. Br Ind. vi. 310; Brandis Ind. Trees 641. Vern. *Ram-dataun,* U. P.

A large prickly climber, stem sometimes exceeding 1 in. in diam. *Leaves* ovate or orbicular, 6-18 in. long, thinly coriaceous, cuspidate, shining above; nerves 5-7 from the rounded or subcordate base; petiole stout 1-1·5 in. long, the lower half narrowly sheathing. *Umbels* 2-3, many-flowered; male peduncle slender, ·5-1·5 in. long, pedicels not exceeding ·3 in., stout in fruit. *Sepals* ·2 in. long, linear. *Stamens* as long as the sepals. *Stigmas* 3, sessile. *Berries* round, ·3-1·5 in. diam.

Fairly common in the Sál forests of the SIWALIK DIVISION.

The stem has a strong fibre which can be used for brushes. The thinner stems are used as tooth-sticks.

Fl. rainy season. Fr. cold weather.

2. **S. prolifera,** Roxb.; Fl. Br. Ind. vi. 312; Brandis Ind. Trees 641; Gamble Man. Ind. Timb. 724. Vern. *Ramdataun,* U. P.

A stout climbing shrub with prickly stem, occasionally up to 1 in. diameter. *Leaves* 4-8 by 2-6 in., oblong, ovate or orbicular, coriaceous; nerves 3-7 from above the rounded or sub-cordate base; petiole ·5-1·5 in. long, often auricled at the base round the stem; tendrils 2-4 in. long. *Umbels* 30-40-flowered; peduncles ·7-1·5 in.; pedicels ·5 in. *Sepals* ·1 in., oblong-lanceolate. *Petals* as long, but narrower. *Stamens* 6, ·1-in. long; staminodes of fem. fls. 3. *Ovary* oblong; stigmas deciduous. *Berries* round, red when ripe, ·3 in. diam.

Economic uses as of the preceding species.

Common in the SIWALIK DIVISION, especially in Sâl forests. Also in the OUTER HIMALAYAS.

Fl. Aug., Sept. Fr. Dec.-Feb.

Several other species of *Smilax* are found in the region of this Flora, of which the following deserve mention:—

1. *S. parvifolia*, Wall.; Fl. Br. Ind. vi. 304.—A gregarious undershrub with stiff slender zigzag branches. *Leaves* very variable, 1-3 in. long, ovate or lanceolate, acuminate, membranous; petiole sheathing, ·1 in. long, jointed at the top. *Peduncles* and *pedicels* very slender, ·2-·5 in. long. *Flowers* minute. *Berries* ·3-·5 in. diam. Common in JAUNSAR and TEHRI-GARHWAL, up to 8,500 ft.

2. *S. vaginata*, Dcne.; Fl. Br. Ind. vi. 305.—A plant very similar in appearance to the above, but the petioles are ·3-·7 in. long and jointed below the extremity, and the female flowers solitary. It is found in much the same localities as the above, only ascending somewhat higher, *e.g.*, Deoban—9,000 ft.

3. *S. aspera*, Linn.; Fl. Br. Ind. vi. 306; Brandis Ind. Trees 641.—A large climbing shrub. *Leaves* 1·5-6 in. long, ovate, deltoid or lanceolate, with a hastate or cordate base; petiole ·5-·7 in. long, often prickly; tendrils 2-3 in. *Flowers* white, sweet-scented; buds oblanceoloid, longer than the pedicels. *Berries* ·2-·3 in., bluish. OUTER HIMALAYA and low valleys in JAUNSAR.

2. Asparagus, Linn.; G. P. n. 7.

Erect or straggling shrubs; rootstock generally terminating in a dense fascicle of spindle-shaped farinaceous roots. *Leaves* reduced to scales or spines, with tufts of green needle-like or flattened rudimentary branchlets (cladodes) in the axils, which are likely to be mistaken for the true leaves. *Flowers* axillary, solitary fascicled or racemed. *Perianth* 6-partite; stamens opposite the perianth-segments; style 1; stigmas 3. *Fruit* a globose berry.

Analysis of the Species.

Stem unarmed. Fls. not racemed; cladodes flat. 1. *A. filicinus.*
Stem spinous. Flowers racemed.
Scandent shrub. Cladodes subulate . . 2. *A. racemosus.*
Suberect shrub. Cladodes terete . . . 3. *A. adscendens.*

1. **A. filicinus,** Ham.; Fl. Br. Ind. vi. 314; Brandis Ind. Trees 642. Vern. *Sharánoi, Kaun'a,* Jaunsar.

An erect unarmed shrub. *Cladodes* ·3-·5 in. long, flat, falcate, acuminate. *Flowers* scarcely ·1 in. diam., solitary or in pairs, white; pedicels 0-·7 in., jointed above the middle, very slender. *Berries* ·2-·3 in. diam.

Common in JAUNSAR, up to 9,000 ft., *e.g.*, at Deoban.

The tuberous roots are pickled and are used in medicine. The shoots are eaten as a vegetable.

Fl. May, June.

2. **A. racemosus,** Willd.; Fl. Br. Ind. vi. 316; Brandis Ind. Trees 642; Gamble Man. Ind. Timb. 724. Vern. *Satáwal,* Dún; *Shatánoi,* Jaunsar; *Satmuli,* Hind.

A much-branched scandent shrub with terete stem and triquetrous branchlets; spines ·2-·5 in., straight or slightly recurved. *Cladodes* 2-6 together, ·6-1 in. long, narrowly subulate, falcate and divaricate, channelled beneath. *Racemes* 1-2 in. long; pedicels ·15 in. long, jointed in the middle, slender below the joint. *Flowers* white, ·1-·15 in. diam. *Anthers* purplish. *Berries* ·15-·25 in. diam.

Throughout the DÚN and the PLAINS, ascending to 5,000 ft. in JAUNSAR, *e.g.*, Birálgádh, Dhárágádh, etc.

The tuberous roots of this as well as of the following species have the same use as those of *A. filicinus.*

Fl. Oct., Nov. Fr. Cold season.

3. **A. adscendens,** Roxb.; Fl. Br. Ind. vi. 317. Vern. *Jhirna,* Garhwal; *Hazar-muli,* Hind.

A suberect shrub with stout terete stem and grooved ascending branchlets; spines ·5-·7 in., stout, straight. *Cladodes* 6-20 together, terete and very slender. *Racemes* 1-2 in. long, many-flowered; pedicels ·1-·2 in., jointed. Flowers white, ·1-·15 in. diam. *Berries* ·2-·3 in. diam., 1-seeded.

Common in the DÚN, especially in Sál forests, *e.g.*, Phándowála.

Fl. Autumn. Fr. Cold season.

Urginea indica, Kunth ; Fl. Br. Ind. vi. 347 ; Vern. *Kándá*, Sahéranpur ;—is a small herbaceous plant with long linear leaves, and an erect racemose scape bearing greenish-white flowers. It has a large bitter bulb, which is used by the weavers about Jawálápur to brush and size their fabrics. Found in the SAHÁRANPUR SIWALIKS and also in the TONS VALLEY, *e.g.*, Sendrá, Moiá ál, etc. —*G. P. n. 126.*

Lilium giganteum, Wall. ; Fl. Br. Ind. vi. 349 ; Vern. *Giotru*, Jaunsar, is the largest of all lilies. *Stem* 6-12 ft. long, tapering, hollow. *Leaves* 12-18 in. long, broadly ovate-cordate. *Flowers* 5-7 in. diam., drooping, fragrant ; buds linear-oblong, 3 4 in. long. *Anthers* ·5 in. long, versatile, yellow. *Capsule* 3 in. ; septa feathered. Fairly common in damp ravines in JAUNSAR, 6,-9,000 ft. ; —Deoban, Mundáli, etc. Jaunsari boys make trumpets of the hollow stems, which give a deep bass note. Fl. July, Aug.—*G. P. n. 138.*

Sub-class ii.—*Spadicifloræ.*

Order 1.—PALMALES.

FAM. 78. PALMÆ ; G. P. N. 187.

Shrubs or trees with usually an unbranched cylindrical stem, erect or scandent, filled inside with cellular tissue which is traversed by strands of closed fibrovascular bundles. *Leaves* alternate, pinnatisect or palmatilobed, with numerous nerves parallel to the segments ; petiole broad-based, amplexicaul or sheathing. *Inflorescence* a simple or panicled spike, enclosed in one or more spathes. *Flowers* 1-2-sexual or polygamous, usually 3-bracteate. *Perianth* inferior ; segments 6, in two series, generally persistent, often accrescent in fruit. *Stamens* usually 6 ; anthers versatile, sometimes introrse. *Ovary* 1-3-celled, or of three distinct 1-celled carpels ; stigmas 3, usually sessile. *Fruit* a drupe or berry. *Seeds* with copious albumen which is ruminate or uniform, solid or hollow.

This most important tropical Family is represented within the limits of this Flora by only two Genera.

Analysis of the Genera.

Erect shrubs. Sheaths not armed; fruit naked . 1. PHŒNIX.
Scandent shrubs. Sheaths armed; fruit covered with imbricating adpressed scales . . 2. CALAMUS.

1. Phœnix, Linn.; G. P. n. 80.

Low or tall palms. *Leaves* pinnate; leaflets sessile, linear, entire, rigid, folded, obliquely attached to the rachis, the lowest transformed into strong spines; petiole inarticulate, persistent, with a fibrous amplexicaul sheath. *Flowers* diœcious, sessile; male in compact, female in interrupted, compound spikes; peduncle axillary, compressed. MALE FLS.: *Calyx* cup-shaped, 3-toothed. *Petals* 3, valvate. *Stamens* usually 6. FEMALE FLS.: *Calyx* as of the male, accrescent in fruit. *Petals* 3, imbricate; staminodes 6. *Carpels* 3, free; stigmas sessile. *Fruit* an oblong 1-seeded drupe. *Seed* ventrally grooved; embryo dorsal; albumen even.

Analysis of the Species.

Stem bulbiform. Fruiting peduncle very short . 1. *P. acaulis.*
Stem at length elongate. Fruiting peduncle long. 2. *P. humilis.*

1. **P. acaulis,** Buch.; Fl. Br. Ind. vi. 426; Brandis For. Flora 555. Ind. Trees 645; Gamble Man. Ind. Timb. 731. Vern. *Khajúr, Khajúri,* Hind.

Stem like a bulb, never free above the ground. *Leaves* 2-5 ft. long; rachis laterally compressed; leaflets 9-18 in. long, ·5-·7 in. broad, very strongly nerved, thick, folded at first, opening out when mature; base raised on the side of the rachis and decurrent with it. *Spadix* 6-10 in. long, compressed; branches stout; peduncle of fruiting spadix flat, 6-8 in. long, but generally concealed in the sheaths of the petioles. *Fruit* seated on the spikelets at a narrow vertical angle,

·5-·7 in. long, ovoid-oblong, with a pinkish tip when young, blackish when ripe.

Common in the DÚN and SAHÁRANPUR FORESTS, generally in grass-lands, *e.g.*, Bám Block, Pathri Forest; Doiwála, Jhabráwála, Johrá Block, Bidhálna Block, etc.

The leaves are plaited into a coarse matting, and make excellent brooms for use on fire-traces. The fruit is eaten.

Fl. Dec., Jan. Fr. Apr., May.

2. **P. humilis,** Royle; Fl. Br. Ind. vi. 426; Brandis Ind. Trees 645; Gamble Man. Ind. Timb. 731. Vern. *Khajúr*, Hind.

A low palm with a slender stem 6-8 ft. high. *Leaves* 3-8 ft. long; rachis laterally compressed; leaflets 12-18 in. long, thin, smooth, faintly nerved, always folded, generally scattered, sometimes in opposite pairs; base only slightly raised on the side of the rachis, or not at all raised. *Male spadix* 1 ft. long; *female* somewhat shorter (excluding the peduncle); spikes often paniculately subdivided; peduncles flat, of fruiting spadix 2-2·5 ft. long, ·5-·8 in. broad. *Fruit* almost horizontal, ·5-·7 in. long, ovoid, generally mucronate, red when ripe.

SAHÁRANPUR SIWALIKS, especially towards the crest, but common and of considerable size near Ránipur. It also occurs in the Chir forests of TEHRI-GARHWAL, *e.g.*, in the Lúnágádh and Khúnigádh Blocks.

Economic uses as of *P. acaulis*.

Fl. Dec., Jan. Fr. Apr.-June.

P. sylvestris, Roxb.; Fl. Br. Ind. vi. 425; Brandis For. Flora 554; Gamble Man. Ind. Timb. 419—The Wild Date Palm—Vern. *Khajúr*,—is cultivated in the DÚN, and also in the SAHÁRANPUR DISTRICT. It is often 30-40 ft. high, with a crown 12-15 ft. in diam. *Fruiting peduncle* 2-2·5 ft. by 1-·1·5 in. with a large bunch of spikes. *Fruit* 1-1·2 in. long, yellow while ripening, reddish-brown when fully ripe. *Seeds* furrowed to the centre. In Bengal and in most parts of Madras a sugary sap is extracted from the tree by cuts made near the head. The leaves are made into mats, and the fruit is eaten.

2. Calamus, Linn.; G. P. n. 102.

1. **C. tenuis,** Roxb.; Fl. Br. Ind. vi. 447; Brandis Ind. Trees 652; Gamble Man. Ind. Timb. 735. Vern. *Bet, Beṇt.* Hind.

A climbing palm, growing in clumps from underground rhizomes; the upper part covered with sheaths of leaves. *Leaves* pinnate, 1·5-2·5 ft. long. *Leaflets* many, equidistant, gradually smaller towards the top, 4-12 by ·3-·5 in., linear-lanceolate, acuminate, 3-nerved, the nerves and margins with bristles or prickles; petiole with straight spines; rachis with one row of short recurved conical prickles; sheath with adpressed flat spines and with a whip-like long thong armed with recurved prickles. *Spadices* axillary, decompound, of various sizes according to position; spathes tubular, lower 6-10 in. long, armed with recurved prickles, upper scurfy. *Flowers* small, in pairs, male in scorpioid spikelets, female pedicellate and somewhat accrescent in fruit, both on the same spike. *Calyx* campanulate, 3-toothed. *Petals* 6, valvate. *Stamens* 6. *Ovary* 3-celled. *Fruit* ·5 in. long, elliptic, clothed with closely-imbricating adpressed reflexed scales with dark-brown margins. *Seeds* ovoid-oblong, ·4 in. long.

Marshy places in the DÚN, *e.g.*, Gángbhewá, Mothronwála, Gularghâti, Nakraunda, Jogiwála, Khairi, etc.

The cane is locally used for various purposes, chiefly for chairs and morahs. It is, however, inferior in quality to the canes used for the same purposes in Bengal, Assam and Burma, as it becomes brittle very soon, and is not so strong or durable. The leaves are eaten by buffaloes, and the seeds are strung up in rosaries worn by faqirs.

Fl. July, Aug. Fr. Cold season.

FAM. 79. TYPHACEÆ; G. P. N. 190.

Perennial aquatic herbs. *Leaves* linear, sessile, thick, spongy. *Flowers* monœcious, very small, densely crowded in cylindrical or globose spikes, male above the female flowers. *Perianth* 0, or reduced to green scales or hairs. *Stamens* 1 or more. *Ovary* superior, 1-2-celled; styles persistent; stigmas laterally papillose. *Fruit* minute.

A small unimportant Family, of which only one species is briefly noticed :—

1. *Typha elephantina*, Roxb.; Fl. Br. Ind. vi. 489. Vern. *Paterá*, Sahâranpur.—*Leaves* radical, bayonet-shaped, 6-10 ft. long, triquetrous; margins often undulate above the middle. *Female spike* about 1·5 in. diam., brownish-orange, at the end of a long scape. The leaves are made into mats, and are also used for temporary walls. The pollen is said to be made into cakes and eaten. Found in the Pathri Block in the SAHÁRANPUR DISTRICT, where it is rather an important article of minor forest produce. It is also found in swamps in the DÚN.—*G. P. n. 1.*

Order 2.—ARALES.

FAM. 80. ARACEÆ; G. P. N. 191.

Perennial herbs, sometimes scandent. *Leaves* alternate, generally net-veined and sheathing at the base. *Flowers* usually 1-sexual and monœcious, the male above the female, sessile, in fleshy spikes which are more or less enclosed in a green or coloured spathe, and often tailed. *Perianth* 0, or of minute scales. *Anthers* 2-4-celled. *Ovary* sessile, 1-3-celled; stigma discoid or lobed. *Fruit* a berry, free or confluent.

Of this herbaceous Family only two forest plants appear deserving of mention:—

1. *Scindapsus officinalis*, Schott; Fl. Br. Ind. vi. 541. Vern. *Poria-bel*, Dún.—A fleshy climbing shrub, stem reaching 1 inch or more in diam., annulate. *Leaves* 5-12 by 2·5-6 in., ovate or elliptic-ovate, caudate-acuminate; base rather obliquely rounded or subcordate; petiole 3-6 in. long, elbowed at the tip, sheathing, amplexicaul. *Spathe* yellow within. *Berries* fleshy, ovoid or lanceolate, about 6 in. long. It is found in the Sál forsets of the SIWALIK DIVISION, trailing on trees by means of suckers from the nodes. Very common in the Dúdhli Block. The stem is traversed by a strong fibre which is easily separated and can be used for various purposes. The berries are used in country medicine, and the leaves as a vegetable.—*G. P. n. 78.*

2. *Acorus Calamus*, Linn.; Fl. Br. Ind. vi. 555. Vern. *Bach*, Hind. The Sweet Flag. A marsh herb much resembling *Typha* in habit. *Leaves* ensiform, 2-4 ft. by ·5-1 in., with wavy margins. *Spathe* 6 to 18 in. long; spadix 2-3 in. long, ·5-·7 in. in diam., sessile, cylindrical, dense-flowered, flowering upwards. *Flowers* 2-sexual. *Sepals* 6, orbicular. *Stamens* 6; filaments flat. *Ovary* conical, 2-3-celled; ovules many, pendulous. *Fruit* a few-seeded berry. The strongly aromatic fibrous rootstock which has a piquant pungent taste, is much valued as a medicine, specially for cough.—*G. P. n. 97.*

Many plants of this Family are cultivated, chiefly for their starchy corms, of which *Colocasia Antiquorum*, Schott; Fl. Br. Ind. vi. 523; Vern. *Ghuiṇá*, is well known throughout the UNITED PROVINCES, and is extensively cultivated in the PLAINS and up to 6,000 ft. in the HILLS, as an important food-plant.—*G. P. n. 30.*

Sub-class iii.—*Glumifloræ.*

Order 1.—GLUMALES.

FAM. 81. CYPERACEÆ; G. P. N. 199.

The Sedges.

Grass-like herbs; stems solid, generally triquetrous. *Leaves* tristichous; sheaths not split. *Flowers* minute, solitary, subtended by a single glume, in spikes which are variously arranged. *Perianth* 0, or reduced to bristles or scales. *Stamens* 1-3; anthers innate. *Ovary* 1-celled; style 2-3-cleft, branches stigmatose. *Fruit* a compressed or 3-gonous nut. *Embryo* central.

Numerous plants of the Family are found in the region of this Flora, some of which are useful as fodder or for other purposes, but they are beyond the scope of this book. One, however, deserves mention, being noted for its strong fibre :—

Eriophorum comosum, Wall.; Fl. Br. Ind. vi. 664.—*Stem* 6-20 in., slender, tough. *Leaves* serrulate, harsh, overtopping the stems. *Umbels* 2-8 in. diam. *Bracts* 8-12 in. *Glumes* dark-brown, glossy. *Nuts* 3-gonous, beaked, smooth. Common in the SIWALIKS and the HIMALAYAS, and put to much the same uses as the *Bhábar* grass, *Ischæmum angustifolium*, Hack.—*G. P. n. 12.*

FAM. 82. GRAMINEÆ; G. P. N. 200.

The Grasses.

Herbs, shrubs or trees; stem jointed; internodes generally hollow. *Leaves* alternate, simple, entire, closely parallel-nerved; base sheathing, distinct from the blade; sheath almost always split in front to the base, often with a ligule at the apex, sometimes constricted into a petiole and jointed to the blade. *Flowers* usually 2-sexual, in variously arranged spikelets. *Spikelets* with 1-3 empty glumes at the base. *Flowering glumes* distichous, each with a 2-nerved scale at its axil which is called the *palea*. Between the palea and the flowering glume is the true flower consisting of 2 or 3 minute ciliate scales (*lodicules*), and stamens or a pistil, or both. *Stamens* usually 3, rarely 6 or more, hypogynous; anthers versatile. *Ovary* 1-celled; styles 2 or 3, clothed with stigmatose hairs. *Fruit* a 1-seeded caryopsis; embryo erect or oblique, at the base of the grain, with copious mealy albumen.

This large Family is divided into several Tribes of which the most important from a forest point of view is the following:—

TRIBE I. BAMBUSEÆ.

The Bamboos.

This Tribe is distinguished from other Tribes chiefly by comprising all shrubby and tree-like grasses, commonly known as Bamboos,—by the blade of the leaf being petiolate and articulated to the sheath which is variously auricled,—and by being protected, while young, by a second form of sheath which usually produces no true leaf. The flowers, moreover, have generally 6 or more stamens, while those of other grasses have only 3, and the flowering takes place usually at intervals of many years whereas the others flower and generally die every year.

Analysis of the Genera.

Stamens 3; pericarp adnate to the seed. Small bamboos . . . . . . 1. ARUNDINARIA.
Stamens 6. Generally large bamboos.
Pericarp adnate to the seed . . . 2. BAMBUSA.
Pericarp separable from the seed . . 3. DENDROCALAMUS

1. Arundinaria, Michx.; G. P. n. 277.

Small bamboos. *Culms* slender, rarely over 1 in. in diameter, hollow; branches short and fascicled at the nodes. *Culm-sheaths* papery; blade narrow, subulate. *Leaves* usually small, often with transverse veinlets. *Inflorescence* paniculate or racemose. *Spikelets* 1-many-flowered, usually 2-sexual. *Empty glumes* 2, unequal, membranous. *Flowering glumes* longer, many-nerved. *Palea* 2-keeled. *Lodicules* 3, ciliate. *Stamens* usually 3. *Ovary* globose above; stigmas 2-3, plumose. *Grain* dorsally furrowed, included in the persistent flowering glume and palea.

Analysis of the Species.

Rootstock cæspitose; culms crowded.
  Leaves without transverse veinlets . . 1. *A. falcata.*
  Leaves with conspicuous transverse veinlets . 2. *A. spathiflora.*
Rootstock long-creeping; culms distant . . 3. *A. jaunsarensis.*

1. **A. falcata,** Nees; Gamble Bamb. Brit. Ind. 12, t. 11; Man. Ind. Timb. 744, No. 12; Fl. Br. Ind. vii. 381; Brandis For. Flora 562, Ind. Trees 665; Vern. *Go-Ningál,* Jaunsar; *Ringál,* Hind.

A small bamboo. *Culm* 6-10 ft. high, ·3-·6 in. diam., cylindrical, sometimes with a white bloom; nodes much swollen; internodes 6-12 in. long. *Culm-sheaths* scaberulous without, tapering to a truncate tip, 12 by 3 in.; margins ciliate; blade subulate, recurved; ligule toothed. *Leaves* 3-4 by ·2-·5 in., with pellucid glands in rows between the nerves; sheath glabrous. *Flowers* in panicles, on separate leafless stems. *Spikelets* ·5-·7 in., distant or 3-4 together.

Common between 4,000 and 7,500 ft. in JAUNSAR and TEHRI-GARHWAL; more or less gregarious; Korwá, Chakrata; Mautárgádh, etc.

2. **A. spathiflora,** Trin.; Gamble Bamb. Brit. Ind. 17, t. 16, Man. Ind. Timb. 745. No. 16; Fl. Br. Ind. vii. 382; Brandis Ind. Trees 665; Syn.—*Thamnocalamus spathiflorus,* Munro; Brandis For. Flora 563. Vern. *Deo-Ningál,* Jaunsar; *Ringál,* Hind.

Culm 12-20 ft. high, ·5-1 in. diam., smooth, glaucous-green when young; nodes prominent; internodes 6-15 in. long. *Culm-sheaths* loose, glabrous; margins ciliate; blade 2-4 in. long, subulate, erect; ligule fimbriate. *Leaves* 3-5 by ·4-·6 in., linear-lanceolate; margins scabrous; petiole ·1-·2 in.; main nerves joined by numerous transverse veins; sheath 2-3 in. long, truncate; auricles bristly; ligule long-ciliate. *Flowers* in paniculate racemes. *Spikelets* 1-2·5 in. long, pedicelled, 2-3 together in a narrow spathe-like yellow sheath—whence the specific name.

Common in JAUNSAR and TEHRI-GARHWAL, 7,500-9,000 ft., generally above the zone of *A. falcata*; eminently gregarious in habit. It flowered gregariously in JAUNSAR in 1882.

3. **A. jaunsarensis,** Gamble Bamb. Brit. Ind. 23, t. 22, Man. Ind. Timb. 745. No. 23; Fl. Br. Ind. vii. 384. Brandis Ind. Trees 665. Vern. *Ningál* or *Ringál,* Jaunsar.

This handsome little bamboo is easily recognised from *A. spathiflora*, upon whose zone it encroaches, by its single culms arising from a long creeping jointed rhizome. *Culm* 10-15 ft. long, ·5 in. diam., nodes marked by a narrow ring, internodes 9-11 in. long. *Culm-sheath* yellow, glabrous, narrowed to a truncate 2-auricled bristly tip. *Leaves* 4-6 in. long, lanceolate, acuminate, with numerous transverse veins between the nerves. *Flowers* and *spikelets* not seen yet.

I happened to be with Mr. Gamble when he made the discovery of this species in the Tútuágádh Block, Mundáli, in May 1891. It is curious that it has not yet been found in any other locality in JAUNSAR. The flowering cycle is not yet known.

A. Falconeri, Benth. & Hook. f.; Fl. Br. Ind. vii. 383,—is also found in TEHRI-GARHWAL. It closely resembles *A. spathiflora*, but the leaves have no transverse veins, and the spathe-like sheaths are much smaller. It flowered in EASTERN TEHRI-GARHWAL in 1885 and again in 1906, thus indicating a flowering cycle of 21 years.

These small bamboos are used for fishing rods, hooka-pipes, and locally for baskets and similar other purposes. They flower at intervals of 20-30 years.

2. Bambusa, Schreb.; G. P. n. 286.

Large bamboos, usually growing in clumps. *Culm-sheaths* broad; blade often triangular. *Leaves* linear or oblong-lanceolate, acuminate, shortly petioled. *Inflorescence* usually a large leafless panicle bearing heads of spikelets. *Spikelets* 1-many-flowered. *Empty glumes* 1-4. *Flowering glumes* ovate, lanceolate, mucronate. *Palea* 2-keeled. *Lodicules* 3, membranous, ciliate. *Stamens* 6. *Ovary* oblong or obovate; stigmas 2-3. *Grain* furrowed on one side; pericarp thin, adherent.

Analysis of the Species.

Culms distant, unarmed; nodes not much raised; leaves and spikelets long . . . . 1. *B. nutans.*
Culms crowded, armed; nodes prominently raised; leaves and spikelets short . . 2. *B. arundinacea.*

1. **B. nutans,** Wall.; Gamble Bamb. Brit. Ind. 32, t. 30; Man. Ind. Timb. 746; Fl. Br. Ind. vii. 387; Brandis For. Flora 567, Ind. Trees 668. Vern. *Báṇs*, Hind., which is the common name for all large bamboos.

Culms rising from a creeping rhizome, not crowded, 20-40 ft. high, 1·5-3 in. diam., straight, gracefully nodding; nodes not much raised, often hairy; internodes 15-18 in. long, thick-walled, not shining. *Culms-sheaths* 6-9 in. long, top rounded, with adpressed black hairs on the back; blade varying in size according to position in the culm, acute, margins recurved, black-hairy within, with 2 large wavy densely-bristly auricles; ligule narrow, dentate. *Leaves* 6-12 by 1-1·5 in., scabrid at tip and along the midrib and margins; nerves 7-10; tip twisted; base rounded or narrowed; petiole ·1-·2 in.; sheath striate, produced into a falcate auricle which is crowned with long bristles. *Inflorescence* a stiff panicle of spikelike branches which bear interrupted clusters of spikelets. *Spikelets* ·7-1 in. long, glabrous, acute, many empty or with buds inside; axis (*rachillum*) clavate. *Lodicules* 3, fimbriate. *Anthers* apiculate. *Stigmas* 2-3, twisted. *Grain* oblong, hairy on the top.

Cultivated in the DÚN, also in low valleys in JAUNSAR, about villages and in sacred groves; also in gardens for ornament: Barkōt; Káluwála; Ámláwa Valley, etc.

Straight, thick-walled and never crowded, it is a very useful bamboo for use as rafters, and as shafts of dog-carts and *ekkus*.

Flowers at intervals of about 55 years.

2. **B. arundinacea,** Willd.; Gamble Bamb. Brit. Ind. 51, t. 48, Man. Ind. Timb. 748; Fl. Br. Ind. vii. 395; Brandis For. Flora 564, Ind. Trees 671.; Vern. *Kánțá Báņs*, Hind.

A tall thorny bamboo with crowded culms rising from branching rootstocks. *Culms* bright-green, shining, varying in size, the largest 80-100 ft. high, 6-7 in. diam.; nodes prominent, lower with almost leafless spinescent more or less zigzag horizontal branches; internodes up to 18 in. long, somewhat depressed near the base of the branches, thick-walled; cavity small. *Culm sheaths* 12-15 by 9-12 in., together with the blade triangular when flattened out, thickly covered with golden hairs when young; blade 2-4 in. long, triangular, acuminate, glabrous without, matted with dark bristles within; margins wavy, involute, thickly ciliate, auriculate; ligule narrow. *Leaves* 8 by 1 in., often much smaller, linear or linear-lanceolate, glabrous above, glabrate beneath; margins scabrous; tip sharp, stiff; main nerves 4-6, with pellucid glands at intervals; base rounded, often somewhat oblique, ciliate near the petiole; petiole ·1 in., often swollen; sheath with short auricles, thickly ciliate when young. *Inflorescence* an enormous panicle, often comprising the whole culm. *Spikelets* about 5 in a cluster, ·5-·7 in. long, lanceolate, acute, bearing a few male flowers above the 2-sexual ones. *Lodicules* 3, small, fimbriate. *Stamens* slender, drooping; anthers obtuse. *Grain* ending in a short beak formed by the base of the style.

Cultivated in the DEHRA DÚN and SAHÁRANPUR DISTRICTS: Ájabpur, Mothroņwála, etc.

Its great strength and superior size make it eminently fit for all building purposes, but owing to the thorns and the crowded condition of the clumps, it is extremely difficult to pull the bamboos out except in very small pieces.

Appears to flowers gregariously at intervals of 30-40 years.

3. Dendrocalamus, Nees; G. P. n. 289.

Unarmed bamboos, often of very large size. *Culm-sheaths* usually elongate; blade narrowly triangular. *Leaves* short-petioled, often with pellucid glands. *Spikelets* few-flowered, in congested globose clusters, on the long branches of a compound panicle. *Flowers* usually 2-sexual. *Empty glumes* 2-3, ovate, acute or mucronate. *Flowering glume* like the empty glumes. *Palea* of lower flowers 2-keeled, ciliate,—of the uppermost flowers rounded on the back and not ciliate. *Lodicules* usually none. *Stamens* 6. *Ovary* hairy above; style long; stigma simple. *Grain* small, surrounded by a crustaceous pericarp.

Analysis of the Species.

A middle-sized bamboo. Spikelets spinescent, lanceolate, green, not depressed . . . . 1. *D. strictus.*
A large bamboo. Spikelets soft, ovoid, purple, depressed . . . . 2. *D. Hamiltonii.*

1. **D. strictus,** Nees; Gamble Bamb. Brit. Ind. 78, t. 68, 69, Man. Ind. Timb. 751; Fl. Br. Ind. vii. 404; Brandis For. Flora 569, Ind. Trees 675. The Male Bamboo. Vern. *Bāṇs*, Hind.

A densely-tufted gregarious bamboo, deciduous in dry climates or in years of drought. *Culms* variable in size according to climate from 20 to 50 ft. in height, and 1 to 3 in. in diam., dark-green, with a white waxy bloom when young, yellowish when old, characteristically crooked and twisted in congested clumps; nodes somewhat swollen, lower often rooting; internodes 10-15 in. long, solid or with a small cavity. *Culm-sheaths* variable in size, 3-12 in. long, paraboloidal, glabrous or with yellowish-brown hairs on the back; top rounded, ciliate, slightly auricled; blade triangular, hairy, especially within: ligule narrow. *Leaves* very variable in size, between 10 by 1·2 in. and 1 by ·2 in., generally about 6 in. long, linear-lanceolate, rough and more or less hairy on both surfaces, scabrous on the edges; midrib prominent, lateral nerves 3-6 pairs; base abruptly rounded; tip twisted; petiole ·1-·2 in.; sheath hairy at first, terminating in a prominent callus; auricle short, ciliate; ligule narrow, serrate. *Panicle* large; clusters of spikelets 1-1·5 in. diam., 1-2 in. apart. *Spikelets* ·3-·5 in. long, ·1-·2 in. diam., usually hairy outside, with 2-3 fertile and many sterile flowers; glumes all spinescent. *Palea* emarginate. *Stamens* long-exserted; filaments fine; anthers ·2-·3 in. long. *Grain* ovoid, beaked, hairy above.

Indigenous and gregarious in the SIWALIKS, especially towards Hardwar; cultivated in the DÚN.

In North-West India this is the only bamboo that is found wild in any quantity and is therefore used for a variety of purposes. It is strong and durable and, but for its small size, would easily be the best bamboo in India. It supplies many industries, *e.g.*, basket-making at Hardwar, and the manufacture of furniture at Bareilly.

A few clumps in a forest, or a few culms in a clump here and there, flower every year; but at the interval of a certain number of years it flowers gregariously over large areas. One such gregarious seeding took place towards Ránipur in 1884.

Fl. Nov.-Apr. Fr. June.

2. **D. Hamiltonii,** Nees & Arn.; Gamble Bamb. Brit. Ind. 84, t. 74, Man. Ind. Timb. 752; Fl. Br. Ind. vii. 405; Brandis For. Flora 570, Ind. Trees 676. Vern. *Kághzi-Baṇs*, Hind.

An ugly-looking bamboo with stems slanting on all sides or curved downwards. *Culms* up to 80 ft. in height and 4-7 in. diam., with long stout branches above, adpressedly densely white-pubescent when young, dull-green when old; nodes marked with root-scars; internodes 12-20 in. long; walls ·5 in. thick. *Stem-sheaths* glabrous or with patches of adpressed hairs; auricles acute; blade lanceolate, with incurved margins; ligule ·2 in., smooth, entire. *Leaves* variable, up to 15 by 2·5 in., broadly lanceolate, cuspidate, smooth above, rough beneath, minutely serrulate at the edges; main lateral nerves 6-17 pairs, secondary nerves with pellucid glands between; base often unequal-sided, rounded; petiole short; sheath glabrous within, with adpressed white hairs without, slightly keeled below the callus; ligule broad. *Panicle* very large, branches furrowed on one side; clusters of spikelets ·5-1·5 in. diameter, ·5-1 in. apart, supported by scarious bracts. *Spikelets* ·4 in. long, ovoid, depressed, purple, glabrous; glumes membranous; flowers 2-4, all fertile. *Stamens* exserted, pendulous; anthers purple, with a hairy tip. *Grain* broadly ovoid, beaked.

Cultivated in the DÚN, and about villages in the MUSSOORIE and JAUNSAR HILLS. It seems to thrive well.

Being thin-walled and rather soft, it is not very good for building purposes, but is much used for basket and mat-work. The young shoots are eaten as a vegetable. The Gáros cook rice in the hollow internodes which they place over fire in a slanting position, and keep turning at short intervals until the outside is all charred; then they split the bamboo open to take out the rice.

It flowers both annually and gregariously like *D. strictus*.

Besides the cultivated cereal crops which supply the staple food of man throughout the world, there are hundreds of grasses of great forest interest, some yielding fibre and paperstock, others supplying forest industries, others again useful as soil-binders, while a great many are indispensable for fodder. But they are obviously beyond the scope of this little Flora. Only a few forest grasses are mentioned below :—

1. *Coix Lachryma-Jobi*, Linn.; Fl. Br. Ind. vii. 100. Job's Tear. Vern. *Sankru*, Hindi. Remarkable from the fact that the female spikelets are enclosed in a bract which, when the grain ripens, becomes like a polished hardened nut, open only by a small aperture at the apex. *Stem* 3-5 ft. *Leaves* 6-18 by 1-2 in. with wavy margins and cordate base; sheaths smooth; ligule short, glabrous. *Grain* about ·3 in. long, ovoid, bluish-grey, hard, smooth and shining. Fairly common in grass-lands in the DÚN and the HILLS. Often cultivated for the sake of the grains which are used for food or for brewery purposes. The leaves and stems are good for cattle fodder and the latter is used in S. China as a material for matting. *G. P. n. 32.*

2. *Thysanolæna Agrostis*, Nees; Fl. Br. Ind. vii. 61. Vern. *Pirlú*, Dún and Sahåranpur. The Broom-grass. This is a tall grass up to 12 ft. high, with a dense bushy fox-tail-like terminal panicle. *Spikelets* very minute, sometimes viviparous. The large broad leaves somewhat resemble those of bamboos. It is often used for brooms, and the stems furnish the reed-pens used in vernacular writing. Deep ravines and shady places up to 5,000 ft.—*G. P. n. 58.*

3. *Saccharum arundinaceum*, Retz.; Fl. Br. Ind. vii. 119; Vern. *Múnj*, *Sarwár*, Hind.—A tall grass up to 20 ft. high, with a much-branched grey or greyish-brown silky panicle, and a glabrous stem. In the SAHÁRANPUR DISTRICT the stem which is used for chiks, morahs, etc., is called *bind*; the flowering scape, which is used for winnowing trays and for light covers over carts (*sirki*), is called *tilú*; and the sheath next to the scape which is twisted into cordage and from which a neat durable matting is made, is called the *múnj* proper, after which the grass has been named. Common along ráus and the foot of the HILLS in the SAHÁRANPUR DISTRICT.—*G. P. n. 75.*

4. *Ischæmum angustifolium*, Hack.; Fl. Br. Ind. vii. 129; Vern. *Bhábar*, Sahåranpur; *Báib*, *Bábai*, Hind.—Perhaps the most important of all forest grasses. *Stems* 3-5 ft. long, wiry, woolly at the base; leaves about ·1 in. broad, convolute, very fibrous. *Spikes* simple or compound, 1-2 in. long, golden- or rusty-villous. Throughout the United Provinces the grass is made into ropes which are used for various purposes. It is also in great demand for paper-making at Lucknow and Calcutta. Common in the SAHÁRANPUR SIWALIKS.—*G. P. n. 91.*

5. *Andropogon Schœnanthus,* Linn.; Fl. Br. Ind. vii. 204; Vern. *Mirchá-gandh,* Sahåranpur.—A handsome grass 3-6 ft. high. *Spikes* inside a reddish-brown spathe. Base of leaf-blade rounded or cordate and amplexicaul. When the stems are cut away, the rootstocks get covered with curly posthumous leaves. It is the famous Rusa-grass from which an aromatic oil is extracted. The roots are used in medicine, and the rootstock is largely purchased by a certain class of pilgrims at Hardwar, probably as a souvenir for friends at home. Common in the plains portion of the Ránipur Range, SIWALIK DIVISION.—*G. P. n. 94.*

6. *Andropogon Nardus,* Linn.; Fl. Br. Ind. vii. 205.—An aromatic grass much resembling *A. Schœnanthus,* but the leaves are not rounded nor amplexicaul at the base, and the spathes much smaller. Also it has a somewhat different habitat, being found in the DÚN, and also in JAUNSAR up to 7,500 ft. (No. 25,006 of Mr. Gamble's collection, Mátkángrá, Jaunsar) as well as in the SAHÁRANPUR SIWALIKS.

7. *Anthistiria gigantea,* Cav.; Fl. Br. Ind. vii. 216; Vern. *Dhá'á-ghás,* Dún; *Kumria,* Garhwal. The Spear-grass—A tall grass 8-16 ft. high, with a hard solid compound stem, notorious for its long-awned dark-brown hairy seed which readily get into clothes and are not easily got rid of. Common in the SIWALIK DIVISION, especially in coppice areas and blanks.—*G. P. n. 97.*

8. *Arundo Donax,* Linn.; Fl. Br. Ind. vii. 302. Vern. *Nal,* Hind.—A tall reed with hollow stems. *Leaves* tapering from an amplexicaul base. Axis of spikelets (*rachillum*) elongate, glabrous; flowering glume silky-hairy. *Panicle* thyrsiform. Found along streams and in shady ravines in the SIWALIK DIVISION.—*G. P. n. 211.*

9. *Phragmites communis,* Trin.; Fl. Br. Ind. vii. 303. Vern. *Nal,* Hind. This is a hollow reed found above 3,000 ft. in the HILLS, *e.g.,* Thadiár and other places in GARHWAL. It is used for a kind of coarse matting.—*G. P. n. 212.*

10. *Phragmites Karka,* Trin.; Fl. Br. Ind. vii. 304. Vern. *Nal,* Hind. This reed is a native of the plains of India and is found at Pathri near Hardwar and such other water-logged localities. The stems are of a larger size but softer-walled than those of *P. communis,* and make a neater kind of matting.

The Genus *Phragmites* differs from *Arundo* by the leaves not being amplexicaul at the base, by short silky rachilla, and by glabrous flowering glumes.

GYMNOSPERMS.

FAM. 83. GNETACEÆ G. P. N. 164.

TREES or shrubs with articulated branches. *Leaves* opposite, large or quite rudimentary, exstipulate. *Flowers* monœcious or diœcious, in axillary or terminal spikes or cones. MALE FLS. tubular or of 2-4 sepals; *anthers* 2-8, on a column of the connate filaments. FEMALE FLS. a naked erect ovule with several coats, one of which is produced into a style-like tube; *stigma* 0. *Fruit* dry or succulent, enclosed in the persistent bracts; seeds 1 or 2; cotyledons 2.

1. Ephedra, Linn.; G. P. n. 2.

1. **E. vulgaris,** Rich.; Fl. Br. Ind. v. 640; Brandis For. Flora 501, Ind. Trees 688; Gamble Man. Ind. Timb. 693. Vern. *Tút-ganthá,* Jaunsar.

A small shrub; branches opposite or whorled, green, striate; nodes 1-2 in. long; bark on old stems grey. *Leaves* scale-like; scales connate into a 2-lobed sheath, yellow or brown. *Spikes* ·1-·3 in. long, often in whorled clusters; fruiting spikes red, often succulent. *Fruit* ·3 in. long, ovoid, red and sweet when ripe; seeds 2.

Dry southern exposures of the Deoban Ridge, JAUNSAR; 8,000 to 9,500 ft., *e.g.*, Gidi Khad, below Karamba Peak, etc.

Wood yellowish-white, very close-grained, with inconspicuous pores. Goats browse on the branches, and the fruit is eaten in some places.

Fl. Apr.-June. Fr. Aug.-Oct.

FAM. 84. CONIFERÆ; G. P. N. 165.

Trees or shrubs with monopodial stems, generally evergreen; wood without pores on a cross section;

annual rings very distinct. *Leaves* alterate, or in alternate fascicles, rigid, generally acicular, exceptionally scale-like or linear, exstipulate. *Flowers* monœcious or diœcious; *perianth* none. MALE FLS. in deciduous catkins; *anthers* 1-or more-celled, adnate to the scales of the catkin, or on a column of connate filaments. FEMALE FLS. of 1, 2, or more naked ovules on a carpellary scale, which is free or adnate to the scales of a spike, the whole becoming a cone in fruit; *stigma* none. *Seeds* usually winged; cotyledons generally more than two.

Analysis of the Genera.

Ovules erect.
- Female cone with only 1 flower; scales imbricate, basifixed; lvs. linear, not adpressed . 3. TAXUS.
- Female cone few-flowered, scales decussately opposite, peltate; leaves scale-like or subulate, adpressed.
  - Scales woody, separating in mature fruit; seeds winged . . . . . . 1. CUPRESSUS.
  - Scales succulent, connate in mature fruit; seeds not winged . . . . 2. JUNIPERUS.

Ovules pendulous.
- (Female cone many-flowered, scales imbricate, basifixed; leaves, generally known as *needles*, not adpressed.)
  - Leaves fascicled.
    - Lvs. long (in the Indian species), in fascicles of 2-5; scales of cone persistent . . . . . . 4. PINUS.
    - Lvs. short, in fascicles of many at least in buds; scales of cones deciduous. 5. CADRUS.
  - Leaves distant.
    - Leaves acicular, multifarious; cones pendulous, scales persistent . . 6. PICEA.
    - Leaves flat, bifarious; cones erect, scales deciduous . . . . . 7. ABIES.

1. Cupressus, Linn.; G. P. n. 6.

1. **C. torulosa,** Don; Fl. Br. Ind. v. 645; Brandis' For. Flora 533, Ind. Trees 693; Gamble Man. Ind. Timb. 696. The Himalayan Cypress. Vern. *Leuri, Leauri,* Jaunsar; *Devidiar, Deviduár,* carpenters of Dún and Sahâranpur.

A large* evergreen tree with a pyramidal crown and drooping branchlets; bark greyish-brown, peeling off in long thin strips. *Leaves* opposite, amplexicaul, scale-like, ·05 in. long, triangular, more or less closely adpressed, with a gland on either side of the midrib. *Male catkins* terminal, cylindrical, with decussately opposite peltate scales, each with 2-6 anther-cells near the edge. *Female fl.* a globose cone consisting of 6-10 decussately-opposite peltate scales, the middle scales bearing 4-6 erect ovules at the base. *Mature cone* ·5 in. diameter, bluish; scales rugose, separating in drying into hexagons. *Seeds* compressed, with an orbicular wing, ·2 in. diam. including the wing; cotyledons 2-3.

JAUNSAR and TEHRI-GARHWAL, 6,-9,000 ft., generally on limestone formations, often crowning rugged limestone precipices. Abundant on N.-E. aspects between the Lakándi and Moilá Peaks, JAUNSAR.

Heartwood light-brown with darker streaks, moderately hard; medullary rays fine, numerous; weight 39 lbs. per c. ft. It is used at Náini Tál for building, and is an excellent timber for sleepers, experiments carried out at the Forest College having proved it to be even more durable than Deodar. It is burnt as an incense in temples.

Fl. Jan., Feb. Fr. Oct., Nov. but remains long on the tree.

C. sempervirens, Linn., is an ornamental tree cultivated in gardens throughout India, which differs from *C. torulosa* by having a cylindrical crown and branches with erect tips, and a larger cone with tubercled scales.

2. Juniperus, Linn.; G. P. n. 7.

The Junipers.

Evergreen trees or shrubs. *Leaves* either all linear or pungent and whorled, or dimorphous, those on

* There is a tree near the Temple at Deota, TEHRI-GARHWAL, 9,000 ft., which measured 22 ft. in girth and 154 ft. in height in May 1896.

lower branches or luxuriant shoots being subulate and pungent, and on upper branches scale-like and closely adpressed. *Flowers* monœcious or diœcious. MALE FLS. in small cylindrical or ovoid catkins; scales whorled, imbricate, each with 3-6 anther-cells. FEM. FLS. in small fleshy globose cones consisting of 3-6 connate carpellary scales, berry-like when mature. *Seeds* 1-5, with a thick hard testa, not winged; cotyledons 2-3.

Analysis of the Species.

A shrub. Leaves linear, pungent; seed solitary . . . . . . 1. *J. recurva.*
A small tree. Leaves dimorphous; seeds 2 or more . . . . . . 2. *J. macropoda.*

1. **J. recurva,** Ham., var. **squamata,** Parlat.; Fl. Br. Ind. v. 647; Brandis For. Flora 538, Ind. Trees 694; Gamble Man. Ind. Timb. 698. The Weeping Blue Juniper. Vern. *Gúggul,* U. P.

A bushy prostrate shrub. *Leaves* in whorls of 3, ·15-·2 in. long, linear, pungent, somewhat narrowed at the base, flat and bluish-green above, convex and light-green beneath, often incurved. *Catkins* at the ends of short lateral branches; the *male* ovoid, yellow; the *female* small; ovules erect. *Fruit* an oblong berry, ·3-·5 in. diam., with the tips of the scales protruding at the apex, the rest cohering into one mass, dark-purple, smooth, shining when ripe. *Seed* solitary, oblong, not winged.

TEHRI-GARHWAL, from 12,000 ft. upwards: Chánsil, Gangottari, etc. On the Chur mountain, SIMLA HILL STATES.

Sapwood white; heartwood light-red, very fragrant; weight 40 lbs. per c. ft. It is chiefly used for fuel and burnt as an incense.

Fl. June, July. Fr. Aug.-Oct. of the second year.

2. **J. macropoda,** Boiss.; Fl. Br. Ind. v. 647; Brandis Ind. Trees 694; Gamble Man. Ind. Timb. 698. Syn.—*J. excelsa,* M. Bieb.; Brandis For. Flora 538. The Himalayan Pencil Cedar. Vern. *Dhúp,* U. P.

A moderate-sized tree with thin reddish-brown fibrous bark; trunk generally gnarled; branchlets slender. *Leaves* of two kinds,—

of the lower branches up to ·3 in. long, subulate, pungent,—of the upper, scale-like and closely adpressed (resembling those of *Cupressus torulosa*), ovate, acute, with a large dorsal gland,—all of a light-green colour. *Male catkins* terminal, on a scaly peduncle. *Berry* ·2-·3 in. diam., subglobose, glaucous, black when ripe, very resinous; tips of the scales forming transverse ridges; seeds 2-5.

TEHRI-GARHWAL along the Jádgangá, a tributary of the Bhágirathi (*Rai Bahadur Keshavánand*).

Sapwood large, white; heartwood dark-red, even- and close-grained, with a scent similar to that of the pencil-cedar; weight about 32 lbs. per c. ft. It is used for fuel and occasionally burnt for incense.

3. Taxus, Tourn.; G. P. n. 13.

1. **T. baccata,** Linn.; Fl. Br. Ind. v. 648; Brandis For. Flora 539, Ind. Trees 696; Gamble Man. Ind. Timb. 701. The Yew. Vern. *Thúner, Thúniára*, Jaunsar.

An evergreen tree, generally middle-sized, but sometimes very large, with a large spreading crown; bark reddish-grey, thin, smooth, peeling off in longitudinal shreds. *Leaves* distichous, 1-1·5 by ·1 in., linear, often cuspidate-acuminate, dark-green and shining above, brownish-yellow and somewhat mealy beneath, 1-nerved, narrowed into a short petiole. *Flowers* usually diœcious, axillary. *Male fl.* a pedicelled whorl of 3-8 anther-cells on peltate scales. *Female fl.* a single erect ovule surrounded by a disk, at the apex of a scaly peduncle. *Fruit* an ovoid berry, ·3-·4 in. long, the disk developing into a fleshy covering which overtops and nearly conceals the compressed wingless olive-green seed; cotyledons 2.

JAUNSAR and TEHRI-GARHWAL, 6,-10,000 ft., generally in shady ravines; common, but not abundant: Jádi Block, Deoban; Tútuá Block, Mundáli; Lambátách; Rikhshin, etc.

Sapwood white; heartwood orange-red, close-grained, hard, smooth, elastic, works and polishes extremely well, but somewhat slow to season. Annual rings wavy. Medullary rays extremely fine, very numerous. Weight 44 lbs. per c. ft. The wood is eminently fit for cabinet-work, and is used for bows, carrying-poles and furniture. The bark is used by Kunawaris as a substitute for tea, this accounting for the long blazes usually seen on road-side trees. The fruit is eaten.

Fl. Mar.-May. Fr. Sept.-Nov.

4. Pinus, Linn.; G. P. n. 26.

Evergreen trees; branches whorled and generally horizontal. *Leaves* of two kinds: on seedlings and luxuriant shoots single and short; on older shoots and trees in bundles of 2-5 and usually long, the latter at first from the axils of the former. *Male catkins* crowded at the base of the current year's shoots. *Anther-cells* in pairs, on a short column, connected at the back by a scale-like connective which is produced at the tip, several such pairs being imbricately close-packed in each catkin. *Female cones* globose or ovoid, generally at the end of the current year's shoots; scales spirally imbricate, open at first, but closing after fertilization; ovules 2 at the axil of each scale, inverted. *Ripe cones* ovoid oblong or cylindrical, usually at the base of the current year's shoots; scales thickened and woody, beaked or with a square knob at the apex. *Seeds* with a hard woody shell, in pairs at the base of each scale, oily, generally winged; cotyledons usually more than two.

Analysis of the Species.

Leaves in clusters of 5, bluish-green; cone cylindrical, with scales not much thickened at the apex . . . . . . 1. *P. excelsa.*

Leaves in clusters of 3, light-green; cone ovoid, with scales much thickened at the apex . . . . 2. *P. longifolia.*

1. **P. excelsa,** Wall.; Fl. Br. Ind. v. 661; Brandis For. Flora 510, Ind. Trees 689; Gamble Man. Ind. Timb. 704. The Blue Pine. Vern. *Káil*, Hind.; *Chil*, Jaunsar.

A large tree; bark smooth slate-coloured and leathery on young stems, grey or greyish-brown corky and with shallow fissures on mature trees. *Leaves* in bundles of 5, 6-8 in. long, slender, triquetrous, glaucous on the inner faces (giving the foliage its characteristic bluish colour); sheaths entire, deciduous. *Male catkins* ·3-·4 in. long, ovoid or oblong. *Cones* generally 2-3 together, 6-12 in. long when ripe, on peduncles 1-3 in. long, cylindrical, erect before fertilization, afterwards pendulous; scales 2-2·5 in. long, 1-1·5 in. broad near the end, spathulate, not much thickened at the end, rhomboid at the back. *Seeds* blackish, ovoid, acute at both ends, compressed, ·25-·35 in. long; wing about three times as long, obliquely truncate; cotyledons usually 9.

JAUNSAR and TEHRI-GARHWAL, 6,-10,000 ft., generally as a companion of Deodar, for which species, if properly guarded against, it is an excellent nurse in early life. In JAUNSAR it is seldom gregarious above 8,500 ft. Occasionally as low down as 4,000 ft., *e.g.*, in the Giri valley, SIMLA HILLS.

Heartwood pinkish-brown, moderately hard; annual rings distinct, marked by a line of compact wood at the outer edge; medullary rays very fine and very numerous; resin ducts smaller than those of *P. longifolia*; weight 30 lbs. per c. ft. The wood is more durable than that of chir, and is altogether a much better timber, but is seldom used beyond the hills, the plains people being doubtful of its qualities, probably from its lighter weight. The sapwood gives a resin, which, though smaller in yield per individual tree, is much superior in quality to that of *P. longifolia*. The wood of the stumps is used for torches, and tar and pitch can be extracted from it by destructive distillation. The leaves may be used to stuff cushions. In certain years a sweet liquid, commonly known as honey-dew, is secreted by some Aphids which infest the leaves of the pines and occasionally of other Coniferous trees. This sweet substance is collected and eaten by the inhabitants of the Himalaya. The bark of poles is used like slate for roofing temporary huts. The seeds are sometimes eaten, although too resinous to be much relished.

Fl. Apr.-June. Fr. ripens Sept.-Nov. of the second year.

2. **P. longifolia,** Roxb.; Fl. Br. Ind. v. 652; Brandis For. Flora 506; Ind. Trees 690; Gamble Man. Ind. Timb. 706. The Long-leaved Pine. Vern. *Chír*, Hind.; *Sarol, Sirli, Kulháin*, Garhwal and Jaunsar.

A large light-loving tree with a clear straight bole; bark 1-2 in. thick, outer corky and in thin crisp plates, reddish-brown,—inner brick-red, vertically and spirally furrowed; branches rough, soon corky. *Leaves* in bundles of 3, 9-12 in. long, obscurely triquetrous, light-green; sheath greyish-brown, persistent, fimbriate. *Male catkins* ·3-·6 in. long, ovoid-cylindric. *Cones* solitary or 3-5 together, 4-8 by 3-5 in. near the base, ovoid, on short stout stalks; scales 1-2 by ·7 in., beak 4-6-gonous, reflexed, much thickened, generally with a sharp black tip. *Seeds* ·3-·45 in. long, obliquely oblanceolate, compressed, with a membranous wing, which is rather longer than the seed; cotyledons about 12.

Throughout the SIWALIK and JAUNSAR DIVISIONS, between 2,000 and 6,500 ft.; generally gregarious, often forming extensive pure forests. SAHÁRANPUR SIWALIKS, 2,-3,000 ft.; Láduákôt in the MÁLKŌT HILLS, 4,-6,000 ft.; Tons and other valleys in JAUNSAR and TEHRI-GARHWAL, 3,-6,500 ft.

The heartwood is soft, reddish; annual rings well-marked by a compact belt of darker colour at the outer edge, inner zone spongy; medullary rays fine, numerous; resin-ducts prominent on a vertical section; weight about 41 lbs. per c. ft. The wood is not durable, specially when exposed to wet. It is, however, used in the hills, and is rising in the estimation of the plains people of the Punjab, where it is largely exported for building and other purposes. The sapwood yields large quantities of resin, from which turpentine and rosin are manufactured. The charcoal of the bark is much prized by Jaunsari blacksmiths. The seeds are eaten by the hill-people. Other economic uses are similar to those of Káil, excepting that the bark is never used for roofing.

Fl. Feb.-Apr. Seeds shed Apr.-May next year. The dry cones remain long on the tree.

The important article of food known throughout Northern India as *Chilghōzá* is the seed of a pine tree, *P. Gerardiana*, Wall.; Fl. Br. Ind. v. 652,—which is a native of AFGHANISTAN, KAFIRISTAN and ARID HIMALAYA. *Seeds* about ·8 in. long, oblanceoloid, terete.

5. Cedrus, Loud.; G. P. n. 27.

1. **C. Libani**, Barrel., var. **Deodara**, Hook. f.; Fl. Br. Ind. v. 653; Gamble Man. Ind. Timb. 710. Syn.—*Cedrus Deodara*, Loud.; Brandis For. Flora 516, Ind. Trees 691. The Himalayan Cedar. Vern. (*Devadáru*, Sans., whence) *Deodár*, *Dedwár*, *Dewár* Hind.; *Keloṇ*, Jaunsar.

A very large and tall gregarious tree, probably the largest and longest-lived in India,* noted for its great beauty; branches and branchlets horizontal, tips slender and nodding; crown from pyramidal in early life to spherical when mature; bark greyish- or reddish-brown, with vertical and diagonal fissures. *Leaves* 1-1·5 in. long, acicular, triquetrous, glaucous-green, mostly in dense fascicles, with a few solitary ones scattered between the fascicles. *Male catkins*

* There is a section in the Forest College Museum, 27 ft. in girth, the age of which is estimated to be over 800 years.

solitary, at the ends of the branchlets, usually ·3-·4 in. long, ovoid. *Anthers* as in *Pinus*. *Ovules* inverted, 2 at the base of each scale. *Cones* always erect, 4-5 in. long by 3-4 in. near the base, ovoid or pyramidal; scales fan-shaped, imbricate, transversely closely-packed in the cone so as to expose only the outer edges; margins thin. *Seeds* ·35-·5 in. long, triangular or broadly crescent-shaped; wing triangular, ·6-·7 in. long; cotyledons about 10.

Deodar is found in a distinct zone of its own, which in JAUNSAR and TEHRI-GARHWAL is between 7,000 and 8,500 ft. In the lower limit the Blue Pine, and elsewhere the Spruce Fir and the Mōru Oak are its constant companions.

Heartwood light yellowish-brown, fine- and even-grained, moderately hard, strongly scented. Annual rings very distinct, being marked at the outer edge by a fine line of darker colour. Medullary rays generally very fine but of unequal width; no visible resin ducts. Weight 35-40 lbs. per c. ft. Deodar is one of the three most important timber trees of India, the other two being Teak and Sál. The wood is extremely durable, and is proof against white-ants, and to some extent against wet, on account of the oil which it contains. It is extensively used for building, is very much in demand for sleepers, and is the best wood for shingles in North-Western India. The oil is extracted from it by destructive distillation, and is used as a remedy for ulcers and eruptions, and also for rubbing on *sarnáis* (inflated skins used for crossing rivers) to keep them from rotting. The wood is a bad fuel.

Male fl. Sept., Oct. The cones do not begin to grow until April; they ripen and shed seeds in Oct., Nov., *i.e.*, about 13 months after flowering.

6. Picea, Link.; G. P. n. 28.

1. **P. Morinda**, Link.; Fl. Br. Ind. v. 653; Brandis Ind. Trees 692; Gamble Man. Ind. Timb. 716. Syn.—*Abies Smithiana*, Forbes; Brandis For. Flora 525. The Himalayan Spruce. Vern. *Roi*, *Rái*, Jaunsar.

A lofty tree,* with rough greyish-white bark, exfoliating in thin orbicular scales about 1 in. in diam.; branches horizontal; branchlets slender, pendulous. *Leaves* 1-1·5 in. long, 4-sided, acicular, stiff, scattered in multifarious spirals round the branchlets (which

* Trees up to 24 ft. in girth and 210 ft. in height have been measured near Mundáli, JAUNSAR, 8,800 ft.

look somewhat like bottle brushes). The bud-scales cohere to form a conical cap which falls off when the leaves open. *Male catkins* single, about ·4 in. long, ovoid, in the axils of the leaves ; anther-cells adnate to the stipitate scales. *Ovules* inverted, in pairs behind the carpellary scale, and in the axils of the imbricating scales of the spike which afterwards becomes the cone. *Cones* terminal, 4-6 in. long, 1·5-2 in. diam., cylindric, pendulous after fertilization, dark-brown when ripe ; scales with a thin edge, smooth outside, concave, broadly obovate ; base cuneate. *Seeds* about ·15 in. long, obliquely oblong, dark-grey, with a broad spathulate obliquely-truncate wing which is about ·5 in. long ; cotyledons 8-10.

JAUNSAR and TEHRI-GARHWAL, 7,-11,000 ft., associated in Deodar forests with that species and the Mōru Oak, and in higher elevations with Silver Fir and the Kharshu Oak,—generally affecting sunny aspects.

Wood white with a brownish tinge, rather soft ; medullary rays very fine and very numerous ; resin-ducts scanty ; weight 30 lbs. per c. ft. It is used for planks and packing-cases, and for shingles in the hills. It is an indifferent fuel, but the charcoal is fairly good. The bark is used for roofing huts, and to make water-troughs.

Fl. April. Cones ripen in Oct.-Nov.

7. Abies, Juss. ; G. P. n. 31.

1. **A. Webbiana,** Lindl. ; Fl. Br. Ind. v. 654 ; Brandis For. Flora 528, Ind. Trees 692 ; Gamble Man. Ind. Timb. 718. The Himalayan Silver Fir.

A lofty tree with a dense cylindrical crown, pre-eminently shade-enduring ; branches pendulous, branchlets stout, stiff, spreading horizontally ; bark smooth on young stems, dark-brown or grey and split into long and narrow scales on old trees. *Leaves* 1-2 by ·1 in., flat, narrow-linear, narrowed into a short petiole, spirally arranged but declinate on two sides to appear distichous, glossy dark-green above with two faint white lines on either side of the midrib beneath, persistent for at least three years ; tip emarginate, generally with two sharp cusps. *Cones* always erect, oblong or cylindrical, 2-4 in. long, 1·5-3 in. diam., dark-purple when ripe ; scales closely imbricate, obovate ; edge rounded, thin. *Seeds* ·15-·2 in. long, obovoid ; wing twice as long, broadly obovate, truncate ; cotyledons 5-6.

TEHRI-GARHWAL, 8,-13,000 ft., generally in moist shady northern aspects and ravines.

Wood white, soft; medullary rays extremely fine and too weak to bind together the annual rings which often separate to form cupshakes. Weight 29 lbs. per c. ft. It is not very durable when exposed to wet but seems to last well as shingles, and is used locally for construction in many parts of the Himalaya.

Fl. Apr. Cones ripen in Sept.-Oct.

Var. **Pindrow,** Brandis; Fl. Br. Ind. v. 655. Vern *Morindá*, Jaunsar,—differs from the type by having longer leaves (2-3 in.), and more slender cylindrical cones (about 1·5 in. in diam.).

This lofty and graceful tree is common in JAUNSAR and TEHRI-GARHWAL, 8,-10,000 ft., generally on northerly aspects and in shady localities, and often attains an enormous size, trees up to 250 ft. in height and 25 ft. in girth having been found at Mundáli. It is important in the Deoban Range as a fuel tree.

INDEX TO BOTANICAL NAMES.

*** Generic names printed in heavy types are those which have been incorporated in the Analyses, but page numbers have been omitted in the case of those Genera whose characters have not been separately described. Genera in ordinary small types are those which are not included in the Analyses and whose species are only briefly noticed. Names in small Italics are synonyms not accorded precedence in this Flora. Divisions and Families are in Roman capitals, while Orders are in Italic capitals.

INDEX TO EUROPEAN AND VERNACULAR NAMES.

*** The letters affixed to names denote the localities or languages to which they belong. Thus *As.* stands for Assam ; *B.* for Bengal; *D.* for Dehra Dún; *E.* for English or European, also for Eastern; *G.* for Garhwal; *H.* for Hindi or Hindustani; *J.* for Jaunsar; *K.* for Kumaun; *Ka.* for Kálsi; *Ma.* for Málkōt; *Mu.* for Mussoorie; *N. I.* for Northern India; *P.* for the Punjab; *R.* for Rajpur; *S.* for Sahåranpur; *Sans.* for Sanskrit; *T. V.* for the Tons Valley; *U. I.* for Upper India; *U. P.* for the United Provinces of Agra and Oudh ; and *W.* for Western.